SAS® Visual Analytics for
SAS® Viya®

SAS Institute Inc.

§.sas.

sas.com/books

The correct bibliographic citation for this manual is as follows: SAS Institute Inc. 2020. *SAS® Visual Analytics for SAS® Viya®*. Cary, NC: SAS Institute Inc.

SAS® Visual Analytics for SAS® Viya®

Copyright © 2020, SAS Institute Inc., Cary, NC, USA

ISBN 978-1-952365-13-3 (Hardcover)
ISBN 978-1-952365-09-6 (Paperback)
ISBN 978-1-952365-10-2 (Web PDF)
ISBN 978-1-952365-11-9 (EPUB)
ISBN 978-1-952365-12-6 (Kindle)

Contents

About This Book

What Is This Book About?

SAS Visual Analytics is a web-based product that leverages SAS High-Performance Analytics technologies to empower organizations to explore huge volumes of data very quickly to identify patterns, trends, and opportunities for further analysis. SAS Viya modernizes the SAS Platform with features like high availability for always-on answers, faster in-memory processing, and native cloud support. Resilient and scalable, SAS Visual Analytics on SAS Viya can handle more users, more data, and a wide range of BI and analytical workloads in a consistent and governed manner.

The book covers the material included in the SAS® Certified Specialist: Visual Business Analytics 7.5/8.3 exam, which is designed for analysts who are using SAS Visual Analytics to analyze data and design reports. It covers the following three main areas:

- Adding and manipulating data items within SAS Visual Analytics
- Analyzing data with SAS Visual Analytics
- Designing and sharing reports using SAS Visual Analytics

Is This Book for You?

SAS Visual Analytics with SAS Viya is written for anyone in an organization who wants to create, share, and collaborate on insights from data with SAS Visual Analytics, including decision makers, business analysts, report creators, and citizen data scientists. No SAS programming skills are necessary.

The first part of the book introduces the basics needed to prepare and explore your data, make discoveries, and create a report in SAS Visual Analytics. The second section introduces more advanced topics, including using automated explanation and creating advanced interactive reports with parameters using SAS Visual Analytics

What Should You Know about the Examples?

This book includes demonstrations and practices for you to follow to gain hands-on experience with SAS Visual Analytics.

Software Used to Develop the Book's Content

SAS Visual Analytics on SAS Viya (Version 8.5 and 8.3).

Example Code and Data

The data sets used in the book's demonstrations and practices are provided to download.

You can access the example code and data for this book by linking to its author page at support.sas.com/sasinstitute.

We Want to Hear from You

SAS Press books are written **by** SAS Users **for** SAS Users. We welcome your participation in their development and your feedback on SAS Press books that you are using. Please visit sas.com/books to do the following:

- Sign up to review a book
- Recommend a topic
- Request information on how to become a SAS Press author
- Provide feedback on a book

Do you have questions about a SAS Press book that you are reading? Contact the author through saspressinfo@sas.com or https://support.sas.com/author_feedback.

SAS has many resources to help you find answers and expand your knowledge. If you need additional help, see our list of resources: sas.com/books.

Acknowledgments

This book is based on the SAS training courses:

SAS® Visual Analytics 1 for SAS® Viya®: Basics

SAS Visual Analytics 2 for SAS® Viya®: Advanced

developed by Nicole Ball. Additional contributions were made by Richard Bell, Beth Hardin, Lynn Matthews, Theresa Stemler, and Stacey Syphus. Design, editing, and production support was provided by the SAS Press team: Robert Harris, Catherine Connolly, Suzanne Morgen, and Denise Jones. Special thanks to Rick Cornell for editorial support.

Chapter 1: Introduction to SAS Visual Analytics

1.1 Introduction

This chapter gives you an overview of SAS Visual Analytics and explains the main difference in architecture between SAS Visual Analytics and SAS Visual Analytics in SAS Viya. We then describe the different roles or levels of permission available in Visual Analytics and introduce the business scenario and data that are used in the first part of the book.

Each chapter contains demos to reinforce the content and a quiz or exercises, and practices so you can test your new skills. The solutions of the quizzes, exercises, and practices can be found at the back of the book.

SAS Visual Analytics

SAS Visual Analytics enables you to explore and analyze massive amounts of data, easily create reports, and share insights.

In traditional reporting, the resulting output is well defined up front. That is, you know what you are looking at and what you need to convey. However, data discovery invites you to plumb the data, its characteristics, and its relationships. Reports can then be made available on a mobile device or on the web. In addition, users can create powerful statistical models (if SAS Visual Statistics is licensed) and work with factorization machines, forests, gradient boosting, neural networks, and support vector machines (if SAS Visual Data Mining and Machine Learning is licensed).

Figure 1.1: SAS Visual Analytics Features

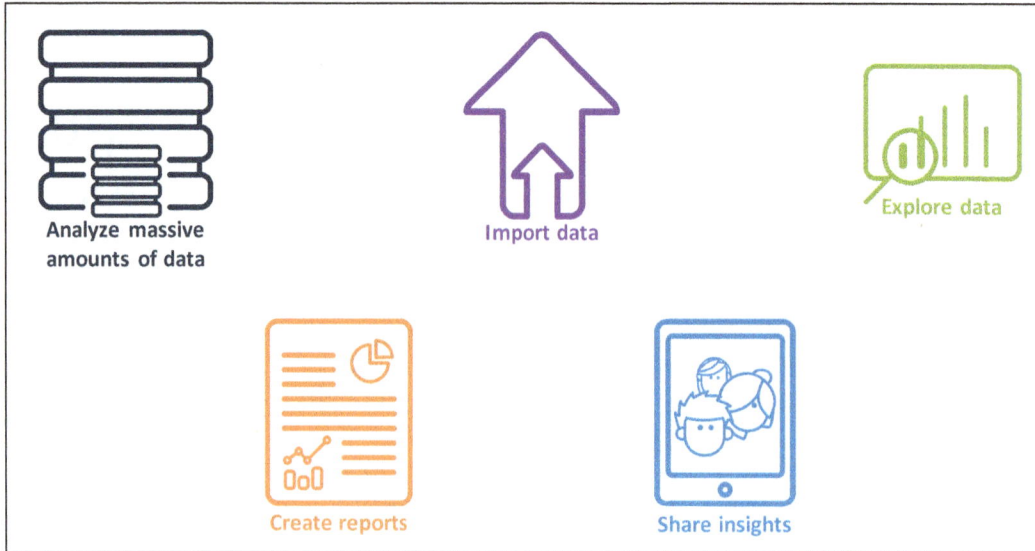

SAS Visual Analytics in SAS Viya

SAS Viya is an open, cloud-enabled, analytic run-time environment with a number of supporting services, including SAS Cloud Analytic Services (CAS). CAS is the in-memory engine on the SAS Platform.

With SAS Visual Analytics in SAS Viya, the compute engine of SAS Visual Analytics 7.x, SAS LASR Analytic Server, has been replaced by the CAS server. The main difference from the SAS LASR Analytic Server is that data preparation is no longer executed by a SAS program on the head node. The CAS server brings its own data preparation capabilities, spreading its workload to all workers across a distributed environment. This enables data management transformations to take place on larger data volumes with short execution times because the operations are done in parallel across the worker nodes.

SAS Viya Architecture

At the heart of SAS Viya, CAS provides the run-time environment for data management and analytics. It uses scalable, high-performance, multi-threaded algorithms to rapidly perform analytical processing on in-memory data of any size. CAS is designed to run in a single-machine symmetric multiprocessing (SMP) or a multi-machine massively parallel processing (MPP) configuration, supporting multiple platform and infrastructure configurations.

Figure 1.2: SAS Viya Architecture

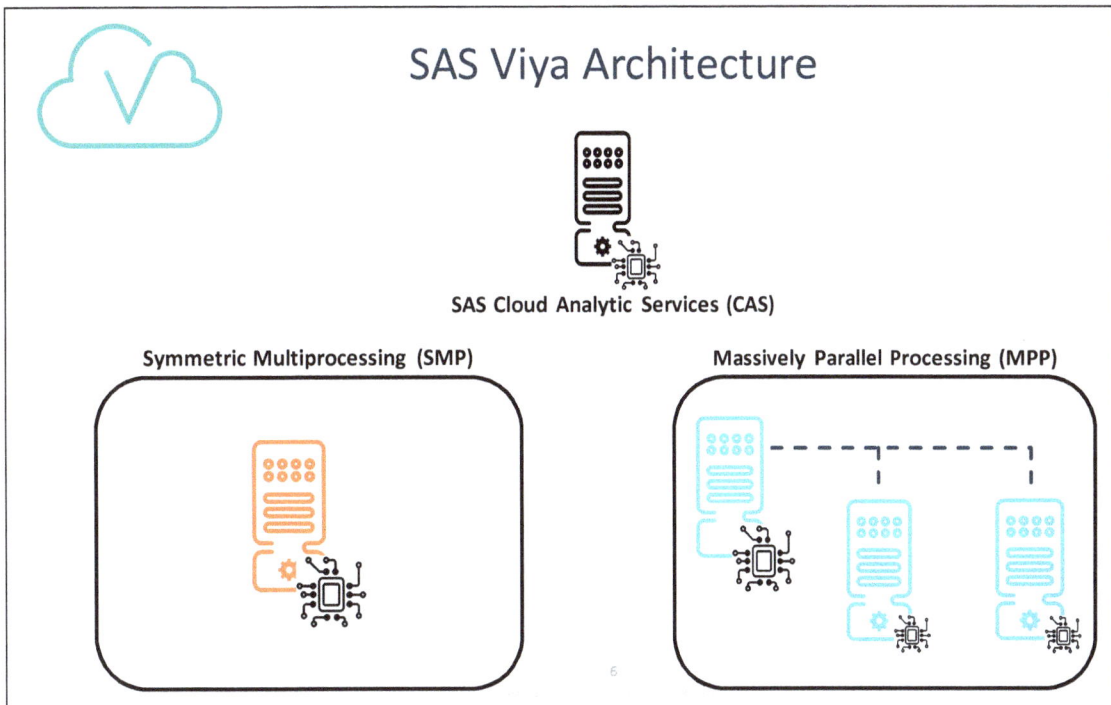

SAS Viya Applications

SAS Drive is a hub for the SAS Viya applications that enables you to easily view, organize, and share your content from one place.

The availability of the features in SAS Drive depends on the applications that have been installed, and the features and permissions that have been specified by your administrator. To access SAS Drive, enter the URL provided by your administrator (for example, https://prod.host.com/SASDrive). SAS Drive is always available from the Applications menu in the upper left. From SAS Drive, you can access your installed applications, including those in Table 1.1 below.

Table 1.1: SAS Viya Applications

Application	Description
SAS Drive	Collaborative interface for accessing, organizing, and sharing content
SAS Visual Analytics	Visualize data interactively, create interactive reports, build statistical models, view reports in a browser
SAS Visual Analytics App	View reports on a mobile device or tablet
SAS Data Studio	Prepare data using data transforms
SAS Graph Builder	Create customized graph objects
SAS Environment Manager	Manage the environment
SAS Theme Designer	Create custom themes for the application or reports

Application	Description
SAS Cloud Analytic Services (CAS)	Cloud-based, run-time environment server for data management and analytics
SAS Studio	Perform programming tasks
SAS Data Explorer	View, reload, and import data to CAS
SAS Lineage Viewer	View and understand relationships between objects (tables, plans, reports)

1.2 SAS Visual Analytics Process

To help you make sense of the growing data within your organization, SAS Visual Analytics provides an interactive user experience that combines advanced data visualization, an easy-to-use interface, and powerful in-memory technology. This enables a wide variety of users to visually explore data, execute analytics, and understand what data means. Then they can create and deliver reports wherever needed via the web, mobile devices. or Microsoft Office applications.

Figure 1.3: SAS Visual Analytics Methodology

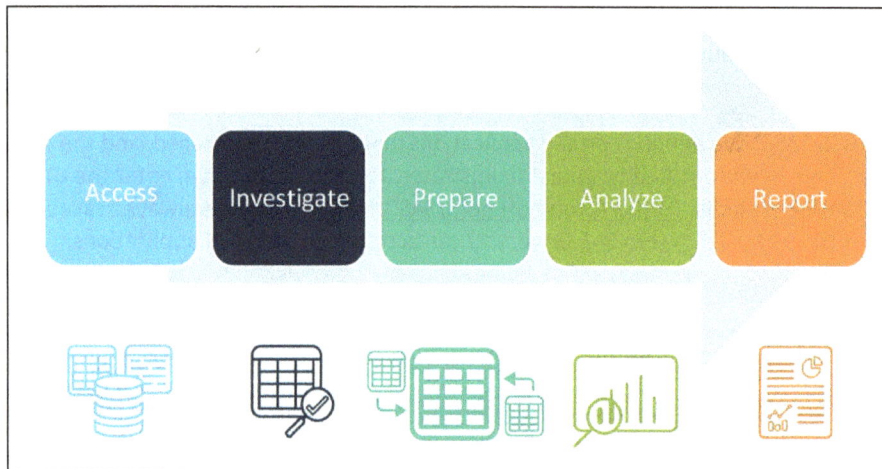

Table 1.2: SAS Visual Analytics Methodology Phases

Phase	Description
Access	In the Access phase, you identify analysis tables that will be used in Visual Analytics and load those tables into CAS.
Investigate	In the Investigate phase, you inspect the tables to determine whether any changes are needed for data items due to data inconsistencies or data quality issues, as well as identify any new data items that need to be calculated.
Prepare	In the Prepare phase, you correct any data quality issues and create any new calculated items needed for analysis.

Phase	Description
Analyze	In the Analyze phase, you explore the data to identify any patterns, relationships, and trends.
Report	In the Report phase, you develop interactive reports that can be shared via the web or a mobile device.

Understanding Roles

Not all users have all permissions to carry out all parts of the process above. Your capabilities from SAS Drive are based on the role that your SAS Visual Analytics administrator assigned to you. The roles exist to define how users interact with the application. For example, a user assigned the consumer role reviews reports or analyses. In contrast, they don't need to access the advanced functionality. SAS provides an initial set of rules to control your users' access to functionality. By default, initial rules are created at installation for the following users:

- ***All authenticated users*** – Users can access selected functions within applications, such as the Dashboard, Data, Servers, and Content pages in SAS Environment Manager and functionality in SAS Visual Analytics. Users can also perform operations on folders and on the objects that the folders contain.

- ***SAS administrators*** – Users can access everything that is under the control of the general authorization system.

Figure 1.4: SAS Visual Analytics Users

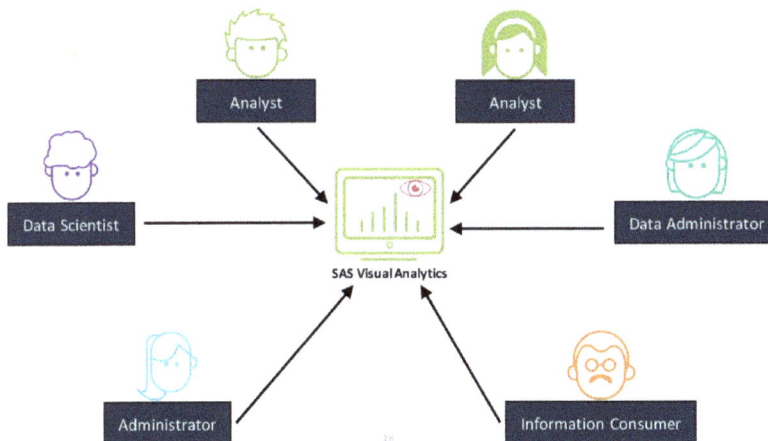

Table 1.3: SAS Visual Analytics User Roles

Role	Description
Consumer	Views the reports, analytics, and dashboards for content. Can use a desktop or mobile device to consume the reports. Consumers might be internal or external to the organization based on how SAS Visual Analytics is configured.
Content Builder	Such as an analyst or data scientist. Creates content like reports, explorations, and dashboards for consumers. This role might produce the data sets or use those made available from the data administrator.

Role	Description
Data Administrator	Schedules and loads data tables into SAS Visual Analytics. Makes data from multiple data sources available to the application.
Platform Administrator	Manages the SAS Visual Analytics environment and platform, which includes controlling the folder structure, user accounts, and access to the content.

Depending on an organization's size, some users might fill more than one role. In a smaller organization, one person might be responsible for creating content and administering the system. In larger organizations, there might be entire departments devoted to each role.

For more information about managing roles and their capabilities, refer to the SAS Visual Analytics Administration Guide for your release.

Introducing the Data

The data used in the first part of this book is taken from a sports store called Orion Star Sports & Outdoors. The business scenario we use is that you have been hired as an analyst and report designer at the store, and you will be asked to explore and build certain reports from the data. We explore and report on the variables such as products, suppliers, customers, orders, and employees.

Figure 1.5: Orion Star Sports & Outdoors

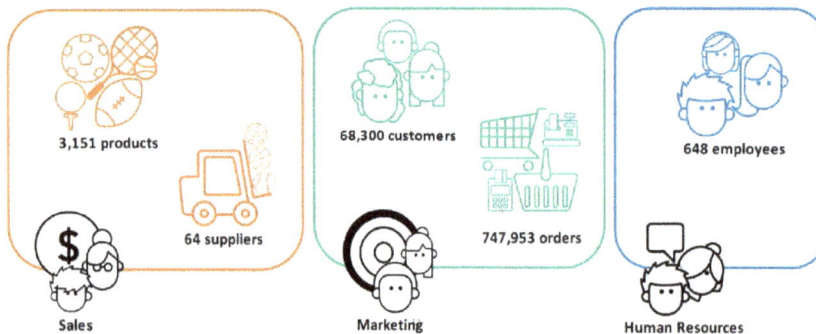

You have been hired as an analyst and report designer at Orion Star Sports & Outdoors.

3,151 products
64 suppliers
Sales

68,300 customers
747,953 orders
Marketing

648 employees
Human Resources

Before getting into the data, let's start by signing in and exploring the components of SAS Drive with a short demo.

Demo 1.1: Exploring SAS Drive

This demonstration illustrates signing in and exploring the components of SAS Drive.

1. From the browser window, sign in to SAS Viya.

   SAS Drive is displayed by default.

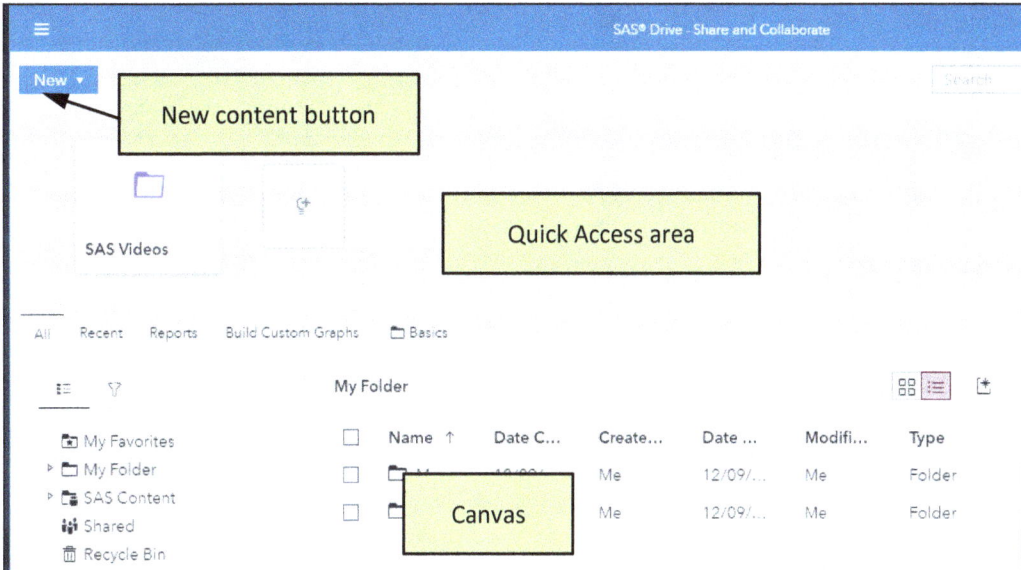

2. In the upper right corner, click ⋮ (**Menu**) and select **Manage tabs**.

3. In the Displayed tabs list, select **Projects**.

4. Click ⟪▬ (**Remove all**) to hide all the displayed tabs.

   Note: All tabs are moved except the All tab and the Recent tab.

5. In the Hidden tabs pane, double-click **Reports** and **Build Custom Graphs** to add them to the Displayed tabs pane.

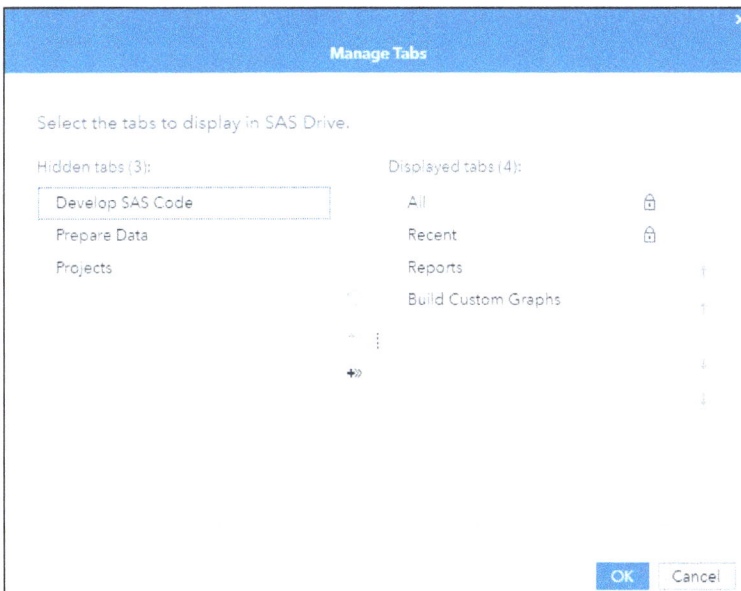

6. Click **OK**.

   SAS Drive displays the tabs that you specified.

7. View the Quick Access area.

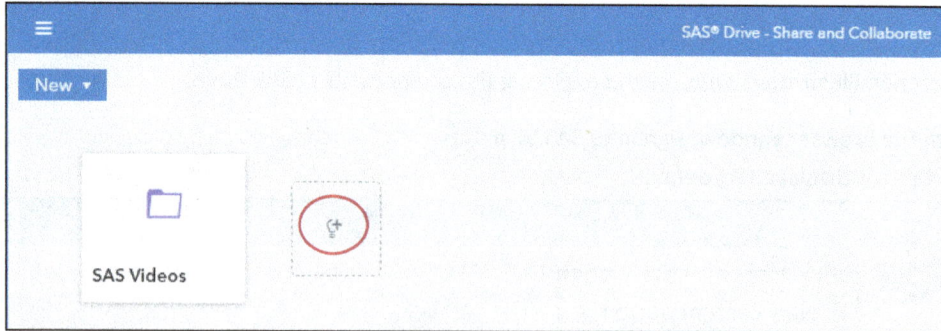

The Quick Access area is a location in SAS Drive where you can add content that you frequently access. Included in the Quick Access area is **Add recommendations**. This automatically adds recently viewed or accessed reports to the Quick Access area.

8. In the upper right corner, click the double arrow to hide the Quick Access area.

SAS Drive should resemble the following:

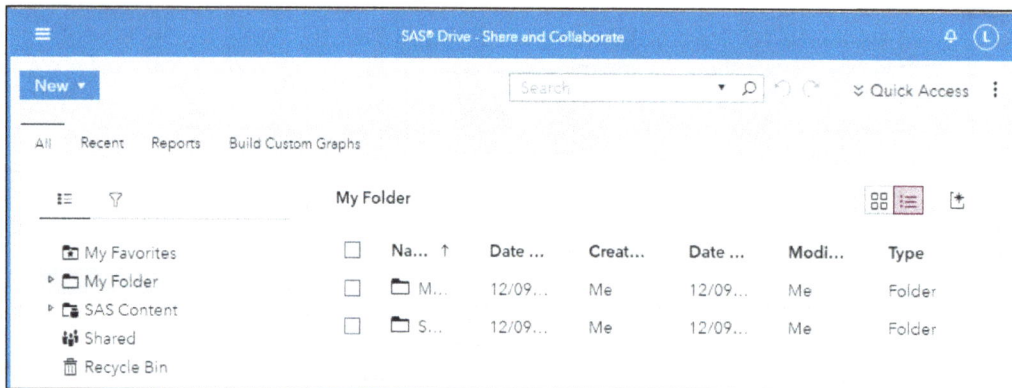

9. In the upper left corner, click (**Show list of applications**) to view the available applications.

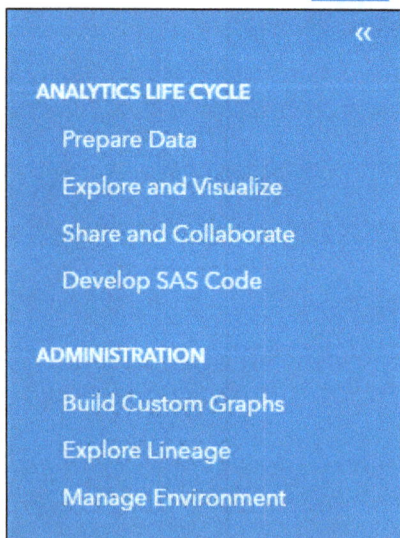

10. Click (**Hide applications menu**) to close the applications menu.

11. On the All tab, in the right corner, click (**Tile view**).

12. On the All tab, expand **SAS Content** ⇨ **Courses** ⇨ **YVA185**.

13. Select the **Basics** folder.

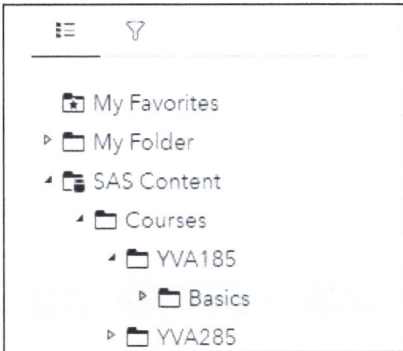

The Basics folder contains two folders and four reports.

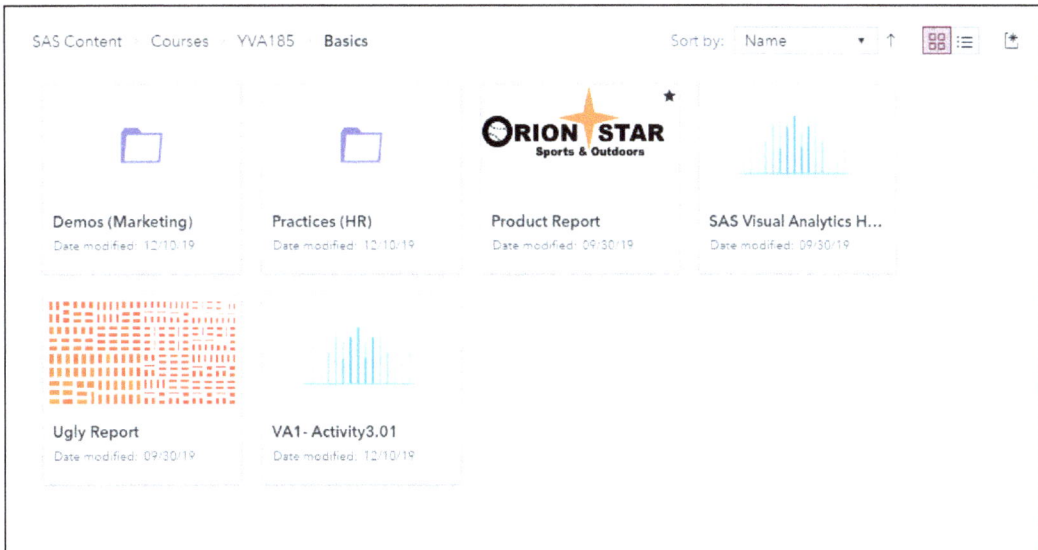

14. In the navigation pane, right-click the **Basics** folder and select **Make this a tab**.

    A new tab is added to the canvas.

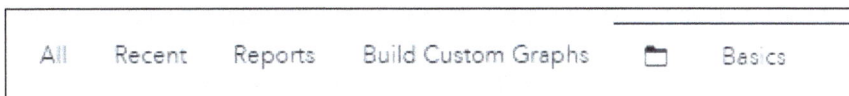

15. Right-click **Product Report** and select **Add to Favorites**.

    A message appears.

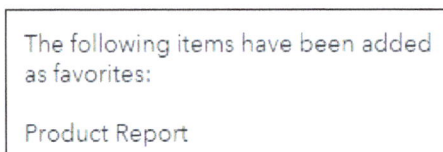

A favorites indictor (⭐) is added to the Product Report tile.

16. Click the **All** tab and select the **My Favorites** folder.

    Product Report is added to the My Favorites folder.

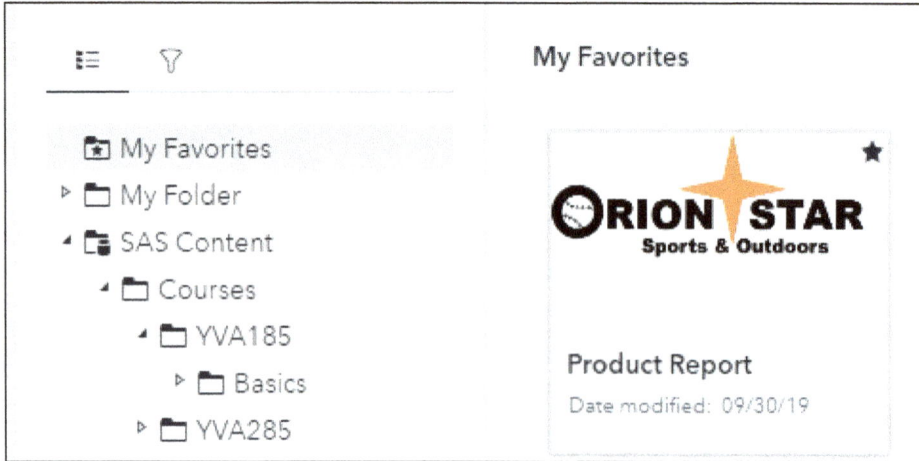

17. View settings.

18. In the upper right corner, select **

19. If necessary, in the Global section, select **General**.

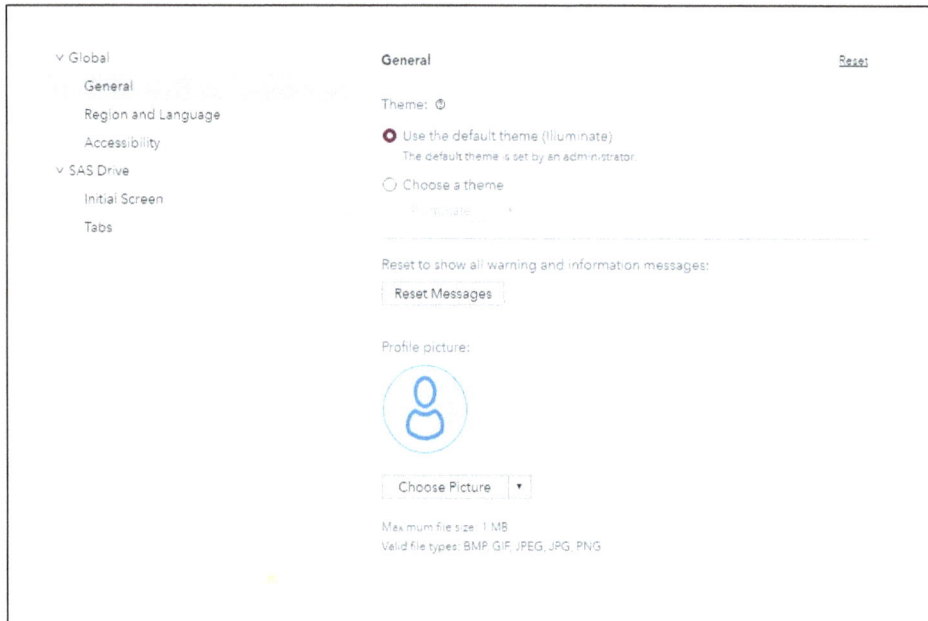

Global settings apply to all the SAS Viya applications.

20. In the SAS Drive section, select **Initial Screen**.

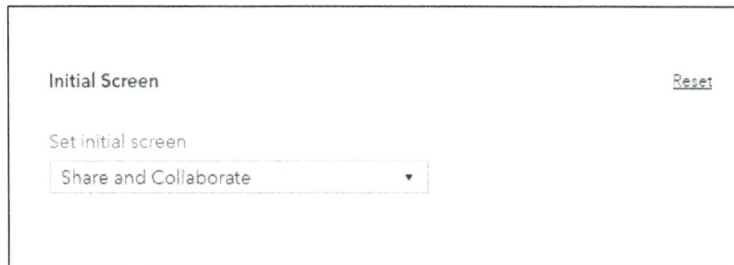

You can set the screen that appears when you sign in to SAS Viya.

21. Select **Tabs**.

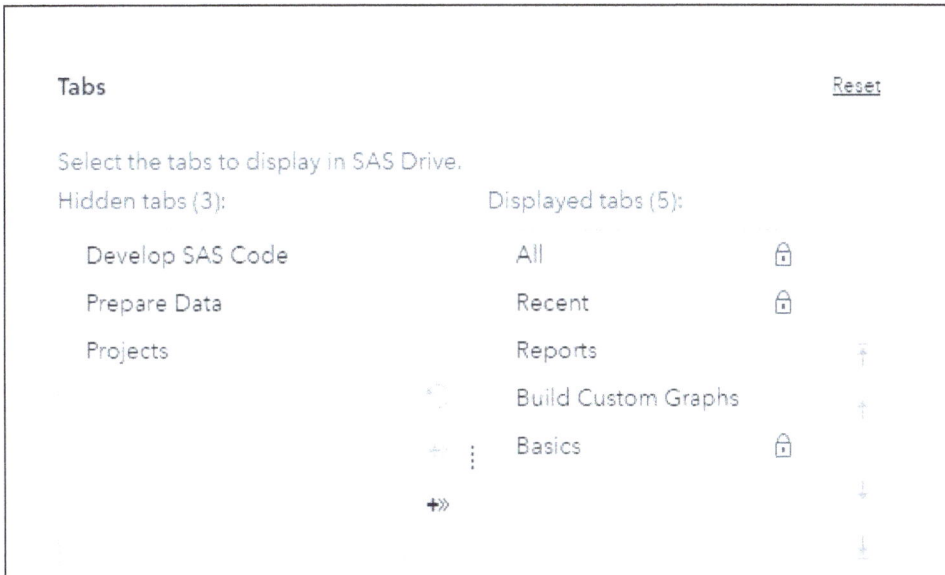

> Tabs   Reset
>
> Select the tabs to display in SAS Drive.
>
> Hidden tabs (3):   Displayed tabs (5):
>
>   Develop SAS Code   All   🔒
>
>   Prepare Data   Recent   🔒
>
>   Projects   Reports
>
>   Build Custom Graphs
>
>   ⋮   Basics   🔒
>
> +»

The Displayed tabs list reflects the changes that you made earlier using **Manage tabs** and includes the new tab created from the Basics folder.

22. Click **Close**.

End of Demonstration

1.3 Viewing SAS Visual Analytics Reports

SAS Report Viewer (the report viewer) enables users who are not report designers or consumers to view a report using a web browser. To open a report in the report viewer from SAS Drive, double-click the report. Because the report viewer is not supported on mobile devices, mobile users are redirected to SAS Visual Analytics Apps when opening a report. SAS Visual Analytics Apps (formerly called SAS Mobile BI) are free mobile apps. You can download the apps from the following locations:

- Apple App Store (supported on iPhones and iPads)
- Google Play (supported on Android devices)
- Microsoft Store (supported on PCs and tablets running Windows 10)

Using these apps, you can view and interact with SAS Visual Analytics reports, as well as share comments and observations with others. The apps support all charts and graphs that are available in SAS Visual Analytics.

You can customize the apps by using the SAS SDK.

In our example, the Product Report contains three visible pages: Report Overview, Supplier Analysis, and Product Analysis.

- The **Report Overview** page gives an overview of the report and describes the other pages of the report.
- The **Supplier Analysis** page gives details about the suppliers for Orion Star, including information about locations, the products manufactured, the quantity sold, and profit generated by each supplier.
- The **Product Analysis** page gives details about the products sold by Orion Star, including information about product categories and groups, the top 10 cities by orders and profits, and historical details.

Figure 1.6: Product Report

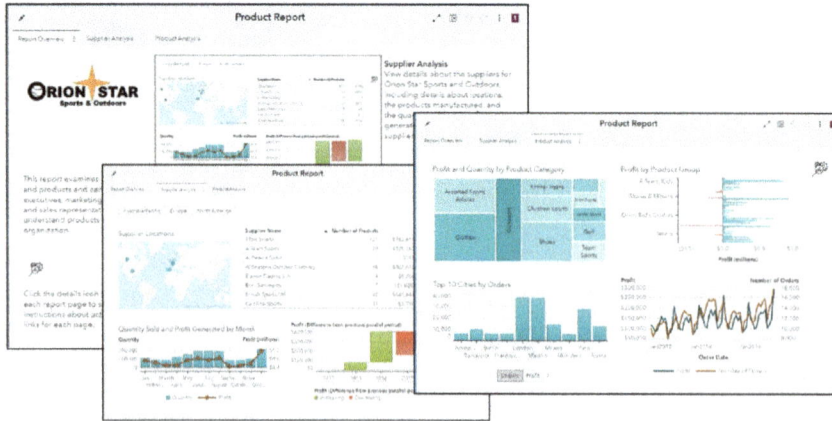

Note: Only users who have the appropriate capabilities can edit the report.

You can print or generate a link to a report or object from SAS Visual Analytics. In addition, an application administrator can distribute a report from SAS Visual Analytics.

Demo 1.2: Viewing Reports

This demonstration illustrates how to view a report in Visual Analytics.

1. From the browser window, sign in to SAS Viya.

   SAS Drive is displayed by default.

2. View and interact with the Product Report.

   a. In the Quick Access area, double-click **Product Report** to open the report.

   The Product Report opens in Visual Analytics.

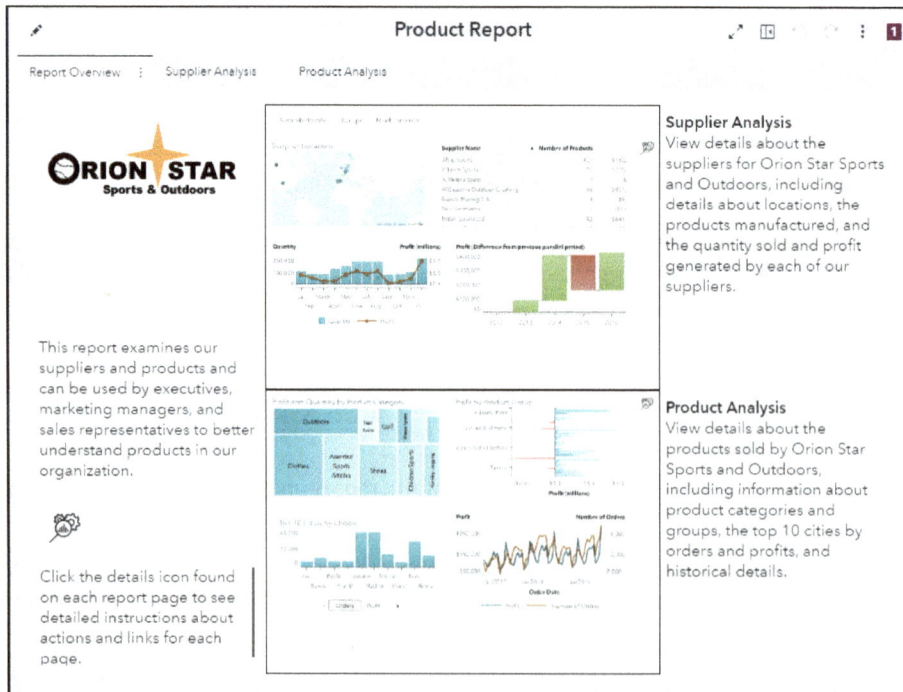

The initial section of the report is an overview section that describes the report and the pages within the report.

b. Click the image next to the Supplier Analysis information or click the **Supplier Analysis** tab at the top of the report to view the page.

   Note: A page link action is established between the images on the Report Overview page and the Supplier Analysis and Product Analysis pages, respectively.

   The Supplier Analysis page should resemble the following:

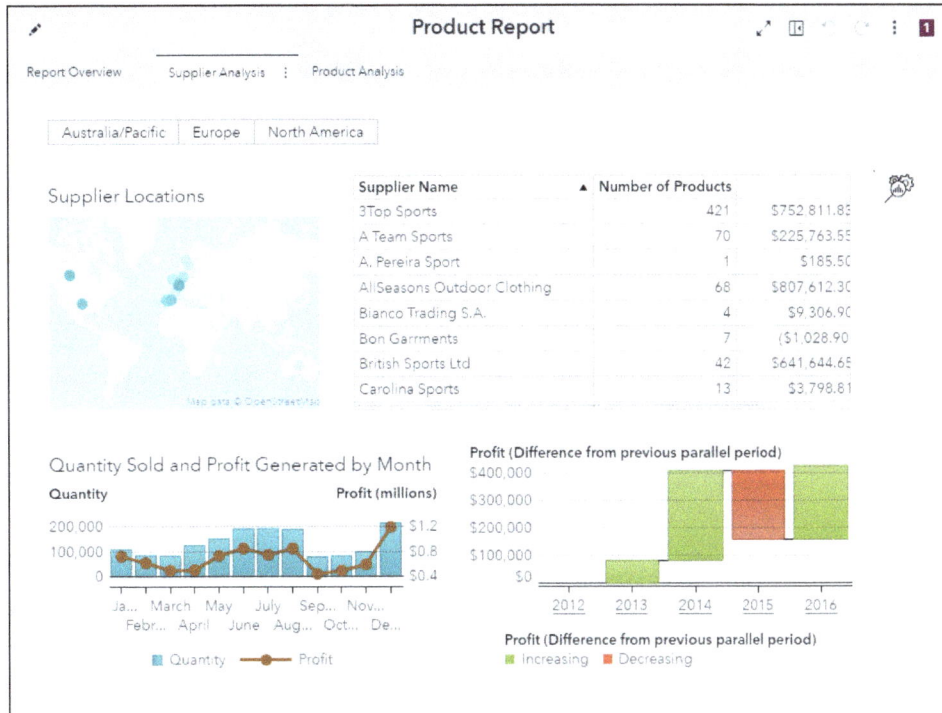

This page uses a button bar as a page prompt to filter data by continent.

The Supplier Analysis page contains several report objects and filters.

-   A geo map shows countries where suppliers for Orion Star are located. The locations are colored by the average number of products produced by suppliers in that country. Darker colors indicate a higher average number of products. Placing your cursor over a country in the geo map displays a data tip with the number of suppliers in that country and the average products produced by supplier.

-   A list table displays the names of suppliers, the number of products produced, and the total profit generated by each supplier. A gauge display rule indicates whether the profit values are below average (red), average (yellow), or above average (green).

-   A dual axis bar-line chart shows the total quantity sold and the total profit generated by month.

-   A waterfall chart displays the change in profit from the previous parallel period. This chart uses a hierarchy, so you can view information by year and by month.

c. In the upper right corner of the page, click [icon] (**Click here for more information about this page**).

   Note: The [icon] icon is an image object with a link to a hidden page. This icon is used throughout the course to link to information about the page.

A hidden page is displayed as a pop-up window. This hidden page includes information about the page, including details about the report objects, actions, and links.

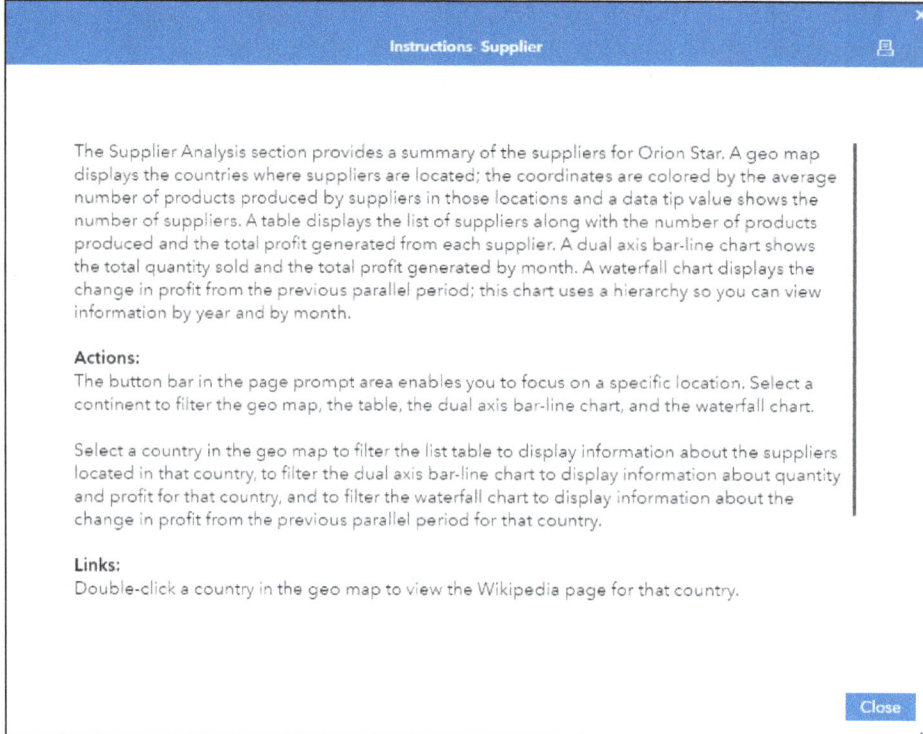

Note: You can resize this window by clicking and dragging [icon] in the lower right corner.

d. Click **Close** to close the hidden window.

3. View information about objects, and work with interactions and links.

a. Move the cursor to the upper right corner of the geo map and click [icon] (**Maximize**).

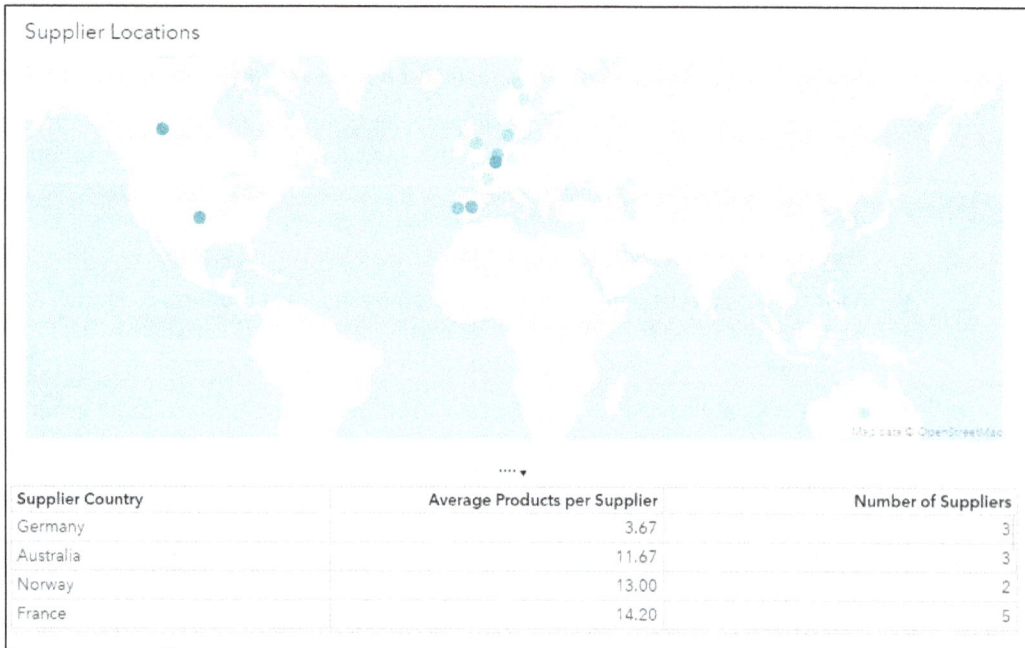

Supplier Country	Average Products per Supplier	Number of Suppliers
Germany	3.67	3
Australia	11.67	3
Norway	13.00	2
France	14.20	5

A table of detail data appears below the geo map, showing the average products produced per supplier and the number of suppliers in each country.

b. Scroll through the list and select the row for **France**.

The country is highlighted in the geo map.

Supplier Locations

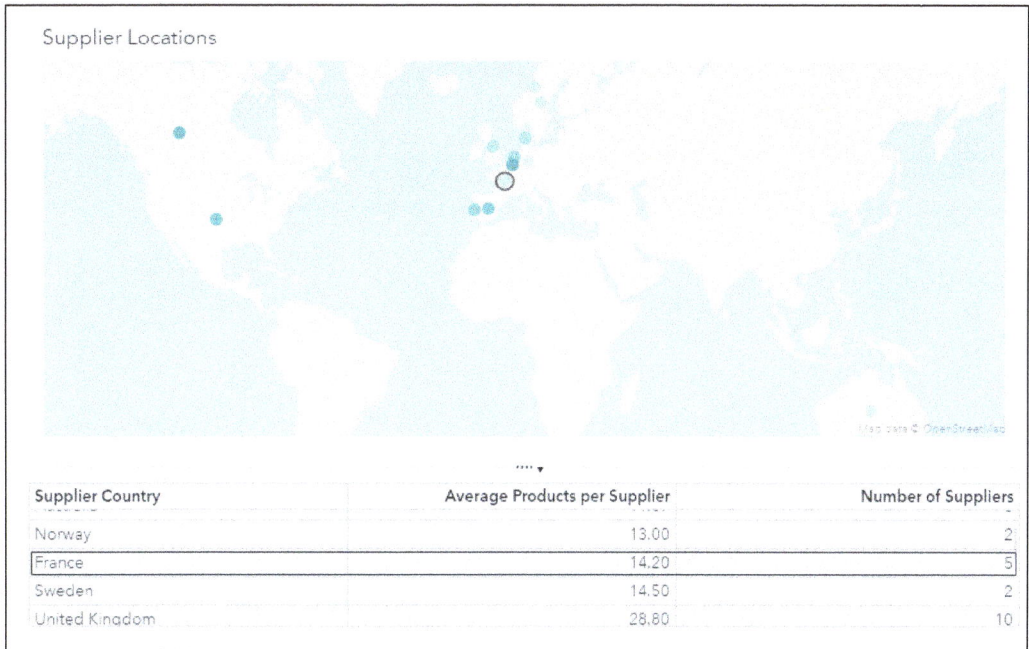

Supplier Country	Average Products per Supplier	Number of Suppliers
Norway	13.00	2
France	14.20	5
Sweden	14.50	2
United Kingdom	28.80	10

On average, each supplier in France produces about 14 products. When compared to other countries in Europe, we can see that although France has a larger number of suppliers, its production is not as diverse.

c. In the upper right corner of the geo map, click [icon] (**Restore**).

With **France** selected, the other objects in the section are updated to show information about suppliers in France.

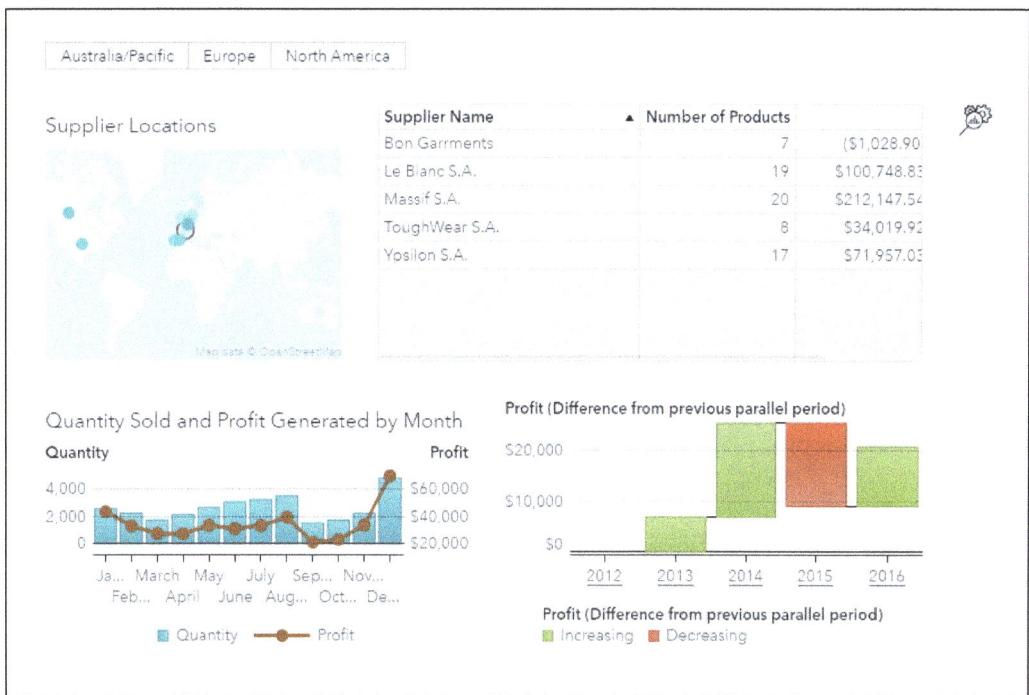

| Australia/Pacific | Europe | North America |

Supplier Locations

Supplier Name	▲ Number of Products	
Bon Garrments	7	($1,028.90
Le Blanc S.A.	19	$100,748.83
Massif S.A.	20	$212,147.54
ToughWear S.A.	8	$34,019.92
Ypsilon S.A.	17	$71,957.03

Quantity Sold and Profit Generated by Month

Profit (Difference from previous parallel period)

d. In the upper right corner, click [icon] (**Show side pane**).

The side pane appears on the right.

e. In the side pane, click **Data**.

The Data Settings pane displays the data items associated with each role for the geo map.

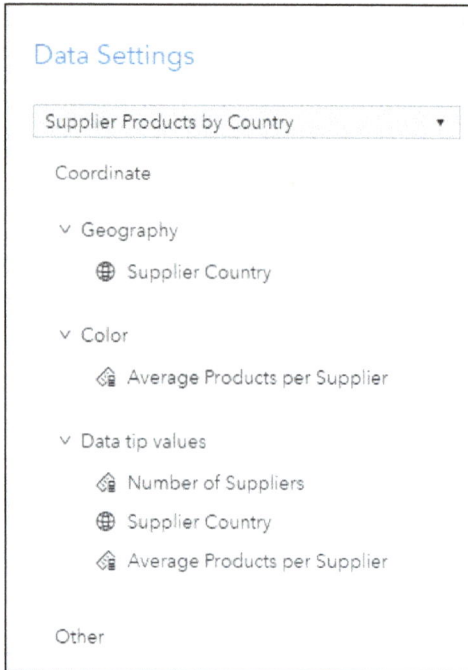

Data Settings

| Supplier Products by Country ▾ |

Coordinate

ⱽ Geography

⊕ Supplier Country

ⱽ Color

◬ Average Products per Supplier

ⱽ Data tip values

◬ Number of Suppliers

⊕ Supplier Country

◬ Average Products per Supplier

Other

Due to the Viewer Customization level set for the Product Report (**Comprehensive edits**), viewers can view, but not modify, data assignments.

f. In the side pane, click ⟫ (**Collapse**).

g. In the list table, resize the **Supplier Name** column.

Supplier Name	⇐Number of Products		⋮
Bon Garrments	7	($1,028.90)	▬
Le Blanc S.A.	19	$100,748.83	▬
Massif S.A.	20	$212,147.54	▬
ToughWear S.A.	8	$34,019.92	▬
Ypsilon S.A.	17	$71,957.03	▬

h. Select the **Profit** column and drag it to the left of **Number of Products**.

Supplier Name ▲	Profit	Number of Produc	⋮
Bon Garrments	($1,028.9⊕		7
Le Blanc S.A.	$100,748.83		19
Massif S.A.	$212,147.54		20
ToughWear S.A.	$34,019.92		8
Ypsilon S.A.	$71,957.03		17

i. In the side pane, click **Rules**.

The Display Rules pane provides details about the display rules used in the list table and enables viewers to subscribe to alerts based on those rules, if any.

j. In the side pane, click ⟫ (**Collapse**).

k. In the list table, double-click **Bon Garrments**.

A hidden window displays information about products produced by that supplier.

Because the list table and the objects in the hidden window are based on the same data source, an automatic filter is applied.

Bon Garrments produces seven products in two product lines: Clothes & Shoes and Sports. The list table displays details about each product along with total quantity sold, total profit generated, and total number of orders for each product.

l. Click the row for the **Holmes Super Break Bag**.

A linked selection action is established between the treemap and the list table. Selecting a row in the list table highlights the associated tile in the treemap, and selecting a tile in the treemap highlights the associated rows in the list table.

Enter a string to search by product name:

Enter Search Parameter...

Number of Products by Product Line

Supplier Name	Product Group	Product Name	▲	Quantity
Bon Garrments	Stockings & Socks	Double Layer Ankle Socks		300
Bon Garrments	Stockings & Socks	Fitness Slouch Socks		207
Bon Garrments	Stockings & Socks	Forrest Backpacking Socks		348
Bon Garrments	Stockings & Socks	Grizzly Hiking		344
Bon Garrments	Assorted Sports articles	Holmes Super Break Bag		370
Bon Garrments	Stockings & Socks	Maxrun 'Liner Socks		180
Bon Garrments	Stockings & Socks	Sports Training Socks		477
			Sum:	2,226 Sum

Sports

Clothes & Shoes

Close

m. In the list table, scroll to the right to view details about the product.

Group	Product Name	▲	Quantity	Profit	Number o Orders
s & Socks	Double Layer Ankle Socks		300	$420.00	188
s & Socks	Fitness Slouch Socks		207	$393.30	128
s & Socks	Forrest Backpacking Socks		348	$596.30	224
s & Socks	Grizzly Hiking		344	$516.00	232
Sports articles	Holmes Super Break Bag		370	($3,922.00)	215
s & Socks	Maxrun 'Liner Socks		180	$252.00	114
s & Socks	Sports Training Socks		477	$715.50	299
		Sum:	2,226 Sum:	($1,028.90) Total:	1,397

A majority of products produced by this supplier are profitable, except for the Holmes Super Break Bag, which generates large losses. Because this is the only product in the Assorted Sports Articles product line produced by this supplier, this might indicate high costs to break into this segment. It might be a good business decision for this supplier to specialize in the Stockings & Socks group, where they make average profits.

n. Click **Close** to close the hidden window.

o. In the list table, double-click **Massif S.A.**.

A hidden window displays information about products produced by that supplier.

p. In the **Enter a string to search by product name** field, enter **Jacket** and press the Enter key.

The list table is updated to show information about products that contain the string *Jacket*.

Supplier Name	Product Group	Product Name	Quantity	
Massif S.A.	Ski Dress	Massif Men's Monitor Bomber Jacket	304	$9,
Massif S.A.	Knitwear	Massif Men's Polar Fleece Jacket	533	$2,
Massif S.A.	Ski Dress	Massif Men's Pro Jacket	207	$15,
Massif S.A.	Ski Dress	Massif Men's Shell Jacket	195	$13,
			Sum: 1,239	Sum: $40,

Note: Parameters are used to search the list table. The parameter is updated with the input value, and the list table is filtered for product names that contain that value. The search is case sensitive.

q. Click **Close** to close the hidden window.

r. On the waterfall chart, double-click the bar for **2013**.

The waterfall chart displays information about changes in profit from the same month in 2012.

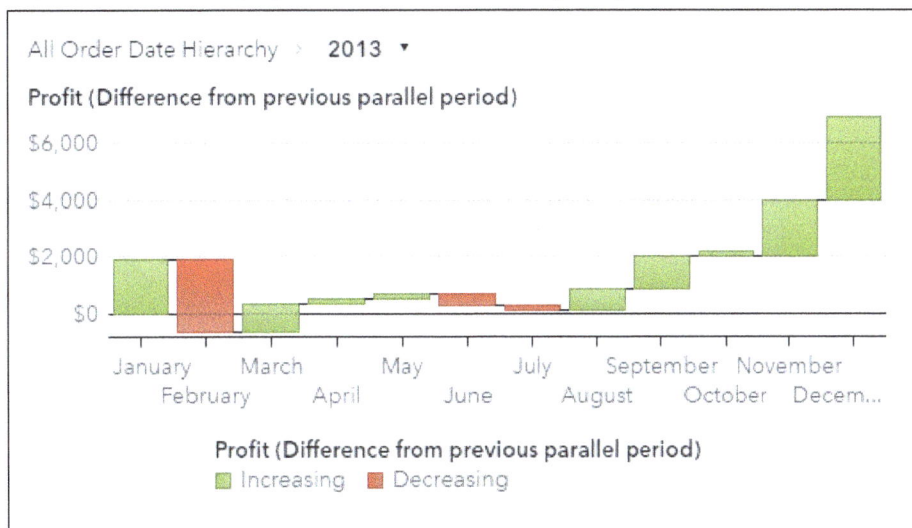

s.   Right-click the waterfall chart and select **Change Waterfall chart to** ⇨ **Crosstab**.

Order Year	▲	Profit (Difference from previous parallel period)
2012	>	.
2013	>	$6,881.95
2014	>	$18,381.09
2015	>	($16,255.64)
2016	>	$11,684.14

Due to the Viewer Customization level set for the Product Report (**Comprehensive edits**), viewers can change chart types.

4.   Investigate printing options.

a.   In the upper right corner of the report, click ⋮ (**Menu**) and select **Print**. The Print to PDF window appears.

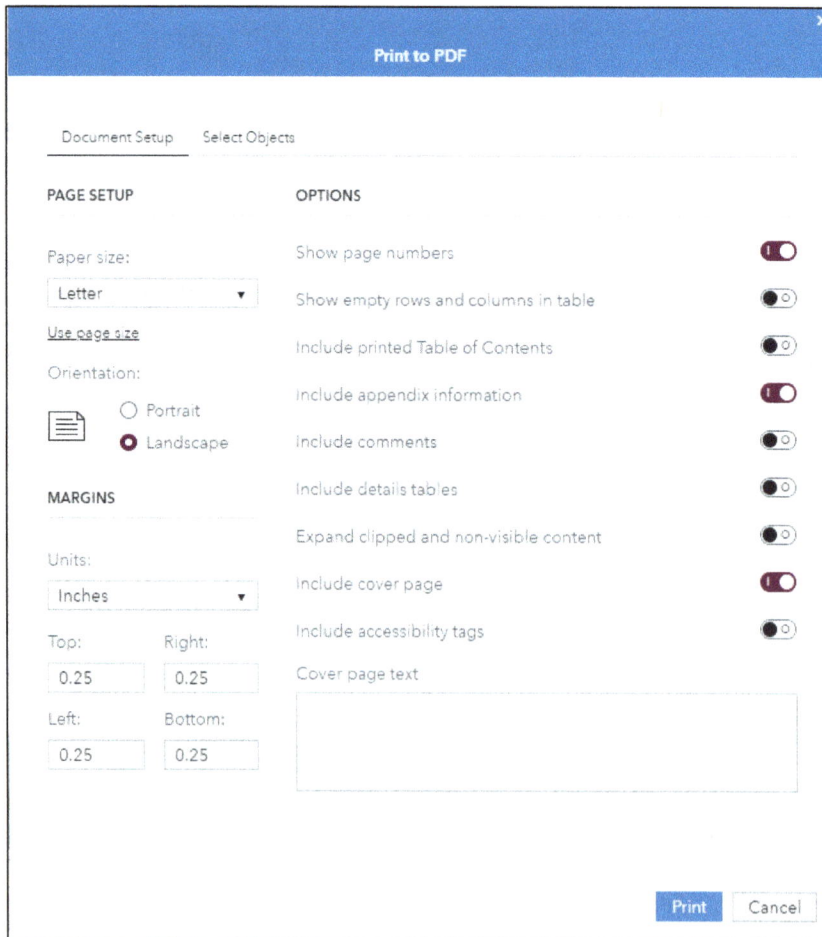

Print to PDF   ✕

Document Setup   Select Objects

PAGE SETUP   OPTIONS

Paper size: Show page numbers   ⬤▯

Letter ▾   Show empty rows and columns in table   ▯⚪

Use page size   Include printed Table of Contents   ▯⚪

Orientation: Include appendix information   ⬤▯

○ Portrait   Include comments   ▯⚪

◉ Landscape   Include details tables   ▯⚪

MARGINS   Expand clipped and non-visible content   ▯⚪

Units: Include cover page   ⬤▯

Inches ▾   Include accessibility tags   ▯⚪

Top: Right: Cover page text

0.25   0.25

Left: Bottom:

0.25   0.25

[Print]   [Cancel]

You can specify options for the PDF document, including whether a table of contents and page numbers are displayed. You also have the option of choosing which objects appear in the PDF.

    b. In the PAGE SETUP area, select **Use page size**.

        Note: The **Use page size** option lets you print a report based on the current size of your browser window.

    c. In the OPTIONS area, turn off the following options:

        Show page numbers

        Include cover page

    d. Click **Print**.

        A message appears.

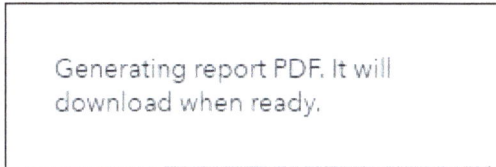

> Generating report PDF. It will download when ready.

    e. At the bottom of the window, click **Product Report on *mm-dd-yyyy*** to open the PDF.

        The report opens in a new tab in the browser.

    f. Close the tab and return to Visual Analytics.

5.   In the upper right corner of the report, click ⋮ (**Menu**) and select **Restore default report state**.

6.   Click ⋮ (**Menu**) and select **Close**.

    Note: It is a best practice to close a report when you are finished viewing it to conserve resources.

    The home pane appears, and the Product Report is listed under **Recent**.

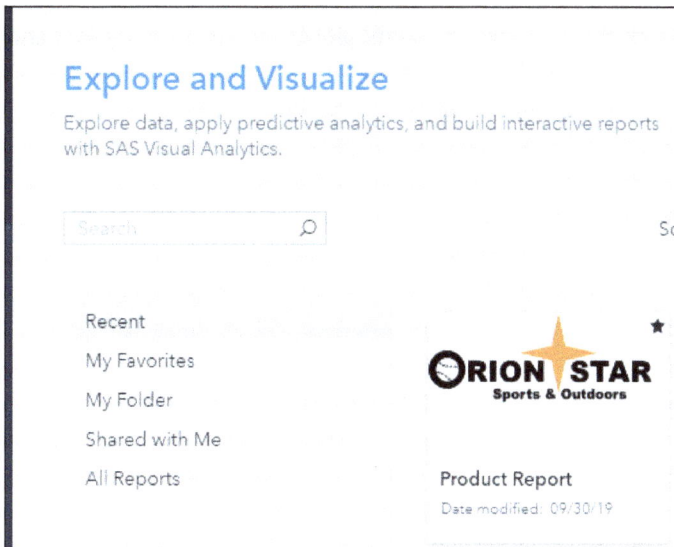

7.   Double-click **Product Report** to reopen the report.

    When you close a report that you were viewing, the viewer state is remembered. This includes the current page, any hierarchy drill-downs, selected filters, and so on. This means that the next time that you open the same report, you return to the same part of the report with all previous selections and actions in place. To prevent this, click **Menu** and select **Restore default report state** before closing the report.

End of Demonstration

Practice 1.1

1. **Viewing a Report in Visual Analytics**

a.   Open the browser and sign in to SAS Viya.

b.   Open and view the Product Report in Visual Analytics.

c.   View the Product Analysis page.

    i.   View information about the page and answer the following question:

        What links are available for the Product Analysis page?

        Answer:

    ii.   View report objects and use actions between the graphs to answer the following questions:

        Which product category has the fewest number of orders? The lowest total profit?

        Answer:

        Which product groups are included in the Indoor Sports category?

        Answer:

        How many products are in the Fitness product group?

        Answer:

        Do any fitness products generate a loss?

        Answer:

        What are the top two cities by orders for fitness products? By profit?

        Answer:

    iii.   Export the data for the dual axis time series plot filtered by *Indoor Sports* and *Fitness*.

d.   Close the report.

End of Practices

Quiz 1.1

Which of the following statements is true?

    a.   All users have the ability to create reports.

    b.   Administrators control access to reports.

    c.   Only administrators can create reports.

Chapter 2: Accessing and Investigating Data

2.1 Introduction

In this chapter, we discuss importing the data into SAS Visual Analytics, perform data transforms, and look at some of the exploration tools available.

2.2 Accessing the Data

Your data sources available in SAS Visual Analytics can be prepared by a data administrator or analyst so that you can easily create a report. Alternatively, if you have the required permissions, you are able to upload your own data sources. The data administrator role can load tables into memory. Analysts can use SAS Data Studio to prepare data, perform data transforms, and view table profiles. For information about SAS Data Studio, see *SAS Data Studio: User's Guide*.

This is known as the *Access* phase of the Visual Analytics methodology. You identify the analysis tables that will be used in Visual Analytics and load those tables into CAS. To identify the analysis tables, you need to discuss the intended uses for the tables with your analysts. Once you understand their goals, you can locate the tables and load them into CAS for immediate use. Tables can be loaded into CAS in many different ways. The method that you choose depends on your role and the types of changes that you need to make to the table before it is loaded. If no changes need to be made to the table, an administrator could import it into CAS using SAS Environment Manager.

Sometimes, administrators configure a feature called *self-service import*, which enables analysts and data scientists to import the data themselves using Visual Analytics. Self-service import makes it easy for the users to access data quickly and easily. With this feature, they can import many different types of data, including local files (like Microsoft Excel spreadsheets, text files, SAS data sets, or data from the clipboard), server data (like Teradata, Oracle, Hadoop, or Impala), or social media data (like Facebook, Google Analytics, Twitter, or YouTube).

However, if data changes need to be made, other methods can be used. For example, a data administrator can use SAS Data Studio to create a CAS table after a series of transforms have been applied. In addition, any users can write code to modify a table and load the result into CAS. This code can be SAS code written in SAS

Studio or SAS Enterprise Guide, or code written in any supported open-source languages such as Python, Lua, and Java.

The left pane of the designer is where you can access an inventory of objects, the data sets that you are working with, and even other reports. This area is where you begin when starting to build reports. In order to start developing a report, you need both data and objects. The object is the chart, table, or control that must be associated with data in order to display information.

The Data pane is used to add or import data sources. SAS Visual Analytics on SAS Viya supports a large variety of file formats in a standard configuration. Data can be imported from your local file system or from social media, or you can choose from data that is already available on the server.

Importing Local Files

Local files are files that can be accessed via the operating system of the machine on which you are running your browser to access SAS Visual Analytics. The following file formats can be imported from your local file system:

- Comma-separated values (CSV) files or TXT files.

- SAS data sets (SASHDAT or SAS7BDAT). SAS data set views (SAS7BVEW) cannot be loaded into CAS tables.

- Microsoft Excel workbook (XLSX) files and Excel 97-2003 workbook (XLS) files. You cannot import XLST, XLSB, XLSM, or other Excel file types. You cannot import pivot tables. To import native Microsoft Excel files, SAS Data Connector to PC File Formats is required.

Importing Social Media Data

With regard to social media, SAS Visual Analytics on SAS Viya supports the following data imports:

- Twitter
- Facebook
- Google Analytics
- YouTube
- Google Drive

To load data from the different social media channels, you must allow SAS Visual Analytics to access your account.

Accessing Server Files

If your data is already loaded onto the CAS server, it can be accessed via the Available data pane in the Open Data Source window. Data that is already physically stored on the CAS server, but not yet loaded into memory, can be opened using the Data Sources pane of the same window. After you click **Data Sources**, a list of available caslibs is displayed. Drilling down into one of these caslibs shows all available tables within that library. The icon beneath the table name indicates the table type.

- CAS table (a table already in the specific CAS format with the extension .sashdat)

- Physical table (a text file usually in CSV format or a SAS 9 file with the extension .sas7bdat)

- In-memory table (a table already loaded into memory on the CAS server; this file does not have any extension).

For more information about loading and preparing your data into Visual Analytics, this SAS Global Forum paper provides a good overview: https://www.sas.com/content/dam/SAS/support/en/sas-global-forum-proceedings/2018/1826-2018.pdf

Note: If you can import data sources, then the Open Data Source window includes an Import tab. For more information about importing, see Import Tab: Work with Local Files, Social Media Content, or Esri Data in *SAS Data Explorer: User's Guide*.

Table 2.1: Data Types That Can Be Imported to CAS Using Self-Service Import

Data Type	Description
Documents Directory	You can extract text and metadata from a collection of documents in a caslib and write this information to a table that can be analyzed using SAS Visual Text Analytics. For more information, see "Working with Data in CAS" in the SAS Visual Analytics: SAS Data Explorer documentation.
Local	You can import data from a Microsoft Excel spreadsheet (XLS or XLSX), a text file (CSV or TXT), or a SAS data set (SASHDAT or SAS7BDAT).
Server	After providing connection information, you can import a table into CAS from a database (Teradata, Oracle, Hadoop, and so on) or from the SAS LASR Analytic Server.
Social Media	After authenticating with Facebook, Google Analytics, Twitter, YouTube, or Google Drive and providing search criteria (where applicable), you can import data to the CAS server. **Note:** Your access to, and use of, social media data through a social media provider's public APIs are subject to the social media provider's applicable license terms, terms of use, and other usage terms and policies.
Folders	You can import text files, SAS data sets, and Microsoft Excel files that were saved to a SAS folder. For more information, see "Making Data Available to CAS" in the SAS Visual Analytics: SAS Data Explorer documentation.

2.3 Investigating the Data

After you load the data, you need to inspect or explore the data. This is known as the *Investigate* phase of the Visual Analytics methodology. Specifically, you are interested in understanding your data in broad terms. You will want to note the size (the number of rows and columns), the shape (whether the table is wide or narrow), and the contents (the number of character, datetime, and numeric variables in the table). In this phase, you also look at the detail data to determine whether there are any data changes that are needed. These data changes could be the result of data quality issues in the data or variables with a significant number of missing values. These could be signs of faulty data preparation and need to be detected (and fixed) as early as possible. The data changes can also include new data items that need to be created for the analysis. For example, if you want to analyze delivery times, but your table contains only delivery dates and order dates, you need to calculate the number of days for delivery.

All data sources contain data items, which can refer to calculations or columns in physical data (tables). Reports can include query results from more than one data source. Each data source that is available in SAS Visual Analytics includes one or more data items that you can use in reports. For example, a data source named **Order Information** might include standard data items such as **Order ID**, **Product ID**, **Unit Cost**, **Order**

Date, and **Order Amount**. You decide which data items to use. You can select all of the data items in the data source or a subset of the data items. Most tasks related to data sources and data items are initiated from the Data pane. For more information, see About the Data Pane.

Data items or variables are classified into types such as category, measure, or hierarchy. In Visual Analytics, character and datetime data items are treated as *categories*—that is, data items whose distinct values can be used to group and aggregate measures. In the Data pane, distinct counts are displayed for each category data item. Numeric data items are treated as *measures*—that is, data items whose values can be used in computations.

Figure 2.1: Data Types in Visual Analytics

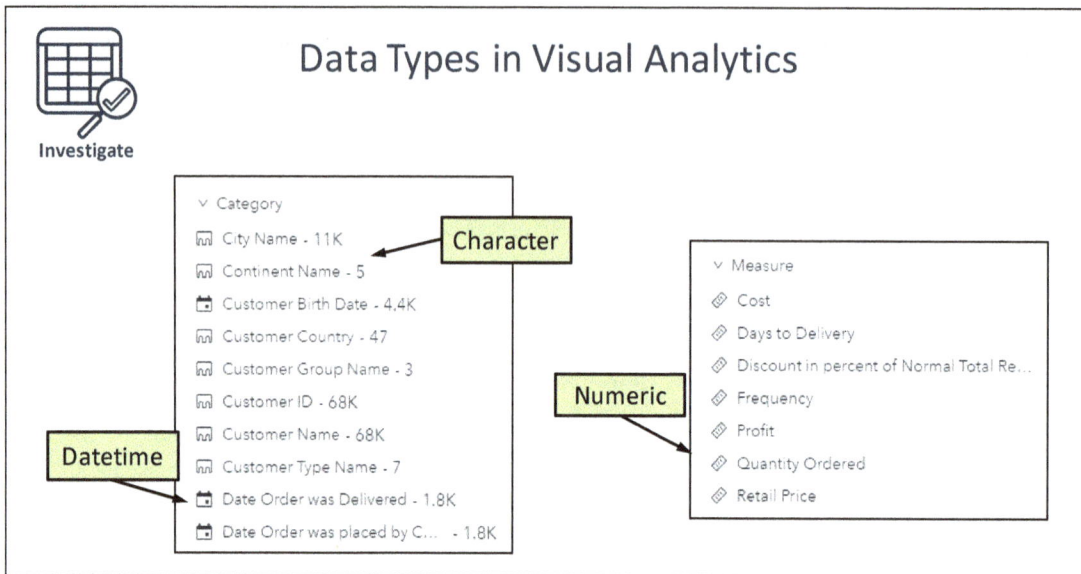

In the Data pane, an icon next to each data item indicates the type of that item. Table 2.2 shows the data items that are available.

Table 2.2: Data Items

Item		Description
Category	ᵔᵕ	A data item whose distinct values are used to group and aggregate measures. There are five types of categories: alphanumeric, date, datetime, time, and numeric.
Date and Time	📅	A category data item whose distinct values are used to group and aggregate measures. There are three types of date categories: date, datetime, and time.
Custom Category	ᵔᵕ	A data item that can be created based on either a category or numeric data item. A custom category is always a category data item with alphanumeric values.
Calculated (category)	ᵔᵕ	A data item that is calculated from existing data items using an expression and returns an alphanumeric value.

Item		Description
Calculated (datetime)		A data item that is calculated from existing data items using an expression and returns a datetime value. Calculated dates and times are treated as categories with distinct values being governed by the chosen date or time format.
Geography		A category data item whose values are mapped to geographical locations or regions. These data items can be used to show data on a geographic map.
Hierarchy		A data item with a predefined arrangement of category data items, typically whose values are arranged with more general information at the top and more specific information at the bottom. The first level of the hierarchy is known as the *root* level.
Geographic Hierarchy		A hierarchy whose members are all geographic data items.
Interaction Effect		A user-created data role that can be used when there is a nonadditive relationship between two variables (the effect of one variable on a model changes as another variable changes). SAS Visual Statistics must be licensed for you to create and use an interaction effect.
Measure		A data item whose values can be used in computations. These values are numeric. By default, almost all measures have a default aggregation of Sum, but the aggregation can be modified.
Calculated (measure)		A data item that is calculated from existing data items using an expression and returns a numeric value. Numeric data items are treated as measures (with an aggregation type of Sum), or they can be changed to category data items.
Frequency		A measure data item whose value represents the number of observations in the selected data source. This data item is automatically added to the Data pane under the Measure group. You cannot change the classification for this data item. This data item is automatically assigned to some report objects when no measure is assigned.
Frequency Percent		A measure data item whose value represents the percentage of observations in the selected data source. This data item is automatically added to the Data pane under the Aggregated Measure group. You cannot change the classification for this data item.
Aggregated Measure or Time Period Calculation		A data item that represents special predefined operations, like distinct count, percentage of totals, percentage of subtotals, or frequency percent. Users can also create their own aggregated measure calculations. Aggregated measures cannot be used in all report objects, filters, controls, spark lines, or time series graphs. Some aggregated measures cannot be used in a detail rank. Percentage of subtotal items can be used only in a crosstab.

Item		Description
Parameter	x	A variable whose values can be changed and that can be referenced by other objects. You can use parameters in calculations, display rules, filters, and ranks.
Spline Effect		A spline function is a piecewise polynomial function in which the individual polynomials have the same degree and connect smoothly at certain points. Spline functions are used to fit smooth curves to a wide variety of data. SAS Visual Statistics must be licensed to create and use a spline effect.

A custom category is a data type that can be created based on either a category or numeric data item. A custom category is always a category data item with alphanumeric values. For example, in our Orion Star Sports & Outdoor data source,

Profit is calculated as **Retail Price (Total Revenue) – Cost (Unit Cost) * Quantity Ordered**

Days to Delivery is calculated as **Date Order was Delivered – Date Order** (that is, the date on which the order was placed by the customer)

Customer Age is calculated as (**Today's Date – Customer Birth Date**)/365.25.

As part of the Investigate phase, you need to determine the contents of the analysis table (that is, the number of character, datetime, and numeric variables in the table). Remember, in Visual Analytics, character and datetime data items are treated as categories. These are data items whose distinct values can be used to group and aggregate measures. In Visual Analytics, distinct counts are displayed for each category data item. This is useful for understanding your data and pinpointing any values that might need to be addressed. For example, if you have a **Gender** data item with six distinct values, your data might need to be cleaned before it can be used for analysis. Numeric data items, however, are treated as measures. These are data items whose values can be used in computations. In Visual Analytics, you can see descriptive statistics for measures, including the minimum, maximum, standard deviation, skewness, and kurtosis. These descriptive statistics are useful for understanding the range of your measures and can be helpful in building models.

2.4 Objects

Objects is the term used for the different charts, tables, and graphs available in Visual Analytics. The *Objects tab* is where you can drag the various objects to the body of a report. This tab is broken into the categories of objects that include tables, graphs, controls, containers, and others. All the objects can go into the body of the canvas, but only control objects can go into the prompt areas. We discuss objects in more detail in Chapter 4, but for now, we will look at tables and automatic charts.

Tables and automatic charts are useful for another part of the Investigate phase: viewing your data to better understand the size, structure, and data values. There are many report objects available for viewing and understanding your data, but perhaps the easiest object to use is the list table. We discuss tables in more detail below.

Tables

There are two types of tables in Visual Analytics: list tables and crosstabs.

A list table can be used to view summary or detail data. This is especially useful when you are viewing the data for the first time. It gives you an idea about the values for each column and the range of values that you can expect to see. Viewing data in a list table is an easy way to spot obvious data quality issues.

Another great object for learning about your data is the crosstab. This object is especially useful for viewing distinct values for category data items and summary information for your measures. It can also be helpful in spotting data quality issues and for gaining a broader insight into your data. When you use a crosstab, it is recommended that lower cardinality categories (that is, categories with few distinct values) be placed in the Columns role and higher cardinality categories (that is, categories with many distinct values) be placed in the Rows role. This enables users to quickly and easily read the table without too much scrolling.

Table 2.3 Using List Tables and Crosstabs

List table	By default, the list table contains aggregated data with one row for each distinct combination of category values. If the Detail data option has been selected, then every row of the data source is displayed. **Note:** By default, the list table is sorted in ascending order by the first column. **Note:** To change the sorting, click the heading for the column on which you want to sort. An arrow appears in the column heading to indicate the sorting. If the arrow points up, the sort is ascending. If the arrow points down, the sort is descending. **Note:** To sort on multiple columns, hold down the Ctrl key and click the columns to sort by, in order. **Note:** If detailed data is displayed in the list table, it cannot be the source of an action or link.
Crosstab	Each cell of the crosstab contains the aggregated measure values for a specific intersection of category values. You should consider placing lower cardinality (fewer distinct values) categories in the Columns role and higher cardinality (more distinct values) categories in the Rows role.

Figure 2.2: Tables

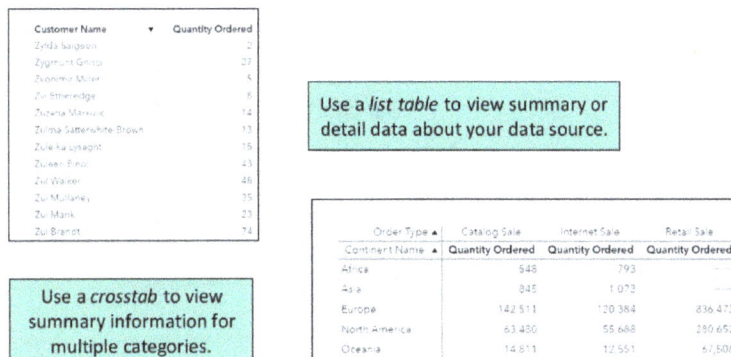

Use a *list table* to view summary or detail data about your data source.

Use a *crosstab* to view summary information for multiple categories.

Automatic Chart

You can use an automatic chart to get a quick view of your data. Depending on the number of measures and categories, Visual Analytics chooses the best chart to represent the data automatically.

Figure 2.3: Automatic Chart

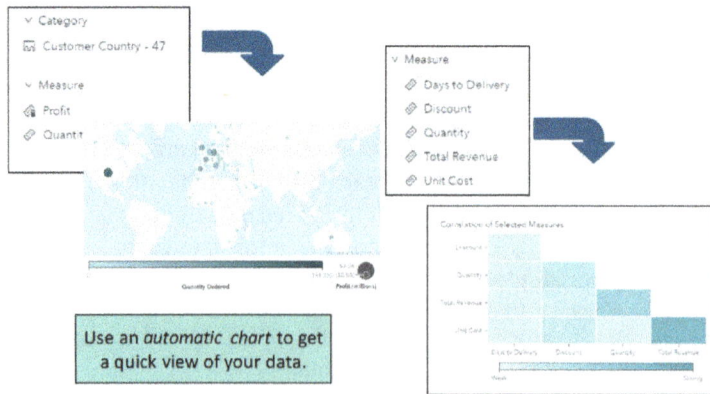

Use an *automatic chart* to get a quick view of your data.

The automatic chart is a special type of report object that selects the chart type based on the data that is assigned to it. For example, if you assign a Geography data item and two measures to the automatic chart, you get a geo map where the bubble placement indicates the geographic location, the size of the bubble represents one measure, and the color of the bubble represents the other measure. Conversely, if you were to assign five measures to the automatic chart, you get a correlation matrix where the color of the cells indicates the linear relationship between those measures. This is a great chart type to use to compare data items when you are not sure of the best way to do so.

Table 2.4: Automatic Chart Assignments

Data Items	Chart Type
One measure	Histogram
One category and any number of measures	Bar chart
One datetime category and any number of measures	Time series plot
One date or datetime category and one or more categories	List table
One geography and up to two measures	Geo map
One geography and three or more measures	Bar chart
One hierarchy and any number of measures	Bar chart
One hierarchy, one or more categories, and any number of other data items	Crosstab
Two or more hierarchies and any number of other data items	Crosstab
Two or more categories and any number of measures	List table
Two or three measures	Scatter plot or heat map*

Data Items	Chart Type
Four or more measures	Scatter plot matrix or correlation matrix*

* The actual chart type depends on the cardinality of the data.

Suggested objects are generated in the following ways:

- **Correlated measures** – A correlation query runs against the data source. The suggested object has the lowest cardinality data item and the two most correlated measures. This can generate a butterfly chart, a dual axis bar chart, or a dual axis bar-line chart.

- **Lowest cardinality** – The lowest cardinality data item, a category with at least six distinct values, in the data source is used to create the suggested object using frequency. This can generate a bar chart, a dot plot, a line chart or needle plot, a pie chart, a treemap, or a word cloud.

- **Custom data items** – Custom data items are detected in the following order: hierarchies, custom categories, calculated items. Suggested objects are generated for each custom data item. The generated objects are the same as those listed for lowest cardinality.

- **Date data items** – If the data source contains a date or time data item, a suggested object (typically a time series plot) is generated using a random measure.

- **Single measures** – A histogram or key value object is generated for a single measure.

Note: The Suggestions pane is not available if the **Bypass retrieving cardinality values for the Data pane** or **Bypass retrieving correlation values for the Data pane** settings are selected.

Demo 2.1: Accessing and Investigating Data

This demonstration illustrates how to access data in Visual Analytics through self-service import and how to investigate data for the business scenario.

1. From the browser window, sign in to SAS Viya.

2. In the upper left corner, click ☰ (**Show list of applications**) and select **Explore and Visualize**. SAS Visual Analytics appears.

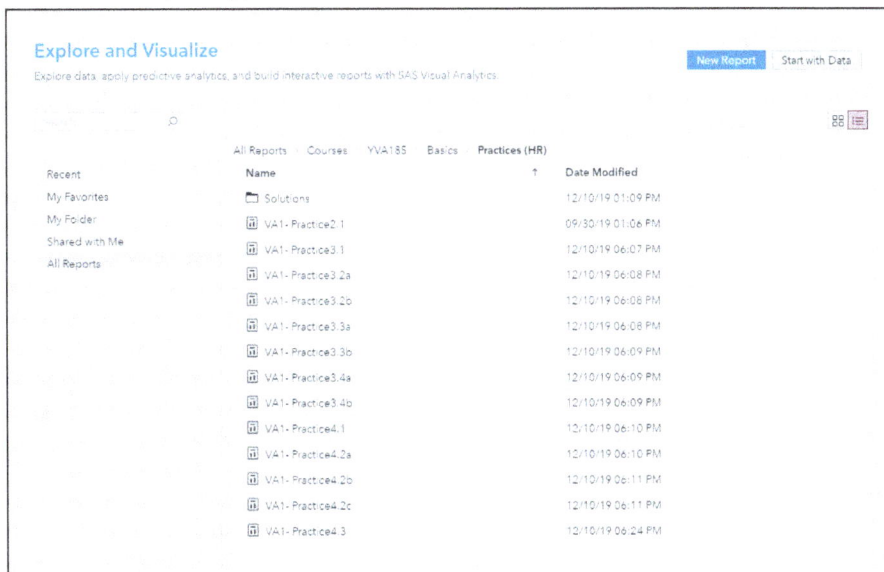

3. Click **All Reports**.

   a. Navigate to **Courses/YVA185/Basics/Demos(Marketing)**.

   b. Double-click the **VA1- Demo2.1** report to open it.

   c. Verify that you are editing the report.

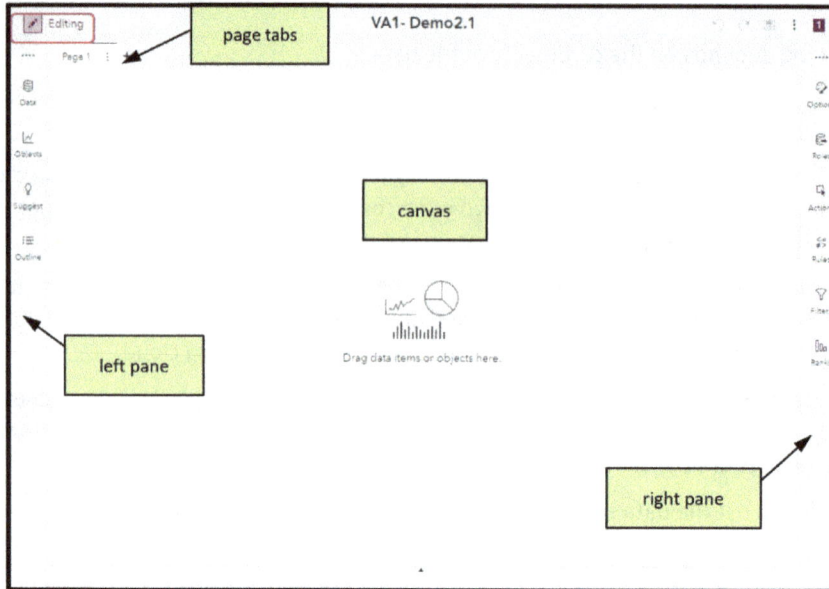

The left pane contains the following icons:

Data	The Data pane enables you to work with data sources, create new data items (hierarchy, calculated item, aggregated measure, geography, parameter), add a data source filter, and view and modify properties for data items.
Objects	The Objects pane provides a list of tables, graphs, controls, analytics, containers, and content objects that can be included in the report. If your site licenses SAS Visual Statistics and SAS Visual Data Mining and Machine Learning, additional objects are available.
Suggest	The Suggestions pane provides a list of suggested objects to help you analyze your data.
Outline	The Outline pane enables you to view and work with pages and objects in your report.

The right pane contains the following icons:

Options	The Options pane lists the options and styles available for the currently selected report, page, or object.
Roles	The Roles pane enables you to add or modify role assignments for the currently selected object.
Actions	The Actions pane enables you to create links, filter actions, and link selection actions between objects.
Rules	The Rules pane enables you to view, add, or modify display rules (expression, color-mapped values, and gauge) for the selected object.
Filters	The Filters pane enables you to view, add, or modify filters for the selected object.
Ranks	The Ranks pane enables you to view, add, or modify rankings for the selected object.

4. Check the general settings for SAS Visual Analytics.

    a. In the upper right corner, select ***<user name>*** ⇨ **Settings**.
        The Settings window appears.

    b. Under **SAS Visual Analytics**, select **General**.

    c. Scroll down to **Default titles for new objects**.

    Default titles for new objects:

    Tables:

    | No title ▾ |

    Graphs:

    | Automatic title ▾ |

    Controls:

    | No title ▾ |

    Content:

    | No title ▾ |

    Analytics:

    | No title ▾ |

    d. Click ⑦ (**More information about this option**).

    The automatic title option might not apply to some objects, such as key value.

    These options enable you to add automatic titles, customize titles, or suppress titles for specific objects in your report. Notice that automatic titles are added to all graph objects.

    e. Click **Close** to close the Settings window.

5. View the data for the report.

    a. In the left pane, click **Data**.

    b. View the list of data items in the Category group.

    ∨ Category

    ⊞ City Name - 11K

    ⊞ Continent Name - 5

    ▦ Customer Birth Date - 4.4K

    ⊞ Customer Country - 47

    ⊞ Customer Group Name - 3

    ⊞ Customer Name - 68K

    ⊞ Customer Type Name - 7

    ▦ Date Order was Delivered - 1.8K

    ▦ Date Order was placed by C... - 1.8K

    ⊞ Name of Street - 21K

    ⊞ Order Type - 3

    ⊞ Postal code - 19K

    ⊞ State Name - 272

Character variables and numeric variables with a date format associated with them appear as categories in Visual Analytics. Distinct counts appear next to each category.

c.   Scroll down in the Data pane to view the list of data items in the Measure group.

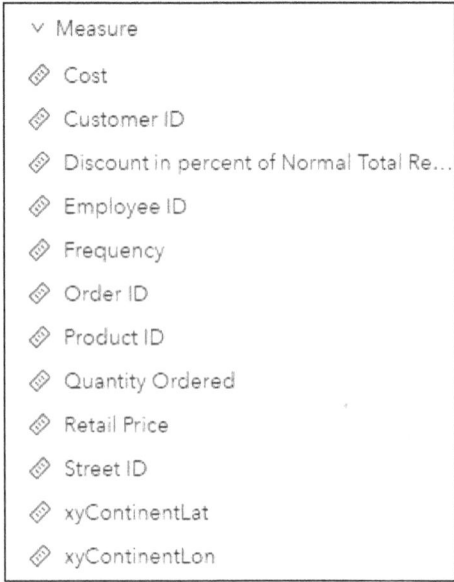

> ∨ Measure
> ◈ Cost
> ◈ Customer ID
> ◈ Discount in percent of Normal Total Re...
> ◈ Employee ID
> ◈ Frequency
> ◈ Order ID
> ◈ Product ID
> ◈ Quantity Ordered
> ◈ Retail Price
> ◈ Street ID
> ◈ xyContinentLat
> ◈ xyContinentLon

Numeric variables appear as measures in Visual Analytics. By default, all measures have an aggregation of Sum.

6.   Use a list table to view the imported table.

a.   In the left pane, click **Objects**.

b.   Drag the **List table** object, from the Tables group, to the canvas.

c.   In the right pane, click **Roles**.

d.   For the **Columns** role, click **Add**.

e.   Select all data items *except* **Frequency** and **Frequency Percent**.

   Note: To make multiple consecutive selections, click the first column, hold down the Shift key, and click the last column.

f.   Click **OK**.

The list table should resemble the following:

City Name ▲	Continent Name	Customer Birth Date	Customer Country	Customer Group Name	Customer Name	Cust
	Europe	08May1953	United Kingdom	Orion Club Gold members	Natalie Pedder	Orio
	Europe	08May1953	United Kingdom	Orion Club Gold members	Natalie Pedder	Orio
	Africa	07Apr1953	South Africa	Orion Club members	Johann Adams	Orio
	Europe	07Oct1938	United Kingdom	Orion Club members	James Dunkin	Orio
	Europe	12Jan1958	Austria	Orion Club members	Richard Finster	Orio
	Africa	07Apr1953	South Africa	Orion Club members	Johann Adams	Orio
	Europe	08May1953	United Kingdom	Orion Club Gold members	Natalie Pedder	Orio
	Europe	08May1953	United Kingdom	Orion Club Gold members	Natalie Pedder	Orio
	Europe	08May1953	United Kingdom	Orion Club Gold members	Natalie Pedder	Orio
	Europe	08May1953	United Kingdom	Orion Club Gold members	Natalie Pedder	Orio
	Europe	08May1953	United Kingdom	Orion Club Gold members	Natalie Pedder	Orio
	Europe	07Oct1938	United Kingdom	Orion Club members	James Dunkin	Orio
	Europe	08May1953	United Kingdom	Orion Club Gold members	Natalie Pedder	Orio
	Europe	07Oct1938	United Kingdom	Orion Club members	James Dunkin	Orio
	Europe	07Oct1938	United Kingdom	Orion Club members	James Dunkin	Orio
	Europe	08May1953	United Kingdom	Orion Club Gold members	Natalie Pedder	Orio
	Europe	12Jan1958	Austria	Orion Club members	Richard Finster	Orio
	Europe	08May1953	United Kingdom	Orion Club Gold members	Natalie Pedder	Orio
	Africa	07Apr1953	South Africa	Orion Club members	Johann Adams	Orio
	Europe	04Dec1990	Ireland	Orion Club Gold members	Flor Donnolly	Orio
	Europe	12Jan1958	Austria	Orion Club members	Richard Finster	Orio
	Europe	08May1953	United Kingdom	Orion Club Gold members	Natalie Pedder	Orio

g. Scroll through the columns to view the data.

The Marketing team has asked for customer data to analyze profits for loyalty club members and non-members for specific age groups.

The Shipping team has requested information about delivery times.

Some data items (**Profit**, **Age Group**, **Loyalty Member**, and **Days to Delivery**) are not in the table but are needed for the analysis. The table below shows the existing data items that can be used to create the new data items.

New Data Item	Contributing Data Items
Profit	**Cost** (unit cost), **Quantity Ordered**, **Retail Price** (total revenue)
Age Group	**Customer Birth Date**
Loyalty Member	**Customer ID** (If **Customer ID** has *99* at the end, then **Loyalty Member=Yes**. If **Customer ID** has *00* at the end, then **Loyalty Member=No**.)
Days to Delivery	**Date Order was Delivered**, **Date Order was placed by Customer**

7. In the upper left corner next to Page 1, click ➕ (**New page**).

8. Use a crosstab to view distinct values for **Order Type**.

    a. In the left pane, click **Objects**.

    b. Drag the **Crosstab** object, from the Tables group, to the canvas.

    c. If necessary, in the right pane, click **Roles**.

    d. For the **Rows** role, select **Add** ⇨ **Order Type**.

    e. Click **OK**.

    The crosstab should resemble the following:

Order Type ▲	Frequency
Catalog Sale	127,129
Internet Sale	108,570
Retail Sale	715,970

    Order Type contains the method in which the order was placed: catalog, internet, or retail.

9. Use the automatic chart to view quantity ordered by customer.

    a. In the left pane, click **Data**.

    b. Select the following data items in the Measures group (in the order specified):

    Customer ID

    Quantity Ordered

    c. Drag the selected items to the right of the crosstab.

Order Type ▲	Frequency		
Catalog Sale	127,129		
Internet Sale	108,570		
Retail Sale	715,970		➕ Auto chart

The automatic chart should resemble the following:

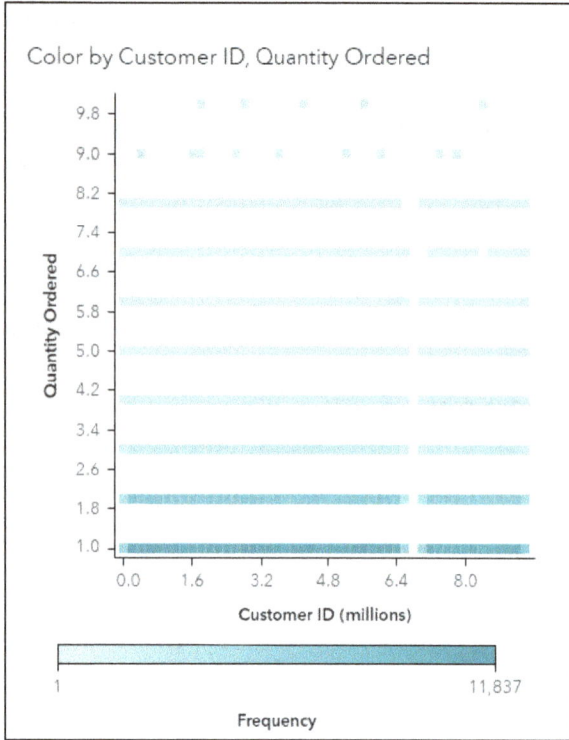

In Visual Analytics, all ID data items are classified as measures by default. An automatic chart of **Customer ID** and **Quantity Ordered** (two measures) yields a heat map that displays the relationship between the data items.

An automatic title is added to the chart by default.

10. View descriptive information for the measure data items.

    a.   In the left pane, click **Data**.

    b.   Click ▦ (**Actions**) and select **View measure details**.

    The Measure Details window displays descriptive statistics for each measure.

Name	Minimum	Maximum	Average	Sum
Cost	0.40	1,583.60	77.76	73,997,879.26
Customer ID	100.00	9,425,499.00	4,544,126.80	4,324,504,609,920.00
Discount in percent of Normal Total Retail Price	0.30	0.60	0.38	3,503.90
Employee ID	120,121.00	99,999,999.00	24,857,697.64	23,656,300,254,058.00

Note: Customer ID, Employee ID, Order ID, and **Product ID** are numeric values and are classified as measures by default. They should be classified as categories because they should not be used in calculations. The results of summing or averaging these data items returns meaningless information.

c. With **Cost** selected, view the More information area.

∨ More information	
Standard Deviation:	85.28
Standard Error:	0.09
Variance:	7,272.08
Distinct Count:	1,883
Number Missing:	0
Total Observations:	951,669
Skewness:	3.7038
Kurtosis:	28.7836
Coefficient of Variation:	109.6721
Uncorrected Sum of Squares:	12,674,377,403.50
Corrected Sum of Squares:	6,920,605,729.76
T-statistic (for Average=0):	889.5021
P-value (for T-statistic):	<0.0001

Note: The number of rows (total observations) in the **CUSTOMERS** table appears in this list along with additional descriptive statistics for **Cost**.

d. View the graph on the right.

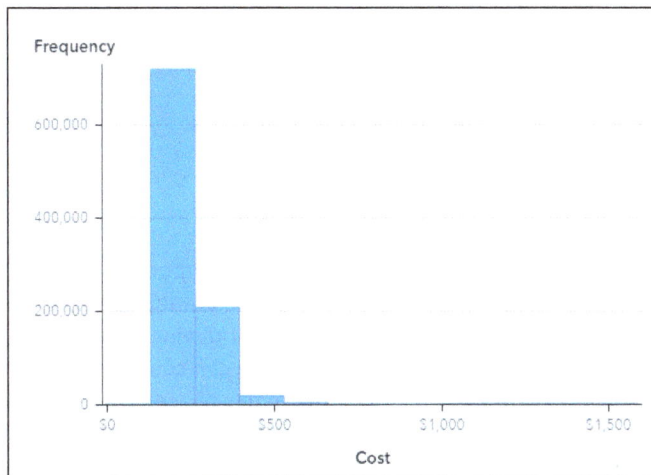

Note: The histogram displays the distribution of the **Cost** values.

e. Click **Close** to close the Measure Details window.

11. Save the report.

End of Demonstration

Practice 2.1

1. Accessing and Investigating Data
   a. Open the browser and sign in to SAS Viya.
   b. Access SAS Visual Analytics.
   c. Open the **VA1- Practice2.1** report in the **Courses/YVA185/Basics/Practices (HR)** folder.

    d.   View the Data pane and answer the following questions:

        How many unique values does **Company** have? **Job Title**?

        Answer:

        What is the type (or classification) of **Employee ID**?

        Answer:

    e.   View the list table of all data items on Page 1 and answer the following questions:

        What is the case of **Employee Country**?

        Answer:

        Which employee represents sales over the internet or through the catalog?

        Answer:

        Which data item can be used to determine whether an employee is active (currently employed) or retired (formerly employed)?

        Answer:

    f.   View the crosstab of **Department** and **Job Title** on Page 2 and answer the following question:

        Which department contains the missing job title?

        Answer:

    g.   Create an auto chart of **Company** (on the right side of the crosstab) and answer the following questions:

        What is the largest company, based on the number of employees? The smallest?

        Answer:

    h.   View the measure details (from the Data pane) and answer the following questions:

        What is the minimum total profit generated by an employee? The maximum? The average? The total profit generated by all employees?

        Answer:

    i.   Save the report.

End of Practices

2.5 Transforming Data Using SAS Data Studio

After you load the data and explore it, you need to prepare it for analysis and reporting. This is known as the *Prepare* phase of the Visual Analytics methodology. In this phase, you create the tables needed for analysis. This can be done by combining tables, correcting data quality issues, and modifying existing or creating new data items. If the data that you need currently exists in multiple tables, you can combine them. Tables can be combined horizontally (using joins) or vertically (using appends). Also, in this phase, data quality issues can be corrected. These issues can be fixed by changing the case of columns, changing the data type or format, renaming columns, removing white space, or standardizing, parsing, or clustering the data. Some data quality transforms require an additional license.

In addition, you can create new calculated columns in this phase by splitting, with an expression or with custom code. You can use SAS Data Studio to prepare tables for Visual Analytics by creating plans that apply the necessary transforms to the table. These plans can then be executed at any time or scheduled to run periodically to create your analysis tables.

SAS Data Studio is the data preparation application in SAS Viya. Using SAS Data Studio, you can view metrics about your tables and apply transforms to the tables by creating plans. Before data can be prepared using SAS Data Studio, the table must first be loaded into CAS. Then you can view details about the table. You can see a sample of the columns and rows, generate a profile of the table to view metrics, and view metadata information. The table sample gives you an idea about the individual data values and can be used to view changes applied to the table when transforms are added. Profile metrics give you an idea about the structure of the table and can be used to identify data quality issues. Profiles can be run on the source table and on the table created from the plan. You can use these profiles to compare metrics over time to ensure that your data quality has improved. Some profile metrics require an additional license. Metadata information shows details about the columns, like the type, length, and format. This can be used to understand your data at a high level.

Figure 2.4: SAS Data Studio Table Values

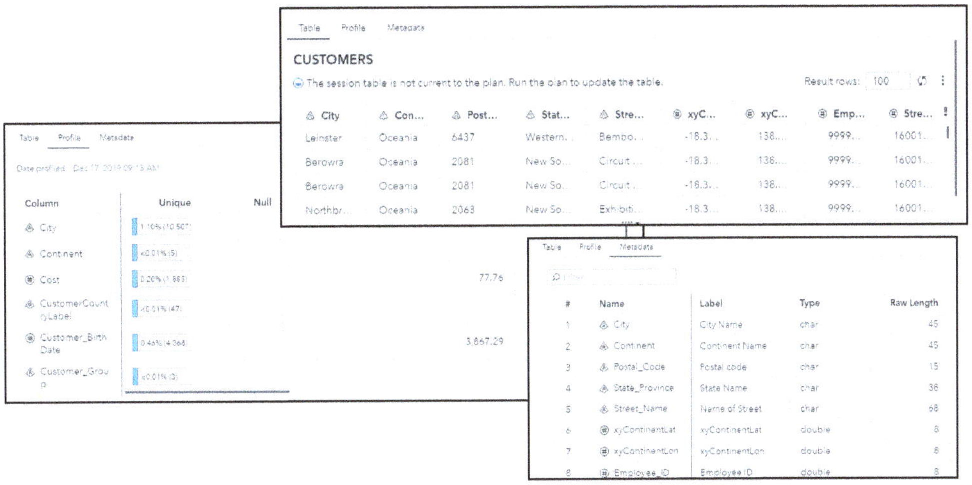

Note: Only the first 300 columns are displayed in the workspace. However, this does not affect your ability to work with all the data in the table. Any changes that are made apply to the entire table, not just the columns that are displayed.

Activity 2.1

Given the values for **Quantity**, **Total Revenue**, and **Unit Cost**, how would you calculate **Profit**?

Quantity	Total Revenue	Unit Cost
1	$191.00	$160.90
4	$499.20	$107.20
1	$173.00	$145.50
1	$56.90	$51.90
4	$740.40	$155.40

Demo 2.2: Preparing Data

This demonstration illustrates how to view table and column profile information and view plan actions in SAS Data Studio.

1. From the browser window, sign in to SAS Viya.
2. Open the **VA1- Demo2.2** plan in SAS Data Studio.
   a. In SAS Drive, click the **All** tab.
   b. Navigate to the **Courses/YVA185/Basics/Demos (Marketing)** folder.

c.   In the workspace, double-click **VA1- Demo2.2** to open the plan in SAS Data Studio. The plan is opened in SAS Data Studio, and the steps of the plan are executed.

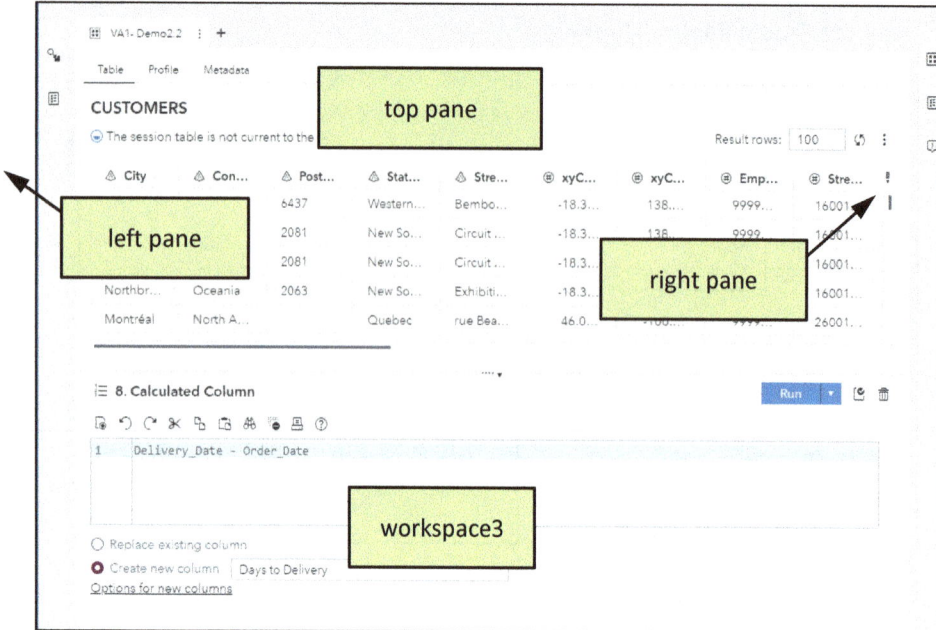

The left pane contains the following icons:

Transforms	The Transforms pane enables you to add column, custom, data quality, multi-input, and row transforms to the plan. Data quality transforms are available only if SAS Data Preparation is licensed at your site.
Properties for the source table	The Properties for the source table pane provides details about the input table (number of rows and columns, size, location, date created and modified, encoding, and tags).

The right pane contains the following icons:

Plan	The Plan pane displays the list of transforms added to the plan.
Properties for the result table	The Properties for the result table pane provides details about the output table (number of rows and columns, size, location, date created and modified, encoding).
Status	The Status pane enables you to view the status of our plans.

3.   View metadata, profile, and table information for the source table.

a.   In the top pane, click **Metadata**.

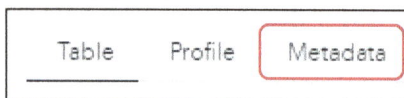

The Metadata view shows a list of columns (and their types) for the source table.

#	Name	Label	Type	Raw Length
1	City	City Name	char	45
2	Continent	Continent Name	char	45
3	Postal_Code	Postal code	char	15
4	State_Province	State Name	char	38
5	Street_Name	Name of Street	char	68
6	xyContinentLat	xyContinentLat	double	8
7	xyContinentLon	xyContinentLon	double	8
8	Employee_ID	Employee ID	double	8

b. In the top pane, click **Profile**.

c. If necessary, click **Run Profile** to execute the profile.

Column	Unique	Null	Blank	Pattern Count	Mean	Median	Mc
City	1.10% (10.507)						
Continent	<0.01% (5)						
Cost	0.20% (1.883)				77.76		
CustomerCountryLabel	<0.01% (47)						
Customer_Birth Date	0.46% (4.368)				3.867.29		
Customer_Group	<0.01% (3)						

Basic profile metrics (Unique, Mean, Standard Deviation, Standard Error, Minimum, Maximum, Data Type, and Data Length) appear for all the columns in the **CUSTOMERS** data source.

Note: Advanced profile metrics (Null, Blank, Pattern Count, Median, Mode, Actual Type, Minimum Length, Maximum Length, Ordinal Position, Primary Key Candidate, and Non-null Count) appear if SAS Data Preparation is licensed at your site.

d. In the top pane, click **Table**.

CUSTOMERS

The session table is not current to the plan. Run the plan to update the table.   Result rows: 100

City	Con...	Post...	Stat...	Stre...	xyC...	xyC...	Emp...	Stre...
Leinster	Oceania	6437	Western...	Bembo...	-18.3...	138...	9999...	16001...
Berowra	Oceania	2081	New So...	Circuit ...	-18.3...	138...	9999...	16001...
Berowra	Oceania	2081	New So...	Circuit ...	-18.3...	138...	9999...	16001...
Northbr...	Oceania	2063	New So...	Exhibiti...	-18.3...	138...	9999...	16001...

A sample of rows from the **CUSTOMERS** data source is displayed. These results might vary.

4. In the left pane, click ⊞ (**Properties for the source table**).

Source Table - CUSTOMERS

Columns	Rows	Size
24	951.7 K	530.2 MB

Label:
(not available)

Location:
cas-shared-default/Public

Date created:
Dec 16, 2019 01:00 PM

Date modified:
Dec 16, 2019 01:00 PM

Date last accessed:
Dec 17, 2019 09:29 AM

Source table:
CUSTOMERS.sashdat

Source CAS Library:
Public

Encoding:
utf-8

Tags (0):
No items have been added.

5. In the right pane, click ⊞ (**Plan**) to view details about the steps performed in the plan.

Plan

Name: VA1- Demo2.2

Modified: 12/17/19 09:29 AM

1. Rename

2. Convert Column

3. Trim Whitespace

4. Trim Whitespace

5. Split

6. Remove

7. Calculated Column

8. Calculated Column

6. With step 8 selected, **Calculated Column**, view the calculation in the workspace.

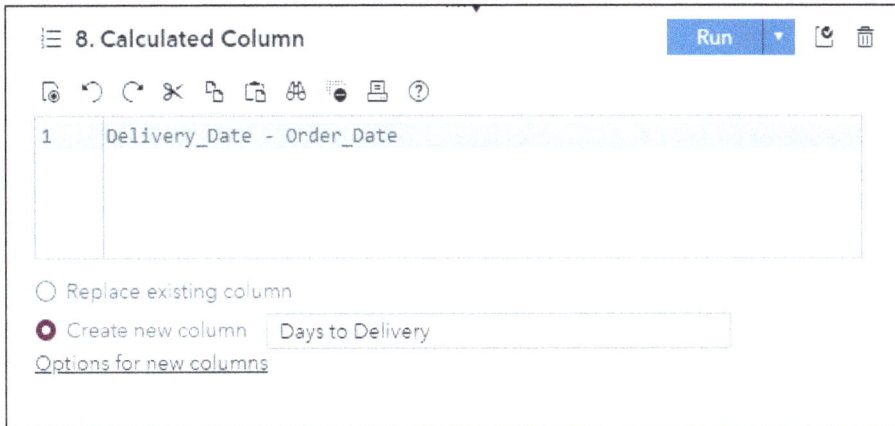

> ☰ **8. Calculated Column**   **Run** ▾ ⌂ 🗑
>
> 🔄 ↶ ↷ ✂ 🗎 🗎 🔍 ● 🖳 ⑦
>
> 1   Delivery_Date - Order_Date
>
> ○ Replace existing column
> ● Create new column | Days to Delivery |
> <u>Options for new columns</u>

This step calculates **Days to Delivery** by subtracting **Order_Date** from **Delivery_Date**.

7. In the right pane, click ⊞ (**Plan**).

8. Select step 7, **Calculated Column**, and view the calculation in the workspace.

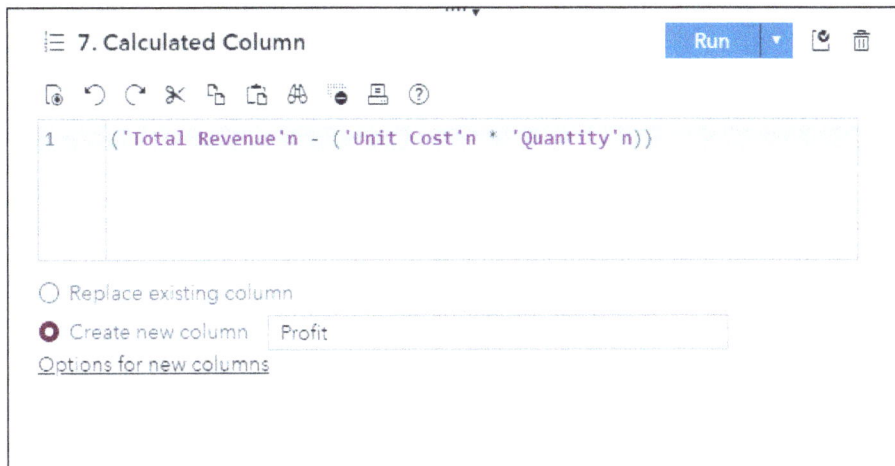

> ☰ **7. Calculated Column**   **Run** ▾ ⌂ 🗑
>
> 🔄 ↶ ↷ ✂ 🗎 🗎 🔍 ● 🖳 ⑦
>
> 1   ('Total Revenue'n - ('Unit Cost'n * 'Quantity'n))
>
> ○ Replace existing column
> ● Create new column | Profit |
> <u>Options for new columns</u>

This step calculates **Profit** by subtracting **Total Cost** (**Unit Cost** times **Quantity**) from **Total Revenue**.

Note: In order to reference a column name that contains blanks, you need to use the following syntax: '*Column Name*'n.

a. Click **Options for new columns**.

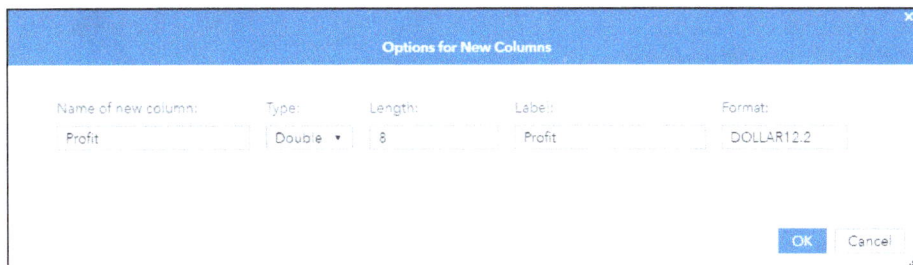

> **Options for New Columns**   ✕
>
> Name of new column: Type: Length: Label: Format:
> Profit   Double ▾   8   Profit   DOLLAR12.2
>
>   OK   Cancel

The new column displays dollar signs and two decimals.

b. Click **Cancel**.

9. Select step 5, **Split**, to view the transformation.

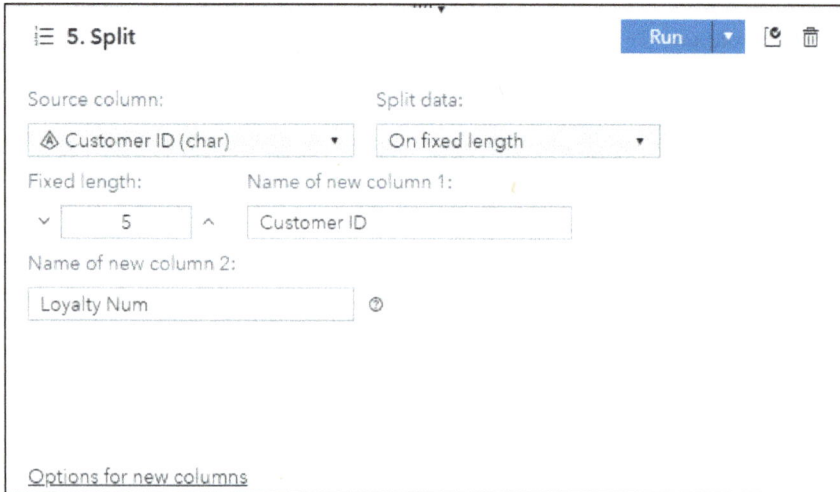

This step splits **Customer_ID** into two new columns. The first five characters represent **Customer_ID** and the last two characters represent **Loyalty Num**.

10. Click the down arrow ▼ and select **Run from beginning** to execute all the steps of the plan.

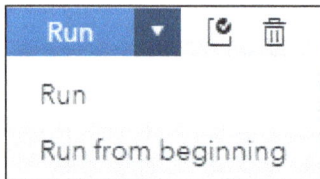

11. View the location of the plan and the name of the result table.

   a. Click ▦ (**Plan**).

   b. In the upper right corner of the plan, click ⋮ (**Options**) and select **Save as**.

   c. In the **Name** field, verify that **VA1 - Demo2.2** is specified.

   d. Below the **Name** field, verify that **Save plan and target table** is selected.

   e. In the **Target table name** field, verify that **CUSTOMERS_CLEAN** is specified.

   f. For the **If the name of the target table already exists** option, verify that **Replace table** is selected.

   The bottom portion of the Save As window should resemble the following:

   g. Click **Cancel**. You do not need to save the plan.

   Note: When a plan is saved, the result table is automatically loaded to the CAS server.

   Note: You can open the result table for the plan in Visual Analytics by clicking ⋮ (**Options**) and selecting **Actions** ⇨ **Saved table** ⇨ **Explore and visualize**.

   End of Demonstration

Practice Scenario

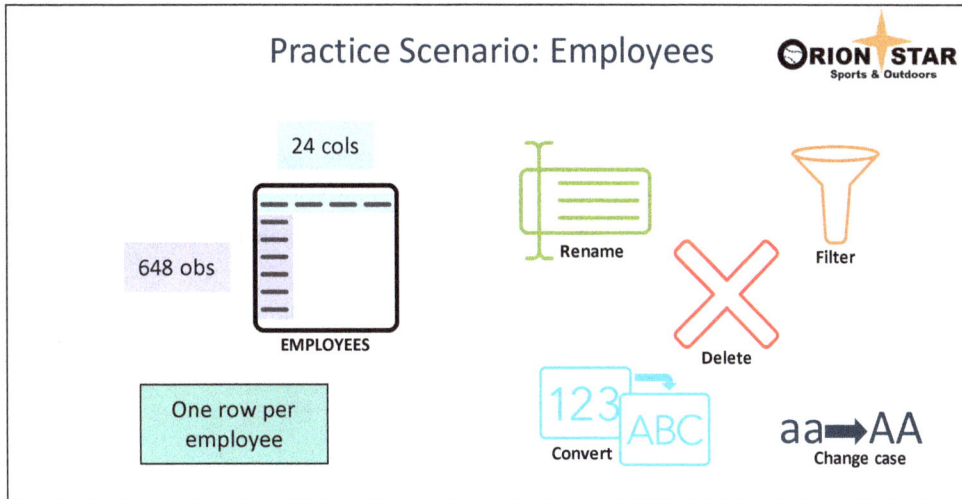

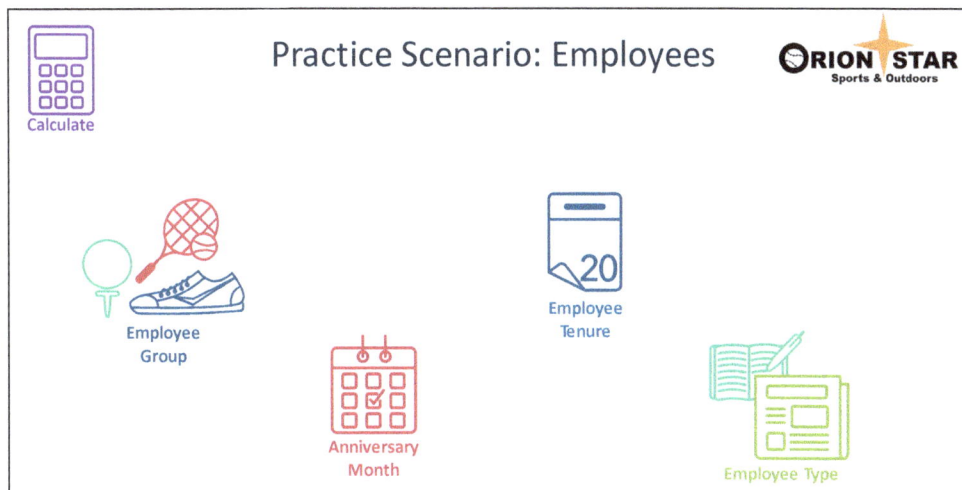

Note: The following data items are not needed for the analysis and will be removed: **Employee Birth Date, Section, Total Customers, Total Products Ordered, Total Quantity Ordered, Levels of Management, Manager at 2. level, Manager at 3. level, Manager at 4. level, Manager at 5. level**, and **Manager at 6. level**.

Note: **Anniversary Month** is calculated in SAS Data Studio. **Employee Tenure** is calculated in Visual Analytics using the NOW operator, so the years of service value updates every time that the report is opened. **Employee Type** can be calculated in SAS Data Studio using custom code. These data items can also be calculated in SAS Visual Analytics, which you see in a later lesson.

Anniversary Month is calculated as the name of the month in which the employee was hired.

Employee Tenure is calculated as (**Employee Termination Date – Employee Hire Date**)/365.25 for retired employees and as (**Today's Date – Employee Hire Date**)/365.25 for active employees.

Employee Type is *Retired* if the termination date is not missing and *Active* if the termination date is missing.

Note: The actual calculations are more complex and are discussed in more detail in later sections.

Practice 2.2

1. Preparing Data
    a. Open the browser and sign in to SAS Viya.
    b. Open and run the **VA1- Practice2.2** plan in the **Courses/YVA185/Basics/Practices (HR)** folder.
    c. View properties for the result table and answer the following question:

    How many rows are in the **EMPLOYEES** table after the actions of the plan are applied?

    Answer:
    d. View details about the steps performed in the plan and answer the following questions:

    How many convert column actions were performed? On which column (or columns)?

    Answer:

    Which column was changed to uppercase?

    Answer:

    What filter was applied to the table?

    Answer:

    What is the name of the new output table created from the plan?

    Answer:

    Hint: Select **Plan** in the right pane to get to **Options**. Click ⋮ (**Options**) and select **Save as** to view the name of the output table.

    Note: You do not need to save the plan.

    End of Practices

Chapter 3: Analyzing Data Using SAS Visual Analytics

3.1 Introduction

In this chapter we cover the *Analyze* phase of the Visual Analytics methodology, where you explore the data to identify any patterns, relationships, and trends that might exist. During this phase, you might need to make changes to the data items for your analysis. This can consist of modifying data item properties (like the names, formats, and aggregations), creating new data items, and applying filters that are needed for the analysis. Then, after the data meets your specifications, you can begin to explore relationships using charts and graphs and discover trends and patterns with analytics. Lastly, you can create, test, and compare models on the patterns that you discovered using SAS Visual Statistics and SAS Visual Data Mining and Machine Learning.

SAS Data Studio Versus SAS Visual Analytics

Remember that SAS Data Studio uses a CAS table as input and creates a CAS table as output from the plan. Alternatively, SAS Visual Analytics uses a CAS table as input and creates a report that can be viewed in the Report Viewer or the SAS Visual Analytics app. Any changes that are made to data items in Visual Analytics are applied to the report only and do not affect the CAS table. However, beginning with Visual Analytics 8.3, report data views can be created to save and apply data changes for a CAS table.

Figure 3.1: SAS Data Studio Versus SAS Visual Analytics

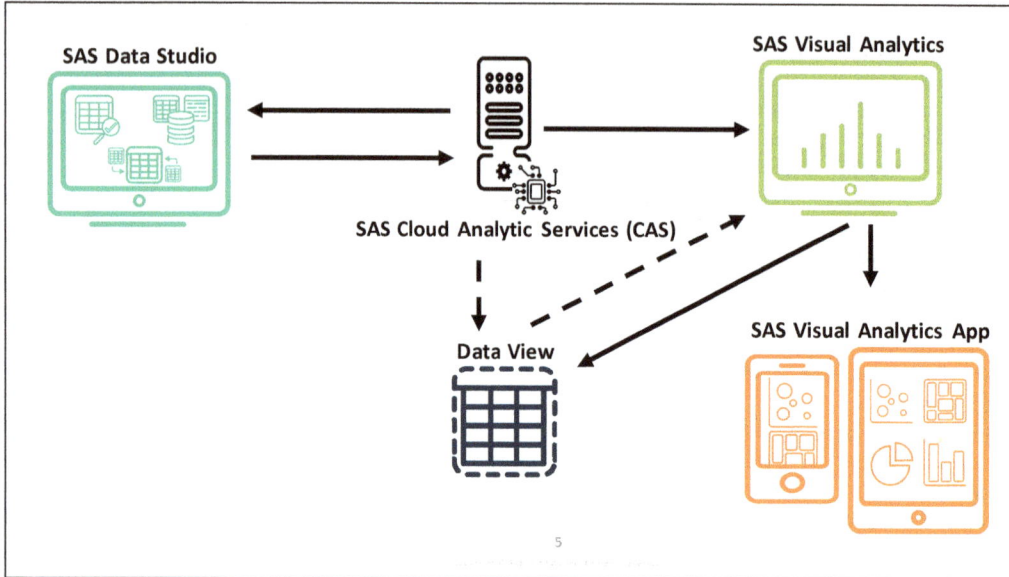

Data Views

Beginning with Visual Analytics 8.3, report data views can be created to save and apply settings for a data source. A data view acts as a template for any settings that are modified, including data property changes, data source filters, hierarchies, geography data items, calculated items, and more. A data view does not update the CAS table. *If the view is updated, your reports are not automatically updated with the new settings.* Data views are saved separately from your reports. If you create a data view in one report, you can apply it to other reports that use the same data source.

Data views can also be shared by an application administrator so that other users can apply them to the data source. A data source can have a default view as set by an application administrator. You can also set the default view for yourself. A default data view is automatically applied anytime that you add the data source to a report. For more information about data views, see "Working with Data Views in Reports" in the *SAS Visual Analytics: Working with Report Data* documentation.

Demo 3.1: Working with Data Items

This demonstration illustrates how to modify data item properties (name, format, aggregation) in Visual Analytics.

1. From the browser window, sign in to SAS Viya.
2. In the upper left corner, click ≡ (**Show list of applications**) and select **Explore and Visualize**.
   SAS Visual Analytics appears.
3. Click All Reports.
   a. Navigate to the **Courses/YVA185/Basics/Demos (Marketing)** folder.
   b. Double-click the **VA1-Demo3.1** report to open it.

4. In the left pane, click **Data**.

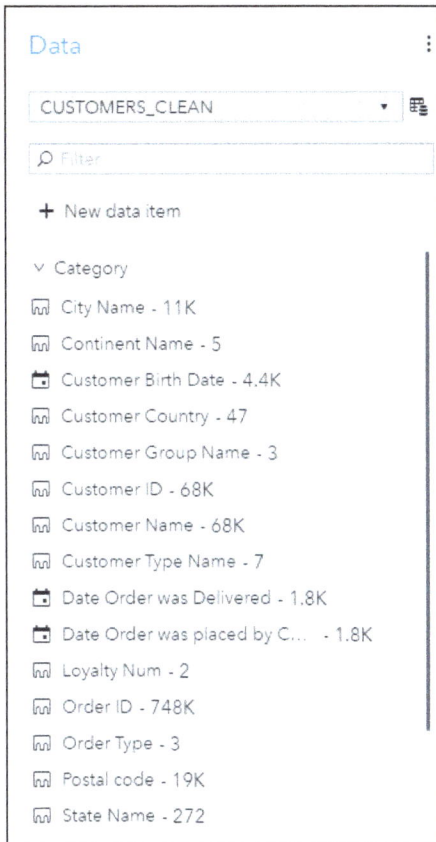

The Data pane contains a list of data items from the **CUSTOMERS_CLEAN** table.

5. Verify that **Customer ID** and **Order ID** appear in the Category group, because the data type was changed to character in SAS Data Studio.

   Note: Character and datetime data items appear as categories in Visual Analytics.

6. Verify that the new column created in SAS Data Studio (**Loyalty Num**) appears in the Category group.

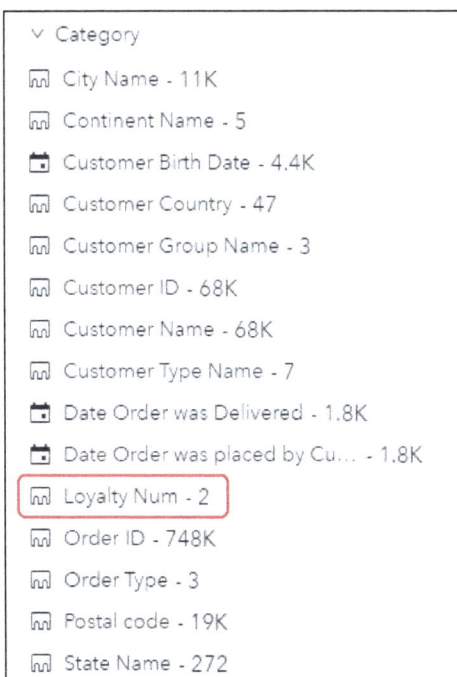

7. Verify that the new columns created in SAS Data Studio (**Days to Delivery** and **Profit**) appear in the Measure group.

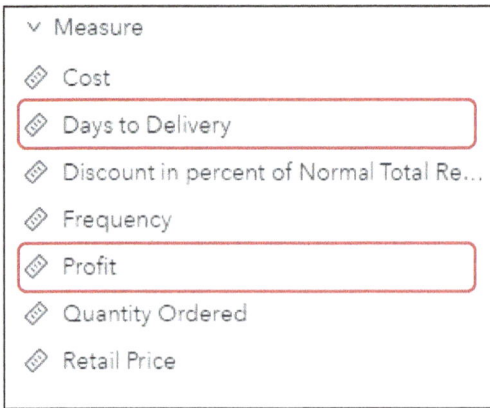

> ∨ Measure
> ⬧ Cost
> ⬧ Days to Delivery
> ⬧ Discount in percent of Normal Total Re...
> ⬧ Frequency
> ⬧ Profit
> ⬧ Quantity Ordered
> ⬧ Retail Price

Note: Numeric (double) data items appear as measures in Visual Analytics.

Note: **Cost** and **Retail Price** were renamed in SAS Data Studio to **Unit Cost** and **Total Revenue**, respectively. Those new names are not reflected because Visual Analytics displays labels, not data source names.

8. Modify properties for a data item, **Date Order was Delivered**.
   a. In the Category group, right-click **Date Order was Delivered**.
   b. Select Format ⇨ MMMYYYY (MONYY7).
   c. Next to Date Order was Delivered, click ⌄ (Edit properties).
   d. In the Name field, enter **Delivery Date** and press the Enter key.

9. Modify properties for a data item, **Discount in percent of Normal Total Retail Price**.
   a. In the Measure group, next to **Discount in percent of Normal Total Retail Price**, click ⌄ (Edit properties).
   b. For the Aggregation field, select **Average**.
   c. In the Name field, enter **Discount** and press Enter.

10. Modify the aggregation for a data item, **Days to Delivery**.
    a. In the Measure group, next to **Days to Delivery**, click ⌄ (**Edit properties**).
    b. For the **Aggregation** field, select **Average**.
    c. In the **Name** field, enter **Average Days to Delivery** and press Enter.

11. Rename data items.
    a. In the Category group, next to **Date Order was placed by Customer**, click ⌄ (**Edit properties**).
    b. In the **Name** field, enter **Order Date** and press Enter.
    c. In the Measure group, next to **Cost**, click ⌄ (**Edit properties**).
    d. In the **Name** field, enter **Unit Cost** and press Enter.
    e. In the Measure group, next to **Quantity Ordered**, click ⌄ (**Edit properties**).
    f. In the **Name** field, enter **Quantity** and press Enter.
    g. In the Measure group, next to **Retail Price**, click ⌄ (**Edit properties**).
    h. In the **Name** field, enter **Total Revenue** and press Enter.

12. Create a data view.

    a. At the top of the Data pane, next to the table name, click ⊞ (**Actions**) and select **Save data view**.

    b. For the **Name** field, verify that **CUSTOMER_CLEAN_View_1** is specified.

    c. In the **Description** field, enter **Modified data item properties (renamed, changed formats, changed aggregations)**.

    d. Click **Save**.

13. Save the report.

End of Demonstration

Practice 3.1

1. Working with Data Items

    a. Open the browser and sign in to SAS Viya.

    b. Open the **VA1-Practice3.1** report from the **Courses/YVA185/Basics/Practices (HR)** folder.

    c. View the data items in the Data pane and answer the following questions:

       What is the classification of **Employee ID**? **Manager at 1. level**?

       Answer:

       What does the **Frequency** data item represent?

       Answer:

    d. Change the classification for **Manager at 1. level** to **Category**.

    e. Change the format for **Annual Salary** to **Dollar13.2**.

    f. Rename the following data items:

Old name	New name
Employee ID	ID
Employee Name	Name

Old name	New name
Manager at 1. level	Manager ID
Frequency	Number of Employees

Note: Click 🖽 (**Actions**) and select **Refresh EMPLOYEES_CLEAN** at the top of the Data pane to collapse the data item properties.

g.   Save the report.

End of Practices

3.2 Exploring Data with Charts and Graphs

Typically, the first part of the *Analyze* phase is gaining a better understanding of your data items in broad terms or getting a good feel for the data, that is, understanding the ranges of values and totals for specific groups or subgroups. This can be accomplished with descriptive graphs (histograms, box plots, and bar charts).

Histograms and Box Plots

Histograms can be used to view the distribution of a single measure. A histogram consists of a series of bars where the height represents the number of observations that fit in a specific range. Histograms are ideal for gauging the overall range of a measure and for identifying values that contain a high number of observations. Histograms can also be used to determine whether a measure is normally distributed, which can be very helpful in modeling.

Figure 3.2: Descriptive Graphs

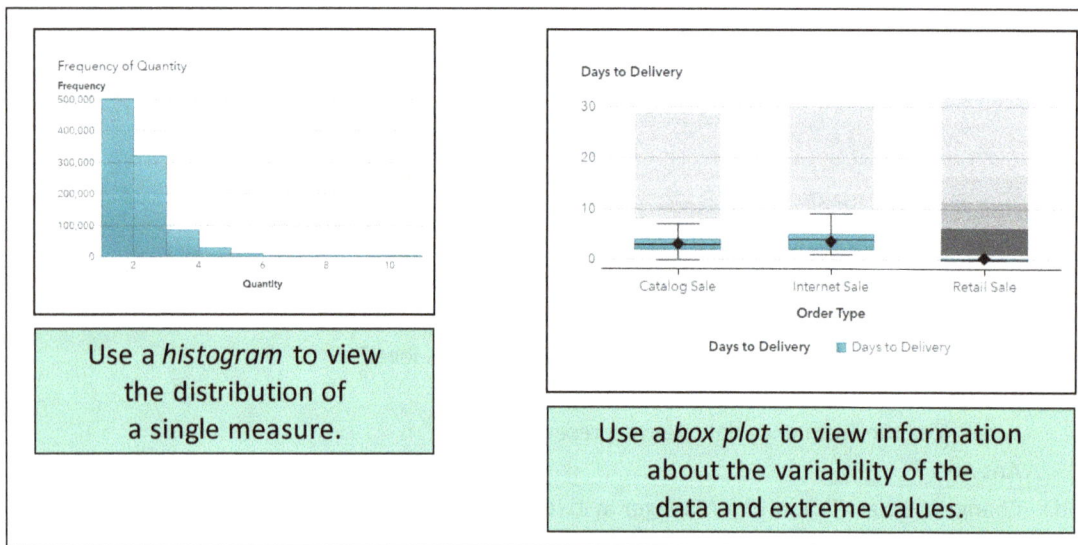

Alternatively, box plots can be used to view information about the variability and extreme values of a measure for distinct values of a category data item. In the box plot, the size and location of the box indicate the range of values between the 25th and 75th percentile for that group. The diamond marker indicates the Mean value and the line inside the box indicates the Median value. You can also modify the options to display outliers in the plot. Outliers are data points whose distances from the interquartile range are more than 1.5 times the size of the interquartile range. The whiskers can indicate either the Minimum and Maximum values or the range of values that are outside the interquartile range, but close enough to not be considered outliers. If there are many outliers, the range of values are shown as a bar that is colored to represent the number of values within that range (as seen above). Box plots are extremely useful for determining the differences between groups.

Bar Charts

Another excellent way to view differences is using bar charts to compare summarized data. Bar charts display aggregated data for the distinct values of a category. They are probably one of the most versatile, and most used, graphs available. Bar charts can be used to compare nominal values (categories that have no particular order), time series data, to show rankings (like the top or bottom values), and to show parts of a whole.

Figure 3.3: Bar Charts

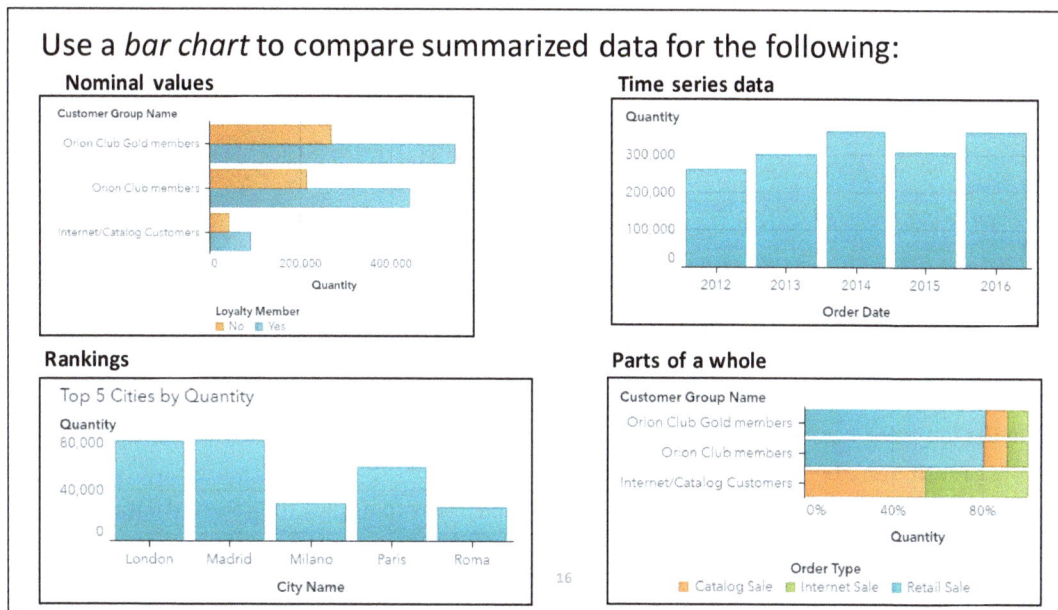

Use a *bar chart* to compare summarized data for the following:

Demo 3.2: Exploring Data - Part 1

This demonstration illustrates how to use the automatic chart to explore data and modify roles and options for charts and graphs in Visual Analytics.

1. From the browser window, sign in to SAS Viya.
2. In the upper left corner, click ☰ (**Show list of applications**) and select **Explore and Visualize**.
3. SAS Visual Analytics appears.
4. Click **All Reports**.
   a. Navigate to the Courses/YVA185/Basics/Demos (Marketing) folder.
   b. Double-click the VA1-Demo3.2a report to open it.
5. Turn off automatic graph titles.
   a. In the upper right corner, select *<user name>* ⇨ **Settings**.
   b. On the left side of the window, select **General** under **SAS Visual Analytics**.
   c. Scroll down to **Default titles for new objects**.
   d. For Graphs, change **Automatic title** to **No title**.

Default titles for new objects:

Tables:

No title ▾

Graphs:

No title ▾

Controls:

No title ▾

Content:

No title ▾

Analytics:

No title ▾

    e. Click **Close**.

6. Create an automatic chart.

    a. In the left pane, click **Data**.

    b. Drag **Profit** from the Data pane to the canvas.

       The automatic chart functionality determines the best way to display the selected data.

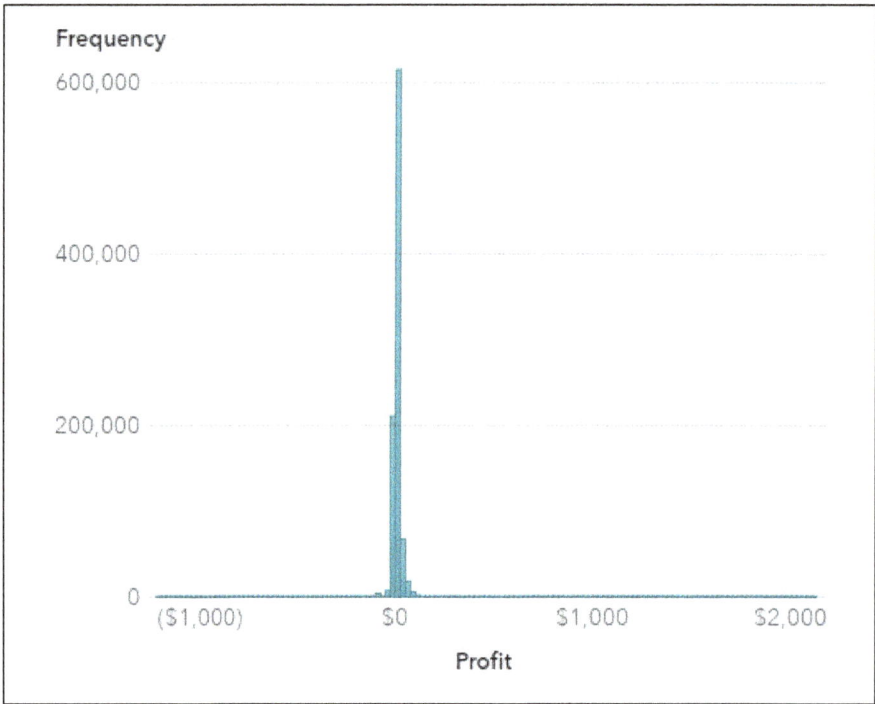

Frequency

600,000	
400,000	
200,000	
0	

($1,000) $0 $1,000 $2,000

Profit

       A histogram is used to display the distribution of profits.

    c. In the right pane, click **Roles**.

Data Roles

Histogram - Profit 1   ▾

⌄ Measure

    ⬗ Profit

⌄ Frequency

    ⬗ Frequency

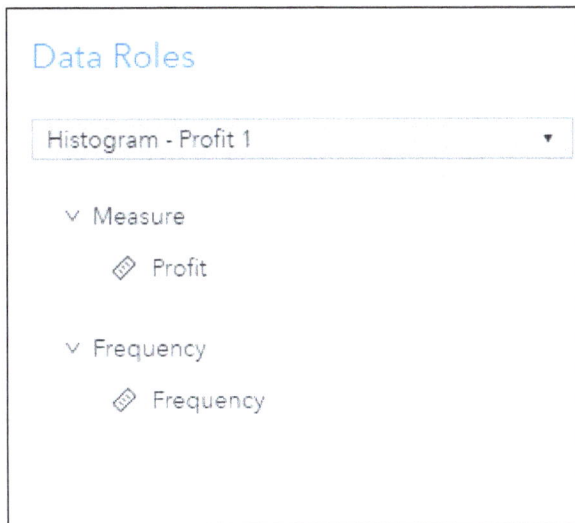

A histogram accepts two roles, Measure and Frequency.

d.   For the Frequency role, select **Frequency** ⇨ **Frequency Percent**.

The histogram is updated to use frequency percent for the Y axis.

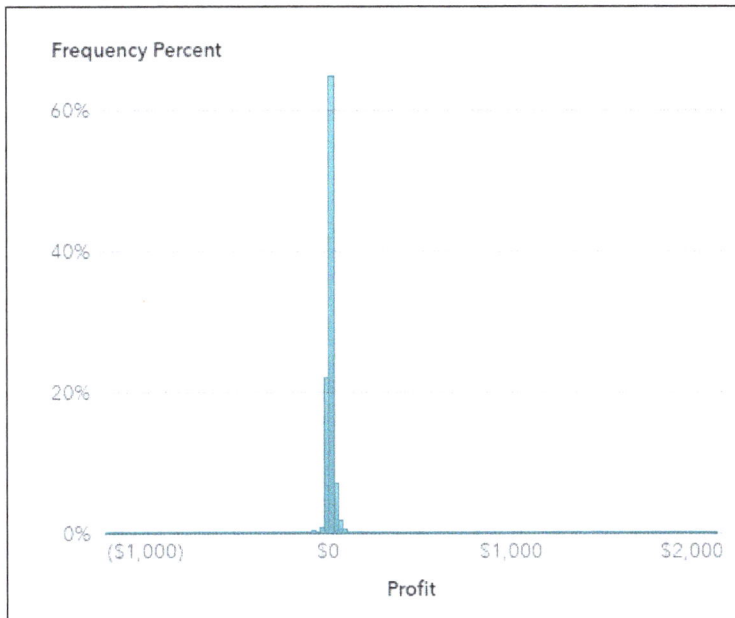

e.   In the right pane, click **Options**.

7.   Expand the **Object** group.

8.   In the **Name** field, enter **Distribution of Profit**.

⌄ Object

   Name:

   Distribution of Profit

   Title:

   No title   ▾

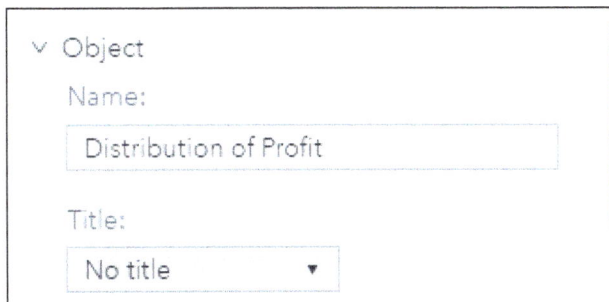

Note: The **Automatic title** setting was turned off for Graph objects in an earlier demo. You can turn it on for this graph by selecting **Automatic title**, or you can create a custom title by selecting **Custom title**.

Title:

No title ▼
Custom title
Automatic title
No title

a. In the upper right corner of the histogram, click ↗ (**Maximize**) to view additional details.
A table of data values is displayed at the bottom of the chart.

Frequency Percent

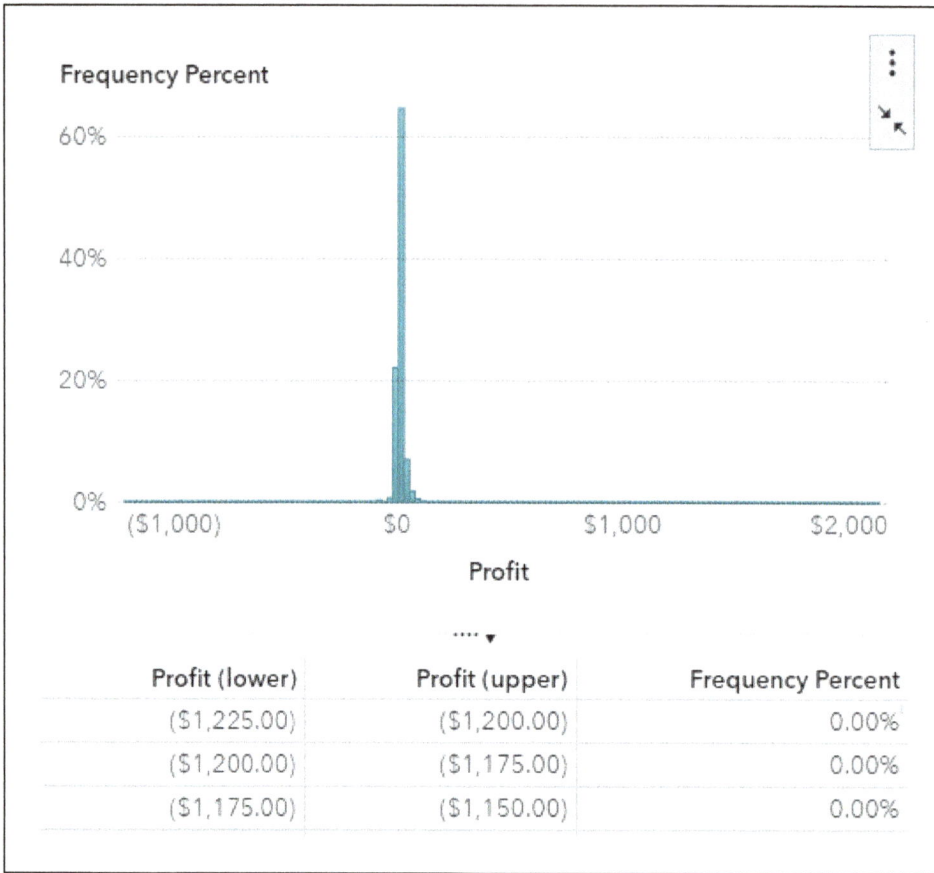

Profit (lower)	Profit (upper)	Frequency Percent
($1,225.00)	($1,200.00)	0.00%
($1,200.00)	($1,175.00)	0.00%
($1,175.00)	($1,150.00)	0.00%

b. Click the highest bar in the graph.
c. Scroll through the table to find the highlighted row.

Profit (lower)	Profit (upper)	Frequency Percent
($50.00)	($25.00)	0.88%
($25.00)	$0.00	22.23%
$0.00	$25.00	64.65%
$25.00	$50.00	7.16%

A majority of the products ordered are low-profit items, in the $0 to $25 range. Also notice that more than 20% of items result in a loss. Why is this problem occurring? Are these products ordered from a similar product area, geographical area, or order type? Could the costs be too high in these areas? What can we do to reduce costs?

d. In the upper right corner, click ⬎ (**Restore**).

9. Create a crosstab.
   a. In the left pane, click **Objects**.
   b. Drag the **Crosstab** object, from the Tables group, to the bottom of the canvas.
   c. In the right pane, click **Roles**.
   d. For the **Rows** role, select **Add** ⇨ **Order Type** and click **OK**.
   e. For the **Measures** role, select **Frequency** ⇨ **Profit**.

   The Roles pane should resemble the following:

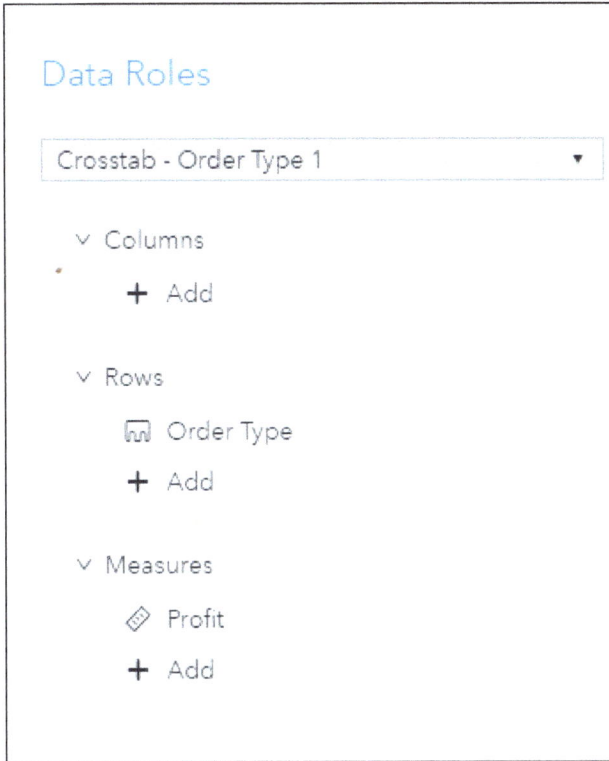

   Data Roles

Crosstab - Order Type 1	▼

   ⌄ Columns

       + Add

   ⌄ Rows

       🔲 Order Type

       + Add

   ⌄ Measures

       ◇ Profit

       + Add

   Note: The Measures role is required for the crosstab object.

   The crosstab should resemble the following:

Order Type ▲	Profit
Catalog Sale	$1,153,380.79
Internet Sale	$981,170.49
Retail Sale	$6,124,855.53

   Profits are much lower in the internet and catalog channels. A company-wide policy mandates that we need to try to improve profits for orders through these channels.
   f. On the Roles tab, for the **Columns** role, select **Add** ⇨ **Continent Name** and click **OK**.

   The updated crosstab should resemble the following:

Continent Name ▲	Africa	Asia	Europe	North America	Oceania
Order Type ▲	Profit	Profit	Profit	Profit	Profit
Catalog Sale	$730.56	$7,564.99	$670,252.82	$423,428.89	$51,403.52
Internet Sale	($858.24)	$7,938.71	$559,663.83	$370,621.44	$43,804.75
Retail Sale	——	——	$4,429,533.94	$1,327,595.24	$367,726.36

   g. In the right pane, click **Options**.
   h. Expand the **Totals and Subtotals** group.

i.   Select the **Totals** check box.

By default, totals are added to rows and columns.

j.   Next to the **Totals** field, select **Columns**.

k.   For the Background color field, click ☐ (Select a color).

l.   Select Pale blue.

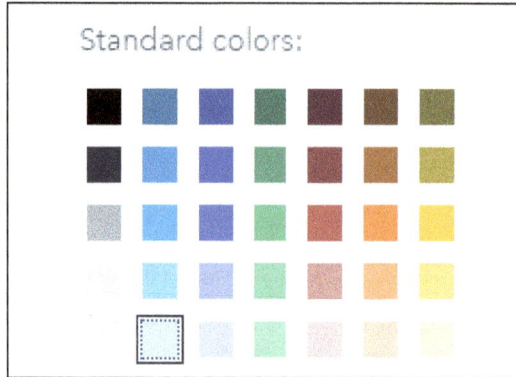

m. For the **Format** field, verify that **B** (**Bold**) is selected.

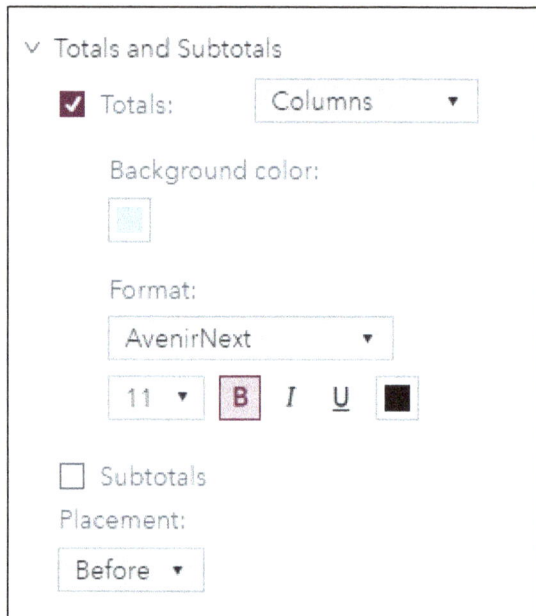

The updated crosstab should resemble the following:

Continent Name ▲	Africa	Asia	Europe	North America	Oceania
Order Type ▲	Profit	Profit	Profit	Profit	Profit
Total	($127.68)	$15,503.70	$5,659,450.59	$2,121,645.57	$462,934.63
Catalog Sale	$730.56	$7,564.99	$670,252.82	$423,428.89	$51,403.52
Internet Sale	($858.24)	$7,938.71	$559,663.83	$370,621.44	$43,804.75
Retail Sale	——	——	$4,429,533.94	$1,327,595.24	$367,726.36

Profits are much lower in North America than in Europe. Because our corporate office is located in North America, we would expect higher profits. Also notice the loss in Africa for internet sales. Why is this loss occurring? Is this due to start-up operations (for example, building distribution facilities in Africa)? Are the losses consistent over time or has this changed over time?

10. Change the crosstab to a bar chart.
    a. Right-click the crosstab and select **Change Crosstab to** ⇨ **Bar chart**.
       The bar chart should resemble the following:

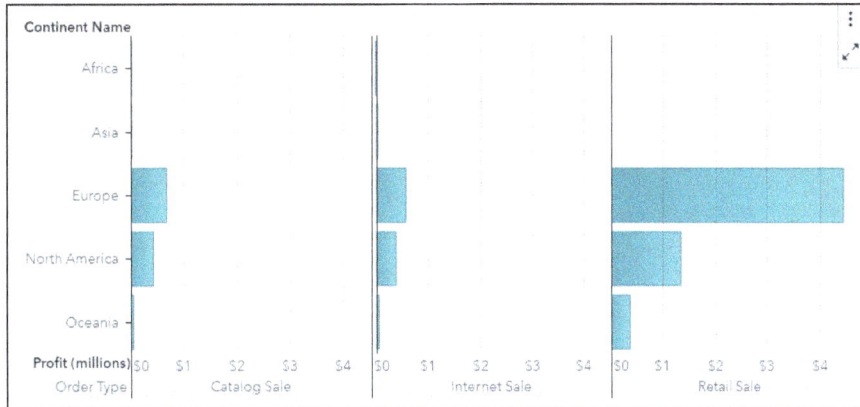

    b. In the right pane, click **Roles**.

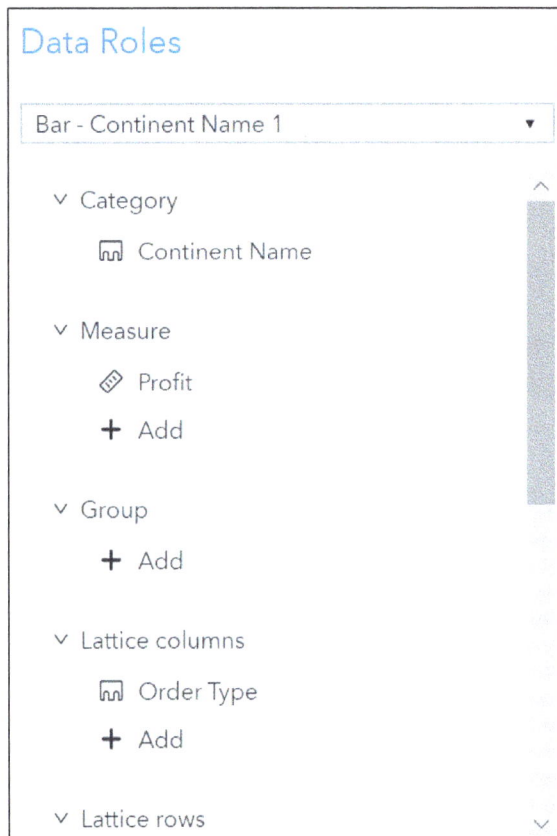

    The bar chart has many more roles available.

- Category data items can be added to the Group role to show additional bars for each category, or to the Lattice columns and Lattice rows roles to add additional bar charts for each distinct category.

- Category and Measure data items can be added to the data tip values role to show additional information when a bar is selected.

- Datetime data items can be added to the Animation role to animate the bar chart.

- Category or date data items can be added to the Hidden role for mapping data sources, adding color-mapped display rules, or adding external links.

c.   Drag **Order Type**, from the **Lattice columns** role, to the **Group** role.

The bar chart should resemble the following:

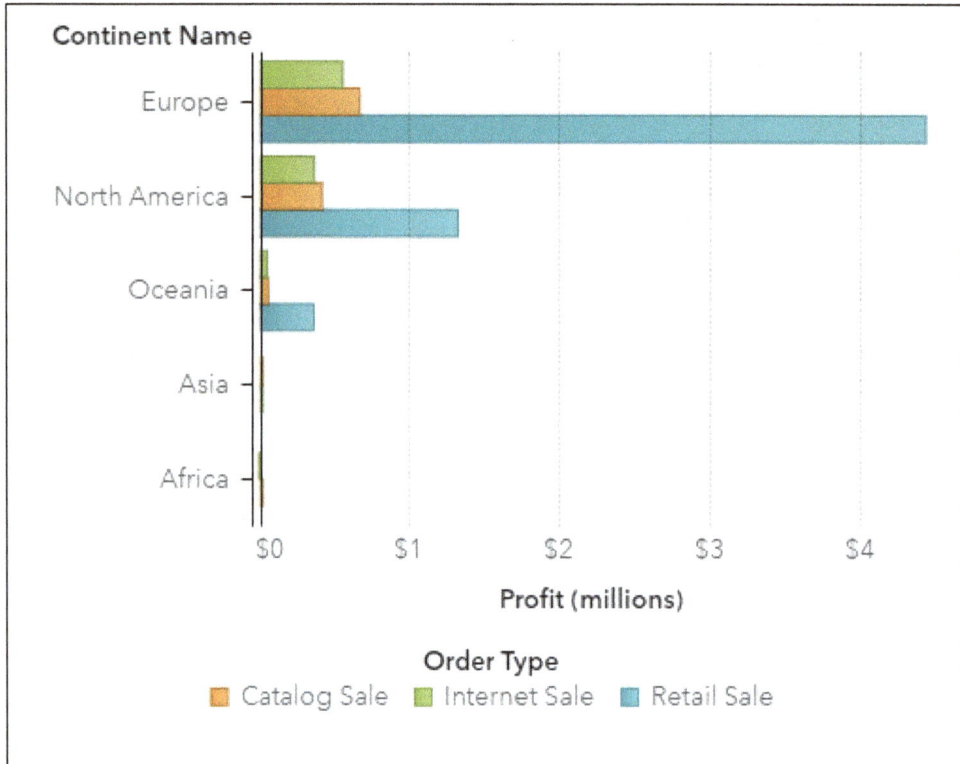

d.   In the right pane, click **Options**.

e.   In the Object group, for the **Name** field, enter **Profit by Continent and Order Type**.

f.   In the Bar group, for the **Grouping style** field, click [|ı|] (**Stacked**).

g.   Select **Data labels**.

h.   For the **Text style** field, select **9**.

The Bar group should resemble the following:

The updated bar chart should resemble the following:

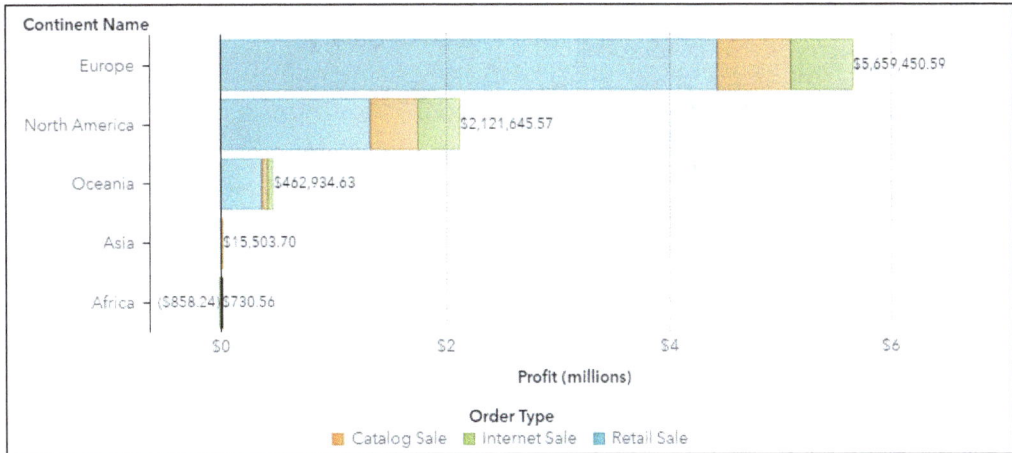

Profits in North America are less than half of total profits in Europe. We need to understand why this discrepancy exists and try to improve profits in non-European countries.

11. In the left pane, click **Outline**.

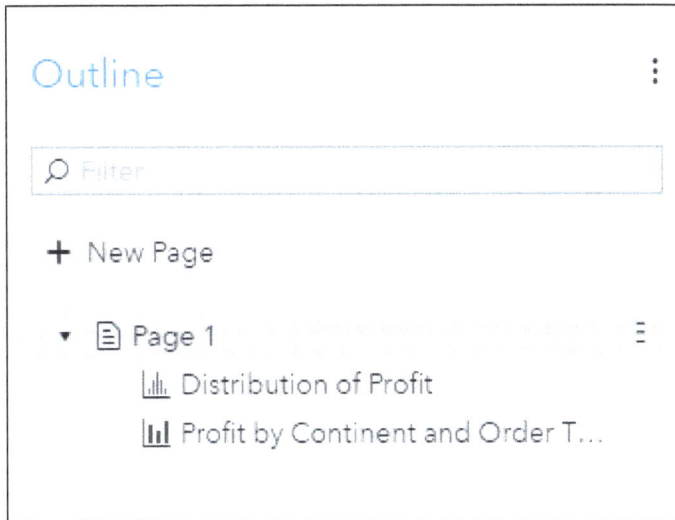

The Outline pane displays a list of all pages and objects in the report.

12. Save the report.

End of Demonstration

 Practice 3.2

1. Exploring Data: Part 1
   a. Open the browser and sign in to SAS Viya.
   b. Open the **VA1-Practice3.2a** report from the **Courses/YVA185/Basics/Practices (HR)** folder.
   c. Create an automatic chart using the following data items:
      Annual Salary
      Frequency Percent

d. Modify the following options for the automatic chart:

Name	Distribution of Salary
Bin range	Measure values
Set a fixed bin count	\<selected\>
Bin count	4

The automatic chart should resemble the following:

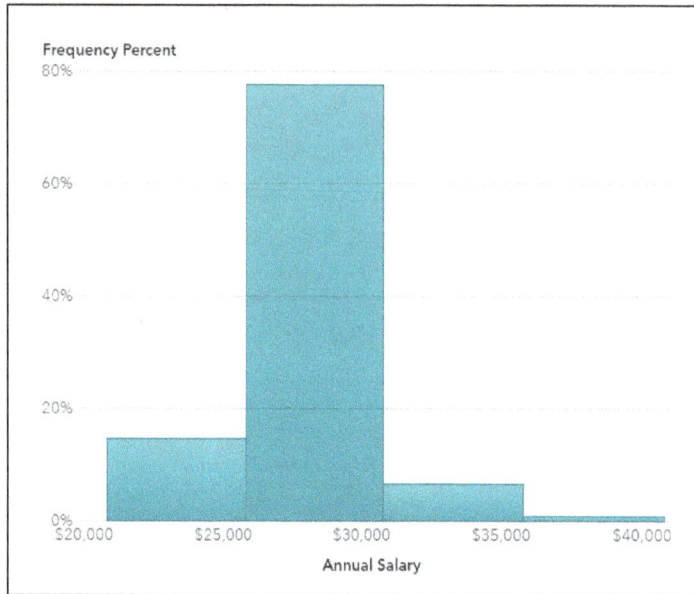

e. Maximize the histogram to answer the following question:

Into which range do the majority of salaries fall?

Answer:

Hint: After answering the question, click [icon] (**Restore**) in the upper right corner.

f. Add a bar chart on the right of the automatic chart by assigning the following data items to the specified roles:

Category	Job Title
Measure	Annual Salary
Group	Department

g.

h. Specify **Total Salary by Job and Department** as the name of the bar chart.

The bar chart should resemble the following:

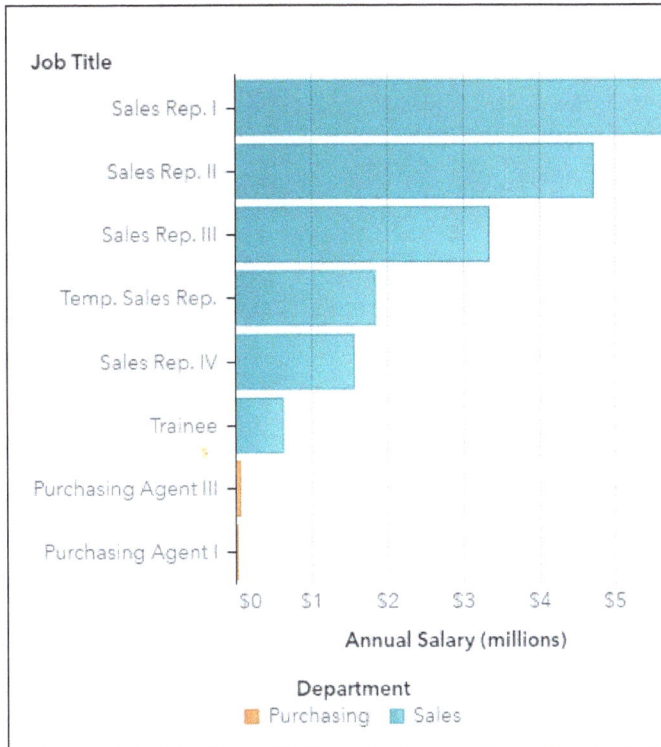

i. Answer the following questions:

In which department are a majority of our salary costs spent? For which job title?

Answer:

What could be some reasons why salary costs are so much higher for this group?

Answer:

j. Save the report.

End of Practices

Demo 3.3: Exploring Data - Part 2

This demonstration illustrates how to use box plots to explore data in Visual Analytics.

1. From the browser window, sign in to SAS Viya.
2. In the upper left corner, click ☰ (**Show list of applications**) and select **Explore and Visualize**.
3. SAS Visual Analytics appears.
4. Click **All Reports**.
    a. Navigate to the Courses/YVA185/Basics/Demos (Marketing) folder.
    b. Double-click the VA1-Demo3.2b report to open it.
5. In the upper left corner of the report, click the **Page 2** tab.

6. Create a box plot.

    a. In the left pane, click **Objects**.

    b. Drag the **Box plot** object, from the Graphs group, to the left side of the canvas.

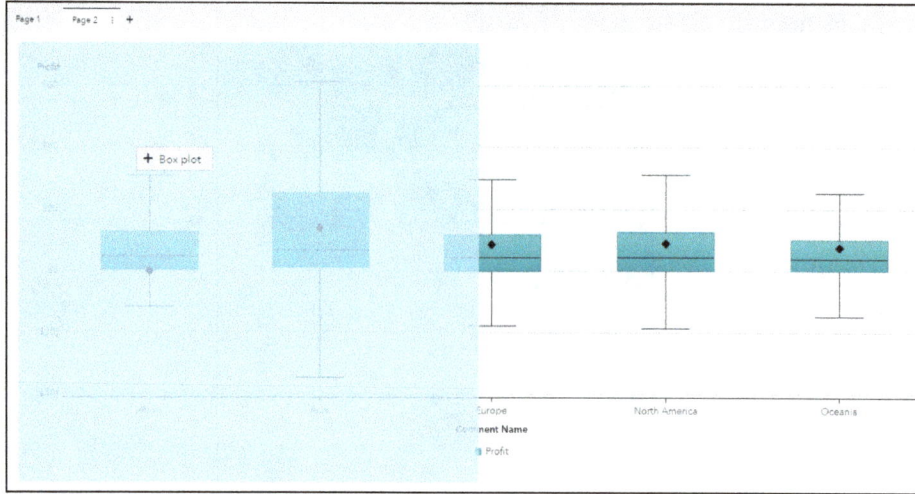

    c. In the right pane, click **Roles**.

    d. For the **Category** role, select **Add** ⇨ **Order Type**.

    e. For the **Measures** role, select **Add** ⇨ **Profit** and click **OK**.

       The Roles pane should resemble the following:

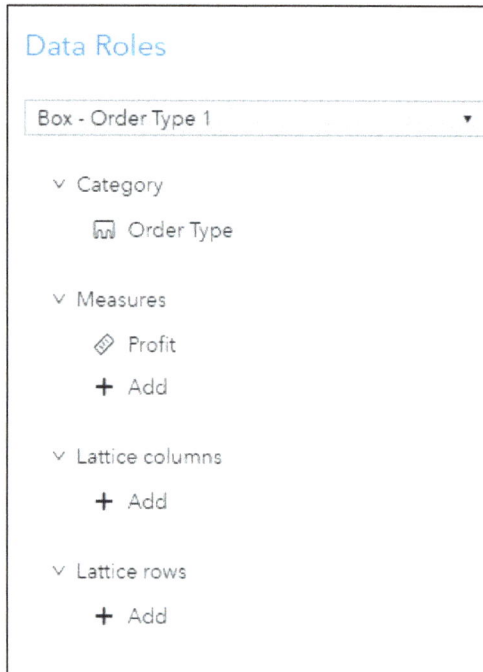

The box plot should resemble the following:

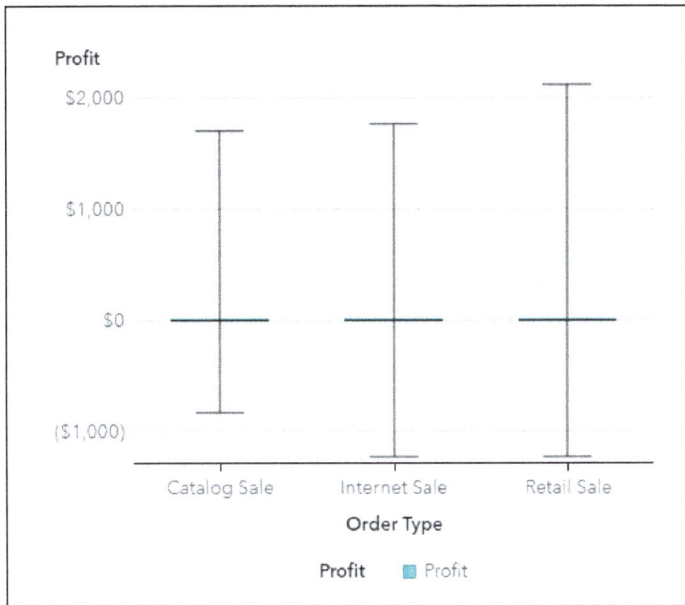

Profit

$2,000

$1,000

$0

($1,000)

Catalog Sale   Internet Sale   Retail Sale

Order Type

Profit   ■ Profit

f.   In the right pane, click **Options**.
g.   In the Object group, for the **Name** field, enter **Profit by Order Type**.
h.   In the Box Plot group, for the **Outliers** field, select **Ignore Outliers**.
i.   Select the check box for **Averages**.

∨ Box Plot

Box direction:

⇒ ⇡

Measure layout:

Automatic   ▼

Outliers:

Ignore Outliers   ▼

☐ Outlier bin outlines
☑ Averages

The box plot should resemble the following:

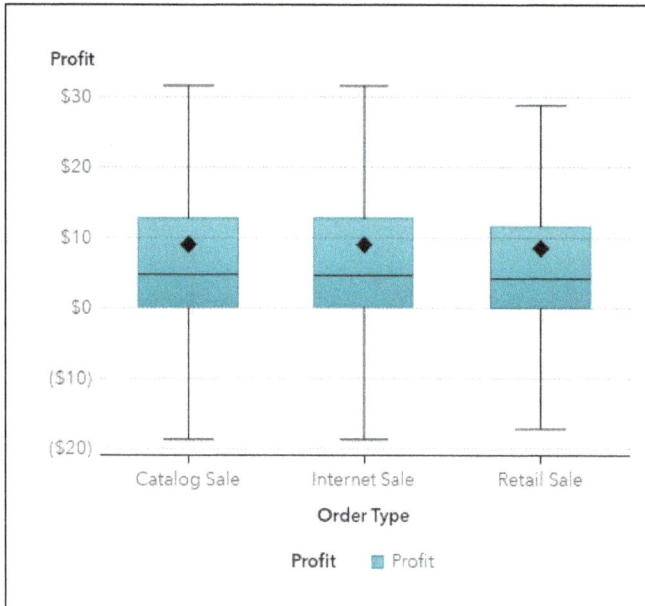

In the upper right corner of the box plot, click ⬈ (**Maximize**) to view additional details.

The detail table displays descriptive statistics for **Profit** for each order type.

Order Type	Minimum	Lower Whisker	First Quartile	Average	Median	Third Quartile
Catalog Sale	($826.26)	($18.63)	$0.20	$9.07	$4.80	$12.80
Internet Sale	($1,222.48)	($18.63)	$0.20	$9.04	$4.70	$12.80
Retail Sale	($1,222.48)	($17.13)	$0.10	$8.55	$4.25	$11.60

Even though total profits are highest for the retail sales channel, averages across all channels are very similar, but are a bit higher for catalog and internet sales. This reinforces our company-wide policy to try to increase profits in these channels. Total profits might be higher in retail because there are more customers or more orders for that channel.

j. In the upper right corner, click ⬔ (**Restore**).

k. In the upper right corner of the **Profit by Continent** box plot, click ⬈ (**Maximize**) to view additional details.

The detail table displays descriptive statistics for **Profit** for each continent.

Continent Name	Minimum	Lower Whisker	First Quartile	Average	Median	Third Quartile	U
Africa	($374.42)	($11.70)	$0.30	($0.17)	$4.80	$12.60	
Asia	($258.84)	($34.62)	$1.00	$13.97	$6.80	$25.20	
Europe	($1,222.48)	($17.82)	($0.10)	$8.66	$4.40	$11.80	
North America	($1,222.48)	($18.63)	$0.10	$9.00	$4.50	$12.60	
Oceania	($646.40)	($14.80)	$0.20	$7.66	$3.90	$10.20	

Even though total profits are highest for Europe, averages are higher in North America and Asia. Because our corporate office is located in North America, we will start by focusing on increasing profits in North America. Total profits might be higher in Europe because there are more customers or more orders for that continent. Also, note the negative average profits in Africa. Why is this occurring? What can we do to increase profits for that continent?

l. In the upper right corner, click ⬔ (**Restore**).

m. Save the report.

End of Demonstration

Practice 3.3

1. Exploring Data: Part 2
    a. Open the browser and sign in to SAS Viya.
    b. Open the **VA1-Practice3.2b** report from the **Courses/YVA185/Basics/Practices (HR)** folder.
    c. On Page 2, create a box plot by assigning the following data items to the specified roles:

Category	Job Title
Measures	Annual Salary

    d. Modify the following options for the box plot:

Name	Salary Analysis by Job Title
Outliers	Show Outliers
Averages	<selected>

The box plot should resemble the following:

    e. Maximize the box plot to answer the following questions:

    Which job title has the highest average salary? The lowest?

    Answer:

    Which job title has the largest number of outliers?

    Answer:

    Hint: After answering the question, click [⬎] (**Restore**) in the upper right corner.

    f. Save the report.

    End of Practices

3.3 Creating Data Items and Applying Filters

Creating Data Items

In Visual Analytics, you can create many different types of data items to aid your analysis or for use in your reports. Some data items can be created before the data is imported to CAS (like a custom category, a duplicate data item, and calculated items). Others must be created in Visual Analytics (like a geography, hierarchies, parameters, aggregated measures, derived items, and distinct counts).

Figure 3.4: Creating Data Items

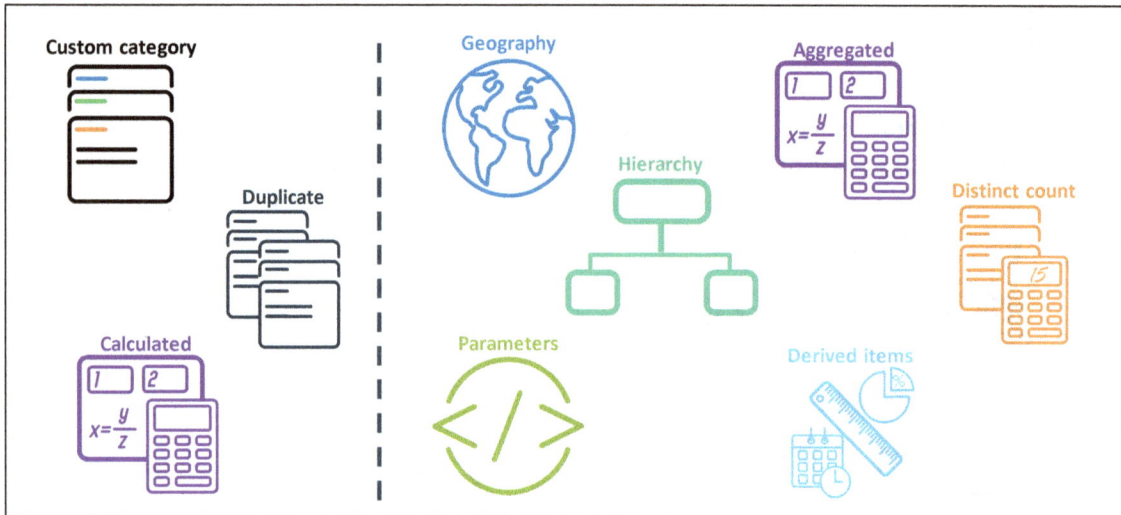

Calculated Items Versus Aggregated Measures

In Visual Analytics, two different types of calculated items can be created: calculated data items or aggregated measures. Calculated data items are created by performing mathematical calculations on numeric values or by performing operations on datetime data items or categories. All calculations are performed on unaggregated data. That is, the expression is evaluated for each row in the data source. For example, you can create a new calculated item (New Salary) by multiplying Salary and Increase. For each row in the data source, the operation is evaluated, and the new data item is created. Then, when that data item is used in a graph (for example, with Gender) the values for New Salary are totaled for each gender.

Figure 3.5: Example of a Calculated Item

Calculated items are created by performing operations on unaggregated data.

(Salary * Increase)

Country	Salary	Increase	New Salary
US	40,000	1.05	42,000
UK	65,000	1.10	71,500
UK	32,000	1.05	33,600
US	80,000	1.10	88,000
UK	56,000	1.15	64,400

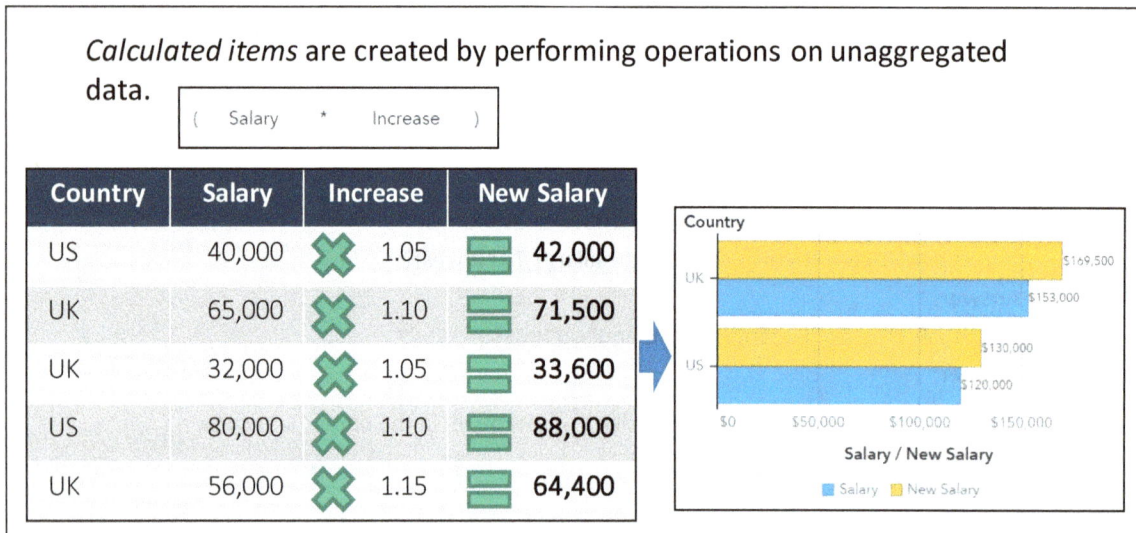

Conversely, aggregated measures enable you to use aggregated values to calculate new data items. These data items are created by first aggregating values, and then by performing the operation. With aggregated measures, the calculation changes depending on other data items that are available in the graph. For example, you can create a new aggregated measure (Salary (Percent of total)) by dividing the Sum of the Salary for each group by the Sum of the Salary for all groups. In this instance, because Salary (Percent of total) is paired with Gender, salaries are first totaled for each gender. Next, salaries are totaled for all genders. Then, the operation is evaluated for each gender to show the contribution to total profit. You could take the same aggregated measure and pair it with Country to see the contribution of each country to total profit. The dynamic nature of aggregated measures makes them extremely useful for analysis and reporting.

Figure 3.6: Example of an Aggregated Measure

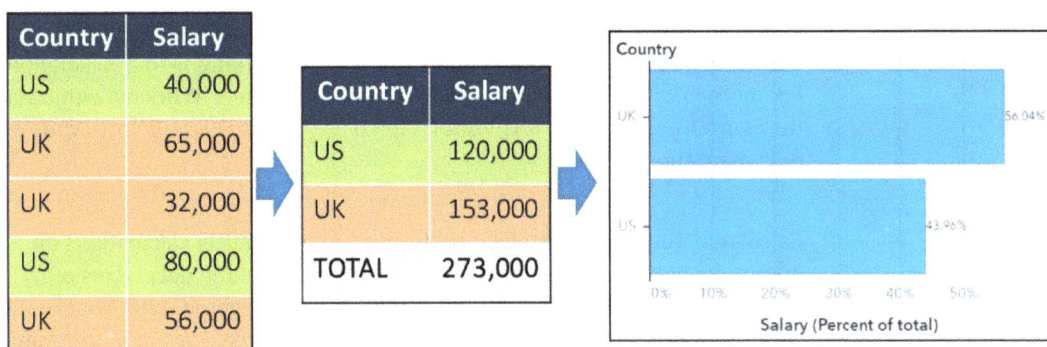

Aggregated measures are created by aggregating first and then performing the operation.

Aggregated measures enable you to calculate new data items using aggregated values. This means that the calculation changes depending on the other data items available in the graph. For example, you can see the profit margin for each region or by each store. For more information about creating calculated data items, see "Working with Calculated Items in a Report" in the *SAS Visual Analytics: Working with Report Data* documentation.

Activity 3.1

Match each new data item with the type of calculation.

_ Gross Profit margin (Total Profit / Total Revenue)
_ Date (from month, day, year)
_ Hemisphere (from continents)
_ GDP Growth (year-over-year)
_ Number of Employees (distinct count)
_ State Abbreviations (uppercase)

A calculated item   **B** aggregated measure

The following types of data items can be created in SAS Visual Analytics, using code, or in SAS Data Studio or SAS Enterprise Guide:

Table 3.1: Data Items in Visual Analytics, Data Studio, or Enterprise Guide

Data Item	Description
Custom category	A custom category creates labels for groups of values of category or measure data items. When you create a custom category from a measure data item, you can use intervals or distinct values to group the data. For more information about custom categories, see "Working with Custom Categories in a Report" in the *SAS Visual Analytics: Working with Report Data* documentation.

Data Item	Description
Duplicate	Both measures and categories can be duplicated (copied) in Visual Analytics. Duplicating measures enables you to compare the data using different aggregations in a table or graph or change the classification to a category for grouping other values in tables or graphs. Duplicating datetime values enables you to apply different formats to the values for use in tables or graphs. Duplicating calculated items enables you to make variations to a calculation. For more information about duplicating data items, see "Working with Data Items in a Report" in the *SAS Visual Analytics: Working with Report Data* documentation.
Calculated item	Calculated items are created by performing mathematical calculations on numeric values, or by performing operations on datetime data items or categories. All calculations are performed on unaggregated data. That is, the expression is evaluated for each row in the data source. For more information about creating calculated data items, see "Working with Calculated Items in a Report" in the *SAS Visual Analytics: Working with Report Data* documentation. For more information about operators, see "Reference: Operators for Data Expressions" in the *SAS Visual Analytics: Working with Report Data* documentation.

The following types of data items need to be created in Visual Analytics:

Table 3.2: Data Items in Visual Analytics

Data Item	Description
Geography	A geography data item is a category whose values are mapped to geographical locations or regions. Geography data items can be used with geo maps and other report objects. Geography data items can be created using predefined roles (for example, country names), by associating latitude and longitude coordinates with the values (custom), or by associating polygon data from a separate data source with map regions (custom). For more information about creating geography data items, see "Working with Geography Data Items" in the *SAS Visual Analytics: Working with Report Data* documentation.
Aggregated Measure	Aggregated measures enable you to calculate new data items using aggregated values. This means that the calculation changes depending on the other data items available in the graph. For example, you can see the profit margin for each region or by each store. For more information about creating calculated data items, see "working with calculated Items in a Report" in the *SAS Visual Analytics: Working with Report Data* documentation.

Data Item	Description
Hierarchy	A hierarchy is a defined arrangement of category data items based on a parent-child relationship. In many cases, the levels of the hierarchy are arranged with the more general information at the top (for example, year) and the more specific information at the bottom (for example, month). Hierarchies enable you to add drill-down functionality to graphs and tables. Hierarchies that consist of all geographic data items are considered geographic hierarchies and can be used in geo maps. **Note:** You can create a date hierarchy from a date data item. The date hierarchy, by default, has levels for year, quarter, month, and day. A date hierarchy created from a datetime data item has levels, by default, for year, quarter, month, day, hour, minute, and second. For more information about hierarchies, see "Working with Hierarchies in a Report" in the *SAS Visual Analytics: Working with Report Data* documentation.
Distinct count	A distinct count counts the number of distinct values of a category data item as an aggregated measure. This means that the calculation changes depending on the other data items available in the graph. For example, you can see the number of orders placed for each age group or the number of orders placed for each country by creating a distinct count from Order ID. For more information about creating distinct counts, see "Working with Data Items in a Report" in the *SAS Visual Analytics: Working with Report Data* documentation. **Note:** If the category contains missing values, the distinct count is increased by one. A configuration setting can modify this behavior.
Parameter	A parameter is a variable whose value can be changed and that can be referenced by other report objects. Parameters can be used in control objects in Visual Analytics. When the value of the control changes, the parameter is updated with that value, and any report objects that reference that parameter are updated as well. Parameters can be used in calculations, display rules, filters, ranks, URLs, and text objects. For more information about parameters, see "Working with Parameters in Reports" in the *SAS Visual Analytics: Working with Report Data* documentation.
Derived item	Derived data items are aggregated measures that display values for the measure and the formula type on which the derived item is based. For more information about derived items, see "Working with Data Items in a Report" in the *SAS Visual Analytics: Working with Report Data* documentation.

The following types of derived items can be created from category data items.

Table 3.3: Derived Data Items from Category Data Items

Derived Item	Description
Distinct count	Displays the number of distinct values for the selected category. For more information, see the distinct count row in Table 3.2.
Count	Displays the number of nonmissing values for the selected category.
Number missing	Displays the number of missing values for the selected category.

The following types of derived items can be created from measure data items.

Table 3.4: Derived Data Items from Measure Data Items.

Derived Item	Description
Cumulative total	Displays a running total of all the values for the measure on which it is based.
Data suppression	Obscures aggregated data if individual data values could easily be inferred. Data suppression replaces all values for the measure on which it is based with an asterisk (*) unless a value represents the aggregation of a specified minimum number of values. For more information, see "Reference: Operators for Data Expressions" in the SAS Visual Analytics 8.3: Working with Report Data documentation.
Difference from previous period	Displays the difference between the value for the current time period and the value for the previous time period.
Difference from previous parallel period	Displays the difference between the value for the current time period and the value for the previous parallel time period within a longer time interval.
Moving average	Displays a moving average (rolling average) for the measure on which it is based. The moving average calculates the average for each value with the specified number of preceding values.
Percent difference from previous period	Displays the percentage difference between the value for the current time period and the value for the previous time period.
Percent difference from previous parallel period	Displays the percentage difference between the value for the current time period and the value for the previous parallel time period within a longer time interval.
Percent of subtotals	Displays the percentage of the subtotal value for the measure on which it is based. You can create a percentage of subtotal only when the source data item has an aggregation of Sum or Count. **Note:** The Percent of subtotals derived item is available only for use in crosstabs. **Note:** The Percent of subtotals derived item is relative to the subset of data that is selected by your filters and ranks.
Percent of total - sum	Displays the percentage of the total value for the measure on which it is based. You can create a percentage of total only when the source data item has an aggregation of Sum or Count. **Note:** The Percent of total – sum derived item is relative to the subset of data that is selected by your filters and ranks.
Period to date	Displays the aggregated value for the current time period and all of the previous time periods within a larger time interval.

Derived Item	Description
Year to date	Displays the aggregated value for the current time period and all of the previous time periods within the year. The year-to-date calculation subsets the data for each year using today's date (where today is evaluated each time you view the report).
Year to date growth	Displays the percentage difference between the year-to-date value for the current time period and the year-to-date value for the same time period of the previous year. The year-to-date calculation subsets the data for each year using today's date (where today is evaluated each time you view the report).
Year over year growth	Displays the percentage difference between the current time period and an equivalent time period from the previous year. The year-over-year calculation subsets the data for each year using today's date (where today is evaluated each time you view the report).

Example: Calculating Customer Age

Given the values of **Customer Birth Date** and today's date, how would you calculate **Customer Age**?

Figure 3.7: Calculated Columns: Customer Age

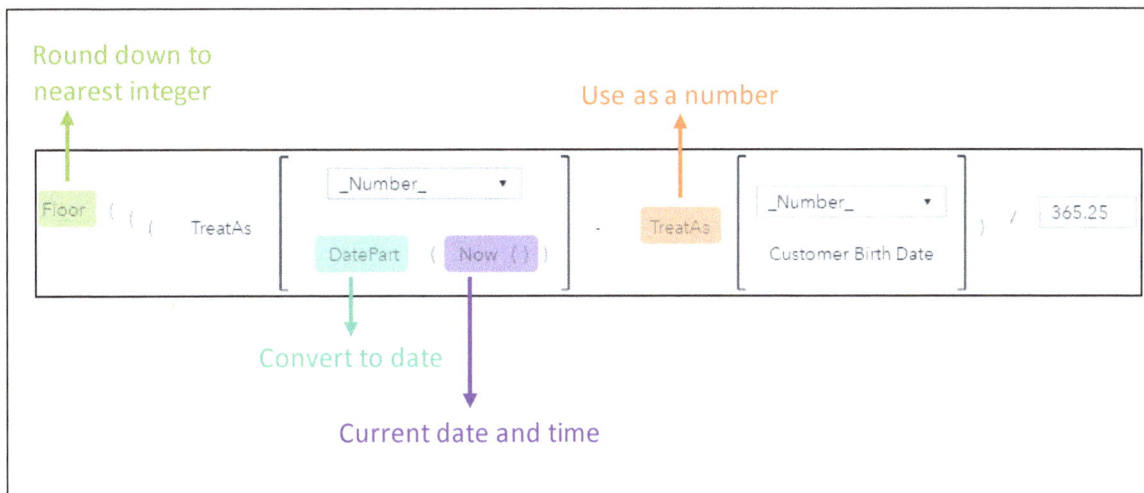

Ages are best calculated in Visual Analytics because you can use operators to ensure that they are updated each time a report is opened. To calculate **Customer Age**, you can use the expression shown below.

Customer Age = (Today - Customer Birth Date) / 365.25

The Now operator creates a Datetime value. It uses the current date and time, where the current date and time is evaluated every time you view the report. The DatePart operator then converts that Datetime value to a Date value. The TreatAs operator enables a Numeric, or Datetime, value to be used as a different data type for the operation. In this case, the dates are treated as numbers for the expression. The Numeric value of a date represents the number of days since January 1, 1960. When both dates are converted to numbers, the Birth Date is subtracted from the current date to return the age of the person in days. To convert to years, this number is divided by 365.25. Because people often don't state their ages in decimals, the Floor operator is used to round the number down to the nearest integer. This type of calculation can also be used to calculate the age of a company, tenure (or the length of time at a company), or the number of years between two dates.

Note: Creating calculated items and aggregated measures is discussed in more detail in Chapter 11.

Custom Category

Sometimes, you might need to create labels for groups of category or measure data items. This can be accomplished with calculated items. However, custom categories can do the same thing but are a bit easier to create. When you create a custom category from a measure data item, you can use intervals or distinct values to group the data. For example, you can create a custom category that shows discount ranges by assigning labels to ranges of discount values. The same grouping could be accomplished with a calculated item, but the expression is much more complex. When you create a custom category from a category data item, you can use distinct values to group the data. For example, you can create a custom category that groups continents into hemispheres. Again, the same grouping could be accomplished with a calculated item, but it is a bit more difficult to implement.

Figure 3.8: Example of a Custom Category

Custom categories create labels for groups of category or measure data items.

Custom category

Value Groups

ˇ Northern

  Asia

  Europe

  North America

ˇ Southern

  Africa

  Oceania

Calculated item

IF   Continent Name   In   (multiple selected)

                               (Asia, Europe, North America)

RETURN   Northern

ELSE   Southern

This calculated item and custom category produce equivalent results.

Demo 3.4: Creating Data Items

This demonstration illustrates how to create new data items (distinct counts, custom categories) in Visual Analytics.

1. From the browser window, sign in to SAS Viya.
2. In the upper left corner, click ☰ (**Show list of applications**) and select **Explore and Visualize**. SAS Visual Analytics appears.

3. Click All Reports.
   a. Navigate to the Courses/YVA185/Basics/Demos (Marketing) folder.
   b. Double-click the VA1-Demo3.3a report to open it.
4. In the upper left corner of the report, click the **Page 3** tab.
5. View new calculated items (**Number of Orders**, **Customer Age**, and **Customer Age Group**).
   a. In the left pane, click **Data**.
   b. In the Aggregated Measure group, view **Number of Orders** (new derived data item).

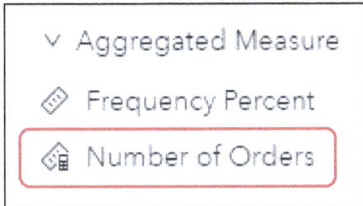

   > ∨ Aggregated Measure
   >
   > ◇ Frequency Percent
   >
   > 🖩 Number of Orders

   Note: You can view the calculation by right-clicking the calculated item and selecting **Edit**.

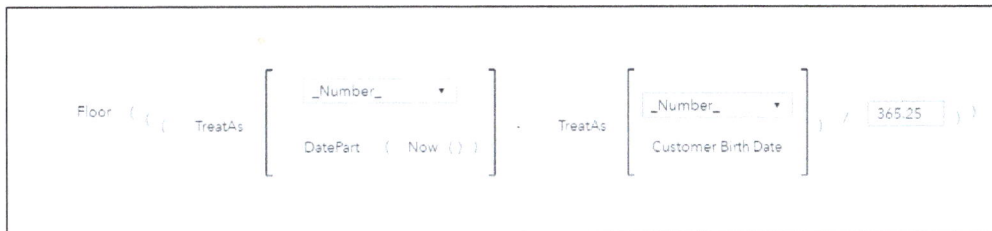

   Distinct   _ByGroup_   ▾   (Order ID   )

   c. In the Measure group, view **Customer Age** (new calculated data item).

   > ∨ Measure
   >
   > 🖩 Customer Age
   >
   > ◇ Days to Delivery
   >
   > ◇ Discount

   Note: You can view the calculation by right-clicking the calculated item and selecting **Edit**.

   Floor ((TreatAs [_Number_ ▾ / DatePart (Now ( ))] - TreatAs [_Number_ ▾ / Customer Birth Date]) / 365.25))

d. In the Category group, right-click **Customer Age Group** and select **Edit**.
    The expression should resemble the following:

IF (Customer Age <= 29)

RETURN " 29 and below "

IF Customer Age BetweenInclusive [30 / 44]

RETURN " 30-44 years "

ELSE

IF Customer Age BetweenInclusive [45 / 59]

RETURN " 45-59 years "

ELSE

IF Customer Age BetweenInclusive [60 / 74]

ELSE

RETURN " 60-74 years "

ELSE " 75 and above "

e. Click **Cancel** to close the Edit Calculated Item window.

6. Create new distinct count data items.

a. In the Category group, right-click **Customer ID** and select **New calculation**.

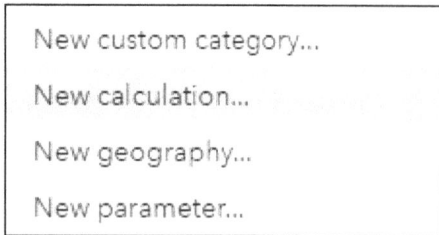

New custom category...

New calculation...

New geography...

New parameter...

b. In the **Name** field, enter **Number of Customers**.

c. For the **Type** field, verify that **Distinct count** is selected.

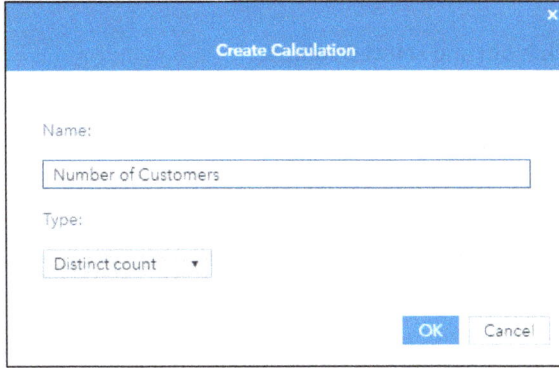

d. Click **OK**.

The new data item, **Number of Customers**, is added to the Aggregated Measure group.

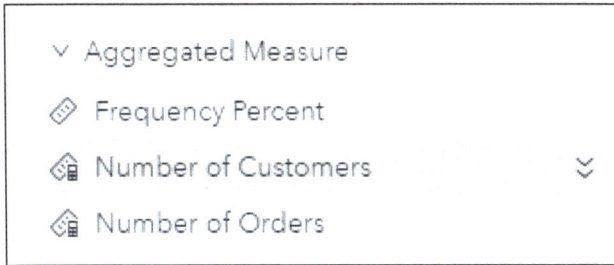

7. Create an automatic chart.

a. In the Data pane, select the following data items:

Number of Orders

Order Type

Note: Number of Customers should already be selected.

b. Drag the columns to the left side of the canvas.

The automatic chart functionality determines the best way to display the selected data.

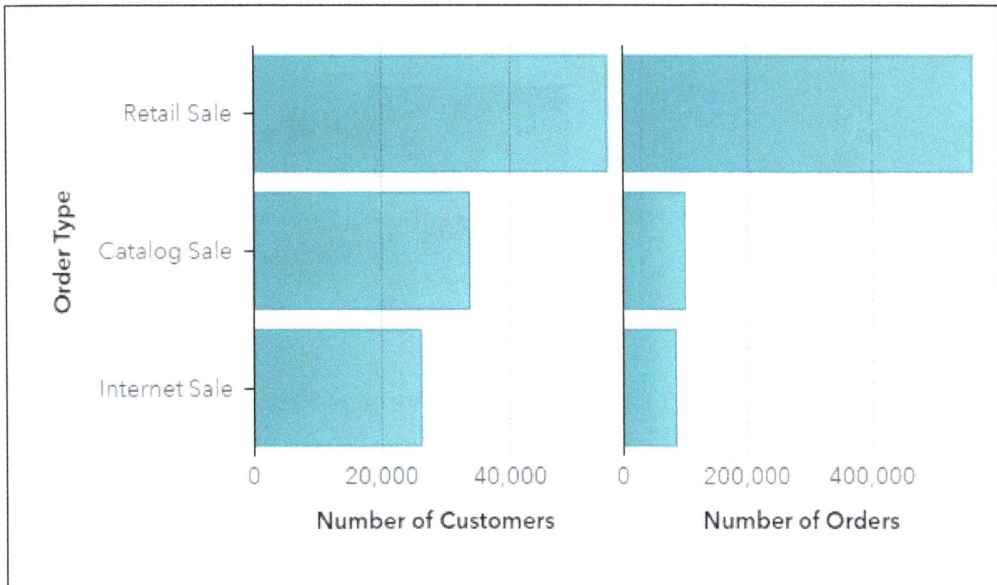

Total profit is lower in the internet and catalog channels because there are fewer customers that place orders through those channels. There are also significantly lower orders placed through those channels.

c. In the right pane, click **Options**.

d. In the Object group, for the **Name** field, enter **Customers and Orders by Order Type**.

8. Duplicate a data item and modify data item properties.

    a. In the left pane, click **Data**.

    b. In the Measure group, right-click **Profit** and select **Duplicate**.

    c. Next to the new data item, **Profit (1)**, click ⌄ (**Edit properties**).

    d. For the **Aggregation** field, select **Average**.

    e. In the **Name** field, enter **Average Profit** and press Enter.

9. Modify the Average Profits by Order Type and Continent bar chart.

    a. In the canvas, click the **Average Profit by Order Type and Continent** bar chart to make it active.

    b. In the right pane, click **Roles**.

    c. In the left pane, click **Data**.

    d. Drag **Average Profit** on top of **Profit** to replace the measure in the Roles pane.

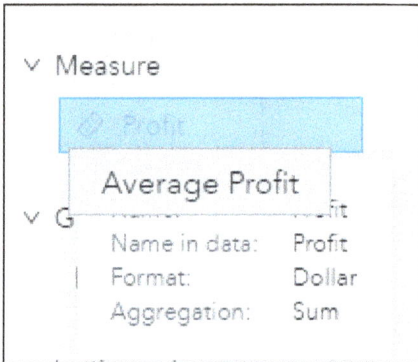

The bar chart should resemble the following:

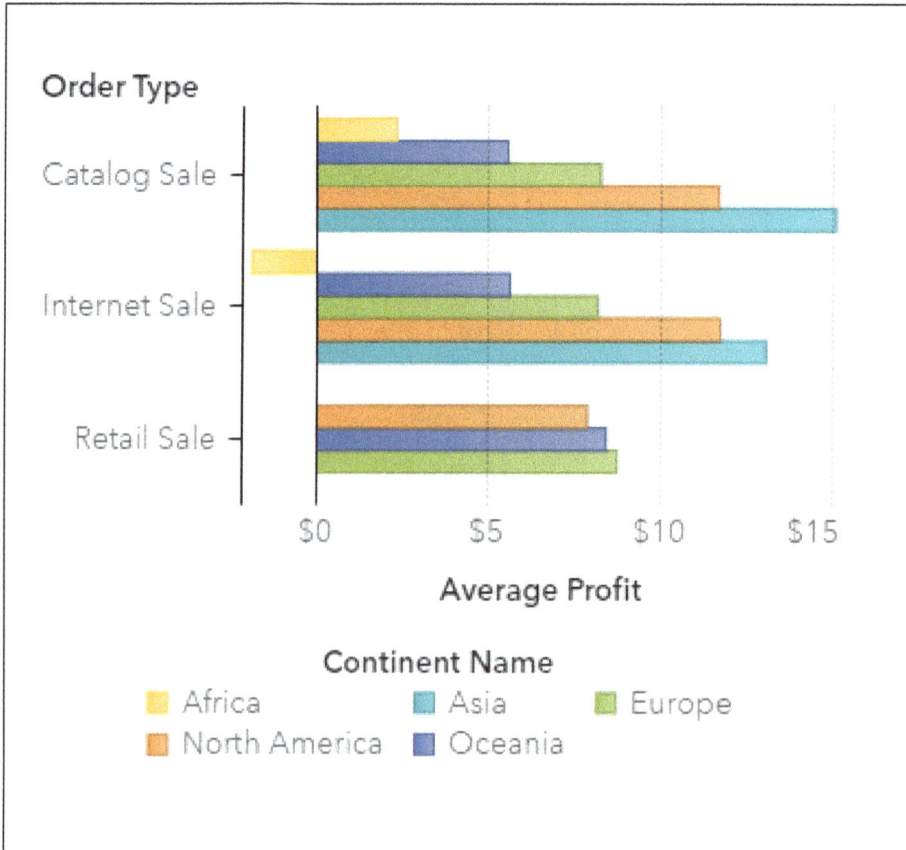

Ideally, we would want to increase orders placed for existing customers that produce the highest average profit. In this example, that would be Asian customers who order through the catalog. However, because corporate headquarters is located in North America, management has decided that the initial marketing strategy should focus on increasing sales among North

American customers who order through the catalog and internet. Then, if the marketing strategy is successful, it is implemented in other locations.

10. Create a new custom category, **Loyalty Member**.

   a. In the Data pane, select **New data item** ⇨ **Custom category**.

   b. In the New Custom Category window, in the **Name** field, enter **Loyalty Member**.

   c. For the **Based on** field, select **Loyalty Num**.

   d. Select **Value Group 1** to edit the group name.

   i. Type **No** and press Enter.

   ii. In the left pane, click **00** and drag to the **Drag values here** area on the right.

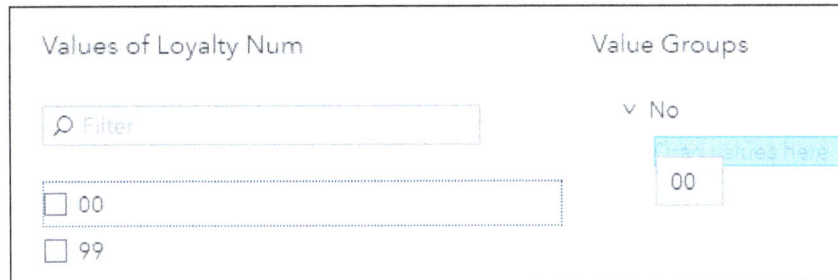

Values of Loyalty Num	Value Groups
🔍 Filter	∨ No
☐ 00	Drag values here
☐ 99	00

   e. Drag **99** to the **Click or drag values here to add a value group** area.

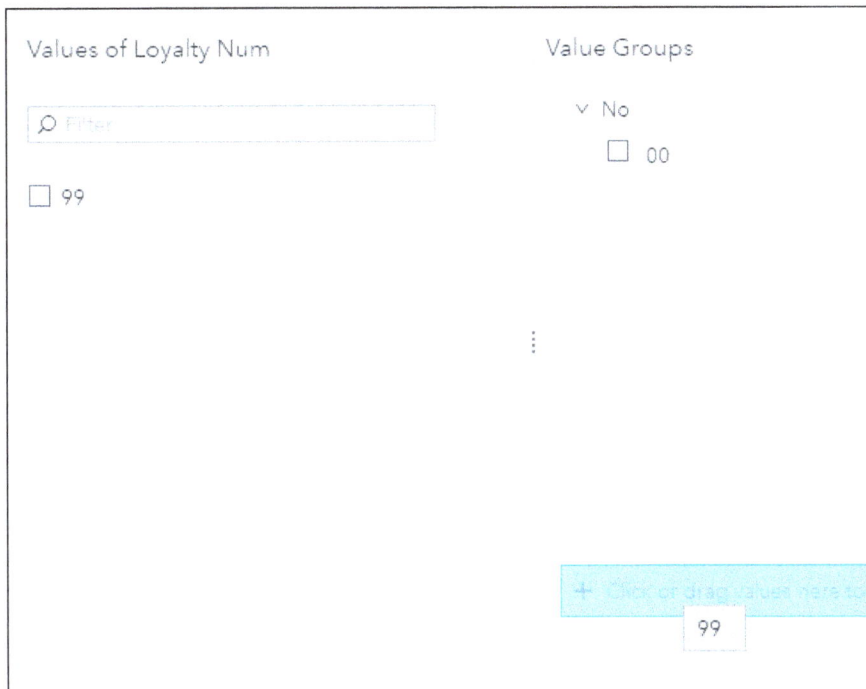

Values of Loyalty Num	Value Groups
🔍 Filter	∨ No
☐ 99	☐ 00
	⋮
	+ Click or drag values here to...
	99

   i. Select **Value Group 1**.

   ii. Type **Yes** and press Enter.

The Value Groups area should resemble the following:

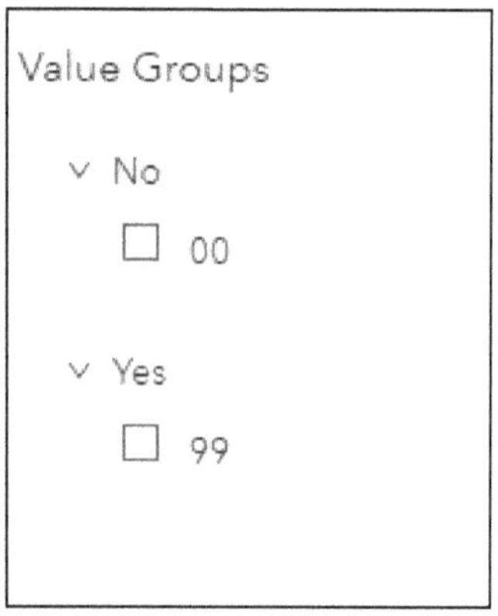
Value Groups
No
00
Yes
99

a. In the Remaining Values area, for the **Group as** field, verify that **Other** is specified.

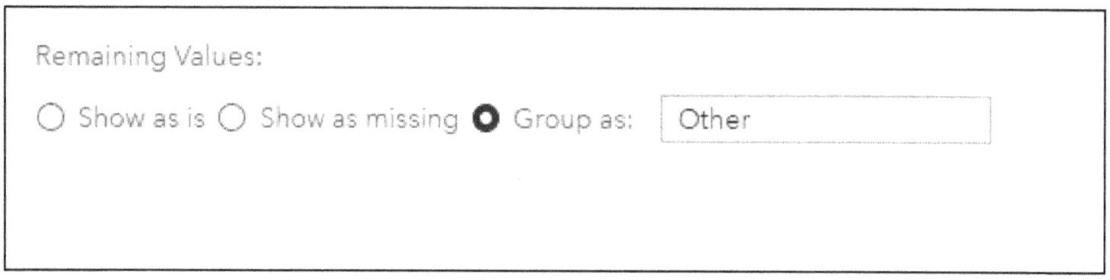
Remaining Values:
Show as is
Show as missing
Group as:
Other

b. Click **OK** to create the new custom category.

Note: As an alternative, you can also create a calculated data item with the following expression:

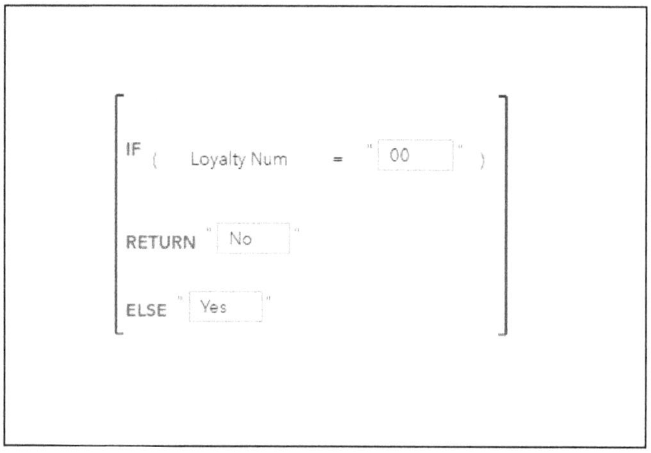
IF
Loyalty Num
=
00
RETURN
No
ELSE
Yes

The new data item, **Loyalty Member**, should appear in the Category group.

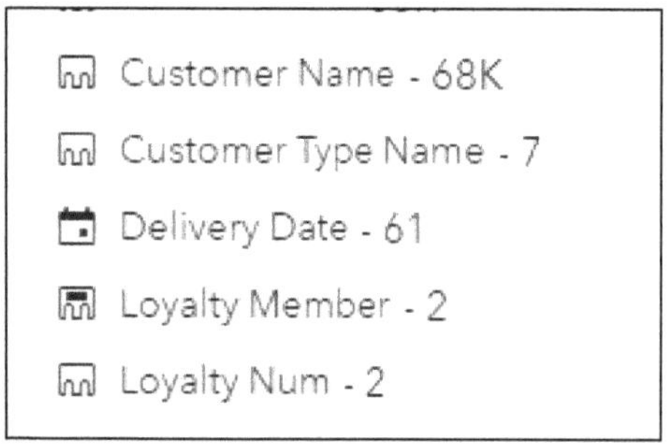
Customer Name - 68K
Customer Type Name - 7
Delivery Date - 61
Loyalty Member - 2
Loyalty Num - 2

11. Duplicate the **Average Profits by Order Type and Continent** bar chart.
    a. In the canvas area, right-click the **Average Profits by Order Type and Continent** bar chart and select **Duplicate** to copy the bar chart.
    b. Click ▪▪▪▪ above the new bar chart and drag to the drop zone to the bottom of the **Average Profits by Order Type and Continent** bar chart.
    c. In the right pane, click **Roles**.
    d. For the **Category** role, select **Order Type** ⇨ **Loyalty Member**.

e. For the **Group** role, select **Continent Name** ⇨ **Customer Age Group**.

f. In the right pane, click **Options**.

g. In the Object group, for the **Name** field, enter **Average Profits by Loyalty Membership and Age Group**.

h. In the Bar group, for the **Direction** field, click [icon] (**Vertical**).

The bar chart should resemble the following:

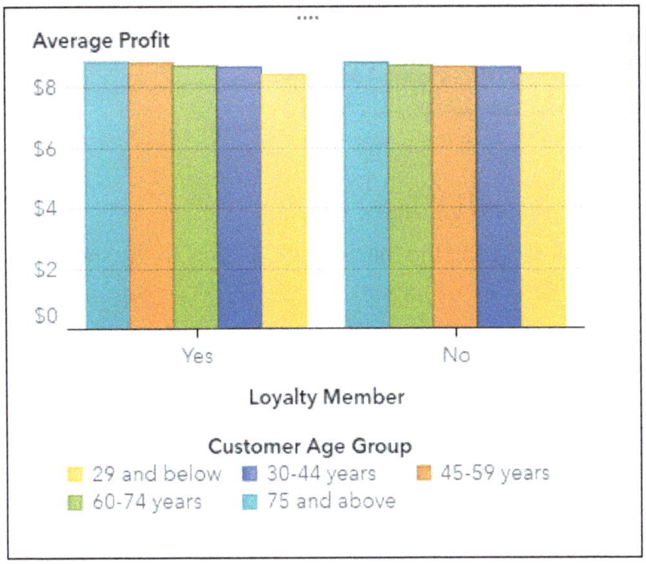

Average profits are similar across loyalty members and non-loyalty members. Average profits are slightly higher for loyalty members in the 75 and above age group.

12. Save the report.

End of Demonstration

Activity 3.2

Given the values of **Employee Hire Date** and **Employee Termination Date**, how would you calculate **Years of Service**?

Employee Hire Date	Employee Termination Date
01Dec2004	28Feb2007
01Nov2005	.
25Jan2005	.
01Mar2005	28Feb2010
31May2005	31May2012
11Dec2005	.
01Sep2002	.

Practice 3.4

1. Creating Data Items
    a. Open the browser and sign in to SAS Viya.
    b. Open the **VA1-Practice3.3a** report from the **Courses/YVA185/Basics/Practices (HR)** folder.
    c. Create a new data item, **Employee Status**, by assigning the following labels to the values:

Employee Status (label)	Employee Termination Date (value)
Active	.
Retired	<all remaining values>

    d. On Page 3, create a bar chart by assigning the following data items to the specified roles:

Category	Job Title
Measure	Years of Service
Group	Employee Status

    e. Specify **Years of Service by Job Title and Status** as the name of the bar chart.
    f. Change the aggregation for **Years of Service** to **Average**.

    The bar chart should resemble the following:

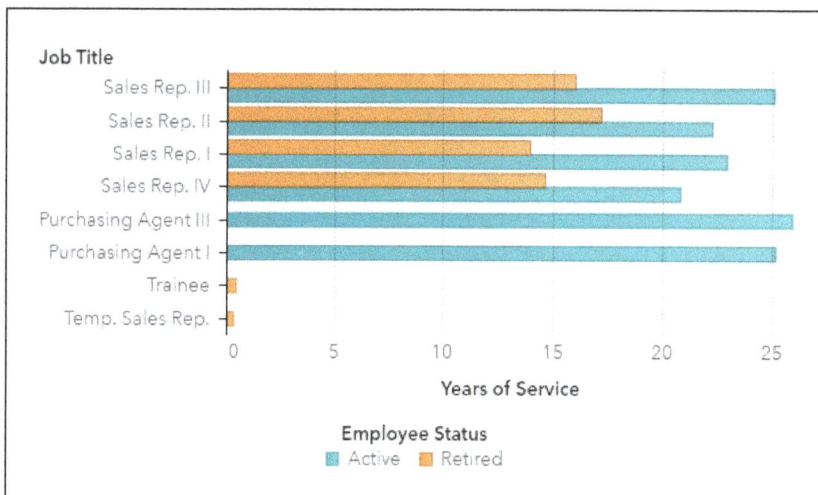

    g. Answer the following questions:

    Which job title has the highest average years of service among active employees? Among retired employees?

    Answer:

    h. Save the report.

End of Practices

Filters

Many different types of filters can be created to subset data in Visual Analytics. In general, these filters are split between those that can be modified by only the Report Designer and those that can also be modified by the Report Viewer. In this chapter, we focus on filters that can be modified by the Report Designer. These filters can be classified into two types:

- Detail report filters
- Post-aggregate report filters

Detail report filters look at the individual values for data items, but post-aggregate report filters look at the aggregated, or total, values. Detail report filters can be split between those that are applied at a global level and those that are applied at a local level. At the global level, a data source filter can be added to subset the entire report. This filter is applied to every object that uses the data source. It acts as a pre-filter by filtering the data before it is brought into Visual Analytics. This can be seen in the updated cardinality values in the Data pane after the filter is applied.

Figure 3.9: Filtering Data

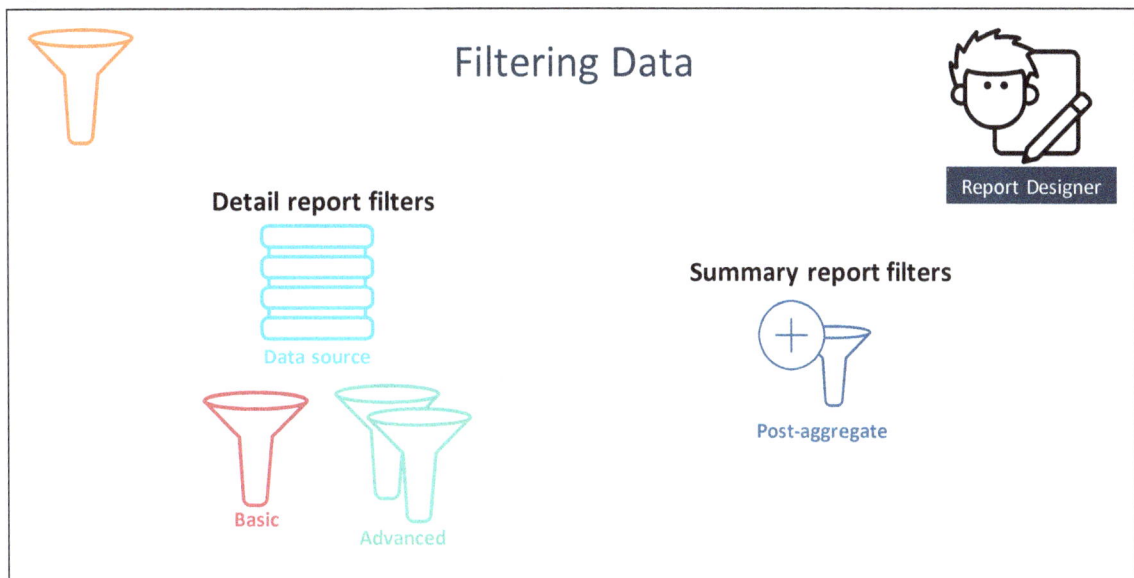

At the local level, Basic and Advanced report filters can be added to subset individual report objects. The Basic report filter subsets the object using a single data item and an equality condition, while the Advanced report filter subsets the object using any number of data items and operators in the same expression. Each of these local filters subsets the data using detail data or individual values for data items. The Post-aggregate report filter subsets the report object using aggregated values, not individual values. These aggregated values are evaluated in the report object and are used to specify the minimum and maximum values in the selectable range. Filters can be very helpful to focus on anomalies or inconsistencies that are discovered during analysis.

Note: Distinct counts and derived data items are special types of aggregated measure.

Note: SAS Visual Analytics treats datetime values as character data. To use numeric operators with datetime values, the TreatAs operator is required.

The following types of filters can be created and modified only by the report designer:

Table 3.5: Filters

Filter	Description
Data source filter	Subsets the data for the entire report and is applied to every report object that uses that data source. The data source filter acts as a pre-filter by filtering the data before it is brought into Visual Analytics. This can be seen by the updated cardinality values in the Data pane after the filter has been applied.
Basic report filter	Subsets the data for individual report objects by using a single data item.
Advanced report filter	Subsets the data for individual report objects by using any number of data items and operators in the same expression.
Post-aggregate report filter	Subsets the data for individual report objects by using aggregated values, not summarized values. Post-aggregate report filters are available only for measure data items.

For more information about filters that can be created and modified by the report designer, see "Working with Report Filters" in the *SAS Visual Analytics: Working with Report Data* documentation.

Filters that can be modified by report viewers are discussed in more detail in a later section. Filters are applied in the following order:

- data source filter (or filters)
- basic or advanced report filter/ post-aggregate report filter
- prompts and actions

Note: More advanced filtering techniques are discussed in Chapter 12.

Geography Maps and Data Item

When location is a critical component of your analysis, geo maps can be very helpful. A geo map overlays data on a geographic map. Four different types of geo maps can be created in Visual Analytics: Coordinate, Region, Bubble, and Contour.

Figure 3.10: Geo Maps

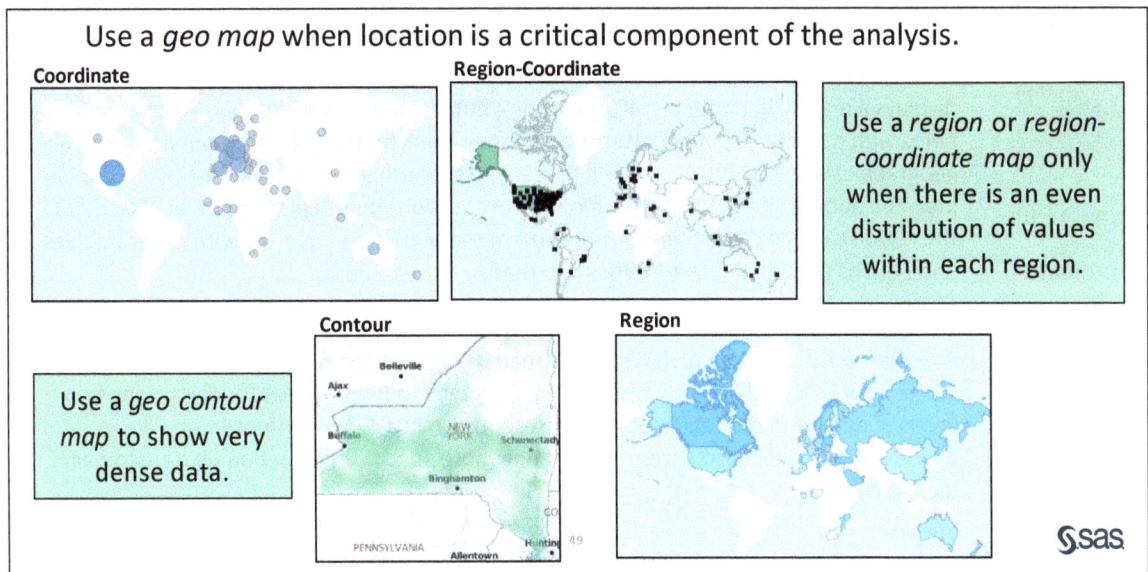

Coordinate maps (also known as dot distribution maps or dot density maps) help with detecting spatial patterns and understanding the distribution of data over a geographic region. These maps use clustered points to help reveal patterns. Region maps (also known as choropleth maps) use colors to show variations by location. With region maps, larger regions seem more emphasized than smaller ones, which can skew your analysis. Geo region or coordinate maps should be used only when there is an even distribution of values within each region. Alternatively, geo bubble maps can be used even when data is not evenly distributed. This is because bubble maps can compare two measures. One is used for the size of the bubble and one is used for the color of the bubble. Bubble maps also have another advantage over region maps. The bubble size helps with comparing regions without the size of the region itself causing distortions. Sometimes, however, the size of the bubble can overlap with other bubbles making the chart difficult to read. Contour maps display shaded regions over a geographic region. These are best used to show very dense data.

When you create geo maps, a geography data item is needed. A geography data item is a category whose values are mapped to geographic locations or regions. Geography data items can be created using predefined roles (for example, country names), by associating latitude and longitude coordinates with the values, or by associating polygon data from a separate data source with regions.

Table 3.6: Geo Map Types

Map Type	Description
Geo map	A geo map overlays data on a geographic map. Data can be displayed using colored regions, coordinates, or regions and coordinates, as a contour plot, or as a network. In order to display data on a geo map, at least one category data item must have values that are mapped to geographical locations or regions.
Region	A regions geo map (also known as a *choropleth map*) uses colors to show variations by location. However, larger regions appear more emphasized than smaller ones, which can affect perceptions of colors.

Map Type	Description
Coordinate	A coordinates geo map (also known as a *dot distribution map* or a *dot density map*) displays a map with either a scatter plot or a bubble plot of coordinates. This type of map helps with detecting spatial patterns and understanding the distribution of data over a geographical region, which can help reveal patterns using clustered points. For a bubble plot, the bubble size helps with comparing proportions over regions without the size of the region causing distortions, but the size of the bubble can overlap with other bubbles and regions making the chart difficult to read.
Region-Coordinate	A region-coordinate geo map displays a map using both colored regions and either a scatter plot or bubble plot of coordinates. This type of map is great for comparing two levels of data with the region colors representing more general information (like countries) and the coordinates representing more specific information (like customer locations).
Contour	A contour geo map displays shaded regions over a geographical region. Contour maps are best used to show very dense data.
Network	A network geo map displays a network diagram overlaid on a map. Network maps are helpful for understanding how location affects the relationships in the network. Network geo maps are discussed in more detail in a later lesson.

For more information about creating geography data items, see "Working with Geography Data Items" in the *SAS Visual Analytics: Working with Report Data* documentation.

Note: By default, Visual Analytics supports country- and state-level polygons for regional overlays in geo maps. An administrator can define a custom polygon provider to create regional overlays for other types of data. For more information about how to define a custom polygon provider, see "Loading Geographic Polygon Data as a CAS Table" in *SAS Visual Analytics: Administration Guide*.

Hierarchies

A hierarchy is a defined arrangement of category data items based on a parent-child relationship. In many cases, the levels of the hierarchy are arranged with more general information at the top and more specific information at the bottom. Hierarchies enable you to add drill-down functionality to graphs and tables. Hierarchies that consist of all geographic data items are considered geographic hierarchies and can be used in geo maps.

Figure 3.11: What Is a Hierarchy?

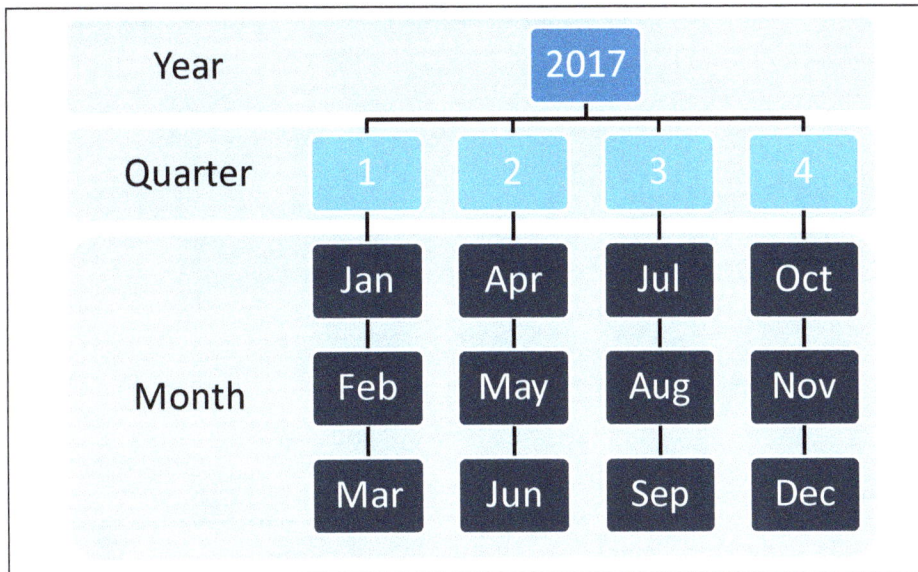

The following demonstration shows how to build a hierarchy as a new data item, create and use geographic data items and charts, and apply filters.

 Demo 3.5: Applying Filter

This demonstration illustrates how to create new data items (geographic data items, hierarchies) and apply filters in Visual Analytics.

1. From the browser window, sign in to SAS Viya.
2. In the upper left corner, click ☰ (**Show list of applications**) and select **Explore and Visualize**.
   SAS Visual Analytics appears.
3. Click All Reports.
   a. Navigate to the Courses/YVA185/Basics/Demos (Marketing) folder.
   b. Double-click the VA1-Demo3.3b report to open it.
4. In the upper left corner of the report, click the **Page 4** tab.
5. Create new data items.
   a. In the left pane, click **Data**.
   b. In the Category group, next to **State Name**, click ⌄ (**Edit properties**).
   c. For the **Classification** field, select **Geography**.
      i. For the Geography data field, verify that Geographic name or code lookup is selected.
      ii. For the Name or code context field, select **US State Names**.
         The map on the right shows that 19% of state names are mapped.

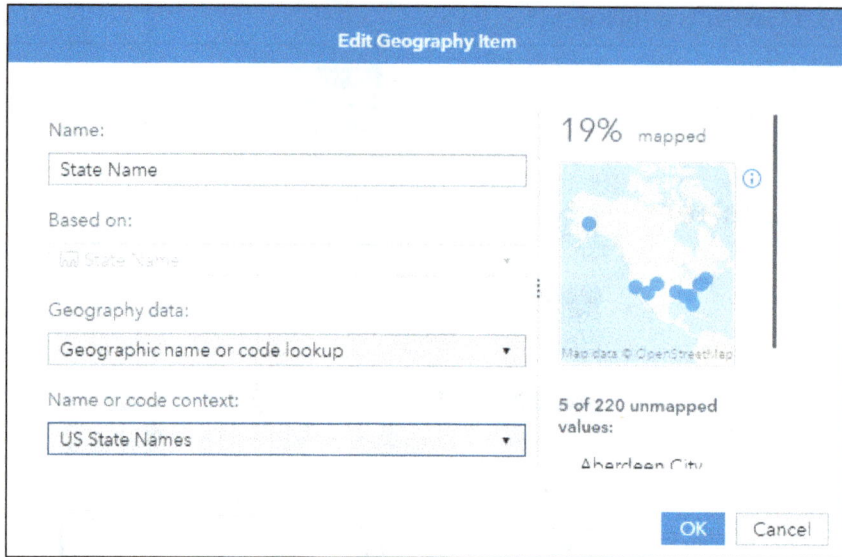

6. View the list of unmapped values.

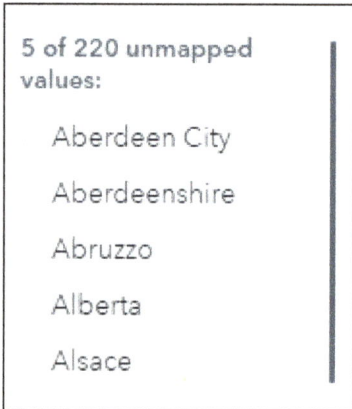

These values represent states and provinces in other countries. Later, we add a data source filter to focus on the United States.

7. Click **OK**.

A new group, **Geography**, is added to the Data pane.

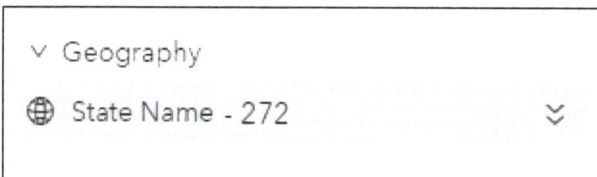

a. In the Data pane, next to **Postal code**, click ⟱ (**Edit properties**).

b. For the **Classification** field, select **Geography**.

i. For the Geography data field, verify that Geographic names or code lookup is selected.

ii. For the Name or code context field, select US ZIP Codes.

iii. Click OK.

The Geography group should resemble the following:

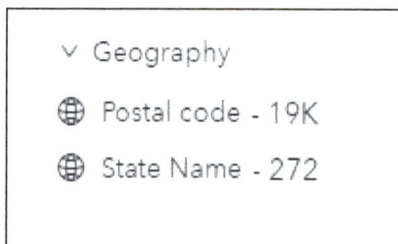

    c.   In the Data pane, select **New data item** ⇨ **Hierarchy**.

        i.   In the New Hierarchy window, for the **Name** field, enter **US Hierarchy**.

        ii.   Double-click the following data items in the Available items list, in the specified order, to move them to the Selected items list:

           State Name

           Postal code

           The New Hierarchy window should resemble the following:

Name:	
US Hierarchy	
Available items (15):	**Selected items (2):**
🔲 City Name - 11K	⊕ State Name - 272
🔲 Continent Name - 5	⊕ Postal code - 19K

8.   Click **OK**.

    A new group, **Hierarchy**, is added to the Data pane.

∨ Hierarchy
🧑 US Hierarchy   ≫

9.   Add a data source filter.

    a.   In the Data pane, click 🗒 (**Actions**) and select **Apply data filter**.

       Note: Because the new geography data items cover only the United States, a data source filter is added to include only the data for products ordered in the United States.

    b.   On the left, verify that **Data Items** is selected.

    c.   Expand the **Character** group.

    d.   Select **Customer Country**.

    e.   In the Conditions area, double-click **Customer Country In (x)** to add it to the expression area.

Customer Country	In	(none selected)

    f.   In the expression area, click **(none selected)**.

    g.   In the Select Data Values window, double-click **United States** to move it from the Available items list to the Selected items list.

Available items (46):	**Selected items (1):**
🔍 Filter	United States
Andorra	
Australia	

    h.   Click **OK**.

       The expression should resemble the following:

Customer Country	In	United States

The bottom of the Apply Data Filter window should resemble the following:

Returned observations: 232,258	Total observations: 951,669

Note: 232,258 observations have a value of *United States* for **Customer Country**.

   i.   Click **OK** to apply the data source filter.

The Data pane should resemble the following:

```
∨ Category

🔲 City Name - 4.5K

🔲 Continent Name - 1

🔲 Customer Age Group - 5

📅 Customer Birth Date - 4.3K

🔲 Customer Country - 1

🔲 Customer Group Name - 3
```

The data source filter updates the cardinality values that appear in the Data pane and is applied to every report object that uses this data source.

10. Create a geo map.

   a.   In the left pane, click **Objects**.

   b.   Drag the **Geo coordinate** object, from the Geographic group, to the canvas.

   c.   In the right pane, click **Roles**.

   d.   For the **Geography** role, select **Add** ⇨ **US Hierarchy**.

   e.   For the **Size** role, **Add** ⇨ **Frequency**.

   f.   For the **Color** role, select **Add** ⇨ **Profit**.

The Roles pane should resemble the following:

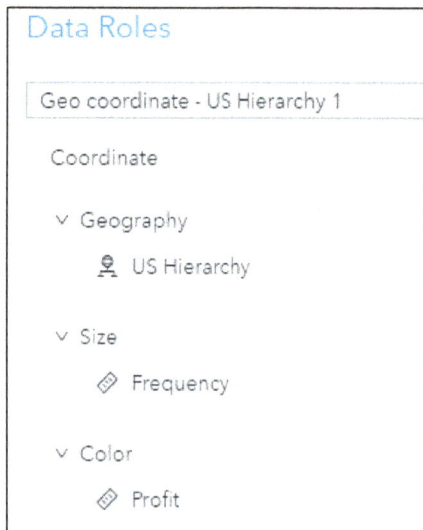

```
Data Roles

Geo coordinate - US Hierarchy 1

Coordinate

  ∨ Geography
      📍 US Hierarchy

  ∨ Size
      ◇ Frequency

  ∨ Color
      ◇ Profit
```

The geo coordinate map requires a geography data item for the Geography role. A measure data item can be added to the Color role to color the coordinates based on the measure. The geo map should resemble the following:

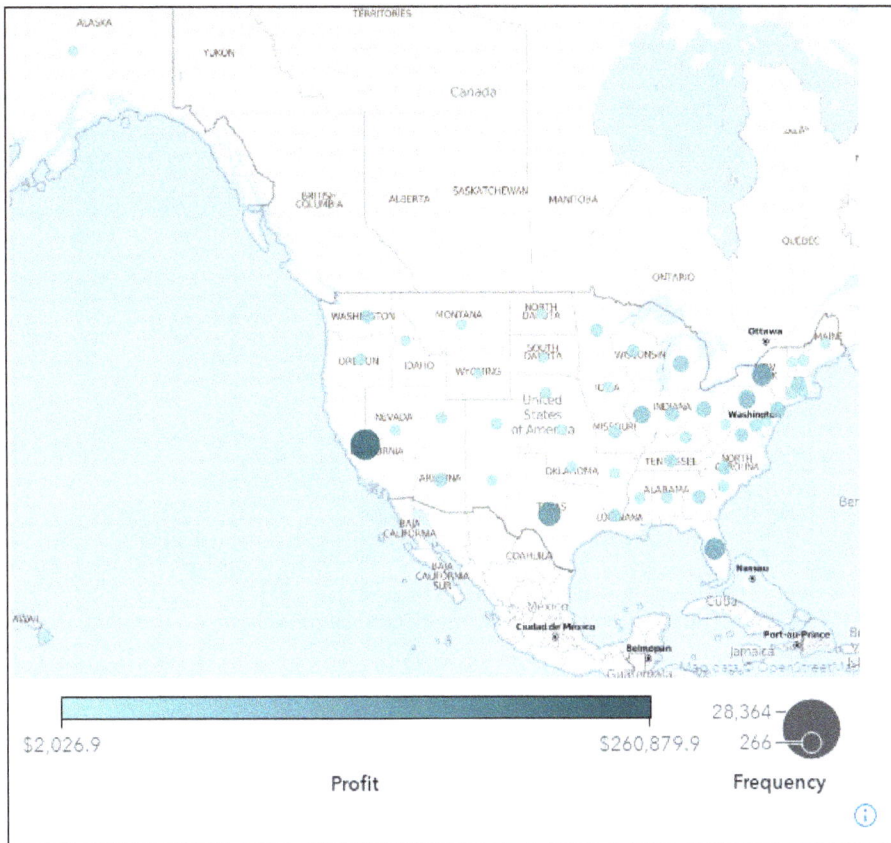

g. Place your cursor over ⓘ in the lower right corner of the geo map to view the warning.

> No matches were found for supplied geography data items: PR
> Some features may not be displayed on the map because of missing location information in the data.

Note: *PR* is not found in the US State Names predefined geographic role. You can filter this value out if you do not want to see the warning.

h. In the right pane, click **Options**.

i. In the Object group, for the **Name** field, enter **Profit by Location**.

j. In the Coordinate group, verify that **Scatter** is selected for the **Data layer render type** field.

k. For the **Initial marker shape** field, select **Diamond**.

l. For the **Marker size** field, select **30**.

The Options pane should resemble the following:

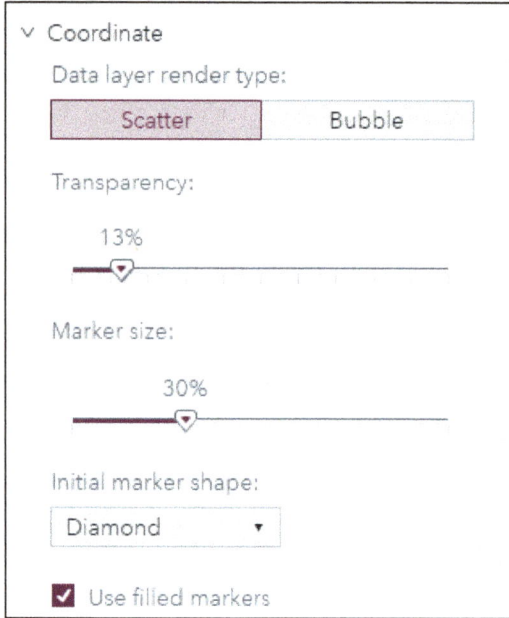

> ∨ Coordinate
>
> Data layer render type:
>
> | Scatter | Bubble |
>
> Transparency:
>
> 13%
>
> Marker size:
>
> 30%
>
> Initial marker shape:
>
> Diamond ▾
>
> ☑ Use filled markers

m. In the Legend group, for the **Placement** field, choose the middle on the right side.

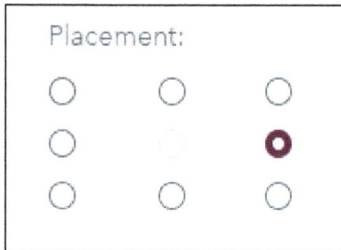

> Placement:
>
> ○   ○   ○
>
> ○   ●
>
> ○   ○   ○

The updated geo map should resemble the following:

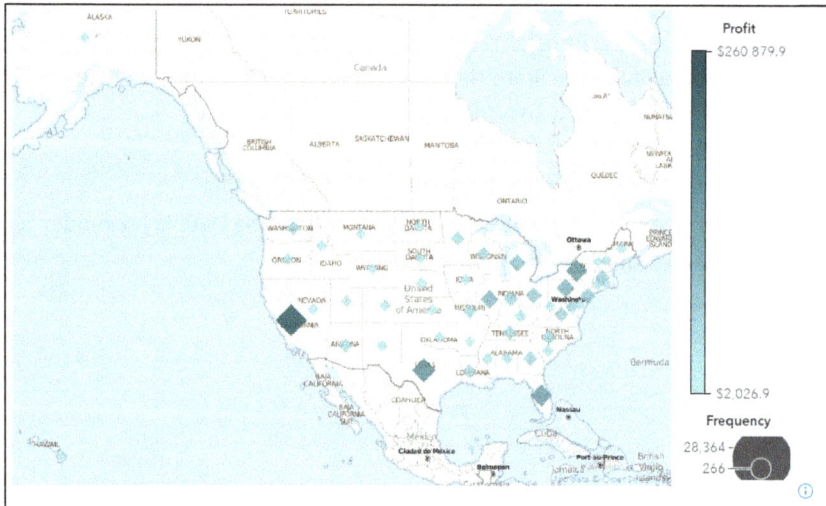

Highest total profits seem to be in larger states (California, Texas, and Florida), most likely because there are more customers and more orders placed in those states. Looking at average profits by location can give greater insight into orders placed in the United States.

n. Right-click the Geo coordinate map object and select Remove data ⇨ Frequency

o. Right-click the Geo coordinate map object and select Replace data ⇨ Profit.

p.   Select Average Profit.

The updated geo map should resemble the following:

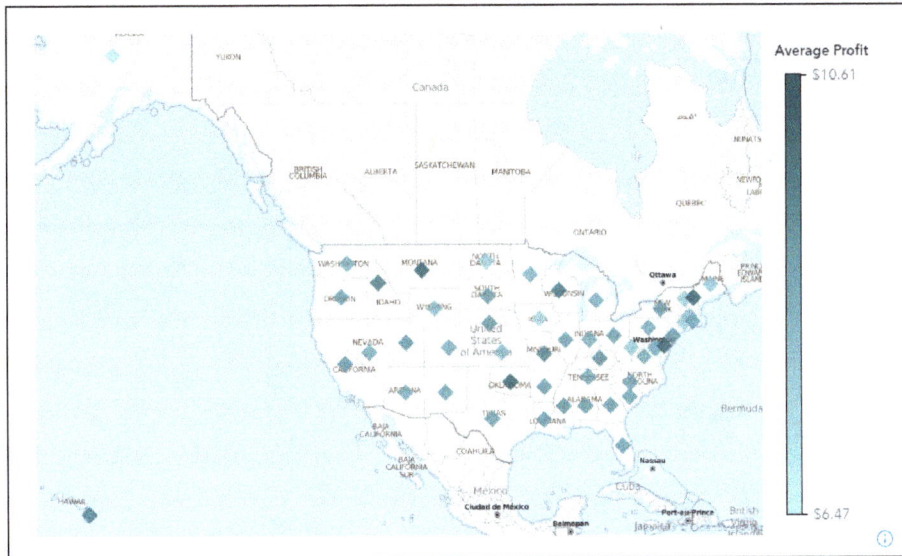

When looking at averages, there does not seem to be any clusters of higher average profits in any one location in the United States. High average profits seem to be evenly distributed across the United States.

q.   Double-click the marker for **Texas**.

The geo map displays markers for all postal codes in Texas where products were ordered.

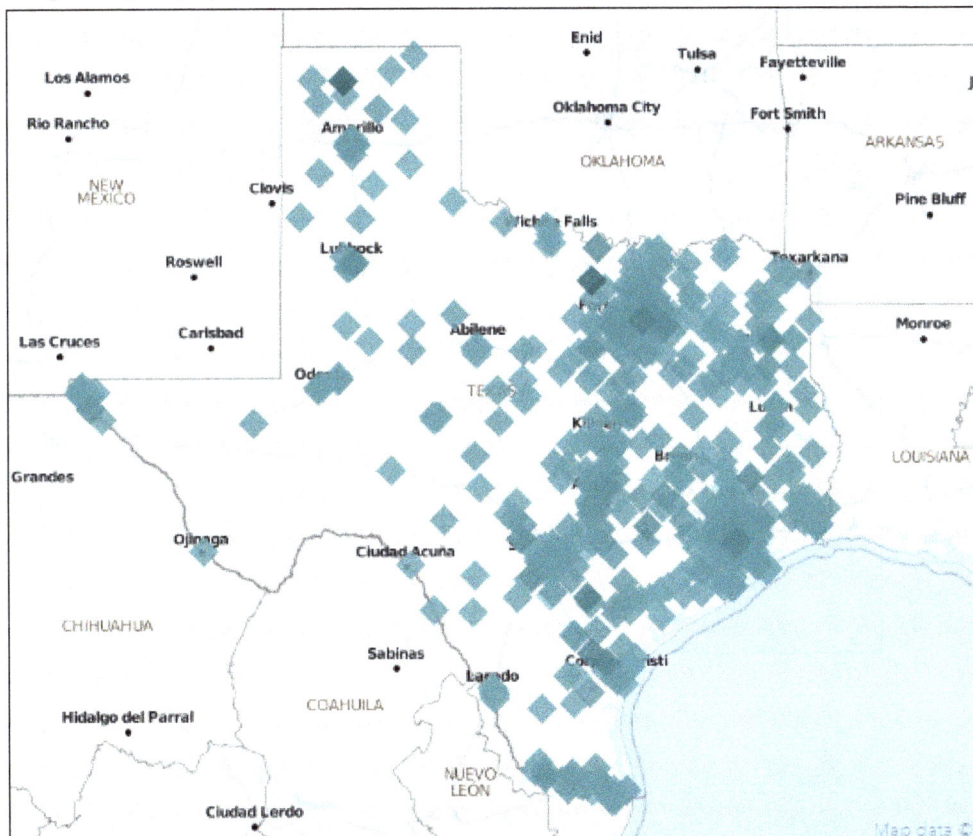

r.   In the upper left corner, click [📍] (**Location**).

s.   In the **Search** field, enter **Austin, TX**.

t. Double-click the first value in the search list, **Austin TX, USA**.

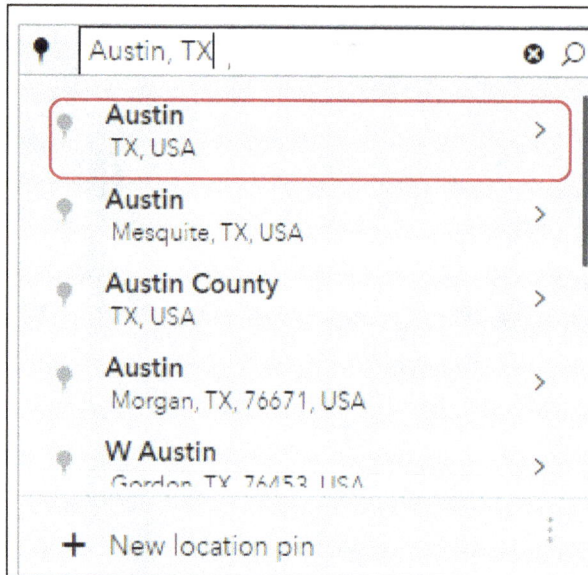

All locations containing combinations of **Austin, TX** are listed in the search. The location of Austin, Texas is marked on the geo map with a 1.

u. Select Geographic selection.

11. For the **Type** field, verify that **Distance** is selected.

12. For the **Unit** field, verify that **Miles** is selected.

13. For the **Distance** field, enter **50**.

The Geographic Selection window should resemble the following:

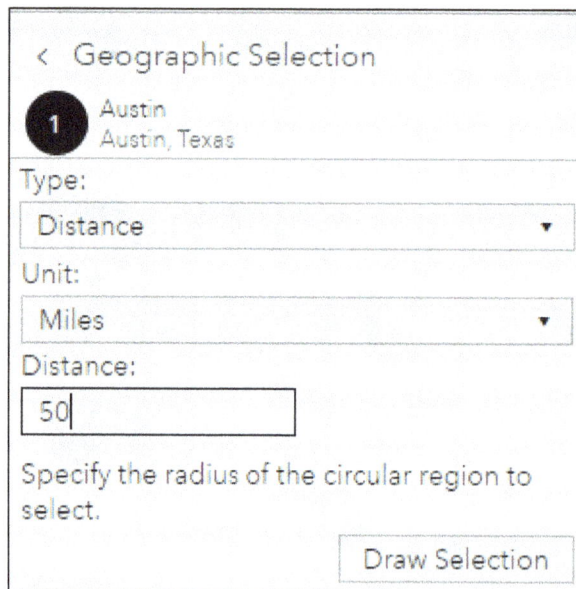

14. Click **Draw Selection**.

All customers within a 50-mile radius of Austin, TX, are highlighted.

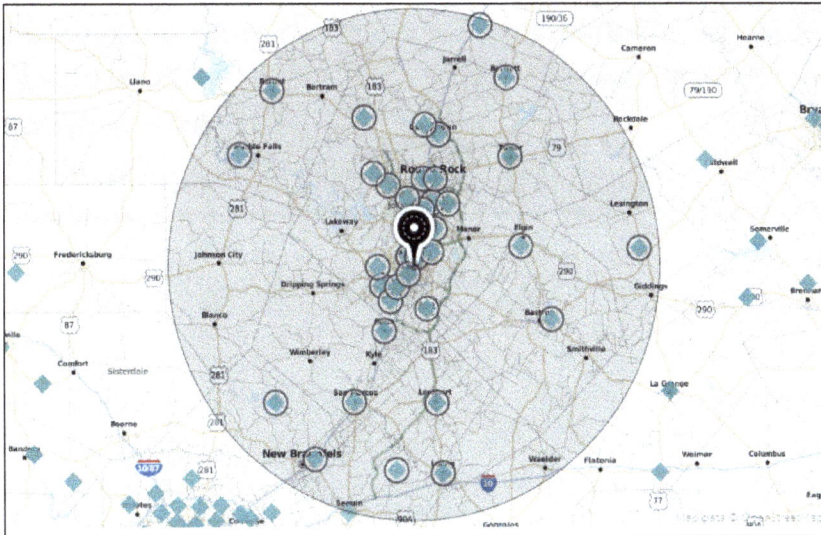

a. Right-click the Geo coordinate map and select **New filter from selection** ⇨ **Include only selection**.

b. In the right pane, click **Filters** to show the applied filter.

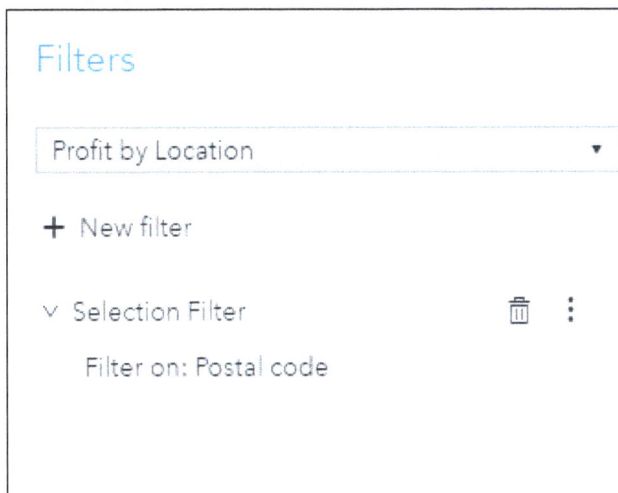

15. Save the report.

End of Demonstration

 Practice 3.5

1. Applying Filters

   a. Open the browser and sign in to SAS Viya.

   b. Open the **VA1-Practice3.3b** report from the **Courses/YVA185/Basics/Practices (HR)** folder.

   c. Add a data source filter to filter for active employees in the Sales Department.

   Note: Use the AND operator (in the Boolean group) to filter for multiple conditions. After the data source filter is applied, 429 observations should be returned.

   d. Change the classification for **Employee Country** to **Geography** ⇨ **Country or Region ISO 2-Letter Codes**.

e. On Page 4, create a geo coordinate map by assigning the following data items to the specified roles:

Category	Employee Country
Size	Total Profit
Color	Number of Employees

The geo map should resemble the following:

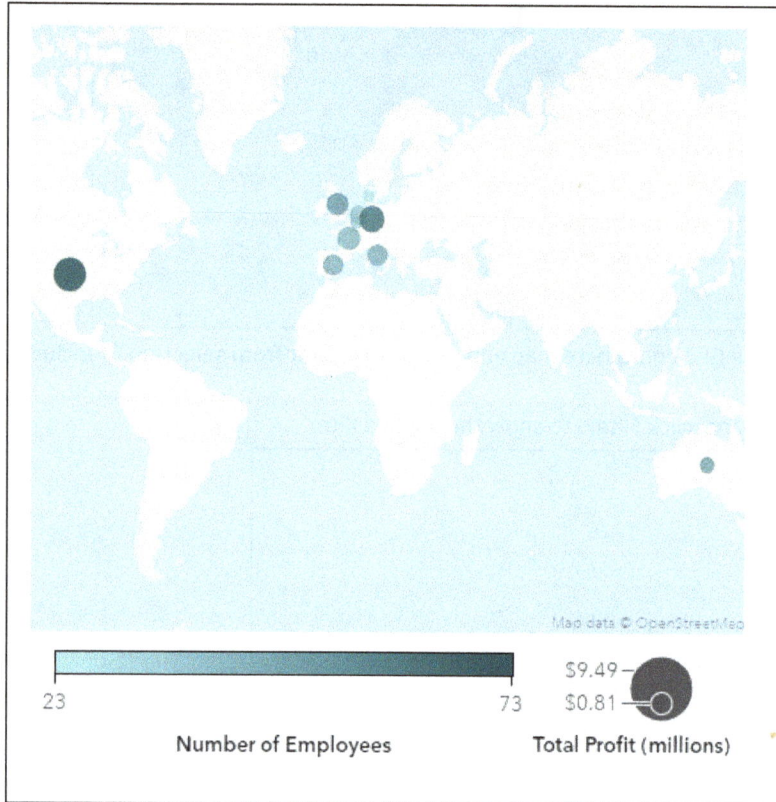

f. Maximize the geo map to answer the following questions:

Management has decided that one possible criterion for promotion is profit generated. Which two countries generate the highest profit? Why do they have such high profits?

Answer:

Hint: After answering the questions, click [icon] (**Restore**) in the upper right corner.

g. In the geo map, specify **Average Profit** for the **Size** role.

h. Specify **Average Profit and Number of Employees by Country** as the name of the geo map.

The updated geo map should resemble the following:

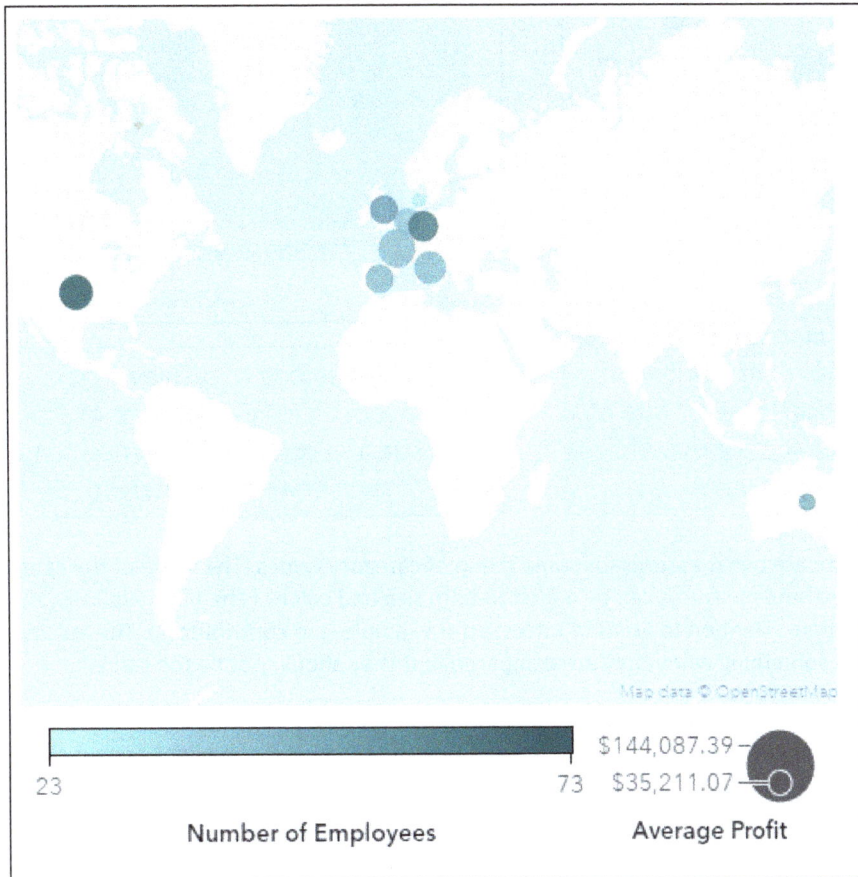

i. Maximize the geo map to answer the following question:

Which country has the highest average profit? Highest number of employees?

Answer:

Hint: After answering the question, click ⬚ (**Restore**) in the upper right corner.

j. Save the report.

End of Practices

3.4 Performing Data Analysis

The next section describes the objects that you can use to begin your analysis of the data.

Bubble Plots and Tree Plots

As part of your analysis, you might be interested in viewing differences between groups. This can be accomplished with analysis graphs (like bubble plots and treemaps). Bubble plots are useful for displaying three dimensions of data (horizontal location, vertical location, and size of bubble) for some group of category values. A bubble plot compares at least three measures by using markers of varying sizes in a scatter plot. The values of two measures determine the location of the bubble in the plot, and the value of the third measure determines the size of the bubble. Bubble plots can also be animated to show changes in data over time. For animated bubble plots, you want to focus on bubbles that act differently than the others. That is, bubbles that are stationary while others are moving or bubbles that are moving in a different direction from the rest of the group. Conversely, treemaps can be used to display lots of information in a small amount of space.

Figure 3.12: Analysis Graphs

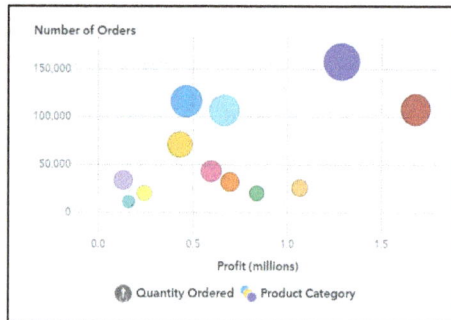

Use a *bubble plot* to display three dimensions of data (horizontal location, vertical location, size of bubble) for some group of category values.

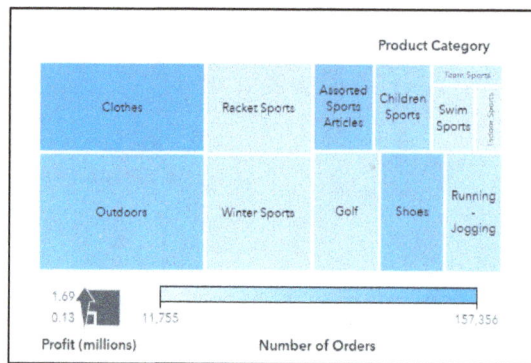

Use a *treemap* to display a lot of information in a small amount of space. Use size and color to draw attention to specific areas of interest.

A treemap can compare two measures for some group of category values. The value of the category is represented by tiles, and measures can be added to both size and color of the tiles. Typically, the size and color are used to draw attention to areas of interest (for example, top contributors). The measures that are used should mean something when they are compared, but they should not be the same.

Note: The layout of the tiles in the treemap is dependent on the size of the display area because it uses a space-filling algorithm to lay the tiles out. This means that the same treemap might appear slightly different while editing a report than it does while viewing a report or in the Visual Analytics app.

Demo 3.6: Analyzing Data

This demonstration illustrates how to analyze data with graphs in Visual Analytics.

1. From the browser window, sign in to SAS Viya.
2. In the upper left corner, click ☰ (**Show list of applications**) and select **Explore and Visualize**. SAS Visual Analytics appears.
3. Click All Reports.
   a. Navigate to the **Courses/YVA185/Basics/Demos (Marketing)** folder.
   b. Double-click the **VA1-Demo3.4a** report to open it.
4. In the upper left corner of the report, click the **Page 4** tab.

5. View the **Delivery Days by Order Type and Continent** bar chart.

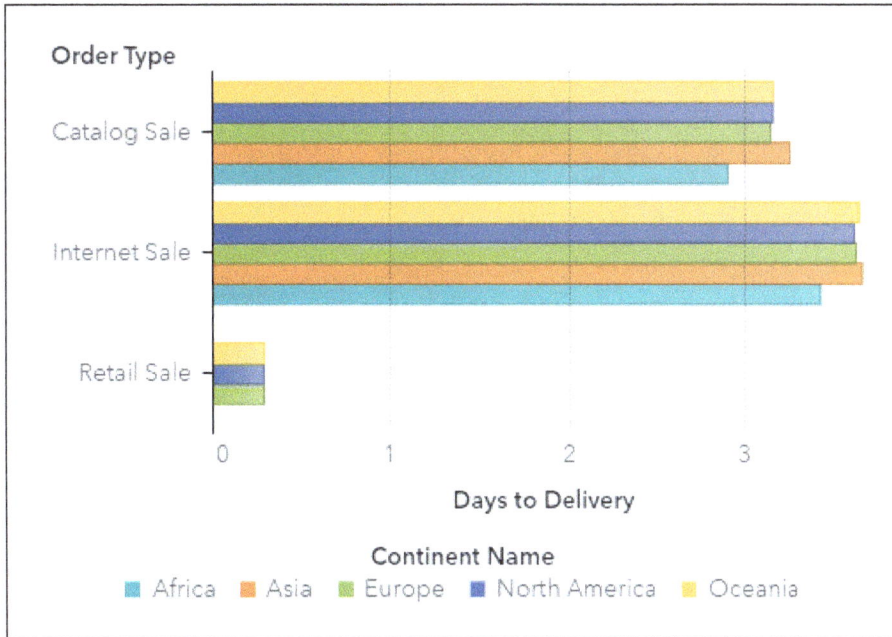

In general, catalog sales take slightly less time to be delivered than internet sales. We might need to look at our internet process to try to minimize the difference. For most continents, the average days to delivery are the same, except that Africa has lower delivery times than other continents. This could be because there are no retail stores in Africa, but that does not explain why Asia has higher delivery times. We might need to look at our distribution facilities in Africa and Asia to determine the discrepancy.

6. Create a bubble plot.

   a. In the left pane, click **Objects**.

   b. Drag the **Bubble plot** object, from the Graphs group, to the right side of the canvas.

   c. In the right pane, click **Roles**.

   d. For the **Group** role, select **Add** ⇨ **Customer Hierarchy**.

   e. For the **X axis** role, select **Add** ⇨ **Days to Delivery**.

   f. For the **Y axis** role, select **Add** ⇨ **Number of Orders**.

   g. For the **Size** role, select **Add** ⇨ **Average Profit**.

   The Roles pane should resemble the following:

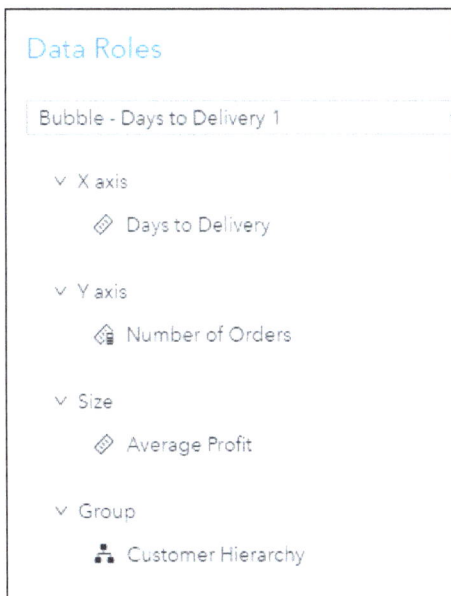

Measure data items can be added to the X axis and Y axis roles to determine the placement of the bubble. A measure data item can be added to the Size role to determine the size of the bubble.

The bubble plot should resemble the following:

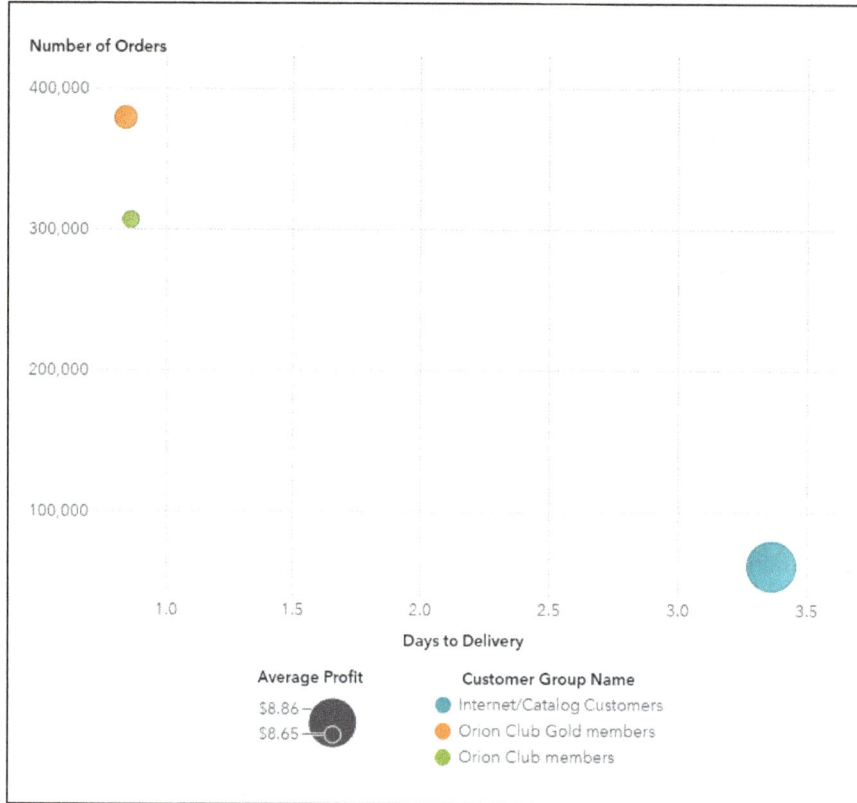

h. In the right pane, click **Options**.

i. In the X Axis Options group, select Fixed minimum.

ii. In the Fixed minimum field, enter 0.

iii. Select Fixed maximum.

iv. In the Fixed maximum field, enter 5.

i. In the bubble plot, double-click the **Internet/Catalog Customers** bubble.

j. Double-click the **Yes** bubble.

The bubble plot should resemble the following:

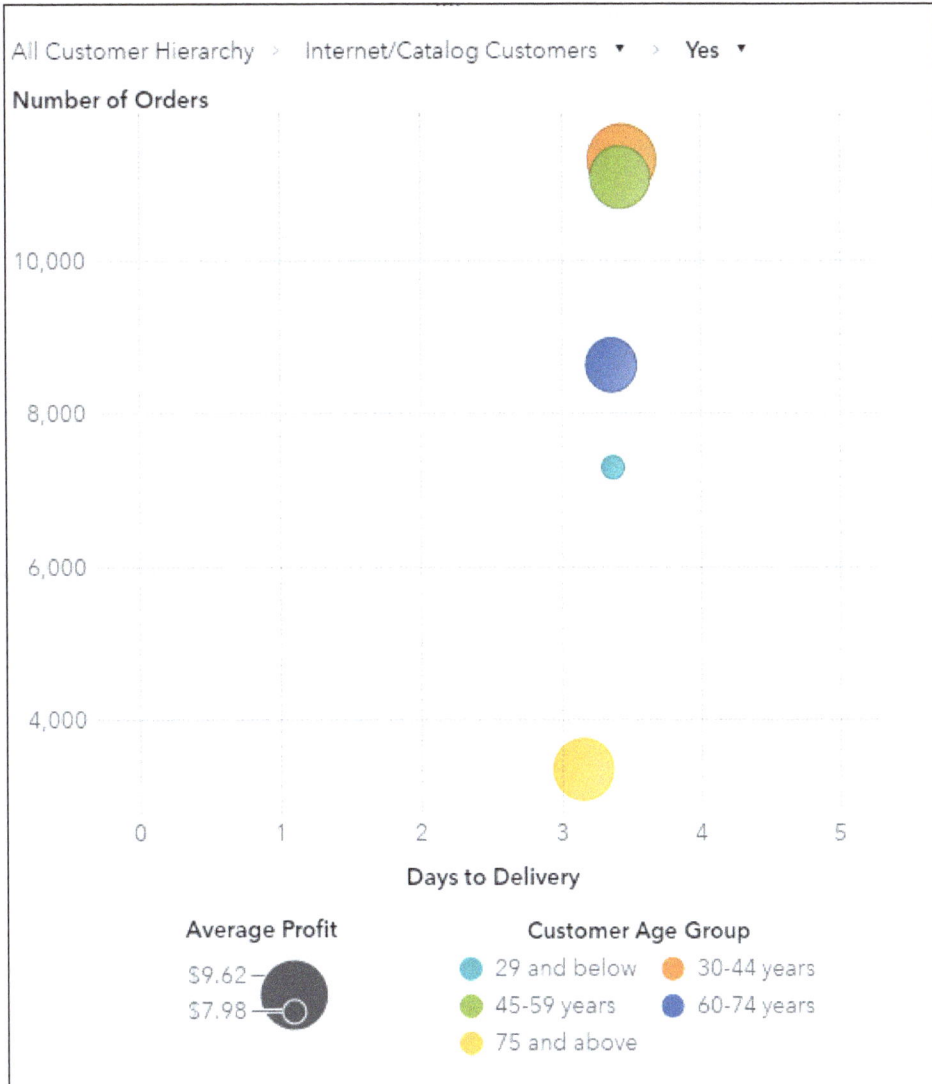

Next, we can analyze customers to determine which groups our marketing strategy can focus on. For internet/catalog orders among female customers, it seems the older age groups (60-74 years and 75 and above) place the fewest orders, but the oldest age group (75 and above) has the highest average profit. We should create marketing materials specifically for these groups to try to increase the number of orders.

7. Animate the bubble plot.

    a. In the right pane, click **Roles**.

    b. For the **Animation** role, select **Add** ➪ **Order Year**.

        The updated bubble plot should resemble the following:

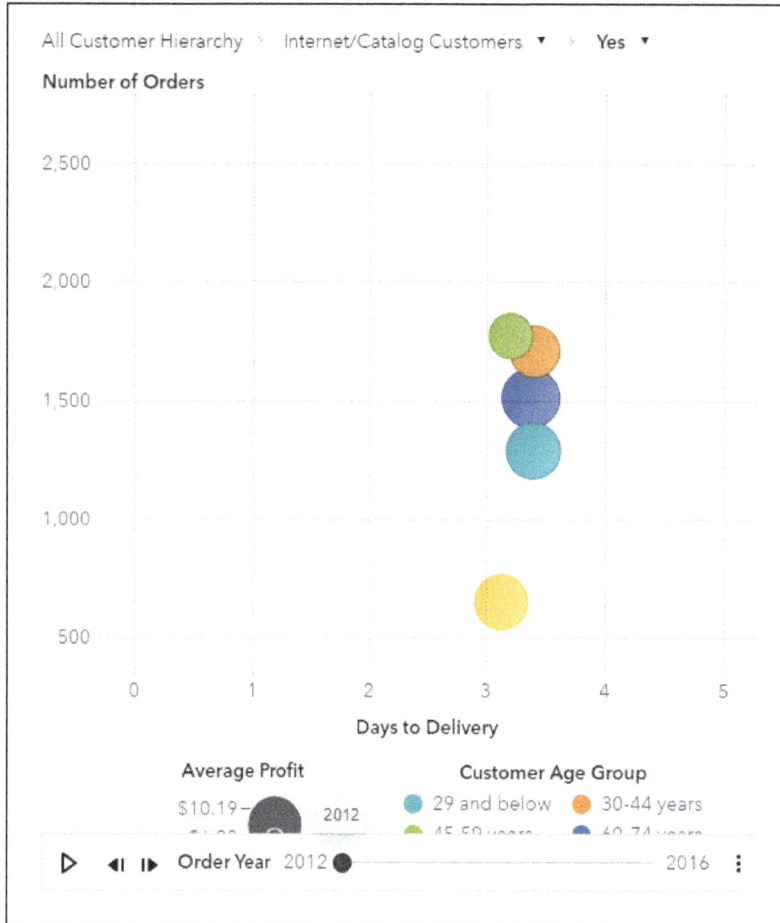

    c. In the lower left corner, click ▷ to play the animation.

        For loyalty customers who have placed internet/catalog orders, the days to delivery remain nearly constant over the years. However, the number of orders has a marked increase in 2014 for customers in the 30–44 age group and a slight drop in 2015, and then seems to remain constant. For the older age groups (60–74 years and 75 and above), the number of orders remains fairly constant, but average profit decreases over time.

8. Save the report.

End of Demonstration

Practice 3.6

1. Analyzing Data

    a. Open the browser and sign in to SAS Viya.

    b. Open the **VA1-Practice3.4a** report from the **Courses/YVA185/Basics/Practices (HR)** folder.

c. On Page 5, create a treemap by assigning the following data items to the specified roles:

Tile	Company
Size	Years of Service
Color	Average Profit
Data tip values	Add Number of Employees

The treemap should resemble the following:

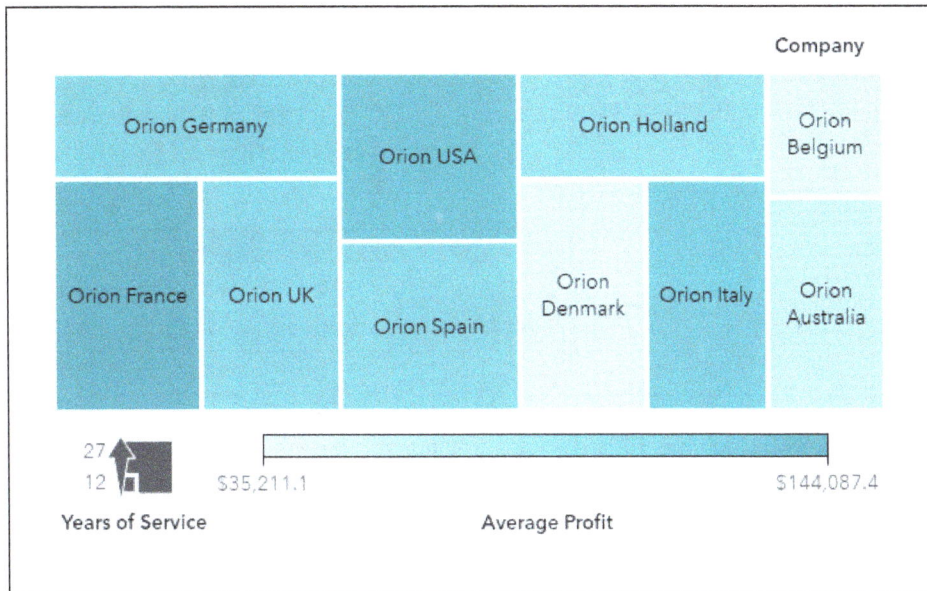

d. Create a new hierarchy (**Employee Hierarchy**) that contains the following categories:

Company

Job Title

Group

e. In the treemap, specify **Employee Hierarchy** for the **Tile** role and navigate through the hierarchy to answer the following questions:

Which two companies have the highest average profit generated (one possible criterion for promotion)?

Answer:

For these two companies, which job titles have the highest average years of service and average profit generated?

Answer:

f. Save the report.

End of Practices

Relationship Plots

As part of your analysis, you might also be interested in viewing relationships between measures. This can be accomplished with relationship plots (like a correlation matrix, a scatter plot, or a heat map). A correlation matrix can be used to evaluate the Linear relationship between multiple measures. It displays the degree of correlation as a matrix of rectangular cells. Each cell represents the intersection of two measures, and the color of the cell indicates the degree of correlation between those measures. The correlation values are calculated by using Pearson's correlation coefficient. They are identified as Weak (if the absolute value of the correlation is 0.3 or lower), Moderate (if the absolute value of the correlation is greater than 0.3 and less than or equal to 0.6), or Strong (if the absolute value of the correlation is greater than 0.6). Positive correlation values indicate that as one measure increases, so does the other, whereas Negative correlation values indicate that as one measure increases, the other decreases. Although two measures seem to have a weak relationship, this does not mean that they have no relationship.

Figure 3.13: Relationship Plots

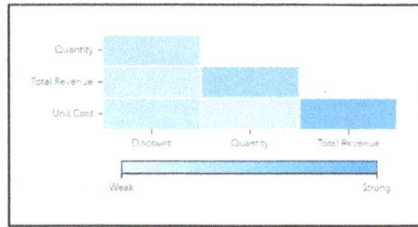

Use a *correlation matrix* to evaluate the linear relationship between measures.

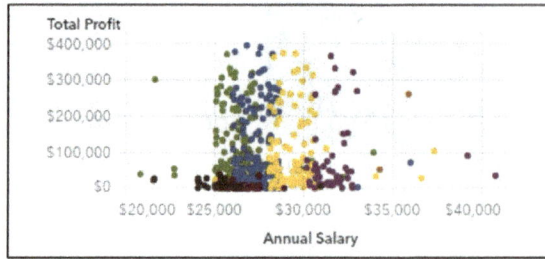

Use a *scatter plot* to evaluate the relationship between two measures.

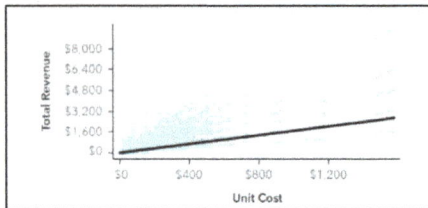

Use a *heat map* to evaluate the relationship between two high-cardinality measures, between two categories, or between a category and a measure.

Remember that the correlation measures the linear relationship between measures. The actual relationship could be more complex. These non-linear relationships can best be displayed with a scatter plot or a heat map. Both can be used to visualize trends between measures and to pinpoint possible outliers. The scatter plot works best with low-cardinality measures and the heat map works best with high-cardinality measures. Scatter plots can be used to evaluate the relationship between measures by displaying the values of two measures using markers. Heat maps can be used to evaluate the relationship between two high-cardinality measures, between two categories, or between a category and a measure. A heat map displays the distribution of values for two data items by using a table with colored cells.

Note: Scatter plots do not use aggregated data. Because of this, you get an error message if you attempt to create a scatter plot using more than 40,000 rows of data. For more information about data limits, see "High-Cardinality Thresholds for Objects" in the *SAS Visual Analytics: Reference* documentation.

Activity 3.3

Each report object has a threshold for how much data it can visually display. Many report objects will not display high-cardinality data items with a large number of unique data.

What are some examples of high-cardinality data items?

What are some examples of low-cardinality data items?

Fit Lines

Fit lines can be added to scatter plots and heat maps to plot the relationship between variables. When adding a fit line, you can select the type of relationship to plot: linear, quadratic, cubic, best fit, or PSpline. A linear relationship is plotted as a straight line that represents the relationship between the measures. For this method, correlation information is automatically added to the plot. A quadratic relationship is plotted as a line with a single curve that represents the relationship between the measures. This method produces a line with the shape of a parabola. A cubic relationship is plotted as a line with two curves that represents the relationship between the measures. This method often produces a line with an S shape. Best fit selects the most appropriate model (linear, quadratic, or cubic) for your data. This method uses backward variable selection to select the highest-order model that is significant. Because of this, best fit often selects more complex models over simpler models. A PSpline relationship creates a penalized BSpline. This is a smoothing spline that closely fits the data. This method can display a complex line with many changes in its curvature. Fit lines are great for quantifying the relationship between measures.

Figure 3.14: Fit Lines

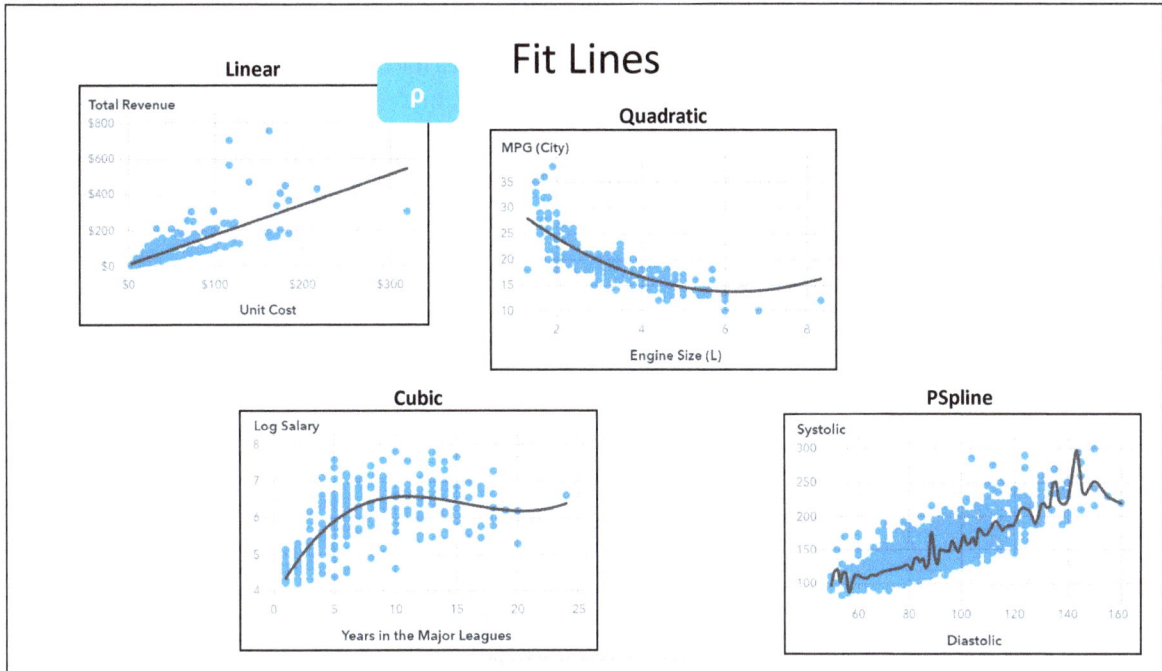

Time Plots

As part of your analysis, you might be interested in viewing relationships over time. This can be accomplished with time plots (like a time series plot or a line chart). A time series plot can be used to show trends in measures over time by displaying data using a line that connects data values. Time series plots are excellent for identifying seasonal peaks or troughs in your data. Line charts can also be used to show trends in measures over time but can be used for any ordinal values (like age groups or loyalty levels). This can be helpful for identifying patterns among or between ordinal groups.

Figure 3.15: Time Plots

Use a *time series plot* to show trends of measures over time.

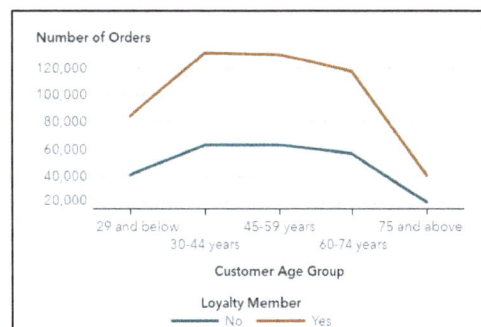

Use a *line chart* to show trends over some ordinal variable (time, age group).

Forecasting

After you identify historical trends in your data, you might want to try to predict future values by forecasting. The forecasting object uses the statistical trends in your data to predict future values. It displays a line with predicted values and a colored band that represents the confidence interval. By default, the next six periods are forecasted, and the 95% confidence interval is displayed. Historical values for the forecasting model are displayed as markers only (without a line). Historical predicted values (hindcast) are displayed as part of the forecast line. Visual Analytics automatically tests several forecasting models against your data and select the best model:

- ARIMA

- Damped-trend exponential smoothing

- Linear exponential smoothing

- Seasonal exponential smoothing

- Simple exponential smoothing

- Winters method (additive)

- Winters method (multiplicative)

Figure 3.16: Forecasting Object

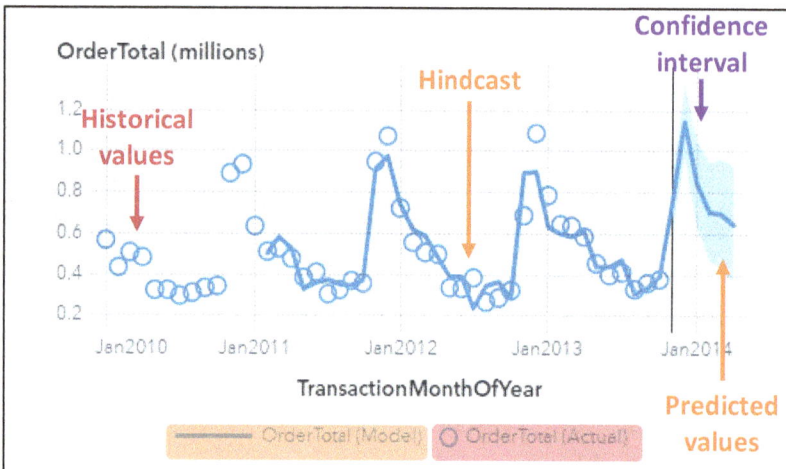

Visual Statistics and Visual Data Mining and Machine Learning give you the added ability to create your own models instead of relying on the model that is automatically selected for forecasting. Visual Forecasting, on the other hand, gives you the power to produce large-scale time series analyses and hierarchical forecasts.

Note: Forecasting accounts for cyclical patterns by using standard intervals of time (for example, 60 minutes in an hour, 24 hours in a day, and so on). If your data uses nonstandard values (for example, 48 thirty-minute cycles per day), then cyclical patterns are not considered in the forecast.

Demo 3.7: Adding Data Analysis

This demonstration illustrates how to add data analysis to graphs in Visual Analytics.

1. From the browser window, sign in to SAS Viya.

2. In the upper left corner, click ☰ (**Show list of applications**) and select **Explore and Visualize**. SAS Visual Analytics appears.

3. Click All Reports.
   a. Navigate to the **Courses/YVA185/Basics/Demos (Marketing)** folder.
   b. Double-click the **VA1-Demo3.4b** report to open it.
4. In the upper left corner of the report, click the **Page 5** tab.
5. Create a correlation matrix.
   a. In the left pane, click **Objects**.
   b. Drag the **Correlation matrix** object, from the Graphs group, to the top of the canvas.
   c. In the right pane, click **Roles**.
   d. For the **Measures** role, click **Add**.
   e. In the Add Data Items window, select the following measures:

      Days to Delivery

      Discount

      Total Revenue

      Unit Cost
   f. Click **OK**.

      The Roles pane should resemble the following:

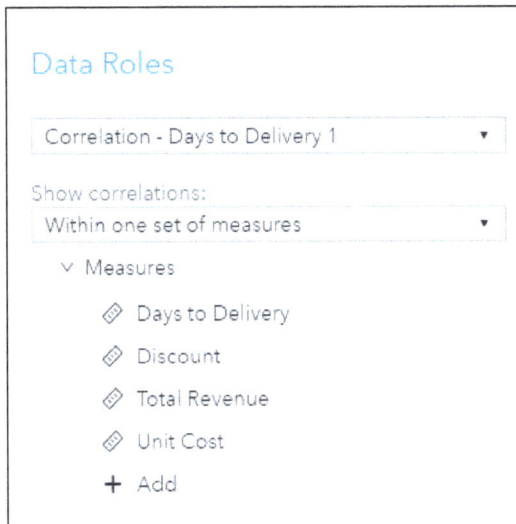

      Only measure data items can be used for the correlation matrix.

      The correlation matrix should resemble the following:

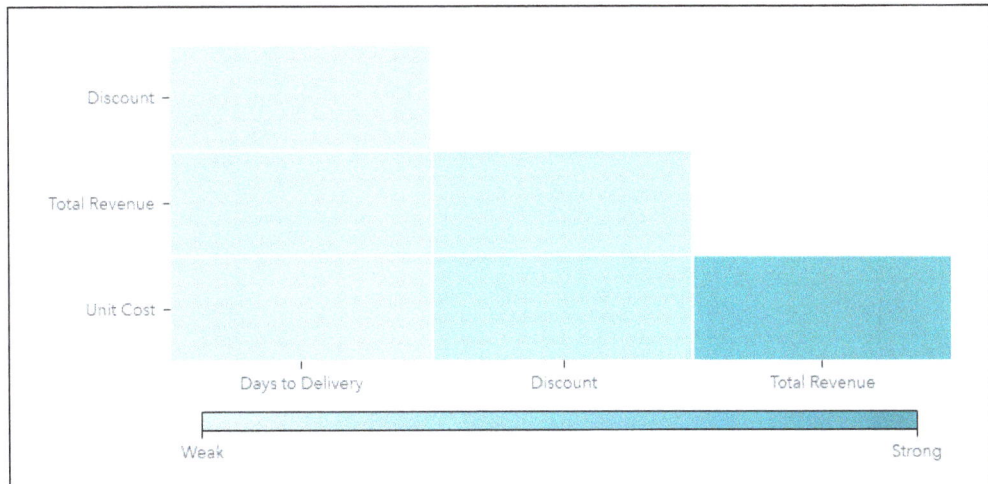

      There is a strong relationship between **Unit Cost** and **Total Revenue**. Placing your cursor over the cell shows a correlation of 0.7790, meaning that as **Unit Cost** increases, so does **Total Revenue**. We should examine these two measures more closely to better understand the relationship.

g. Select the cell for **Unit Cost** and **Total Revenue**.

h. Right-click the correlation matrix and select **New object from selection** ⇨ **Heat map**.

   A heat map is created below the correlation matrix.

i. Drag the heat map to the right of the correlation matrix.

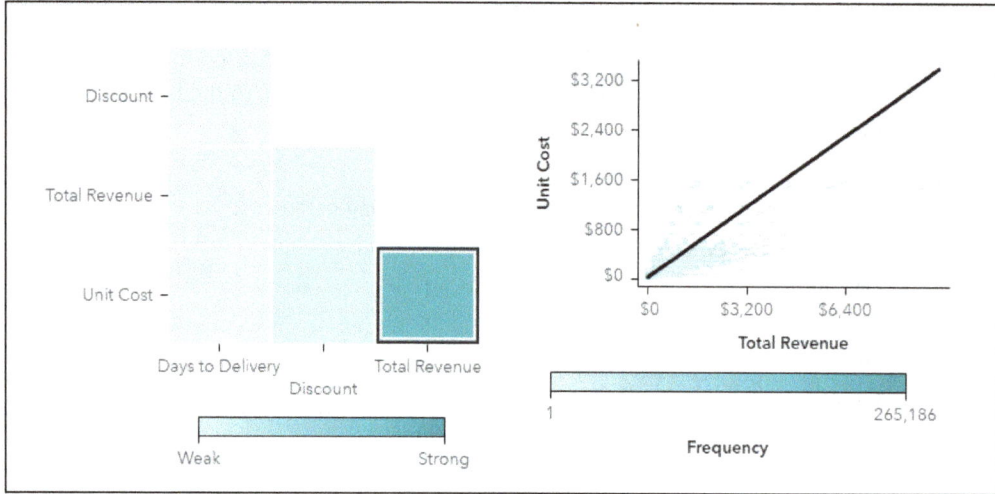

We want to move **Unit Cost** to the horizontal axis because we want to see how a unit change in cost affects **Total Revenue**.

j. If necessary, click the heat map to select it.

k. In the right pane, click **Roles**.

l. Select **Unit Cost** and drag it above **Total Revenue**.

m. In the upper right corner of the heat map, click ⬈ (**Maximize**) to view additional details.

n. In the detail table below the chart, click **Unit Cost, Total Revenue analysis**.

Unit Cost, Total Revenue	Unit Cost, Total Revenue analysis
Property	**Value**
Model type	Linear
Model description	The linear fit is the straight line that best represents the relationship betwe...
R-square value	0.6068
Correlation	A correlation of 0.78 suggests there is a strong linear relationship between...
Correlation help	A positive correlation value means that as one variable increases, the seco...
Slope	1.6966
Function	f(x)=8.0391 + 1.6966x
Average x	77.76
Average y	139.96
Standard deviation x	85.2765
Standard deviation y	185.7319
Observations	951,669

The linear fit line between unit cost and total revenue indicates that a dollar increase in costs increases revenues by $1.69.

o. In the upper right corner, click ⬐ (**Restore**).

6. Modify the time series plot.
   a. Click the time series plot to select it.
   b. Right-click the time series plot and select **Change Time series plot to** ⇨ **Forecasting**.
   c. In the right pane, click **Options**.
   d. In the Time Series group, for the **Binning interval** field, select **Automatic**.

   ```
   ∨ Time Series

       Binning interval:

         Automatic        ▼
   ```

   e. Increase the size of the Forecast object to see the forecasted values.

   The forecast plot should resemble the following:

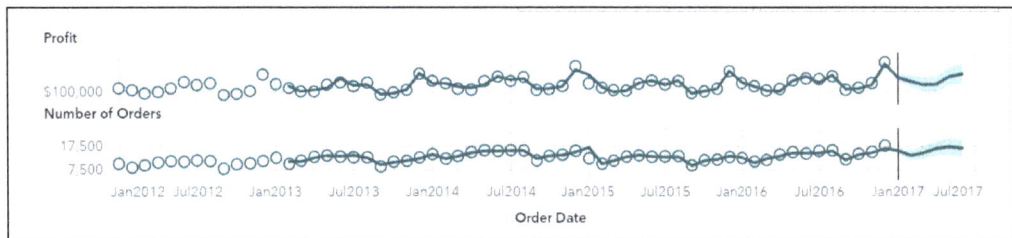

   We can see that **Profit** and **Number of Orders** are closely related. When the number of orders rise, so do profits. The forecast shows that this trend is expected to continue in the near future.

   f. In the upper right corner of the forecast plot, click ⬈ (**Maximize**) to view additional details.
   g. Scroll to the bottom of details table below the chart.

Order Date	Profit (Model)	Profit (Actual)	Lower Confidence Interval	Upper Confidence Interval	Number of Orders
Nov2016	$137,377.61	$149,117.28	.	.	14,639
Dec2016	$273,803.86	$284,648.43	.	.	16,409
Jan2017	$184,241.94	.	$157,588.93	$210,894.95	15,466
Feb2017	$160,011.07	.	$122,318.02	$197,704.12	13,551
Mar2017	$139,309.78	.	$93,145.41	$185,474.15	14,609
Apr2017	$141,069.26	.	$87,763.24	$194,375.29	16,465
May2017	$190,606.43	.	$131,008.48	$250,204.37	17,154
Jun2017	$207,670.00	.	$142,383.72	$272,956.28	16,576

Results   Dependent Variables Results   Forecast Summary

   The forecasted values for profit and number of orders, along with values for the lower and upper confidence intervals, are displayed.

   h. Click **Dependent Variables Results** in the table of data values below the chart.

Results   Dependent Variables Results   Forecast Summary

Dependent Variable	Algorithm
Profit	ARIMA: Profit ~ P = (12) D = (1,12) NOINT
Number of Orders	ARIMA: Number of Orders ~ P = (12) D = (1,12) NOINT

   Visual Analytics has determined that the ARIMA algorithm best forecasts profit and number of orders. This algorithm cannot be changed.

i. Click **Forecast Summary** in the table of data values below the chart to view the Forecast Summary.

> Results   Dependent Variables Results   Forecast Summary
>
> **Forecast Summary**
>
> The forecasting object uses statistical trends in your data to predict future values. It automatically tests multiple forecasting models against the specified data items and then selects the best model for each one.
>
> The selected model for Profit is ARIMA: Profit ~ P = (12) D = (1,12) NOINT, displayed with a 95% confidence interval. A 95% confidence interval is the predicted data range that will contain future values of Profit with 95% confidence.
>
> Historical values of Profit are displayed as markers only, without a line. The chart displays predicted values (hindcast) as part of the forecast line. Some forecasting models include delayed effects, in which case the hindcast will not begin at the start of the MONTH axis.

j. In the upper left corner, click ⬚ (**Restore**).

7. Save the report.

End of Demonstration

Practice 3.7

1. Adding Data Analysis

    a. Open the browser and sign in to SAS Viya.

    b. Open the **VA1-Practice3.4b** report from the **Courses/YVA185/Basics/Practices (HR)** folder.

    c. On Page 6, create a correlation matrix by assigning the following data items to the specified roles:

Measures	Annual Salary
	Total Orders
	Total Profit
	Years of Service

The correlation matrix should resemble the following:

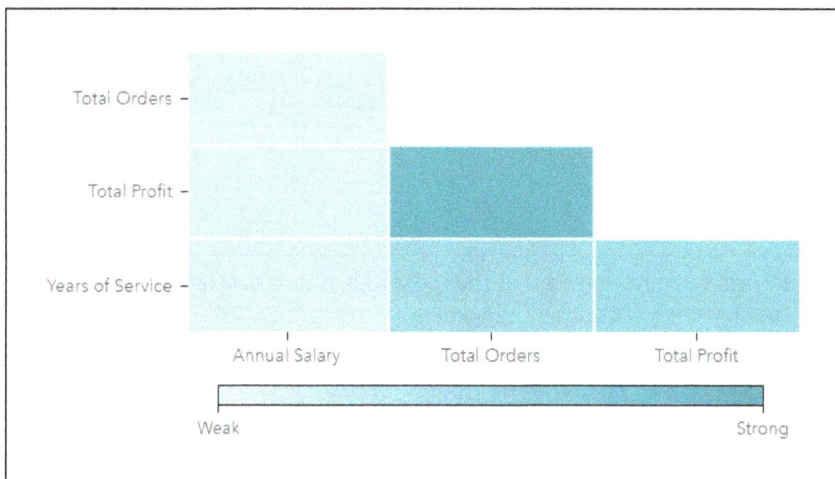

d. Answer the following question:

What is the degree of correlation between **Total Orders** and **Total Profit**?

Answer:

e. Create a scatter plot, on the right of the correlation matrix, by assigning the following data items to the specified roles:

Measures	Total Profit
	Years of Service
Color	Job Title

The scatter plot should resemble the following:

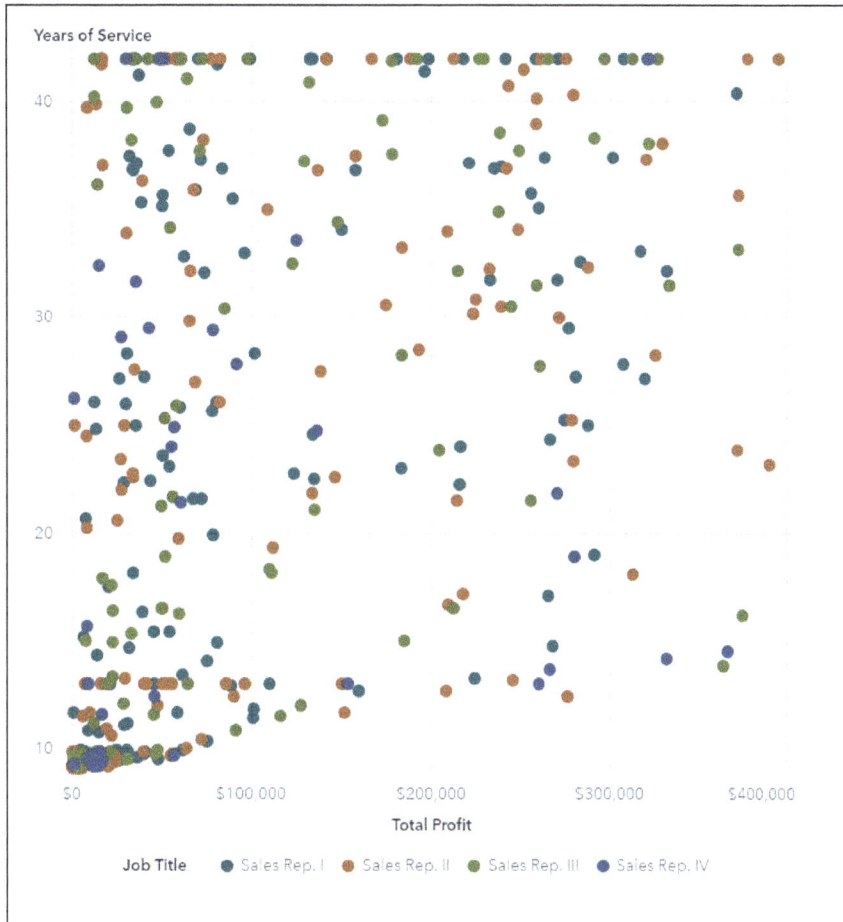

f. Answer the following question:

Using years of service and profit generated as promotion criteria, do you notice any differences between job titles?

Answer:

g. Save the report.

End of Practices

Quiz 3.1

1. Which graph would help you determine whether a measure is normally distributed?
   a. distribution plot
   b. box plot
   c. histogram
   d. normality plot

2. Which object can use a data item that has a classification type of geography?
   a. crosstab
   b. geo map
   c. table
   d. bar chart

Chapter 4: Creating a Simple Report

4.1 Introduction

In the *Report* phase of the Visual Analytics methodology, you need to create reports that are based on your discoveries. Reports should be organized, easy to navigate, versatile, and attractive. You can organize content by adding multiple pages to your reports. Your reports should focus on telling a single data story. Pages can then be used to tell parts of that story (like chapters in a book). You can make your reports easy to navigate by adding descriptions to define the purpose and instructions to describe the features of your report. You can make your reports versatile (or interactive) by adding animations, ranks, prompts, actions, and links. Finally, you can add styles and display rules to make your reports more attractive. After the reports are available, they can be shared with anyone, anywhere via the web or a mobile device.

Activity 4.1

Sign in to SAS Viya.

Open **Ugly Report** (located in the **Courses/YVA185/Basics** folder). What are your first impressions of this report?

Do you think it can be improved? If so, how?

Here are some tips to make a good report:

- Understand the audience.
- Make accessible to all.
- Tell a single data story.
- Use visually appealing, easy-to-understand objects.
- Use the simplest graph.
- Use consistent fonts.
- Limit the number of objects.
- Limit the number of pages.

For more information about how to create effective reports, see www.sas.com/beautifulreports.

4.2 Graphs

During the Report phase, you want to use graphs that convey information to your audience in a pleasing and clear fashion. One way to accomplish this could be with pie charts, donut charts, or word clouds.

Pie Charts

A pie chart is best used to compare a few groups whose values vary greatly. These charts display the relative contribution of each group to the whole using a circle that is divided into multiple slices. Pie charts are popular, but be aware that it is very difficult to compare the relative sizes of slices in the chart. Because of this, pie charts should be used sparingly and only in special circumstances. For example, pie charts would work well to highlight large differences in groups or to show the relative contributions of a few groups. Donut charts are similar to pie charts but have a hole in the center. This hole makes it easier to compare relative slices because it forces the viewer to focus on reading the lengths of the arcs rather than the proportions of the slices. Neither of these charts can show a slice with a zero or negative response, so if your data has these values, another chart type should be used.

Fig 4.1: Graphs

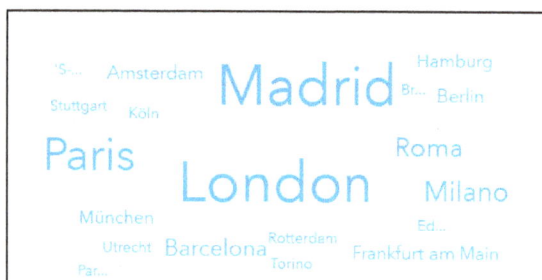

Use a *word cloud* to show summary information in an appealing fashion.

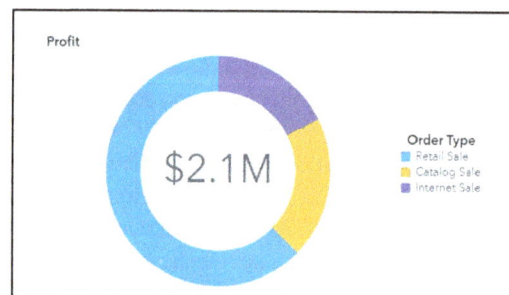

Use a *donut chart (pie chart)* to compare a few groups whose values vary greatly.

Word Clouds

Word clouds can be used to show summary information in an appealing fashion. A word cloud analyzes each value of a category data item as a single text string. The value of one measure can be used to size the word, and the value of another measure can be used to color the word. Word clouds should be avoided if analytical accuracy is desired because it is difficult to compare the relative sizes of different words. Words that have more letters often seem larger than words that have fewer letters. In addition, words that contain large letters (like o, m, and w) will generally receive more attention than words that contain smaller letters (like l, i, and f). Lastly, words whose letters contain ascenders (the part of a lowercase letter that projects above the body of the letter: like b, d, or h) or descenders (the part of a lowercase letter that projects below the body of the letter: like g, p, or q) receive more attention than words that do not. For these reasons, word clouds are mostly used for aesthetic purposes.

Dual Axis Charts

When you want to compare two series with different ranges, dual axis charts can be very effective. Dual axis charts display each series on a separate axis, which makes it easy to see relationships between the series when the ranges are very different. Four types of dual axis charts can be created in Visual Analytics: a dual axis bar chart, a dual axis bar-line chart, a dual axis line chart, and a dual axis time series plot.

Figure 4.2: Dual Axis Graphs

Use *dual axis* charts and plots to compare two series with different ranges.

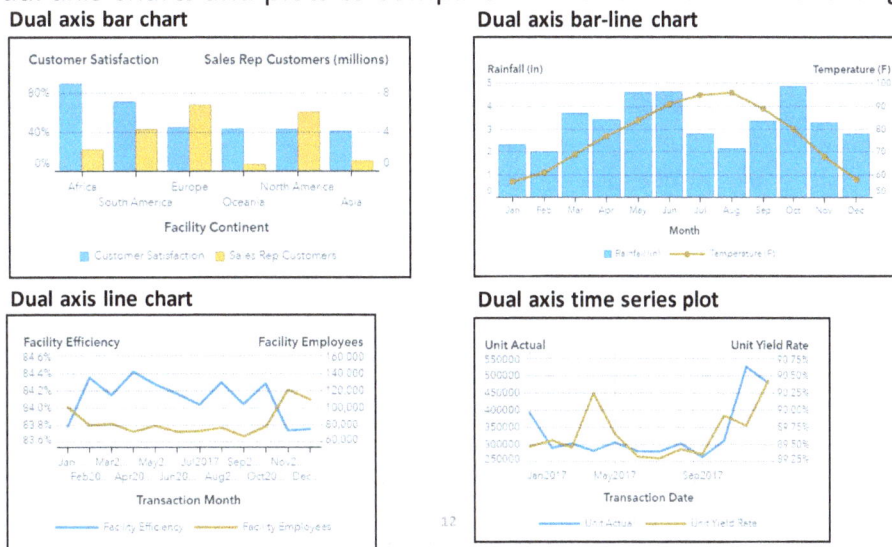

A dual axis bar chart displays two bar charts with a shared category axis and separate response axes. Use a dual axis bar chart when the current value for both measures does not depend on the prior value. For example, in the top left chart in Figure 4.2, customer satisfaction and the numbers of sales representatives' customers for South America are not impacted by the values for Africa.

A dual axis bar-line chart combines a bar chart and a line chart on a shared category axis. The bar chart and the line chart have separate response axes. For the bar, use a measure whose current value does not depend on the prior value. For the line, use a measure whose current value does depend on the prior value. For example, in the top right chart in Figure 4.2, the value of temperature for February depends on the value from January. However, the value of rainfall for February does not depend on the value from January.

A dual axis line chart displays data by using two lines that connect the data values for a shared category axis on separate response axes. Use a dual axis line chart when the current value for both measures depends on the prior value. For example, in the bottom left chart in Figure 4.2, the values of facility efficiency and facility employees in February are impacted by the values from January. This chart is an excellent example of why separate axes can show relationships that a single axis does not. If both series were placed on the same axis, the line for facility efficiency would appear as a straight line near 1. However, because these series are plotted on separate axes, you can see the inverse relationship between the series. When the number of employees increases, efficiency declines and when the number of employees decreases, efficiency improves.

A dual axis time series plot displays two time series with a common time axis on separate response axes. Dual axis time series plots are good for spotting seasonal movements for two sets of time series data. For example, in the bottom right chart in Figure 4.2, you can see that the values for unit actual and unit yield rate tend to stay flat in the middle of the year and show a pronounced increase toward the end of the year. This is likely the result of increased purchases during the holidays.

Demo 4.1: Creating a Simple Report

This demonstration illustrates how to create a simple report in Visual Analytics.

1. From the browser window, sign in to SAS Viya.
2. In the upper left corner, click ☰ (**Show list of applications**) and select **Explore and Visualize**. SAS Visual Analytics appears.
3. Click **All Reports**.
   a. Navigate to the **Courses/YVA185/Basics/Demos (Marketing)** folder.
   b. Double-click the **VA1- Demo4.1** report to open it.
4. Change the settings to add custom titles for all graph objects.
   a. In the upper right corner, select **<user name>** ⇨ **Settings**.
   b. On the left side of the window, select **General** under **SAS Visual Analytics**.
   c. Scroll down to Default titles for new objects.
   d. For Graphs, change No title to Custom title.

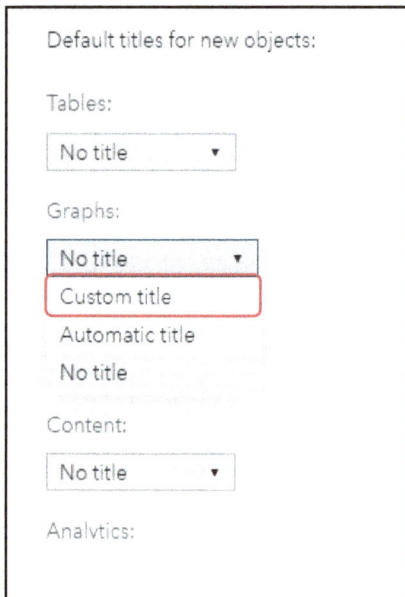

   e. Click **Close**.
5. Hide data items.
   a. In the left pane, click **Data**.
   b. In the upper right corner of the Data pane, click ⋮ (**Actions**) and select **Show or hide data items**.
   c. Click ◀— (**Remove all**) to move all data items to the Available items list.
   d. Double-click the following data items to add them to the Selected items list:
      Customer Age Group
      Frequency
      Number of Orders
      Order
      Month
      Profit

The Selected items list should resemble the following:

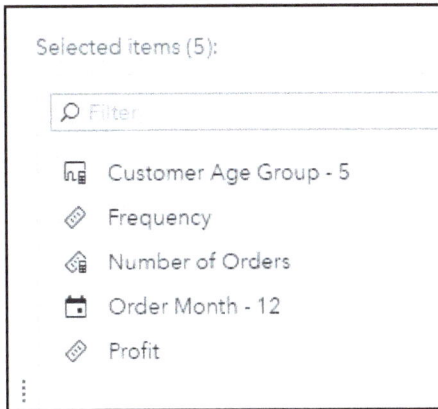

Selected items (5):

🔍 Filter

- 🔢 Customer Age Group - 5
- ◈ Frequency
- ⬗ Number of Orders
- 📅 Order Month - 12
- ◈ Profit

e. Click **OK**.

The Data pane should resemble the following:

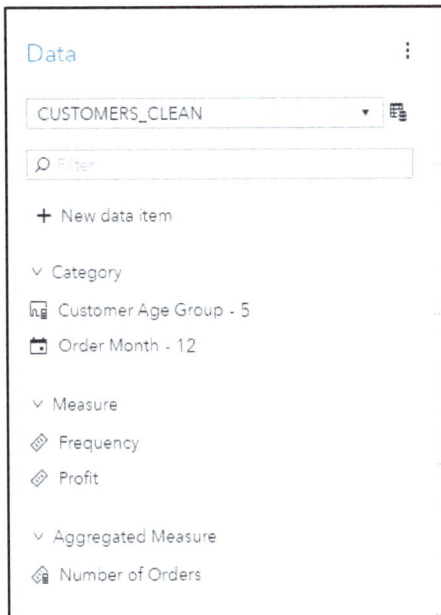

Data   ⋮

CUSTOMERS_CLEAN   ▾ 🗃

🔍 Filter

+ New data item

⌄ Category
- 🔢 Customer Age Group - 5
- 📅 Order Month - 12

⌄ Measure
- ◈ Frequency
- ◈ Profit

⌄ Aggregated Measure
- ⬗ Number of Orders

6. Create a pie chart.

a. In the left pane, click **Objects**.

b. Drag the **Pie chart** object, from the Graphs group, to the top of the canvas.

c. In the right pane, click **Roles**.

d. For the **Category** role, select **Add** ⇨ **Customer Age Group**.

e. For the **Measure** role, select **Frequency** ⇨ **Number of Orders**.

The pie chart should resemble the following:

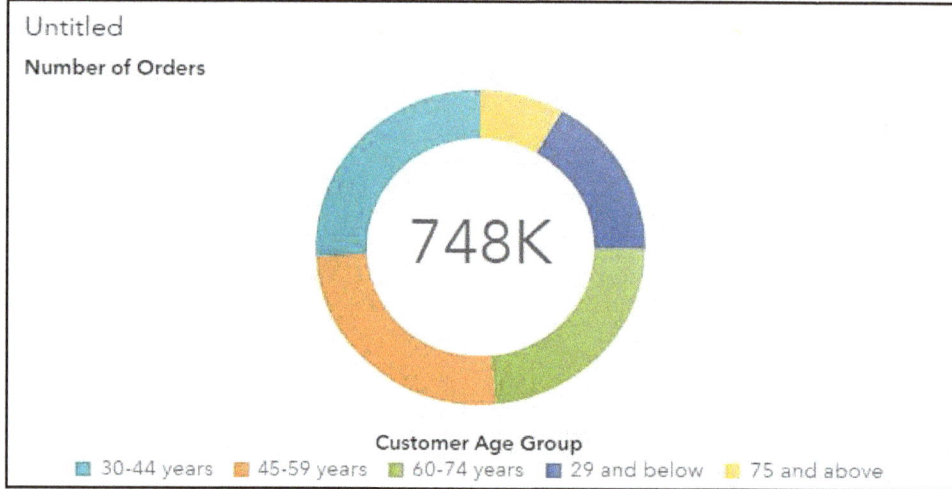

By default, the slices in a pie chart are sorted by the measure in descending order.

f. Below the pie chart, right-click **Customer Age Group** and select **Sort** ⇨ **Customer Age Group**: **Ascending**.

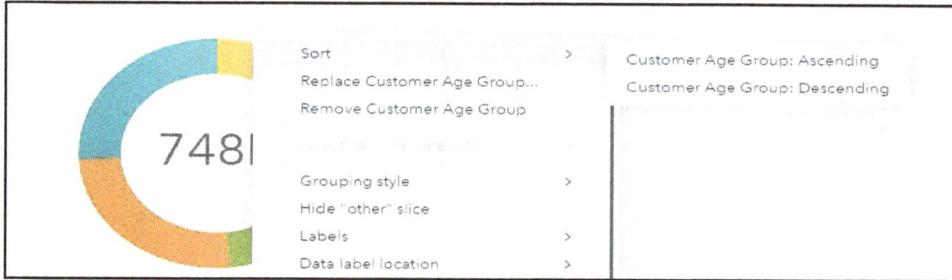

The updated pie chart should resemble the following:

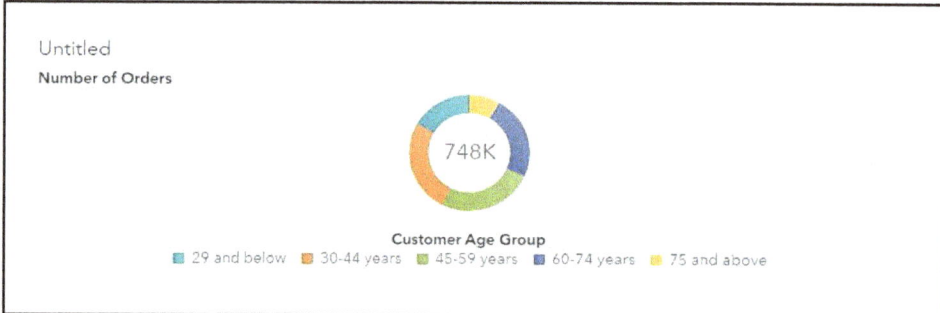

g. Double-click the title, **Untitled**.

A font formatting tool appears that you can use to format the title.

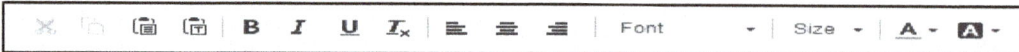

h. Enter **Number of Orders by Customer Age Group** as the title.

i. In the right pane, click **Options**.

j.   In the Object group, for the **Name** field, enter **Orders by Age Group**.

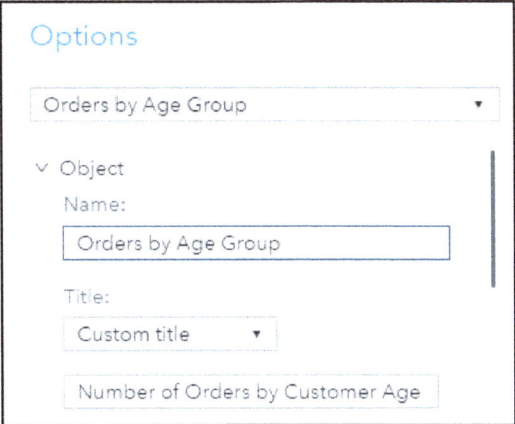

Options

Orders by Age Group   ▼

∨ Object
    Name:
        Orders by Age Group

    Title:
        Custom title   ▼

        Number of Orders by Customer Age

k.   In the Pie group, clear **"Other" slice**.

l.   Clear **Pielabel**.

The updated pie chart should resemble the following:

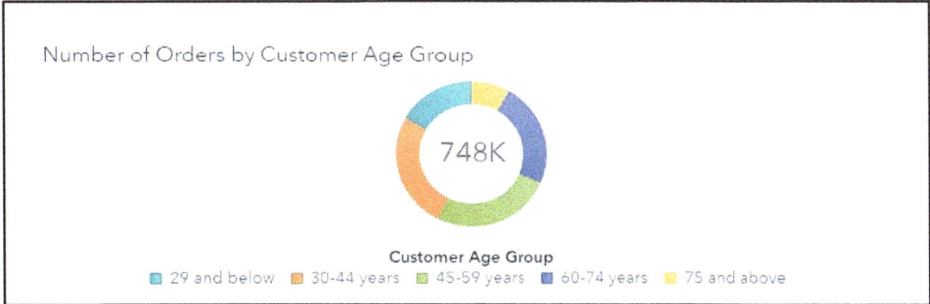

Number of Orders by Customer Age Group

748K

Customer Age Group
■ 29 and below   ■ 30-44 years   ■ 45-59 years   ■ 60-74 years   ■ 75 and above

7.   Create a bar chart.

a.   In the left pane, click the **Objects** tab.

b.   Drag the **Bar chart** object, from the Graphs group, to the drop zone on the right side of the pie chart.

c.   In the right pane, click **Roles**.

d.   For the **Category** role, select **Add** ⇨ **Order Month**.

e.   For the **Measure** role, select **Frequency** ⇨ **Profit**.

For the **Measure** role, select **Add** ⇨ **Number of Orders** and click **OK**. The bar chart should resemble the following:

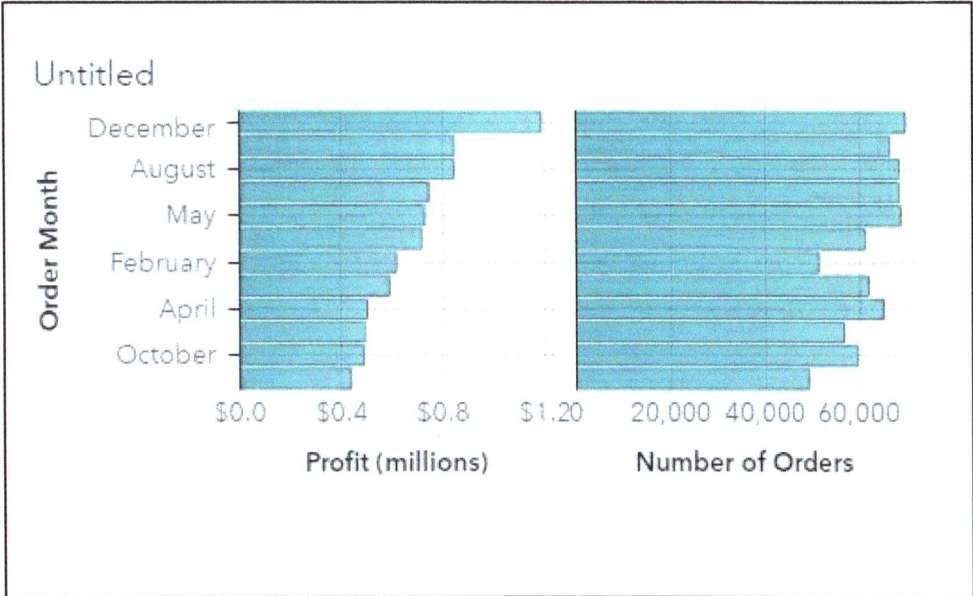

Untitled

Order Month	Profit (millions)	Number of Orders
December		
August		
May		
February		
April		
October		

Profit (millions): $0.0 $0.4 $0.8 $1.20
Number of Orders: 20,000 40,000 60,000

Because **Profit** and **Number of Orders** have different ranges, they are displayed in different bar charts. You can change to a dual axis bar chart to display both measures together.

f. Right-click the bar chart and select **Change Bar chart to** ⇨ **Dual axis bar chart**. **Note:** This option is not available if the object is maximized.

g. In the dual axis bar chart, on the horizontal axis, right-click **Order Month** and select **Sort** ⇨ **Order Month: Ascending.**

h. In the right pane, click **Options**.

i. In the Object group, for the **Name** field, enter **Profit and Orders**.

j. For the **Title** field, enter **Profit and Number of Orders by Month**.

k. In the X Axis Options group, clear **Axis label**.

The updated dual axis bar chart should resemble the following:

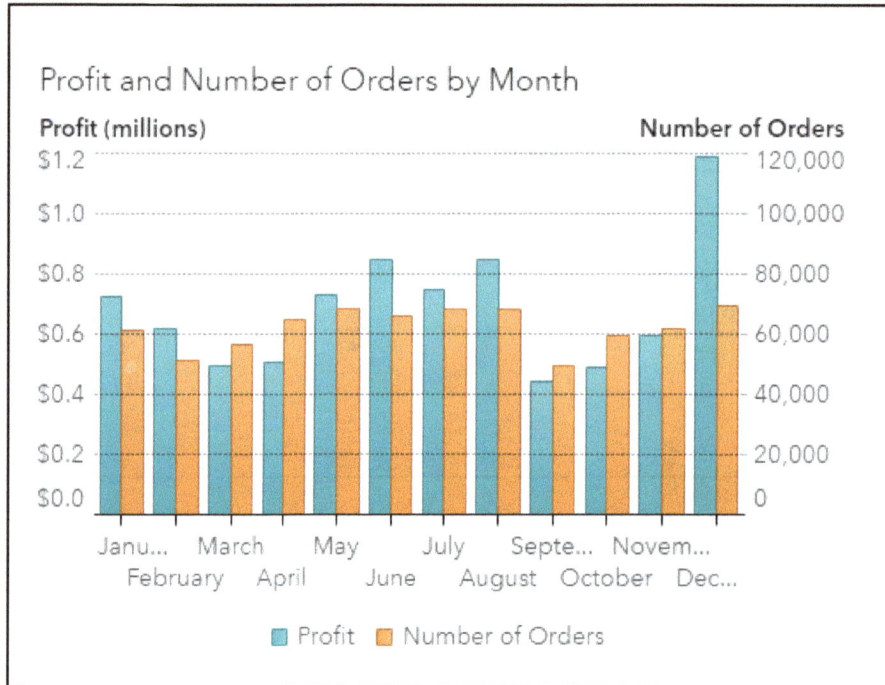

The report should resemble the following:

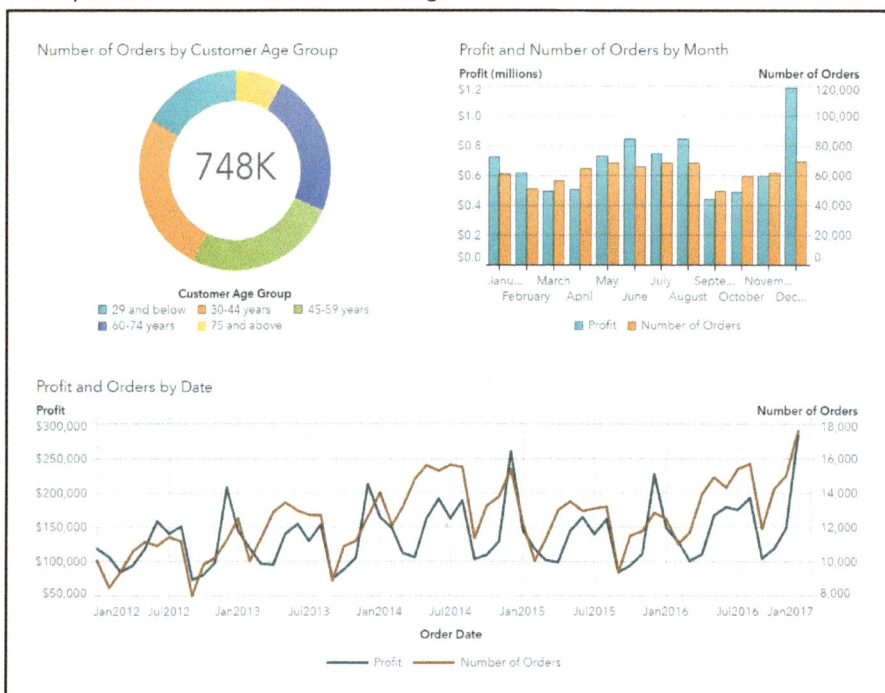

8. Save the report.

End of Demonstration

Practice 4.1

1. Creating a Simple Report
    a. Open the browser and sign in to SAS Viya.
    b. Open the **VA1-Practice4.1** report from the **Courses/YVA185/Basics/Practices (HR)** folder.
    c. Create a geo coordinate map to the left of the bar chart.
    d. Modify the following options for the geo map:

Object: Name	Average Profit by Country
Object: Custom Title	Average Profit by Country
Object	Geo Coordinate
Legend: Visibility	Off

    e. Assign the following data items to the specified roles:

Geography	Employee Country
Color	Average Profit
Data tip values	Number of Employees

    The geo map should resemble the following:

    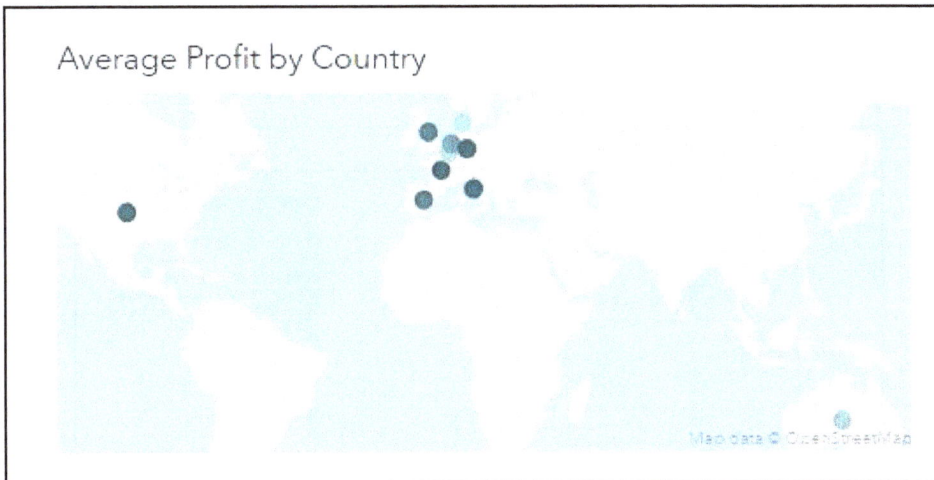

    f. Maximize the geo map and answer the following questions: Which country has the highest average profit? The lowest?
        Answer:
        Which country has the highest number of employees? The lowest?
        Answer:

g. Create a dual axis bar-line chart at the bottom of the canvas. Assign the following data items to the specified roles:

Category	Anniversary Month
Measure (bar)	Number of Employees
Measure (line)	Average Profit

h. Modify the following options for the dual axis bar-line chart:

Object: Name	Employees and Profit by Anniversary Month
Object: Custom Title	Employees and Profit by Anniversary Month
Line: Markers	<selected>

i. Sort the bars by **Anniversary Month** in ascending order. The dual axis bar-line chart should resemble the following:

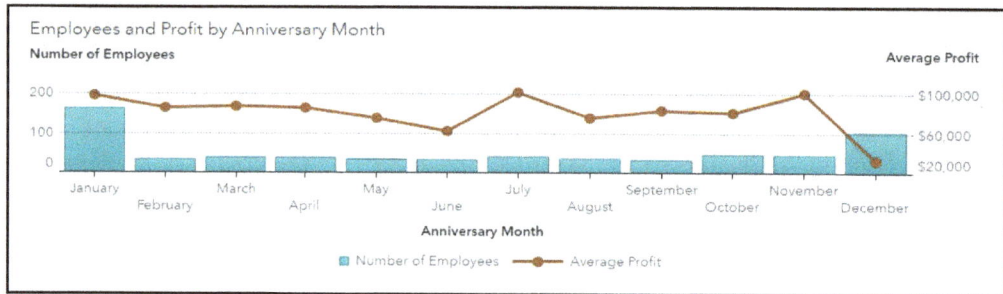

j. Maximize the dual axis bar-line chart and answer the following questions: In which month were the most employees hired?

Answer:

Which anniversary month contains employees that generate the highest average profit?

Answer:

The report should resemble the following:

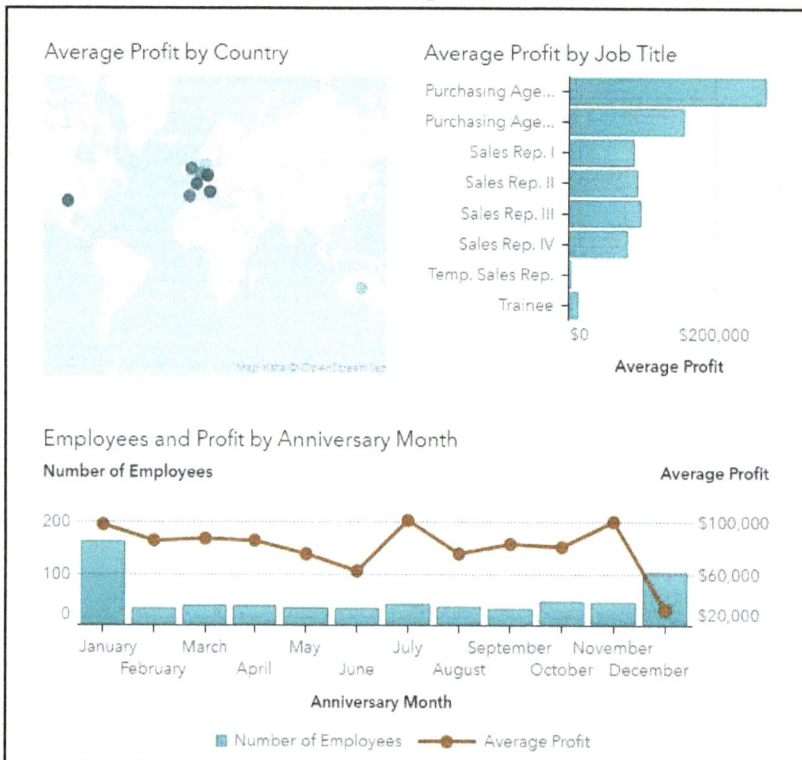

    k.   Save the report.

    End of Practices

4.3 Creating Interactive Reports

Beginning in SAS Visual Analytics 8.4, the types of changes a report viewer can make to a report can be set using the Viewer Customization option at the report level.

The available levels of permissions are as follows:

Simple edits	Enables report viewers to make changes that do not change the original intent for the report content. For example, report viewers can change how the data is sorted or change legends and value labels.
Comprehensive edits (default)	Enables report viewers to make changes that might alter the original intent of the report. For example, report viewers can change object types.
Data edits	Enables report viewers to change the data for objects in the report. For example, report viewers can change data assignments, filters, and ranks.

Remember that the goal of reporting is to tell a single data story. Many times, that story can be told in multiple parts. That's where multiple pages are useful.

Multiple Pages

Each page in your report should focus on one aspect of the story and tell that piece with a limited number of objects. Not only that, you must ensure that each page can stand on its own. Viewers should not be expected to remember details from one page to understand the concepts that are communicated on another page. Basically, you want to ensure that each page communicates one point that will advance your data story.

Figure 4.3: Creating Reports with Multiple Pages

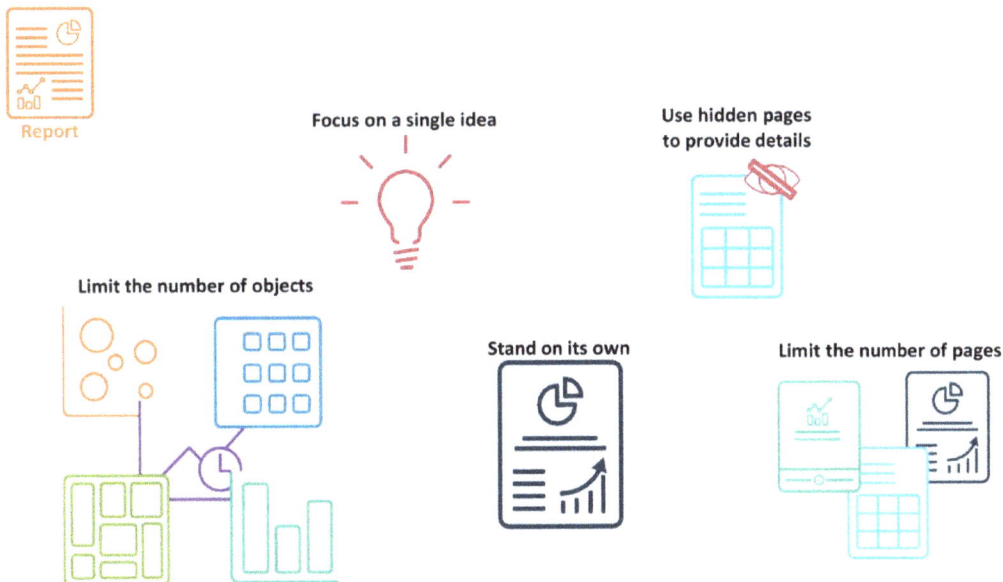

In addition to adding multiple pages to your report, you can create pages that are hidden from report viewers. These hidden pages can be useful to communicate details about the report to other designers or they can be linked to from an object on a regular page to enable viewers to see additional details. There is no limit to the number of pages that can be added to a report or the number of objects that can be added to a page. However, it is a good idea to limit the number of pages to make your report easier to access, easier to navigate, and easier to understand. If you need more than six or seven visible pages to tell your data story, you should consider creating multiple reports and use links between them to provide additional information.

Each page in your report can use one or more data sources and can contain one or more report objects. There is no limit to the number of pages that can be added to a report. However, it is a good idea to limit the number of pages in a report to make your report easier to access, easier to navigate, and easier to understand. If you need more than six or seven visible pages to tell your data story, you should consider creating multiple reports and use links between reports to provide additional information.

Note: Links are discussed in more detail in a later section.

Demo 4.2: Working with Pages and Ranks

This demonstration illustrates how to create new pages, how to move graphs between pages, and how to apply ranks to graphs in Visual Analytics.

1. From the browser window, sign in to SAS Viya.
2. In the upper left corner, click ▤ (**Show list of applications**) and select **Explore and Visualize**. SAS Visual Analytics appears.
3. Click **All Reports**.
   a. Navigate to the **Courses/YVA185/Basics/Demos (Marketing)** folder.
   b. Double-click the **VA1-Demo4.2a** report to open it.
4. Change the viewer customization level.
   a. In the right pane, click **Options**.
   b. Use the drop-down list on the top of the Options pane to select the report.

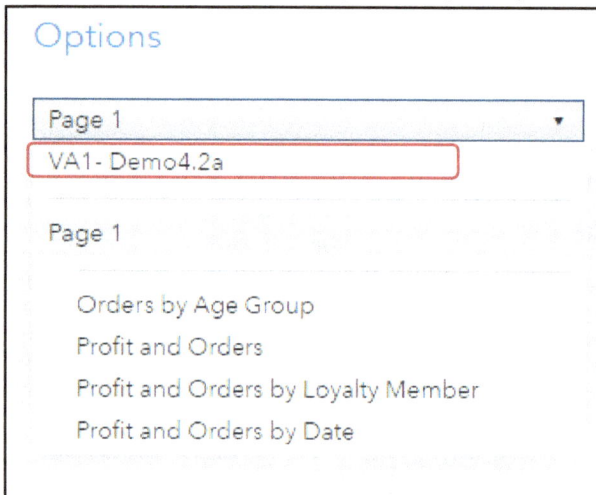

c. In the Viewer Customization group, select **Data edits**.

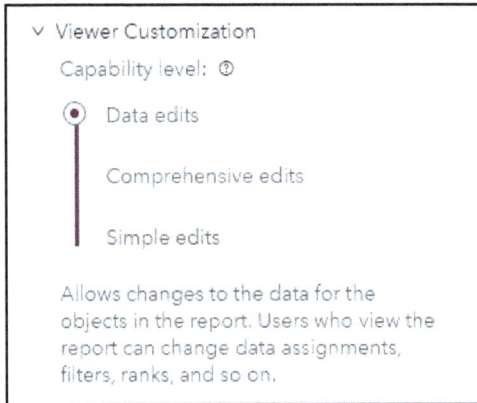

> ∨ Viewer Customization
>
> Capability level: ⓘ
>
> ⦿ Data edits
>
> Comprehensive edits
>
> Simple edits
>
> Allows changes to the data for the
> objects in the report. Users who view the
> report can change data assignments,
> filters, ranks, and so on.

This option enables viewers to make changes to the data used in objects, as well as the filters and ranks applied to objects.

5. Create a new page.

a. In the upper left corner of the report, next to **Page 1**, click ➕ (**New page**).

b. Double-click the **Page 2** heading to make it editable.

c. Enter **Delivery Analysis** and press Enter.

d. Click **Page 1** to make it active.

e. Right-click **Page 1** and select **Rename page**.

f. Enter **Customer Order Analysis** and press Enter.

6. Move the **Profit and Orders by Month** bar chart to the new page.

Right-click the **Profit and Orders by Month** bar chart and select **Move to** ⇨ **Delivery Analysis.**

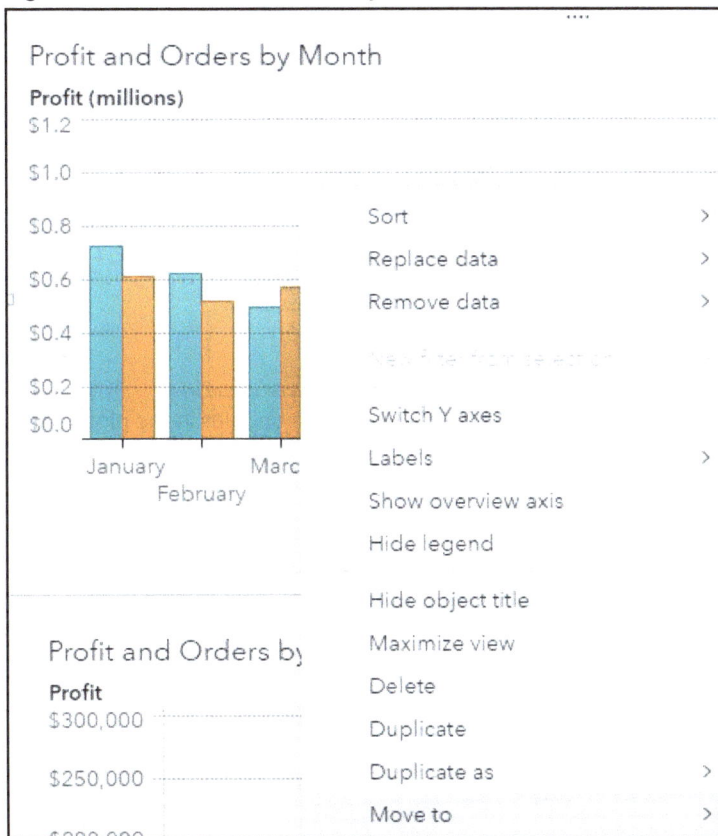

Profit and Orders by Month

Profit (millions)

$1.2	
$1.0	
$0.8	Sort >
	Replace data >
$0.6	Remove data >
$0.4	
$0.2	
$0.0	Switch Y axes
January Marc	Labels >
February	Show overview axis
	Hide legend
	Hide object title
Profit and Orders by	Maximize view
Profit	Delete
$300,000	Duplicate
$250,000	Duplicate as >
	Move to >

Note: You can also drag an object and drop it onto the new page tab. Alternatively, objects can be moved from one page to another using the Outline pane.

7. Click the **Customer Order Analysis** tab to make it active.

8. Rearrange the graphs on the Customer Order Analysis page so that it resembles the following:

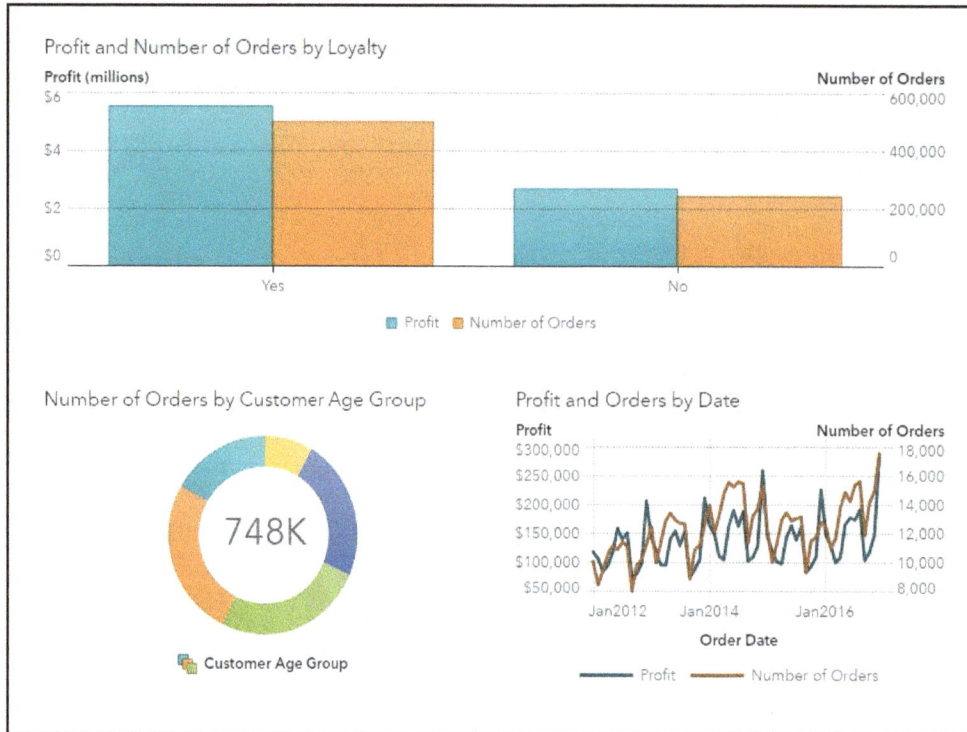

Profit and Number of Orders by Loyalty

Profit (millions)   Number of Orders

Number of Orders by Customer Age Group   Profit and Orders by Date

9. Create a bubble plot.
   a. Click the **Delivery Analysis** tab to make it active.
   b. In the left pane, click **Objects**.
   c. Drag the **Bubble plot** object, from the Graphs group, to the left side of the canvas.
   d. In the right pane, click **Roles**.
   e. For the **Group** role, select **Add** ⇨ **City Name**.
   f. For the X axis role, select **Add** ⇨ **Days to Delivery**.
   g. For the Y axis role, select **Add** ⇨ **Number of Orders**.
   h. For the **Size** role, select **Frequency** ⇨ **Profit**.

      A warning appears in the lower right corner of the bubble plot.

      > No data appears because too many values were returned from the query. Filter your data to reduce the number of values.

      There are too many distinct values of **City Name** to display as bubbles in the plot. Later, you add a rank to reduce the number of bubbles.
   i. For the Animation role, select **Add** ⇨ **Order Month**.
   j. In the right pane, click **Options**.
   k. In the Object group, for the **Name** field, enter **Order Information by Month**.
   l. For the Title field, enter **Top 10 Cities by Number of Orders**.
   m. In the right pane, click **Ranks**.
   n. In the Ranks pane, select **New rank** ⇨ **City Name**.
   o. Verify that **Top count** is specified.
   p. For the **Count** field, verify that **10** is specified.
   q. For the **By** field, select **Number of Orders**.

r. Select the box for **Ties**.

The bubble plot should resemble the following:

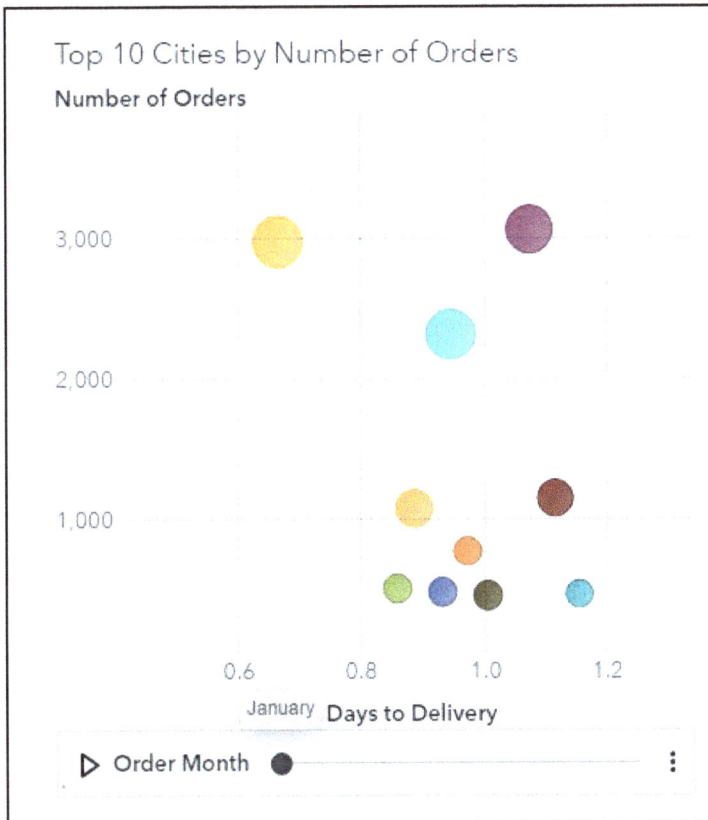

s. In the lower left corner of the bubble plot, click ▷ to play the animation.

10. Save the report.

11. View the report.

a. In the upper left corner, click (**View report**) to view the report.

b. Right-click the dual axis bar chart and select **Replace data** ⇨ **Number of Orders**.

c. Select **Days to Delivery**.

d. Right-click the dual axis bar chart and select **Sort** ⇨ **Order Month: Ascending**.

The dual axis bar chart should resemble the following:

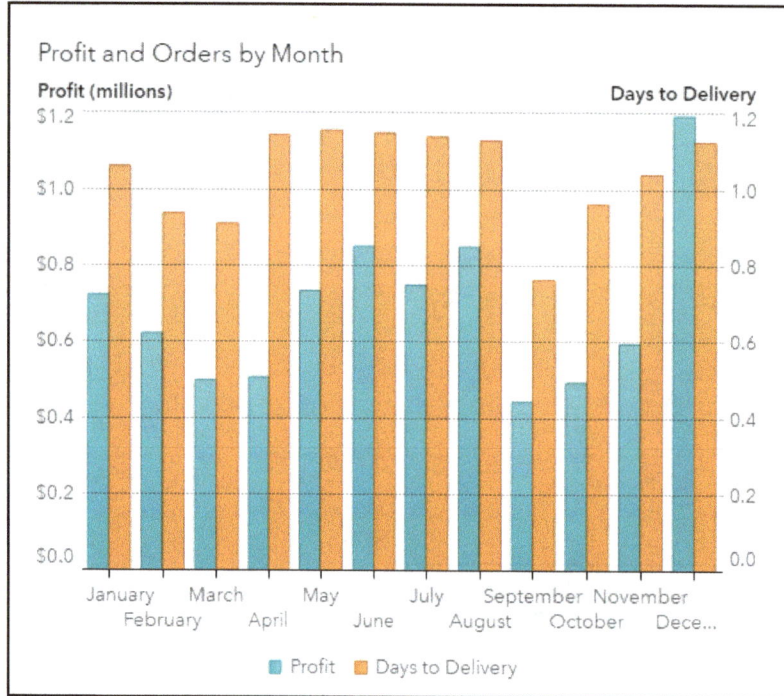

Because the Viewer Customization level for the report was set to **Data edits**, users can change the data used in each report object while viewing the report.

12. Save a copy of the report.

a. In the upper right corner, click ⋮ (**Menu**) and select **Save a copy**.

When anyone saves a copy of a report while viewing it, that user cannot choose a name or a location for the saved report.

The following message appears:

> "VA1- Demo4.2a updated 12/26/2019 3:56:11 PM" saved to My Folder. View ✕

The report is saved to My Folder with a name that includes the date and time at which the copy was created. This copy can then be shared with other users.

13. In the upper right corner, click ⋮ (**Menu**) and select **Close** to close the rep

End of Demonstration

Practice 4.2

1. Working with Pages

   a. Open the browser and sign in to SAS Viya.

   b. Open the **VA1-Practice4.2a** report from the **Courses/YVA185/Basics/Practices (HR)** folder.

   c. Set the Viewer Customization level so that users cannot change the data or the type of chart used in the report.

   d. Add a new page to the report.

   - Change the name of the new page to **Profit Analysis**.

   - Change the name of **Page 1** to **Employee Analysis**.

e. Create a bar chart on the Profit Analysis page by assigning the following data items to the specified roles:

Category   Group

Measure   Total Profit

f. Specify **Total Profit by Group** as the name and title of the bar chart.

g. Sort the bars by **Group** in ascending order.

The Profit Analysis page should resemble the following:

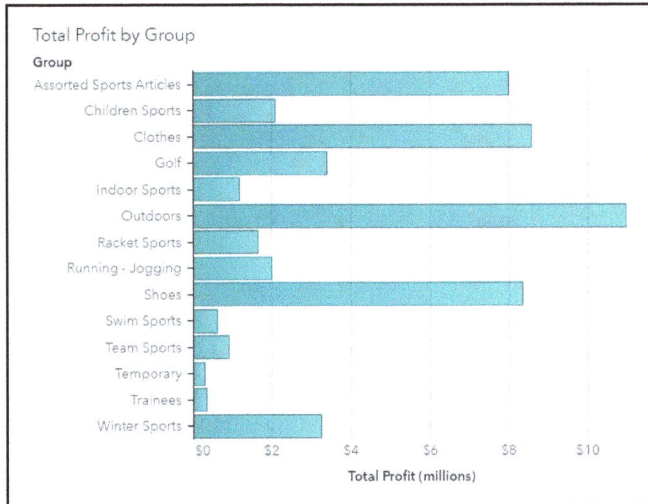

h. Maximize the bar chart and answer the following questions: Which group produces the highest total profit?

Answer: ___

Which group produces the lowest total profit?

Answer: ___

i. Save the report.

j. View the report.

k. On the Profit Analysis page, sort the bars by **Total Profit** in descending order and show data labels.

l. Close the report.

End of Practices

Filtering

Many types of filters can be created to subset data in Visual Analytics. In general, these filters are split between those that can be modified by only the report designer and those that can also be modified by the report viewer. In this lesson, we focus on filters that can be modified by the report viewer. These filters can be classified into three types: prompts, actions, and links. Prompts enable you to subset all data in the report or on a page. Actions, however, can be used to subset specific objects. You can add two types of prompts to a report: report prompts or page prompts. Report prompts filter all objects in the report, and page prompts filter all objects on a single page. Selections that are made in report prompts also filter the values that are available in page prompts. In this example, the year 2014 is selected in the drop-down list in the report prompt area. All objects in the report are filtered to show data for 2014, including the slider control in the page prompt area. In addition, Europe is selected on the button bar in the report prompt area. All objects in the report, including the text input control in the page prompt area, are filtered to show data for Europe. Both types of prompts automatically filter all objects.

Figure 4.3: Filtering Data

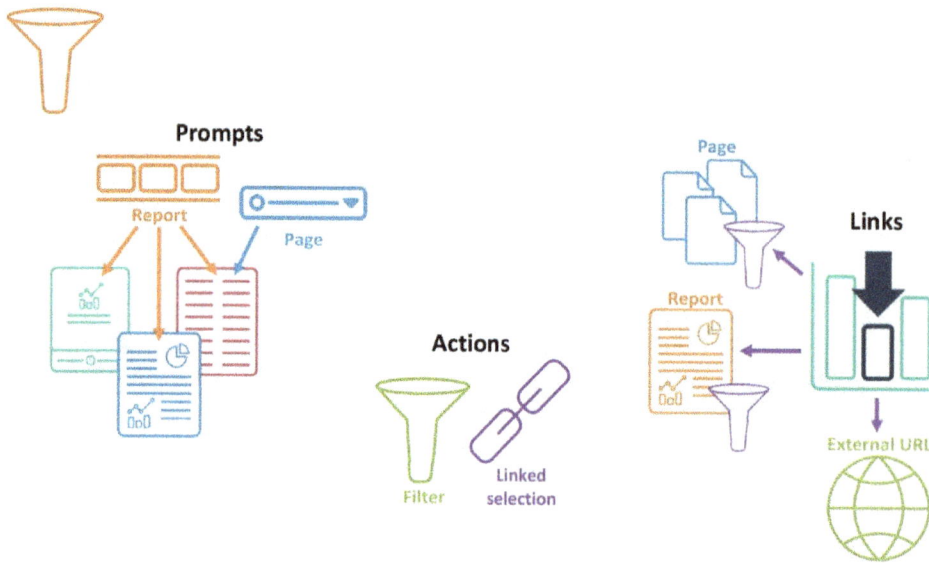

If you prefer to focus the filter on specific objects, you can use actions. The filter action subsets the data in specific objects on the page, based on selections in a source object. Links can be used to subset another report, another page in the same report, or an external URL based on selections in a source object. Link actions will automatically filter the target object if both the source and the target use the same data source. Filters enable you to create general reports that can be widely used for diverse areas of interest by empowering viewers to find answers to their unique questions.

The following types of filters can be modified by report viewers:

Table 4.1: Filters

Filter Type	Description
Report prompt	Automatically subsets the data for all objects in the report if the report object uses the same data source as the prompt. *
Page prompt	Automatically subsets the data for all objects on the page if the report object uses the same data source as the prompt. *
Filter action	Subsets the data in the target object based on selections in a source object.
Linked selection action	Highlights the data in the target object based on selections in a source object.
Links	Subsets the report, page, or an external URL based on the selections in a source object. Links pass a value to filter the target object (report or page) when the source and target are based on the same data source.

* For all prompts and actions, if the report objects use different data sources, automatic mappings are applied. You can modify the data source mappings by right-clicking the control and selecting **Edit data source mappings**. For more information about mapping data sources, see "Map Data Sources for Actions and Links" in the SAS Visual Analytics: Working with Report Data documentation.

For more information about prompts, see "Working with Controls" in the *SAS Visual Analytics: Working with Report Content* documentation.

For more information about actions and links, see "Working with Report Actions and Links" in the *SAS Visual Analytics: Working with Report Data* documentation.

Controls and Prompts

Both report and page prompts can be created by using controls. A control is a report object that can be used to filter or narrow the scope of the data that is used in the report. Controls provide a way for report viewers to focus on a specific area of interest. To use controls effectively, you need to select the appropriate control for your data. One option is to use auto controls. Auto controls can be created by dragging data items to the report or page prompt area. Visual Analytics chooses the appropriate control based on the type and the cardinality of the data item. For more information about the type of control that is selected using auto controls with specific data assignments, see the Resource section of this lesson. Alternatively, you can select your own control object. When selecting control objects, you need to consider the type and cardinality of the data item.

Figure 4.4: Report Controls

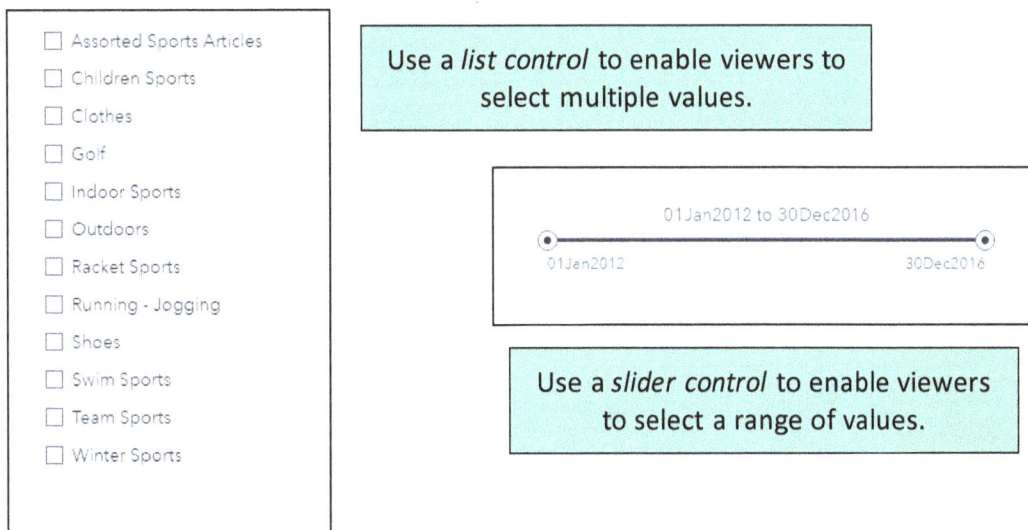

Use a *list control* to enable viewers to select multiple values.

01Jan2012 to 30Dec2016
01Jan2012   30Dec2016

Use a *slider control* to enable viewers to select a range of values.

For date and measure data items, a slider control should be used. This control enables a viewer to move a selector horizontally or vertically to select a single value or a range of values. For category data items, the control that you use will depend on whether you want the viewer to select multiple values or a single value. To select multiple values, a list control should be used. This object enables a viewer to select one or more category values from a list. To select a single value, you also need to consider the cardinality. Remember that the cardinality measures the number of distinct values for a category data item. Categories with few distinct values (less than 5) can be used with a button bar. A button bar displays buttons in a vertical or horizontal layout. Categories with a moderate number of distinct values (between 5 and 40) can be used with a drop-down list. Categories with many distinct values (more than 40) can be used with a text input control. A text input control enables a viewer to enter text in a field. As text is entered, the list of available values is updated.

A control is a report object that filters or narrows the scope of the data viewed in the report. Controls provide a way for report viewers to focus on specific areas of interest.

Note: When multiple control object are used to filter values, the AND operator is used for the filter.

List   A list control enables a viewer to select one or more category values from a list.

           Note: List controls can be used as a report prompt or page prompt only if it is located inside a prompt container or if the report or page control placement option is set to left or right.

Slider   A slider control enables a viewer to move a selector horizontally or vertically to select a single value or a range of values. A slider control accepts only date time or measure data items.

Note: When a parameter is used with a slider control, the control is converted to a single-point slider.

A control is a report object that filters or narrows the scope of the data viewed in the report. Controls provide a way for report viewers to focus on specific areas of interest.

Note: When multiple control objects are used to filter values, the AND operator is used for the filter.

Figure 4.5: Report and Page Prompts

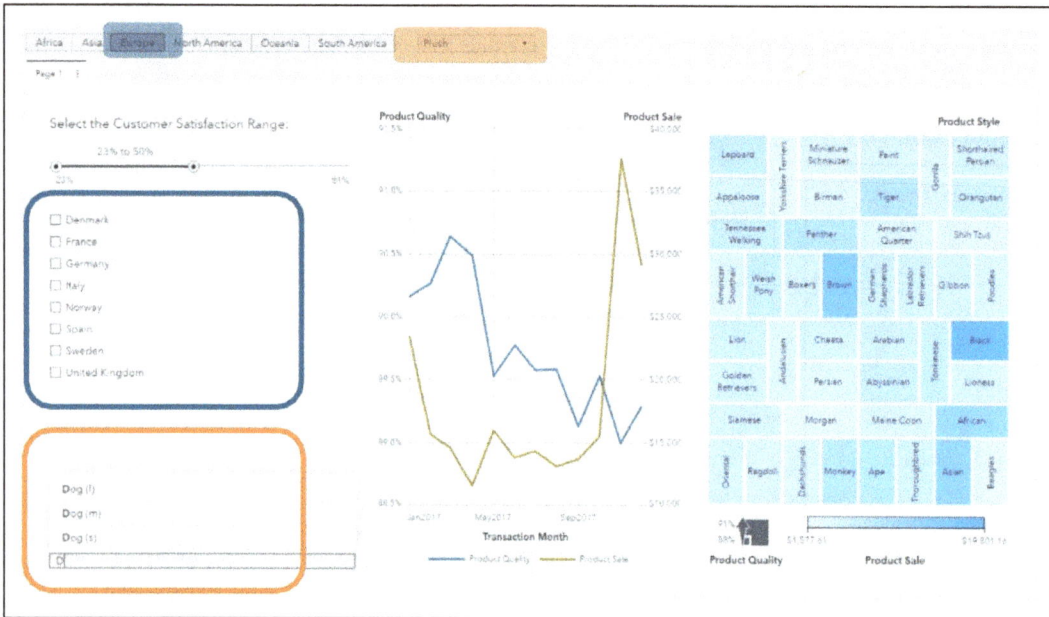

In the display capture above, page controls are placed on the left side of the page. Beginning in SAS Visual Analytics 8.4, report designers can change the position of report and page controls. The **Placement** option enables you to place the controls at the top, bottom, left, or right. If you want reports that you create to have the same placement for controls, you can use the **Default report controls placement** and **Default page control placement** settings for Visual Analytics. If the report or page controls are placed on the left or right, you can add a list control to the prompt area (as seen above).

Note: Report and page prompt areas are not displayed by default when editing a report.

Note: Auto controls can be created by dragging data items to the report or page prompt area.

Data Items	Control Type
Category with 1–4 distinct values	Button bar
Category with 5–40 distinct values	Drop-down list
Category with more than 40 distinct values	Text input
Datetime	Slider

Data Items	Control Type
Measure	Slider

Actions

One way to create interactive reports is with actions. Actions are used to direct a report viewer's attention to specific results in a report. Two types of actions are available: linked selections and filters. A linked selection action enables you to show the same data highlighted simultaneously in two or more objects. The data for the linked selection has the same appearance in each object. This makes it easy for the report viewer to identify and compare the values. A filter action, on the other hand, enables you to restrict the data displayed in other objects. Filters make it easy for the report viewer to focus on specific areas of interest. In this example, the list control filters the geo map, so only countries in Europe are displayed. The geo map then filters both the bar chart and the list table, so only details about products in Italy are shown. A linked selection is also established between the bar chart and the list table, so when a specific product line is selected in one object, it is highlighted in the other.

Figure 4.5: Actions

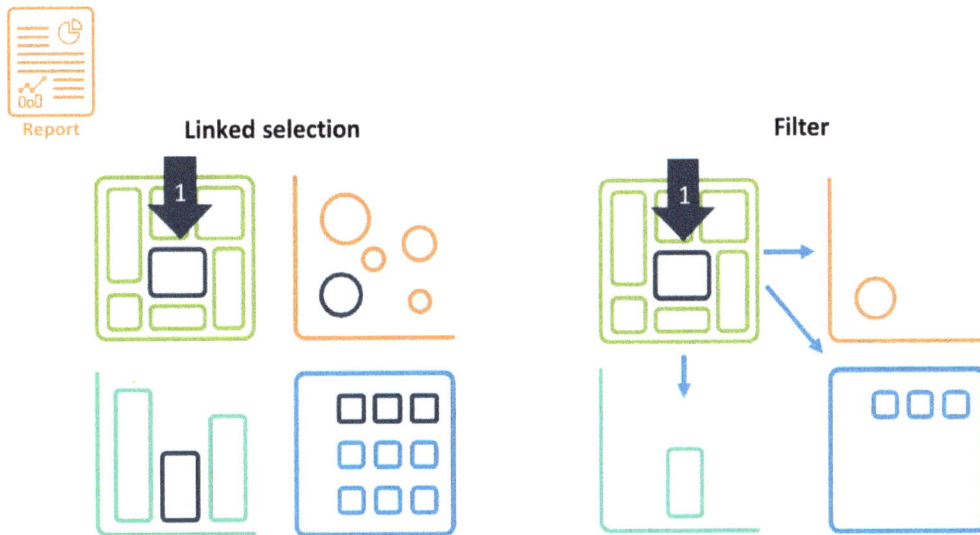

Actions are used to direct a report viewer's attention to specific results in a report.

The following actions are available:

Table 4.2: Actions

Action	Description
Linked selection	A linked selection action enables you to show the same data highlighted simultaneously in two or more tables, graphs, or controls on the same page. The data for the linked selection action has the same appearance in each object, which makes the data easily apparent to report viewers.
Filter	A filter action enables you to restrict the data displayed in other objects on the page. A viewer can select a subset of data in the source object and see the restricted data for any target objects.

Figure 4.6: Adding Actions to a Page

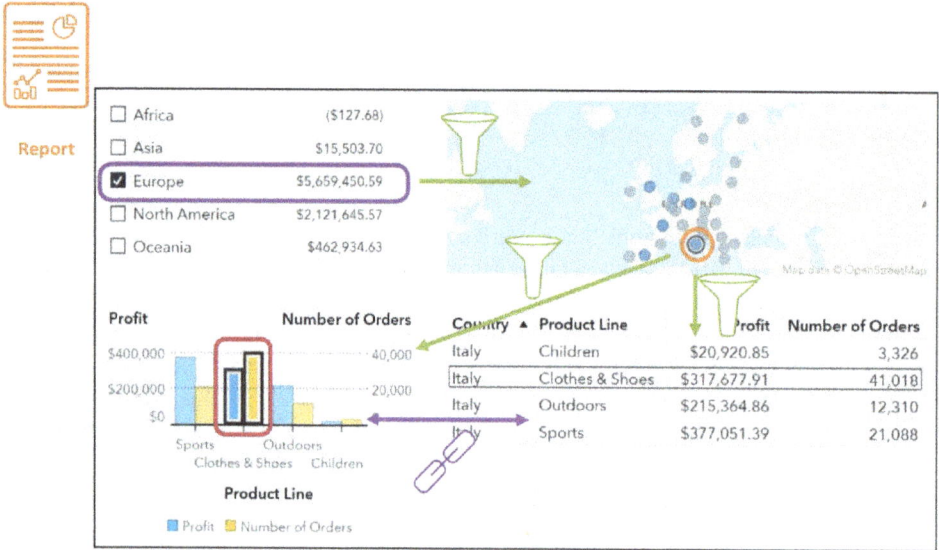

Demo 4.3: Working with Prompts and Actions

This demonstration illustrates how to add page prompts and actions to create interactive reports in Visual Analytics.

1. From the browser window, sign in to SAS Viya.
2. In the upper left corner, click ☰ (**Show list of applications**) and select **Explore and Visualize**. SAS Visual Analytics appears.
3. Click **All Reports**.
   a. Navigate to the **Courses/YVA185/Basics/Demos (Marketing)** folder.
   b. Double-click the **VA1- Demo4.2b** report to open it.
4. Add a page prompt to Customer Order Analysis.
   a. If necessary, click the **Customer Order Analysis** page to make it active.
   b. On the Customer Order Analysis tab, click ⋮ (**Options**) and select **Expand page controls**.

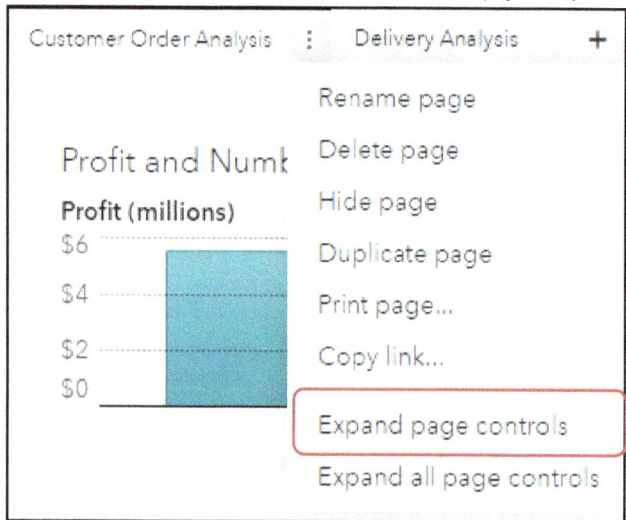

The page prompt area is shown on the page:

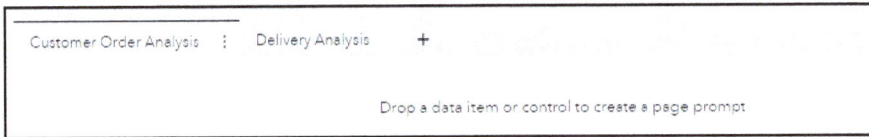

Customer Order Analysis ⋮	Delivery Analysis +	
		Drop a data item or control to create a page prompt

Note: You can also display report controls and all page controls for the report. To display the report controls, click ⋮ (**Menu**) and select **Expand report controls**. To display both report and page controls, click ⋮ (**Menu**) and select **Expand report controls** and all page controls.

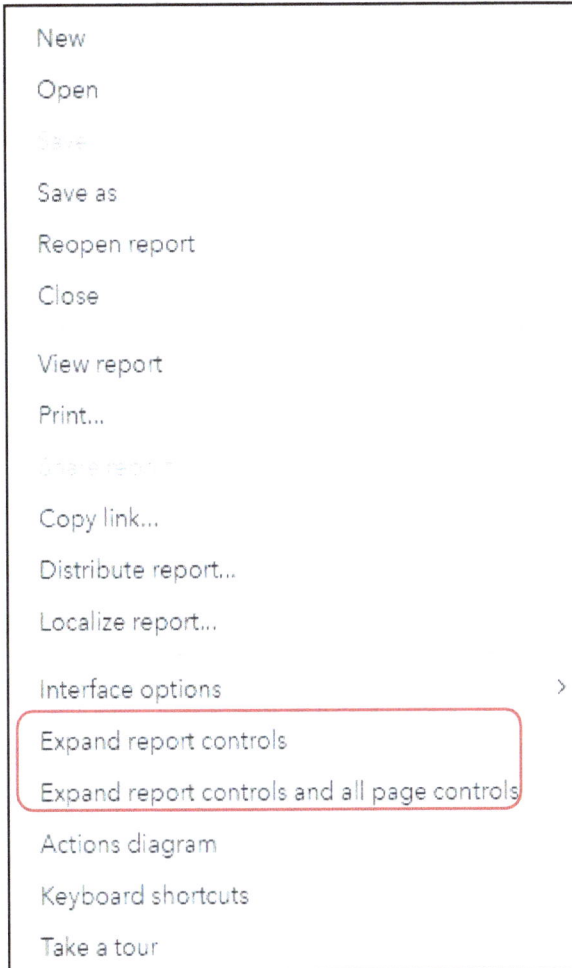

New

Open

~~Save~~

Save as

Reopen report

Close

View report

Print...

~~Share report...~~

Copy link...

Distribute report...

Localize report...

Interface options   >

Expand report controls

Expand report controls and all page controls

Actions diagram

Keyboard shortcuts

Take a tour

Note: In the general settings for Visual Analytics, you can specify whether to expand report and page controls by default for new pages.

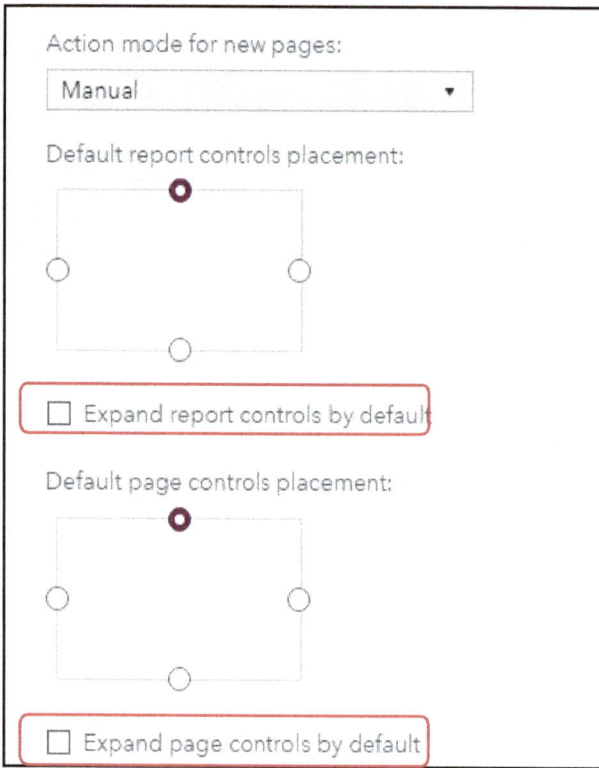

Action mode for new pages:

```
Manual                              ▼
```

Default report controls placement:

☐ Expand report controls by default

Default page controls placement:

☐ Expand page controls by default

c. In the left pane, click **Data**.

d. Drag **Order Type**, from the Category group, to the **Drop a data item or control to create a page prompt** area.

An auto control determines the best control object to use for the selected data.

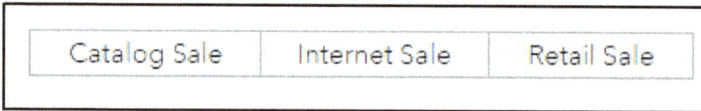

Catalog Sale	Internet Sale	Retail Sale

e. In the right pane, click **Options**.

f. In the Object group, for the **Name** field, enter **Order Type Selector**.

g. For the **Title** field, select **Custom title**.

h. For the **Title** field, enter **Select an order type:**. The auto control should resemble the following:

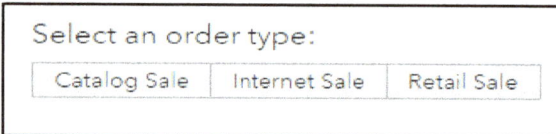

Select an order type:

Catalog Sale	Internet Sale	Retail Sale

i.   For the control, click **Catalog Sale** to filter the objects on the page. The Customer Order Analysis section should resemble the following:

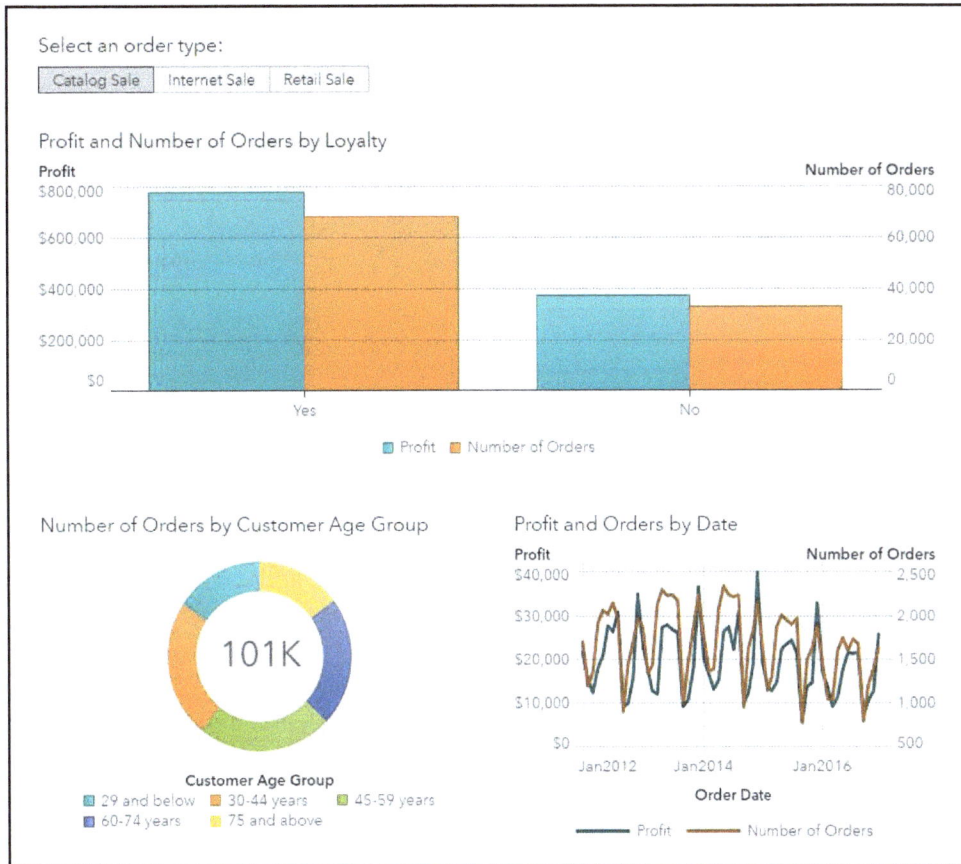

Select an order type:

| Catalog Sale | Internet Sale | Retail Sale |

Profit and Number of Orders by Loyalty

Number of Orders by Customer Age Group

Customer Age Group
■ 29 and below ■ 30-44 years ■ 45-59 years
■ 60-74 years ■ 75 and above

Profit and Orders by Date

j.   For the control, click **Catalog Sale** to deselect it.

5.   Add actions between objects on the Delivery Analysis page.

   a.   Click the **Delivery Analysis** page to make it active.

   b.   In the canvas, click the drop-down list control to select it.

   c.   In the right pane, click **Actions**.

   d.   In the Object Links group, select **Profit and Orders** (the dual axis bar chart).

   e.   Verify that [⛛ ▾] (**Filter**) is selected.

   f.   Select **Order Information by Month** (the bubble plot).

   g.   Click [⛛ ▾] (**Filter**) and select **Linked selection**.
        The Actions pane should resemble the following:

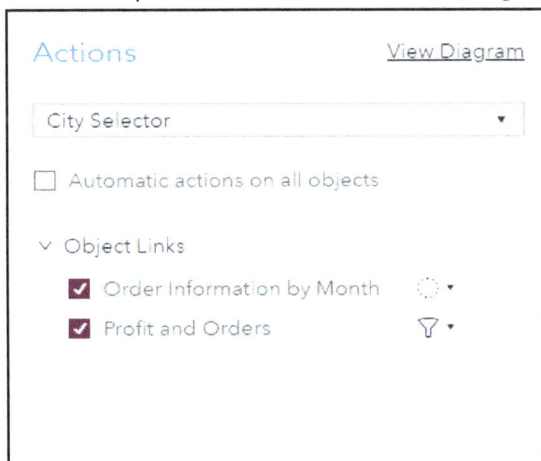

h. In the Actions pane, click **View Diagram**. The Actions Diagram window appears.

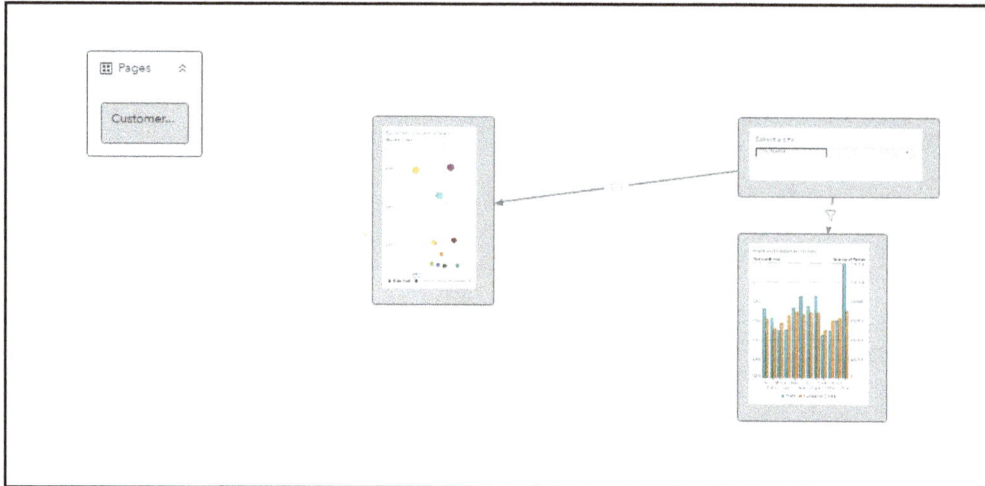

Note: The Actions Diagram window can also be used to create actions between objects. Simply click and drag between objects to create the action.

6. Click **Close**.

7. Save the report.

8. View the report.

a. In the upper left corner, click (**View report**) to view the report.

b. At the top of the report, click the **Customer Order Analysis** tab to make the page active.

c. In the button bar, click **Internet Sale**.

The Customer Order Analysis page updates to show information about internet products ordered.

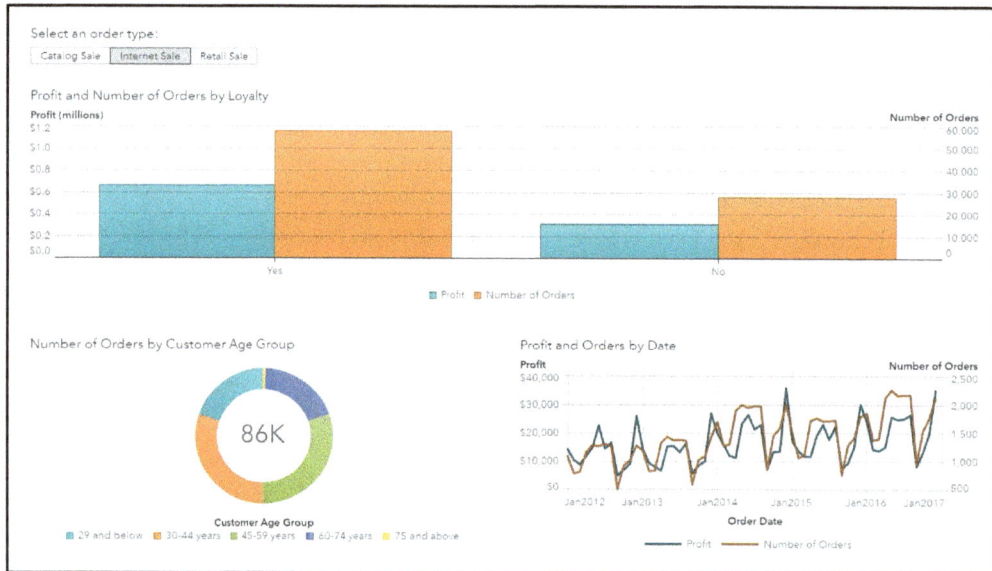

d. In the upper right corner of the pie chart, click [↗] (**Maximize**).

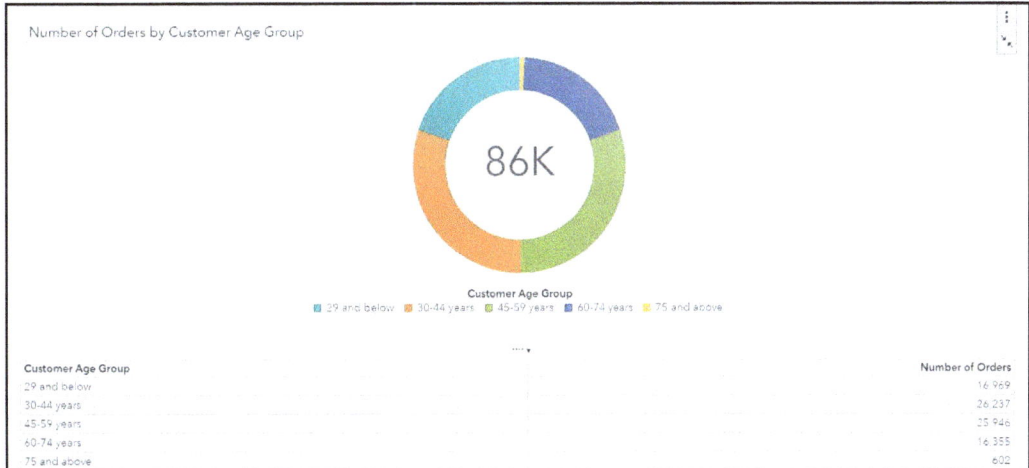

Number of Orders by Customer Age Group

86K

Customer Age Group
■ 29 and below ■ 30-44 years ■ 45-59 years ■ 60-74 years ■ 75 and above

Customer Age Group	Number of Orders
29 and below	16,969
30-44 years	26,237
45-59 years	25,946
60-74 years	16,355
75 and above	602

A lower percentage of all internet orders is placed by customers in the older age groups (60-75 years and 75 and above) compared to younger age groups. This appears to be a generational difference. How do we plan for this difference in ordering patterns among different age groups? Do we expect this difference to continue over time, or do we expect the difference to eventually get smaller?

e. In the upper right corner of the pie chart, click [↘] (**Restore**).

f. In the dual axis bar chart, click the bars for **Yes**.

g. In the pie chart, click the slice for **30–44 years** (orange slice). The dual axis time series plot should resemble the following:

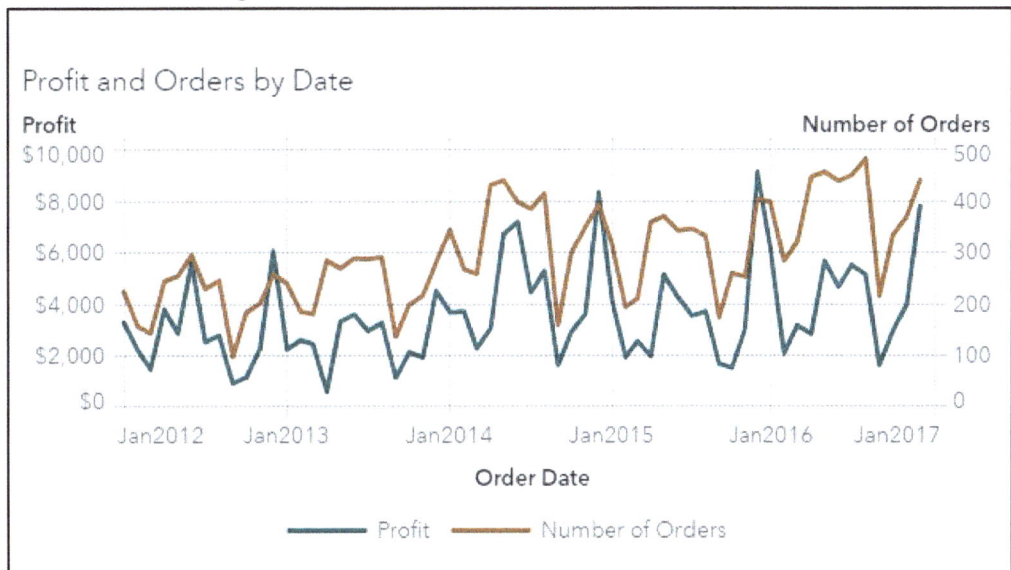

Profit and Orders by Date

Profit		Number of Orders
$10,000		500
$8,000		400
$6,000		300
$4,000		200
$2,000		100
$0		0

Jan2012   Jan2013   Jan2014   Jan2015   Jan2016   Jan2017

Order Date

——— Profit   ——— Number of Orders

h. At the top of the report, click the **Delivery Analysis** tab to make the page active.

i. In the drop-down list control, select **Madrid**.

The bubble for Madrid is highlighted in the bubble plot, and the dual axis bar chart is filtered to show profit and orders by month for Madrid.

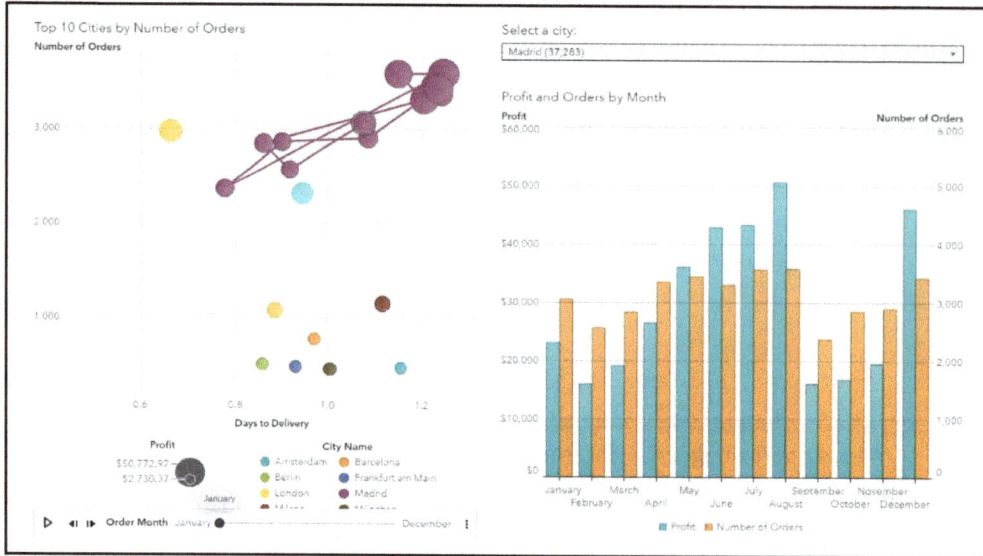

Looking at the bubble plot, you can see a positive association between the number of orders and the days to delivery for Madrid. As the number of orders increase, so does the time it takes to receive the delivery. Looking at the dual axis bar chart, you can see that the number of orders peak around the summer and winter months. This could indicate more interest in buying sports and outdoor products during this time. However, notice that profits spike in August and December. Why are profits so much higher in those specific months?

j. In the upper right corner, click ⋮ (**Menu**) and select **Close** to close the report.

End of Demonstration

Practice 4.3

1. Working with Prompts and Actions

    a. Open the browser and sign in to SAS Viya.

    b. Open the **VA1- Practice4.2b** report from the **Courses/YVA185/Basics/Practices (HR)** folder.

    c. Add a report prompt that uses a button bar to select the employee status.

    d. Modify the following options for the button bar:

    Name   Employee Status Selector

    Title   Select an employee status:

    The button bar should resemble the following:

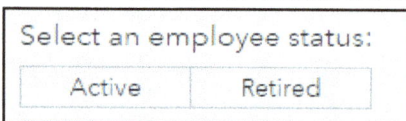

Select an employee status:	
Active	Retired

    e. Add the following actions between objects on the Employee Analysis page:

    - The geo map filters the bar chart and the dual axis bar-line chart.

    - The bar chart highlights the dual axis bar-line chart.

f. On the Profit Analysis page, add a rank to the list table to show the top five employees by Total Profit.

   Hint: Add a rank for *all* visible categories. The list table should resemble the following:

Top 5 Employees by Total Profit Generated	
Name	**Total Profit ▼**
Agnes de Fourtou	$395,552.03
Christelle Bourrier	$390,366.78
Eric Golliot	$322,279.04
Cedric Desqueyroux	$312,768.37
Marie-Christine Le Bihen	$312,696.37

The Profit Analysis page should resemble the following:

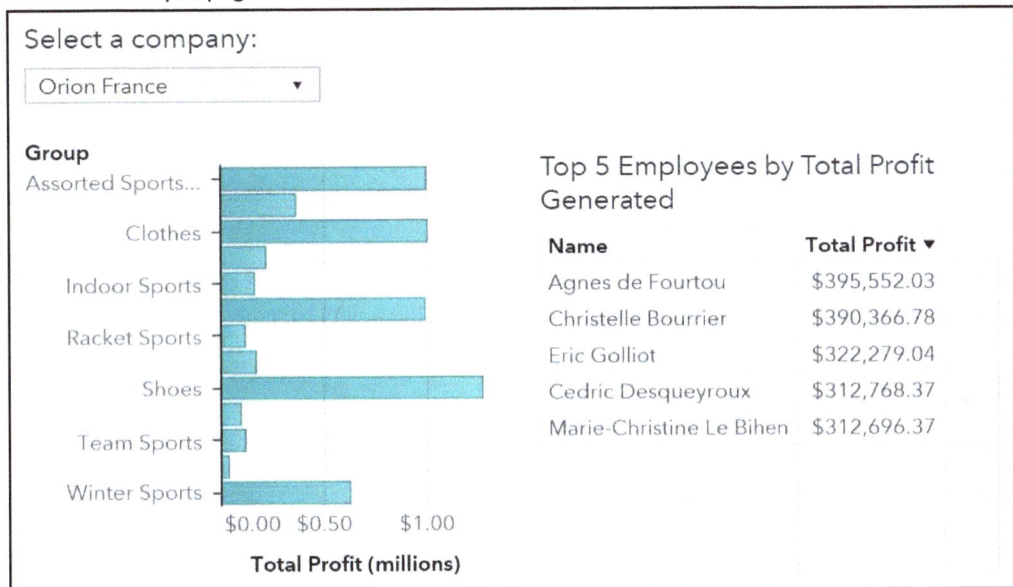

g. Save the report.
h. View the report and answer the following questions:

   Which job title has the highest average profit among active employees in Australia?

   Answer:

   For Orion USA, which active sales representative had the highest total profit generated for the Indoor Sports group?

   Answer:

   For Orion France, how many active sales representatives sold items for the Racket Sports group?

   Answer:

i. Close the report.

   End of Practices

Adding Links

Another way to create interactive reports is with links. Links have elements of both a filter and an action. Three types of links are available: page links, report links, and URL links. Page links enable you to access another page in the same report, and report links enable you to access another report.

Figure 4.7: Adding Page Links

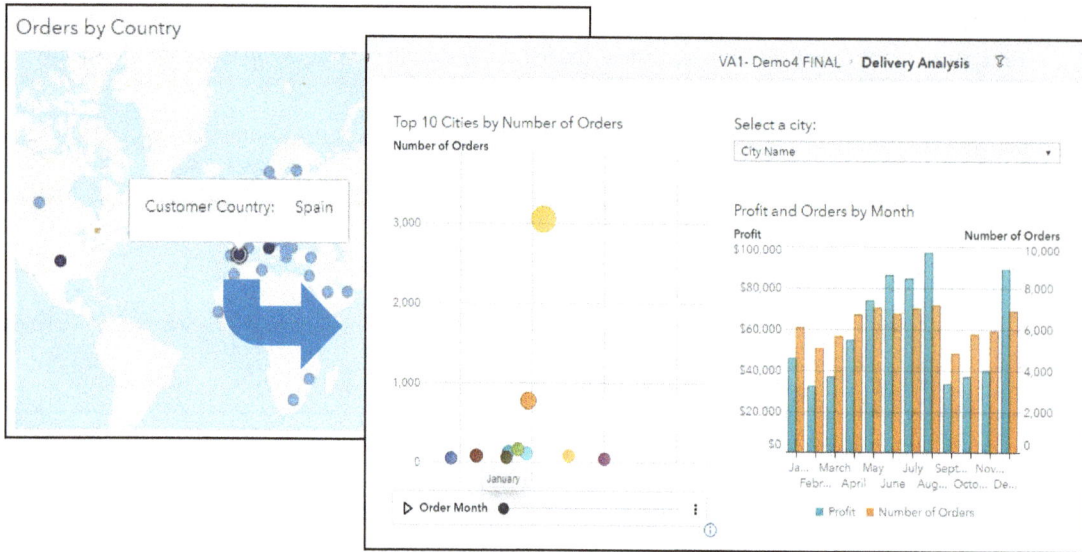

Linking has elements of both a filter and an action. A page that is the target of a link is filtered by the values selected in the linked report object.

If the source and the target use the same data source, an automatic filter is passed through the link. If the source and the target use different data sources, you have the ability to map data sources, so a filter is passed through the link.

Figure 4.8: Adding Report Links

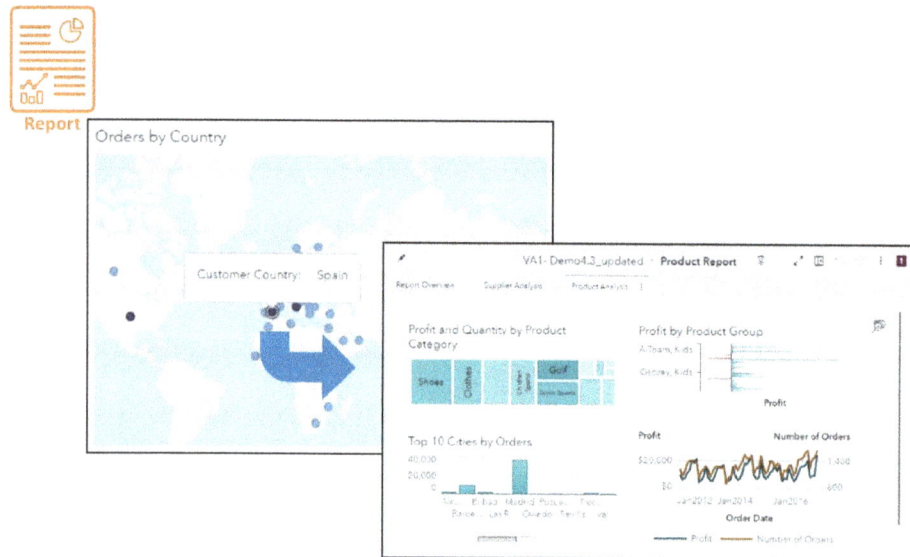

If the destination report contains multiple pages, then when you define the link, you can choose the initial page of the destination report that opens first.

Figure 4.9: Adding URL Links

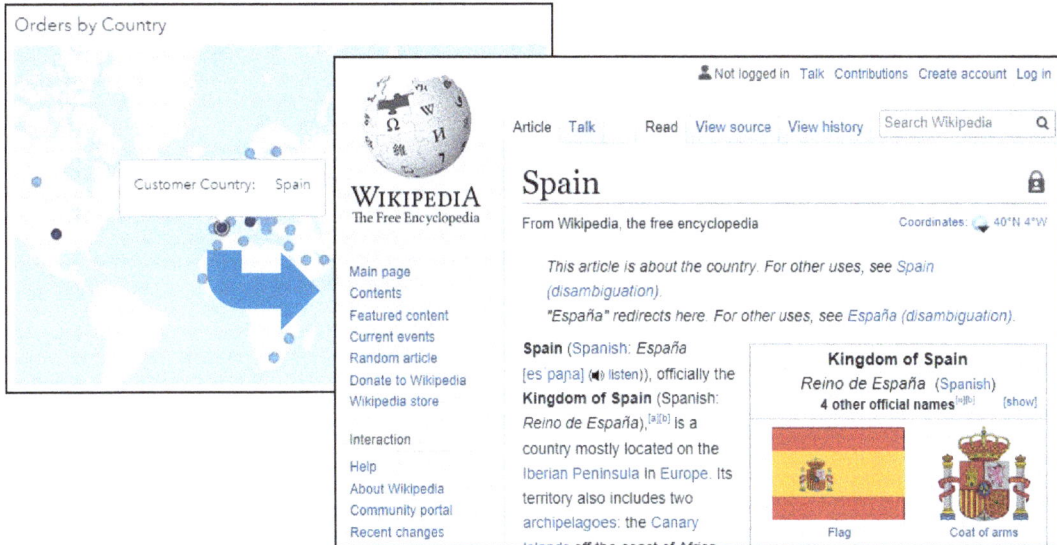

If the source and the target of the link use the same data source, an automatic filter is passed through the link. In this example, a page link was added to the report. Double-clicking the bubble for Spain opens another page in the same report and subsets the page to show details about Spain. In this example, a report link was added to the report. Double-clicking the bubble for Spain opens another report and subsets the report to show details about Spain. Alternatively, you can specify a URL link, which enables you to access and view an external web page. For URL links, you have the added ability to specify parameters that pass data item values to the URL. In this example, a URL link with parameters was added to the report. Double-clicking the bubble for Spain opens the Wikipedia page for Spain.

Demo 4.4: Working with Hidden Pages and Page Links

This demonstration illustrates how to create hidden pages and how to add page links to create interactive reports in Visual Analytics.

1. From the browser window, sign in to SAS Viya.
2. In the upper left corner, click ☰ (**Show list of applications**) and select **Explore and Visualize**. SAS Visual Analytics appears.
3. Click All Reports.
   a. Navigate to the **Courses/YVA185/Basics/Demos (Marketing)** folder.
   b. Double-click the **VA1-Demo4.2c** report to open it.
4. Change the name of Page 3 and hide the page.
   a. Click the **Page 3** tab to make the page active.
   b. Double-click the **Page 3** heading to make it editable.
   c. Enter **Customer Details** and press Enter.
   d. Click ⋮ (**Options**) and select **Hide page** to make the page hidden.
      Note: Hidden pages do not appear when viewing the report unless they are linked to.
5. Modify the size of the hidden page.
   a. In the right pane, click **Options**.
   b. In the General group, for the **Window width (percentage)** field, enter **75**.

c.　For the **Window height (percentage)** field, enter **75**. The Options pane should resemble the following:

Options

Customer Details

∨ General
　　Name: *
　　Customer Details

　　☑ Hide and link to page as pop-up window
　　Window width (percentage):
　　75

　　Window height (percentage):
　　75

　　☐ Periodically reload page data

6.　Add links between objects.
　　a.　Click the **Customer Order Analysis** page to make it active.
　　b.　In the canvas, click the pie chart to make it active.
　　c.　In the right pane, click **Actions**.
　　d.　In the Actions pane, expand **Page Links**.
　　e.　Select Customer Details.

　　　　The Actions pane should resemble the following:

Actions　　　　　View Diagram

Orders by Age Group　　　▼

☐ Automatic actions on all objects

∨ Object Links
　☑ Profit and Orders by Date　　▽ ·

∨ Page Links
　☐ Delivery Analysis
　☑ Customer Details　　　　⋮

> Report Links
> URL Links

7.　Save the report.
8.　View the report.

　　a.　In the upper left corner, click ▱ (**View report**) to view the report.
　　b.　In the button bar, select **Internet Sale**.
　　c.　In the dual axis bar chart, select **Yes**.

d. In the pie chart, double-click the slice for **45–59 years** (green slice).

The Customer Details hidden page appears as a pop-up window and shows details about female customers in the 45-59 age group who placed orders via the internet.

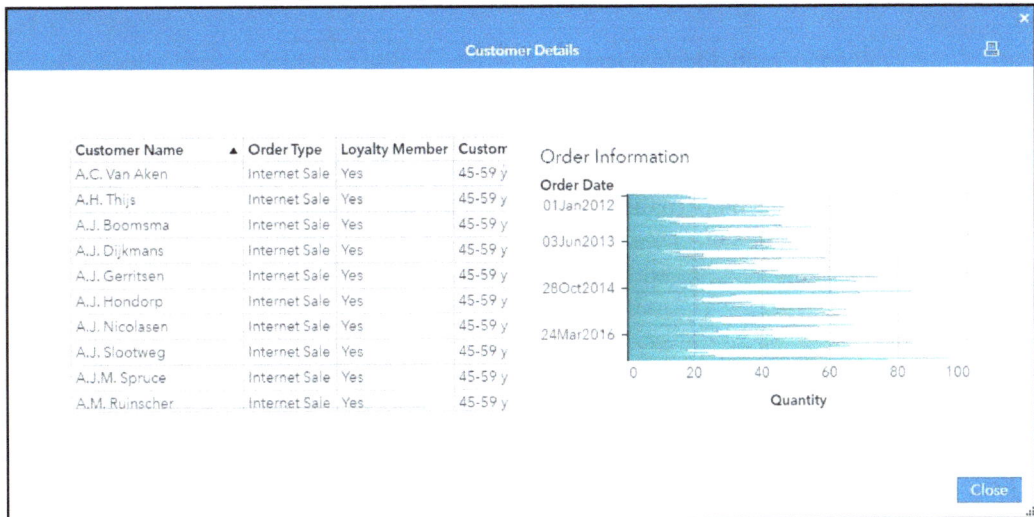

e. In the list table, select the row for **Ada Harsen**. The hidden window should resemble the following:

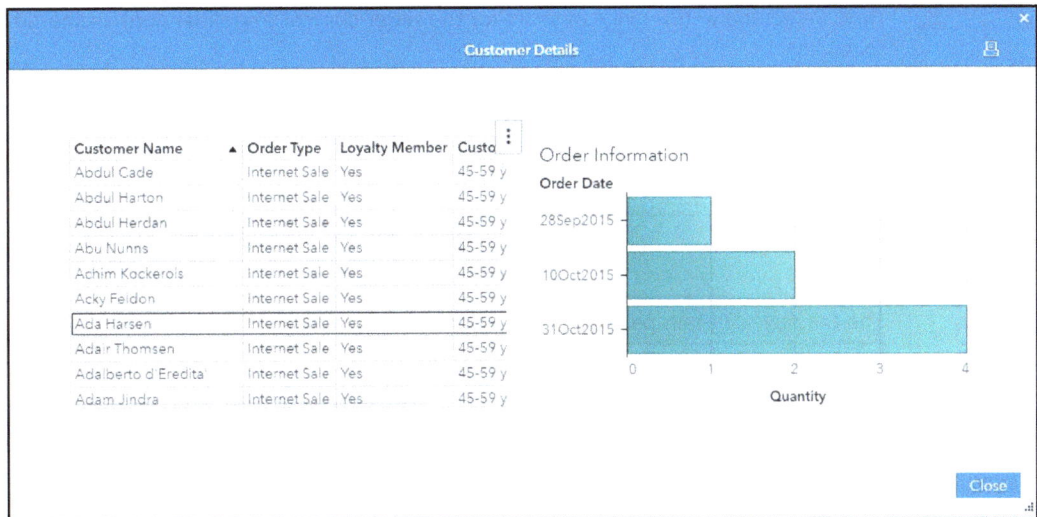

Ada seems to place a lot of orders in the same time frame (fall). Why does she place orders during the same time period? Does her birthday or a friend's birthday fall near this time? If so, we might want to try to offer her discounts at other times of year to increase her orders.

f. Click **Close** to close the hidden window.

g. In the upper right corner, click ⋮ (**Menu**) and select **Close** to close the report.

End of Demonstration

Practice

1. Working with Hidden Pages and Page Links

    a. Open the browser and sign in to SAS Viya.

    b. Open the **VA1-Practice4.2c** report from the **Courses/YVA185/Basics/Practices (HR)** folder.

    c. Hide **Page 3** and rename the page as **Employee Details**.

d. Modify the following options for the hidden page, Employee Details:

Window width (percentage)	75
Window height (percentage)	75

e. Add a page prompt to the Employee Details page that uses a slider control to select a range of values for years of service.

f. Modify the following options for the slider control:

Object: Name	Years of Service Selector
Object: Custom Title	Select a range of years:
Slider: Act on aggregated data in filtered objects	<selected>
Slider: Minimum	0
Slider: Maximum	45

Hint: Select the entire range of years for the slider control. The slider control should resemble the following:

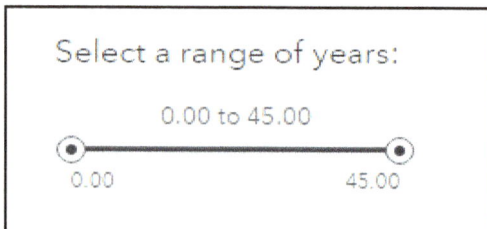

The Employee Details page should resemble the following:

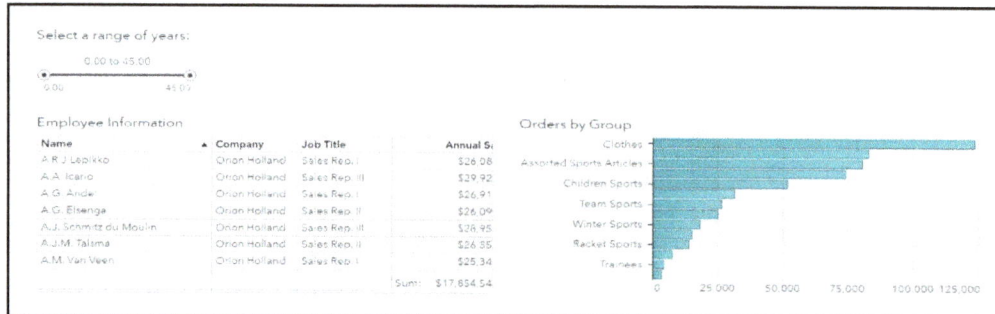

g. Add a page link from the bar chart on the Employee Analysis page to the Employee Details page.

h. Save the report.

i. View the report and answer the following questions:

How many employees retired in Italy with the Sales Rep. III job title?

Answer:

Management has decided to start promotions with active employees in the United States with the Sales Rep. I job title. Of the active employees with 25 or more years of service, how many generate a total profit more than $200,000?

Answer:

j. Close the report.

End of Practices

4.4 Working with Display Rules

Display rules enable you to use colors to identify specific areas of interest. Display rules can be added for a specific object or to the entire report.

Table 4.3: Display Rules

Display Rule	Description
Expression	Expression display rules are based on the value of a measure data item. For a list table, the expression display rule can be applied to the measure used in the expression, to another column in the table, or to the entire row. Crosstabs accept only expression display rules. If the crosstab contains a hierarchy or totals and subtotals are displayed, you can specify the hierarchy levels or intersections where the display rule will be applied.
Color-mapped values	Color-mapped values display rules are based on the value of a category data item. For a list table, the color-mapped values display rule can be applied to any column in the table or to the entire row.
Gauge	Gauge display rules are based on intervals for a measure data item. For a list table, the gauge display rule can be added to any column in the table. The display rule can be displayed to the left or to the right of the value, or it can replace the value.

Graph Level

For most graph objects, two types of display rules can be added: expression display rules or color-mapped values display rules. Expression display rules are based on the value of a measure data item. For the graph, the display rule can be applied to the background of the graph (shown in Figure 4.10) or to the graph itself. Expression display rules are great for showing values that outperform or underperform a specific target or for easily identifying the range in which the actual values occur. In this example, an expression display rule indicates which categories produce low, medium, or high average profits. Color-mapped values display rules are based on the value of a category data item (shown here). These display rules are excellent for associating colors with specific values. (For example, coal is gray.) They can be used to add consistency to your reports. In this example, a color-mapped values display rule is applied to color the group sports brown, individual sports blue, and other items gray.

Figure 4.10: Graph-Level Display Rules

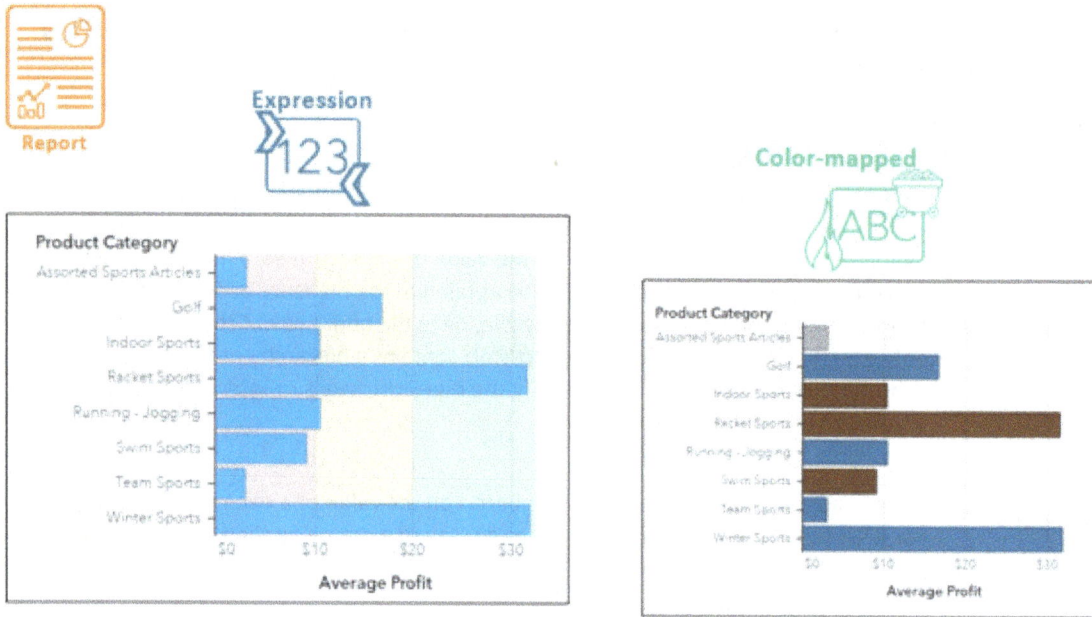

Table Level

Display rules can use colors in table objects to identify specific areas of interest. For list tables, three types of display rules are available: expression, color-mapped values, and gauge. Expression display rules are based on the value of a measure data item. For a list table, the display rule can be applied to the measure that is used in the expression, to another column in the table, or to the entire row. Expression display rules are excellent for showing values that outperform or underperform a specific target or for easily identifying the range in which the actual values fall.

In the example shown in Figure 4.11, an expression display rule indicates which product lines and order types have profits below $50,000. Color-mapped values display rules are based on the values of a category data item.

For a list table, the display rule can be applied to any column in the table or to the entire row. Color-mapped values display rules are great for associating colors with specific values. (For example, coal is gray.) They can be used to add consistency in your reports. In Figure 4.11, a color-mapped values display rule is applied to color the outdoors line orange and the sports line blue. Gauge display rules are based on intervals for a measure data item. For a list table, the display rule can be added to any column in the table. It can be displayed to the left or to the right of the value, or it can replace the value. Gauge display rules are ideal for showing the overall performance of a measure with a single glance, without having to focus on details. In this example, a gauge display rule indicates which product lines and order types have low, medium, or high order numbers.

Figure 4.11: Table-Level Display Rules

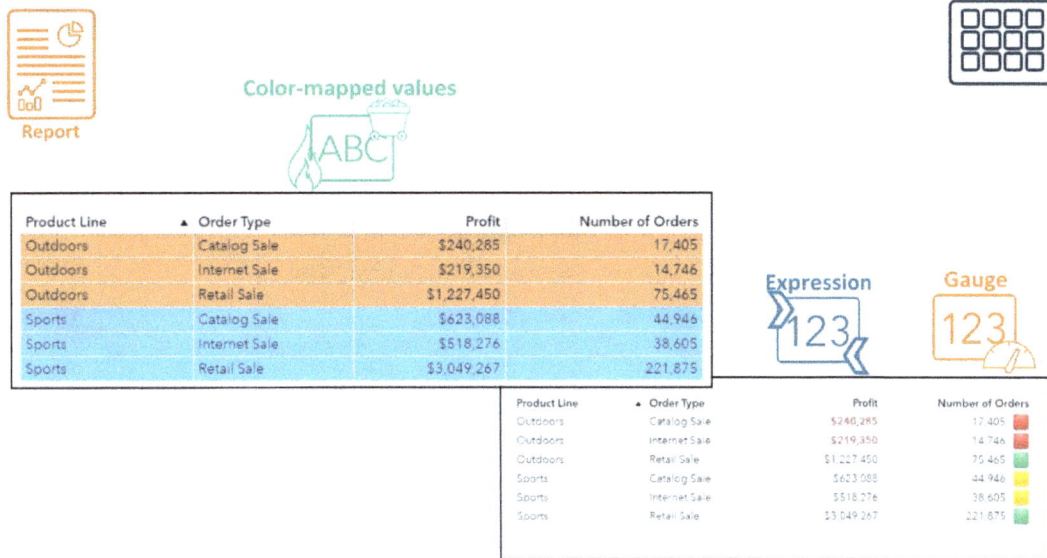

Product Line	▲ Order Type	Profit	Number of Orders
Outdoors	Catalog Sale	$240,285	17,405
Outdoors	Internet Sale	$219,350	14,746
Outdoors	Retail Sale	$1,227,450	75,465
Sports	Catalog Sale	$623,088	44,946
Sports	Internet Sale	$518,276	38,605
Sports	Retail Sale	$3,049,267	221,875

Report

Color-mapped values

ABC

Expression
123

Gauge
123

Product Line	▲ Order Type	Profit	Number of Orders	
Outdoors	Catalog Sale	$240,285	17,405	
Outdoors	Internet Sale	$219,350	14,746	
Outdoors	Retail Sale	$1,227,450	75,465	
Sports	Catalog Sale	$623,088	44,946	
Sports	Internet Sale	$518,276	38,605	
Sports	Retail Sale	$3,049,267	221,875	

Crosstabs, on the other hand, only accept expression display rules. In Figure 4.12, an expression display rule highlights profits that are less than $100,000 for specific order types and years.

Figure 4.12: Crosstab Table-Level Display Rules

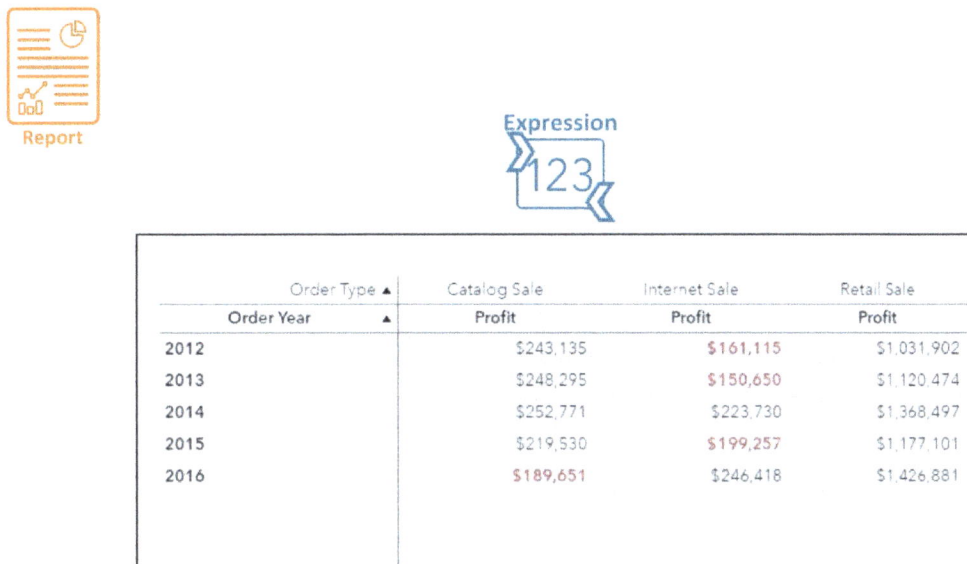

Report

Expression
123

Order Type ▲	Catalog Sale	Internet Sale	Retail Sale
Order Year ▲	Profit	Profit	Profit
2012	$243,135	$161,115	$1,031,902
2013	$248,295	$150,650	$1,120,474
2014	$252,771	$223,730	$1,368,497
2015	$219,530	$199,257	$1,177,101
2016	$189,651	$246,418	$1,426,881

Report Level

A report-level display rule applies to all objects in the report.

Figure 4.13: Report-Level Display Rules

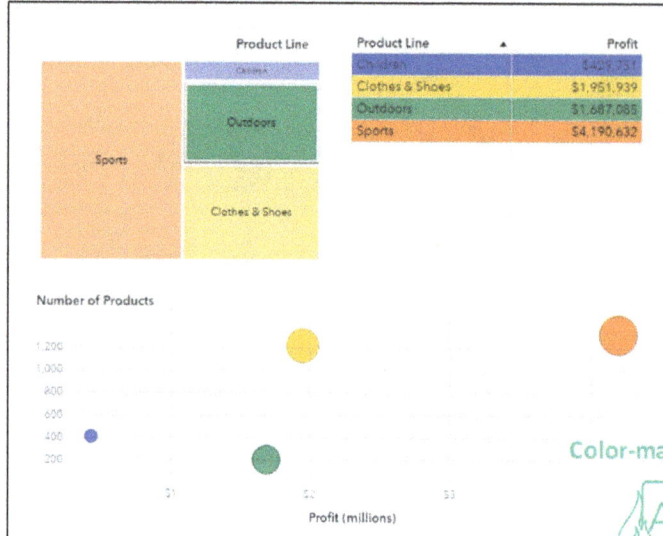

Demo 4.5: Working with Graph-Level Display Rules

This demonstration illustrates how to add graph-level display rules in Visual Analytics.

1. From the browser window, sign in to SAS Viya.
2. In the upper left corner, click ▤ (**Show list of applications**) and select **Explore and Visualize**. SAS Visual Analytics appears.
3. Click **All Reports**.
   a. Navigate to the **Courses/YVA185/Basics/Demos (Marketing)** folder.
   b. Double-click the **VA1-Demo4.3** report to open it.
4. Add a custom sort for **Order Type**.
   a. In the left pane, click **Data**.
   b. Right-click **Order Type** and select **Custom sort**.
      The Add Custom Sort window appears.
      i. Double-click the following values, in order, to add them to the Sorted Items list:
         Retail Sale
         Catalog Sale
         Internet Sale

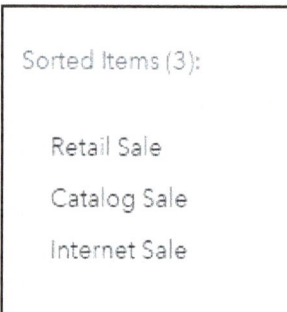

Sorted Items (3):

Retail Sale

Catalog Sale

Internet Sale

ii.   Click **OK**.

The button bar, in the page prompt area, is updated to reflect the custom sort.

Select an order type:

| Retail Sale | Catalog Sale | Internet Sale |

5.   Change the style of the button bar.

a.   In the page prompt area, select the button bar.

b.   In the right pane, click **Options**.

c.   In the Button Bar group, for the **Background color** field, click ☐ (**Select a color**).

d.   Select **Pale blue**.

Standard colors:

e.   For the Background selection color field, click ☐ (**Select a color**).

f.   Select **Gray**.

Standard colors:

The button bar should resemble the following:

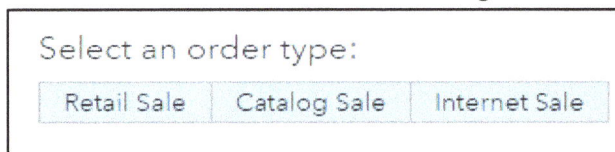

Select an order type:

| Retail Sale | Catalog Sale | Internet Sale |

6. Change the color of a slice in the piechart.
   a. In the canvas, click the **Number of Orders by Custer Age Group** pie chart to make it active.
   b. In the right pane, click **Options**.
   c. Expand the **Style** group.

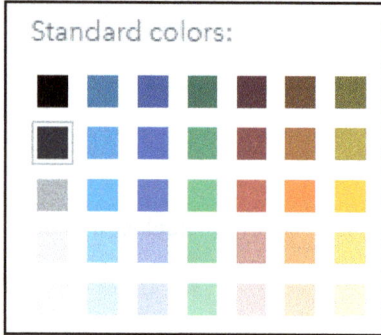

   Standard colors:

   d. In the Fill section, select the yellow box and change the color to **Deep gray.**
   e. For the **Data skin** field, select **Flat**.

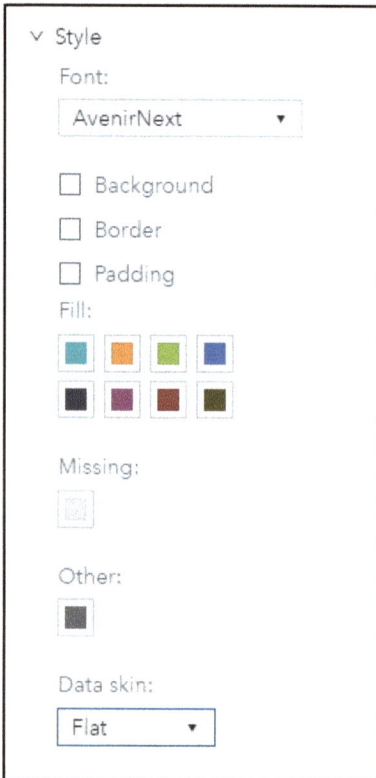

The pie chart should resemble the following:

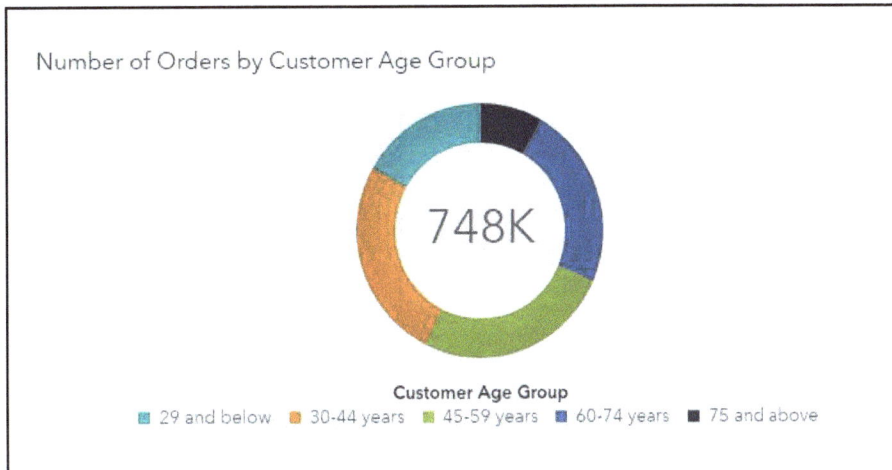

Number of Orders by Customer Age Group

748K

Customer Age Group
■ 29 and below ■ 30-44 years ■ 45-59 years ■ 60-74 years ■ 75 and above

7. Add a display rule to the list table on the Customer Details page.

   a. Click the **Customer Details** page to make it active.

   b. In the canvas, click the list table to make it active.

   c. In the right pane, click **Rules**.

   d. In the Display Rules pane, select **New rule** ⇨ **Profit**.

     i. In the New Display Rule window, for the **Rule Type** field, verify that **Expression** is selected.

     ii. For the **Operator** field, select **<** (lessthan).

     iii. For the **Value** field, verify that **0** is specified.

     iv. In the **Format** area, click ▱ (**Select a fontcolor**).

Format:

AvenirNext ▾   **B** *I* <u>U</u>   ▱

     v. Select **Red**.

Standard colors:

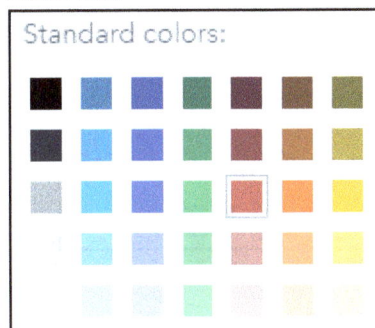

     vi. For the **Background color** field, click ▱ (**Select a background color**).

vii.   Select **Light gray**.

Standard colors:

viii.   For the **Placement** field, verify that **Row** is specified.
        The New Display Rule should resemble the following:

New Display Rule

Profit

Rule Type:

Expression ▾

Operator:

< ▾

Value:

0 ▾

Format:

AvenirNext ▾   **B** *I* U ▮

Background color:

Placement:

Row ▾

☐ Allow alerts for this rule

OK   Cancel

ix.   Click **OK**.

The Display Rules pane should resemble the following:

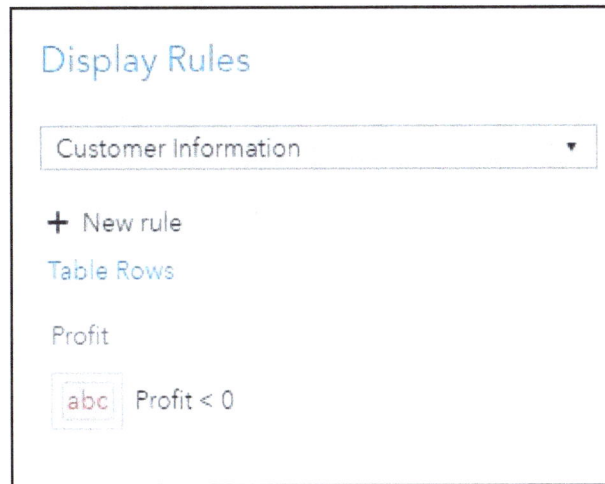

Display Rules

Customer Information ▾

+ New rule

Table Rows

Profit

abc Profit < 0

e. If necessary, scroll down in the list table to find a row where **Profit** is less than 0.

Customer Name ▲	Order Type	Loyalty Member	Customer Age Group
©ime Rituper	Catalog Sale	Yes	60-74 years
©tefka Tertnik	Internet Sale	No	60-74 years
A Amanda Mitchell	Retail Sale	Yes	60-74 years
A R J Swart Rc	Catalog Sale	Yes	29 and below
A R J Swart Rc	Internet Sale	Yes	29 and below
A.A. Broekhuisen	Catalog Sale	No	75 and above
A.A. Broekhuisen	Retail Sale	No	75 and above
A.A. Busselaar	Internet Sale	Yes	29 and below
A.A. Busselaar	Retail Sale	Yes	29 and below
A.A. Duim	Internet Sale	No	30-44 years
A.A. Duim	Catalog Sale	No	30-44 years
A.A. Duim	Retail Sale	No	30-44 years
A.A. Hautvast	Retail Sale	No	75 and above
A.A. Hilhorst	Retail Sale	Yes	60-74 years

8. Save the report.

9. View the report.

   a. In the upper left corner, click ✎ (**View report**) to view the report.

   b. At the top of the report, click the **Customer Order Analysis** tab to make the page active.

   c. In the button bar, select **Retail Sale**.

   The geo map should resemble the following:

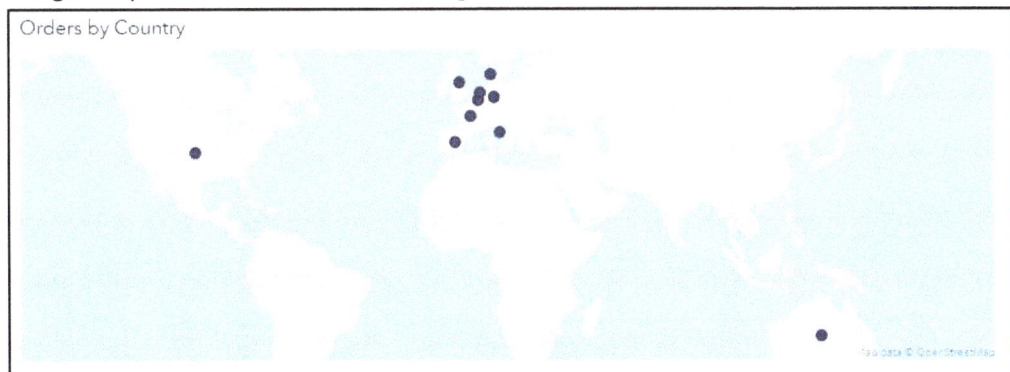

Orders by Country

There are no retail sales in a number of countries because we have stores in only a few countries: Australia, Belgium, Denmark, France, Germany, Italy, Netherlands, Spain, United

Kingdom, and United States. If we wanted to expand our retail stores to new countries, Canada might be a logical choice.

d. In the button bar, select **Internet Sale**.

The geo map should resemble the following:

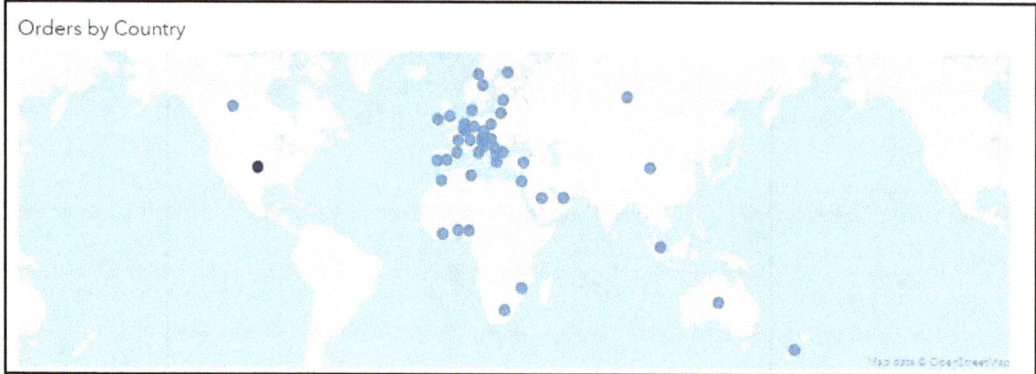

A display rule has been added to the geo map to show countries with more than 100,000 orders as dark blue. Currently, only the United States has more than 100,000 orders.

However, notice that, through the internet, we can reach more countries and more customers. Perhaps we can start marketing campaigns in South America as we currently have no customers in that continent.

e. In the geo map, select **Saudi Arabia**.

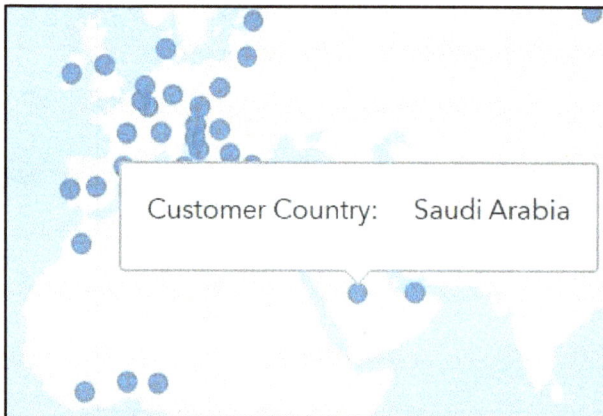

The page updates, and the other objects are filtered to show product orders in Saudi Arabia.

f. In the upper right corner of the dual axis bar chart, click [icon] (**Maximize**).

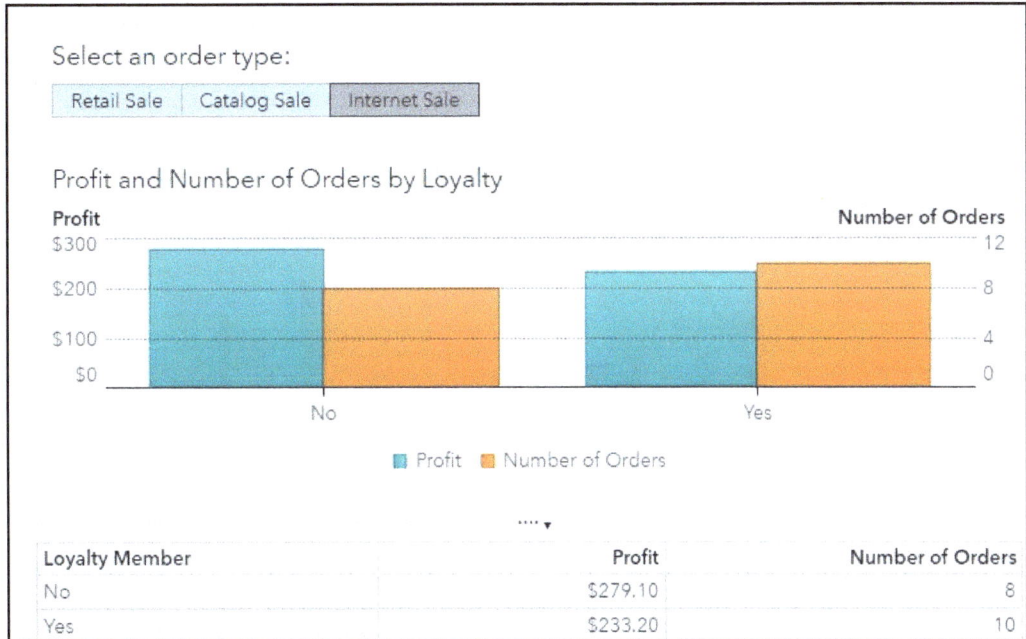

Select an order type:

| Retail Sale | Catalog Sale | Internet Sale |

Profit and Number of Orders by Loyalty

Loyalty Member	Profit	Number of Orders
No	$279.10	8
Yes	$233.20	10

In Saudi Arabia, profits are higher for loyalty members. This is one of the only countries where orders placed by non-loyalty members are more profitable than those placed by loyalty members. What is Saudi Arabia doing to generate this behavior? Are they targeting their marketing campaigns toward non-loyalty members? Why would they do this? This might be something to investigate to try to increase profits from loyalty members in this country.

g. In the upper right corner of the dual axis bar chart, click [icon] (**Restore**).

h. In the geo map, double-click **Canada**.

The Delivery Analysis page is displayed and filtered to show information about Canada.

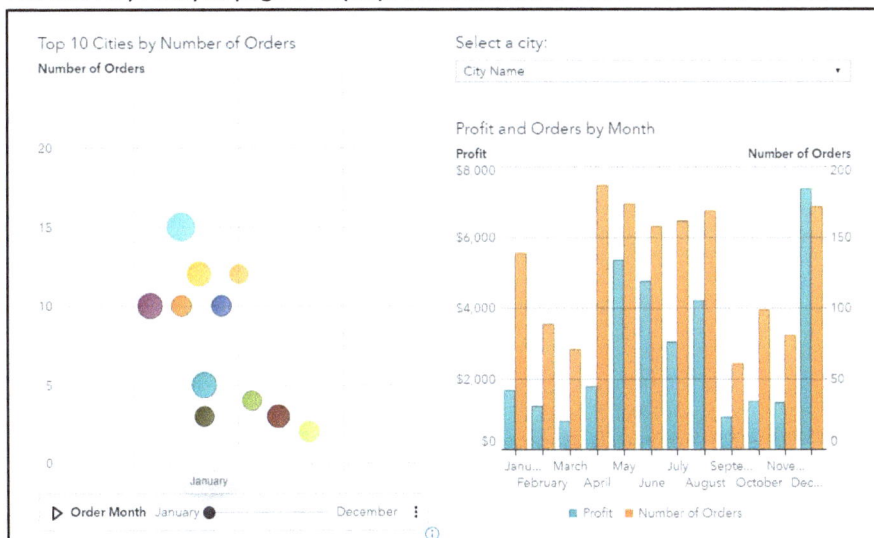

The monthly profits and orders in Canada seem to follow a similar trend to other countries (higher in the summer and winter months). However, it is interesting to note that there seems to be a strong uptick in profits in December. Why does this happen?

i. In the drop-down list control, select **Calgary**.

The page is updated to resemble the following:

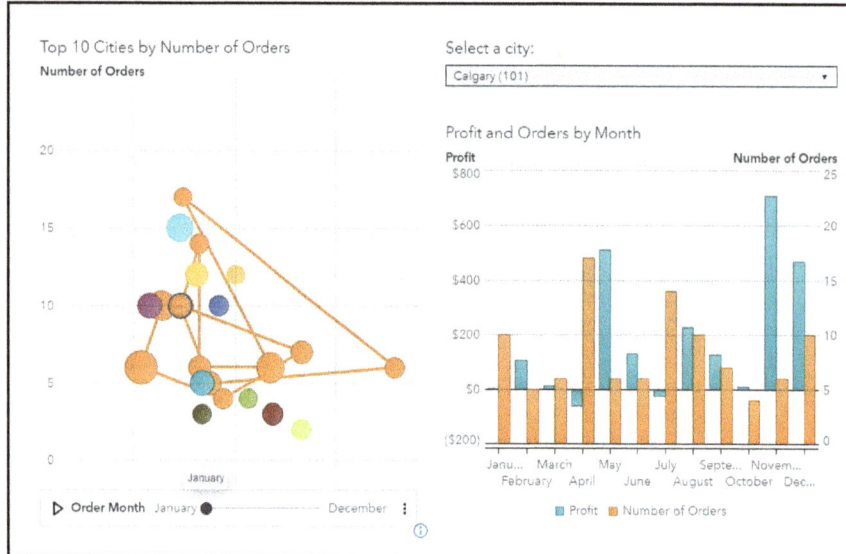

Internet orders placed in Calgary do not always produce a profit. Most notable is the negative profits in both April and July, even though orders are quite high for those months.

Conversely, profits in November and December are high even though the number of orders are pretty low. Is it the types of items that are ordered in those months that are creating this phenomenon?

j. At the top of the report, click the report name (**VA1-Demo4.3**) to return to the page.

k. In the dual axis bar chart, select **Yes**.

l. In the pie chart, double-click the **75 and above** slice (gray slice).

The Customer Details hidden window appears and shows details about Canadian loyalty customers in the 75 and above age group who placed orders via the internet.

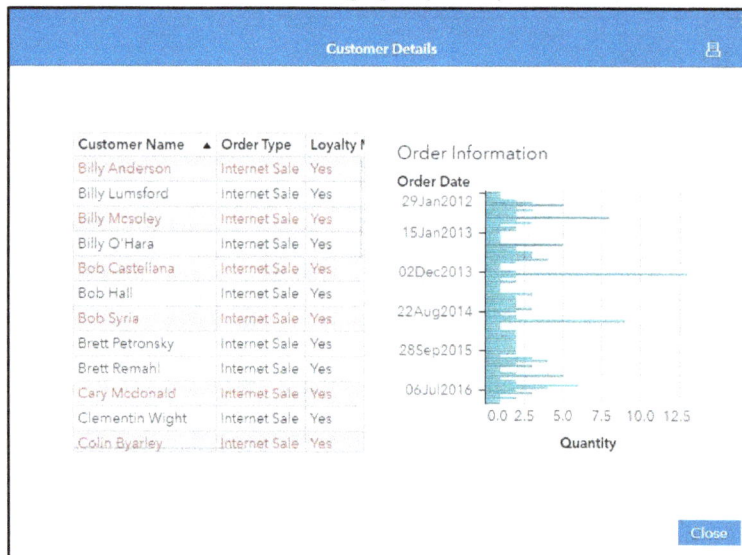

m. In the list table, select the row for **Julie Barham**.

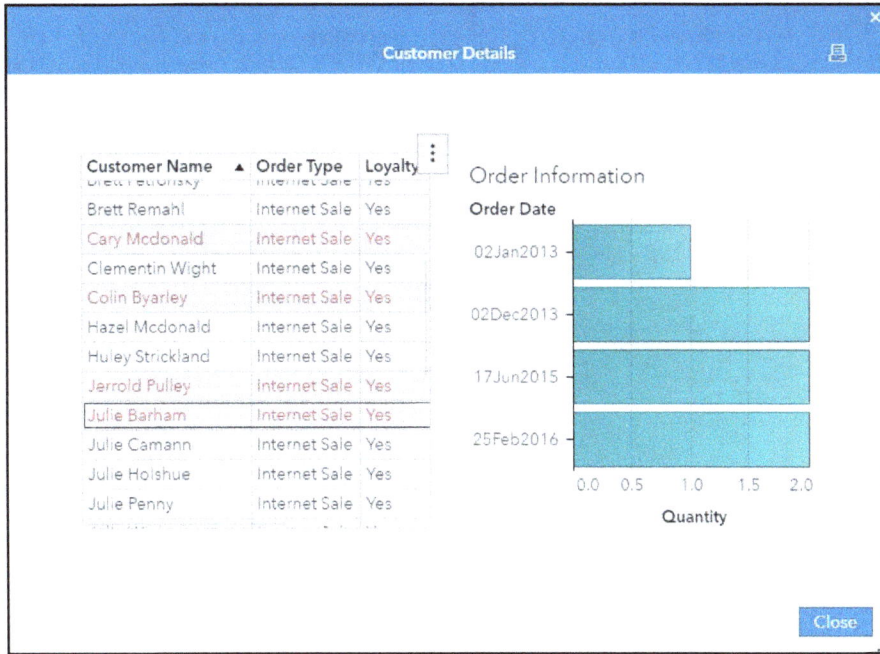

Julie has placed a number of orders through the internet but has generated a negative profit for the company. It might be worth investigating the orders to understand why this occurs.

n. Click **Close** to close the hiddenwindow.

o. In the upper right corner, click ⋮ (**Menu**) and select **Close** to close the report.

End of Demonstration

Practice 4.5

1. Working with Report-Level and Graph-Level Display Rules

    a. Open the browser and sign in to SAS Viya.

    b. Open the **VA1-Practice4.3** report from the **Courses/YVA185/Basics/Practices (HR)** folder.

    c. Add a report-level display rule for job title by assigning the following colors to the values:

Job Title	Color
Sales Reps I, II, III, IV	Deep blue
Temp. Sales Rep, Trainee, Purchasing Agent I, Purchasing Agent III	Deep orange

The Employee Analysis page should resemble the following:

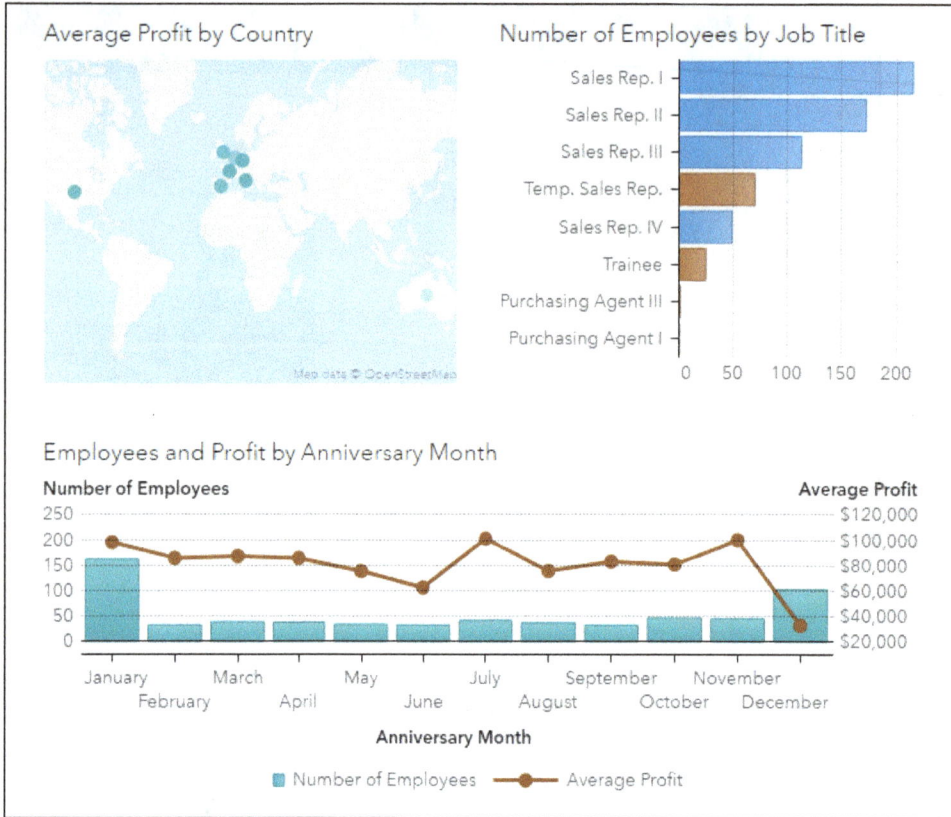

Average Profit by Country

Number of Employees by Job Title

Employees and Profit by Anniversary Month

d. Add three expression display rules to the bar chart on the Profit Analysis page by assigning the following colors to the ranges of **Total Profit**:

Total Profit Ranges	Color
Total Profit < 200,000	Red
200,000 <= Total Profit <= 500,000	Yellow
Total Profit > 500,000	Green

Note: Apply the display rule to the bars of the chart.

The Profit Analysis page should resemble the following:

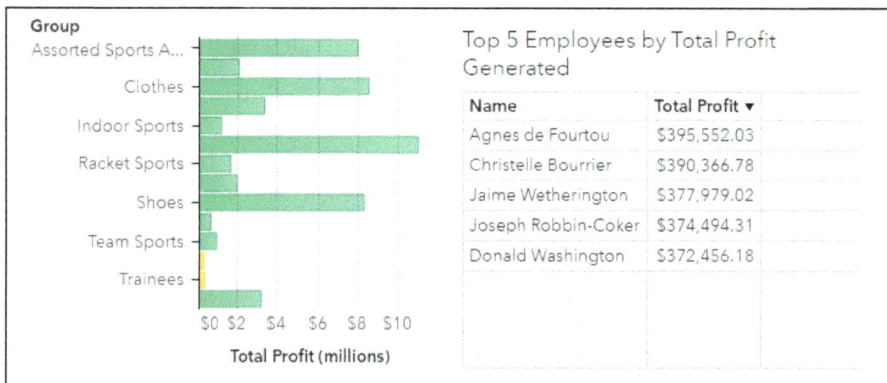

e. Save the report.

f. View the report and answer the following questions:

How many employees retired in Spain? How many retired with the Sales Rep. I job title?

Answer:

View the Profit Analysis page. Among active employees in Orion Spain, how many groups generated a total profit above $500,000?

Answer:

g. Close the report.

End of Practices

Quiz 4.1

What type of chart would you use to show profit information by continent?

a. Bubble plot
b. Pie chart
c. Bar chart
d. Treemap

Continent	Profit
Africa	($127.68)
Asia	$15,503.70
Europe	$5,659,450.59
North America	$2,121,645.57
Oceania	$462,934.63

Chapter 5: Advanced Topics – Automated Explanations

5.1 Introduction

In the following section we describe some advanced techniques possible in Visual Analytics for SAS Viya. Specifically, we will cover the following:

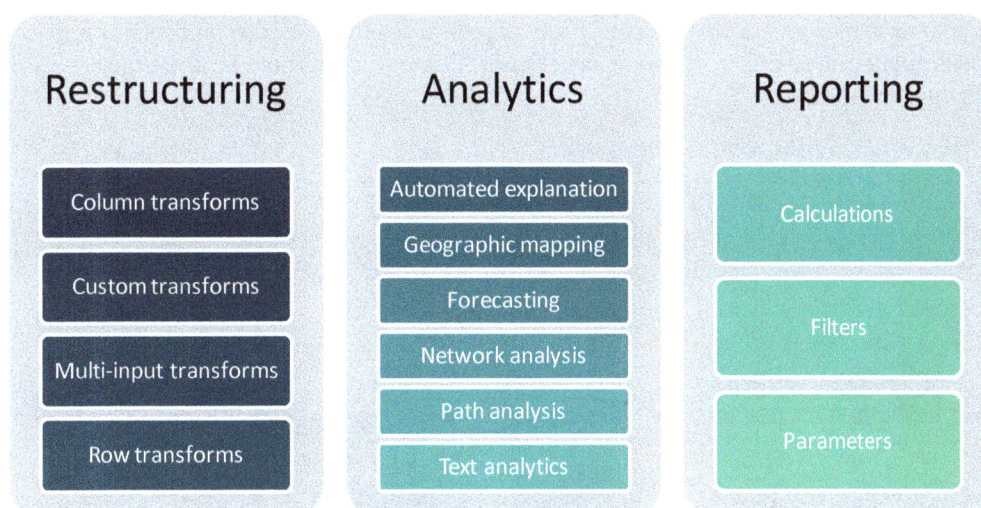

Restructuring	Analytics	Reporting
Column transforms	Automated explanation	Calculations
Custom transforms	Geographic mapping	Filters
Multi-input transforms	Forecasting	Parameters
Row transforms	Network analysis	
	Path analysis	
	Text analytics	

Note: Data quality transforms are available in SAS Data Studio if SAS Data Preparation is licensed at your site.

In this section we will be using a new data set, Parks, and business scenario, consisting of information about the animals in a national park, and how endangered their species is.

5.2 Automated Explanation

Automated analysis is a new feature in SAS® Visual Analytics that uses machine learning to automatically suggest business intelligence (BI) visualizations for you. Powered by the analytics platform, this analysis is performed quickly so that results are interactive. Once you choose a variable that you are interested in, the most relevant factors are automatically identified and easy to compare. As a business analyst or manager, you can immediately understand the results in a report by using the automated narratives and familiar BI visualizations. Figure 5.1 shows how to select the measure data that you want to explore.

Figure 5.1: Select a Measure Data Item That You Want to Understand

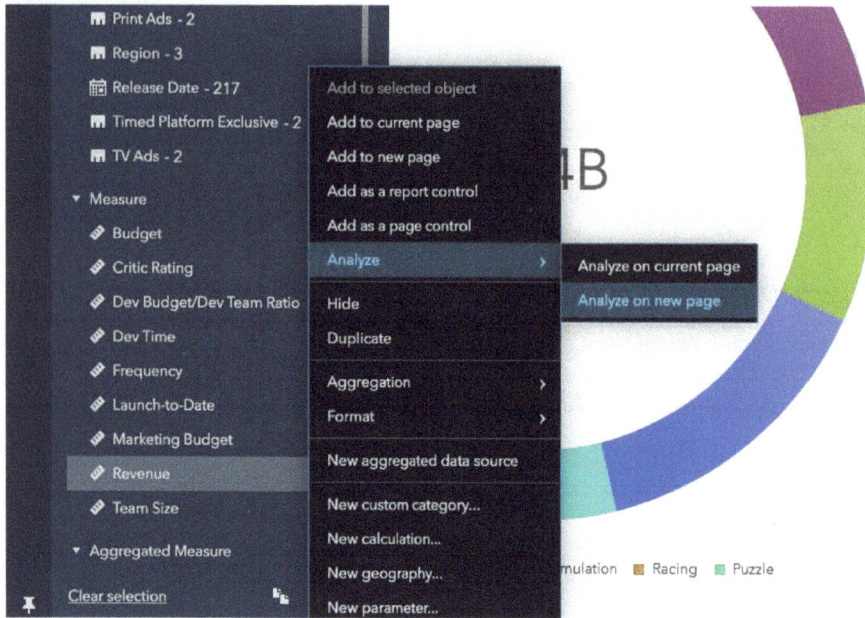

Automated analysis quickly determines the most important underlying factors for a specific outcome. Often, the outcome of interest is a key metric (for example, hospital patient readmission rate, units of inventory, percentage of sales quota, and so on). In the example in Figure 5.2, we want to know what are the key characteristics of days to delivery.

Figure 5.2: Objects - Automated Explanation

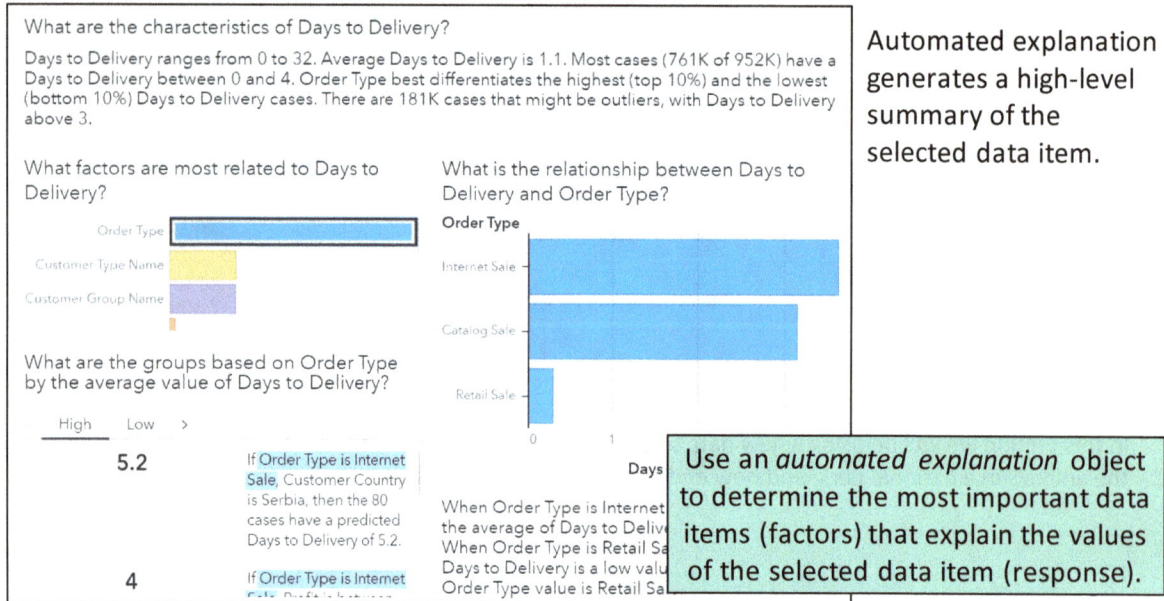

Automated explanation generates a high-level summary of the selected data item.

Use an *automated explanation* object to determine the most important data items (factors) that explain the values of the selected data item (response).

A good introduction to the automated analysis can be found in this 2019 SAS Global Forum Paper, https://www.sas.com/content/dam/SAS/support/en/sas-global-forum-proceedings/2019/3526-2019.pdf.

The automated explanation object determines the most important underlying factors for a specific response variable using most of the data items in the table.

Note: Aggregated measures, date and time values, and automatically computed values such as frequency, hierarchies, filter items, interaction effects, and spline effects are not added as underlying factors. Variables that are identical to the response variable, variables that have excessive missing values, or variables that have high cardinality are added as underlying factors but are subsequently rejected during variable screening.

The automated explanation displays the following information:

- Summary information about the response factor.

- A relative importance score for each underlying factor (factors bar chart). The most important underlying factor is assigned a score of 1, and all other scores are proportional to that value.

- Groups calculated based on the selected underlying factor (groups list). Several decision trees are run on the specified response variable and each group describes a leaf from one of those decision trees. For measure responses, the three groups that result in the highest average values of the response are displayed on the High tab and the three groups that result in the lowest average values of the response are displayed on the Low tab. For category responses, the three groups that contain the highest percentage of the selected event level of the response are displayed on the High tab and the three groups that contain the lowest percentage of the selected event level of the response are displayed on the Low tab.

- The relationship between the response factor and the selected underlying factor (relationship plot). The contents of this plot depend on the variable type for both the response variable and the selected underlying factor.

Demo: 5.1 Using Automated Explanation: Threat Level

This demonstration illustrates how to use automated explanation in Visual Analytics to understand the underlying factors for **Threat Level**.

1. From the browser window, sign in to SAS Viya.
2. In the upper left corner, click ☰ (**Show list of applications**) and select **Explore and Visualize**. SAS Visual Analytics appears.
3. Click **All Reports**.
   a. Navigate to the **Courses/YVA285/Advanced/Demos** folder.
   b. Double-click the **VA2-Demo1.2** report to open it.
4. View the custom category of grouped threat levels.
   a. In the left pane, click **Data**.
   b. In the Category group, right-click **Threat Level** and select **Edit**.
   c. At the top of the window, for the **Based on** field, verify that **Conservation Status** is selected.

Name:	Based on:
Threat Level	⌂ Conservation Status - 12 ▾

   d. Verify that the Values of Conservation Status area (on the left side of the window) resembles the following:

```
Values of Conservation Status

  🔍 Filter

  ☐ (missing)

  ☐ Species of Concern
```

   Note: A conservation status of *(missing)* indicates that the species has not been identified as not threatened, threatened, or extinct.

   Note: A conservation status of *Species of Concern* indicates that the species might need proactive protection, but there is insufficient information available to list the species as endangered.

e. Verify that the Value Groups area (on the right side of the window) resembles the following:

∨ Not Threatened

☐ Breeder

☐ In Recovery

☐ Migratory

☐ Resident

☐ Under Review

∨ Threatened

☐ Endangered

☐ Proposed Endangered

☐ Proposed Threatened

☐ Threatened

∨ Extinct

☐ Extinct

Note: You might need to scroll down to see all the values.

f. In the Remaining Values area (at the bottom of the window), verify that **Show as is** is selected.

Remaining Values:

⦿ Show as is ◯ Show as missing ◯ Group as: Other

g. Click **Cancel** to close the custom category without saving any changes.

5. Use automated explanation to explain the characteristics and contributing factors for threatened species.

a. In the Data pane, right-click **Threat Level** and select **Explain** ⇨ **Explain on current page**.

Threat Level is specified as the response level, and most of the remaining data items in the table are automatically added as underlying factors. For more information about which data items are not added as underlying factors and which data items are likely to be rejected during variable screening, see "About Automated Explanation Objects" in the *SAS Visual Analytics: Working with Report Content* documentation.

An automated explanation object is added to the current page to explain **Threat Level**.

b. In the right pane, click **Filters**.

c. Select New filter ⇨ Threat Level.

d. Clear **Include missing values**.

The Filters pane should resemble the following:

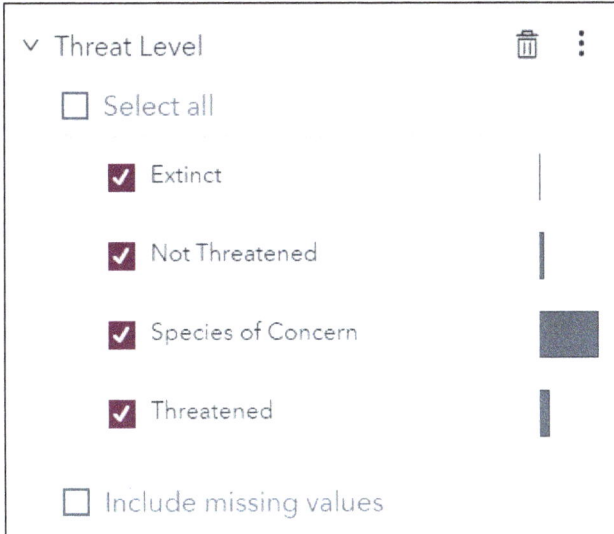

The automated explanation should resemble the following:

What are the characteristics of Threat Level?

Threat Level has a 0.02% chance (1 of 4.7K) of being Extinct. It's the least common Threat Level value.

What factors are most related to Threat Level?

What is the relationship between Threat Level and Category?

What are the groups based on Category by the chance of Threat Level being Extinct?

2.04% If Category is Crab/Lobster/Shrimp, Fish, Invertebrate, or Spider/Scorpion, Park Name is Biscayne National Park, Black Canyon of the Gunnison National Park, Cuyahoga

When Category is Fish, the total count of Extinct is 1.0. When Category is other value, the total count of Extinct is 0. The most common Category value is Bird.

Because the response variable (**Threat Level**) is a category, in the upper right corner of the automated explanation object, you can select the event level to describe.

e. In the upper right corner of the automated explanation, select **Threatened**.

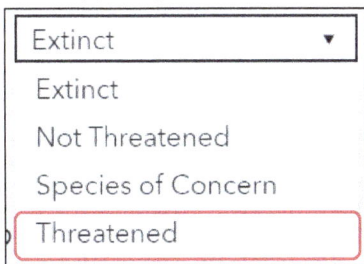

The automated explanation should resemble the following:

What are the characteristics of Threat Level? | Threatened ▼

Threat Level has a 12.48% chance (589 of 4.7K) of being Threatened. It's the second most common Threat Level value.

What factors are most related to Threat Level?

- Order
- Category
- Park Name
- Abundance

What is the relationship between Threat Level and Category?

Category

Vascular Plant
Mammal
Reptile
Invertebrate
Slug/Snail
Spider/Scorpion
Nonvascular Plant

0   500   1,000 1,500 2,000 2,500

Frequency

■ Threatened   ■ NOT Threatened

What are the groups based on Category by the chance of Threat Level being Threatened?

< High   Low   >

82.08% | If Category is Vascular Plant, Park Name is Haleakala National Park or Hawaii Volcanoes National Park, then Threat Level has a 82.08% chance (87 out of 106 cases) of being

When Category is Vascular Plant, the total count of Threatened is a high value; when Category is Reptile, Insect, Invertebrate, Amphibian, Slug/Snail, Spider/Scorpion, Crab/Lobster/Shrimp or Fungi, the total count of Threatened is a low value. The most common Category value is Bird.

6. View the details for the automated explanation.

    a. In the upper right corner of the automated explanation object, click ⤢ (**Maximize**).

    b. View the **Explanation Description** tab.

Explanation Description	Screening Results	Relative Importance

1. Select response for Automated Explanation.	A report author selected Threat Level as the response.
2. Screen factors.	Automated Explanation modified or removed 5 of 13 factors. See the Screening Results tab for details.
3. Determine most related factors.	Automated Explanation used a one-level decision tree for each factor to determine its relative importance to Threat Level. For example, the input Category has a relative importance of 0.64 which means it is 0.64 times as important as Order.
4. Find groups based on selected related factor.	Automated Explanation ran 7 decision trees with response Threat Level. The trees used Category and another important factor as predictors. The trees had 6 levels and 2 branches. Each group

    c. Click the **Screening Results** tab.

Explanation Description	Screening Results	Relative Importance

Factor	Action Taken
Abundance	
Category	
Common Names	The category was rejected because too many distinct levels were detected.
Conservation Status	The category was rejected because it is a subset of the response.
Family	The category was rejected because too many distinct levels were detected.
Nativeness	

d. Click the **Relative Importance** tab.

Explanation Description	Screening Results	Relative Importance
Factor	**Importance**	
Order	1.0000	
Category	0.6423	
Park Name	0.5418	
Abundance	0.3359	
Occurrence	0.3242	
Seasonality	0.2850	

The relative importance score for each underlying factor is displayed in the factors bar chart. The most important underlying factor is assigned a score of 1, and all other scores are proportional to that value.

e. In the upper right corner of the automated explanation object, click [⬎] (**Restore**).

7. View the results of the automated explanation.

a. View the characteristics for the response variable (**Threat Level**).

> What are the characteristics of Threat Level?
>
> Threat Level has a 12.48% chance (589 of 4.7K) of being Threatened. It's the second most common Threat Level value.

b. View the factors for **Threat Level**.

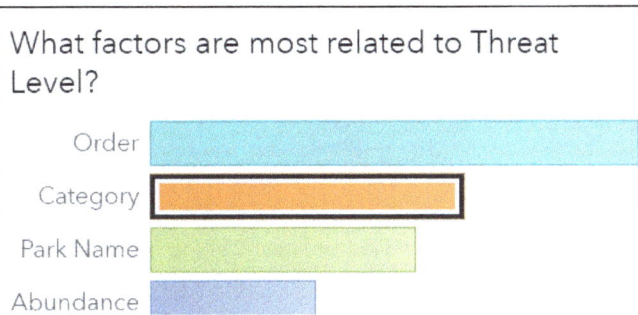

> What factors are most related to Threat Level?
>
> Order
> Category
> Park Name
> Abundance

Order is the most important underlying factor to explain **Threat Level**.

c. If necessary, select **Category** in the factors bar chart.

d. View the relationship plot between **Threat Level** and the selected underlying factor (**Category**).

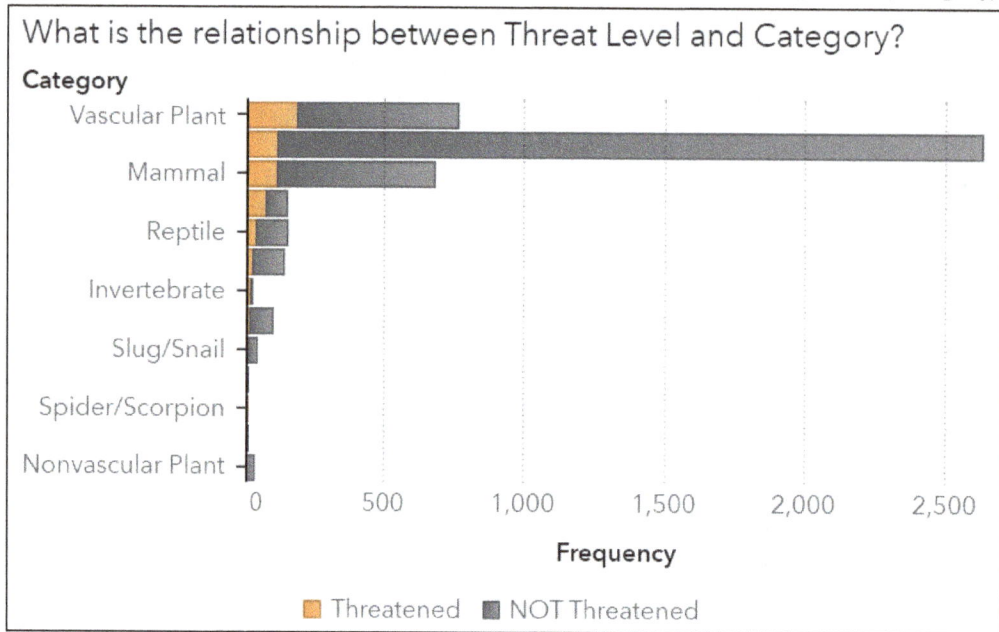

The relationship plot displays a stacked bar chart of the selected underlying factor (**Category**). Each bar is split to show the portion of each level that has contains threatened species (orange bars) and the portion that contains non-threatened species (gray bars).

When **Category** is *Vascular Plant*, the total count of threatened species is a high value.

e. View the groups list for **Threat Level** based on the selected underlying factor (**Category**).

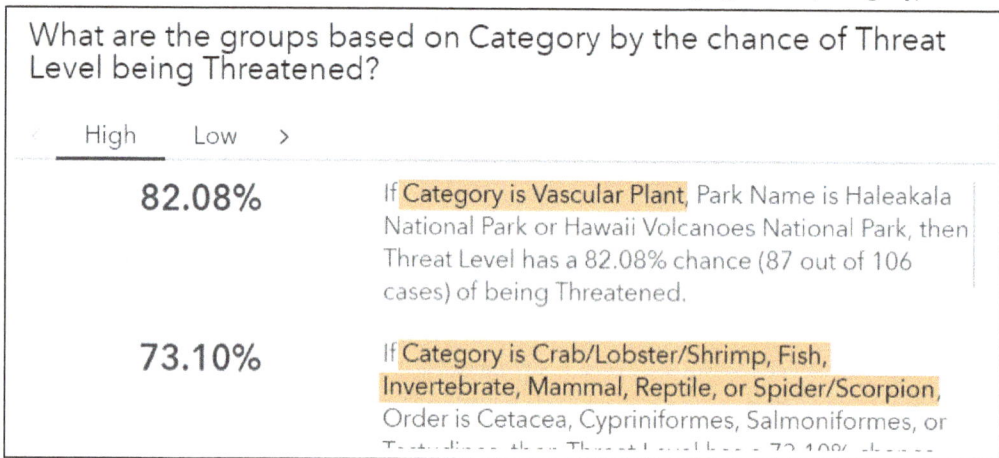

Groups are calculated based on the selected underlying factor (**Category**) in the factors bar chart. Several decision trees are run on the specified response variable (**Threat Level**), and each group describes a leaf from one of the decision trees.

The High tab lists the three groups that are likely to have the highest chance of being threatened, and the Low tab lists the three groups that are likely to have the lowest chance of being threatened. You can use these groups to determine which species could be threatened in the future.

f. Select the highest group (82.08%).

g. Right-click the group and select **Derive group item**.

h. In the left pane, click **Data**.

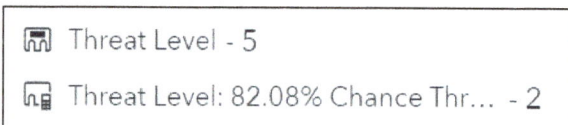

A new calculated item is added to the Data pane. This data item has two distinct values: *In* (if the species is in the group) or *Out* (if the species is not in the group).

8. View a list of species that have a high change of being threatened.

    a. In the Data pane, select the following columns:

      Park Name

      Common Names

    b. Right-click and select **Add to new page**.

      A list table is added to a new page that shows the species present in each park.

Park Name	▲ Common Names
Acadia National Park	Flatstem Pondweed
Acadia National Park	Narrow-Leaved Vetch
Acadia National Park	Cardinal Flower
Acadia National Park	Shore Sedge
Acadia National Park	Black Nightshade
Acadia National Park	Canada Goose, Eastern Canada Goose

    c. In the canvas, click the list table to select it, if necessary.

    d. In the right pane, click **Filters**.

    e. Select **New Filter** ⇨ **Threat Level: 82.08% Chance Threatened Group**.

    f. Clear **Out**.

    g. Clear **Include missing values**.

      The Filters pane should resemble the following:

∨ Threat Level: 82.08% Chance Thre... 🗑 ⋮	
☐ Select all	
☑ In	│
☐ Out	▮
☐ Include missing values	

The list table should resemble the following:

Park Name	▲ Common Names
Haleakala National Park	`Ahinahina, Haleakala Silversword, Hawai'i Silversword
Haleakala National Park	`Aiea
Haleakala National Park	`Akala
Haleakala National Park	`Akia
Haleakala National Park	`Anunu
Haleakala National Park	`Awa-Kanaloa, Makou
Haleakala National Park	`Oha Wai, Oahu Clermontia

h. In the right pane, click **Roles**.

i. For the **Columns** role, click **Add**.

j. Select **Threat Level** and click **OK**.

The list table should resemble the following:

Park Name	▲ Common Names	Threat Level
Haleakala National Park	`Ahinahina, Haleakala Silversword,...	Threatened
Haleakala National Park	`Aiea	Threatened
Haleakala National Park	`Akala	Species of Concern
Haleakala National Park	`Akia	Threatened
Haleakala National Park	`Anunu	Species of Concern
Haleakala National Park	`Awa-Kanaloa, Makou	Threatened
Haleakala National Park	`Oha Wai, Oahu Clermontia	Threatened

Some species are already on the threatened list.

k. Click **Threat Level** to sort the list in ascending order.

Park Name	Common Names	Threat Level
Haleakala National Park	`Akala	Species of Concern
Haleakala National Park	`Anunu	Species of Concern
Haleakala National Park	Alani	Species of Concern
Haleakala National Park	Fringed Spleenwort	Species of Concern
Haleakala National Park	Haha, Haha-Nui	Species of Concern
Haleakala National Park	Haleakala Stenogyne	Species of Concern
Haleakala National Park	Monterey Pine	Species of Concern

The species that have a high chance of being threatened, but are not yet classified as threatened, are displayed at the top of the list table.

9. Save the report.

End of Demonstration

Practice 5.1

1. Using Automated Explanation: Customer Satisfaction
    a. Open the browser and sign in to SAS Viya.
    b. Open the **VA2-Practice1.2** report in the **Courses/YVA285/Advanced/Practices** folder.
    c. Create an automated explanation to explain **Customer Satisfaction**.
    d. Answer the following questions:

       What is the average **Customer Satisfaction** value?

       Answer:

       What are the top three factors most related to **Customer Satisfaction**?

       Answer:
    e. Remove the following underlying factors from the automated explanation:

       xyCustomer Lat

       xyCustomer Lon
    f. Answer the following question:

       Which factor best differentiates the highest and lowest **Customer Satisfaction** values?

       Answer:
    g. View the groups and relationship plot for the underlying factor, **Customer Distance**.
    h. Answer the following questions:

       What is the customer distance for the highest predicted customer satisfaction (96%)? For the lowest predicted customer satisfaction (31%)?

       Answer:

       Which range of **Customer Distance** contains the most observations?

       Answer:
    i. From the automated explanation of customer distance, explain **Product Sale** (an underlying factor) on a new page.

       Note: Alternatively, in the Data pane, you can right-click **Product Sale** and select **Explain** ⇨ **Explain on new page**.
    j. Answer the question:

       Which factor best differentiates the highest and lowest **Product Sale** values?

       Answer:
    k. Save the report.

       End of Practices

Activity 5.1

Sign in to SAS Viya. Edit the **VA2-Activity1.01** report (in the **Courses/YVA285/Advanced** folder).

What is the predicted customer satisfaction for the following factors?

Factor	Value
Customer Country	AR (Argentina)
Product Line	Figurine
Product Cost of Sale	15
Customer Distance	2
Product Price (target)	4

Chapter 6: Advanced Topics – Restructuring Data for Geographic Mapping

6.1 Introduction

Adding analytic graphs to your reports can help enhance your results and provide deeper insights into your data. Each of these objects, however, requires the data to be shaped in a certain way. Before you can use analytic objects in your reports, you will need to ensure that the table is in the correct form. If not, you might need to transform the data. This could mean joining or appending tables, creating new columns or extracting information from a column, filtering tables, or restructuring data. In this chapter, we discuss the various types of analytic objects: geo maps, forecasts, network analysis, path analysis, and text analytics; and you will learn more about geographic maps. First, we see how SAS Data Studio can be used to restructure data and prepare data for Visual Analytics. Then, we learn more about geo maps, the data needed to create these graphs, and see how to restructure the data for Visual Analytics. Finally, you will use the restructured data to add geo maps to a report.

6.2 SAS Data Studio

SAS Data Studio is the data preparation application in SAS Viya. Using SAS Data Studio, you can view details about your tables and apply transforms to the tables by creating plans. In Data Studio, you create plans that modify your data for analysis and reporting. These plans use a CAS table as input and create a CAS table as output. Plans can modify existing or create new data items, combine tables, filter data, restructure the data, or improve data quality. You can use column transforms to modify existing columns in the table (by changing the case, converting columns, renaming columns, splitting columns, or trimming white space). In addition, you can use custom transforms to create new columns or add custom code to the plan.

Figure 6.1: Plans

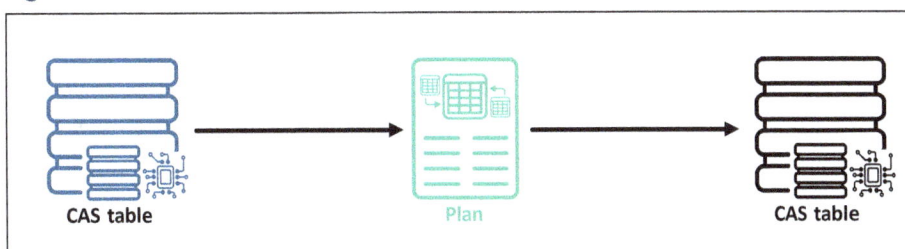

Before a table can be used as a data source for a new plan, it must be loaded in CAS. However, if you open an existing plan that uses a table that is not currently loaded, it is automatically loaded to the CAS server. If the data that you need currently exists in multiple tables, you can use multi-input transforms to combine them together. Tables can be combined horizontally (using joins) or vertically (using appends). You can use row transforms to add filters to subset the data to a specific group or subgroup or transpose the data.

Additional row transforms are also available for Visual Statistics and analytics objects. The analytic partitioning transform can be used to divide a table into training, validation, and test for modeling. The unique identifier transform can be used for text analytics to create a column that contains a unique value for each row in the table. In addition, a number of data quality transforms are available to improve the quality of your data. These transforms are only available if SAS Data Preparation is licensed at your site. For more information about the types of transforms available in SAS Data Studio, see the Resources section of this book.

Table 6.1: SAS Data Preparation Options

Data Transform	Description
Modify columns	Columns can be modified by changing the case, changing the data type, changing formats, removing white space, removing columns, or renaming column headings. For more information about modifying columns, see "Working with Columns" in the *SAS Data Studio: User's Guide*.
Create new columns	New columns can be created by splitting columns, by creating calculated columns with an expression, or by writing custom code. For more information about splitting columns, see "Splitting Columns" in the *SAS Data Studio: User's Guide*. For more information about creating calculated columns with an expression, see "Creating Calculated Columns" in the *SAS Data Studio: User's Guide*. For more information about writing custom code, see "Creating Custom Code" in the *SAS Data Studio: User's Guide*. Additional columns can be created for analytics. For more information about these columns, see "Creating a Partition Column" and "Generating a Unique Identifier" in the *SAS Data Studio: User's Guide*.
Combining tables	Tables can be combined horizontally (using joins) or vertically (using appends). For more information about joins, see "Working with Joins" in the *SAS Data Studio: User's Guide*. For more information about appends, see "Appending Data to a Table" in the *SAS Data Studio: User's Guide*.
Filter data	Data can be filtered by specifying conditions to restrict the data. For more information about filtering, see "Filtering Data" in the *SAS Data Studio: User's Guide*.
Restructure data	Data can be restructured by transposing columns. For more information about transposing columns, see "Transposing Columns" in the *SAS Data Studio: User's Guide*.
Improve data quality	Data quality can be improved by changing casing, parsing data, performing field extraction, performing gender analysis, performing identification analysis, performing match operations using matchcodes, removing duplicates, standardizing data, and working with matching and clustering. For more information about improving data quality, see "Working with Data Quality" in the *SAS Data Studio: User's Guide*. **Note:** Data quality transforms are available if SAS Data Preparation is licensed.

You can create jobs from plan actions that can be scheduled with SAS Job Monitor. For more information about creating jobs, see "Creating Jobs for Scheduling" in the *SAS Data Studio: User's Guide*. For more information about scheduling jobs, see the *SAS Viya Administration: Jobs* documentation.

Activity 6.1

Sign in to SAS Viya. Open the **VA2-Activity2.01** plan (in the **Courses/YVA285/Advanced** folder).

Which options are available for modifying the case of columns?

Casing Transforms

Casing transforms are used to change the case of your data. If you have SAS Data Preparation licensed, two casing transforms are available: Change Case (in the Column Transforms group) and Casing (in the Data Quality Transforms group). Both transforms change the case of your data, but they differ in their complexity. For example, let's say I have an input string Sas institute. Using the Chase Case transform, I can either lowercase the string or uppercase the string. The Casing transform (in the Data Quality Transforms group) provides some additional options, such as propercasing and propercasing based on the type of data. In this example, I could use the Proper (Organization) definition to get the correct casing for the string.

Figure 6.2: Casing Transforms

Input data
Sas institute

Transform	Definition	Output data
Change Case	Lowercase	sas institute
Change Case	Uppercase	SAS INSTITUTE
Casing	Proper	Sas Institute
Casing	Proper (Organization)	SAS Institute

Note: If SAS Data Preparation is licensed at your site, then you have access to more advanced options using the Casing transform.

6.3 Restructuring Data

Quite often to build the report, you need to first restructure the data. For example, suppose that the US National Park Service has asked for a map that shows the locations of all national parks and lists the species located in each park. Currently, we have a table that contains information about the parks (like size, location, name) and another table that contains information about the species (like type, location, name). We need to join the tables together to produce the desired map. In addition, we will need to modify the case for the State field, create Park ID using the first four characters of the Species ID field, and remove a column from the result table. We will create a plan that performs these tasks and creates a new CAS table (parks_loc) that can be used in Visual Analytics to create our geo map.

Figure 6.3: Business Scenario: Parks

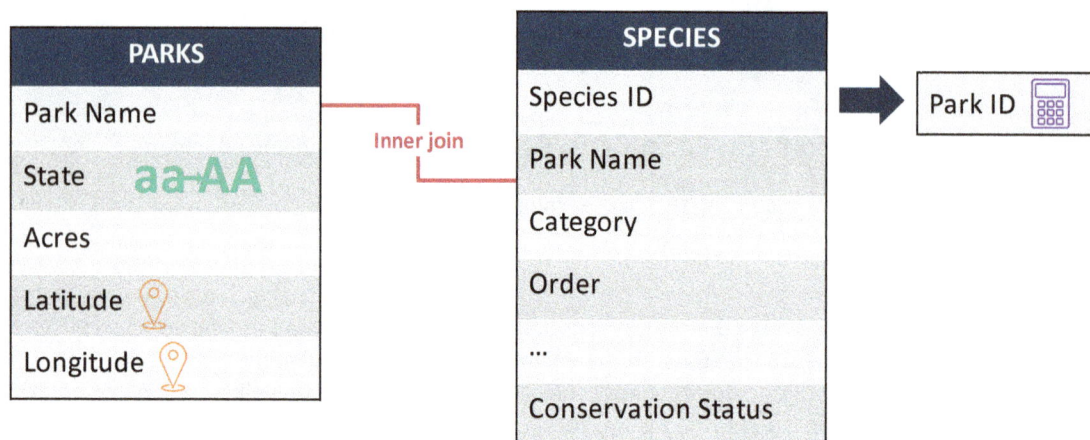

In the following demonstration, we perform the following steps:

1. Convert **State** to uppercase.
2. Create an inner join of the **PARKS** table and the **SPECIES** table (using Park Name).
3. Remove a column from the result table (**Park Name** from the **SPECIES** table).
4. Calculate **Park ID** from the first four characters of **Species ID**.

The plan creates a new CAS table (**PARKS_LOC**) that is used in a later section.

Latitude and longitude values are required for geographic selections that are not predefined. If the data does not contain latitude and longitude values, a data join can be used to add latitude and longitude values. For more information about using latitude and longitude in data, see "Working with Geography Data Items" in the *SAS Visual Analytics: Working with Report Data* documentation.

A geographic data provider is required for custom polygonal shapes. For more information about adding custom polygons, see "Loading Geographic Polygon Data as a CAS Table" in the *SAS Viya Administration: Data Administration* documentation.

Demo 6.1: Creating a Geographic Data Source

This demonstration illustrates how to explore a data source and use transforms (Change Case, Join, and Calculated Column) to create a geographic data source in SAS Data Studio.

1. From the browser window, sign in to SAS Viya.
2. In the upper left corner, click ☰ (**Show list of applications**) and select **Prepare Data**.
   SAS Data Studio appears.

3. Click **Open Plan**.
    a. Navigate to the **Courses/YVA285/Advanced/Demos** folder.
    b. Double-click the **VA2-Demo2.2** data plan to open it.
       The plan is opened in SAS Data Studio.

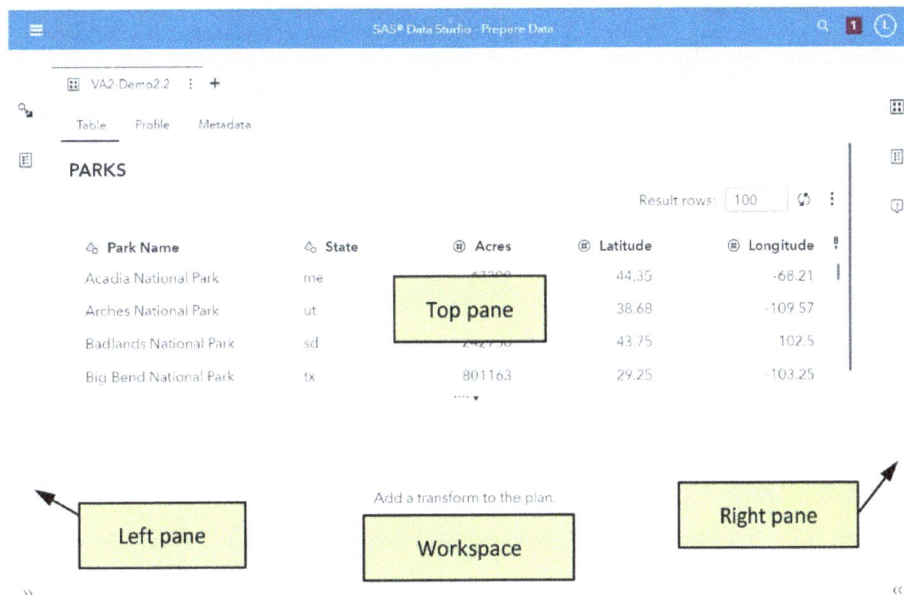

The top pane contains the following information:

Table	The Table tab displays a sample of rows of the result table. **Note:** Only the first 300 columns are displayed in the workspace. However, this does not affect your ability to work with all of the data in the table. Any changes made are applied to the entire table, not just the columns that are displayed.
Profile	The Profile tab displays column metrics for the source and result tables. **Note:** If SAS Data Preparation is licensed at your site, advanced column metrics are displayed.
Metadata	The Metadata tab displays a list of column attributes (including name, label, type, and length).

Note: After you run a transform, the Table, Profile, and Metadata views reflect the current state of the table, including any changes that have been made.

The left pane contains the following icons:

Transforms	The Transforms pane displays a list of all transforms available for the plan.
Source Table	The Source Table pane displays properties of the source table.

Note: If SAS Data Preparation is licensed at your site, a third icon appears in the left pane, Suggestions. The Suggestions pane displays a list of suggested actions to perform on the active table of the plan.

The right pane contains the following icons:

Plan ⊞   The Plan pane displays a list of all actions associated with the plan.

Result Table ⊞   The Result Table pane displays properties of the result table.

Status 🗩   The Status pane displays the status of the plan.

4.   In the left pane, click ⊞ (**Properties for the source table**) to show details about the source table.

> **Source Table - PARKS**   ⟳
>
> | Columns | Rows | Size |
> |---|---|---|
> | 5 | 56 | 14.6 KB |
>
> Label:
> (not available)
>
> Location:
> cas-shared-default/Public
>
> 👤   Date created:
>
> 👤   Date modified:
>
> Encoding:
> (not available)
>
> Tags (0):
>   No items have been added.   🏷

5.   View metadata, profile, and table information for the source table.

    a.   In the top pane, click **Metadata**.

> ⊞ VA2-Demo2.2   ⋮ +
>
> Table   Profile   Metadata

A list of column attributes (including name, label, type, and length) appears in the top pane.

	Table	Profile	Metadata					

#	Name	Label	Type	Raw Length	Formatted Length	Format	
1	Park Name		varchar	46	46		
2	State		varchar	10	10		
3	Acres		double	8	12		
4	Latitude		double	8	12		
5	Longitude		double	8	12		

b. In the top pane, click **Profile**.

c. Click **Run Profile** to execute the profile, if necessary.

Table   Profile   Metadata

Date profiled: Dec 17, 2019 12:17 PM   Input table (PARKS) ▼   Run Profile

Column	Unique	Null	Blank	Pattern Count	Mean	Median
Acres	98.21% (55)				927,929.14	
Latitude	94.64% (53)				41.23	
Longitude	98.21% (55)				-113.23	
Park Name	100.00% (56					

Notice that the **Park Name** column has a uniqueness of 100%, meaning that this table contains one row for each national park in the United States.

Basic profile metrics (Unique, Mean, Standard Deviation, Standard Error, Minimum, Maximum, Data Type, and Data Length) appear for all the columns in the **PARKS** data source.

Note: Advanced profile metrics (Null, Blank, Pattern Count, Median, Mode, Actual Type, Minimum Length, Maximum Length, Ordinal Position, Primary Key Candidate, and Non-null Count) appear if SAS Data Preparation is licensed at your site.

d. In the top pane, click **Table**.

Table   Profile   Metadata

PARKS

Result rows: 100

Park Name	State	Acres	Latitude	Longitude	
Acadia National Park	me	47390	44.35	-68.21	
Arches National Park	ut	76519	38.68	-109.57	
Badlands National Park	sd	242756	43.75	-102.5	
Big Bend National Park	tx	801163	29.25	-103.25	

A sample of rows from the **PARKS** data source is displayed.

6. Add transforms to the plan.

   a. In the left pane, click ▣ (**Transforms**) to view the available transforms.

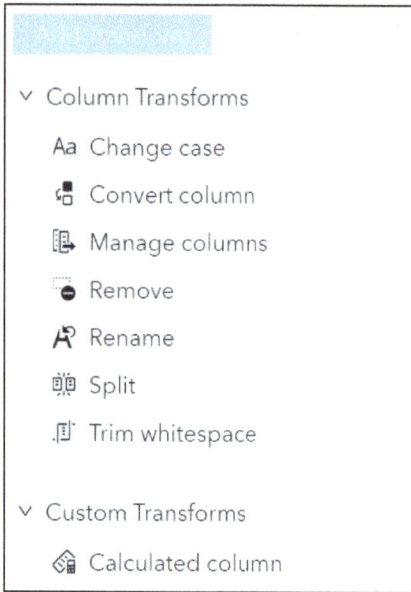

   ∨ Column Transforms

      Aa Change case

         Convert column

         Manage columns

         Remove

         Rename

         Split

         Trim whitespace

   ∨ Custom Transforms

         Calculated column

   b. In the Column Transforms group, double-click **Change case** to add the transform to the plan.

   Note: As an alternative, you can right-click a column in the table in the top pane to add transforms to the plan.

   Note: The Casing transform, in the Data Quality Transforms group, provides advanced options for casing (such as proper casing using Quality Knowledge Base (QKB) definitions), but the SAS Data Preparation license is required.

   c. In the workspace, the Change Case transform is added to the plan.

   Change Case - Step 1 of 1   ↺   **Run** ▾   Save ⋮

   ① Change Case

   Source column: Case:

   🔤 Park Name   ▾   Uppercase   ▾ ⓘ

   ⦿ Replace source column
   ○ Create new column

       i. Click ⑦ (**How do I change the case in columns?**) to view information about using the transform.

   ### Changing the Case in Columns

   You can change the case of column data to all uppercase or all lowercase characters. To change the case of column data, select a column from the **Source column** drop-down menu, and then select **Uppercase** or **Lowercase** in the **Case** drop-down menu. The **Source column** drop-down menu includes columns that contain character data only. You cannot change the case for columns that contain numeric data.

       ii. For the **Source column** field, select **State**.

       iii. For the **Case** field, verify that **Uppercase** is selected.

       iv. Verify that **Replace source column** is selected.

The Change Case transform should resemble the following:

☰ 1. Change Case	
Source column:	Case:
⚘ State ▾	Uppercase ▾ ⓘ
⦿ Replace source column	
○ Create new column	

v. In the upper right corner of the workspace, click **Run** to execute the transform on the data.

A sample of rows is displayed in the Table view on the top pane. The **State** column is updated to reflect the change.

⚘ State
ME
UT
SD
TX

d. In the left pane, double-click the **Join** transform, in the Multi-input Transforms group, to add it to the plan.

The Join Tables window appears.

Join Tables	
Join Tables	
Table 1 (T1):	Table 2 (T2):
PARKS (session) ⓘ	✎ ▦
⚘ T1.Park Name ▾ = ▾	+
☑ Select all columns	
☐ No duplicate rows	

i. For Table 1 (**PARKS**), verify that **T1.Park Name** is selected.

ii. For Table 2, click ✎ (**Edit**).

a. In the Choose Data window, verify that **Available** is selected.

b. Select the **SPECIES** table.

Details about the table appear on the right side of the window. This is the same information that you can see in the plan using the top pane and the left pane.

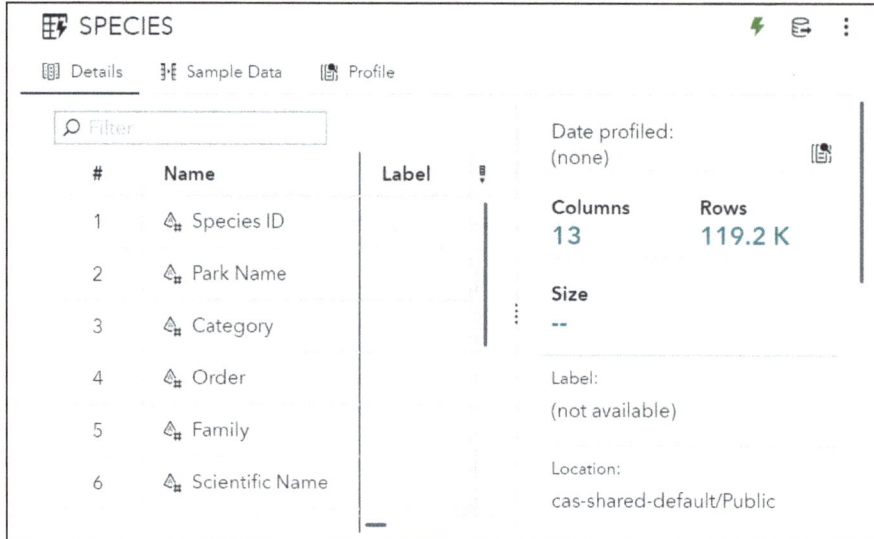

Note: If the **SPECIES** table is not available, on the Data Sources tab, do the following:

- Double-click the CAS server.

- Double-click the library.

- Scroll through the list of tables and select **SPECIES.sashdat**.

- In the upper right corner, click [⚡] (**Load into memory**).

- When the load is complete, click **OK** at the bottom of the window to add the data source to the plan.

iii.   For Table 2 (**SPECIES**), verify that **T2.Park Name** is selected as the column.

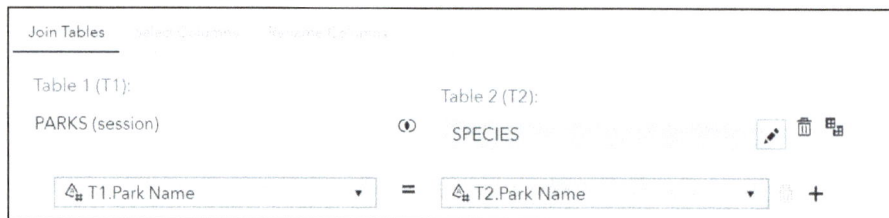

Note: The two tables are joined using an inner join by default. You can click [⬤] (**Click to select the join type**) to change the join type to Left, Right, or Full.

Note: You can click [⊞] (**Add a table to the join**) to join additional tables.

Note: The two tables are joined on one column by default. You can click [+] (**Add a join condition**) to join on additional columns.

iv.   At the bottom of the window, clear **Select all columns**.

At the top of the window, the Select Columns and Rename Columns tabs become active.

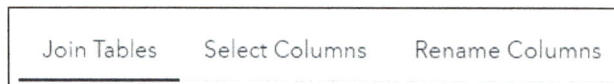

v.   Click the **Select Columns** tab.

vi.   For the **Table** field, verify that **All** is selected.

vii.   In the Selected items area, select **T2.Park Name_1** and click ⬅ (**Remove**).

Select one or more columns for inclusion in the join.

Table:

| All ▾ |

Available items (1):   Selected items (17):

🔍 Filter   △ T1.Park Name

△ T2.Park Name_1   ⋮ +»   △ T1.State

                                                                  ⊞ T1.Acres

viii.   At the bottom of the window, click **OK** to close the Join Tables window.

ix.   In the upper right corner of the workspace, click **Run** to execute the join.

x.   In the Table view, scroll to the right to view the new columns from the **SPECIES** data source.

♧ Species ID	♧ Category	♧ Order	♧ Family
KOVA-1473	Vascular Plant	Malpighiales	Salicaceae
KOVA-1474	Vascular Plant	Malpighiales	Salicaceae
KOVA-1475	Vascular Plant	Malpighiales	Salicaceae
BADL-1327	Fish	Cypriniformes	Catostomidae

The first four characters of **Species ID** represent the park code where the species is located.

Note: The table previews displayed in SAS Data Studio might not match what is displayed in the course notes.

e.   In the left pane, double-click the **Calculated column** transform, in the Custom Transforms group, to add it to the plan.

i.   In the code area, enter substr('Species ID'n, 1, 4).

Note: The SUBSTR function extracts a substring from an argument. Here is the syntax for this function: **substr(***column-name, position, length***)**.

- *column-name* specifies the name of the column in the source table.

- *position* specifies the beginning position of the extraction.

- *length* specifies the length of the string (how many characters) to extract.

Note: To use a column name that contains blanks in the code area, use the following syntax: '*Column Name*'n

Note: For more information about DATA step expressions, see "Dictionary of SAS DATA Step Statements."

Note: In this example, the Split transform (with a hyphen delimiter) can also be used to calculate the new column.

ii.   Below the code area, select **Create new column**.

iii.   For the name of the new column, enter **ParkID**.

iv.   Click Options for new columns.

a.   For the **Name of new column** field, verify that **ParkID** is specified.

b.   For the **Type** field, select **Char**.

c.   For the **Length** field, enter **4**.

d.   For the **Label** field, enter **Park ID**.

The Options for New Columns window should resemble the following:

Name of new column:	Type:	Length:	Label:
ParkID	Char ▾	4	Park ID

e. Click **OK**.

f. In the upper right corner of the workspace, click **Run** to create the new column.

The **ParkID** column is added to the Table view in the top pane.

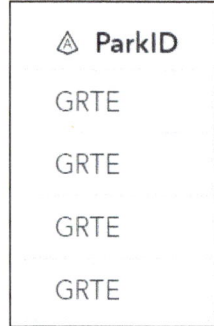

⚠ **ParkID**

GRTE

GRTE

GRTE

GRTE

7. In the right pane, click ⊞ (**Plan**) to view the steps of the plan.

Plan

▷ ⎗ 🖫 ⋮

Name: VA2-Demo2.2

Modified: 12/17/19 12:38 PM

📇 📇 ↑ ↓ 🗑

Aa 1. Change Case ✓

🔲 2. Join ✓

🔷 3. Calculated Column ✓

8. In the right pane, click ⊞ (**Properties for the result table**) to show details about the result table.

Result Table - PARKS (session) ↺

Columns	Rows	Size
18	119.2 K	44.5 MB

Label:

(not available)

Location:

cas-shared-default/Public

Date created:
Dec 17, 2019 12:38 PM

Date modified:
Dec 17, 2019 12:38 PM

9. Save the plan and the result table.

   a. In the right pane, click ▦ (**Plan**).

   b. In the upper right corner of the Plan tab, click ⋮ (**Options**) and select **Save as**.

   The bottom part of the Save As window displays the name of the table created from the plan:

Name:		Type:	
VA2-Demo2.2		Data plan	▾

   ● Save plan and target table   ○ Save plan   ○ Save target table

Target table name: *	Label:	Format: ⓘ	Library:
PARKS_LOC	Enter label	sashdat ▾	cas-shared-default/Public 🗄

   ☐ Save as an in-memory table only

   If the name of the target table already exists: ○ Cancel save ● Replace table

   c. Click **Save**.

   Note: If necessary, click **Yes** to replace the file.

   A note appears at the bottom of the workspace.

   > The table "PARKS_LOC" in plan "VA2-Demo2.2" was successfully saved.

   Note: When the plan is saved, the result table is automatically loaded to the CAS server.

   Note: You can open the result table for the plan in Visual Analytics by clicking ⋮ (**Options**) and selecting **Actions** ⇨ **Saved table** ⇨ **Explore and visualize**.

   End of Demonstration

Practice 6.1

The head of operations for Orion Star has requested a map of facility locations in North and South America. Currently, you have a table that contains information about all facilities across the world. You need to filter the table to include details only about facilities in North and South America. You will create a plan that filters the data and creates a new CAS table (facility_toy_america) that can be used in Visual Analytics to create the requested geo map.

Note: Beginning with Visual Analytics 8.3, users can create data views to save data settings (hierarchies, filters, calculated columns, parameters, and more) for a table. For more information about data views, see "Working with Data Views in Reports" in the *SAS Visual Analytics: Working with Report Data* documentation.

Figure 6.3: Practice Scenario - Facilities

Facility	FacilityLat	FacilityLon	...	FacilityContinent	...
ARBUENOS0118	-34.629791	-58.462157		South America	
~~AUSYDNEY0142~~	~~33.866995~~	~~151.207237~~		~~Oceania~~	
~~CNBEIJIN0127~~	~~39.889142~~	~~116.338605~~		~~Asia~~	
~~DEHAMBUR0107~~	~~53.567292~~	~~9.941885~~		~~Europe~~	
MXGUADAL0037	20.678052	-103.335076		North America	
~~ZAJOHANN0144~~	~~-26.204920~~	~~28.040020~~		~~Africa~~	

Filter the **FACILITY_TOY** table to include only facilities located in North America or South America. The plan creates a new CAS table (**FACILITY_TOY_AMERICA**) that is used in a later section.

1. Creating a Geographic Data Source
   a. Open the browser and sign in to SAS Viya.
   b. Open the **VA2-Practice2.2** plan in the **Courses/YVA285/Advanced/Practices** folder.
   c. View the source table properties and answer the following questions:
      What is the name of the source table for the plan?
      Answer:
      How many rows are in the source table? How many columns?
      Answer:
   d. View profile information about the source table and answer the following questions:
      How many unique values exist for **Facility Continent**?
      Answer:
      What is the average number of products produced (**UnitActual**) by each unit? The minimum? The maximum?
      Answer:
   e. Add a filter to the plan to include only facilities located in North America or South America.
   f. Save the plan.
   g. View the result table properties and answer the following question:
      How many rows are in the result table?
      Answer:
   h. View profile information about the result table and answer the following questions:
      What is the name of the result table for the plan?
      Answer:
      How many unique values exist for **Facility Continent**?
      Answer:
      What is the average number of products produced (**UnitActual**) by each unit? What does this tell you about production in the Americas compared to production in other continents?
      Answer:

Alternate Practices (Optional)

1. Creating Report Data Views in SAS Visual Analytics
   a. Open the browser and sign in to SAS Viya.
   b. Open the **VA2-Practice2.2 (Alternate)** report in the **Courses/YVA285/Advanced/Practices** folder.
   c. Answer the following questions:

      How many observations are in the **FACILITY_TOY** data source?

      Answer:

      How many unique values exist for **Facility Continent**?

      Answer:
   d. Add a data filter to include only facilities located in North America or South America.
   e. Answer the following questions:

      How many observations are returned after the data filter is applied?

      Answer:

      How many unique values exist for **Facility Continent**?

      Answer:
   f. Save the data changes as a data view (**FACILITY_TOY_View**). Make the data view the default.

      Note: Selecting **Default data view** automatically applies the view anytime that the data source is added to a report.

      Note: An administrator has an option (**Shared data view**) that makes the view available to other users, not just the user who created the view.
   g. Save the report.
   h. Create a new report using the **FACILITY_TOY** data source.
   i. Answer the following questions:

      How many observations are in the **FACILITY_TOY** data source? Why?

      Answer:

      How many unique values exist for **Facility Continent**? Why?

      Answer:

      Note: You do not need to save the new report.

2. **Creating Data Joins in SAS Visual Analytics**
   a. Open the browser and sign in to SAS Viya.
   b. Open the **VA2-Demo2.2 (Alternate)** report in the **Courses/YVA285/Advanced/Practices** folder.
   c. Create a new data join for the report with the following specifications:

Name	Parks_Species
Join type	Inner
Data source 1	PARKS
Data source 2	SPECIES

      Both the **PARKS** and **SPECIES** tables contain a column named **Park Name**.

      Select all columns, from both tables, except the **Park Name** column from the **SPECIES** table.

      Note: Create a new data join from the Data pane by clicking [image] (**Actions**) and selecting **New data join**.
   d. Rename the **State** column to **State (lower)**.
   e. Create a new data item, **State**, that is the uppercase version of **State (lower)**.
   f. Create a new data item, **Park ID**, that consists of the first four characters of **Species ID**.

g. Verify the results by adding a list table to the canvas that displays the following columns:

State

State (lower)

Park Name

Species ID

Park ID

h. Save the report.

`End of Practices`

6.4 Analyzing Geographic Information

The US National Park Service has asked for a map that shows the locations of all national parks and lists the species located in each park. They would like a report that shows each park location on a map. When a user selects a park, they would like to see a list of all species found in that park. To create this report, we will need to create a geographic data item and use that data item in a geo map.

Figure 6.4: Objects: Graphs (Geography)

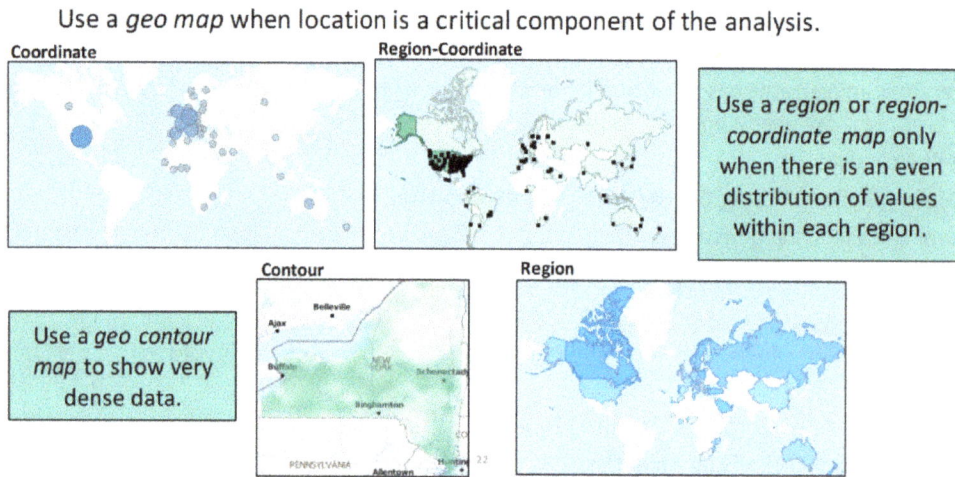

Use a *geo map* when location is a critical component of the analysis.

Use a *region* or *region-coordinate map* only when there is an even distribution of values within each region.

Use a *geo contour map* to show very dense data.

A geo map overlays data on a geographic map. Data can be displayed using colored regions, coordinates, or regions and coordinates, as a contour plot, or as a network. In order to display data on a geo map, at least one category data item must have values that are mapped to geographical locations or regions

Table 6.2: Geo Map Types

Geo Map	Description
Region	A regions geo map (also known as a *choropleth map*) uses colors to show variations by location. However, larger regions appear more emphasized than smaller ones, which can affect perceptions of colors.

Geo Map	Description
Coordinate	A coordinates geo map (also known as a *dot distribution map* or a *dot density map*) displays a map with either a scatter plot or a bubble plot of coordinates. This type of map helps with detecting spatial patterns and understanding the distribution of data over a geographical region, which can help reveal patterns using clustered points. For a bubble plot, the bubble size helps with comparing proportions over regions without the size of the region causing distortions, but the size of the bubble can overlap with other bubbles and regions making the chart difficult to read.
Region-Coordinate	A region-coordinate geo map displays a map using both colored regions and either a scatter plot or bubble plot of coordinates. This type of map is great for comparing two levels of data with the region colors representing more general information (like countries) and the coordinates representing more specific information (like customer locations).
Contour	A contour geo map displays shaded regions over a geographical region. Contour maps are best used to show very dense data.
Network	A network geo map displays a network diagram overlaid on a map. Network maps are helpful for understanding how location affects the relationships in the network.

For more information about creating geography data items, see "Working with Geography Data Items" in the *SAS Visual Analytics: Working with Report Data* documentation.

Figure 6.5: Uses for Geo Maps

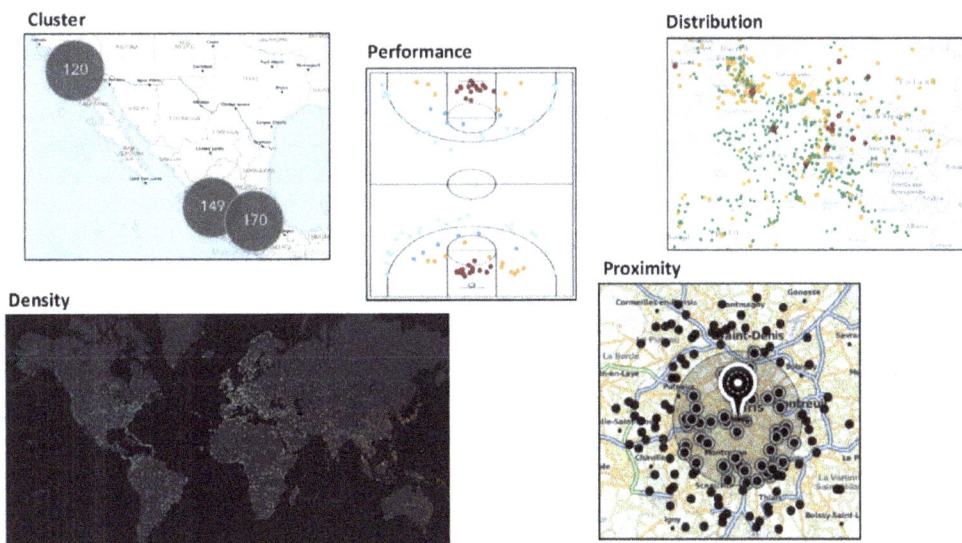

Demo 6.2: Analyzing a Geographic Data Source

This demonstration illustrates how to explore and visualize a geographic data source using SAS Visual Analytics.

1. From the browser window, sign in to SAS Viya.

2. In the upper left corner, click ☰ (**Show list of applications**) and select **Explore and Visualize**. SAS Visual Analytics appears.

3. Click **All Reports**.

    a. Navigate to the **Courses/YVA285/Advanced/Demos** folder.

    b. Double-click the **VA2-Demo2.3** report to open it.

4. In the left pane, click **Data**.

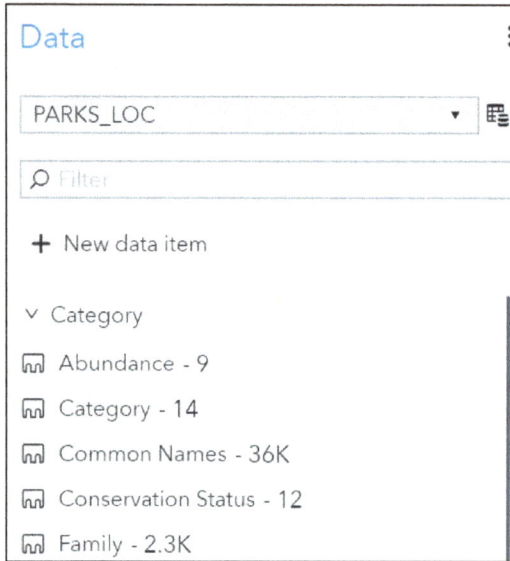

5. Create geography data items.

    a. In the Data pane, right-click **Park Name** and select **New geography**.

       Note: This creates a duplicate of the data item that is a geographic data item.

        i.   In the New Geography Item window, in the **Name** field, enter **Park Location**.

        ii. For the **Based on** field, verify that **Park Name** is specified.

        iii. For the Geography data field, select Latitude and longitude in data.

        iv. For the **Latitude (y)** field, select **Latitude**.

        v.   For the **Longitude (x)** field, select **Longitude**.

        vi. For the Coordinate Space field, verify that World Geodetic System (WGS84) is selected.

The map on the right shows that 100% of park locations are mapped.

vii.   At the bottom of the window, click **OK**.

A new group, Geography, is added to the Data pane.

> ∨ Geography
>
> ⊕   Park Location - 56   ≫

6.   Create a geo map.

a.   In the canvas, click the geo map object to select it.

b.   Click Assign Data.

i.   For the **Geography** role, select **Add ⇨ Park Location**.

ii.   For the **Size** role, right-click **Frequency** and select **Remove Frequency**.

Note: Data does not appear in the geo map until it is changed to a coordinate map.

iii.   Click **Close**.

c.   In the right pane, click **Options**.

i.   In the Coordinate group, for the **Data layer render type** field, select **Scatter**.

The geo map should resemble the following:

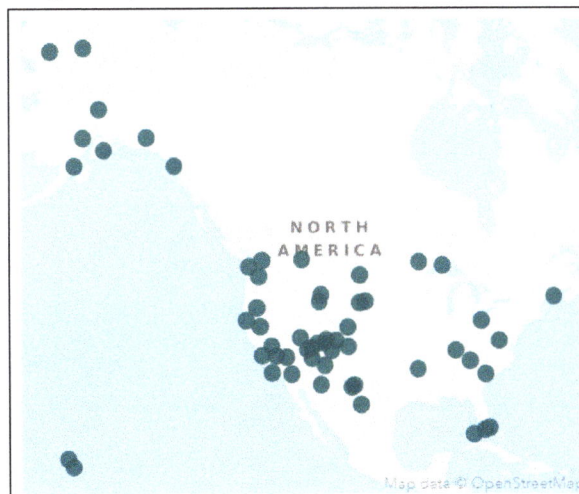

7. Search for parks within 500 miles of Flagstaff, AZ.

    a. In the upper left corner of the geo map, click ⬛ (**Location**).

    b. In the **Search** field, enter **Flagstaff, AZ**.

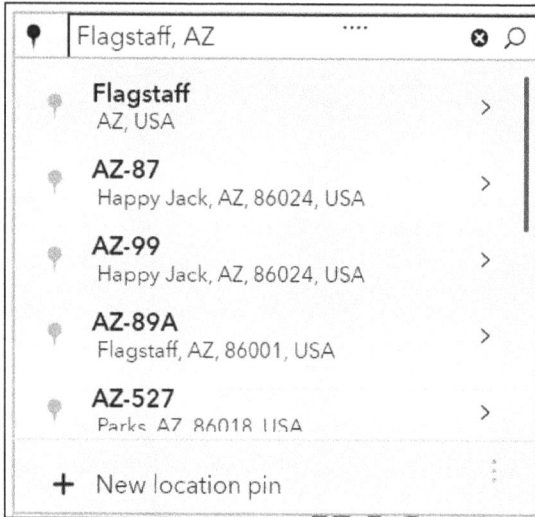

    c. Double-click the search result for **Flagstaff AZ, USA**.

    d. Click **Geographic selection**.

    e. For the **Type** field, verify that **Distance** is selected.

    f. For the **Unit** field, verify that **Miles** is selected.

       Note: The default distance unit can be modified by changing the Geographic Mapping settings for Visual Analytics.

    g. For the **Distance** field, enter **500**.

       The Geographic Selection window should resemble the following:

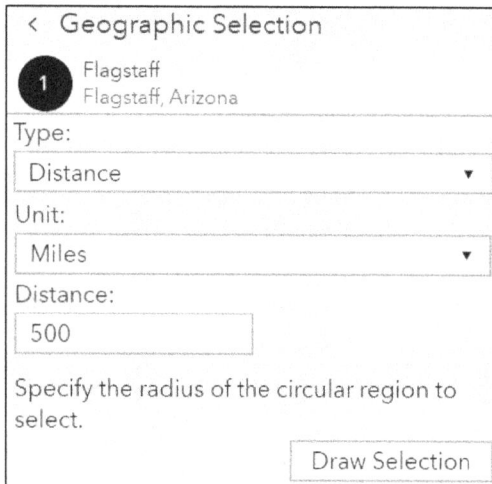

h. Click **Draw Selection**.

All parks within a 500-mile radius of Flagstaff, AZ, are highlighted.

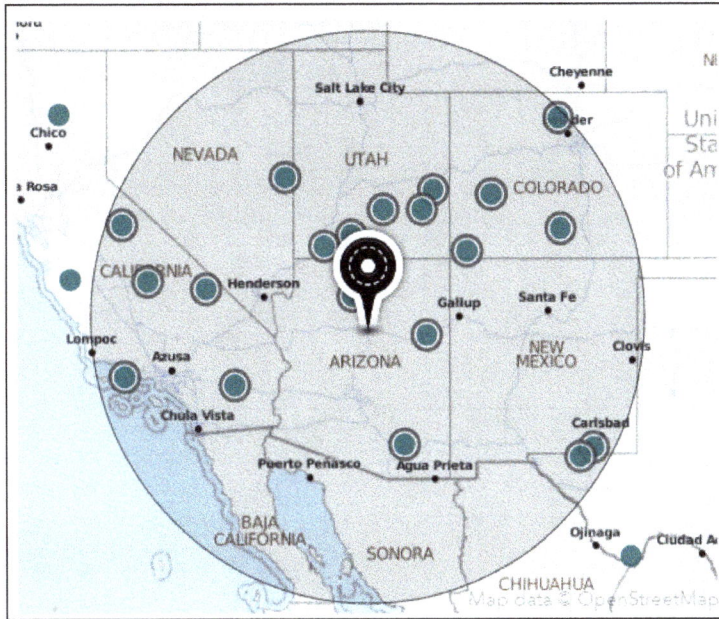

The list table on the right shows all the species located in the selected parks.

Category ▲	Common Names
Algae	None
Algae	Bull Kelp
Algae	Giant Kelp
Algae	Colander Weed
Algae	Bladder Chain Kelp
Algae	Snot Weed
Algae	Feather Boa

8. In the geo map, click the bubble for **Big Bend National Park** (in Texas).

The list table on the right is updated to show all the species in Big Bend National Park.

Category ▲	Common Names
Amphibian	American Bullfrog
Amphibian	Barred Tiger Salamander
Amphibian	Canyon Treefrog
Amphibian	Couch's Spadefoot
Amphibian	Great Plains Narrow-Mouthed Toad
Amphibian	Green Treefrog
Amphibian	Mexican Spadefoot
Amphibian	Red-Spotted Toad

9.   Save the report.

End of Demonstration

Practice 6.2

The head of operations for Orion Star has requested a map of current facility locations in North and South America. Specifically, she wants to see the production and number of employees in each facility location. She will use this information to determine which facilities need to be expanded and which facilities need to be shut down. To create this report, we will need to create two geographic data items, create a geographic hierarchy, and use the hierarchy in a geo map.

1.   Analyzing a Geographic Data Source

   a.   Open the browser and sign in to SAS Viya.

   b.   Open the **VA2-Practice2.3** report in the **Courses/YVA285/Advanced/Practices** folder.

   c.   Change the classification for **Facility Country** to **Geography** using **Geographic name or code lookup** predefined geographic data.
   What percentage of data items are mapped?
   Answer:

   d.   Change the classification for **Facility** to **Geography** using the latitude and longitude in the data source.

   e.   Create a geographic hierarchy (**Facility Hierarchy**) of the geographic data items.

   f.   Create a geo map by assigning the following data items to the specified roles:

Category	Facility Hierarchy
Size	Facility Employees
Color	Unit Actual

   g.   Answer the following question:
   How many facilities are in the United States within 250 miles of Topeka, KS?
   Answer:

   h.   Save the report.

   End of Practices

Quiz 6.1

To create a geo map, you need a geographic data item.

Which geographic areas would require a geographic data provider or latitude and longitude in data? (Select all that apply.)

1. Voting districts
2. Cities
3. Sales regions
4. School districts

Chapter 7: Advanced Topics – Restructuring Data for Forecasting

7.1 Introduction

Exploring historical trends and forecasting help companies analyze past performance and prepare for the future, show them how to be more efficient, help them understand how to better manage their inventory, or help them schedule their processes more effectively. In this chapter, you will learn more about forecasting in Visual Analytics. First, you will learn more about the forecasting object, the data needed to create forecasts, and data structure needed for Visual Analytics. Finally, you will use the restructured data to add forecasts, underlying factors, and a what-if analysis to a report.

7.2 Restructuring Data

To create a forecast in Visual Analytics, you need time series data. That means the rows of your table must represent data over some period of time (date, time, or datetime) and the columns of your table must contain at least one measure data item for forecasting. The data can contain multiple rows for each date. In that case, the forecasted measure will be aggregated for each date before forecasting is performed. If your data contains multiple measures and you think some of those additional measures may contribute to the forecast, you add them as possible underlying factors.

Figure 7.1: Data Shape

Date 📇	123 Forecast	123 Underlying Factor
Jan2000	10	4
Feb2000	12	8
Mar2000	5	2
Apr2000	6	5
May2000	15	12
Jun2000	13	5
Jul2000	10	7
...		
May2019	18	9

Columns contain at least one measure data item for forecasting.

Time series data

Rows represent data over some period of time.

Transposing Data

In some cases, your data might not be structured appropriately for the type of analysis you want to perform. For example, you might have a table that shows data over time, but the date values are stored as columns, and the measures are stored rows. In this case you will need to transform your data so that each row shows data for a single time period and each column displays the different measures. You can create a plan that uses the Transpose transform to restructure your data.

Transposing data takes a wide data set and rotates it to a narrow data set; basically, it turns rows of data into columns of data and columns of data into rows of data. When you transpose data, you need to specify an ID column and the transpose columns. The ID column is the one that contains the rows that you want to become columns. In our example, the Measure column contains values for each of the measures. When the transpose is performed, new columns for each measure will be created. The Transpose columns contain the data that you want to use to populate the rows of the new table. In our example, each of the month columns will be used to populate a new column (Month) and the values of the month columns will be used to populate the new measure columns in the table.

Figure 7.2: Transposing Data

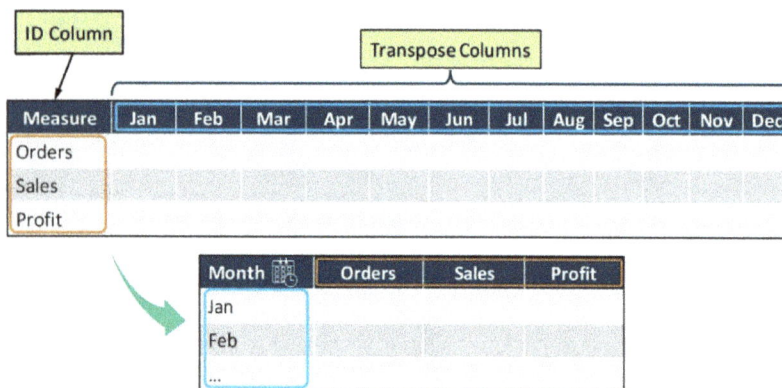

In our example, the Sales team at Orion Star has asked for a forecast of sales for the next six months. We have a table that contains a row for each measure and separate columns for each month. We need to transpose the table to produce a data set suitable for forecasting. We will create a plan that transposes the data and creates a new CAS table (sales_orders) that can be used in Visual Analytics for our forecast.

Figure 7.3: Business Scenario - Sales

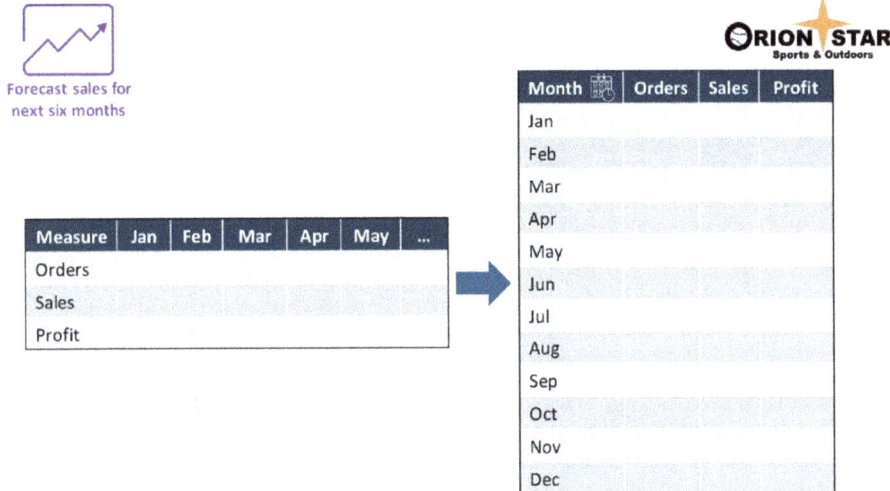

We need to perform the following steps:

1. Transpose the **SALES_ORD_T** table.
2. Convert a character column (**Date**) to a date type (**TransactionDate**).
3. Remove the character column (**Date**).

   The plan creates a new CAS table (**SALES_ORDERS**) that is used in a later section.

Demo 7.1: Creating a Forecasting Data Source

This demonstration illustrates how to explore a data source and use transforms (Transpose, Convert Column, and Remove) to create a forecasting data source in SAS Data Studio.

1. From the browser window, sign in to SAS Viya.
2. In the upper left corner, click ☰ (**Show list of applications**) and select **Prepare Data**.

   SAS Data Studio appears.
3. Click **Open Plan**.
   a. Navigate to the **Courses/YVA285/Advanced/Demos** folder.
   b. Double-click the **VA2-Demo3.1** data plan to open it.

4. In the left pane, click ▦ (**Properties for the source table**) to show details about the source table.

> **Source Table - SALES_ORD_T**   ↺
>
> | Columns | Rows | Size |
> |---------|------|------|
> | 47 | 4 | 13.7 KB |
>
> Label:
> (not available)
>
> ---
> Location:
> cas-shared-default/Public
>
> Date created:
>
> Date modified:
>
> ---
> Encoding:
> (not available)
>
> ---
> Tags (0):
>
> No items have been added.   ⬦

The table contains only four rows of data and 47 columns.

5. In the top pane, verify that **Table** is selected.

> Table   Profile   Metadata
>
> **SALES_ORD_T**
>
> Result rows: 100   ↺   ⋮
>
> | ⚠ Measure | ⊕ JAN2014 | ⊕ JAN2015 | ⊕ JAN2016 | ⊕ JAN2017 | ⊕ FEB2014 |
> |-----------|-----------|-----------|-----------|-----------|-----------|
> | OrderTotal | 434318.79… | 511634.64… | 556871.22… | 646284.68… | 507457.77… |
> | OrderMarketingCost | 20276.497… | 24265.481… | 26471.522… | 30058.668… | 23294.241… |
> | SalesRepActual | 2455110.4… | 2604001.0… | 3338254.9… | 3532498.7… | 2527409.1… |
> | MarketPenetration | 0.0000685… | 0.0000602… | 0.0000658… | 0.0000636… | 0.0000681… |

In order to perform forecasting in Visual Analytics, the table must contain one column for each measure and one row for each month (time series data). This table is not formatted properly and needs to be transposed.

6. Add transforms to the plan.

   a. In the left pane, click 🔍 (**Transforms**) to view the available transforms.

   b. In the Row Transforms group, double-click **Transpose** to add the transform to the plan.

      i. At the top of the window, verify that **ID Columns** is selected.

   > | ID Columns | Transpose Columns | Group By Columns |
   > |------------|-------------------|------------------|

ii.   In the Available items list, double-click **Measure** to add it to the Selected items list.

ID Columns   Transpose Columns   Group By Columns

Available items (46):   Selected items (1):

🔍 Filter   ⓐ Measure

⊕ JAN2014

⊕ JAN2015

For the ID columns, you want to select columns that contain row values that you want to transform into columns. In this example, we would like the new table to contain a column for each distinct value of **Measure**.

iii. For the Rename the _NAME_ column field, enter Date.

Options for Output Column Headings

Include column prefix:

Enter a prefix for the transposed columns

Rename the _NAME_ column:

Date

☐ Eliminate redundant values

NAME is the default column name for the column created by transposing the data. In this example, we want to transpose the month columns, so we name the column **Date**.

iv.   At the top of the window, click **Transpose Columns**.

For the Transpose columns, you want to select columns that contain the data that you want to use to populate the new table. In this example, we would like the new table to use the data from each of the month columns.

v.   In the Available items list, click **JAN2014**, hold down the Shift key, and select **DEC2016**.

vi.   Click ➕ (**Add**) to add the selected columns to the Selected items list.

ID Columns   Transpose Columns   Group By Columns

Available items (1):   Selected items (46):

🔍 Filter   ⊕ JAN2014

                                                  ⊕ JAN2015

ⓐ Measure   ⊕ JAN2016

                                                  ⊕ JAN2017

vii. At the bottom of the window, click **OK**.

viii. In the upper right corner of the workspace, click **Run** to execute the transform. The Table view is updated to reflect the transpose.

| Table | Profile | Metadata |

SALES_ORD_T (session)

⊘ The session table is current to the plan.   Result rows: | 100 |

⚠ Date	⊕ MarketPenetration	⊕ OrderMarketingCost	⊕ OrderTotal	⊕ SalesRepActual
JAN2014	0.0000685895	20276.497916	434318.79866	2455110.4697
JAN2015	0.0000602122	24265.481173	511634.64723	2604001.0721
JAN2016	0.0000658731	26471.522861	556871.22448	3338254.9585
JAN2017	0.0000636889	30058.668071	646284.68963	3532498.7018
FFB2014	0.0000401140	22204.241571	507457.77820	2527400.1701

The **Date** column is classified as a character column. We need to change the classification to **DATE** so that we can use Date functions and calculations in Visual Analytics.

c. On the Transforms pane, in the Column Transforms group, double-click **Convert column** to add the transform to the plan.

   i. For the **Source column** field, verify that **Date** is selected.

   ii. For the **Conversion** field, select **DATE**.

   iii. For the Informat or format field, click 🗀 (Suggestions for informats or formats).

      a. In the Informat or Format window, select **MONYYw**.

      b. For the **Informat or format** field, modify the value to **MONYY7**.

      The informat provides instructions about how to read the data. Because the **Date** column has a three-character month and a four-digit year (JAN2014), we need to specify a width of *7*.

   iv. For the New column field, enter **TransactionDate**.

   v. For the **Length** field, verify that **8** is specified.

   vi. For the **Format** field, enter **DATE9.** as the format.

      The format provides instructions on how to write the data (01JAN2014).

   vii. For the **Label** field, enter **Transaction Date**.

      The transform should resemble the following:

☰ 2. Convert Column   [Run ▾] 🗁 🗑

Source column:		Conversion:		Informat or format:
⚠ Date	▾	DATE	▾	MONYY7. 🗀

New column:	Length:	Format:	Label:
TransactionDate	8	DATE9.	Transaction Date

⊙ +

     viii.   In the upper right corner of the workspace, click **Run** to execute the transform. The new column is added to the Table view.

⊕ TransactionDate
01JAN2014
01JAN2015
01JAN2016
01JAN2017

    d.   On the Transforms pane, in the Column Transforms group, double-click **Remove** to add the transform to the plan.

        i.   For the **Source column** field, select **Date**.

             The transform should resemble the following:

> ☰ **3. Remove**
>
> Source column:
>
> [Ⓐ Date ▼] ⑦ +

        ii.   In the upper right corner of the workspace, click **Run** to execute the transform and remove the column.

             The **Date** column is removed from the Table view.

  7. Save the plan.

End of Demonstration

Practice 7.1

The California Highway Patrol has asked for a forecast of injuries from motor vehicle accidents for the next two years. Currently, we have a table that contains information about the number of injuries, drivers, and vehicles, and a tourism index for California. Our table, however, only has information for the 1990s. We have recently been given an updated table that has information for the 2000s. We need to append the new data to our existing table to create a data set for forecasting. In addition, we want to add a new column (DV Ratio) to the result table that shows the ratio of drivers to vehicles. We will create a plan that appends the new data, creates the calculated column, and creates a new CAS table (mvainjuries) that can be used in Visual Analytics for our forecast.

Date 📅	Injuries	Vehicles	Drivers	...	DV Ratio
MAR1990					
APR1990					
...					

⊕

Date 📅	Injuries	Vehicles	Drivers	...	DV Ratio 🧮
Jan2000					
FEB2000					
...					

Forecast injuries for next two years

In this practice, we perform the following steps:

1. Append the **MVAINJURIES00** table to the **MVAINJURIES90** table.
2. Calculate **DV Ratio** as the ratio of **Drivers** to **Vehicles**.

   The plan creates a new CAS table (**MVAINJURIES**) that is used in a later section.

3. **Creating a Forecasting Data Source**

   a. Open the browser and sign in to SAS Viya.

   b. Open the **VA2-Practice3.1** plan in the **Courses/YVA285/Advanced/Practices** folder.

   c. View the source table properties and answer the following question:

   How many columns are in the source table?

   Answer:

   d. Append the **MVAINJURIES00** data source to the source table (**MVAINJURIES90**).

   Note: The **MVAINJURIES00** data source is defined for the CAS server but is not currently loaded.

   e. Answer the following question:

   How many columns are in the **MVAINJURIES00** table?

   Answer:

   f. Add a new column (**DVRatio**) to the result table that computes the ratio of **Drivers** to **Vehicles**.

   Note: Make sure that you change the type and label of the new column as necessary.

   Note: The resulting table should have 10 columns and 202 rows of data.

   g. Save the plan.

   End of Practices

7.3 Forecasting

Now that you have shaped and transformed your data into a suitable format, you can build your forecast using the forecasting object. This object uses the statistical trends in your data to predict future values. It displays a line with predicted values and a colored band that represents the confidence interval. By default, the next six periods are forecast, and the 95% confidence interval is displayed. Historical values for the forecasting model are displayed as markers only (without a line). Historical predicted values (hindcast) are displayed as part of the forecast line. Visual Analytics automatically tests several forecasting models against your data (ARIMA, damped-trend exponential smoothing, linear exponential smoothing, seasonal exponential smoothing, simple exponential smoothing, Winters method (additive), and Winters method (multiplicative)) and selects the best model.

Figure 7.4: Objects - Analytics (Forecasting)

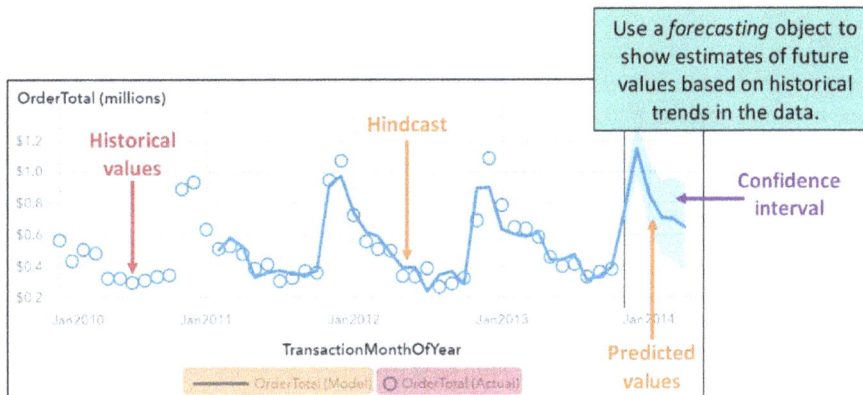

Visual Statistics gives you the added ability to create your own models instead of relying on the model that is automatically selected for forecasting. Forecasts are very useful in planning for the future. For example, you can use a forecast to predict the number of storms for the next six years based on historical storm occurrence. You can also use a forecast to predict the number of injuries from motor vehicle accidents for a specific city. In addition, forecasts can be used to determine high-use periods for electricity so that higher rates can be charged, or so that energy can be redirected to a specific area. Forecasts can also be used to predict future performance, either in terms of sales or the volume of stocks sold.

A forecasting object uses the statistical trends in your data to predict future values. The forecast displays a line with predicted values and a colored band that represents the confidence interval. By default, the next six periods are forecast, and the 95% confidence interval is displayed. Historical values for the forecasting model are displayed as markers only (without a line). Historical **predicted** values (hindcast) are displayed as part of the forecast line. SAS Visual Analytics automatically tests the following forecasting models against your data and selects the best model:

- ARIMA

- damped-trend exponential smoothing

- linear exponential smoothing

- seasonal exponential smoothing

- simple exponential smoothing

- Winters method (additive)

- Winters method (multiplicative)

Note: Forecasting accounts for cyclical patterns by using standard intervals of time (for example, 60 minutes in an hour, 24 hours in a day, and so on). If your data uses nonstandard values (for example, 48 thirty-minute cycles per day), then cyclical patterns are not considered in the forecast.

Note: If SAS Visual Statistics and SAS Visual Data Mining and Machine Learning are licensed at your site, you have the ability to create models instead of relying on the model automatically selected for forecasting.

Note: If SAS Visual Forecasting is licensed at your site, you have the ability to automatically produce large-scale time series analyses and hierarchical forecasts.

Underlying Factors and What-If Analysis

When you create a forecast in Visual Analytics, the predicted values are based solely on historical trends in your data. In some cases, you might be able to improve the forecast by adding underlying factors. These are additional measures that you think may help improve the accuracy of your forecast. As you add these additional measures, Visual Analytics evaluates them to determine whether they contribute to the accuracy of the forecast. If the additional measures do not increase the accuracy, then they are not applied. If they do increase the accuracy, then the forecast is adjusted (to include their impact) and the confidence bands are narrowed. After underlying factors are identified, you can then perform what-if analysis, which looks at changes in the forecasts based on changes in your data from new information.

There are two different types of what-if analysis that can be performed: scenario analysis and goal seeking. With scenario analysis, you modify future values of the underlying factors to see what impact those changes have on the forecast. With goal seeking, you modify the future values of the forecast to see what changes in the underlying factors are needed to reach that goal. In the following example, we have created a forecast for OrderTotal. OrderMarketingCost is identified as an underlying factor. This means that changes in OrderMarketingCost were found to improve the accuracy of the forecast for OrderTotal.

Figure 7.5: Forecasting - Underlying Factors

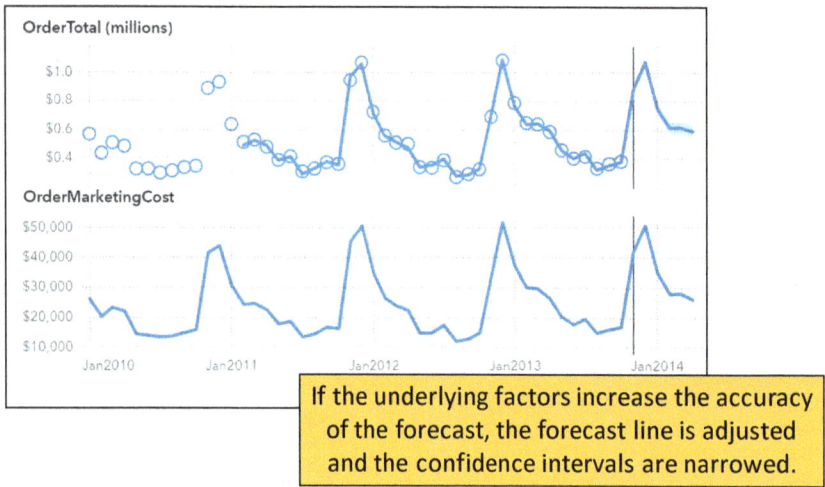

If the underlying factors increase the accuracy of the forecast, the forecast line is adjusted and the confidence intervals are narrowed.

Once an underlying factor is identified, we perform scenario analysis to see how a 20% increase in marketing costs will impact the forecast for OrderTotal. Notice that the future values of OrderTotal are found to increase as well, meaning the more money we spend on marketing, the more orders we are likely to receive in the future.

Figure 7.6: Forecasting - What-If Analysis

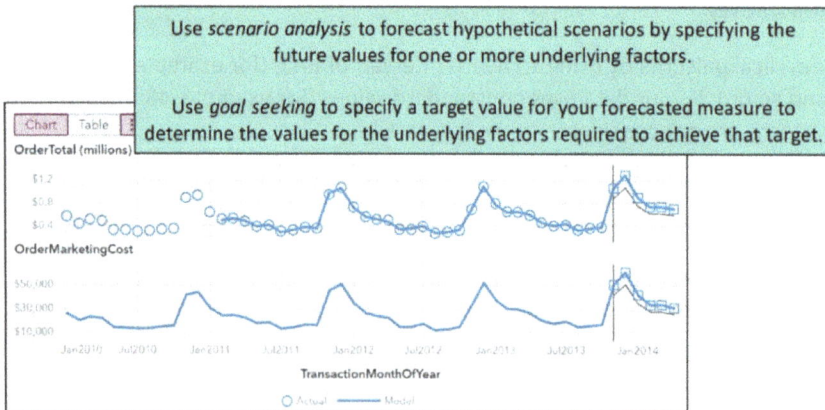

Use *scenario analysis* to forecast hypothetical scenarios by specifying the future values for one or more underlying factors.

Use *goal seeking* to specify a target value for your forecasted measure to determine the values for the underlying factors required to achieve that target.

To perform a what-if analysis for a forecast, measures need to be added to the underlying factors role and found to contribute to the forecast.

Business Scenario

The sales team at Orion Star has asked for a forecast of sales for the next year. They would like to see if marketing costs or market penetration will improve the forecast. They would also like to know how much the underlying factors would need to change to meet their sales goal (a 10% increase). To create this report, we will need to add a forecast for sales, determine if there are any underlying factors for the forecast, and then perform goal seeking to see how we can achieve a 10% increase in sales.

Figure 7.7: Business Scenario - Sales

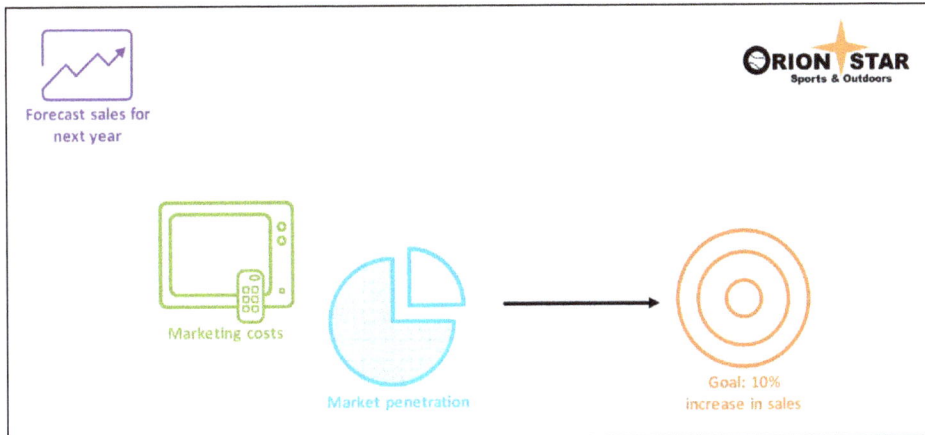

Demo 7.2: Analyzing a Forecasting Data Source

This demonstration illustrates how to add a forecast, underlying factors, and goal seeking using SAS Visual Analytics.

1. From the browser window, sign in to SAS Viya.
2. In the upper left corner, click ☰ (**Show list of applications**) and select **Explore and Visualize**. SAS Visual Analytics appears.
3. Click **All Reports**.
   a. Navigate to the **Courses/YVA285/Advanced/Demos** folder.
   b. Double-click the **VA2-Demo3.2** report to open it.
4. Create a forecast.
   a. In the canvas, click the forecasting object to select it.
   b. In the right pane, click **Roles**.

c.   For the Time axis role, select **Add** ⇨ **Transaction Date**.

d.   For the **Measure** role, click **Frequency** and select **SalesRepActual**.

The forecasting object should resemble the following:

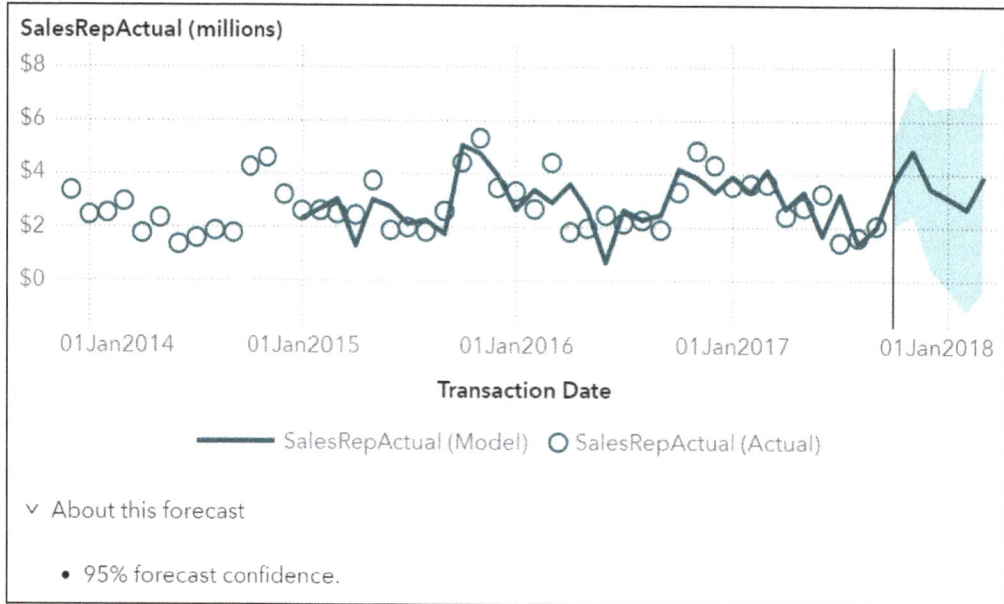

Historical values for **SalesRepActual** are displayed as markers, and historical predicted values (using the selected forecasting algorithm) are displayed as a line.

e.   In the upper right corner of the forecasting object, click [↗] (**Maximize**) to view details about the forecast.

f.   At the bottom of the chart, verify that **Results** is selected.

g.   Scroll through the table to view the forecasted values for **SalesRepActual**.

Results	Dependent Variables Results	Forecast Summary		
Transaction Date	**SalesRepActual (Model)**	**SalesRepActual (Actual)**	**Lower Confidence Interval**	**Uppe**
01Aug2017	$1,384,966.77	$1,628,960.76		
01Sep2017	$2,011,920.97	$2,074,657.61		
01Oct2017	$3,758,104.30		$2,033,637.33	$
01Nov2017	$4,888,167.63		$2,449,403.05	$
01Dec2017	$3,478,785.87		$491,921.46	$,

Historical predicted values and future predicted values are calculated using the forecasted algorithm selected for the data. For future values, a lower and upper confidence interval is also calculated.

h.   At the bottom of the chart, click **Dependent Variables Results** to view details about the forecasting algorithm.

Results	Dependent Variables Results	Forecast Summary
Dependent Variable	**Algorithm**	
SalesRepActual	ARIMA: SalesRepActual ~ P = (12) D = (1,12) NOINT	

SalesRepActual is forecast using an ARIMA algorithm.

The P=(12) indicates the autoregressive term in the model. This means that the forecasted value for the next period of **SalesRepActual** depends on the values for **SalesRepActual** from the last 12 periods.

The D=(1,12) indicates the changes performed on the data to make the forecasted value (**SalesRepActual**) stationary. In this case, a 1-lag difference is needed (the change of **SalesRepActual** from the previous period to this period). The 12 indicates that the forecast is affected by the large changes in **SalesRepActual** from the past 12 periods.

NOINT indicates that no integer is used in the model of **SalesRepActual**.

i.   At the bottom of the chart, click **Forecast Summary** to view details about the forecast.

Results	Dependent Variables Results	Forecast Summary

Forecast Summary

The forecasting object uses statistical trends in your data to predict future values. It automatically tests multiple forecasting models against the specified data items and then selects the best model for each one.

The selected model for SalesRepActual is ARIMA: SalesRepActual ~ P = (12) D = (1,12) NOINT, displayed with a 95% confidence interval. A 95% confidence interval is the predicted data range that will contain future values of SalesRepActual with 95% confidence.

5.   Modify options for the forecasting object.

   a.   In the right pane, click **Options**.

   b.   In the Forecast group, for the **Forecast horizon** field, enter **12**.

   The updated forecast should resemble the following:

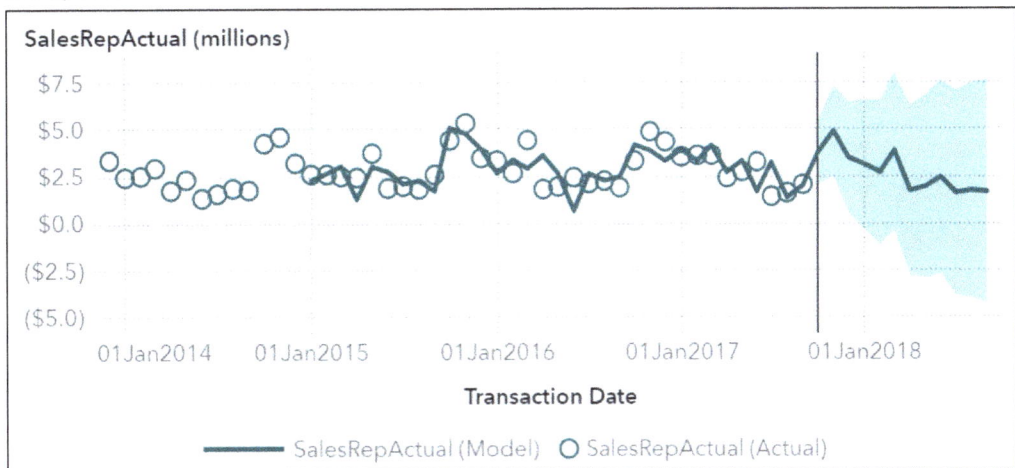

Notice that when we forecast further into the future, the confidence interval increases (and dips into negative values).

6.   Add underlying factors to the forecast.

   a.   In the right pane, click **Roles**.

   b.   For the **Underlying factors** role, click **Add**.

      i.   Select the following data items:

         MarketPenetration

         OrderMarketingCost

ii.   Click **OK**.

The updated forecast should resemble the following:

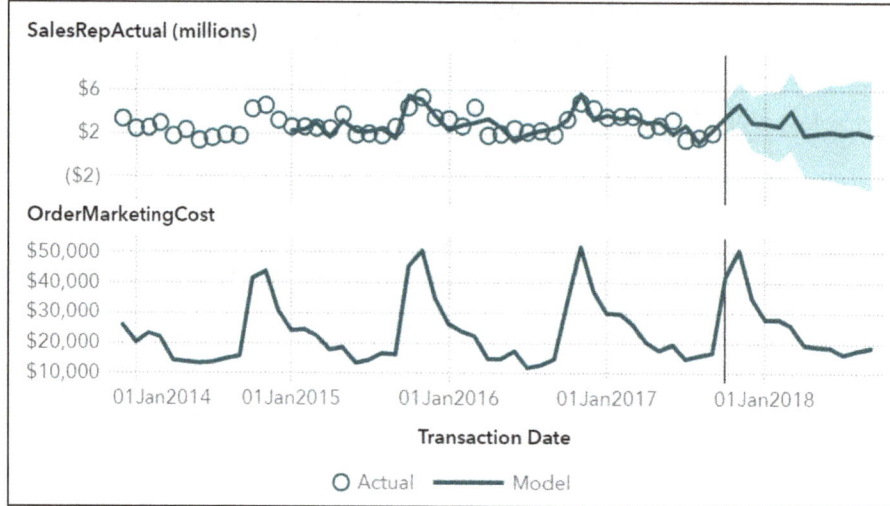

Visual Analytics evaluates the additional measures to determine whether they contribute to the accuracy of the forecast. In this case, **OrderMarketingCost** was found to increase the accuracy of the forecast (as indicated by the narrower confidence interval), so it was added to the model. On the other hand, **MarketPenetration**, was *not* found to increase the accuracy of the forecast, so it was *not* added to the model.

iii.   At the bottom of the chart, click **Dependent Variables Results**.

> Algorithm
>
> ARIMA: SalesRepActual ~ P = (12) D = (1,12) NOINT + INPUT: Dif(1,12) OrderMarketingCost

The forecasting algorithm is updated to reflect the underlying factor (**OrderMarketingCost**).

SalesRepActual is forecast using an ARIMA algorithm.

The Dif(1,12) indicates that the model requires second-order differencing of **OrderMarketingCost** to make the series stationary: one difference term at lag 1 and the other at lag 12.

iv.   In the upper right corner of the forecasting object, click ⬚ (**Restore**).

7.   Perform goal seeking.

a.   In the right pane, click **Roles**.

b.   For the **Forecast** role, click **What If**.

The What-If Analysis window appears.

c.   On the right side of the window, verify that **Goal Seeking** is selected.

Note: It is possible to add bounds for the underlying factors when goal seeking is performed. This ensures that the forecasted values for the underlying factors are not higher (or lower) than acceptable values.

d.   In the upper left corner of the window, click ⠇ (**Menu**) and select **Set series values**.

The Set Series Values window appears.

     i.   For the **Change all future values for the selected series** field, verify that **Forecast: SalesRepActual** is specified.

          Note: We are performing goal seeking, so we must set desired values for the forecasted measure (**SalesRepActual**).

     ii.   For **Adjust series value**, select **By percentage**.

     iii.   In the **By percentage** field, enter **10** and press Enter.

> Change all future values for the selected series:
>
> [Forecast: SalesRepActual ▾]
>
> ○ Set all values to:
>
> Adjust series values
>
> ○ By constant value:
>
> ● By percentage: [10]
>
> ○ Progressively by:

     iv.   Click **OK**.

          As an alternative, you can drag the markers in the chart to set the target values for the forecasted measure or you can enter values directly in the table cells.

e.   On the right side of the window, click **Apply**.

The adjustment is applied to the forecasted measure, and the updated values for the underlying factor are displayed.

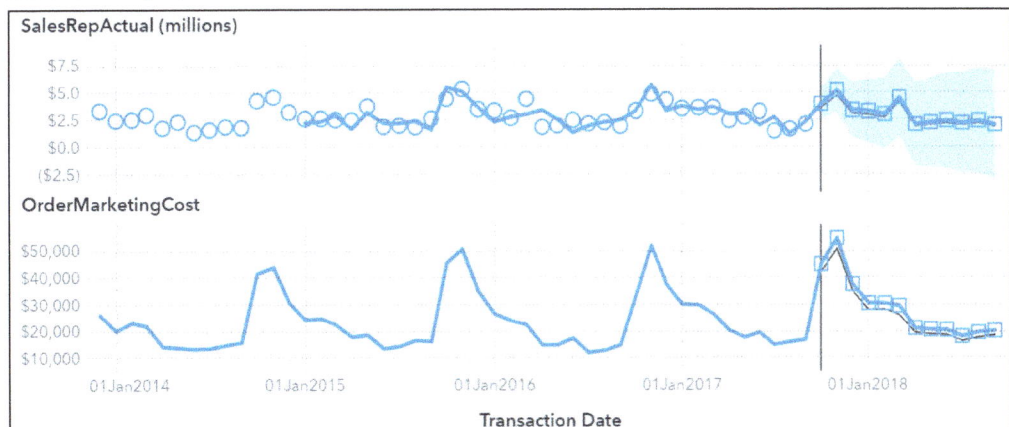

To increase sales rep actual by 10%, marketing costs must increase as well.

f.   Click **Close** to save the results.

The results are applied to the forecasting object in the report.

8.   Save the report.

End of Demonstration

Practice 7.2

The California Highway Patrol has asked for a forecast of injuries from motor vehicle accidents for the next two years. They would like to see if tourism or the driver-to-vehicle ratio will improve the forecast.

Then they want to see how a constant increase in the underlying factor will impact the forecast of injuries. To create this report, we will need to add a forecast for injuries, determine if there are any underlying factors for the forecast, and then perform scenario analysis to see how changes in the underlying factors will change the forecast for injuries.

1.   **Analyzing a Forecasting Data Source**

a.   Open the browser and sign in to SAS Viya.

b.   Open the **VA2-Practice3.2** report in the **Courses/YVA285/Advanced/Practices** folder.

c.   Create a forecast by assigning the following data items to the specified roles:

Time axis	Date
Measure	Injuries from Motor Vehicle Accidents

d.   View details about the forecast and answer the following question:

Which algorithm is selected for the forecast?

Answer:

e.   Modify options for the forecasting object to change the forecast horizon to two years.

f.   Add the following measures to the Underlying factors role in the forecast:

Tourism Index (Difference from previous period)

DV Ratio

Which measures, if any, were selected as underlying factors and applied to the forecast?

Answer:

Which algorithm is now selected for the forecast?

Answer:

g.   Perform scenario analysis on the forecast by increasing the underlying factor by a constant value of 10.

How does increasing the underlying factor impact the forecast?

Answer:

h.   Save the report.

End of Practices

Chapter 8: Advanced Topics – Performing Network Analysis

8.1 Introduction

Today almost everything is connected: people, places, transactions, devices, ideas. With advances in technology, it is now easier than ever to collect data about these connections and use them to make informed decisions. Network diagrams are a great way to look at this information. In this chapter we will learn more about network analysis in Visual Analytics. First, we will look at the different networks, the data needed to create these graphs, and the data structure needed for Visual Analytics. Then, we will use the restructured data to add networks to a report.

8.2 Analytics Network

One way to view the relationship between data is using a network analysis object. A network analysis object displays relationships by using a series of linked nodes. Two types of network analysis objects can be created in Visual Analytics: hierarchical and ungrouped.

A hierarchical network diagram creates a structure using a defined arrangement of category data items. It shows a parent-child relationship where each parent node is linked only to its children. Typically, this type of network diagram will show disconnected clusters of nodes. An ungrouped network diagram, on the other hand, creates a series of linked nodes from a source to a target. A node is created for each value of the source data item, and a link is created from each node to the node that corresponds to the value of the target data item. Vertices and links in this type of diagram represent connections between the nodes. This helps to illuminate types of relationships between groups of entities.

Figure 8.1: Objects: Analytics (Network)

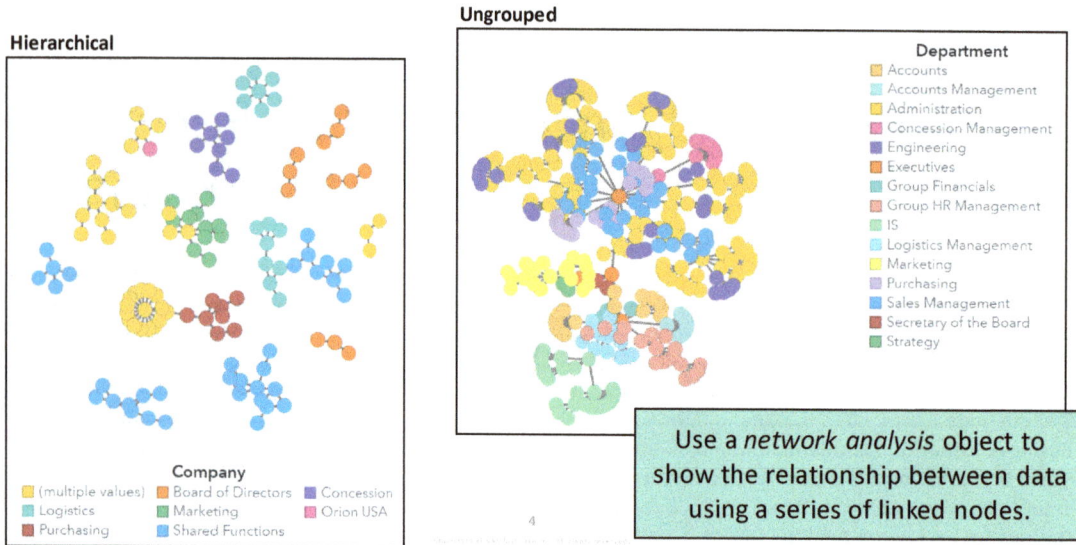

Use a *network analysis* object to show the relationship between data using a series of linked nodes.

Links between nodes in an ungrouped network can either be undirected or directed. Undirected links only display connections between entities, meaning there is no direction to the relationship: node A is related to node B, which implies that node B is related to node A. For example, the "friends" relationship on Facebook is an undirected relationship; that is, the friendship is mutual. Directed links, on the other hand, show the direction of the relationships using arrows, meaning there is a direction to the relationship: node A is related to node B, but node B is not necessarily related to node A. For example, the "follows" relationship on Twitter is a directed relationship: Ross can follow Rachel but that does not mean that Rachel must follow Ross. The type of network analysis object that you create (either hierarchical or ungrouped) is driven by the structure of the CAS table.

A network analysis displays the relationships between the values of categories or hierarchy levels by using a series of linked nodes. The following types of network analysis objects can be created.

Table 8.1: Types of Analytic Networks

Type	Description
Hierarchical	A hierarchical network diagram creates a hierarchical structure using arranged levels of category data items.
Ungrouped	An ungrouped network diagram creates a series of linked nodes from a source node to a target node. A node is created for each value of the source data item, and a link is created from each source node to the node that corresponds to the value of the target data item. Vertices and link lines in the network diagram represent connections and help illuminate types of relationships between groups of entities. Ungrouped network diagrams can be used to interpret a structure of a network by looking at the clustering of nodes, how densely the nodes are connected, and how the diagram layout is arranged. Ungrouped network diagrams can either be undirected (which displays only connections between entities) or directed (which shows the direction of the relationship using arrows).

Note: The network analysis object uses a multi-dimensional force-directed algorithm to layout nodes and links. It attempts to minimize edge length and crossings of links for maximum readability.

Note: If a network analysis object uses geographic data items, the network can be overlaid on a map.

A network consists of nodes (or vertices) and edges (or links). Links can indicate any type of relationship:

Table 8.2: Types of Relationships

Relationship	Description
Directed	A directed (or asymmetric) relationship indicates that there is a direction to the relationship: node A is related to node B, but node B is not necessarily related to node A. For example, the follows relationship on Twitter is a directed relationship.
Undirected	An undirected (or symmetric) relationship indicates that there is no direction to the relationship: node A is related to node B, which implies node B is related to node A. For example, the "friends" relationship on Facebook is an undirected relationship. That is, the relationship is mutual.

Social network analysis can analyze a variety of different social structures, including social media, kinship, disease transmission, and criminal and terrorist networks.

Figure 8.2: Uses for Network Analysis

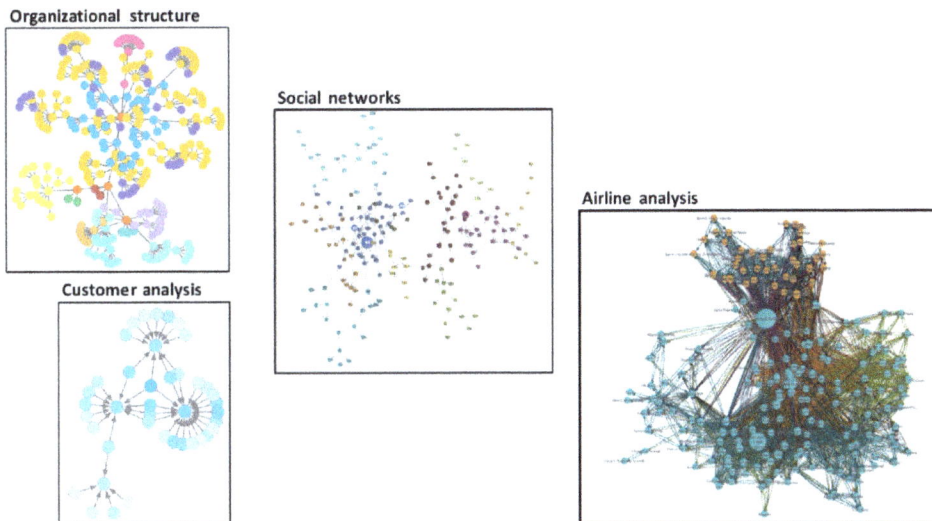

8.3 Data Network Shape

To create an ungrouped network analysis object, the data source must have at least one row for each source-target pair. The target values must be a subset of the source values. For example, let's say I am interested in understanding the texts sent within the members of my family. The table must have one row for each text connection between family members. The source column should have each family member listed at least once.

The target column can either contain all my family members (if all of them text) or be a subset of my family members (if some of them do not text). My grandma does not text, but she is still a member of my family, so she would need to be included in the diagram. I can create a row where my grandma is the source, but because she has no text connections, the target value is missing.

Figure 8.3: Ungrouped Network Analysis - Data Shape

One row for each source-target pair

Source	Target
Me	Dad
Me	Mom
Sister	Me
Sister	Brother
Dad	Mom
Mom	Sister
Brother	Me
Brother	Mom
Grandma	

Each source value must be listed at least once.

Target values are a subset of source values.

Another example is looking at a path or a delivery route. In this case, we would have one row for each destination on the route. Eventually, the route will end. To represent this terminal value, the table must contain a row where the final destination is the value for the source column and the target value is missing. In addition, I can show this route on a geo map. To do so, however, the data source must also contain geographical information for each source and target node.

Figure 8.4: Network Analysis - Data Shape

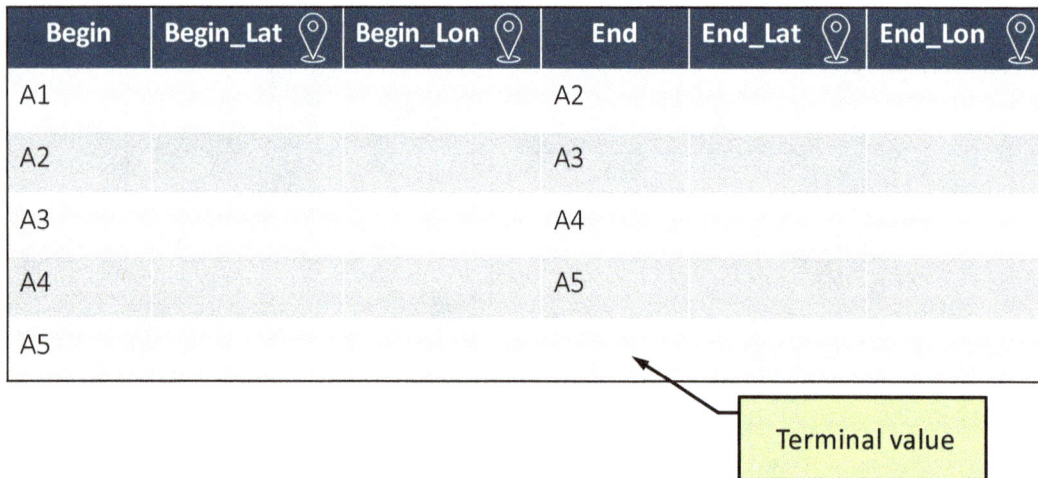

Begin	Begin_Lat	Begin_Lon	End	End_Lat	End_Lon
A1			A2		
A2			A3		
A3			A4		
A4			A5		
A5					

Terminal value

Note: To represent terminal (target-only) values in an ungrouped network analysis, you can add rows to your data where the terminal value is the value for the source data item and the target data item is missing.

8.4 Restructuring Data for Network Analysis

Often the data in your tables is not already in the correct shape in order to create the analytic network, and so you will need to restructure the data before carrying out the analysis. The following section describes some useful techniques available in SAS Data Studio.

Splitting Columns

The Split transform in SAS Data Studio contains many options for splitting your data: on a delimiter, on a fixed length, before a delimiter, after a delimiter, and quick split. The option that you choose will depend on whether or not you want the delimiter to be included in the output and your data values. If you do want the delimiter included in the output, then you can choose either the before a delimiter or after a delimiter option. If you do not want the delimiter included in the output, then the option that you choose will depend on your data value.

For example, let's say I have a column in my data that contains values in a fixed structure: four characters and six digits. I can use the fixed length option to split the data into characters and digits. If my data does not have a fixed structure, then I need to choose between the on a delimiter or quick split options. The Quick split option will split a column using the first delimiter that appears in each cell. In many cases, this may work well for your data. However, consider the following examples. Let's say I have data that contains City Name, State Abbreviation. If I have a data value for Winston-Salem, NC, the Quick split option will not split the values appropriately. It will split based on the first delimiter (-) and not the comma. However, if I use the On a delimiter option and specified comma as the delimiter, the values would be split appropriately. Additionally, if I have a value for San Antonio, TX, the quick split option will split based on the space (not the comma), but the On a delimiter option with the comma as a delimiter, will give the desired result.

Figure 8.5: Splitting Columns

Data	Quick Split		Split (comma)	
Winston-Salem, NC	Winston	Salem, NC	Winston-Salem	NC
Potter, Harry	Potter	Harry	Potter	Harry
San Antonio, TX	San	Antonio, TX	San Antonio	TX
221B Baker St, London	221B	Baker St, London	221B Baker St	London
toto@oz.com	toto@oz	com	toto@oz.com	

> A column can be split based on the following delimiters:
> ! $ % & ( ) * + , - . / ; < |

Note: If your computer uses ASCII characters, the ^ character is also available. For ASCII environments that do not contain the ^ character, the ~ character is available instead.

Note: If your computer uses EBCDIC characters, the ? character is also available.

Custom Code

The Code transform in SAS Data Studio enables you to perform actions on your table that cannot be accomplished with other transforms. For this transform, you can write DATA step code or CASL code. For both versions, you need to ensure that you use specific variable names in place of table names and caslib names. This is because during processing, table names and library names can change. Basically, when a plan is executing, each step of the plan creates a temporary table. The next step then reads that temporary table and creates a new temporary table. Because temporary tables are used, it is impossible to determine the names of those tables. The variable names ensure that the code reads the appropriate table (from the previous step) and creates the appropriate table when the code is processed. For the output table and library, you need to use the variables _dp_outputTable and _dp_outputCaslib respectively. For the input table and library, you need to use the variables _dp_inputTable and _dp_inputCaslib respectively. Starting with version 8.3, Data Studio adds the necessary pieces of the code (with the required variables) by default.

Figure 8.6: Custom Code – DATA Step

```
data {{_dp_outputTable}} (caslib={{_dp_outputCaslib}}
    promote='no');
  set {{_dp_inputTable}} (caslib={{_dp_inputCaslib}});
  length Category $15;
  if Type = 'HU' then Category='Hurricane';
  else if Type in ('TD' 'TS' 'WV')
    then Category='Tropical';
  else if Type in ('SS' 'SD')
    then Category='Subtropical';
  else if Type='EX' then Category='Extratropical';
  else Category='Other';
run;
```

> Because session table names can change during processing, you must use variables for tables and caslibs.

For more information about DATA step, see *Dictionary of SAS DATA Step Statements*.

Note: The PROMOTE= data set option specifies the scope of the CAS table. A value of *yes* specifies that the table from the step is added with a global scope, whereas a value of *no* specifies that the table from the step is added with a session scope. Because this step produces a temporary table (**_dp_outputTable**), PROMOTE= is set to *no* to create a session scope table as output from the step.

Note: You can also create custom code using CASL. For more information about CASL, see "Getting Started with CASL" in the *SAS 9.4 and SAS Viya Programming* documentation.

Business Scenario

The National Oceanic and Atmospheric Administration has asked for a report that shows the path of hurricanes and the category of the hurricane at each point in the path. Currently, we have a table that contains the location of each hurricane at certain times, but the data is not formatted correctly. For example, all details about the origin of the hurricane at each time are displayed in one column as from_loc: from_lat, from_lon. We will need to split this column into three separate columns to create the requested map. In addition, the hurricane type contains codes. We will need to create a new column that classifies each of the hurricane types into one of five categories: Hurricane, Tropical, Subtropical, Extratropical, or Other. We will create a plan that splits the From column, generates the new calculated column, and creates a new CAS table (hurricanes_prep) that can be used in Visual Analytics for our network analysis.

Figure 8.7: Business Scenario: Hurricanes

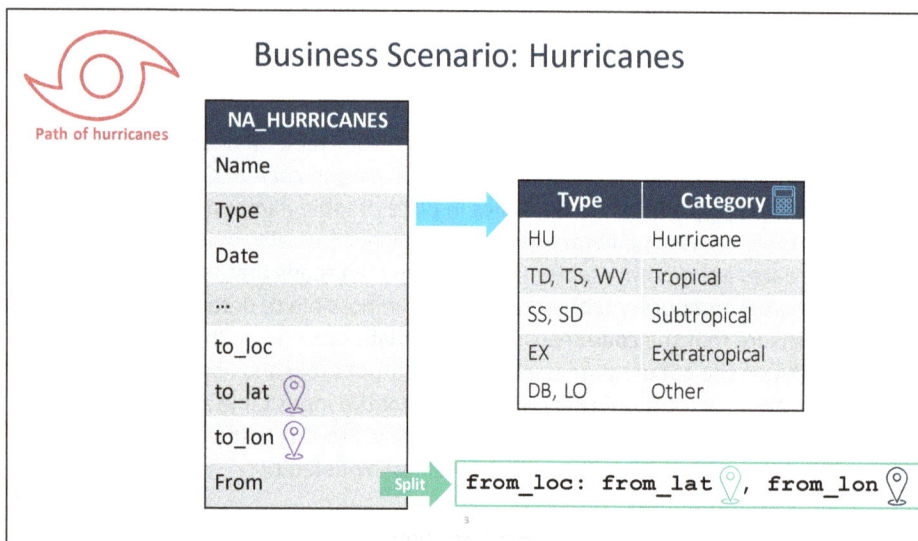

Note: The hurricane data is used by permission of National Oceanic and Atmospheric Administration (NOAA). Please note that NOAA offers no warranty regarding the data. See the disclaimer here: http://www.noaa.gov/disclaimer.

In the following demonstration, we perform the following steps:

1. Split a column into three separate columns (one for the from location, one for the from latitude, and one for the from longitude).
2. Convert character columns to double.
3. Remove unnecessary columns.
4. Add custom code to create a new column.

   The plan creates a new CAS table (**HURRICANES_PREP**) that is used in a later section.

   Note: As an alternative to creating a data plan in SAS Data Studio, users can create a data view in Visual Analytics that performs the necessary steps for this demonstration.

Demo 8.1: Creating a Network Analysis Data Source

This demonstration illustrates how to explore a data source and use transforms (Split, Convert Column, Remove, and Code) to create a network analysis data source in SAS Data Studio.

1. From the browser window, sign in to SAS Viya.
2. In the upper left corner, click ☰ (**Show list of applications**) and select **Prepare Data**.

   SAS Data Studio appears
3. Click **Open Plan**.
   a. Navigate to the **Courses/YVA285/Advanced/Demos** folder.
   b. Double-click the **VA2-Demo4.1** data plan to open it.
4. In the left pane, click ▦ (**Properties for the source table**) to show details about the source table.

Source Table - NA_HURRICANES		
Columns	Rows	Size
14	22.4 K	7 MB

Label:
(not available)

Location:
cas-shared-default/Public

Date created:
Dec 18, 2019 02:47 PM

Date modified:
Dec 18, 2019 02:47 PM

Date last accessed:
Dec 18, 2019 02:47 PM

Source table:
NA_HURRICANES.sashdat

Source CAS Library:
Public

The table contains 14 columns and 22.4K rows of data.

5. In the top pane, click **Table**, if necessary.

    a. Scroll to the right to locate the **to_loc**, **to_lat**, **to_lon**, and **From** columns.

⚠ to_loc	⊞ to_lat	⊞ to_lon	⚠ From
1-2	17.7	-56.3	1-1:17.1,-55.5
1-3	18.2	-57.4	1-2:17.7,-56.3
1-4	19	-58.6	1-3:18.2,-57.4
1-5	20	-60	1-4:19,-58.6

For network analysis, we need a source data item and a target data item. In our table, **to_loc** is the source data item and **to_lat** and **to_lon** contain mapping coordinates for the location. **From**, however, is in the following format: *from_loc: from_lat, from_lon*. We need to split this column into three separate columns to create a network diagram.

6. View the **Split** transform that has been added to the plan.

7. In the upper right corner of the workspace, click **Run** to execute the transform.

    The two new columns (**from_loc** and **from_lat_long**) are added to the Table view from the Split transform.

⚠ from_loc	⚠ from_lat_long
190-13	21.4,-85.2
190-14	21.9,-85.3
190-15	22.4,-85.4
190-16	23,-85.5

Now we need to split the **from_lat_long** column into two new columns that contain the latitude and longitude, respectively. We also need to convert the new columns to doubles (measures) for use in Visual Analytics.

8. Add additional transforms to the plan.

    a. In the left pane, click 🔍 (**Transforms**) to view available transforms.

    b. In the Column Transforms group, double-click **Split** to add the transform to the plan a second time.

        i.   For the Source column field, select from_lat_long.

        ii.   For the **Split data** field, verify that **On a delimiter** is specified.

        iii. For the **Delimiter** field, verify that **Comma** is specified.

        iv.   For the Name of new column 1 field, enter from_latitude.

This is the left column created from the split. Remember that we still need to convert this value to a double (measure), so we give it a temporary name for now.

v.   For the Name of new column 2 field, enter from_longitude.

This is the right column created from the split. Remember that we still need to convert this value to a double (measure), so we give it a temporary name for now.

The Split transform should resemble the following:

☰ 2. Split		Run ▾ ⬀ 🗑
Source column:	Split data:	Delimiter:
⬙ from_lat_long ▾	On a delimiter ▾	Comma ▾
Name of new column 1:	Name of new column 2:	
from_latitude	from_longitude	ⓘ
Options for new columns		

vi.   Click Options for new columns.

For the **from_latitude** column, enter **20** in the **Length** field.

For the **from_longitude** column, enter **20** in the **Length** field.

Name of new column:	Type:	Length:
from_latitude	Char ▾	20
Name of new column:	Type:	Length:
from_longitude	Char ▾	20

From this window, we cannot change the type of the columns. We will add a Convert column transform to change the type to double (measure).

In the bottom right corner of the window, click **OK**.

vii.   In the upper right corner of the workspace, click **Run** to execute the transform.

The two new columns (**from_latitude** and **from_longitude**) are added to the Table view.

⬙ from_latitude	⬙ from_longitude	⬙ from_loc	⬙ from_lat_long
42.5	-33.7	272-40	42.5,-33.7
43.7	-32	272-41	43.7,-32
44.8	-30.3	272-42	44.8,-30.3
45.1	-28.5	272-43	45.1,-28.5

Both columns were created as character columns, but they need to be double for creating a geography data item.

c.   In the left pane, in the Column Transforms group, double-click **Convert column** to add the transform to the plan.

i.   Convert the **from_latitude** column to double.

a.   For the **Source column** field, verify that **from_latitude** is specified.

b.   For the **Conversion** field, verify that **DOUBLE** is specified.

c.   For the **Informat or format** field, verify that **BEST16.** is specified.

d.   In the **New column** field, enter **from_lat**.

e.   For the **Length** field, verify that **8** is specified.

f.   For the **Format** field, verify that **BEST16.** is specified.

The Convert Column transform should resemble the following:

3. Convert Column				Run ▼	
Source column:			**Conversion:**		
⊛ from_latitude	▼		DOUBLE	▼	
Informat or format:			New column:		
BEST16.	🗀		from_lat		
Length:	Format:		Label:		
8	BEST16.			⑦ +	

ii.   Convert the **from_longitude** column to double.

    a.   Click ⊞ (**Add**) to add an additional column to the transform.

    b.   For the Source column field, select from_longitude.

    c.   For the **Conversion** field, verify that **DOUBLE** is specified.

    d.   For the **Informat or format** field, verify that **BEST16.** is specified.

    e.   In the **New column** field, enter **from_lon**.

    f.   For the **Length** field, verify that **8** is specified.

    g.   For the **Format** field, verify that **BEST16.** is specified.

The Convert Column transform should resemble the following:

Source column:			**Conversion:**		
⊛ from_longitude	▼		DOUBLE	▼	
Informat or format:			New column:		
BEST16.	🗀		from_lon		
Length:	Format:		Label:		
8	BEST16.			⑦ 🗑 +	

iii.   In the upper right corner of the workspace, click **Run** to execute the transform.

Two new columns (**from_lat** and **from_lon**) with the type DOUBLE are added to the Table view.

⊞ from_lat	⊞ from_lon
42.5	-33.7
43.7	-32
44.8	-30.3
45.1	-28.5

d.   In the left pane, in the Column Transforms group, double-click **Remove** to add the transform to the plan.

    i.   For the **Source column** field, select **From**.

    ii.   Click ⊞ (**Add**) to add an additional column to the transform.

    iii.   For the **Source column** field, select **from_lat_long**.

    iv.   Click ⊞ (**Add**) to add an additional column to the transform.

    v.   For the **Source column** field, select **from_latitude**.

    vi.   Click ⊞ (**Add**) to add an additional column to the transform.

    vii.   For the Source column field, select **from_longitude**.

The Remove transform should resemble the following:

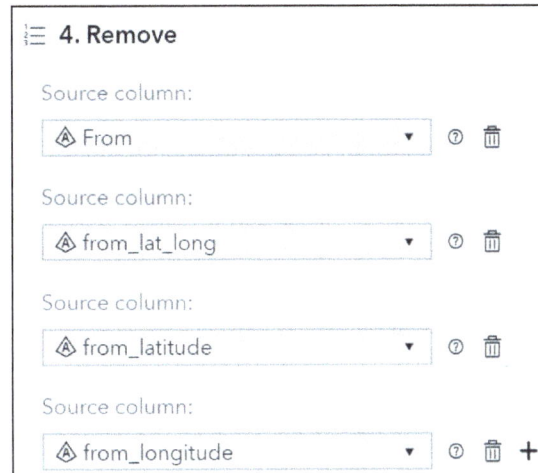

> ≡ **4. Remove**
>
> Source column:
>
> ⬨ From ▾ ⊙ 🗑
>
> Source column:
>
> ⬨ from_lat_long ▾ ⊙ 🗑
>
> Source column:
>
> ⬨ from_latitude ▾ ⊙ 🗑
>
> Source column:
>
> ⬨ from_longitude ▾ ⊙ 🗑 +

    viii.   In the upper right corner of the workspace, click **Run** to execute the transform.

             The columns are removed from the Table view.

  e.   In the Table view, examine the **Type** column.

> ⚠ **Type**
>
> HU
>
> HU
>
> HU
>
> HU

This column keeps track of the type of storm at each stage. It has values such as *HU* for categories of hurricanes, *TD* (tropical depression), *TS* (tropical storm), *WV* (tropical wave), *SS* (subtropical storm), *SD* (subtropical depression), *EX* (extratropical cyclone), *DB* (disturbance), and *LO* (other type).

  f.   In the left pane, in the Custom Transforms group, double-click **Code** to add the transform to the plan.

    i.   On the toolbar above the code editor, click ⑦ (**How do I create custom code?**) to view information about using the transform.

> **Creating Custom Code**
>
> You can create custom code to perform actions or transformations on a table. To create custom code, choose the code language from the drop-down menu, and then enter the code in the text box. The following code languages are available: **CASL** or **DATA step**.
>
> **CAUTION:**
> You must use variables in place of table and caslib names. Errors will occur if you use literal values. This is because session table names can change during processing.
>
> The following variables are available: **_dp_inputCaslib**, **_dp_inputTable**, **_dp_outputCaslib**, and **_dp_outputTable**. For DATA step only, variables must be enclosed in braces, for example, data {{_dp_outputTable}} (caslib={{_dp_outputCaslib}});.
>
> For more information about creating custom code, see Creating Custom Code in *SAS Data Studio: User's Guide*.

Notice that you must use specific variables to represent the input table and caslib and the output table and caslib.

ii.   On the toolbar above the code editor, verify that **DATA step** is specified.

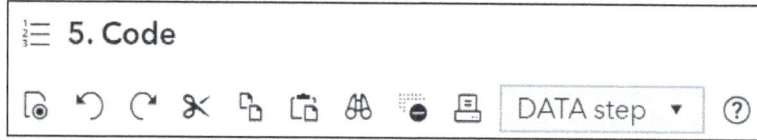

> ≔ **5. Code**
>
> 🔘 ↺ ↻ ✂ � 📋 🔍 ⚬ 🖳 | DATA step ▾ | ⑦

iii.   In the code editor, enter the following after the SET statement:

> **length Category $15;**
> **if Type = 'HU' then Category='Hurricane';**
> **else if Type in ('TD' 'TS' 'WV') then Category='Tropical';**
> **else if Type in ('SS' 'SD') then Category='Subtropical';**
> **else if Type='EX' then Category='Extratropical';**
> **else Category='Other';**

This code creates a new variable (Category) that categorizes each hurricane by type.

iv.   In the upper right corner of the workspace, click **Run** to execute the transform.

The new column (**Category**) is added to the Table view.

> ⚠ **Category**
>
> Extratropical
>
> Extratropical
>
> Tropical
>
> Tropical

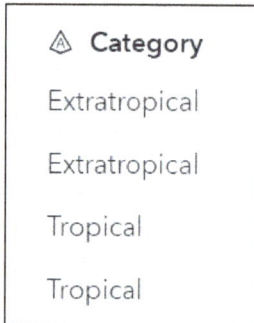

9.   Save the plan.

End of Demonstration

8.5 Creating a Network Analysis Object

As previously described, the basic data role for a hierarchical network analysis object is Levels. The hierarchy in the Levels role specifies the nodes of the network analysis. The basic data roles for an ungrouped network analysis object are Source and Target. The Source specifies a data item that contains all of the node values for the plot. The Target specifies a data item that creates the links between nodes. The Target data item must contain a subset of the values of the Source data item.

In addition to the basic data roles, you can specify the following data roles for a network analysis:

Size

Specifies a measure that determines the size of the nodes in the network analysis.

Note: You can assign internal network metrics to the Size role by using options in your SAS Visual Analytics settings. For more information, see Modify SAS Visual Analytics Settings in SAS Visual Analytics: Designing Reports.

Color

Specifies a data item that determines the color of the nodes in the network.

Note: You can assign internal metrics to the Color role by using options in your SAS Visual Analytics settings. For more information, see Modify SAS Visual Analytics Settings in SAS Visual Analytics: Designing Reports.

Link width	Specifies a measure that determines the width of the links in the network.
Link color	Specifies a data item that determines the color of the links in the network.
Label	Specifies a data item whose values are displayed inside each node if the Node labels option is enabled.
Data tip values	Specifies data items whose values are included in the data tips for the network. Measure values are aggregated by sum.

Options for a Network Analysis Object

In addition to the general options, you can specify object-specific options on the Options pane. For more information about the options available under Network Analysis, see *SAS® Visual Analytics 8.1: Working with Report Content.*

Arranging Nodes in a Network Analysis Object

Once you have created your network analysis object, you can move any node in the network by clicking the node and dragging it. You can move multiple nodes in the network by selecting the nodes that you want to move and dragging them.

Note: The positions of the nodes in your network are saved with your report.

You can refresh your node layout by clicking ![icon]. The network creates a new node layout based on your current node layout. This is especially useful after you have moved nodes manually. Refreshing the node layout adjusts the spacing and orientation of your nodes.

You can select nodes in the network by using any of the following methods:

- If the rectangular selection tool is selected, you can select nodes by clicking and dragging.

- If the rectangular selection tool is not selected, then click ![icon] in the object toolbar, and then select ![icon].

- Hold down the Ctrl key, and click the nodes that you want to select.

- Select a series of linked nodes by setting a node as the source node.

- Select a node, right-click the node, and then select Set as source for selection.

- In the Options pane, specify the range of levels of Predecessors (parents) and Successors (children) of the source node to select. 0 specifies that the source node is selected.

  For example, if you specify a range of 0 to 1 for Predecessors and a range of 0 to 2 for Successors, then the source node, one level of predecessors, and two levels of successors are selected.

Controlling the View of a Network Analysis Object

You can control the view of a network by using the following controls:

Zoom	Zoom in and out at the location of the cursor by scrolling the mouse wheel.
	You can also enable the zoom control by selecting ![icon] from the object toolbar. Click ![icon] to zoom in, or ![icon] to zoom out.

Pan (scroll)	If the pan tool is selected, you can pan (scroll) the map by clicking the map and dragging it. If the pan tool is not selected, then click ⬚ in the object toolbar, and then select ✋ .

Using Maps with the Network Analysis Object

Sometimes you might want to add a background map to a Network Analysis object to better visualize the relationships geographically. Figure 8.8 shows some examples. In the customer analysis, you see the offices and their associated customers. You will need to add the geo-coordinates for each customer/office when you create the data. Then add custom geographic data item for each customer/office based on their postal codes.

Figure 8.8: Using Maps

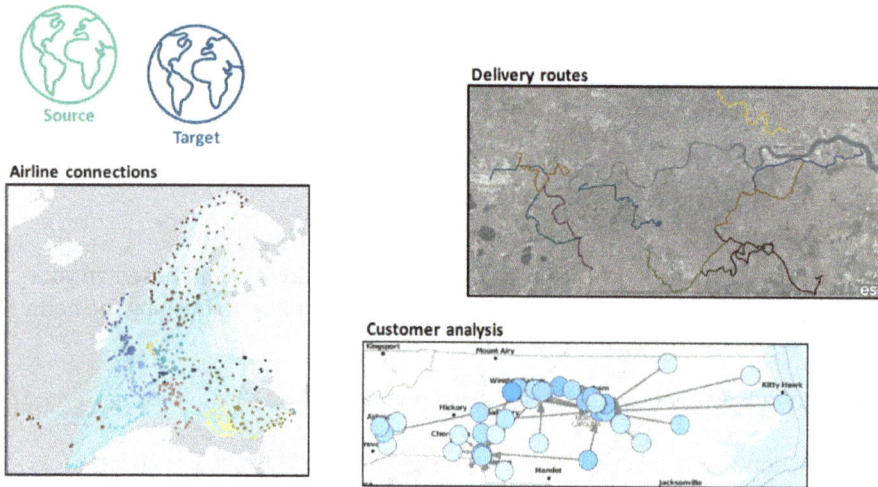

Note: For the network analysis object, you can assign the following centrality metrics to the **Color** role: Community, Disconnected Network ID, Betweenness Centrality, Closeness Centrality, Reach Centrality, and Stress Centrality. You can assign the following centrality metrics to the **Size** role: Betweenness Centrality, Closeness Centrality, Reach Centrality, and Stress Centrality.

For more information about the centrality metrics, see "Working with Network Analysis Objects: Network Metrics" in the *SAS Visual Analytics: Working with Report Content* documentation. Falko Schulz provides an in-depth look at the object in his Exploring Social Networks with SAS Visual Analytics post.

 Practice 8.1

1. Analyzing a Network Analysis Data Source
   a. Open the browser and sign in to SAS Viya.
   b. Open the **VA2-Practice4.2** report in the **Courses/YVA285/Advanced/Practices** folder.

c. Assign the following data items to the specified roles for the network analysis object:

Source	**from_loc**
Target	**to_loc**
Size	**MaxWind**
Color	**Category**

d. Modify options for the network analysis object:

Type	Ungrouped
Link Direction	Target
Map background	*<selected>*

e. Answer the following questions:

Which states did Hurricane Matthew hit in 2016? What was the maximum wind speed? How was Hurricane Matthew categorized?

Answer:

Which states did Hurricane Nicole hit in 2016? What was the maximum wind speed? How was Hurricane Nicole categorized?

Answer:

f. Save the report.

Alternate (Optional)

2. **Creating a Report Data View for Network Analysis**
   a. Open the browser and sign in to SAS Viya.
   b. Open the **VA2-Practice4.2 (Alternate)** report in the **Courses/YVA285/Advanced/Practices** folder.
   c. Create a new character data item, **from_loc**, that consists of the first portion of **From**.

   Hint: **From** is in the following format: *from_loc: from_lat, from_lon*. Make sure that the new data item consists of the values from the first character up to, but not including, the : (colon). Be aware that the length of the value is not consistent throughout the table.

   d. Create a new measure data item, **from_lat**, that consists of the middle portion of **From**.

   Hint: **From** is in the following format: *from_loc: from_lat, from_lon*. Make sure that the new data item consists of the values between the : (colon) to the , (comma). Be aware that the length of the value is not consistent throughout the table.

   Hint: The Parse operator (in the Text (simple) group) can be used to convert a character string to a numeric value.

   e. Create a new measure data item, **from_lon**, that consists of the last portion of **From**.

   Hint: **From** is in the following format: *from_loc: from_lat, from_lon*. Make sure that the new data item consists of the values after the , (comma) to the last character. Be aware that the length of the value is not consistent throughout the table.

Hint: The Parse operator (in the Text (simple) group) can be used to convert a character string to a numeric value.

f.   Hide the data item **From** from the Data pane.

g.   Create a new category data item, **Category**, by assigning the following labels to the values:

Category (label)	Type (value)
Hurricane	HU
Tropical	TD
	TS
	WV
Subtropical	SS
	SD
Extratropical	EX
Other	DB
	LO

h.   Save the data changes as a data view (**NA_HURRICANES_View**). Do *not* make the data view the default.

Note: A data view that is not specified as the default, can be applied to the CAS table after the table has been added to a report by clicking ⊞ (**Actions**) and selecting **Data views**. Multiple data views can be added to a table and are additive when applied, meaning each data view applied adds data changes to the report.

Note: An administrator has an option (**Shared data view**) that makes the view available to other users, not just the user who created the view.

i.   Save the report.

End of Practices

Chapter 9: Advanced Topics – Performing Path Analysis

9.1 Introduction

In some analytical projects, you might be interested in flows of data. This could be flows through steps in a process, flows through different loyalty levels, flows through pages in a website, or flows through product packages. Often, you want to see which path leads to some goal, like completion or buying a product. In this chapter, we will learn more about path analysis in Visual Analytics. Specifically, we will learn about the path analysis object and the data needed to create the graph. Then, we will describe how to add a path analysis object to a report.

9.2 Path Analysis Object

A path analysis object can be used to show flows of data from one event to another as a series of paths. Each path consists of linked nodes, which represent consecutive events in that path. The same event can appear in multiple nodes in the diagram, depending on their position in the path. The links between nodes can be sized either to represent the frequency of the path or the value of weight.

Figure 9.1: Objects – Analytics (Path)

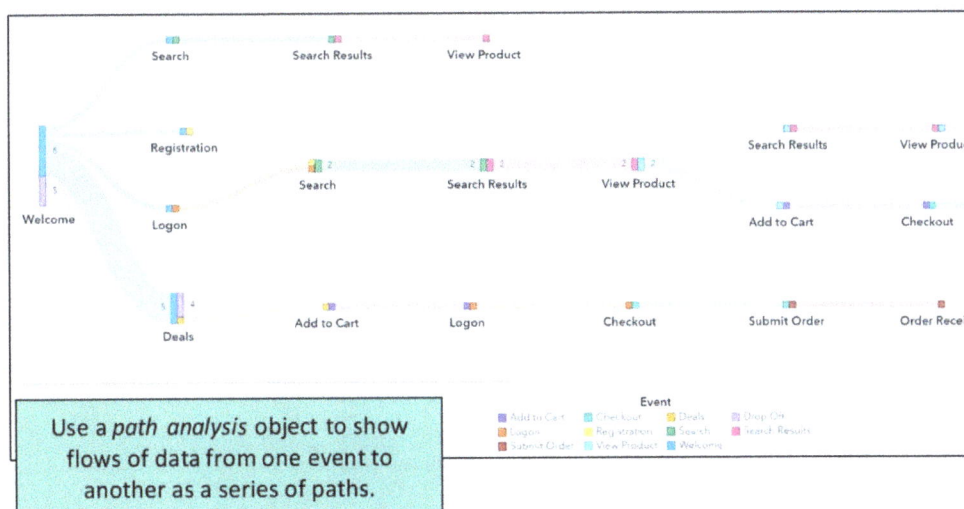

Use a *path analysis* object to show flows of data from one event to another as a series of paths.

Figure 9.2 shows some common examples. The customer journey example shows the web pages visited by customers who made a purchase. Notice that most visitors who purchase an item enter through the Welcome page. The most popular path, in terms of purchase amount, starts at the Welcome page then continues to the

Products page. We can also use path analysis to analyze the customer journey with regard to training courses. Notice, most customers start with the PG1 course. The most popular path, in terms of number of students, starts with PG1 then continues to PG2.

Another example explores the customer attrition, or customer churn, for a fictional internet service provider. In this example, we see all the paths that lead to a cancellation. Notice that most cancellations start with an outage.

Lastly, we can analyze the drug approval process for a pharmaceutical company. In this case, there is one main path; new drugs must go through a rigorous set of steps before they can be brought to the market. For this company, it seems like steps 1 and 2 (animals testing and the IND application) cause the most problems. We can use this information to refine our process so that more drugs reach the approval step. Links can be colored to show each path in a different color, each event in a different color, or to indicate drop offs (where one path ended, and other paths continued). Coloring links by path is useful if you have a small number of paths and you would like to follow each separately. In this example, we can see the web pages visited by customers who made a purchase.

Figure 9.2: Examples of Path Analysis

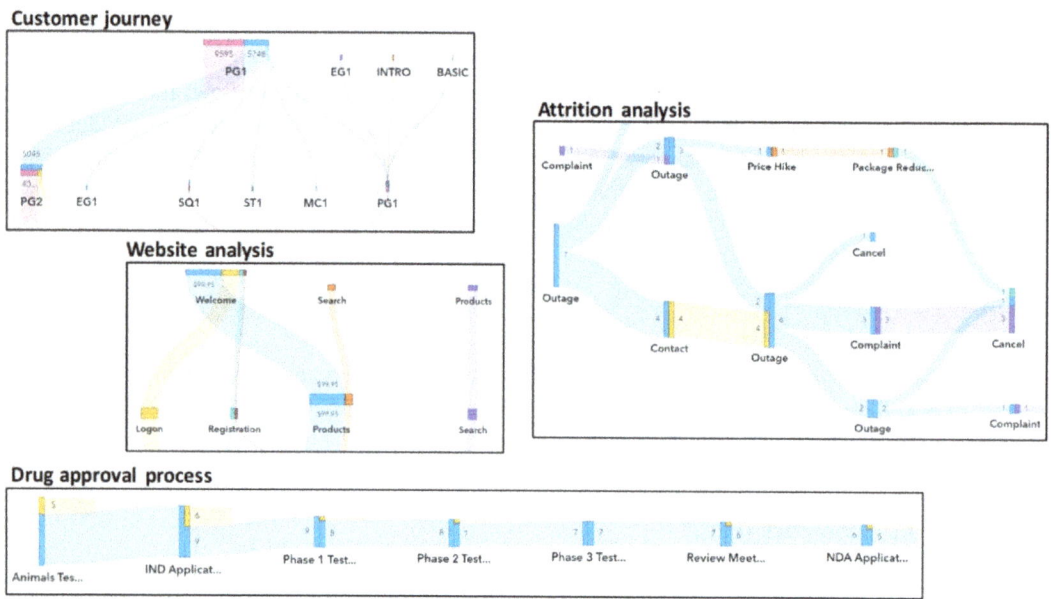

Each path has its own color and each link is sized by the purchase amount. Because each path is assigned a color, we can easily view one path from start to end. Coloring links by event makes it easier to visually compare the same event throughout the diagram. For example, we can analyze the customer journey with regard to training courses. In this diagram, each event has its own color and each link is sized by the number of students on that path. Because each event is assigned a color, we can easily see that PG1 appears in multiple places in this diagram; it's a popular course for our customers. Coloring links by drop off makes it easier to identify where paths frequently end. For example, we can analyze the drug approval process for a pharmaceutical company. In this case, there is one main path; new drugs must go through a rigorous set of steps before they can be brought to the market. Because the links are colored by drop off, we can easily see where in the process we have issues: steps 1 and 2. We can use this information to refine our process so that more drugs reach the approval step.

Figure 9.3: Path Analysis Link Color

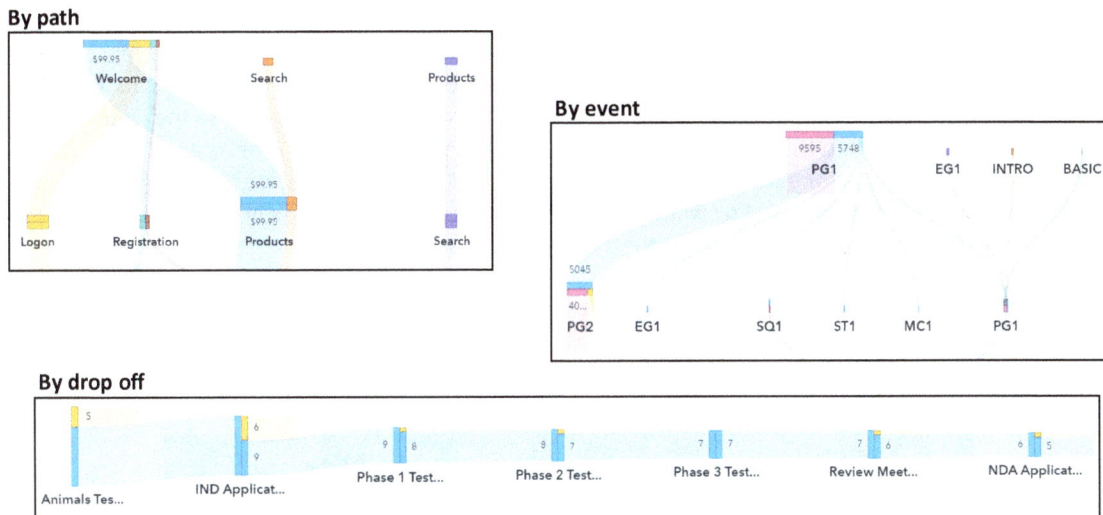

Data Roles for a Path Analysis Object

The basic data roles for a path analysis object are as follows:

Event — specifies a category whose values identify the events that are represented as nodes in the diagram.

Sequence order — specifies a datetime data item or a measure whose values identify the order of the events for each transaction.

Transaction identifier — specifies a data item whose values identify the transactions in the diagram.

Note: The paths in a path analysis object exclude any missing values in the data items that are assigned to the Event, Transaction identifier, or Sequence order role.

In addition to the basic data roles, you can specify the following role:

Weight — specifies a measure for the weight of each event in a transaction. The weight values for each transaction and for each event in a path are aggregated to determine the path weight.

Note: The measure that is assigned to the Weight role must have one of the following aggregation types: sum, average, minimum, or maximum.

Note: For a path analysis that is colored by event or by a drop-off link and where the Weight measure has an aggregation type other than sum, the links at each node overlap. This is because the link widths are not additive.

9.3 Path: Data Shape

As with the network analysis object, before creating the path analysis, you must ensure that the data is in the correct shape.

To create a path analysis object, the data source must have one row for each identifier-event pair. The identifier is a value that uniquely labels each person or object that we would like to analyze. The identifier could be a single student, a single customer, a unique visitor to the website, or a specific drug. The event represents the different nodes in the diagram. The events could be the classes a student takes, the incidents or interactions with a customer, the pages of a website, or the steps in the drug approval process. In addition, each row needs a datetime data item or measure that orders the events for any given identifier. This sequence order value will determine the order of events within any given path.

Optionally, you can have a measure that determines the link width for the object. This measure must be a positive number not equal to zero. If any paths do not have a value greater than zero, they are hidden in the path analysis object. In this example, the ID value is the identifier for each unique visitor to the website, the Page category is the event, and the Time measure is the sequence order. Think of Time as an ordinal value that simply orders the events for each unique visitor; the actual values 100, 101, and 102 have no meaning. The Purchase measure is the optional link width. When we look at only customers who have made a purchase, each link will be sized by the purchase amount for that specific identifier.

Figure 9.4: Path Analysis Data Shape

One row for each identifier-event pair

ID	Page	Time	Purchase
1	Welcome	100	.
1	Deals	101	.
1	Add to Cart	102	.
1	Checkout	103	.
1	Submit Order	104	.
1	Order Receipt	105	12.75

Identifier → (points to ID column)

Event → (points to Page column)

Note: If the link width in the path analysis object represents a weight value, then any paths that do not have a value greater than zero are hidden.

Business Scenario

The web design team at Orion Star has requested an analysis of visits to the website. They would like to see what types of pages were visited by customers and in what order. They also want to view pages visited by customers who bought a product. To create this report, we will need to add a path analysis object, simplify the graph by grouping related web pages, and filter the graph to only show customers who made a purchase.

Demo 9.1: Analyzing a Path Analysis Data Source

This demonstration illustrates how to create a path analysis object in a report.

1. From the browser window, sign in to SAS Viya.
2. In the upper left corner, click ☰ (**Show list of applications**) and select **Explore and Visualize**. SAS Visual Analytics appears.
3. Click **All Reports**.
   a. Navigate to the **Courses/YVA285/Advanced/Demos** folder.
   b. Double-click the **VA2-Demo5.1** report to open it.

4. View the structure of the table.

    a. At the top of the canvas, click the **Details** tab to view the page.

id ▲	page	time ▲	purchase
3	Welcome	120	.
3	Registration	121	.
3	Products	122	.
3	Music	123	.
3	Search	124	.
3	Search Results	125	.
3	Add to Cart	126	.
3	Add to Cart	127	.
3	Add to Cart	128	.
3	Add to Cart	129	.
3	Add to Cart	130	.
3	Checkout	131	.
3	Submit Order	132	.
3	Order Receipt	133	$6.50

This table contains details about visits to a website. Each row represents a page visit for each unique visitor.

The **id** field represents the unique visitors to the website, the **page** field represents the pages visited, and the **time** field represents the time at which each visitor visited each of the pages (ordinally).

The **purchase** field is missing if a visitor did not make a purchase on the visit. If the visitor did make a purchase, the field contains the purchase amount for the Order Receipt page.

    b. Click the **Path Analysis** tab.

5. Create a path analysis object.

    a. On the canvas, click the path analysis object to select it.

    b. In the right pane, click **Roles**.

    c. For the **Event** role, select **Add** ⇨ **page**.

    d. For the **Sequence order** role, select **Add** ⇨ **time**.

    e. For the **Transaction identifier** role, select **Add** ⇨ **id**.

    The path analysis object should resemble the following:

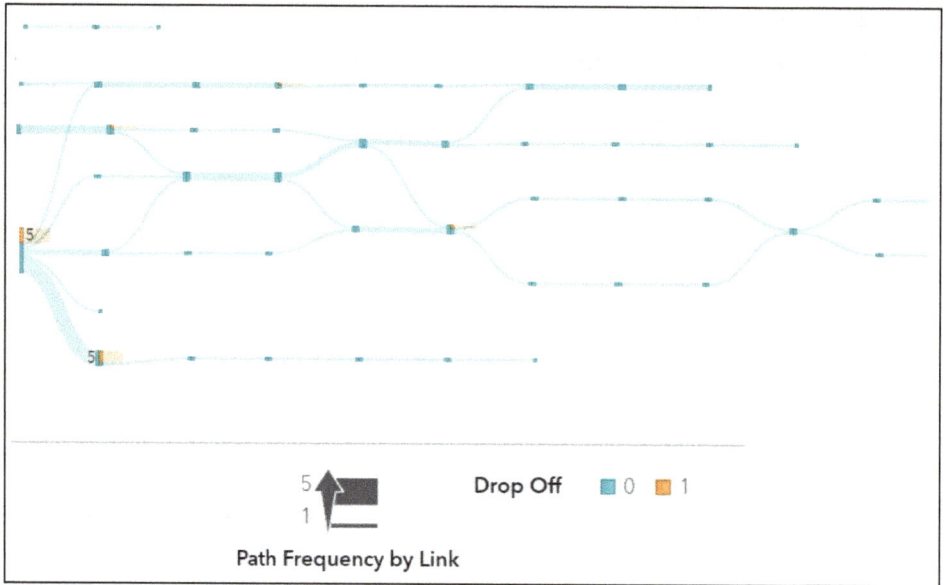

Path Frequency by Link

f. Scroll in to the beginning on the diagram (on the left) to view additional details.

    Note: Use the scroll wheel on your mouse to zoom on the path analysis object.

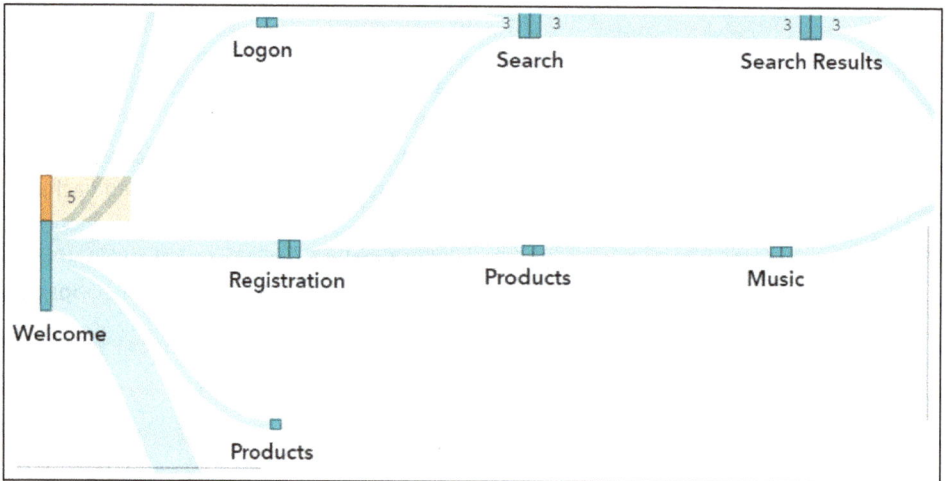

This indicates that of the 15 visitors who entered our website through the Welcome page, 5 immediately left the website. The remaining 10 continued using different paths.

g. Scroll to the right to view terminal nodes for the diagram.

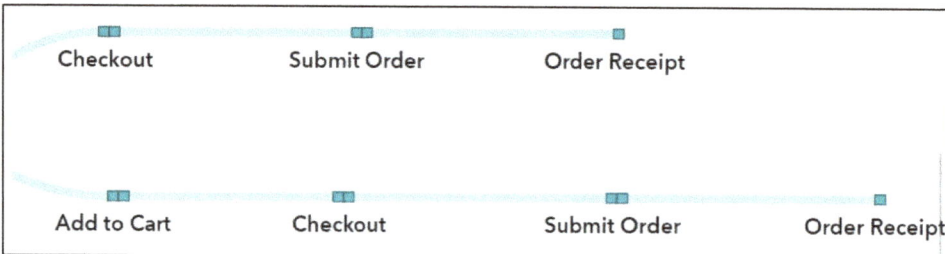

When a customer makes a purchase, he or she views specific pages: Add to Cart, Checkout, Submit Order, and Order Receipt.

We can group the nodes into main events to get a better view of the typical flow through our website. We can group these notes with a custom category.

6. View the custom category of grouped events.
    a. In the left pane, click **Data**.
    b. In the Category group, right-click **Grouped Pages** and select **Edit**.

       The Value Groups area should resemble the following:

       Value Groups

       ∨ Buy

       ☐ Add to Cart
       ☐ Checkout
       ☐ Order Receipt
       ☐ Submit Order

       ∨ Search

       ☐ Search
       ☐ Search Results

       ∨ Products

       ☐ Books
       ☐ Deals
       ☐ Music
       ☐ Products
       ☐ View Product

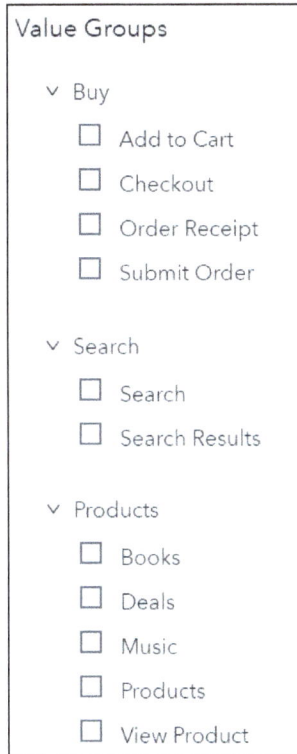

       Note: You might need to scroll down to see all the values.

    c. In the Remaining Values section (at the bottom of the window), verify that **Show as is** is selected.

       Remaining Values:

       ⦿ Show as is ◯ Show as missing ◯ Group as: Other

    d. Click **Cancel** to close the custom category without saving any changes.
7. Modify roles for path analysis object.
    a. In the canvas, select the path analysis object to make it active, if necessary.
    b. In the right pane, click **Roles**.
    c. For the **Event** role, select **page ⇨ Grouped Pages**.

       The path analysis object is updated to use the new custom category:

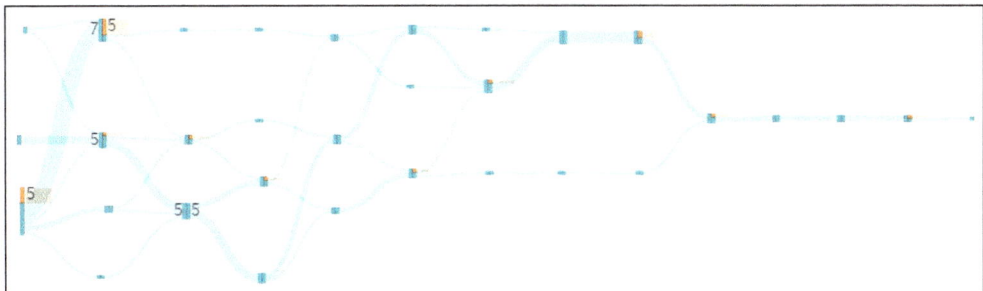

8. Modify options for the path analysis object.

     In the right pane, click **Options**.

     a. In the Path Analytics group, for the **Link color** field, select **Path**.

     The path analysis object should resemble the following:

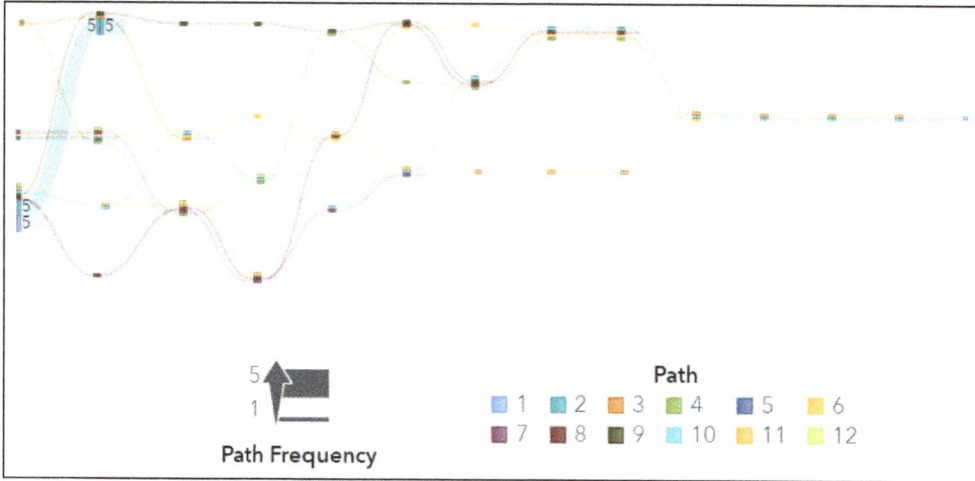

     Each unique path now has a specific color.

     b. In the legend, click **path 6**.

     The path is highlighted in the path analysis object.

     c. Scroll in and view the end of the path.

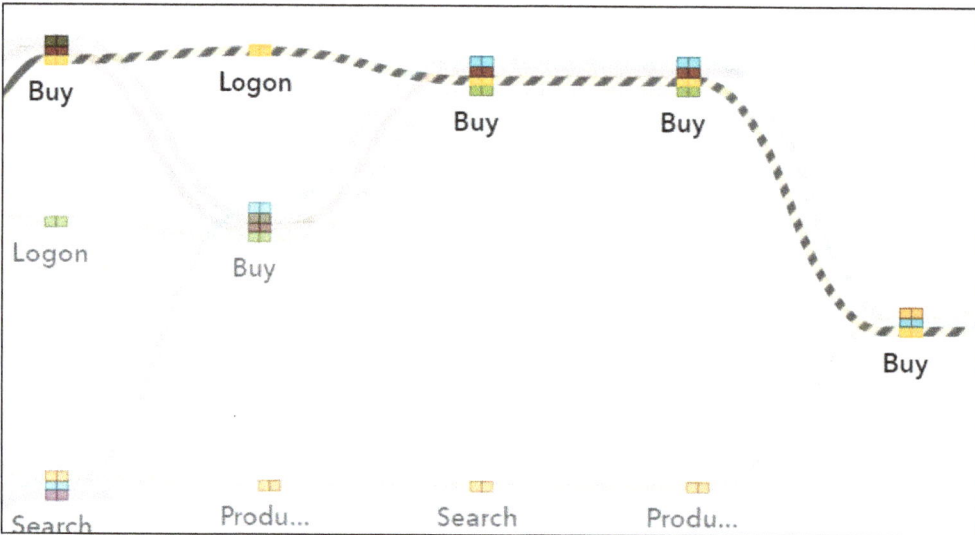

     Because a visitor must view specific pages to purchase a product, this path contains subsequent nodes with the same value.

d. In the Options pane, in the Path Analytics group, select **Compress**.

The path analysis object is updated to combine duplicate nodes.

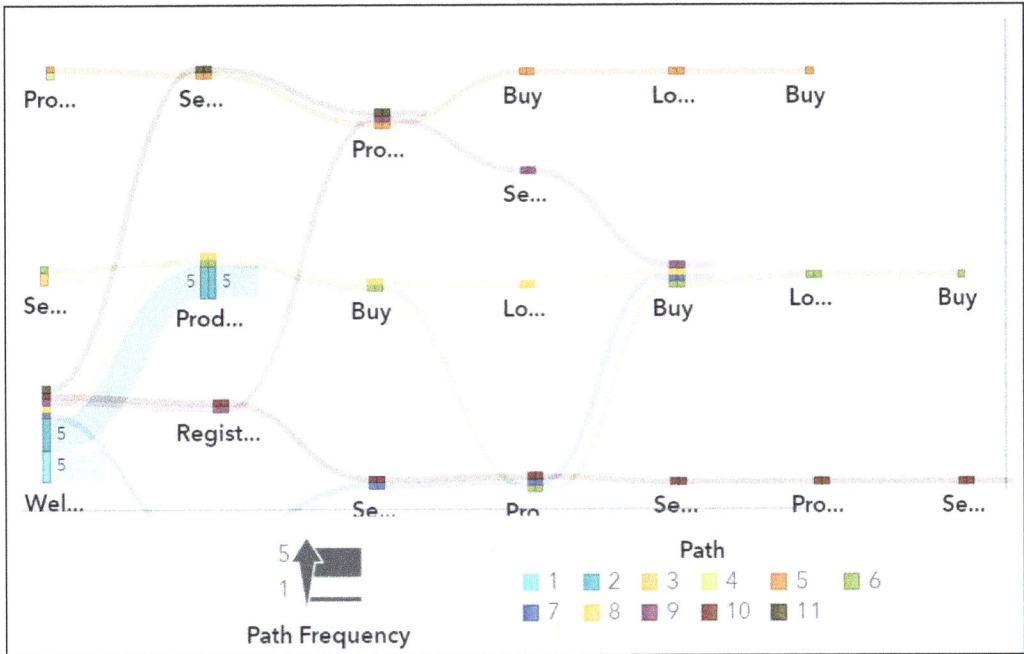

e. In the lower right corner of the object, place your mouse pointer on (i).

> An artificial sequence order was generated for 9 paths that contains simultaneous events.

When we compress the path analysis, similar events are grouped together.

f. On the Options pane, in the Path Display group, select **Vertical layout**.

The orientation of the path analysis object is updated.

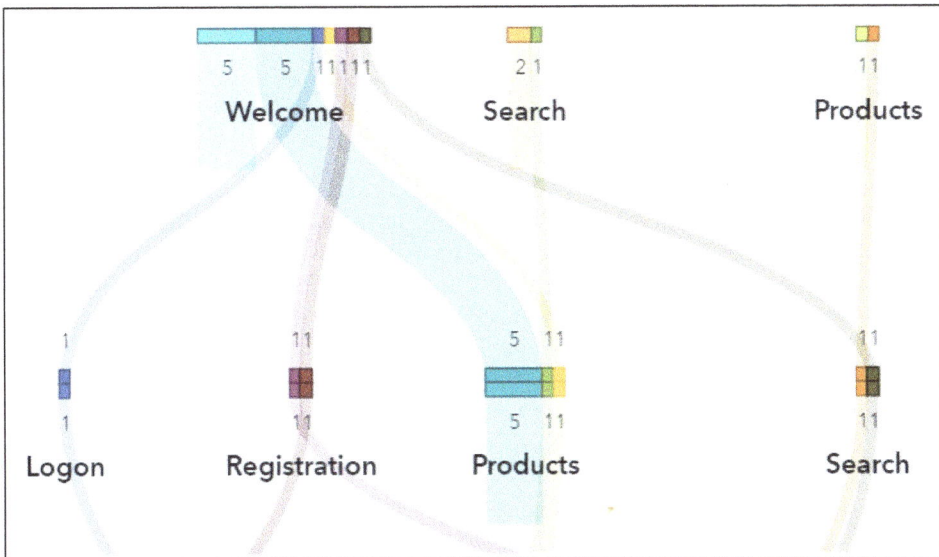

9. View paths for customers who have made a purchase.

a. In the path analysis object, scroll to the bottom and select a terminal **Buy** node.

b. Right-click the node and select New path filter from selection ⇨ Include only ⇨ Paths containing the selected events on any node.

A note is displayed.

> Your selection has been converted to a filter.   ✕

c. In the right pane, click **Filters**.

A new path filter condition was created and added to the path analysis object.

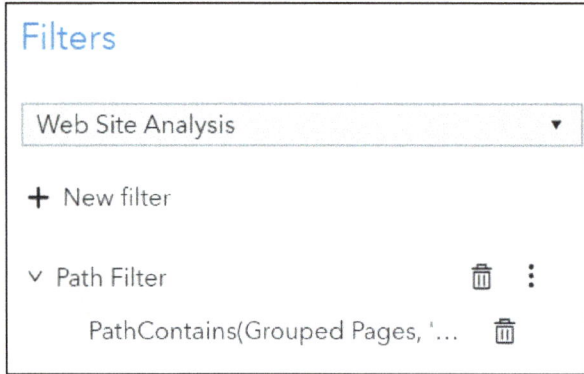

The path analysis object should resemble the following:

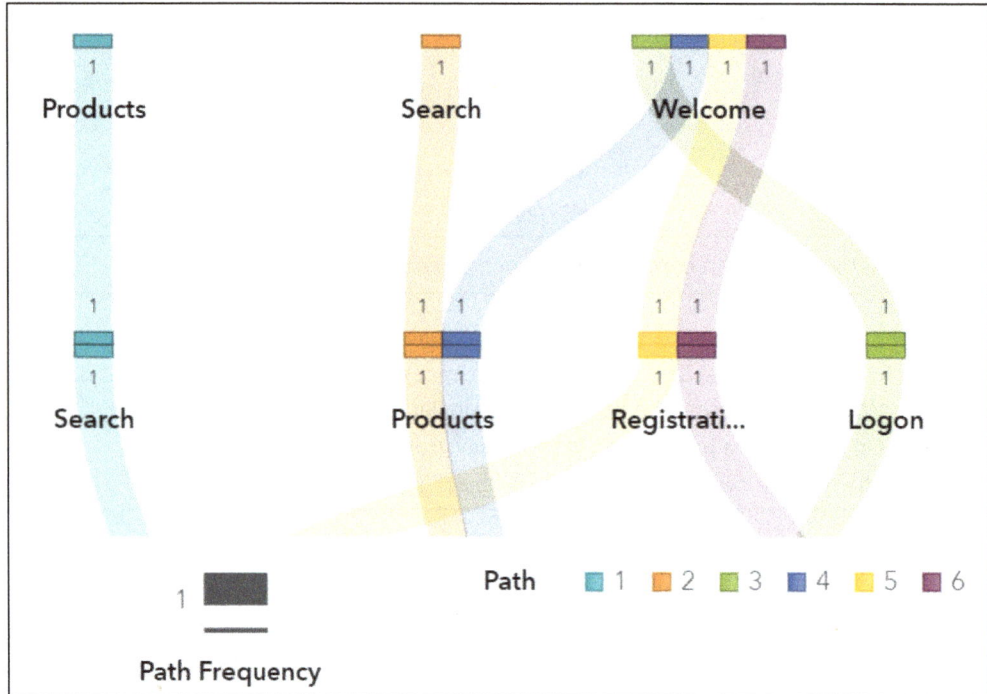

Because the path analysis object shows only those paths where a customer made a purchase, we can now size each path by the purchase amount.

d. In the right pane, click **Roles**.

e.   For the **Weight** role, select **Frequency** ⇨ **purchase**.

Each path is now sized by the purchase amount.

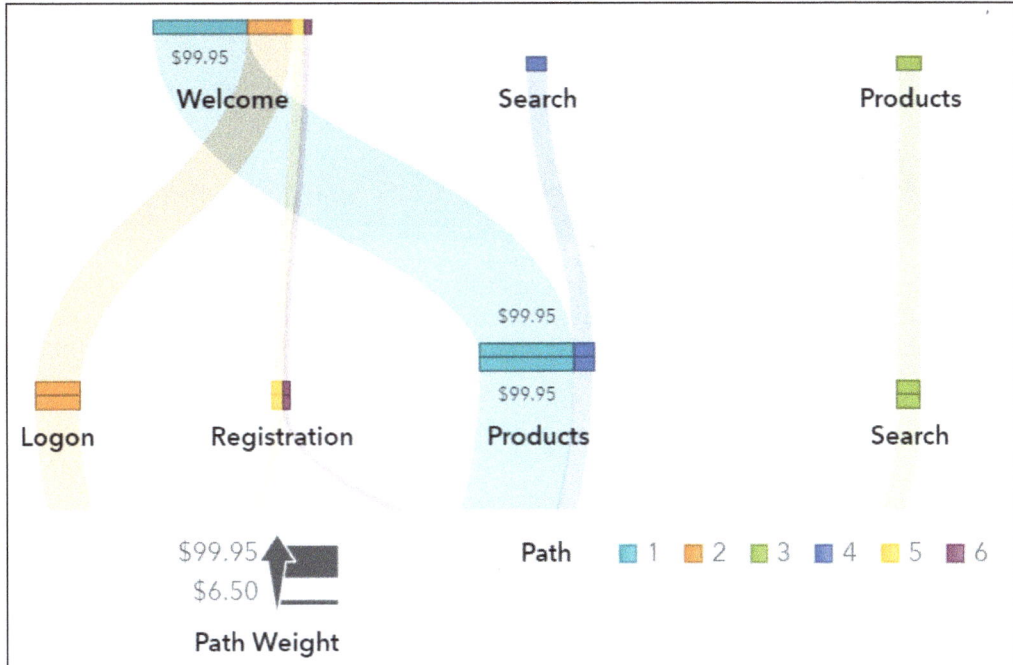

10. Create a visualization for all visitors who started on the Welcome page.

a.   In the path analysis object, select the **Welcome** node.

b.   Right-click in the path analysis object and select **New object from selection** ⇨ **Include only** ⇨ **Selected full paths**.

c.   Drag the list table to the right of the path analysis object.

The list table should resemble the following:

Grouped Pages ▲	time	id	purchase
Buy	746	9	$47.25
Buy	1036	3	$6.50
Buy	642	6	$12.50
Buy	1057	17	$99.95
Logon	263	17	.
Logon	181	9	.
Products	245	3	.

This list table shows details about customers who made purchases and entered the website through the Welcome page. We would like to see purchase amount by customer.

d.   In the canvas, verify that the list table is selected.

e.   In the right pane, click **Roles**.

f.   For the **Columns** role, right-click **Grouped Pages** and select **Remove Grouped Pages**.

g.   For the **Columns** role, right-click **time** and select **Remove time**.

h. Right-click the list table and select **Change List table** to ⇨ **Bar chart** (recommended). The bar chart should resemble the following:

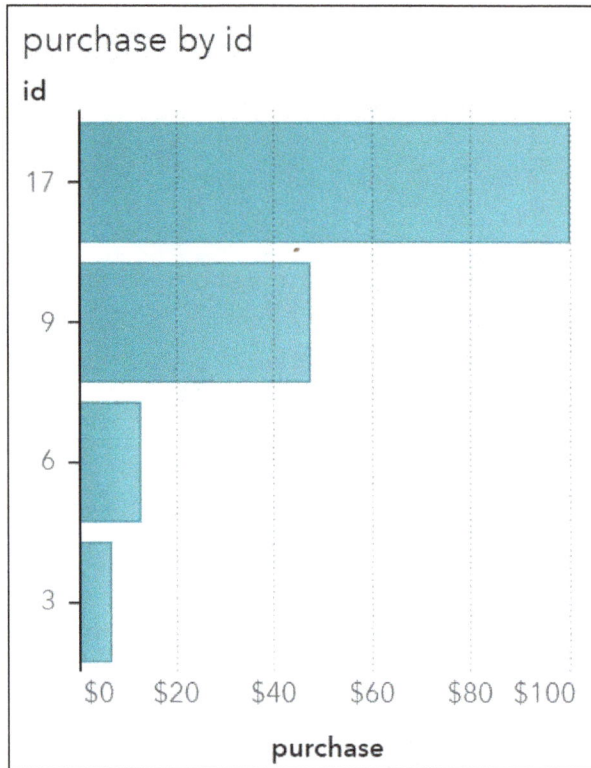

purchase by id

id

The bar chart now shows the total purchase amount by customers who entered on the Welcome page. Total purchase amounts span from $6.50 to $99.95.

11. Save the report.

End of Demonstration

Practice 9.1

1. **Analyzing a Path Analysis Data Source**
    a. Open the browser and sign in to SAS Viya.
    b. Open the **VA2-Practice5.1** report in the **Courses/YVA285/Advanced/Practices** folder.
    c. View data item properties and answer the following question:
        How many unique courses did students attend?
        Answer:
    d. Assign the following data items to the specified roles for the path analysis object:

Event	Course Code
Sequence order	Event Delivered (End) Date
Transaction identifier	Student ID

e. Answer the following question:

    What information is displayed when you place your mouse pointer on ⓘ in the lower right corner of the object? What do you think this means?

    Answer:

f. Modify options for the path analysis object to color each link by event and to show only the top 20 paths. Also change the display to a vertical layout.

g. Answer the following questions:

    With which course do a majority of students begin?

    Answer:

    Of those students who start with PG1, how many have not taken another class?

    Answer:

    Of those students who start with PG1, what is the next course that most are likely to take? How many students take this course?

    Answer:

    Are there any students who take PG1 twice? How many students do this? Why might this be the case?

    Answer:

h. Save the report.

    End of Practices

Chapter 10: Advanced Topics – Performing Text Analytics

10.1 Introduction

When thinking about analyzing data, you usually think of structured tables; data organized into rows and columns. With text analytics, however, it is possible to analyze unstructured columns of text data as well. This could be free-form data like text in comment fields, customer complaints, movie reviews, job descriptions, book summaries, or the contents of health records. In this chapter, we will look at text analysis in Visual Analytics. Specifically, we will learn about the text topics object, the data needed to create the analysis, and how text analysis and sentiment analysis work. Then, we will add a text topics object to a report.

Figure 10.1: Objects - Analytics (Text Topics)

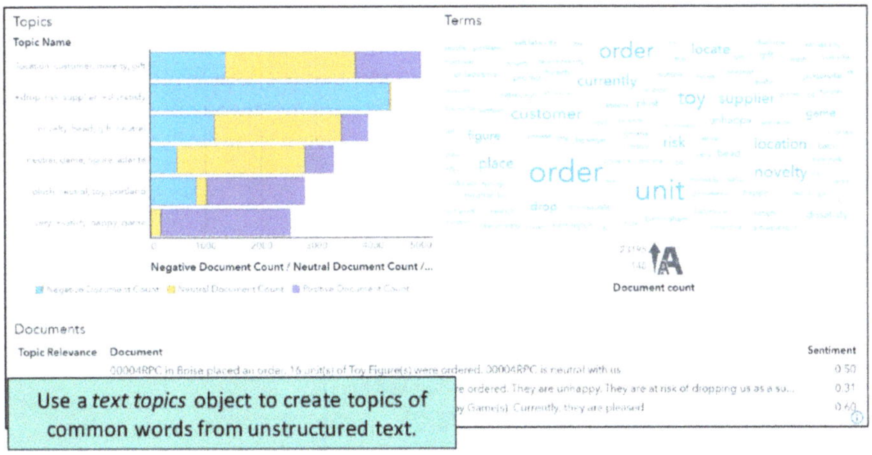

Use a *text topics* object to create topics of common words from unstructured text.

10.2 Text Topics Object

A text topics object displays a set of words from a character data item (unstructured text). For the text topics object, this column of unstructured text is referred to as a *document collection*. The size of each word in the cloud indicates the importance (topic term weight) of the word. A text topics object analyzes each value in a document collection as a text document that can contain multiple words. Words that often appear together in the document collection are identified as *topics* and displayed in a bar chart. For the selected topic, the text topics object displays the terms with the greatest topic term weight values. The topic term weight indicates the importance of the term within the topic. For a selected term, the table lists all documents which contain that term. A text topics object can also display whether the documents in a topic express positive, negative, or neutral sentiment.

Words are typically sized based on the importance of the word. However, the length of the word and the size of the letters that make up the word can make a single word look more (or less) important than an equally sized word.

Text analytics can be used to analyze any unstructured text: customer reviews of products, posts and comments on Facebook, tweets from Twitter, news headlines, or even job descriptions to determine which skills are in demand.

To enable text topics, you must set a unique row identifier for your data source (a data item that contains a unique value for each row of your data source). Depending on the number of rows in your data source and the length of the values in your document collection, it might require a significant amount of time to display a text topics object.

Note: The data source for a text topics object must have UTF-8 encoding. If the data source has a different encoding, then some characters might not be displayed properly, and an error message might appear.

Note: Text topics objects in SAS Visual Analytics use a different algorithm than SAS Text Miner and SAS Visual Text Analytics. Your results might be different from the results that SAS Text Miner and SAS Visual Text Analytics produce.

Note: You can export model score code from the Text topics object by right-clicking the object and selecting **Export Model**. This creates a SAS program that includes all data items used by the model and can be applied to new data sets in a SAS programming environment.

Note: If Visual Text Analytics is licensed at your site, you have additional options for contextual extraction, sentiment analysis, and categorization in Model Studio. For example, you can use Visual Text Analytics to drop terms that are not useful for analysis, create a custom sentiment model, and create custom categories from selected topics.

Sentiment Analysis

Sentiment Analysis is used to categorize documents as generally positive, neutral, or negative. This can be very useful in determining the actions needed to address any issues that are uncovered. For example, while analyzing customer reviews of products, you notice that documents are mostly negative. Text analysis can help you determine if the negative reviews stem from low quality, delivery issues, or some other mitigating factor.

Figure 10.2: Sentiment Analysis

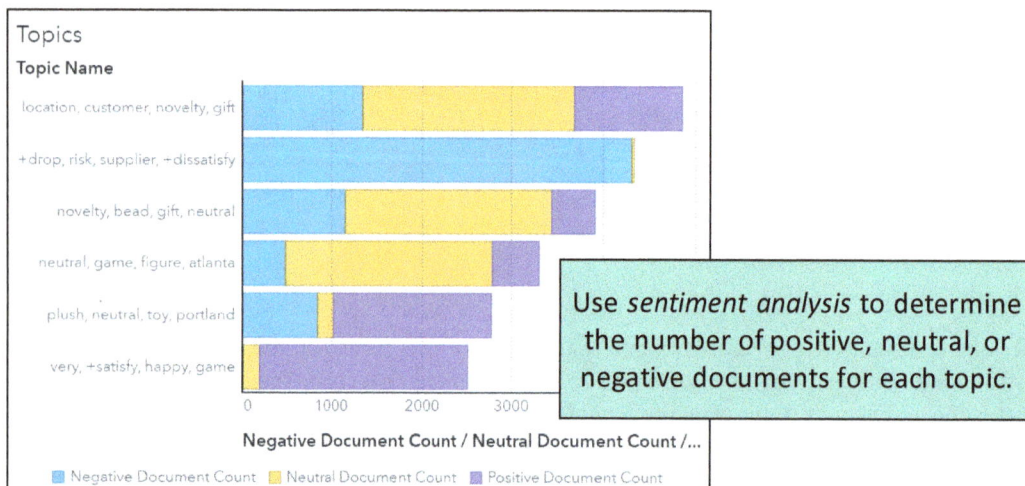

Activity 10.1

Sign in to SAS Viya.

Edit the **VA2-Activity6.01** report (in **Courses/YVA285/Advanced** folder).

Click **Assign Data**. What three things are required for the text topics object?

10.3 Data Shape

To create a text topics object, the data source must have a data item that contains unstructured text (the document collection). In addition, each document must be associated with a unique value (the unique row identifier). If your data source does not contain a unique row identifier, you can create one in Data Studio by adding a unique identifier transform to your plan. In this example, Order is the unique row identifier and OrderNote is the document collection. When we perform text analytics, OrderNote will be analyzed to determine topics (or words that often appear together).

Figure 10.3: Text Analytics - Data Shape

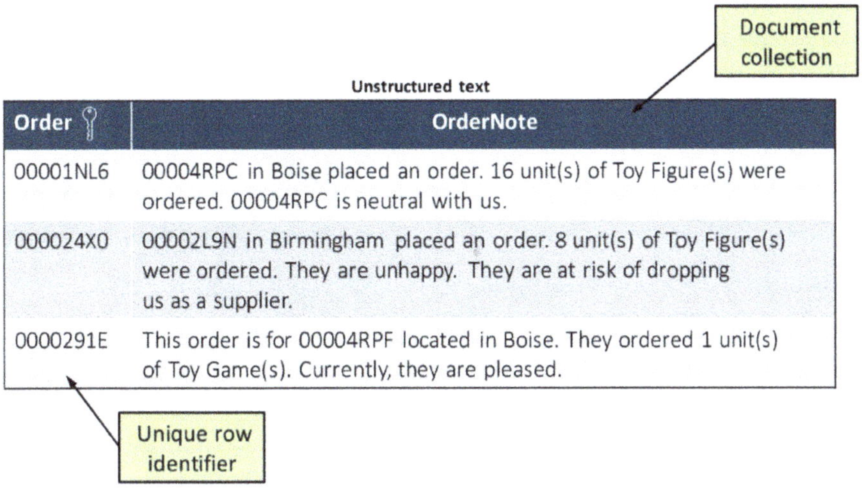

If your data source does not contain a unique row identifier, you can create one using the unique identifier transform, in the Row Transforms group, in SAS Data Studio. For more information about the unique identifier transform, see "Generating a Unique Identifier" in the *SAS Data Studio: User's Guide*.

10.4 Text Analytics: How It Works

You might be wondering how text analytics actually works. Up to this point, it sounds a bit like magic. There are, however, a defined set of steps that are followed whenever a document collection is analyzed. First, each document of unstructured text is parsed into individual terms. Then, these terms are compared with a stop list. A stop list is simply a table of common words that are ignored during text analytics; this is a great way to filter out noise from your analysis. If terms are found in the stop list, they are removed from the analysis. Any remaining terms are then analyzed to determine common topics (or terms that tend to show up together in documents).

Figure 10.4: How Text Analytics Works

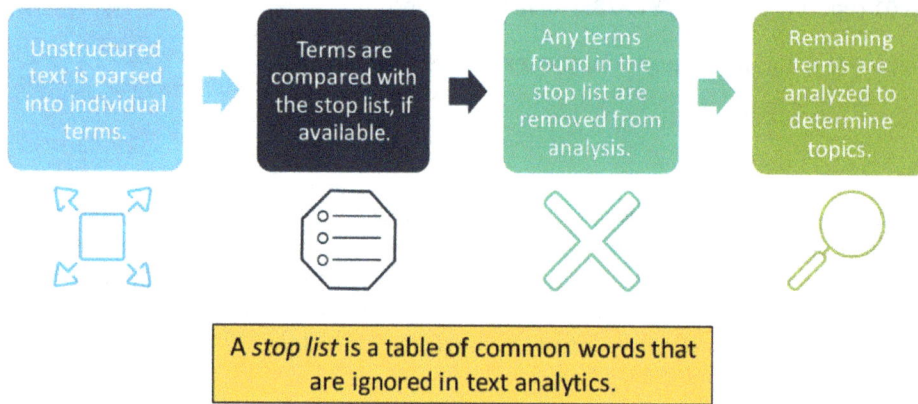

| Unstructured text is parsed into individual terms. | → | Terms are compared with the stop list, if available. | → | Any terms found in the stop list are removed from analysis. | → | Remaining terms are analyzed to determine topics. |

A *stop list* is a table of common words that are ignored in text analytics.

Note: If the stop list is not loaded when text analytics is performed, it will be loaded automatically using just-in-time loading.

Table 10.1 lists common phrases used with text analytics.

Table 10.1: Common Phrases

Phrase	Description
Documents	Unstructured text. These are displayed in the documents list table and are a single row in the data source.
Terms	Words or phrases. These are displayed in the terms word cloud.
Topics	Words that often appear together in documents. These are displayed in the topics bar chart.
Topic term weight	Indicates the importance of the word in the topic.
Term roles	Identifies terms by their parts of speech (noun, verb, adjective), identifies groups of nouns as single terms, and identifies text entities (names, address, phone numbers).
Stem words	Different forms of a given word. For example, *sell* is the stem word of the following: *sell, sells, selling, sold*.

Sentiment Analysis Steps

Adding sentiment analysis requires additional steps. First, all relevant terms are scored for each document. Positive words (like happy, satisfied, wonderful) are given a score of 1. Neutral words (like order, neutral, class) are given a score of 0.5. Negative words (like dissatisfy, risk, angry) are given a score of 0. Scores are then averaged for each document to determine the overall sentiment. A total sentiment score above 0.5 represents a positive document, equal to 0.5 represents a neutral document, and below 0.5 represents a negative document.

Figure 10.5: Sentiment Analysis Scoring

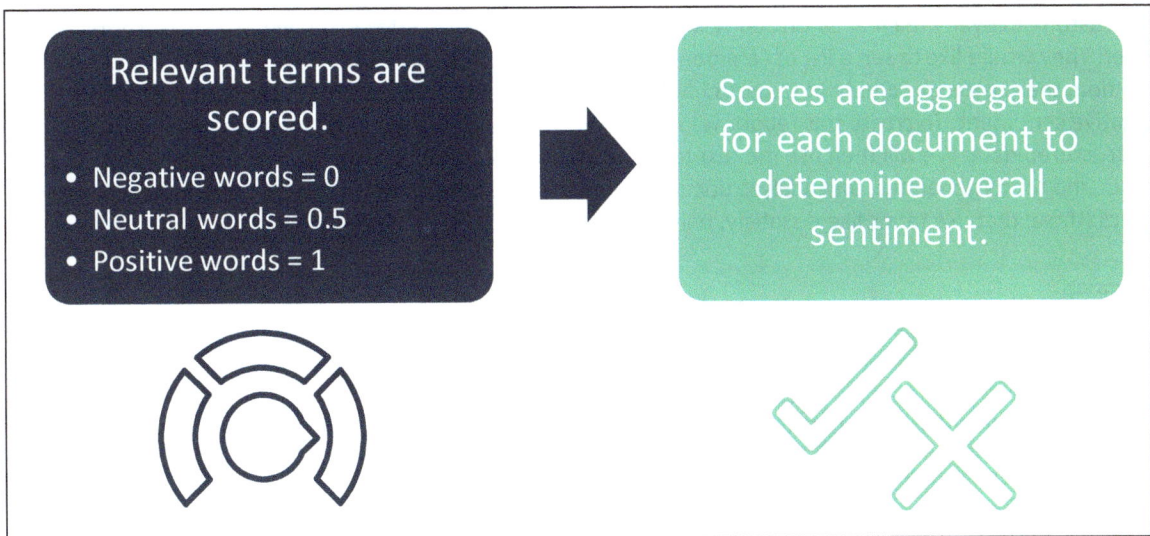

A total sentiment score above 0.5 represents a positive sentiment, equal to 0.5 represents a neutral sentiment, and below 0.5 represents a negative sentiment.

10.5 Derive Topics

After you have completed text analytics, you can create derived data items to further analyze the topics generated. Derived data items can be created from topics and relevance. For derived relevance, the value represents the relevance of the document in that topic. For derived topics, the value is either 1 (if the document is included in the topic) or 0 (if the document is not included in the topic). This derived topic can then be used with other data items in the table to get a better understanding of the subgroup for the topic. For example, we can create a derived topic from the drop, risk, supplier, dissatisfy topic to analyze the locations of customers that have order notes that fall in that topic. We can also use this information to analyze the products, facilities, or manufacturing batches that have negative orders. These derived topics can really help us pinpoint the cause of the dissatisfaction: is it the product itself, the facility that ships the product, or some other factor?

Figure 10.6: Text Analytics Derive Topics

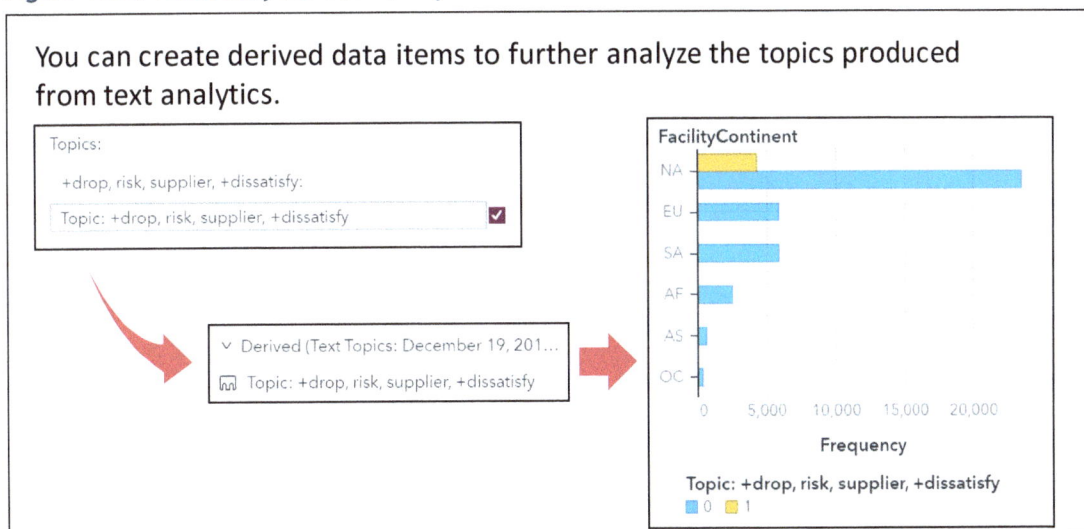

The value of the derived topic is either 1 (if the document is included in the topic) or 0 (if the document is not included in the topic). In addition, you can derive a data item that contains the relevance of the document in the topic.

Business Scenario

The Customer Loyalty team at Orion Star has requested an analysis of notes taken when a customer places an order. They would like to see a list of common topics to determine if there are any reoccurring issues. In addition, the Customer Complaint Department is interested in viewing orders that produced notes with a negative sentiment. To create this report, we need to add a new data source that contains a column of unstructured data. We will then use the text topics object to analyze this unstructured text, view the list of topics and terms generated, and analyze document sentiment. Specifically, we will focus on mostly negative topics (those that use terms like dissatisfy, unhappy, drop, and risk).

Demo 10.1: Analyzing a Text Analysis Data Source

This demonstration illustrates how to create a text topics object in a report.

1. From the browser window, sign in to SAS Viya.
2. In the upper left corner, click ▤ (**Show list of applications**) and select **Explore and Visualize**. SAS Visual Analytics appears.
3. Click **All Reports**.
   a. Navigate to the **Courses/YVA285/Advanced/Demos** folder.
   b. Double-click the **VA2-Demo6.1** report to open it.
4. View the structure of the table.
   a. At the top of the canvas, click the **Details** tab.

Order	▲ OrderNote
00001NL6	00004RPC in Boise placed an order. 16 unit(s) of Toy Figure(s) were ordered. 00004RPC is neutral with us.
000024X0	00002L9N in Birmingham placed an order. 8 unit(s) of Toy Figure(s) were ordered. They are unhappy. They are at risk of dropping us as a supplier.
0000291E	This order is for 00004RPF located in Boise. They ordered 1 unit(s) of Toy Game(s). Currently, they are pleased.
00003MNR	000052GF in Pittsburgh placed an order. 5 unit(s) of Toy Figure(s) were ordered. They are dissatisfied. We are at risk of being dropped as their supplier.
00003NDE	
00003NFX	000052C0 in Pittsburgh placed an order. 4 unit(s) of Toy Figure(s) were ordered. This customer is at risk.
00003NG3	Customer: 000052GL, Location: Pittsburgh. 1 unit(s) of Toy Plush(s) were ordered. Currently, they are unhappy. They are at risk of dropping us as a supplier.

   This table contains details about orders. Each row represents an order placed by a customer. The **Order** field represents the unique order number, and the **OrderNote** field contains a comment about the order (if any).
   b. Click the **Text Topics** tab.
5. View a text topics object.
   a. In the left pane, click **Data**.

   ∨ Category

   ⌂ FacilityContinent - 6

   ⚷ Order - 43K

   ⌂ OrderNote - 23K

The **Order** column is specified as a unique identifier column for the text topics object.

b. On the canvas, click the text topics object to select it, if necessary.

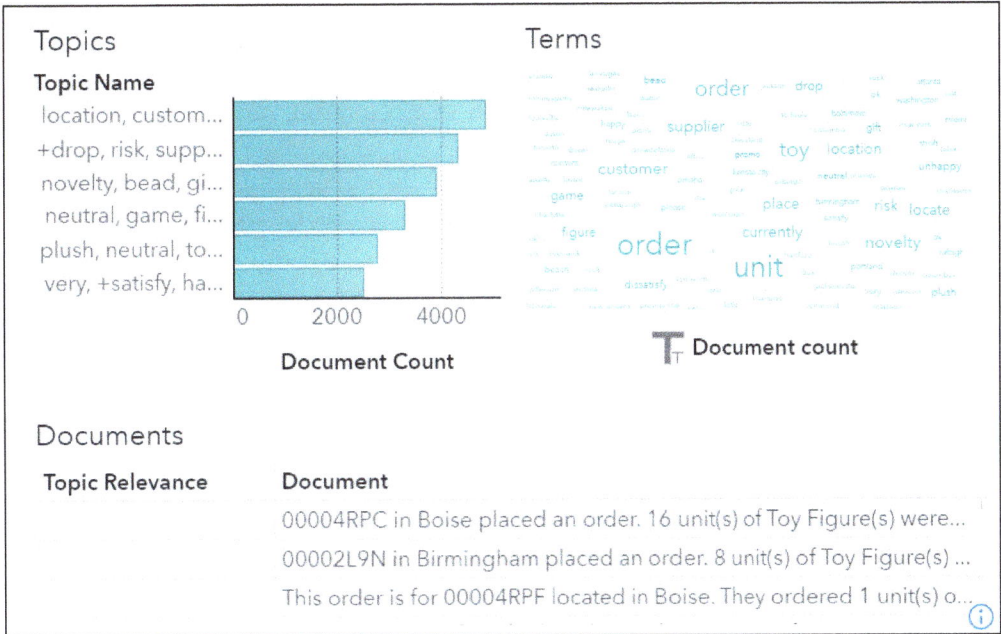

Topics

Topic Name

location, custom...
+drop, risk, supp...
novelty, bead, gi...
neutral, game, fi...
plush, neutral, to...
very, +satisfy, ha...

0   2000   4000

Document Count

Terms

order drop
supplier
customer toy location
game
figure
order currently risk locate
novelty
unit
plush

Document count

Documents

Topic Relevance   **Document**

00004RPC in Boise placed an order. 16 unit(s) of Toy Figure(s) were...

00002L9N in Birmingham placed an order. 8 unit(s) of Toy Figure(s) ...

This order is for 00004RPF located in Boise. They ordered 1 unit(s) o...

The bar chart in the upper left corner shows the topics identified from the **OrderNote** field and displays the document count for each topic.

The word cloud in the upper right corner shows the relevant terms for all documents.

The table at the bottom shows the relevance and document details.

c. In the lower right corner of the text topics object, place your mouse pointer on ⓘ .

> Only the top 1000 documents have been returned.

d. In the upper right corner of the text topics object, click 🡕 (**Maximize**) to view details.

e. At the bottom of the object, verify that **Topics** is selected for the details table.

Topics Terms Text Topics Summary	
Topic Name	**Document Count**
location, customer, novelty, gift	4859
+drop, risk, supplier, +dissatisfy	4331
novelty, bead, gift, neutral	3913
neutral, game, figure, atlanta	3301
plush, neutral, toy, portland	2777

Each topic is listed, as well as the number of documents in that topic.

Note: Additional details, such as the number of negative, neutral, and positive documents, are displayed if sentiment analysis is enabled.

Topics Terms Text Topics Summary				
Topic Name	**Negative Document...**	**Neutral Document...**	**Positive Document...**	**Document Count**
location, customer, novelty, gift	1357	2338	1164	4859
+drop, risk, supplier, +dissatisfy	4306	25	0	4331
novelty, bead, gift, neutral	1160	2280	473	3913
neutral, game, figure, atlanta	485	2302	514	3301
plush, neutral, toy, portland	839	184	1754	2777

f. In the details table, click **Terms**.

Topics Terms Text Topics Summary		
Term	**Document count**	**Role**
order	23195	Verb
unit	23195	Noun
order	15340	Noun
toy	13650	Proper noun
customer	9602	Noun

All terms are listed, as well as the number of documents in which the term appears.

g. In the details table, click **Text Topics Summary** to view details about text topics.

> Topics   Terms   Text Topics Summary
>
> **Text Topics Summary**
>
> The text topics object displays a set of words from a document collection, in this case OrderNote. The size of each term in the cloud indicates its importance. Text topics analyzes each value in the document collection as text containing multiple words. Text topics identifies words used throughout the document collection as relevant terms (omitting common words such as "the"). It defines terms that appear together often in documents as topics. With no selected topic, the word cloud displays the most common terms across the document collection. For example, "order" is the most frequently used term in this document collection.

h. In the upper right corner of the text topics object, click ⬒ (**Restore**).

6. Modify options for the text topics object.

a. In the right pane, click **Options**.

b. For the General group, select **Analyze document sentiment**.

The bar chart updates to show each topic grouped by sentiment.

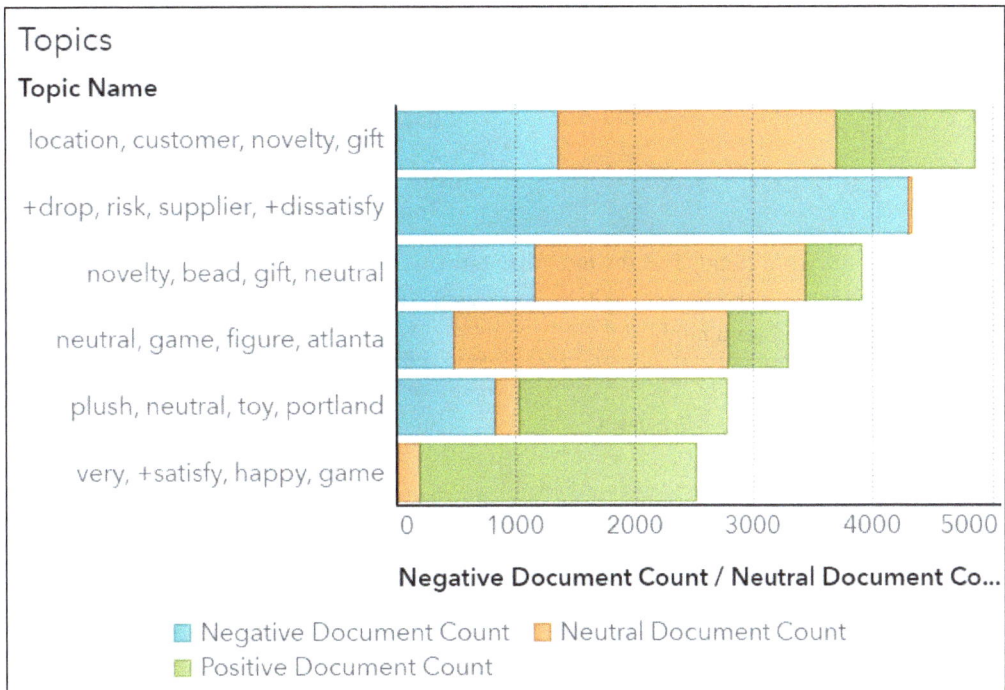

In sentiment analysis, each word in the document is assigned a value based on the connotation of that word. For example, a word like *bad* evokes a negative connotation, whereas a word like *good* evokes a positive connotation. The values are aggregated for the entire document to determine a sentiment score for the document.

A sentiment score of less than 0.5 indicates a negative document, a score of 0.5 indicates a neutral document, and a score greater than 0.5 indicates a positive document.

7. View details about a topic.

   a. In the bar chart, click the bar for the **+drop, risk, supplier, +dissatisfy** topic.

   The word cloud updates to show terms in that topic.

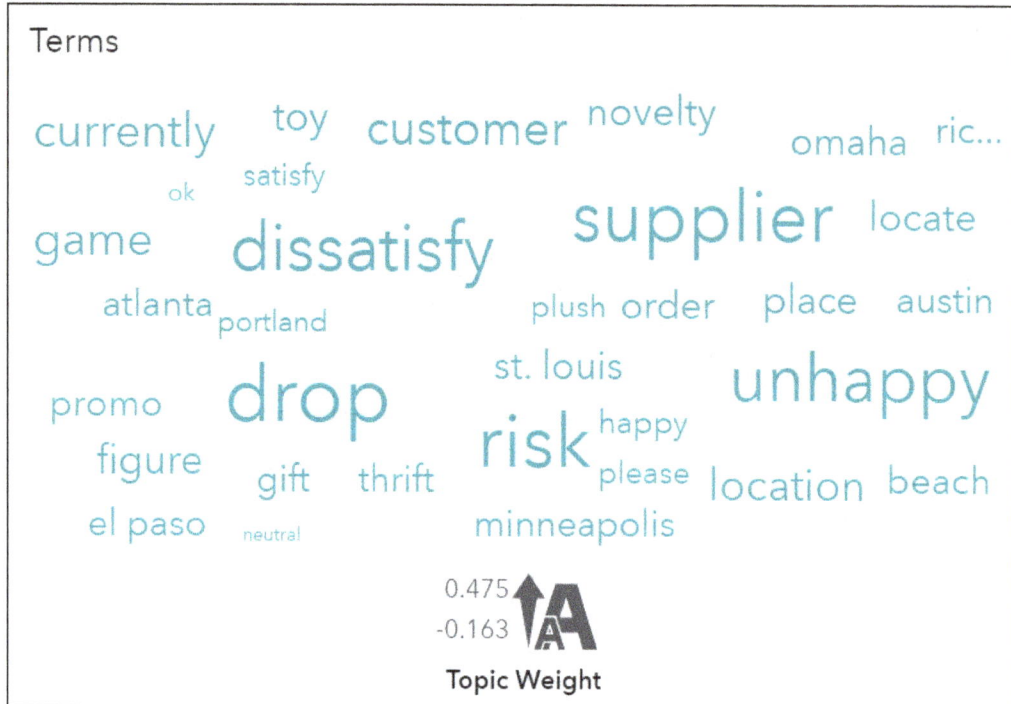

```
Terms

currently      toy   customer   novelty              omaha   ric...
         ok    satisfy
game      dissatisfy              supplier  locate
   atlanta  portland              plush order   place  austin
                                  st. louis
promo    drop              risk  happy      unhappy
figure      gift   thrift        please  location  beach
el paso   neutral          minneapolis

         0.475 ▲A
        -0.163 ▼A

         Topic Weight
```

   b. In the word cloud, click the **dissatisfy** term.

   The table at the bottom updates to show the documents that contain that term and their associated sentiment.

Documents		
Topic Relevance	Document	Sentiment
0.5974	Customer: 000019XB, Location: Raleigh. 3 unit(s) of Toy Game(s) were or...	0.31
0.5949	Customer: 00001OVK, Location: St. Louis. They ordered 4 unit(s) of Toy Fi...	0.31
0.5949	Customer: 00001OYW, Location: St. Louis. They ordered 7 unit(s) of Toy F...	0.31

   We might want to provide some context to these negative documents. We can do this by adding additional data items to the text topics object.

   c. In the right pane, click **Roles**.

   d. For the Document details role, select **Add** ⇨ **OrderTotal** ⇨ **OK**.

   The total order amount is added to the Documents table to put each negative comment into perspective.

Documents			
Topic Relevance	Document	Sentiment	OrderTotal
0.5974	Customer: 000019XB, Location: Raleigh. 3 unit(s) of Toy Game(s) ...	0.31	334
0.5949	Customer: 00001OVK, Location: St. Louis. They ordered 4 unit(s) ...	0.31	244
0.5949	Customer: 00001OYW, Location: St. Louis. They ordered 7 unit(s...	0.31	453

   e. Select the first row in the Documents table (with **OrderTotal=334**).

    f.   Right-click the row and select **View full document**.

       A new window displays the text of the full document.

OrderNote	▲	OrderTotal
Customer: 000019XB, Location: Raleigh. 3 unit(s) of Toy Game(s) were ordered. Currently, they are dissatisfied with us as their supplier. We are at risk of being dropped as their supplier.		334

    g.   Click **Close**.

8.   Derive new data items for topics.

    a.   Right-click the text topics object and select **Derive topics**.

New Topics Items

12 new items will be created: 6 topics and 6 relevance values.

Select the items you want to show in the Data pane.

Topics:

  plush, neutral, toy, portland:

   Topic: plush, neutral, toy, portland ☑

  neutral, game, figure, atlanta:

   Topic: neutral, game, figure, atlanta ☑

  location, customer, novelty, gift:

   Topic: location, customer, novelty, gift ☑

Twelve items can be created, two for each topic created from text analytics: one for topics and one for relevance.

Deriving topics from the text topics object creates a derived data item whose value is 1 (if the document for that row appears in the topic) or 0 (if the document for that row does not appear in the topic).

Deriving relevance from the text topics object creates a derived data item whose value is equal to the relevance of the document in the topic.

    b.   In the New Topics Items window, clear all check boxes except the one next to **Topic: +drop, risk, supplier, +dissatisfy**.

    c.   Click **OK**.

    d.   In the left pane, click **Data**.

       A new group is added to the Data pane.

⌄ Derived (Text Topics: December 19, 2019 …

🔖 Topic: +drop, risk, supplier, +dissatisfy

---

    e.   At the top of the canvas, click the **Details** tab.

    f.   Click the list table in the canvas to select it.

    g.   In the right pane, click the **Roles** tab.

    h.   For the Columns role, select **Add** ⇨ **Topic: +drop, risk, supplier, +dissatisfy**.

i.   Click **OK**.

j.   If necessary, click the **Order** column to sort the list table.

The list table should resemble the following:

Order	▲ OrderNote	Topic: +drop, risk, supplier, +dissatisfy
00001NL6	00004RPC in Boise placed an order. 16 unit(s) of Toy Figure(s) were ordered. 00004RPC is neutral with us.	0
000024X0	00002L9N in Birmingham placed an order. 8 unit(s) of Toy Figure(s) were ordered. They are unhappy. They are at risk of dropping us as a supplier.	1
0000291E	This order is for 00004RPF located in Boise. They ordered 1 unit(s) of Toy Game(s). Currently, they are pleased.	0
00003MNR	000052GF in Pittsburgh placed an order. 5 unit(s) of Toy Figure(s) were ordered. They are dissatisfied. We are at risk of being dropped as their supplier.	1

k.   In the left pane, click **Objects**.

l.   Drag the **Bar chart** object, from the Graphs group, to the right side of the canvas.

m.   In the right pane, click **Roles**.

n.   For the Category role, select **Add** ⇨ **FacilityContinent**.

o.   For the **Measure** role, select **Frequency** ⇨ **OrderTotal**.

p.   For the Group role, select **Add** ⇨ **Topic: +drop, risk, supplier, +dissatisfy**.

The bar chart should resemble the following:

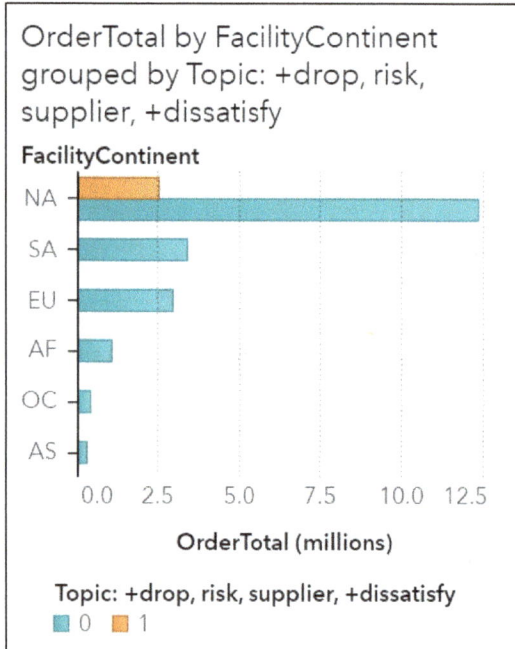

OrderTotal by FacilityContinent grouped by Topic: +drop, risk, supplier, +dissatisfy

FacilityContinent

OrderTotal (millions)

Topic: +drop, risk, supplier, +dissatisfy
◼ 0   ◼ 1

It seems as if all of our comments in the **+drop, risk, supplier, +dissatisfy** topic come from NA (North America).

9.   Save the report.

End of Demonstration

Practice 10.1

1. Analyzing a Text Analysis Data Source

a. Open the browser and sign in to SAS Viya.

b. Open the **VA2-Practice6.1** report in the **Courses/YVA285/Advanced/Practices** folder.

c. View data item properties and answer the following question:

Which data item would be the unique identifier column? The document collection?

Answer:

d. Assign the appropriate data items to the roles for the text topics object.

e. Add sentiment analysis.

f. Answer the following questions:

Which sentiment (negative, neutral, or positive) is assigned to a majority of course descriptions?

Answer:

How many documents are in the **visual, analytics, sas, +teach** topic?

Answer:

What are the top two terms for all topics? Does that make sense given the data?

Answer:

g. Save the report.

End of Practices

Chapter 11: Advanced Topics – Creating Advanced Data Items

11.1 Introduction

As discussed in Chapter 3, SAS Visual Analytics enables you to calculate new data items from your existing data items by using an expression. For example, you might want to calculate a company's profits by subtracting expenses from revenues. In addition to performing mathematical calculations on numeric values, you can use calculated data items to create date and time values. For example, if your data contains separate categories for *month*, *day*, and *year*, then you can calculate a date value from those categories. To recap:

- All calculations are performed on unaggregated data. The calculation expression is evaluated for each row in the data source before aggregations are performed. To perform calculations on aggregated data, see Section 11.3.

- Calculated data items can accept parameters. For more information, see Section 11.2.

- A hierarchy can contain calculated data items as long as they are categories.

- Calculated data items can be changed into geographic data items and used in geo maps.

Figure 11.1: Creating Data Items

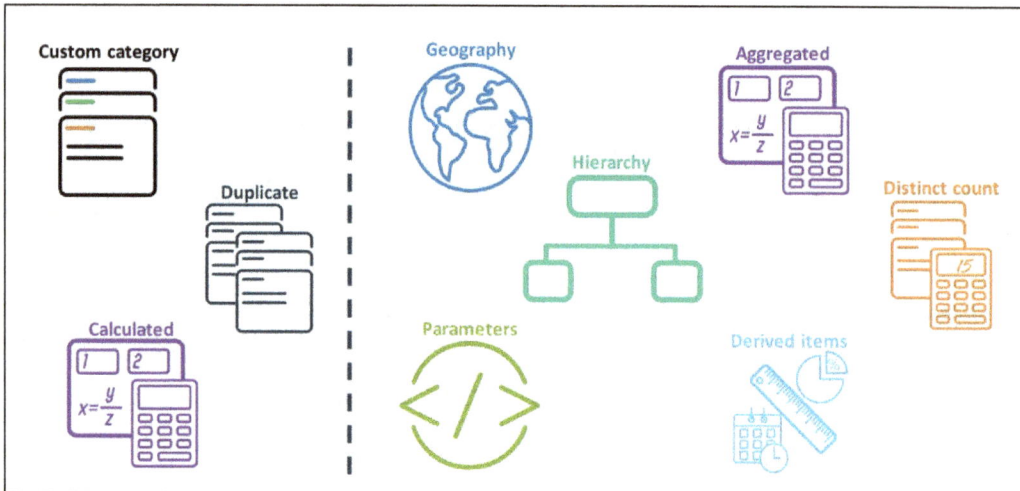

The following types of data items can be created in SAS Visual Analytics using code or in SAS Data Studio or SAS Enterprise Guide.

Table 11.1: Data Items

Item	Description
Custom category	A custom category creates labels for groups of values of category or measure data items. When you create a custom category from a measure data item, you can use intervals or distinct values to group the data. For more information about custom categories, see "Working with Custom Categories in a Report" in the *SAS Visual Analytics: Working with Report Data* documentation.
Duplicate	Both measures and categories can be duplicated (copied) in Visual Analytics. Duplicating measures enables you to compare the data using different aggregations in a table or graph or change the classification to a category for grouping other values in tables or graphs. Duplicating datetime values enables you to apply different formats to the values for use in tables or graphs. Duplicating calculated items enables you to make variations to a calculation. For more information about duplicating data items, see "Working with Data Items in a Report" in the *SAS Visual Analytics: Working with Report Data* documentation.
Calculated item	Calculated items are created by performing mathematical calculations on numeric values or by performing operations on datetime data items or categories. All calculations are performed on unaggregated data. That is, the expression is evaluated for each row in the data source. For more information about creating calculated data items, see "Working with Calculated Items in a Report" in the *SAS® Visual Analytics: Working with Report Data* documentation. For more information about operators, see "Reference: Operators for Data Expressions" in the *SAS® Visual Analytics: Working with Report Data* documentation.

The following types of data items need to be created in Visual Analytics.

Table 11.2: SAS Visual Analytics Data Items

Item	Description
Geography	A geography data item is a category whose values are mapped to geographical locations or regions. Geography data items can be used with geo maps and other report objects. Geography data items can be created using predefined roles (for example, country names), by associating latitude and longitude coordinates with the values (custom), or by associating polygon data from a separate data source with map regions (custom). For more information about creating geography data items, see "Working with Geography Data Items" in the *SAS Visual Analytics: Working with Report Data* documentation.
Aggregated measure	Aggregated measures enable you to calculate new data items using aggregated values. This means that the calculation changes depending on the other data items available in the graph. For example, you can see the profit margin for each region or by each store. For more information about creating calculated data items, see "Working with Calculated Items in a Report" in the *SAS Visual Analytics: Working with Report Data* documentation.
Hierarchy	A hierarchy is a defined arrangement of category data items based on a parent-child relationship. In many cases, the levels of the hierarchy are arranged with the more general information at the top (for example, year) and the more specific information at the bottom (for example, month). Hierarchies enable you to add drill-down functionality to graphs. Hierarchies that consist of all geographic data items are considered geographic hierarchies and can be used in geo maps. **Note:** You can create a date hierarchy from a date data item. The date hierarchy, by default, has levels for year, quarter, month, and day. A date hierarchy created from a datetime data item has levels, by default, for year, quarter, month, day, hour, minute, and second. For more information about hierarchies, see "Working with Hierarchies in a Report" in the *SAS Visual Analytics: Working with Report Data* documentation.
Distinct count	A distinct count counts the number of distinct values of a category data item as an aggregated measure. This means that the calculation changes depending on the other data items available in the graph. For example, you can see the number of orders placed for each age group or the number of orders placed for each country by creating a distinct count from the order ID. For more information about creating distinct counts, see "Working with Data Items in a Report" in the *SAS Visual Analytics: Working with Report Data* documentation. **Note:** If the category contains missing values, the distinct count is increased by one. A configuration setting can modify this behavior.
Parameter	A parameter is a variable whose value can be changed and that can be referenced by other report objects. Parameters can be used in control objects in Visual Analytics. When the value of the control changes, the parameter is updated with that value, and any report objects that reference that parameter are updated as well. Parameters can be used in calculations, display rules, filters, and ranks, URLs, and text objects. For more information about parameters, see "Working with Parameters in Reports" in the *SAS Visual Analytics: Working with Report Data* documentation.

Item	Description
	Derived data items are aggregated measures that display values for the measure and the formula type on which the derived item is based.
	The following types of derived items can be created from category data items:
	Distinct count — Displays the number of distinct values for the selected category. For more information, see the distinct count row above.
	Count — Displays the number of nonmissing values for the selected category.
	Number missing — Displays the number of missing values for the selected category.
	The following types of derived data items can be created from measure data items:
	Cumulative total — Displays a running total of all the values for the measure on which it is based.
Derived item	**Data suppression** — Obscures aggregated data if individual data values could easily be inferred. Data suppression replaces all values for the measure on which it is based with an asterisk (*) unless a value represents the aggregation of a specified minimum number of values. For more information, see "Reference: Operators for Data Expressions" in the *SAS Visual Analytics: Working with Report Data* documentation.
	Difference from previous period — Displays the difference between the value for the current time period and the value for the previous time period.
	Difference from previous parallel period — Displays the difference between the value for the current time period and the value for the previous parallel time period within a longer time interval.
	Moving average — Displays a moving average (rolling average) for the measure on which it is based. The moving average calculates the average for each value with the specified number of preceding values.
	Percent difference from previous period — Displays the percentage difference between the value for the current time period and the value for the previous time period.
	Percent difference from previous parallel period — Displays the percentage difference between the value for the current time period and the value for the previous parallel time period within a longer time interval.

Item	Description
Percent of subtotals	Displays the percentage of the subtotal value for the measure on which it is based. You can create a percentage of subtotal only when the source data item has an aggregation of Sum or Count. **Note:** The Percent of subtotals derived item is available for use only in crosstabs. **Note:** The Percent of subtotals derived item is relative to the subset of data that is selected by your filters and ranks.
Percent of total – sum	Displays the percentage of the total value for the measure on which it is based. You can create a percentage of total only when the source data item has an aggregation of Sum or Count. **Note:** The Percent of total – sum derived item is relative to the subset of data that is selected by your filters and ranks.
Period to date	Displays the aggregated value for the current time period and all of the previous time periods within a larger time interval.
Year to date	Displays the aggregated value for the current time period and all of the previous time periods within the year. The year-to-date calculation subsets the data for each year using today's date (where today is evaluated each time you view the report).
Year to date growth	Displays the percentage difference between the year-to-date value for the current time period and the year-to-date value for the same time period of the previous year. The year-to-date calculation subsets the data for each year using today's date (where today is evaluated each time you view the report).
Year over year growth	Displays the percentage difference between the current time period and an equivalent time period from the previous year. The year-over-year calculation subsets the data for each year using today's date (where today is evaluated each time you view the report).

For more information about derived items, see "Working with Data Items in a Report" in the *SAS Visual Analytics: Working with Report Data* documentation.

11.2 Creating Calculated Items

To recap, calculated data items are created by performing mathematical calculations on numeric values or by performing operations on datetime data items or categories. All calculations are performed on unaggregated data. That is, the expression is evaluated for each row in the data source. For example, you can create a new calculated item (New Salary) by multiplying salary and increase. For each row in the data source, the operation is evaluated, and the new data item is created. Then, when that data item is used in a graph (for example, with Gender) the values for New Salary are totaled for each gender.

Figure 11.2: Example of a Calculated Item

Calculated items are created by performing operations on unaggregated data.

| | (| Salary | * | Increase |) | |

Country	Salary		Increase		New Salary
US	40,000	✖	1.05	▤	**42,000**
UK	65,000	✖	1.10	▤	**71,500**
UK	32,000	✖	1.05	▤	**33,600**
US	80,000	✖	1.10	▤	**88,000**
UK	56,000	✖	1.15	▤	**64,400**

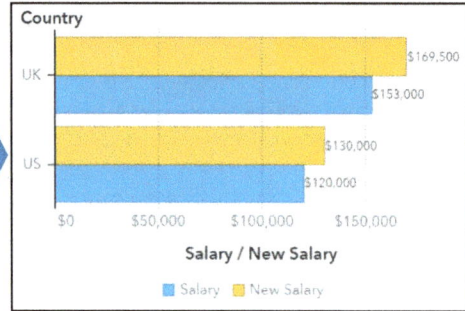

Country

UK: $169,500 / $153,000
US: $130,000 / $120,000

Salary / New Salary

■ Salary ■ New Salary

Vector Plot

A *vector plot* shows the change in the value of two measures using directed line segments (vectors) to represent both the direction and magnitude of the change at each point. Each set of measures shows information about the starting point and the ending point.

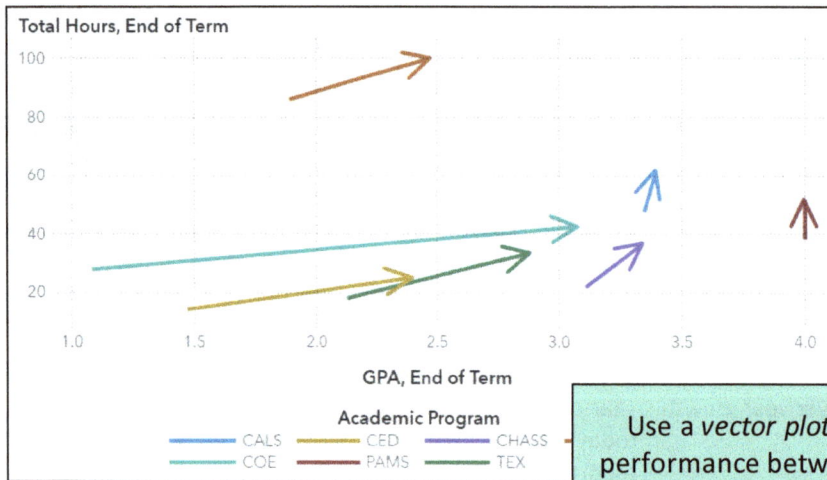

Total Hours, End of Term

GPA, End of Term

Academic Program
— CALS — CED — CHASS
— COE — PAMS — TEX

Use a *vector plot* to view relative performance between two measures from one point in time to another.

Demo 11.1: Creating a Numeric Calculated Item

This demonstration illustrates how to create a numeric calculated item and a vector plot in a report.

1. From the browser window, sign in to SAS Viya.
2. In the upper left corner, click ☰ (**Show list of applications**) and select **Explore and Visualize**. SAS Visual Analytics appears.
3. Click **All Reports**.
   a. Navigate to the **Courses/YVA285/Advanced/Demos** folder.
   b. Double-click the **VA2-Demo7.1a** report to open it.

4. View roles available for the vector plot and the data items available in the table.
    a. In the canvas, click the vector plot to select it.
    b. In the right pane, click **Roles**.

    > ⌄ X axis*
    >
    >   + Add
    >
    > ⌄ Y axis*
    >
    >   + Add
    >
    > ⌄ X Origin*
    >
    >   + Add
    >
    > ⌄ Y Origin*
    >
    >   + Add

    The vector plot requires two groups of measures: one set for the X axis and one set for the Y axis. For each set, a measure is required for the start time (origin) and a measure is required for the end time.

    c. In the left pane, click **Data**.

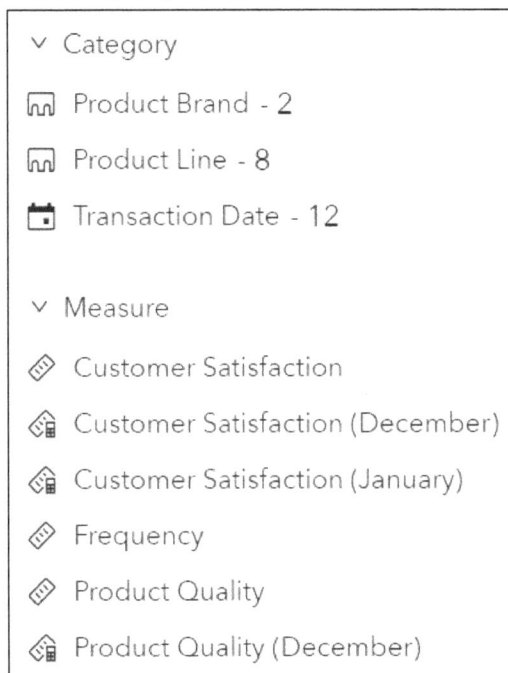

    > ⌄ Category
    >
    > ⌐⌐ Product Brand - 2
    >
    > ⌐⌐ Product Line - 8
    >
    > 🗓 Transaction Date - 12
    >
    > ⌄ Measure
    >
    > ◈ Customer Satisfaction
    >
    > ◈ Customer Satisfaction (December)
    >
    > ◈ Customer Satisfaction (January)
    >
    > ◈ Frequency
    >
    > ◈ Product Quality
    >
    > ◈ Product Quality (December)

    Transaction Date is in the format MMMYYYY. We have customer order information for one year. For the vector plot, we would like to compare **Product Quality** and **Customer Satisfaction** for two points during the year: January and December.

    We have already calculated **Customer Satisfaction** at both time points (January and December) and **Product Quality** for December. We still need to calculate **Product Quality** for January.

5. Calculate **Product Quality** for January.
    a. On the Data pane, select **New data item** ⇨ **Calculated item**.
    b. In the Name field, enter Product Quality (January).
    c. For the **Result Type** field, verify that **Automatic (Numeric)** is selected.

d. For the **Format** field, click  (**Edit**).

   i.   In the Format window, select **Percent**.
   ii. For the **Width** field, verify that **12** is specified.
   iii. For the **Decimals** field, verify that **2** is specified.
   iv. Click **OK**.

e. On the left side of the window, click **Operators**.

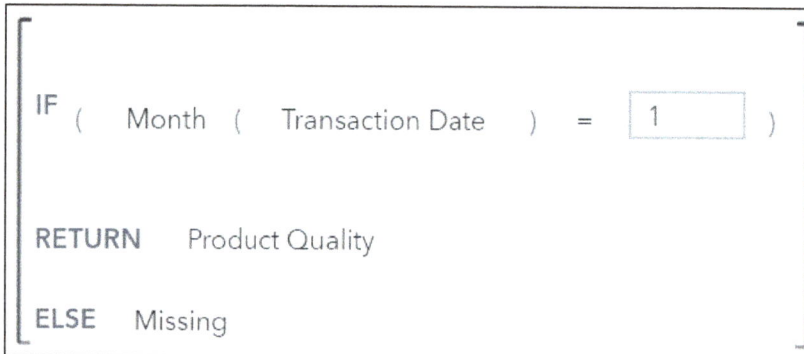

f. Expand the **Boolean** group.

g. Double-click the **IF...ELSE** operator to add it to the expression.

h. Expand the **Comparison** group.

i. Drag **x=y** to the **condition** field in the expression.

j. Expand the **Date and Time** group.

k. Drag **Month** to the **number** field on the left of the equal sign.

l. Right-click the **No selection** field in the expression and select **Replace with** ⇨ **Transaction Date**.

m. Enter **1** in the **number** field on the right of the equal sign.

n. Right-click the **number** field for the RETURN operator and select **Replace with** ⇨ **Product Quality**.

o. Right-click the **number** field for the ELSE operator and select **Replace with** ⇨ **Missing Value**. The expression should resemble the following:

```
IF  (  Month ( Transaction Date ) = [ 1      ]  )



RETURN    Product Quality


ELSE    Missing
```

p. In the lower right corner of the window, click **OK**.

The new data item is added to the Data pane.

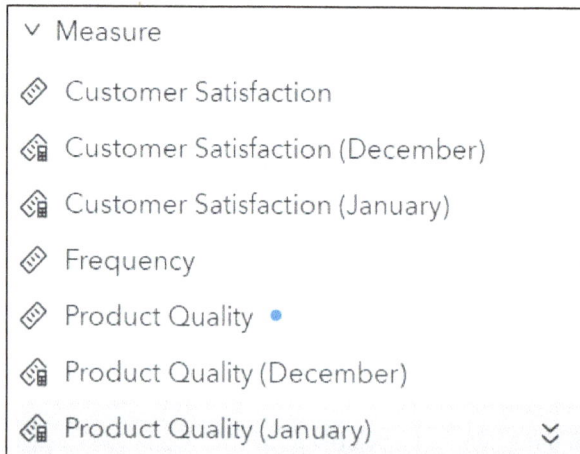

q. Next to Product Quality (January), click ⌄ (**Edit properties**).

r. For the **Aggregation** field, select **Average**.

6. Assign data items to the vector plot.

    a. In the canvas, click the vector plot to select it.

    b. In the right pane, click **Roles**, if necessary.

    c. For the X axis role, select **Add** ⇨ **Product Quality (December)**.

    d. For the Y axis role, select **Add** ⇨ **Customer Satisfaction (December)**.

    e. For the X Origin role, select **Add** ⇨ **Product Quality (January)**.

    f. For the Y Origin role, select **Add** ⇨ **Customer Satisfaction (January)**.

    g. For the **Group** role, select **Add** ⇨ **Product Line**.

    h. For the **Data tip values** role, click **Add**.

    i. Select **Product Brand** and click **OK**.

    The vector plot should resemble the following:

The grouping of arrows in the upper left corner are product lines in the Toy brand. For these product lines, there is a negative change in both quality and satisfaction over the year.

The grouping of arrows in the lower right corner are product lines in the Novelty brand. For these product lines, most have also declined (in both quality and satisfaction) over the year. On the other hand, the Kiosk product line has a marginal improvement in **Product Quality** but still a reduction in **Customer Satisfaction**. We might need to further analyze the products to determine why **Customer Satisfaction** is trending down.

7. Save the report.

End of Demonstration

Business Scenario

As a challenge, you calculate employee tenure. For retired employees, we want to know how many years they worked for the company as of their retirement date. For current employees, we want to know how many years they have worked for the company as of today's date.

Butterfly Chart

A *butterfly chart* (also known as a *tornado chart*) displays two bars with a shared category axis, where the baselines of the two bar charts are located in the center of the chart.

Figure 11.3: Butterfly Chart

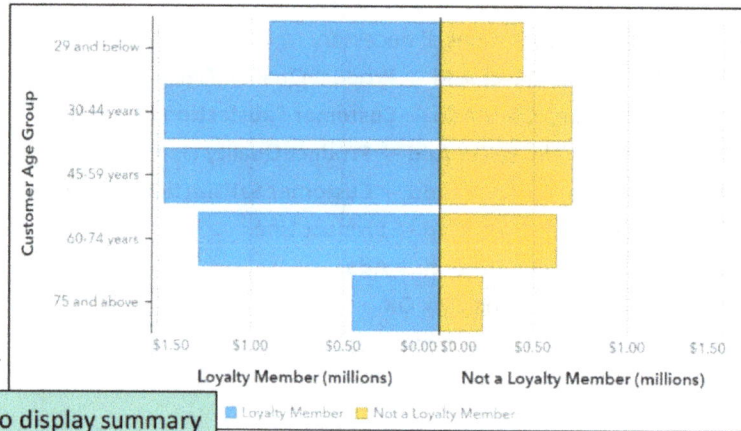

Use a *butterfly chart* to display summary information for two opposing groups.

 Practice 11.1

1. Creating a Numeric Calculated Item
   a. Open the browser and sign in to SAS Viya.
   b. Open the **VA2-Practice7.1a** report in the **Courses/YVA285/Advanced/Practices** folder.
   c. Create a new data item, **Salary (Europe)**, that averages salaries for European employees.
      Hint: **Employee Country** has the two-letter abbreviations for each country and can be used to calculate the new data item. For this data, all countries except Australia (AU) and United States (US) are in Europe.
   d. Assign the following data items to the specified roles for the butterfly chart:

Category	Job Title
Measure (bar)	Salary (Europe)
Measure (bar 2)	Salary (America/Oceania)

   e. Answer the following questions:
      Are there any jobs that do not exist in Europe?
      Answer:
      Are there any jobs in which Europeans make more than other continents (on average)?
      Answer:

The butterfly chart should resemble the following:

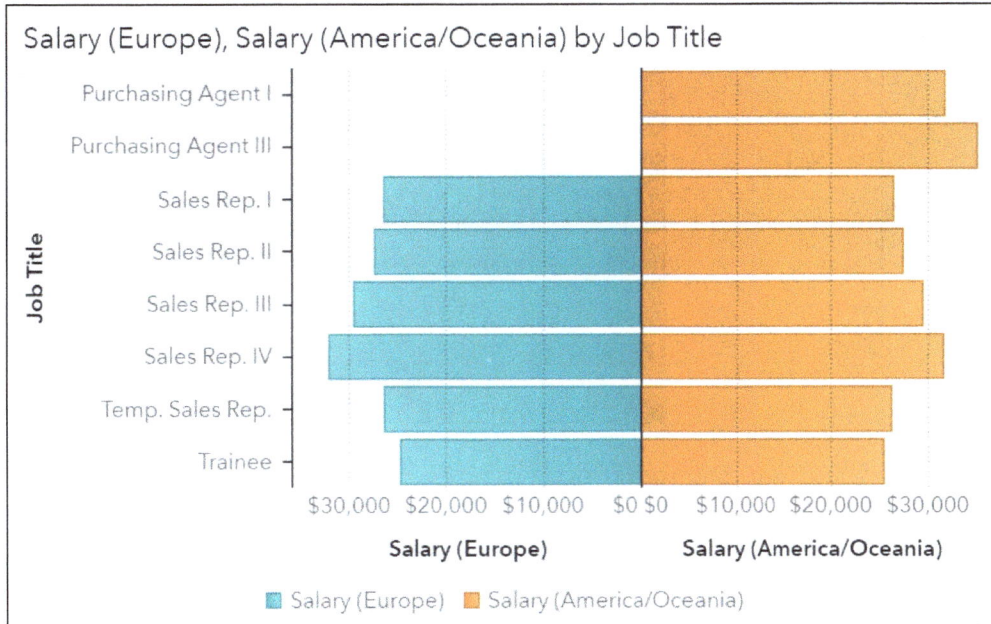

f.   Save the report.

Challenge (Optional)

1.   Creating an Advanced Numeric Calculated Column

   a.   Open the browser and sign in to SAS Viya.

   b.   Open the **VA2-Practice7.1a** report in the **Courses/YVA285/Advanced/Practices** folder.

   c.   Create a new data item, **Employee Tenure**, that calculates how many years each employee has been with the company.

   Hint: For retired employees, we want the number of years at the time of retirement. For active employees, we want the number of years as of today's date.

   Note: In order to match the displayed results, use the FLOOR operator when calculating Employee Tenure.

   d.   Answer the following question:

   What is the average employee tenure for retired Sales Rep. III employees? For retired Temp. Sales Rep. employees?

   Answer:

The bar chart should resemble the following:

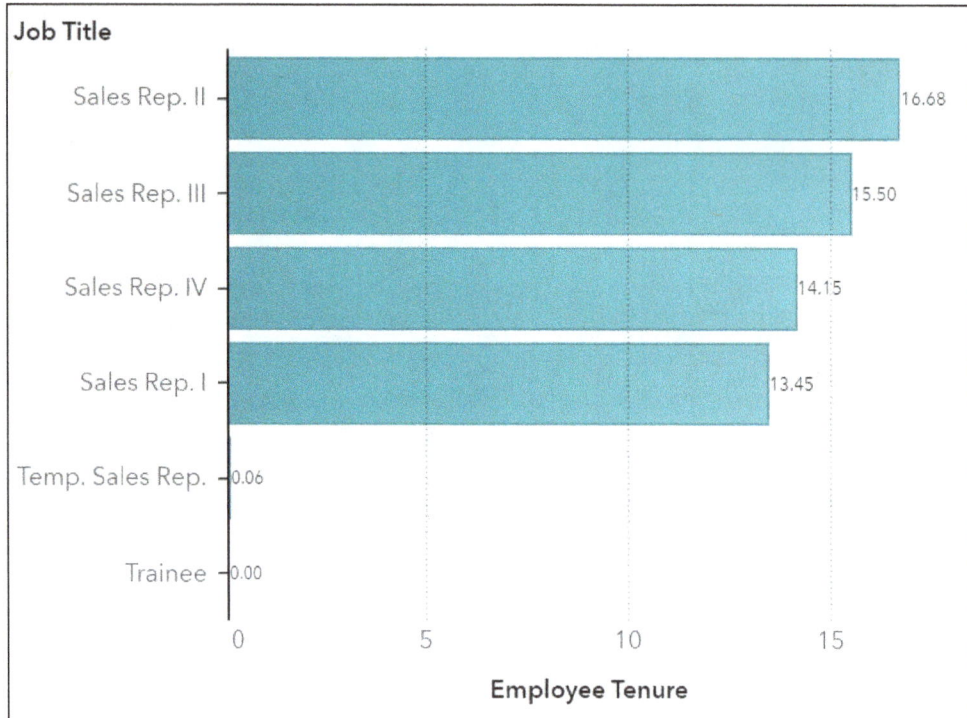

e. Save the report.

End of Practices

Needle Plot

A *needle plot* displays vertical line segments (needles) connected to a horizontal baseline. The horizontal baseline can be at zero (shown above for profit) or can be at some other value (above which signals improvement and below which signals decline). Measures can be assigned to both the vertical and horizontal axis. Needle plots are often used in clinical trials to indicate the effect of drugs on various patients.

Figure 11.4: Needle Plot

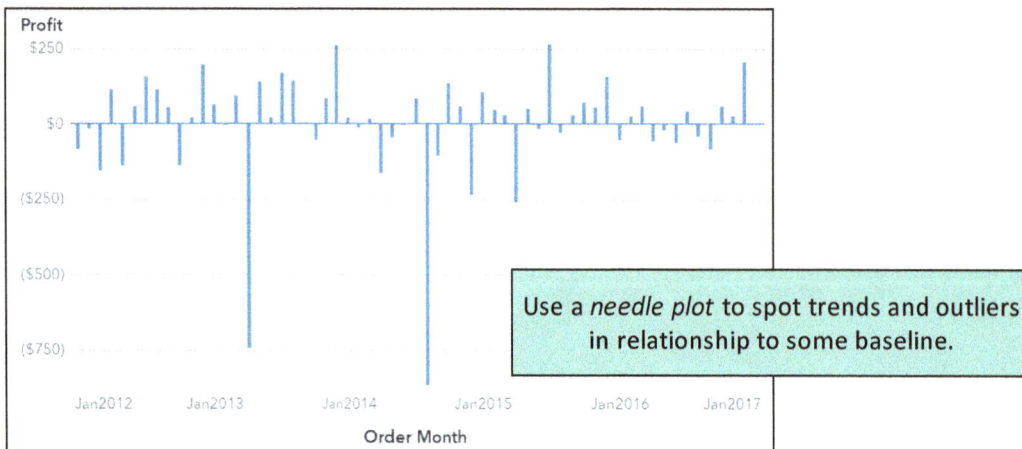

Use a *needle plot* to spot trends and outliers in relationship to some baseline.

Demo 11. 2: Creating a Character Calculated Item

This demonstration illustrates how to create a character calculated item and a needle plot in a report.

1. From the browser window, sign in to SAS Viya.
2. In the upper left corner, click ▤ (**Show list of applications**) and select **Explore and Visualize**. SAS Visual Analytics appears.
3. Click All Reports.
   a. Navigate to the **Courses/YVA285/Advanced/Demos** folder.
   b. Double-click the **VA2-Demo7.1b** report to open it.
4. In the canvas, view the list table.

City	▲	Profit
A&T State University (336)		$14,250
Asheville (828)		$14,250
Black Mountain (828)		$3,000
Bowman Gray School of Med (336)		$35,250
Cary (919/984)		$27,750
Chapel Hill (919/984)		$23,250

City contains the area code of the location in parentheses. Some cities share an area code (for example, Asheville and Black Mountain in the list table above). For the needle plot, we would like to view total profit for each area code.

5. Calculate area codes.
   a. In the left pane, click **Data**.
   b. Select **New data item** ⇨ **Calculated item**.
   c. In the **Name** field, enter **Area Codes**.
   d. For the **Result Type** field, select **Character**.
   e. On the left side of the window, click **Operators**.
   f. Expand the **Text (advanced)** group.
   g. Double-click the **Substring** operator to add it to the expression.
   h. Right-click the **string** field in the expression and select **Replace with** ⇨ **City**.
   i. On the left side of the window, expand the **Text (advanced)** group, if necessary.
   j. Drag the **FindChar** operator to the first **number** field in the expression.
   k. Right-click the first **string** field for the FindChar operator and select **Replace with** ⇨ **City**.
   l. Enter **(** in the second **string** field for the FindChar operator.

m.   Enter **9** in the last **number** field in the expression.

The expression should resemble the following:

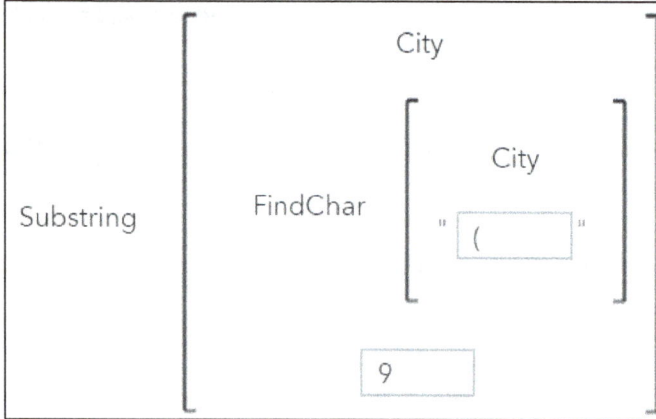

```
Substring   FindChar   City
                       [ City
                         " ( " ]

                       9
```

n.   In the bottom right corner of the window, click **Preview**.

Number of rows to show: 50   ▾   ⓘ

Area Codes	City
(336)	Winston Salem (336)
(336)	Winston-Salem (336)
(336)	Bowman Gray School of Med (336)
(336)	Elon College (336)
(919/984)	Mebane (919/984)

We need to remove the parentheses from the new data item, **Area Codes**. The RemoveChars operator can do this.

o.   Click **Close** to close the Preview Result window.

p.   On the left side of the window, expand the **Text (advanced)** group, if necessary.

q.   Drag the **RemoveChars** operator to the outside of the expression.

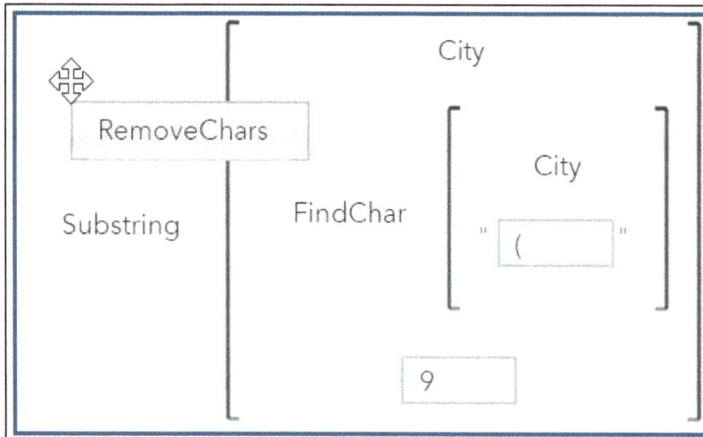

```
RemoveChars   City
              [ FindChar   City
                           [ City
                             " ( " ]
Substring
                           9 ]
```

r.   Enter **()** in the **string** field for the RemoveChars operator.

The expression should resemble the following:

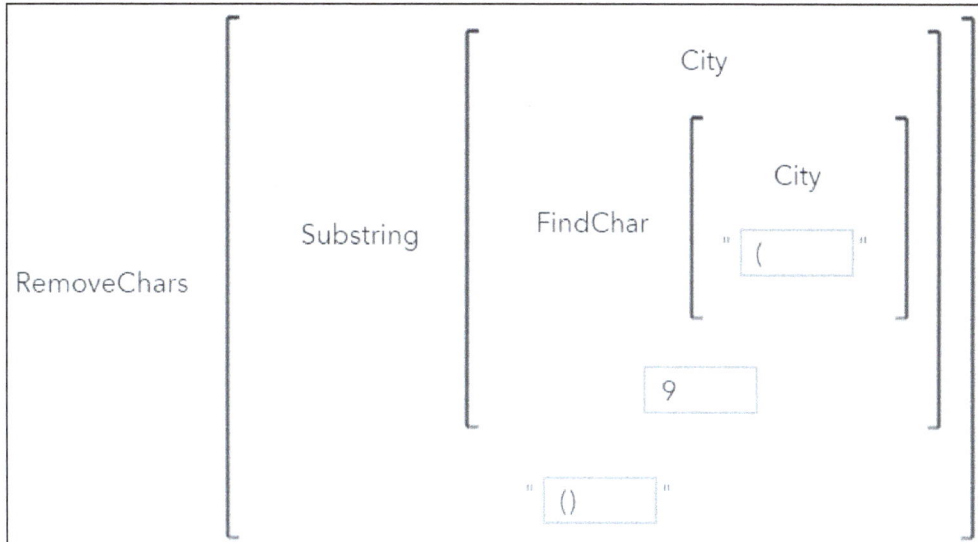

RemoveChars [Substring [FindChar [City [" (" City]] 9] " () "]

s.   In the bottom right corner of the window, click **Preview**.

Number of rows to show: 50   ▼   ⓘ

Area Codes	City
336	Winston Salem (336)
336	Winston-Salem (336)
336	Bowman Gray School of Med (336)
336	Elon College (336)
919/984	Mebane (919/984)

t.   Click **Close** to close the Preview Result window.

u.   In the lower right corner of the window, click **OK**.

The new data item is added to the Data pane.

∨ Category

▥ Area Codes - 6   ⩒

▥ City - 40

▥ Student Location - 41

▥ Training Center Location - 4

6.   Assign data items to the needle plot.

a.   In the canvas, click the needle plot to select it.

b.   In the right pane, click **Roles**, if necessary.

c.   For the **X axis** role, select **Add** ⇨ **Area Codes**.

d. For the **Y axis** role, select **Frequency** ➪ **Profit**.

The needle plot should resemble the following:

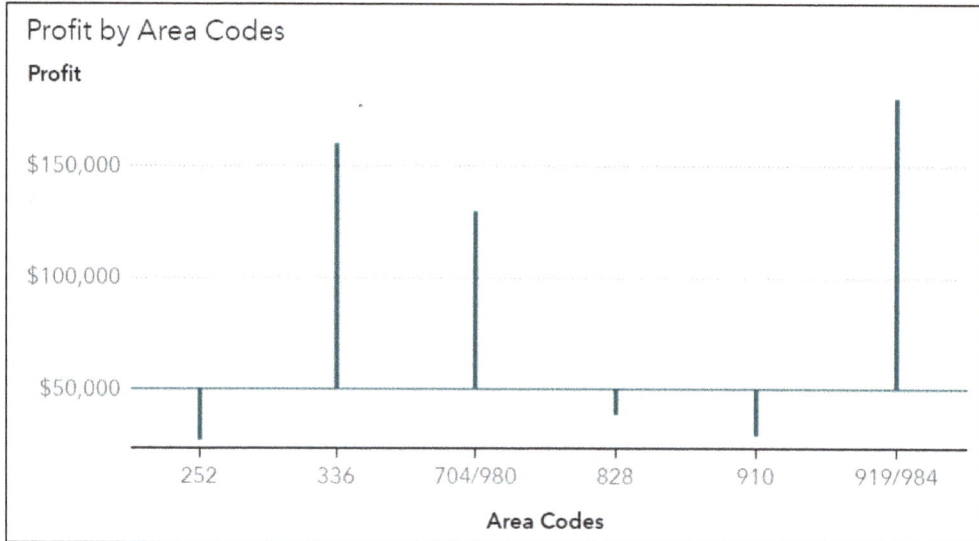

A majority of our profit comes from the area codes 336 and 919/984. Three area codes generate profit below the $50,000 minimum (252, 828, and 910).

7. Save the report.

End of Demonstration

Dot Plot

A dot plot displays data for each value of a category data item using dots. The position of each dot on the response axis represents the summarized value of the measure. Dot plots are similar to bar charts but minimize the amount of chart junk (visual elements in graphs that are not necessary to understand the graph or distract from the main message of the graph). Dot plots are often preferred because bar charts can distort the values if the area of the bars is compared and not the height. Dot plots can also be a good alternative to a bar chart to highlight differences between values that are close together. By starting the vertical axis at a nonzero value (as shown in Figure 11.5), you can more easily compare the differences than you could with a bar chart.

Figure 11.5: Graphs (Dot Plot)

Practice 11.2

1. Creating a Character Calculated Item

a. Open the browser and sign in to SAS Viya.

b. Open the **VA2-Practice7.1b** report in the **Courses/YVA285/Advanced/Practices** folder.

c. Create a new data item, **Product Code**, that takes the following form:

<first eight characters of Facility> – <first three characters of Unit>

Facility	Unit	▲ Product Code
MXMEXICO0038	NBD000020	MXMEXICO-NBD
MXTIJUAN0036	NBD000020	MXTIJUAN-NBD
USATLANT0025	NBD000020	USATLANT-NBD
USAUSTIN0011	NBD000020	USAUSTIN-NBD
USBALTIM0032	NBD000020	USBALTIM-NBD
USCHARLE0030	NBD000020	USCHARLE-NBD
USCHARLO0028	NBD000020	USCHARLO-NBD
USJACKSO0020	NBD000020	USJACKSO-NBD

d. Assign the following data items to the specified roles for the dot plot:

Category	Product Code
Measure	Frequency
Data tip values	Facility City

e. Add a rank to the dot plot to show the top five products by frequency.

f. Answer the following question:

Where are the top five products produced?

Answer:

The dot plot should resemble the following:

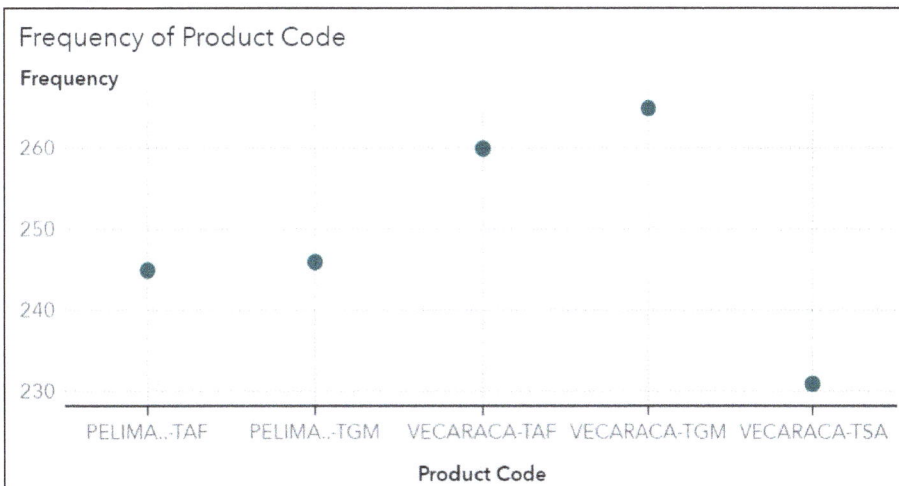

g. Save the report.

Challenge (Optional)

1. Creating a Date Calculated Item

   a. Open the browser and sign in to SAS Viya.

   b. Open the **VA2-Practice7.1b** (Challenge) report in the **Courses/YVA285/Advanced/Practices** folder.

   c. Create a new data item, **Facility Closing Date**, that is 20 years after the facility opened (on December 31).

   d. Assign the following data items to the specified roles for the dot plot:

Category	Facility Closing Date

Measure	Number of Facilities

   e. Answer the following question:

   How many facilities will be closed in 2020?

   Answer:

   The dot plot should resemble the following:

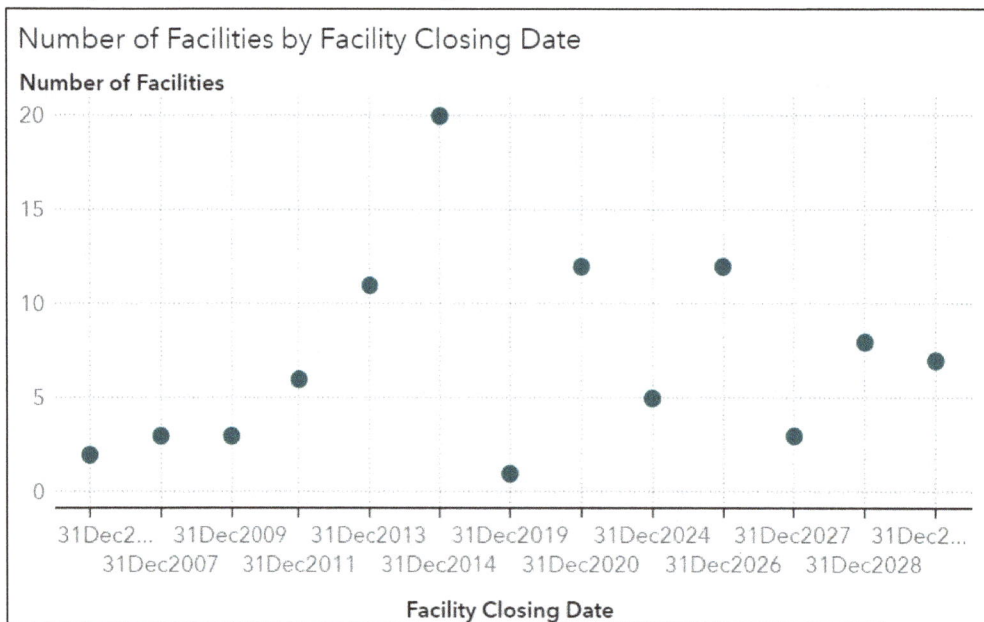

   Number of Facilities by Facility Closing Date

   f. Save the report.

   End of Practices

11.3 Creating Aggregated Measures

Conversely, aggregated measures enable you to use aggregated values to calculate new data items. These data items are created by first aggregating values, and then by performing the operation. With aggregated measures, the calculation changes depending on other data items that are available in the graph. For example, you can create a new aggregated measure (Salary (Percent of total)) by dividing the sum of the salary for each group by the sum of the salary for all groups. In this instance, because Salary (Percent of total) is paired with Gender, salaries are first totaled for each gender. Next, salaries are totaled for all genders. Then, the operation is evaluated for each gender to show the contribution to total salary. You could take the same aggregated measure and pair it with Country to see the contribution of each country to total salary.

When you create aggregated measures, you need to specify specific parameters for each aggregated operator. For simple aggregated operators, the aggregation context is required.

Figure 11.6: Example of an Aggregated Measure

Aggregated measures are created by aggregating first and then performing the operation.

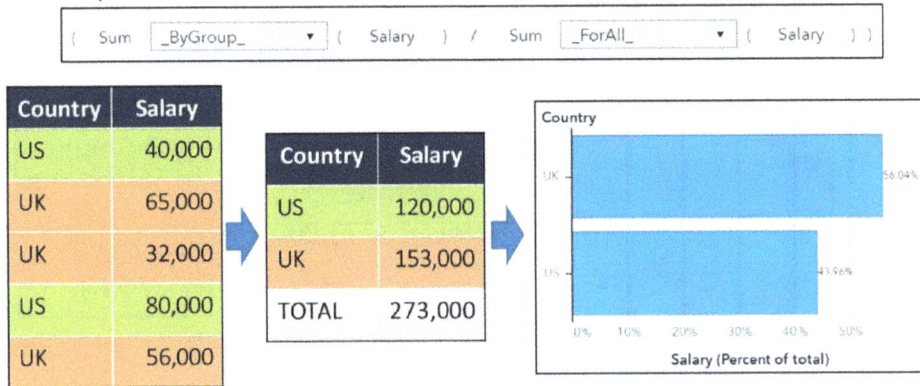

Note: Distinct counts and derived data items are special types of aggregated measures.

The aggregation context is the extent to which the aggregation is calculated. The _ByGroup_ context will aggregate the values for each group (the ones created in the report object), while the _ForAll_ context will aggregate the values for the entire set of data. The dynamic nature of aggregated measures makes them extremely useful for analysis and reporting.

For each aggregation in your expression, select the aggregation context. A drop-down list beside each aggregation enables you to select one of the following context values:

ByGroup

calculates the aggregation for each subset of the data item that is used in a visualization. For example, in a bar chart, an aggregated measure with the ByGroup context calculates a separate aggregated value for each bar in the chart.

ForAll

calculates the aggregation for the entire data item (after filtering). For example, in a bar chart, an aggregated measure with the ForAll context uses the same aggregated value (calculated for the entire data item) for each bar in the chart.

By using the ForAll and ByGroup contexts together, you can create measures that compare the local value to the global value. For example, you might calculate the difference from mean by using an expression such as the following: Avg ByGroup(X) - Avg ForAll(X)

Figure 11.7: Aggregation Context

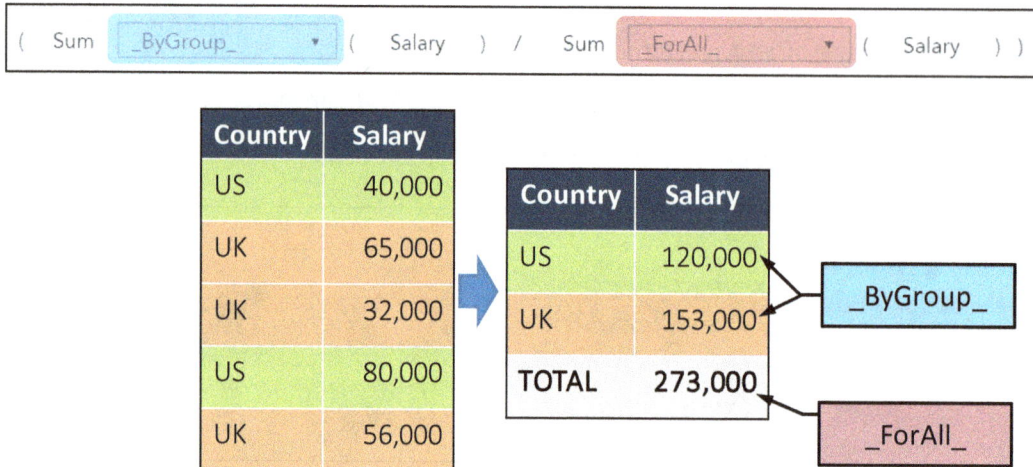

Demo 11.3: Creating an Aggregated Measure

This demonstration illustrates how to create an aggregated measure and a region geo map in a report.

1. From the browser window, sign in to SAS Viya.
2. In the upper left corner, click ☰ (**Show list of applications**) and select **Explore and Visualize**. SAS Visual Analytics appears.
3. Click **All Reports**.
   a. Navigate to the **Courses/YVA285/Advanced/Demos** folder.
   b. Double-click the **VA2-Demo7.2a** report to open it.
4. View details table for the geo map.
   a. In the upper right corner of the geo map, click ⬈ (**Maximize**).
   b. In the details table at the bottom of the window, click **Product Sale** twice to sort in descending order.

Customer Country	Product Sale ▼	Number of Customers
US	$3,570,181	4,295
GB	$352,500	716
ES	$337,595	543
BR	$203,929	663

   The country with the highest sales (US) also has the highest number of customers. Region geo maps should be used with measures that are evenly distributed within each region. We need to create a new aggregated measure that takes the total sales for the region and divides by the number of customers.
   c. In the upper right corner of the geo map, click ⬊ (**Restore**).
5. Calculate a new aggregated measure, **Sales by Customer**.
   a. In the left pane, click **Data**.
   b. Select **New data item** ⇨ **Calculated item**.
   c. In the **Name** field, enter **Sales by Customer**.
   d. For the **Result Type** field, select **Aggregated Measure**.
   e. On the left side of the window, click **Operators**.

    f.   Expand **Numeric (simple)**.

    g.   Double-click the **x/y** operator to add it to the expression.

    h.   Expand **Aggregated (simple)**.

    i.   Drag **Sum** to the **number** field on the left of the division sign.

    j.   Verify that **_ByGroup_** is specified for the Sum operator.

    k.   Right-click the **number** field for the Sum operator and select **Replace with** ⇨ **Product Sale**.

    l.   On the left side of the window, drag **Distinct** to the **number** field on the right of the division sign.

    m.   Verify that **_ByGroup_** is specified for the Distinct operator.

    n.   Right-click the **number** field for the Distinct operator and select **Replace with** ⇨ **Customer**.

        The expression should resemble the following:

| (Sum | _ByGroup_ | ▾ | (Product Sale) | / | Distinct | _ByGroup_ | ▾ | (Customer)) |

6.   In the upper right corner of the window, for the **Format** field, click [✎] **(Edit)**.

    a.   In the Format window, expand **Currency (basic)**.

    b.   Select **Dollar**.

    c.   For the **Width** field, verify that **12** is specified.

    d.   For the **Decimals** field, verify that **2** is specified.

    e.   Click **OK**.

        i.   Click **OK** to create the new aggregated measure.

           The Data pane should resemble the following:

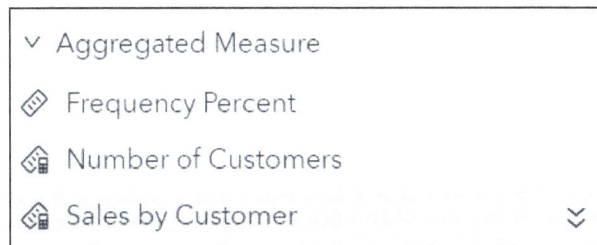

> ∨ Aggregated Measure
>
> ◈ Frequency Percent
>
> ▨ Number of Customers
>
> ▨ Sales by Customer   ⌄

7.   Modify the geo map to use the new aggregated measure.

    a.   In the canvas, click the geo map to select it.

    b.   In the right pane, click **Roles**.

    c.   For the **Color** role, select **Product Sale** ⇨ **Sales by Customer**.

        The geo map should resemble the following:

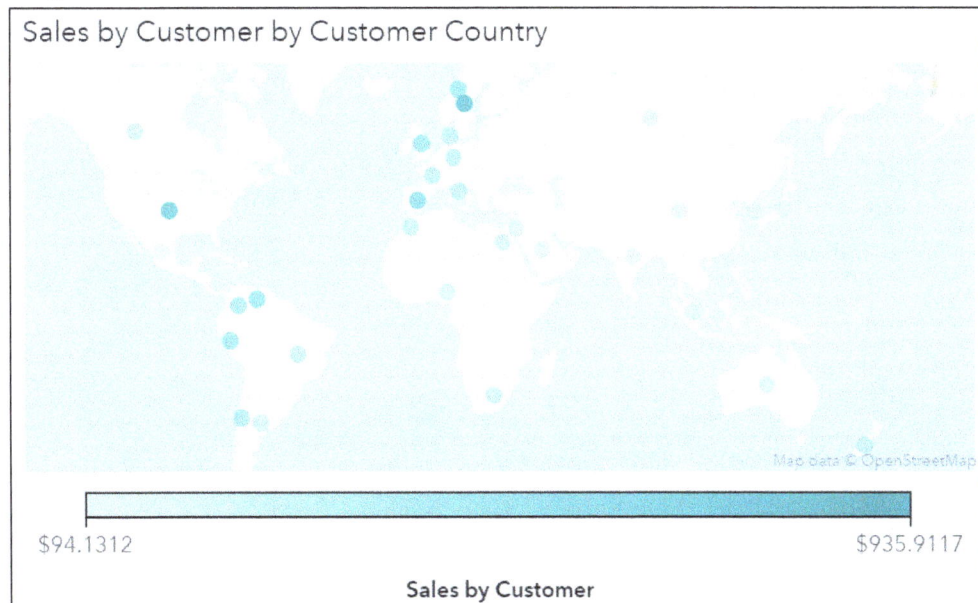

Sales by Customer by Customer Country

$94.1312 $935.9117

Sales by Customer

d. In the upper right corner of the geo map, click ⬈ (**Maximize**).

e. In the details table at the bottom of the window, click **Sales by Customer** twice to sort in descending order.

Customer Country	Sales by Custo... ▼	Number of Customers
SE	$935.91	147
US	$831.24	4,295
ES	$621.72	543
VE	$531.81	309
NO	$509.35	167

If we look at sales by customer, Sweden ranks first and United States ranks second. Now there is an even distribution of the values in the coordinate geo map, and we can more accurately compare countries.

f. In the upper right corner of the geo map, click ⬏ (**Restore**).

8. Save the report.

End of Demonstration

Practice 11.3

1. **Creating an Aggregated Measure**

    a. Open the browser and sign in to SAS Viya.

    b. Open the **VA2-Practice7.2a** report in the **Courses/YVA285/Advanced/Practices** folder.

    c. Create a new aggregated measure (**Yield Rate**) that has the following expression:

     Total production for each group / Total capacity for each group

    d. Add **Yield Rate** to the crosstab.

    The crosstab should resemble the following:

Unit ▲	Unit Actual	Unit Capacity	Yield Rate
Total	176007	429427	40.99%
NBD000020	31	348	8.91%
NBD000028	743	2784	26.69%
NBD000036	1541	2964	51.99%
NBD000044	1773	3048	58.17%
NBD000066	929	1980	46.92%
NBD000094	36	408	8.82%
NBD000111	936	2004	46.71%
NBD000163	933	1956	47.70%

    e. Save the report.

    End of Practices

Periodic Operator

Periodic operators in SAS Visual Analytics enable you to build relative period calculations for month, quarter, and year. For example, you might want to see a metric for every month, the previous month's value next to it, and lastly the difference between the two. The periodic operators have a new additional parameter that controls how filtering on the date data item used in the calculation affects the aggregated measure calculations such as the difference between parallel periods, year to date cumulative calculations, and so on.

Figure 11.8: Relative Period Operator

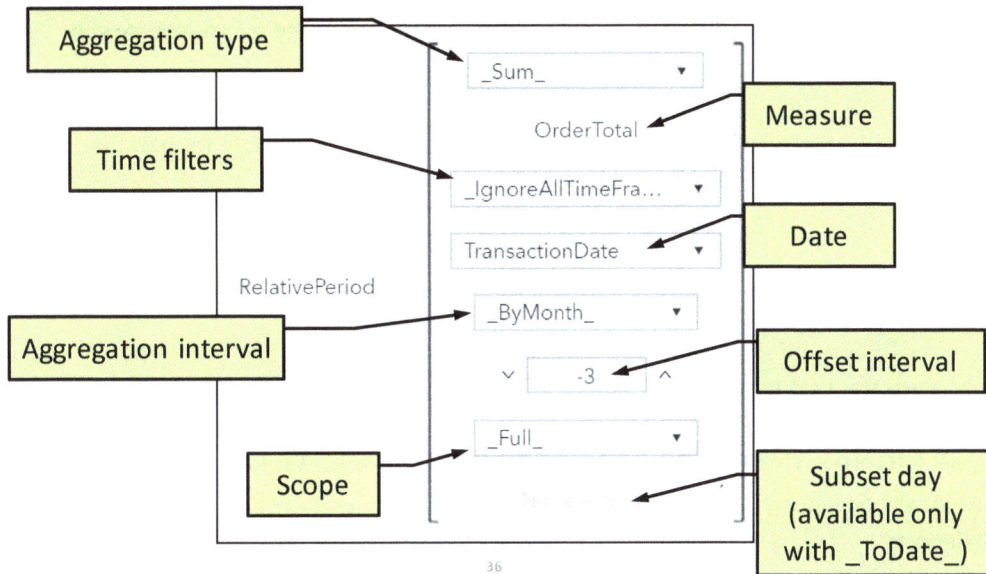

The RelativePeriod operator returns aggregated values for a period of time that is relative to the current period.

Note: The following values for the time filters parameter are available:

Parameter	Description
ApplyAllFilters	Applies all filters (object, prompt, actions) *before* the measure is calculated.
IgnoreAllTimeFrameFilters	Applies all filters (object, prompt, actions) based on the same date data item *after* the measure is calculated.
IgnoreInteractiveTimeFrameFilters	Applies object filters based on the same date data item *before* the measure is calculated, but applies interactive filters (prompt, actions) *after* the measure is calculated.

Note: For the date parameter, only date data items whose formats specify a year are available.

Note: For the aggregation interval parameter, **_Inferred_** automatically selects an interval using the format for date data items used with the aggregated item.

Note: The scope parameter specifies how much of each period is aggregated. The following values are available:

Parameter	Description
Full	Aggregates values for the entire period.
ToDate	Aggregates values up to a specific day within a period.
ToToday	Aggregates values up to the equivalent of today's position in the current interval. The value for today is evaluated dynamically whenever the aggregated measure is viewed in a report.

For more information about Aggregated (Periodic) Operators, see "Reference: Operators for Data Expressions" in the *SAS Visual Analytics: Working with Report Data* documentation.

Demo 11.4: Creating a Periodic Aggregated Measure

This demonstration illustrates how to create and modify a periodic aggregated measure.

1. From the browser window, sign in to SAS Viya.
2. In the upper left corner, click ▤ (**Show list of applications**) and select **Explore and Visualize**. SAS Visual Analytics appears.
3. Click **All Reports**.
   a. Navigate to the **Courses/YVA285/Advanced/Demos** folder.
   b. Double-click the **VA2-Demo7.2b** report to open it.
4. Create a new periodic aggregated measure, **Order Total (3M change)**.
   a. In the left pane, click **Data**.
   b. Select **New data item ⇨ Calculated item**.
   c. In the **Name** field, enter **Order Total (3M change)**.
   d. For the **Result Type** field, select **Aggregated Measure**.
   e. On the left side of the window, click **Operators**.
   f. Expand **Numeric (simple)**.
   g. Double-click the **x-y** operator to add it to the expression.
   h. Expand **Aggregated (periodic)**.
   i. Drag **RelativePeriod** to the **number** field on the left of the minus sign.
   j. For the Aggregation Type operator, verify that **_Sum_** is specified.
   k. Right-click the **number** field for the Measure operator and select **Replace with ⇨ OrderTotal**.
   l. For the Time Filters operator, select **_ApplyAllFilters_**.
   m. For the Date operator, select **Transaction Date**.
   n. For the Aggregation Interval operator, select **_ByMonth_**.
   o. For the Offset Interval operator, verify that **0** is specified.
   p. For the Scope operator, verify that **_Full_** is specified.
   q. Right-click the **RelativePeriod** operator and select **Copy**.
   r. Right-click in the **number** field on the right of the minus sign and select **Paste**.

s. For the Offset Interval operator, on the right of the minus sign, enter **-3**.

The expression should resemble the following:

(	RelativePeriod	_Sum_ ▼ OrderTotal _ApplyAllFilters_ ▼ Transaction Date ▼ _ByMonth_ ▼ ⌄ 0 ⌃ _Full_ ▼	-	RelativePeriod	_Sum_ ▼ OrderTotal _ApplyAllFilters_ ▼ Transaction Date ▼ _ByMonth_ ▼ ⌄ -3 ⌃ _Full_ ▼	)

t. In the upper right corner of the window, for the **Format** field, click 🖊 (**Edit**).

  ii. In the Format window, expand **Currency (basic)**.

  iii. Select **Dollar**.

  iv. For the **Width** field, verify that **12** is specified.

  v. For the **Decimals** field, verify that **2** is specified.

  vi. Click **OK**.

u. Click **OK** to create the new periodic aggregated measure.

The Data pane should resemble the following:

> ∨ Aggregated Measure
>
> ◈ Frequency Percent
>
> 🗔 Order Total (3M change)   ⌄⌄

5. Modify the crosstab to use the new periodic aggregated measure.

  a. In the canvas, click the crosstab to select it.

  b. In the right pane, click **Roles**.

  c. For the **Measures** role, click **Add**.

  d. Select **Order Total (3M change)** and click **OK**.

The crosstab should resemble the following:

Transaction Date ▲	OrderTotal	Order Total (3M change)
Dec2013	$567,120.92	.
Jan2014	$434,318.80	.
Feb2014	$507,457.78	.
Mar2014	$483,017.52	($84,103.40)
Apr2014	$324,288.42	($110,030.38)
May2014	$323,937.28	($183,520.50)
Jun2014	$296,352.29	($186,665.23)
Jul2014	$310,416.38	($13,872.03)

6. Filter the crosstab to view details since January 2016 and modify the periodic aggregated measure.

    a. For the slider control, click (⦿) on the left side of the slider control.

        i.   Click 📅 (Select a month and year).

        ii. For the **Month** field, select **January**.

        iii. For the **Year** field, enter **2016**.

Month:	Year:
January ▾	2016

        iv. Click **OK**.

             The crosstab should resemble the following:

Transaction Date ▲	OrderTotal	Order Total (3M change)
Jan2016	$556,871.22	.
Feb2016	$507,799.87	.
Mar2016	$498,377.75	.
Apr2016	$336,489.84	($220,381.38)
May2016	$332,398.02	($175,401.85)
Jun2016	$385,458.01	($112,919.74)
Jul2016	$267,465.31	($69,024.54)
Aug2016	$287,697.00	($44,701.02)

             Even though the table contains details for **Order Total** in previous months, we specified **_ApplyAllFilters_** for the calculation, which applies the filters first before calculating the aggregated measure.

    b. In the left pane, click **Data**.

    c. Right-click **Order Total (3M change)** and select **Edit**.

        i.   For the Time Filters operator on the left of the minus sign, select **_IgnoreInteractiveTimeFrameFilters_**.

7. For the Time Filters operator on the right of the minus sign, select **_IgnoreInteractiveTimeFrameFilters_**.

    The expression should resemble the following:

(RelativePeriod	_Sum_ ▾		-	RelativePeriod	_Sum_ ▾	)
	OrderTotal				OrderTotal	
	IgnoreInteractiveTi... ▾				_IgnoreInteractiveTi..._ ▾	
	Transaction Date ▾				Transaction Date ▾	
	ByMonth ▾				_ByMonth_ ▾	
	⌄ 0 ⌃				⌄ -3 ⌃	
	Full ▾				_Full_ ▾	
	No selection				No selection	

8. Click **OK** to apply the changes.

The crosstab should resemble the following:

Transaction Date ▲	OrderTotal	Order Total (3M change)
Jan2016	$556,871.22	($389,696.66)
Feb2016	$507,799.87	($563,339.01)
Mar2016	$498,377.75	($224,858.13)
Apr2016	$336,489.84	($220,381.38)
May2016	$332,398.02	($175,401.85)
Jun2016	$385,458.01	($112,919.74)
Jul2016	$267,465.31	($69,024.54)
Aug2016	$287,697.00	($44,701.02)

The _IgnoreInteractiveTimeFrameFilters_ option ignores any interactive filters from prompts and actions that are based on the same date data item used in the calculation.

9. Add a filter to the crosstab to view information about 2017 and modify the periodic aggregated measure.

a. In the canvas, click the crosstab to select it, if necessary.

b. In the right pane, click **Filters**.

c. Select **New filter** ⇨ **Transaction Date**.

d. On the left of the filter, drag ⬤ to **Jan2017**.

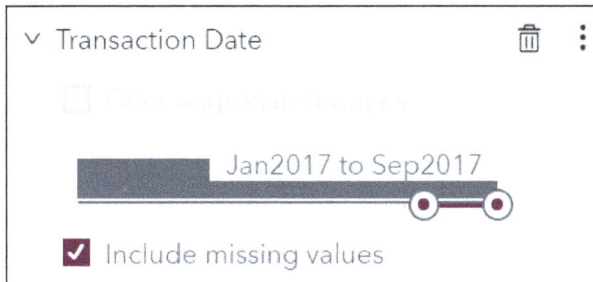

The crosstab should resemble the following:

Transaction Date ▲	OrderTotal	Order Total (3M change)
Jan2017	$646,284.69	.
Feb2017	$638,150.34	.
Mar2017	$586,158.30	.
Apr2017	$456,879.14	($189,405.55)
May2017	$399,074.94	($239,075.40)
Jun2017	$412,108.99	($174,049.30)
Jul2017	$330,220.11	($126,659.03)
Aug2017	$361,144.14	($37,930.81)

The _IgnoreInteractiveTimeFrameFilters_ option ignores only interactive filters before the calculation is performed. Filters specified on the Filters pane are not interactive (that is, report viewers cannot modify them).

e. In the left pane, click **Data**.

    f.   Right-click **Order Total (3M change)** and select **Edit**.

        ii.   For the Time Filters operator on the left of the minus sign, select **_IgnoreAllTimeFrameFilters_**.

        iii.   For the Time Filters operator on the right of the minus sign, select **_IgnoreAllTimeFrameFilters_**.

The expression should resemble the following:

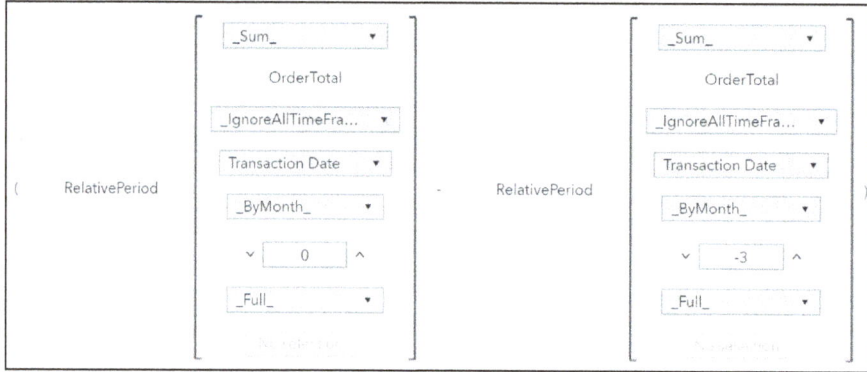

RelativePeriod	_Sum_ OrderTotal _IgnoreAllTimeFra... Transaction Date _ByMonth_ 0 _Full_	-	RelativePeriod	_Sum_ OrderTotal _IgnoreAllTimeFra... Transaction Date _ByMonth_ -3 _Full_

        iv.   Click **OK** to apply the changes.

The crosstab should resemble the following:

Transaction Date ▲	OrderTotal	Order Total (3M change)
Jan2017	$646,284.69	($42,765.73)
Feb2017	$638,150.34	($448,414.02)
Mar2017	$586,158.30	($200,214.63)
Apr2017	$456,879.14	($189,405.55)
May2017	$399,074.94	($239,075.40)
Jun2017	$412,108.99	($174,049.30)
Jul2017	$330,220.11	($126,659.03)
Aug2017	$361,144.14	($37,930.81)

The _IgnoreAllTimeFrameFilters_ option ignores all filters that are based on the same date data item used in the calculation.

10. Save the report.

End of Demonstration

Practice 11.4

    1. **Creating a Periodic Aggregated Measure**

    a.   Open the browser and sign in to SAS Viya.

    b.   Open the **VA2-Practice7.2b** report in the **Courses/YVA285/Advanced/Practices** folder.

    c.   Create a new periodic aggregated measure (**Cumulative Profit**) that calculates a running total for **Profit** over the year.

d. Add **Cumulative Profit** to the list table.

Order Date ▲	Profit	Cumulative Profit
Jan2012	$118,773.87	$118,773.87
Feb2012	$106,735.23	$225,509.10
Mar2012	$84,893.31	$310,402.41
Apr2012	$94,871.26	$405,273.67
May2012	$118,248.93	$523,522.60
Jun2012	$159,343.43	$682,866.04
Jul2012	$140,479.12	$823,345.15
Aug2012	$151,644.75	$974,989.91
Sep2012	$74,120.37	$1,049,110.28
Oct2012	$80,908.90	$1,130,019.18
Nov2012	$98,421.96	$1,228,441.13
Dec2012	$207,711.25	$1,436,152.38
Jan2013	$145,229.98	$145,229.98
Feb2013	$118,856.68	$264,086.66

e. Modify **Cumulative Profit** to calculate a running total for the fiscal year (starting in March). The list table should resemble the following:

Order Date ▲	Profit	Cumulative Profit
Jan2012	$118,773.87	$118,773.87
Feb2012	$106,735.23	$225,509.10
Mar2012	$84,893.31	$84,893.31
Apr2012	$94,871.26	$179,764.57
May2012	$118,248.93	$298,013.50
Jun2012	$159,343.43	$457,356.93
Jul2012	$140,479.12	$597,836.05
Aug2012	$151,644.75	$749,480.81
Sep2012	$74,120.37	$823,601.18
Oct2012	$80,908.90	$904,510.08
Nov2012	$98,421.96	$1,002,932.03
Dec2012	$207,711.25	$1,210,643.28
Jan2013	$145,229.98	$1,355,873.26
Feb2013	$118,856.68	$1,474,729.94

f. Save the report.

Challenge (Optional)

1. Adding Scopes to an Aggregation
    a. Open the browser and sign in to SAS Viya.
    b. Open the **VA2-Practice7.2b (Challenge)** report in the **Courses/YVA285/Advanced/Practices** folder.
    c. Answer the following questions:
        What is the expression for **Average Salary**?
        Answer:

What is the average salary for all employees?

Answer:

d.   Management would like to see the total salary for all employees in the crosstab. Edit the **Average Salary** aggregated measure to add the following scope:

Grand total: <total salary for all employees>

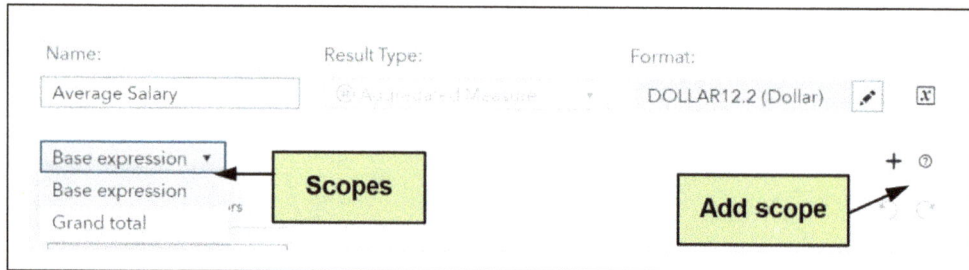

Note: All aggregated measures must have a base expression.

Note: Scopes enable you to apply different expressions for different crossings of categories. The expression for each scope is applied only when that exact crossing of categories is displayed in an object. Wherever that exact crossing of categories is not displayed, the base expression is applied.

The crosstab should resemble the following:

Department ▲	Purchasing	Sales	Total
Job Title ▲	Average Salary	Average Salary	Average Salary
Purchasing Agent I	$31,760.00	———	**$31,760.00**
Purchasing Agent III	$35,070.00	———	**$35,070.00**
Sales Rep. I	———	$26,417.79	**$26,417.79**
Sales Rep. II	———	$27,373.58	**$27,373.58**
Sales Rep. III	———	$29,457.35	**$29,457.35**
Sales Rep. IV	———	$31,880.51	**$31,880.51**
Temp. Sales Rep.	———	$26,317.43	**$26,317.43**
Trainee	———	$25,260.80	**$25,260.80**
Total	**$33,966.67**	**$27,566.22**	**$17,854,545.00**

Total Salary

e.   Save the report.

End of Practices

The Suppress Operator

The Suppress operator hides aggregated values if the specified condition is true. Hidden values are displayed as an asterisk within objects. Suppressed data is commonly used to protect the identity of individuals in aggregated data when some aggregations are sparse. For example, suppose your data contains test scores by school district for various demographics. If one of your demographic categories is represented by only a single student, the value would represent the score for that student. Data suppression hides the test score for the student so that the test score is not publicized. The suppress operator requires several parameters: the suppression condition, the suppressed value, and the suppression application. The suppression condition will determine which rows to hide. In this example, any group that has a count of quantity less than 5 will be hidden. The suppressed value will determine which values to hide. In Figure 11.9, total quantity by group will be hidden if the group contains a count less than 5. All other groups will show the total quantity by group.

Figure 11.9: Aggregated (Advanced) Operators: Suppress

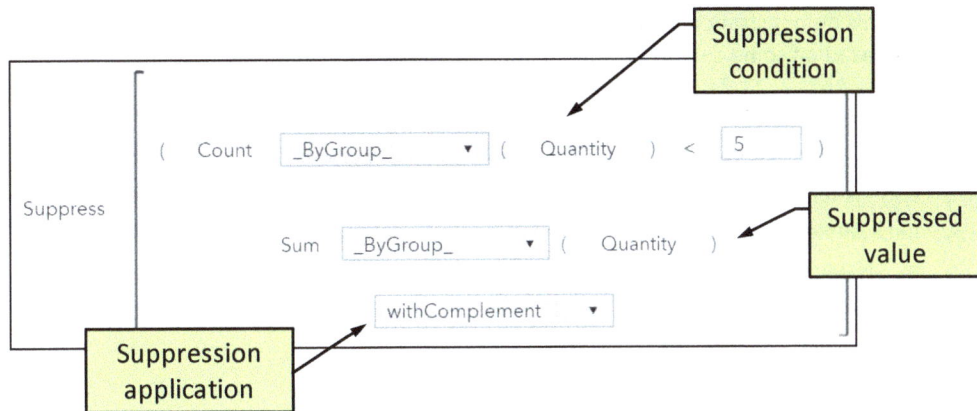

The suppression application specifies whether additional values will be hidden when a single value is hidden for a group or subgroup. The withoutComplement option specifies that only values that meet the suppression condition are hidden, whereas the withComplement option specifies that additional values may be hidden if hidden values can be inferred by totals, subtotals, or other cell values. We will examine these options more in a later demo.

Note: The data item used in the suppression condition and the suppressed value do not have to be the same. For example, you can suppress total profit (suppressed value) for all countries where the number of orders is less than 10 (suppression condition).

When using suppressed data, keep the following best practices in mind:

- Never used the unsuppressed version of the data item in your report, even in filters and ranks. You can hide the unsuppressed version using the Data pane.

- Avoid using suppressed data in any object that is the source or target of a filter action. Filtering can sometimes make it possible to infer the value of suppressed data.

- Avoid assigning hierarchies to objects that contain suppressed data. Expanding or drilling down on a hierarchy can sometimes make it possible to infer the value of suppressed data.

Note: The suppression application parameter can have one of the following values:

withoutComplement	Only values that meet the suppression condition are suppressed.
withComplement	Values that do not meet the suppression condition might be suppressed if the hidden value can be inferred by totals, subtotals, or other cell values.

For more information about aggregated (advanced) operators, see "Reference: Operators for Data Expressions" in the *SAS Visual Analytics: Working with Report Data* documentation.

Demo 11.5: Creating an Advanced Aggregated Measure

This demonstration illustrates how to create an advanced aggregated measure that suppresses data values based on some condition.

1. From the browser window, sign in to SAS Viya.
2. In the upper left corner, click ☰ (**Show list of applications**) and select **Explore and Visualize**. SAS Visual Analytics appears.
3. Click **All Reports**.
   a. Navigate to the **Courses/YVA285/Advanced/Demos** folder.
   b. Double-click the **VA2-Demo7.2c** report to open it.
4. View display rules for the crosstab.
   a. In the canvas, click the crosstab object to select it.
   b. In the right pane, click **Rules**.

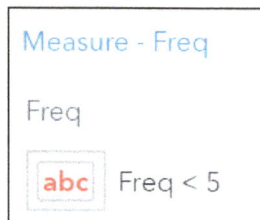

   Measure - Freq

   Freq

   `abc` Freq < 5

   If **Freq** is less than 5, the number is red and bold in the crosstab.
5. Create a new advanced aggregated measure, **Quantity (Suppress)**.
   c. In the left pane, click **Data**.
   d. Select **New data item** ⇨ **Calculated item**.
   e. In the **Name** field, enter **Quantity (Suppress)**.
   f. For the **Result Type** field, select **Aggregated Measure**.
   g. On the left side of the window, click **Operators**.
   h. Expand **Aggregated (advanced)**.
   i. Double-click **Suppress** to add it to the expression.
   j. Expand **Comparison**.
   k. Drag **x<y** to the **condition** area in the expression.
   l. Expand **Aggregated (simple)**.
   m. Drag **Count** to the **number** field on the left of the less than sign.
   n. For the Count operator, verify that **_ByGroup_** is specified.
   o. Right-click the **number** field for the Count operator and select **Replace with** ⇨ **Quantity**.
   p. Enter **5** in the **number** field on the right of the less than sign.
   q. On the left side of the window, expand **Aggregated (simple)** on the left side of the window, if necessary.
   r. Drag **Sum** to the **number** field in the Suppress operator.
   s. For the Sum operator, verify that **_ByGroup_** is specified.
   t. Right-click the **number** field for the Sum operator and select **Replace with** ⇨ **Quantity**.

u. For the Suppress operator, verify that **withComplement** is specified.

The expression should resemble the following:

Suppress	(Count	_ByGroup_ ▾	(Quantity)	<	5	)
	Sum	_ByGroup_ ▾	(Quantity)			
		withComplement ▾				

v. In the upper right corner of the window, for the **Format** field, click [✎] (**Edit**).

    i.   In the Format window, verify that **Comma** is selected as the format.

    ii.   For the **Width** field, verify that **12** is specified.

    iii.   For the **Decimals** field, enter **0**.

    iv.   Click **OK**.

w. Click **OK** to create the new periodic aggregated measure.

The Data pane should resemble the following:

> ∨ Aggregated Measure
>
> ◈ Frequency Percent
>
> ▦ Quantity (Suppress)   ≫

6. Modify the crosstab to use the advanced aggregated measure.

    a.   In the canvas, click the crosstab to select it.

    b.   In the right pane, click **Roles**.

    c.   For the **Measures** role, select **Quantity ⇨ Quantity (Suppress)**.

The crosstab should resemble the following:

Customer Group Name ▲	Internet/Catalog Customers		Orion Club Gold members	
Customer Country ▲	Freq	Quantity (Suppress)	Freq	Quantity (Suppress)
Andorra	-------	*	35	69
Australia	6,106	9,895	30,307	47,472
Austria	170	281	780	1,256
Belgium	1,434	2,468	12,616	21,279
Benin	-------	*	4	*
Bulgaria	1	*	6	8
Canada	405	749	1,762	3,325

When the frequency is less than 5 (including missing values), quantity values are suppressed. For Bulgaria, the quantity is suppressed for internet/catalog customers but not for Orion Club Gold members.

    d.   In the right pane, click **Options**.

e. In the Totals and Subtotals group, select **Totals**.

The crosstab should resemble the following:

| Customer Group Name ▲ | Total | | Internet/Catalog Customers | | Orion Club Gold members |
Customer Country ▲	Quantity (Suppress)	Freq	Quantity (Suppress)	Freq	Quantity (Suppress)
Total	1,597,317	76,965	134,343	483,438	808,676
Andorra	144	———	*	35	69
Australia	94,728	6,106	9,895	30,307	47,472
Austria	2,438	170	281	780	1,256
Belgium	42,109	1,434	2,468	12,616	21,279
Benin	20	———	*	4	*
Bulgaria	25	1	*	6	8
Canada	6,470	405	749	1,762	3,325

When totals are added, it might be possible to infer a hidden value for a group. The withComplement option hides additional values, so hidden values cannot be inferred.

7. Modify the advanced aggregated measure.

a. In the left pane, click **Data**.

b. Right-click **Quantity (Suppress)** and select **Edit**.

c. For the Suppress operator, select **withoutComplement**.

The expression should resemble the following:

Suppress	(Count [_ByGroup_ ▾] (Quantity) < [5])
	Sum [_ByGroup_ ▾] (Quantity)
	[withoutComplement ▾]

d. Click **OK** to apply the changes.

The crosstab should resemble the following:

| Customer Group Name ▲ | Total | | Internet/Catalog Customers | | Orion Club Gold members |
Customer Country ▲	Quantity (Suppress)	Freq	Quantity (Suppress)	Freq	Quantity (Suppress)
Total	1,597,317	76,965	134,343	483,438	808,676
Andorra	144	———	*	35	69
Australia	94,728	6,106	9,895	30,307	47,472
Austria	2,438	170	281	780	1,256
Belgium	42,109	1,434	2,468	12,616	21,279
Benin	20	———	*	4	*
Bulgaria	25	1	*	6	8
Canada	6,470	405	749	1,762	3,325

The withoutComplement option does not hide additional values when a hidden value can be inferred.

8. Save the report.

End of Demonstration

Practice 11.5

1. Creating an Advanced Aggregated Measure

a. Open the browser and sign in to SAS Viya.

b. Open the **VA2-Practice7.2c** report in the **Courses/YVA285/Advanced/Practices** folder.

c. In the list table, replace **Order Date** with **Customer Country.**

   Note: The Cumulative operator works only with date or datetime data items.

d. Create a new advanced aggregated measure (**Aggregate Profit**) that calculates a running total for **Profit** over the countries.

   Hint: Use the AggregateCells operator to create the new aggregated measure.

e. In the list table, replace **Cumulative Profit** with **Aggregate Profit.**

f. Answer the following question:

   What is the total profit for all countries?

   Answer:

   The list table should resemble the following:

Customer Country ▲	Profit	Aggregate Profit
Andorra	$223.60	$223.60
Australia	$461,983.93	$462,207.53
Austria	$7,873.73	$470,081.26
Belgium	$189,299.54	$659,380.79
Benin	$81.00	$659,461.79
Bulgaria	$105.80	$659,567.59
Canada	$60,103.96	$719,671.55

g. Save the report.

Challenge (Optional)

1. **Working with the CumulativePeriod Scope Parameter (_ToDate_)**

a. Open the browser and sign in to SAS Viya.

b. Open the **VA2-Practice7.2c (Challenge 1)** report in the **Courses/YVA285/Advanced/Practices** folder.

c. Answer the following question:

   What is the cumulative profit for Dec2012? Does this match the total profit for 2012 in the Yearly list table?

   Answer:

d. Edit the **Cumulative Period (First Quarter)** data item to aggregate profit through the first quarter only.

e. Answer the following question:

   What is the cumulative profit for Mar2012? Does this match the new total profit for 2012 in the Yearly list table?

   Answer:

f. Save the report.

2. **Working with the First Operator**

   a. Open the browser and sign in to SAS Viya.

   b. Open the **VA2-Practice7.2c (Challenge 2)** report in the **Courses/YVA285/Advanced/Practices** folder.

   c. Create a new aggregated measure (**First Month**) that calculates the order total for the first month of the year only.

   d. Add the new aggregated measure to the Yearly list table.

   e. Answer the following question:

      What is the order total for Jan2014? Does this match the order total for 2014 in the Yearly list table?

      Answer:

   f. Save the report.

   End of Practices

Chapter 12: Advanced Topics – Creating Advanced Filters

12.1 Introduction

In Chapter 3, we discussed basic filters that you can use in SAS Visual Analytics. In this chapter, we explore advanced filters that enable you to create filters that use more than one data item and filters that use data parameters.

The following types of filters can be created and modified only by the report designer.

Table 12.1: Report Designer Filters

Filter	Description
Data source filter	Subsets the data for the entire report and is applied to every report object that uses that data source. The data source filter acts as a pre-filter by filtering the data before it is brought into Visual Analytics. This can be seen by the updated cardinality values in the Data pane after the filter has been applied.
Basic report filter	Subsets the data for individual report objects by using a single data item.
Advanced report filter	Subsets the data for individual report objects by using any number of data items and operators in the same expression.
Post-aggregate report filter	Subsets the data for individual report objects by using aggregated values, not detail values. Post-aggregate report filters are available only for measure data items.

For more information about filters that can be created and modified by the report designer, see "Working with Report Filters" in the *SAS Visual Analytics: Working with Report Data* documentation.

Filters that can be modified by report viewers are discussed in more detail in a later section.

Filters are applied in the following order:

- data source filters

- basic or advanced report filters/ post-aggregate report filters

- prompts and actions

Activity 12.1

Which Date and Time operator could be used to calculate the date value for four years prior to today?

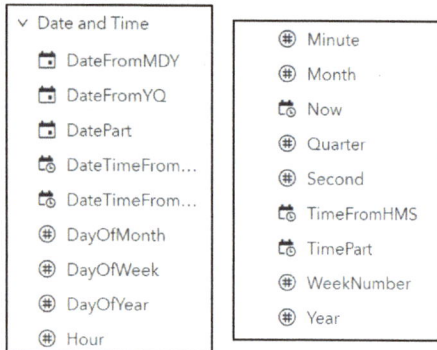

12.2 Post-Aggregate Report Filters

Post-aggregate filters subset the data for individual objects in your reports by using the aggregated values, not the detail data values. You can use the Filters pane to filter data in an object using an aggregated value instead of a detail value. Post-aggregate filters are available only for measure data items. When an object has both ranks and post-aggregate filters applied, the ranks are applied before the post-aggregate filters. The following points should be considered when using post-aggregated filters:

- Post-aggregate filters are not available for objects that use detail data.

- Crosstabs, time series plots, and dual axis time series plots do not support post-aggregate filters.

- Advanced analytics objects do not support post-aggregate filters.

Create a Post-Aggregate Report Filter

1. If it is not already selected, select the object on the canvas that you want to filter. The object must have at least one data item assigned.

2. Tip: Clear the **Auto-update** check box above the report canvas until you are ready to apply your filter changes.

3. If the side pane is not displayed, click ⊞ in the toolbar.

4. Click ▽. The **Filters** pane is displayed.

5. Click **New filter** and select a measure data item from the list. The filter appears in the **Filters** pane.

6. Select the **Filter aggregated values** check box. A slider shows you the maximum and minimum data values that exist for the data item using the current data item format. Use the slider to select a range of target values.

Note: Filtering aggregated values is disabled if hierarchies are assigned to the object.

Hint: Use the arrow to the left of the filter name in the Filters pane to expand or collapse the filter details when you are working with multiple filters.

Demo 12.1: Applying an Advanced Filter

This demonstration illustrates how to apply an advanced filter to a time series plot.

1. From the browser window, sign in to SAS Viya.
2. In the upper left corner, click ☰ (**Show list of applications**) and select **Explore and Visualize**. SAS Visual Analytics appears.
3. Click **All Reports**.
    a. Navigate to the **Courses/YVA285/Advanced/Demos** folder.
    b. Double-click the **VA2-Demo8.1a** report to open it.
4. Create an advanced filter on the time series plot for the past four years from today.
    a. In the canvas, click the time series plot to select it, if necessary.
    b. In the right pane, click **Filters**.
    c. Select **New filter** ⇨ **Advanced filter**.
        i.   In the **Name** field, enter **Filter: Last 4 Years**.
        ii. On the left side of the window, verify that Data Items is selected.
        iii. Expand **Date**.
        iv. Click **Order Date**.
        v.   In the **Conditions** area, double-click **Order Date > 'x'** to add it to the expression.
        vi. In the left side of the window, click **Operators**.
        vii. Expand **Date and Time**.
        viii. Drag **DateFromMDY** to the **No** selection field in the expression.
        ix. Drag **Month** to the first field in the expression.
        x.   Drag **DatePart** to the field for the Month operator in the expression.
        xi. Drag **Now** to the field for the **DatePart** operator in the expression.
        xii. Right-click **Month(DatePart(Now()))** and select **Copy**.
        xiii. Right-click in the second field in the expression and select **Paste**.
        xiv. Right-click the **Month** operator and select **Replace Operator with** ⇨ **DayOfMonth**.
        xv. On the left side of the window, expand **Numeric (simple)**.
        xvi. Drag **x-y** to the last field in the expression.
        xvii. Right-click in the field on the left of the minus sign and select **Paste**.
        xviii. Right-click the **Month** operator and select **Replace Operator with** ⇨ **Year**.
        xix. In the **number** field on the right of the minus sign, enter **4**.

        The expression should resemble the following:

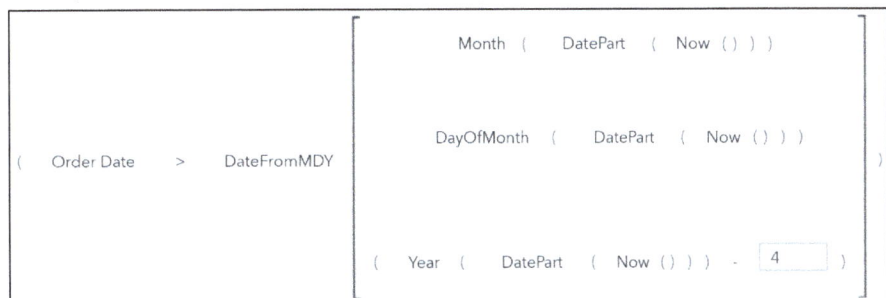

	Month (DatePart (Now ( )))
(Order Date > DateFromMDY	DayOfMonth (DatePart (Now ( )))
	(Year (DatePart (Now ( ))) - [4])

        The bottom of the window should resemble the following:

Returned observations: 210,918	Total observations: 951,669

Note: The number of returned observations might differ based on today's date.

xx.   Click **OK** to create the filter.

The time series plot should resemble the following:

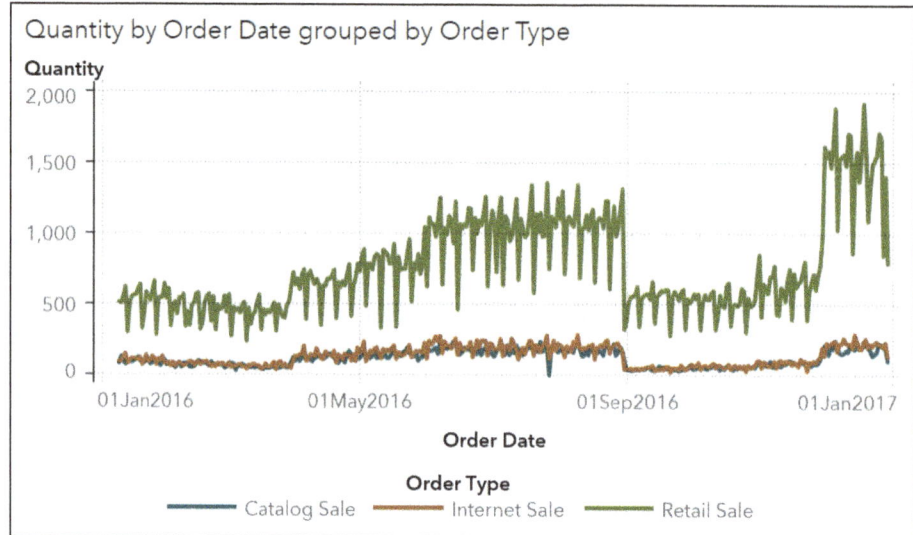

Quantity by Order Date grouped by Order Type

5.   Save the report.

End of Demonstration

Practice 12.1

1.   **Creating a Post-Aggregate Filter**

a.   Open the browser and sign in to SAS Viya.

b.   Open the **VA2-Practice8.1a** report in the **Courses/YVA285/Advanced/Practices** folder.

c.   Add a filter on the list table for **Quantity** and answer the following question:

What is the range for **Quantity**?

Answer:

d.   Change the filter to a post-aggregate filter and answer the following question:

What is the range for aggregate **Quantity**?

Answer:

e.   Filter for countries with a total quantity greater than 100,000 and answer the following question:

How many countries have a total quantity greater than 100,000?

Answer:

f.   Save the report.

End of Practices

Activity 12.2

Which operator enables a numeric or datetime value to be used as a different type for the calculation?

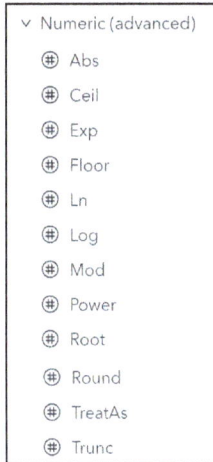

> ∨ Numeric (advanced)
>
>   ⊕ Abs
>
>   ⊕ Ceil
>
>   ⊕ Exp
>
>   ⊕ Floor
>
>   ⊕ Ln
>
>   ⊕ Log
>
>   ⊕ Mod
>
>   ⊕ Power
>
>   ⊕ Root
>
>   ⊕ Round
>
>   ⊕ TreatAs
>
>   ⊕ Trunc

Adding Ranks

You can use Ranks to filter the data by ranking the data in an object to show the top (greatest) count or percent or the bottom (least) count or percent for a category that is based on a measure. For a list table, you can also rank across a set of categories for the top value or bottom value in the set. A rank filters the values of a category based on the aggregated measure by the top or bottom of the values. A rank greatly reduces the visible categories to make it easier to focus on the top value or bottom value that interests a user.

For example, you might create a rank of the top 10 countries by frequency to select the 10 countries that are most represented in your report. As another example, you might create a rank of the top 10 countries by population to select the 10 countries with the greatest populations.

Here are some key points about ranks:

- Controls and gauges support ranks.

- Ranks can accept parameters. For more information, see "Working with Parameters in Reports in SAS Visual Analytics: Working with Report Data" in the *SAS Visual Analytics 8.5* documentation.

- Ranks can be added to an object before the data roles are assigned.

- For slider controls, you cannot assign a rank to a category data item (either a date or a categorical numeric) that is also assigned to the slider itself.

- For time series plots, you cannot assign a rank to the data item that is assigned to the **Time axis** role. If a data item has a rank, then you cannot assign that data item to the **Time axis** role.

Demo 12.2: Applying an Advanced Rank

This demonstration illustrates how to add an advanced rank to a time series plot to view rolling quarters.

1. From the browser window, sign in to SAS Viya.
2. In the upper left corner, click ☰ (**Show list of applications**) and select **Explore and Visualize**. SAS Visual Analytics appears.
3. Click **All Reports**.

    a.   Navigate to the **Courses/YVA285/Advanced/Demos** folder.

    b.   Double-click the **VA2-Demo8.1b** report to open it.

4.   Create a numeric data item from **Order Quarter**.

    a.   In the left pane, click **Data**.

    b.   Select **New data item ⇨ Calculated item**.

    c.   In the **Name** field, enter **Order Quarter (Numeric)**.

    d.   For the **Result Type** field, verify that **Automatic (Numeric)** is selected.

    e.   On the left side of the window, click **Operators**.

    f.   Expand **Numeric (advanced)**.

    g.   Double-click **TreatAs** to add it to the expression.

    h.   Verify that **_Number_** is specified for the TreatAs operator.

    i.   Right-click the **number** field for the TreatAs operator and select **Replace with ⇨ Order Quarter**. The expression should resemble the following:

```
          ┌─                              ─┐
          │  ┌──────────────────────┐      │
          │  │  _Number_          ▼ │      │
TreatAs   │  └──────────────────────┘      │
          │        Order Quarter           │
          └─                              ─┘
```

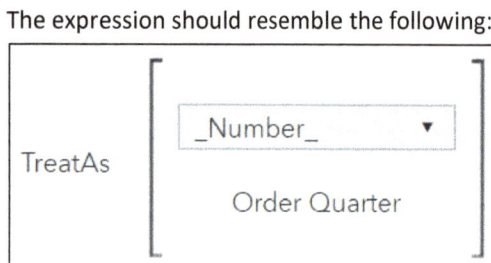

    j.   In the lower right corner, click **Preview**.

Number of rows to show: 50 ▼ ⓘ

Order Quarter (Numeric)	Order Quarter
18,993.00	1st quarter 2012
18,993.00	1st quarter 2012
18,993.00	1st quarter 2012

This expression calculates **Order Quarter** as the number of days since January 1, 1960.

    k.   Click **Close** to close the Preview Result window.

    l.   Click **OK** to create the new calculated item. The Data pane should resemble the following:

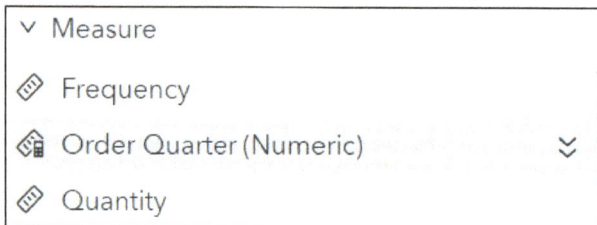

```
⌄ Measure

  ◈  Frequency

  ▦  Order Quarter (Numeric)              ⌄

  ◈  Quantity
```

5.   Add the new data item to the list table.

    a.   In the canvas, click the list table to select it.

    b.   In the right pane, click **Roles**.

    c.   For the **Columns** role, select **Add ⇨ Order Quarter (Numeric)**.

    d.   Click **OK**.

e. Click the **Order Quarter (Numeric)** column to sort in ascending order.

The list table should resemble the following:

Order Quarter	Order Quarter (Numeric) ▲
1st quarter 2012	663,672,399.00
3rd quarter 2012	742,034,150.00
4th quarter 2012	766,595,396.00
2nd quarter 2012	807,062,360.00
1st quarter 2013	818,266,212.00
1st quarter 2015	842,673,283.00

Notice that the quarters are not in the correct order. By default, all numeric columns have an aggregation of Sum. Because some quarters have more days and more orders than others, they are given a higher value. We need to change the aggregation to something that is nonadditive (minimum, medium, or maximum).

f. In the left pane, click **Data**.

g. Next to **Order Quarter (Numeric)**, click ⌄ (**Edit properties**).

h. For the **Aggregation** field, select **Minimum**.

The list table should resemble the following:

Order Quarter	Order Quarter (Numeric) ▲
1st quarter 2012	18,993.00
2nd quarter 2012	19,084.00
3rd quarter 2012	19,175.00
4th quarter 2012	19,267.00
1st quarter 2013	19,359.00

Now **Order Quarter (Numeric)** represents the numeric value of the first day of the quarter in which an order was placed. Therefore, the quarters are sorted appropriately. The numeric value of the first day of the quarter in which an order was placed is the number of days between January 1, 1960, and that date. Notice that as we get farther from 1960, the numeric dates increase.

6. Add a rank to the time series plot to see the last four quarters.

a. In the canvas, click the time series plot to select it.

b. In the right pane, click **Ranks**.

c. Select **New rank** ⇨ **Order Quarter**.

d. Verify that **Top Count** is selected.

Note: This selects the most recent quarters.

e. In the **Count** field, enter **8**.

f. For the **By** field, select **Order Quarter (Numeric)**.

The Ranks pane should resemble the following:

∨ Order Quarter	🗑
Top count	▾
Count:	
8	▾
By:	
Order Quarter (Numeric)	▾
Include:	
☐ Ties	

The time series plot should resemble the following:

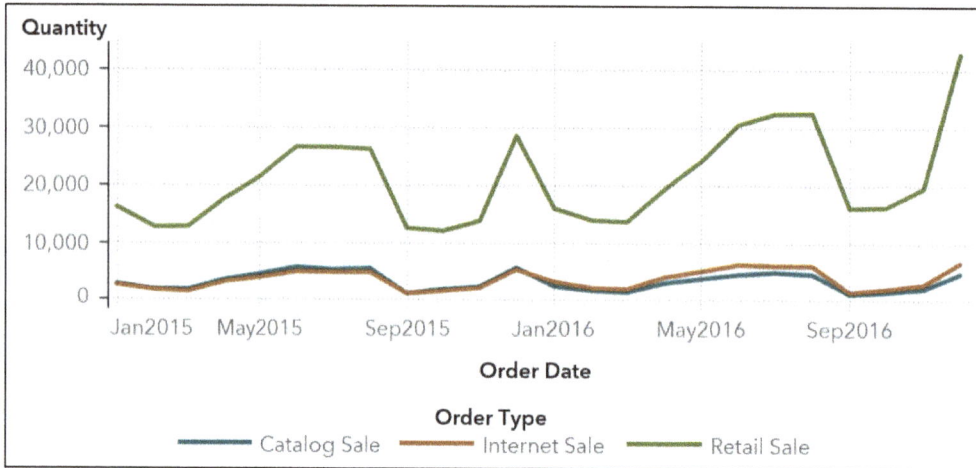

The time series plot shows the last eight quarters (that is, the past two years) of data. The plot updates as new rows are added to the data source.

7. Save the report.

End of Demonstration

12.3 Creating Advanced Interactive Filters

A *parameter* is a variable whose value can be changed and that can be referenced by other objects. SAS Visual Analytics supports parameters for controls in reports. If a control has an associated parameter, then when the value of the control changes, the parameter is assigned that changed value. When the value of the parameter changes, any objects that reference the parameter detect the change accordingly. Whenever a parameter value is updated, then all display rules, ranks, calculations, and filters that use that parameter are updated. Any object in the report that uses the display rule, rank, calculation, or filter is updated accordingly.

Parameters can also be used in the following filters: detail filters, aggregated filters, and data source filters. Multiple-value parameters can be used only with the In, NotIn, and IsSet operators. The data source filter is a special case. Ordinarily, a data source filter applies to all of the objects on the canvas. However, if the data source filter contains a parameter, then the filter is not applied to the control that has that parameter assigned to it.

Links

Links are report actions that are used to direct someone's attention to specific results in a report. (In SAS Visual Analytics 7.4 and earlier releases, actions were known as *report interactions*.) Actions, such as filters, ranks and links, enable users to understand data within a particular context.

Linked selection enables you to show the same data selected simultaneously in two or more tables, graphs, or controls. (In SAS Visual Analytics 7.4 and earlier releases, linked selection was known as *data brushing*.) The linked selection highlights a percentage that reflects the number of shared observations in the data set. The linked selection does not highlight a percentage that corresponds to the aggregated value. The data for the linked selection has the same appearance in each object, which makes the data easily apparent to users.

A link enables single-step access to a report or web page that is related to the current report. You can add a link from an object to another report, to a specific page in the current report, or to an external URL. If a destination report contains multiple pages, then you are able (when defining the link) to choose the initial page of the destination report that you want to open first.

Linking has elements of both a filter and an action. A report page that is the target of a link is filtered by the values that are selected in the linked object. And, like actions, objects that display detail data cannot be the source of a link.

The **Actions** pane in SAS Visual Analytics enables you to specify which actions you want to add to tables, graphs, and controls in a report. It provides an easy way to set up a single filter; a linked selection; or a page, report, or URL link.

The **Actions Diagram** is an alternative to using the Actions pane. In addition to all the features that the Actions pane offers, the Actions Diagram provides a quick, visual way for you to see how multiple actions and links are related or to create many actions at one time.

You can create actions between controls in the page prompt area using either the Actions pane or the Actions Diagram. However, you cannot create actions between objects in the page prompt area and objects on the page using the Actions Diagram. For more information, see "Using the Actions Diagram" in the *SAS Visual Analytics 7.5* documentation.

Figure 12.1: Interactive Filters

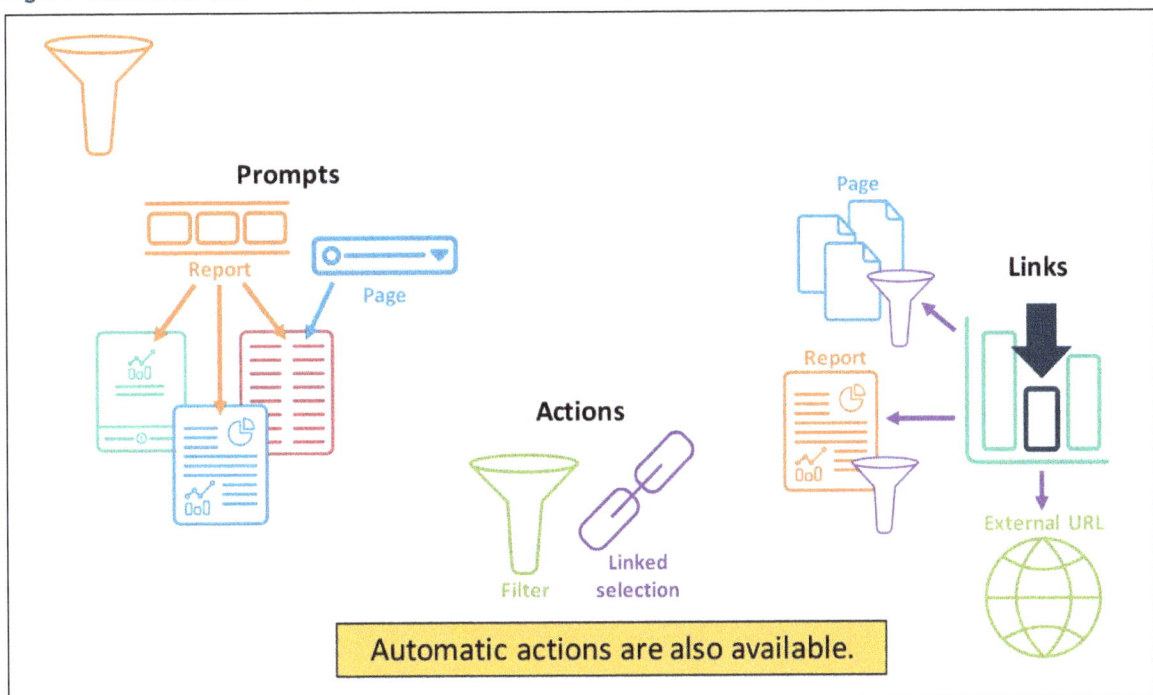

The following types of filters can be modified by report viewers.

Table 12.2: Report Viewer Filters

Filter	Description	
Report prompt	Automatically subsets the data for all objects in the report as long as the report object uses the same data source as the prompt. *	
Page prompt	Automatically subsets the data for all objects on the page as long as the report object uses the same data source as the prompt. *	
Filter action	Subsets the data in the target object based on selections in a source object.	
Linked selection action	Highlights the data in the target object based on selections in a source object.	
Automatic actions	Automatically add actions to objects on a page. The following types of automatic actions are available:	
	One-way filters	Applies filters in the order in which they are selected.
	Two-way filters	Applies filters to all objects on the page, even previously selected objects.
	Linked selections	Simultaneously highlights the same data in all objects on a page based on the selections.
Links	Subsets the report, a page, or an external URL based on the selections in a source object. Links pass a value to filter the target object (report or page) when the source and target are based on the same data source.	

* For all prompts and actions, if the report objects use different data sources, automatic mappings are applied. You can modify the data source mappings by right-clicking the control and selecting **Edit data source mappings**. For more information about mapping data sources, see "Map Data Sources for Actions and Links" in the *SAS Visual Analytics: Working with Report Data* documentation.

For more information about prompts, see "Working with Controls" in the *SAS Visual Analytics: Working with Report Content* documentation.

For more information about actions and links, see "Working with Report Actions and Links" in the *SAS Visual Analytics: Working with Report Data* documentation.

Linked selection automatic actions simultaneously show the same data in multiple objects. The linked selection has the same appearance in each object, which makes the data relationship easily apparent to report viewers. In Figure 12.2, a report viewer selects a bubble in the bubble plot, which highlights the same data in the other objects. Linked selection actions can be applied in any order. For example, if a report viewer selects the bar in the bar chart, the same data would be highlighted in other objects.

Figure 12.2: Automatic Action Linked Selection

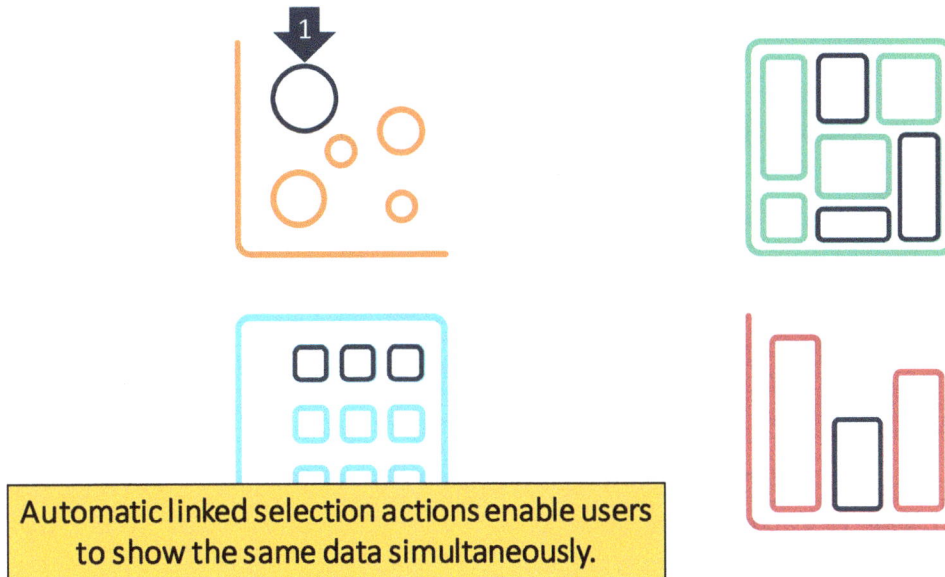

Automatic linked selection actions enable users to show the same data simultaneously.

Demo 12.3: Applying Automatic Actions: Linked Selection

This demonstration illustrates how to apply automatic actions (linked selection) to a report.

1. From the browser window, sign in to SAS Viya.
2. In the upper left corner, click ☰ (**Show list of applications**) and select **Explore and Visualize**. SAS Visual Analytics appears.
3. Click **All Reports**.
   a. Navigate to the **Courses/YVA285/Advanced/Demos** folder.
   b. Double-click **VA2-Demo8.2a** report to open it.
4. Apply automatic actions (linked selection) to the report.
   a. In the canvas, click the crosstab to select it.
   b. In the right pane, click **Actions**.
   c. Select **Automatic actions on all objects**.
   d. Select **Linked selection**.

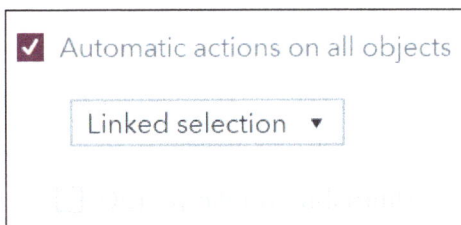

e. In the crosstab, click the cell for **Belgium** and **Catalog Sale**.

The associated data in the other objects is selected.

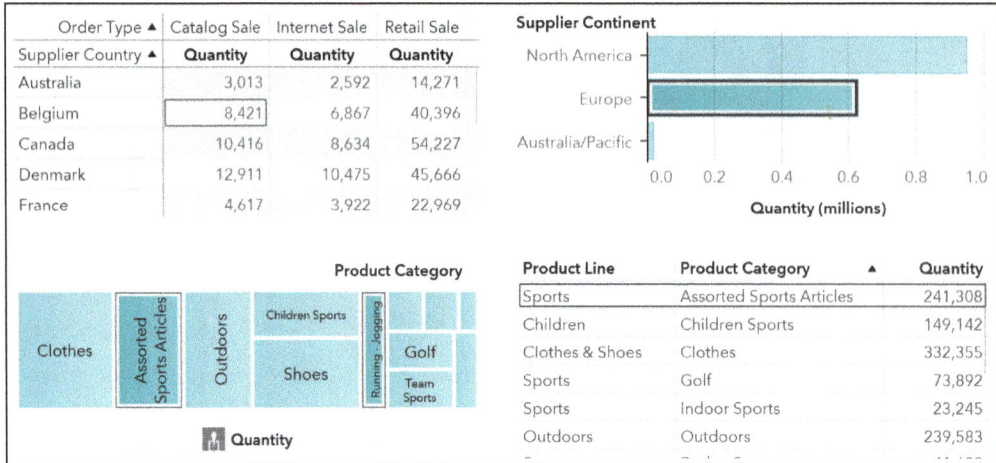

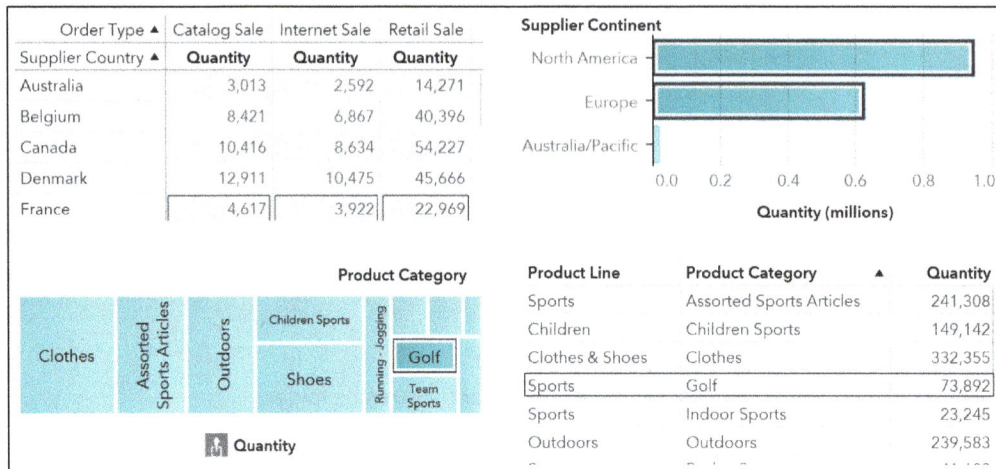

| Order Type ▲ | Catalog Sale | Internet Sale | Retail Sale |
Supplier Country ▲	**Quantity**	**Quantity**	**Quantity**
Australia	3,013	2,592	14,271
Belgium	8,421	6,867	40,396
Canada	10,416	8,634	54,227
Denmark	12,911	10,475	45,666
France	4,617	3,922	22,969

Supplier Continent

North America / Europe / Australia/Pacific — Quantity (millions) 0.0 0.2 0.4 0.6 0.8 1.0

Product Category (treemap): Clothes, Assorted Sports Articles, Outdoors, Children Sports, Shoes, Running - Jogging, Golf, Team Sports — Quantity

Product Line	Product Category ▲	Quantity
Sports	Assorted Sports Articles	241,308
Children	Children Sports	149,142
Clothes & Shoes	Clothes	332,355
Sports	Golf	73,892
Sports	Indoor Sports	23,245
Outdoors	Outdoors	239,583

f. In the treemap, click the **Golf** tile to select it.

The associated data in other objects is selected.

| Order Type ▲ | Catalog Sale | Internet Sale | Retail Sale |
Supplier Country ▲	**Quantity**	**Quantity**	**Quantity**
Australia	3,013	2,592	14,271
Belgium	8,421	6,867	40,396
Canada	10,416	8,634	54,227
Denmark	12,911	10,475	45,666
France	4,617	3,922	22,969

Supplier Continent

North America / Europe / Australia/Pacific — Quantity (millions) 0.0 0.2 0.4 0.6 0.8 1.0

Product Category (treemap): Clothes, Assorted Sports Articles, Outdoors, Children Sports, Shoes, Running - Jogging, Golf, Team Sports — Quantity

Product Line	Product Category ▲	Quantity
Sports	Assorted Sports Articles	241,308
Children	Children Sports	149,142
Clothes & Shoes	Clothes	332,355
Sports	Golf	73,892
Sports	Indoor Sports	23,245
Outdoors	Outdoors	239,583

5. Save the report.

End of Demonstration

One-way filter automatic actions apply filters in the order in which they are selected. In Figure 12.3, a report viewer performs the following actions, in order:

- selects a bubble in the bubble plot (which filters the treemap, the crosstab, and the bar chart)

- selects a bar in the bar chart (which filters the treemap and the crosstab)

- selects a tile in the treemap (which filters the crosstab)

Typically, the one-way filter automatic action is used for objects that are hierarchical or cascading.

Figure 12.3: One-Way Filter Automatic Actions

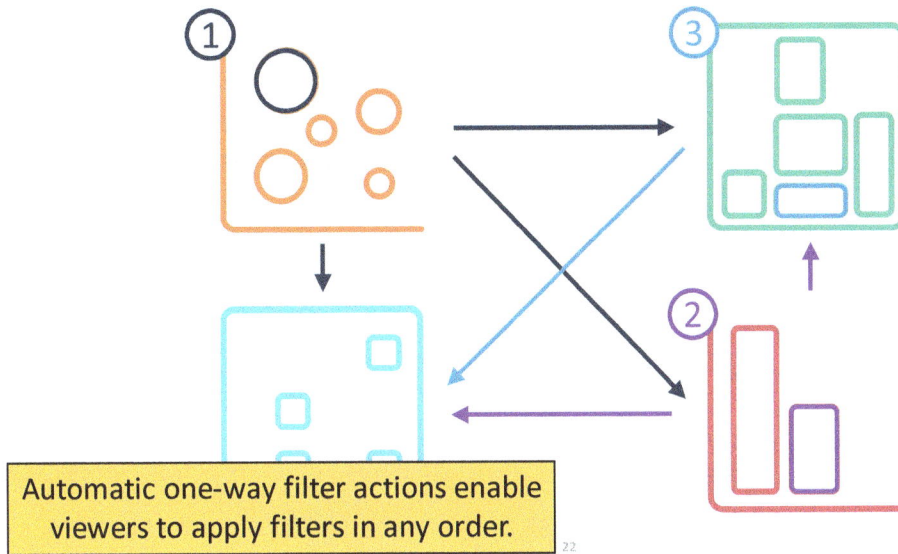

Automatic one-way filter actions enable viewers to apply filters in any order.

Two-way filter automatic actions apply filters to all objects on a page, even previously selected objects. In Figure 12.4, a report viewer performs the following actions, in order:

- selects a bubble in the bubble plot (which filters the treemap, the crosstab, and the bar chart)
- selects a bar in the bar chart (which filters the bubble plot, the treemap and the crosstab)
- selects a tile in the treemap (which filters the bubble plot, the crosstab, and the bar chart)

Note: Only objects that can be the source of a filter can participate in the two-way filter automatic action.

Figure 12.4: Two-Way Filter Automatic Actions

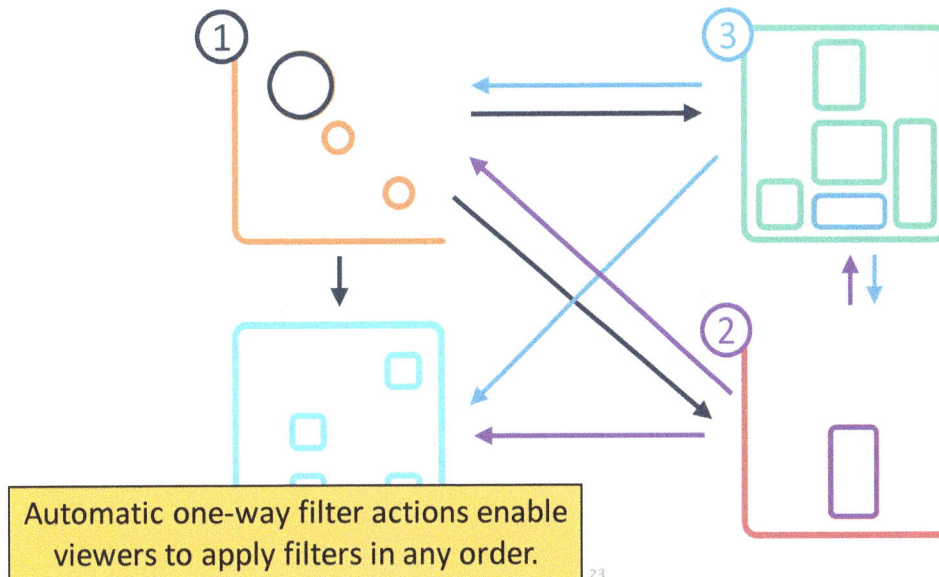

Automatic one-way filter actions enable viewers to apply filters in any order.

 Practice 12.2

1. Applying Automatic Actions: One-Way Filters
   a. Open the browser and sign in to SAS Viya.
   b. Open the **VA2-Practice8.2a** report in the **Courses/YVA285/Advanced/Practices** folder.
   c. Apply a one-way filter automatic action to the report.
   d. Answer the following questions:
      To which product line does the Running - Jogging product category belong?
      Answer:
      Which product groups are in the Running - Jogging product category?
      Answer:
   e. Save the report.

Challenge (Optional)

1. **Applying Automatic Actions: Two-Way Filters**
   a. Open the browser and sign in to SAS Viya.
   b. Open the **VA2-Practice8.2a (Challenge)** report in the **Courses/YVA285/Advanced/Practices** folder.
   c. Answer the following question:
      How many orders were placed for products supplied by Australia/Pacific?
      Answer:
   d. Apply a two-way filter automatic action to the report.
   e. View details about the Sports and Outdoors product lines and answer the following question:
      How many orders were placed for products supplied by Australia/Pacific for the Sports and Outdoors product lines?
      Answer:
   f. View details about the Golf product category and answer the following questions:
      To which product line does the Golf product category belong?
      Answer:
      How many Golf orders were supplied by Australia/Pacific?
      Answer:
   g. View details about Golf orders in North America and answer the following question:
      When you select a row in the list table, are the other objects filtered?
      Answer:
   h. Modify options for the list table so that it does ***not*** show detail data and answer the following question:
      When you select a row in the list table now, are the other objects filtered?
      Answer:
   i. Save the report.
      Note: All of your filters are saved when you save a report. If you do not want the saved report to have the filters applied, then you need to clear the filters before saving the report.

   End of Practices

The training center managers have requested a calendar that shows which courses are being delivered over a 90-day span. Specifically, they would like to specify a date and see all courses scheduled for the 90 days after that date. We will use parameters to create the requested report. Because the user would like to specify a date, we will need to create a date parameter (DateParameter). To populate this parameter, we will use a text input control, so viewers can enter a date directly. We will apply the parameter to an advanced filter that filters the calendar to all courses scheduled for the 90 days after that date.

Using a Parameter in an External Link

This demonstration illustrates how to use parameters in an external URL link.

1. From the browser window, sign in to SAS Viya.
2. In the upper left corner, click ☰ (**Show list of applications**) and select **Explore and Visualize**. SAS Visual Analytics appears.
3. Click **All Reports**.
    a. Navigate to the **Courses/YVA285/Advanced/Demos** folder.
    b. Double-click the **VA2-Demo8.2b** report to open it.
4. View the structure of the link for Amazon.
    a. Open a new tab in the browser.
    b. In the address bar of the browser, enter **www.amazon.com** and press Enter.
    c. In the Search bar, enter **Badminton** and press Enter.

    d. Make a note of the web address: https://www.amazon.com/s?k=Badminton&ref=nb_sb_noss_2
        The web address consists of two parts:
        -   The main portion of the link: https://www.amazon.com/s
        -   The portion of the link referencing parameters: ?k=Badminton&ref=nb_sb_noss_2

        Note: In a web address, the list of parameters follow the ? (question mark). Parameters are specified as a sequence of name=value pairs, separated by the & (ampersand).

        We will combine the main portion of the link, the ? (question mark), and the ref=nb_sb_noss_2 parameter reference. Then we will use k=*parameter* when creating an external link for the report.
5. Add an external link to the list table in the report.
    a. In the browser, click the **VA2-Demo8.2b – SAS Visual Analytics** tab to return to the report.
    b. In the canvas, click the list table to select it.
    c. In the right pane, click **Actions**.
    d. Expand **URL Links**.
        i.   Click New URL Link.
        ii.   In the **Name** field, enter **Link to Amazon**.
        iii. In the **URL** field, enter the following:
              https://www.amazon.com/s/?ref=nb_sb_noss_2
        iv.   Next to **Parameters**, click ➕ (**Add**) to add a new parameter for the link.
        v.   For the **Source** field, verify that **Product Group** is specified.

vi.   In the **Target** field, enter **k**.

Source:

Number of Orders by Product Group

Name: Link to Amazon

URL: https://www.amazon.com/s/?ref=nb_sb_noss_2

Parameters   +

                Source: Target:

                ⌂ Product Group   ▾   k   🗑

vii.   Click **OK** to add the URL link action.

The Actions pane should resemble the following:

Actions   View Diagram

Number of Orders by Product Group   ▾

☐ Automatic actions on all objects

∨ Object Links

> Page Links

> Report Links

∨ URL Links

   Link to Amazon   ⋮
   + New URL Link

6.   Test the link.

    a.   In the page prompt area, click the **Sports** button to filter the page.

    b.   In the treemap, click the **Assorted Sports Articles** tile to filter the list table.

       The report should resemble the following:

Select a product line:

Children	Clothes & Shoes	Outdoors	Sports

Product Category

Running - Jogging

Swim Sports

Racket Sports

Assorted Sports Articles

Golf

Team Sports

Winter Sports

116,267
11,755

Number of Orders

Product Group	▲	Number of Orders
Assorted Sports articles		66,960
Darts		20,404
Petanque - Boule		8,471
Skates		38,142

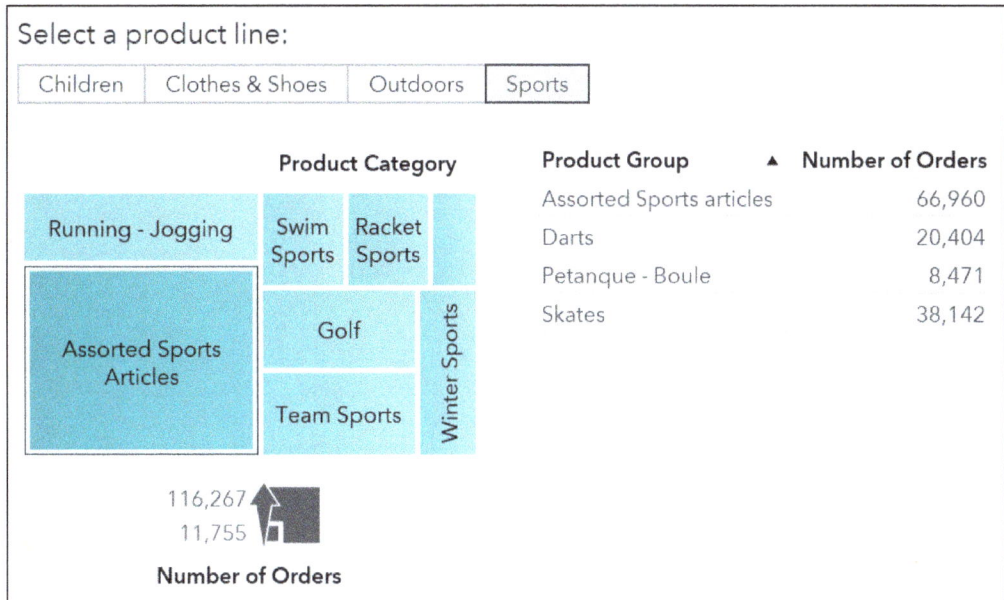

    c.   In the list table, double-click the **Skates** row to link to Amazon.

       Amazon appears, and search results appear for Skates items:

All ▾	Skates	🔍

    d.   In the browser, click the **VA2-Demo8.2b – SAS Visual Analytics** tab to return to the report.

7.   Save the report.

End of Demonstration

Note: Beginning in Visual Analytics 8.3, users can perform a data source join within SAS Visual Analytics without having to use the map data source functionality. For more information about data source joins, see "Working with Data Source Joins in Reports" in the *SAS Visual Analytics: Working with Report Data* documentation.

Practice 12.3

1.   Applying Filters between Two Different Data Sources

    a.   Open the browser and sign in to SAS Viya.

    b.   Open the **VA2-Practice8.2b** report in the **Courses/YVA285/Advanced/Practices** folder.

    c.   Answer the following questions:

       Which data source is used for the treemap?

       Answer:

       Which data source is used for the list table?

       Answer:

       Which data items can be used to map the two data sources?

       Answer:

d. Add a filter action from the treemap to the list table.

    Hint: Be sure to map the two data sources appropriately. Remember, the data items used to map the data sources need to be used in both report objects.

e. View details about employees who sold products in the Indoor Sports product category and answer the following questions:

    Which employee makes the highest salary (of those who sold Indoor Sports products)?

    Answer:

    What is the job title of the above employee?

    Answer:

f. Save the report.

End of Practices

Chapter 13: Advanced Topics – Using Parameters to Create Advanced Reports

13.1 Introduction

Parameters are data set independent dynamic variables in Visual Analytics that can be added to report controls to store user-selected value(s) of lists, buttons, sliders, and other controls into a variable or group of variables. Often underused, parameters provide you with a powerful level of control over the report.

There are three types of parameters available in Visual Analytics:

- Character
- Numeric
- Date/datetime

The types of values that a parameter will accept are self-explanatory. Character parameters can only accept character values, numeric parameters can only accept numeric values, and date/datetime parameters can only accept date or datetime values. Parameters are like categorical, measure, or datetime variables. They work with the same values, can be used in calculated variables, and can be assigned to controls.

There are two differentiating factors that make them such powerful assets in a report:

1. They are data set agnostic: parameters are independent of report data sets
2. They are dynamic: they change values as users interact with them

When you create a parameter, it is tied solely to the report and not any one data set, unlike a calculated variable, which can only be used within the data set in which it was created. Due to this data set independence, parameters require some sort of input to give them a value. This is either a static value that you decide, or a dynamic value that is populated from a control in the report.

Figure 13.1: Steps for Using Parameters

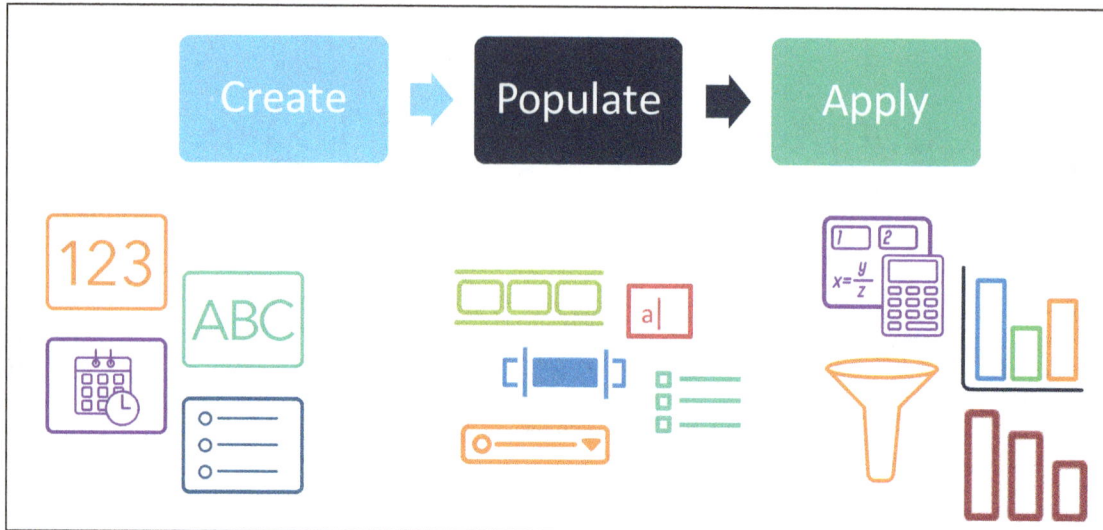

Table 13.1: Steps for Using Parameters

Step	Description
Create	In the Create step, you create the parameter using the Data pane. You need to know what type of parameter (numeric, character, date, multiple values) is needed for your scenario.
Populate	In the Populate step, you add a control object to the canvas so that the report viewer has some method to modify the value of the parameter. The type of control object you can use depends on the type of parameter that was created in the previous step and your scenario.
Apply	In the Apply step, you use the parameter in a calculation, a display rule, a filter, or a rank to make your report more dynamic.

The type of parameter must match the type of data that is required for the control object. The following table lists the supported control objects and parameter types:

Table 13.2: Control Objects and Parameter Types

Control Object	Parameters		
	Character	Numeric	Date/DateTime
Drop-Down List	Yes	No*	Yes
List (multiple values)	Yes	No*	Yes
Button Bar	Yes	No*	Yes
Text Input	Yes	Yes	Yes

Control Object	Parameters		
Slider (single-point only)	No	Yes	Yes

*Numeric parameters can be used with drop-down list, list, and button bar controls only if the underlying category data item is numeric.

13.2 Numeric Parameters

You can create a parameter in three places: from the Data tab's menu by right-clicking on the data item, from the Calculated Item advanced editor, or from the Aggregated Measure advanced editor.

Then you can simply name the parameter, select **Numeric** as the type, enter a minimum, maximum and current value, and select the desired format. Numeric parameters require a current value, which then serves as the default value.

Demo 13.1: Using a Numeric Parameter in a Rank

This demonstration illustrates how to create a numeric parameter, populate the parameter with a control object, and apply the parameter to a rank.

1. From the browser window, sign in to SAS Viya.
2. In the upper left corner, click ≡ (**Show list of applications**) and select **Explore and Visualize**.
   SAS Visual Analytics appears.
3. Click **All Reports**.
   a. Navigate to the **Courses/YVA285/Advanced/Demos** folder.
   b. Double-click the **VA2-Demo9.1** report to open it.
4. View the rank on the time series plot.
   a. On the canvas, click the time series plot to select it, if necessary.
   b. In the right pane, click **Ranks.**

> Ranks
>
> Quantity by Order Type and Date ▾
>
> **+** New rank
>
> ⌄ Order Quarter   🗑
>
>   Top count ▾
>
>   Count:
>
>   8 ▾
>
>   By:
>
>   Order Quarter (Numeric) ▾
>
>   Include:
>   ☐ Ties

The rank shows the most recent eight quarters of data in the table. We would like for the report viewer to choose how many quarters to view.

5. On the canvas, view the list table.

Order Quarter	Order Quarter (Numeric) ▲
1st quarter 2012	18,993.00
2nd quarter 2012	19,084.00
3rd quarter 2012	19,175.00
4th quarter 2012	19,267.00
1st quarter 2013	19,359.00

The dates in the table range from the first quarter in 2012 ...

1st quarter 2016	20,454.00
2nd quarter 2016	20,545.00
3rd quarter 2016	20,636.00
4th quarter 2016	20,728.00

... to the fourth quarter of 2016. That is five years of data, or 20 quarters.

6. Create a numeric parameter.

    a. In the left pane, click **Data**.

    b. Select **New data item ⇨ Parameter**.

        i.   In the **Name** field, enter **RankParameter**.

        ii. For **Type**, verify that **Numeric** is selected.

             Note: Because we want the report viewer to change the number of quarters in the rank, we need a numeric parameter.

        iii. In the **Minimum value** field, enter **2**.

             Note: This is the lowest number of quarters that a viewer can select.

        iv. In the **Maximum value** field, enter **20**.

             Note: This is the total number of quarters available in the table.

        v.   Next to the **Format** field, click [✎] (**Edit**).

             -   For **Format**, verify that **Comma** is selected.

             -   For the **Width** field, verify that **12** is specified.

             -   In the **Decimals** field, enter **0**.

             -   Click **OK**.

        vi. In the **Current value** field, enter **4** and press Enter.

             Note: We enter a value different from the default (8) so that we can see exactly when the parameter is applied.

The New Parameter window should resemble the following:

Name:

> RankParameter

Type:

> Numeric ▾

☐ Multiple values

Minimum value:

> 2

Maximum value:

> 20

Format:

> COMMA12. (Comma)   ✎

Current value:

> 4

vii.   Click **OK** to create the numeric parameter.

The Data pane should resemble the following:

> ∨ Parameter
>
> x RankParameter   ≫

7. Modify the control object to populate the parameter.
    a. On the canvas, click the text input control to select it.
    b. In the right pane, click **Roles**.
    c. For the **Parameter** role, select **Add** ⇨ **RankParameter**.

    The text input control should resemble the following:

> Specify the number of quarters to view (2-20):
>
> 4

Note: The parameter still needs to be applied to the rank on the time series plot.

8. Apply the parameter to the rank on the time series plot.
    a. On the canvas, click the time series plot to select it.
    b. In the right pane, click **Ranks**.

c. For the **Count** field, select **RankParameter**.

The time series plot should resemble the following:

9. In the text input control, enter **12** and press Enter.

The time series plot should resemble the following:

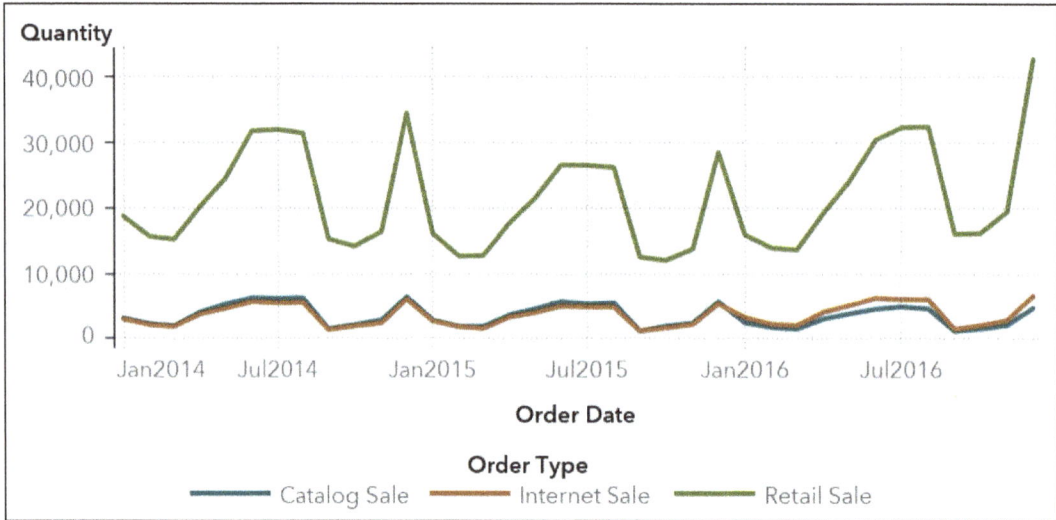

10. Save the report.

End of Demonstration

Practice 13.1

1. **Using a Parameter in a Display Rule**

a. Open the browser and sign in to SAS Viya.

b. Open the **VA2-Practice9.1** report in the **Courses/YVA285/Advanced/Practices** folder.

c. Answer the following questions:

What is the expression for the display rule on the treemap?

Answer:

What is the range of Quantity in the treemap?

Answer:

d. Parameterize the value used in the display rule.

   e.   Answer the following questions:

       What type of parameter did you create? Why?

       Answer:

       How many product groups have a quantity less than 2,500? Less than 500?

       Answer:

   f.   Save the report.

End of Practices

13.3 Character Parameters

Figure 13.2 illustrates an example of using character parameter in a drop-down list control object. First we created the parameter making sure to select parameter type as character.

Figure 13.2: Example of Using a Character Parameter

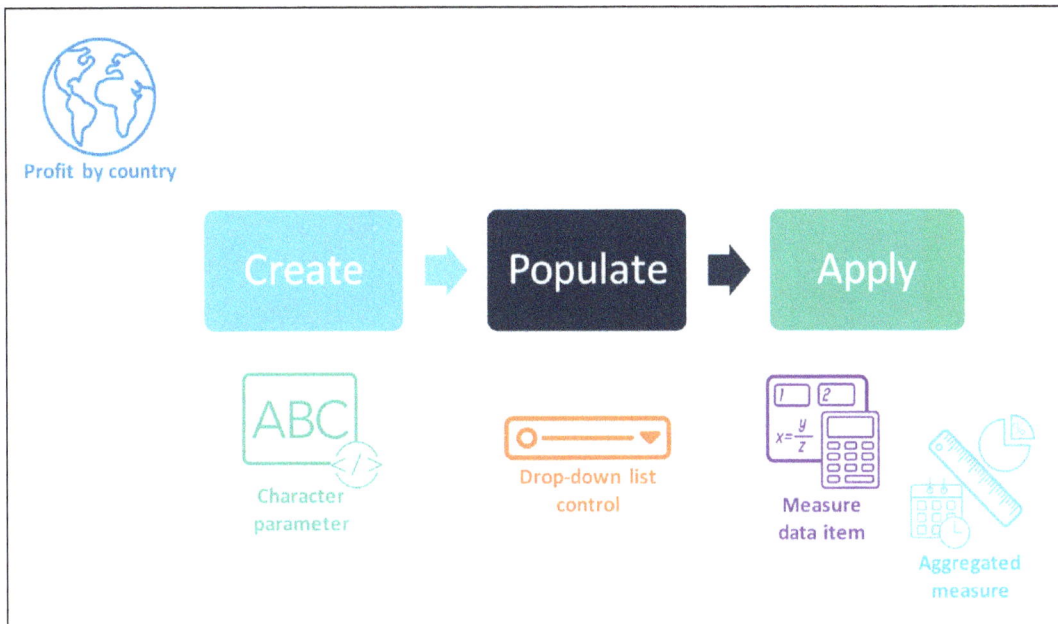

The following demonstration describes in detail how to create a character parameter, populate the parameter with a control object, and apply the parameter to a calculation, as illustrated in Figure 13.3.

Figure 13.3: Using a Character Parameter in a Calculation

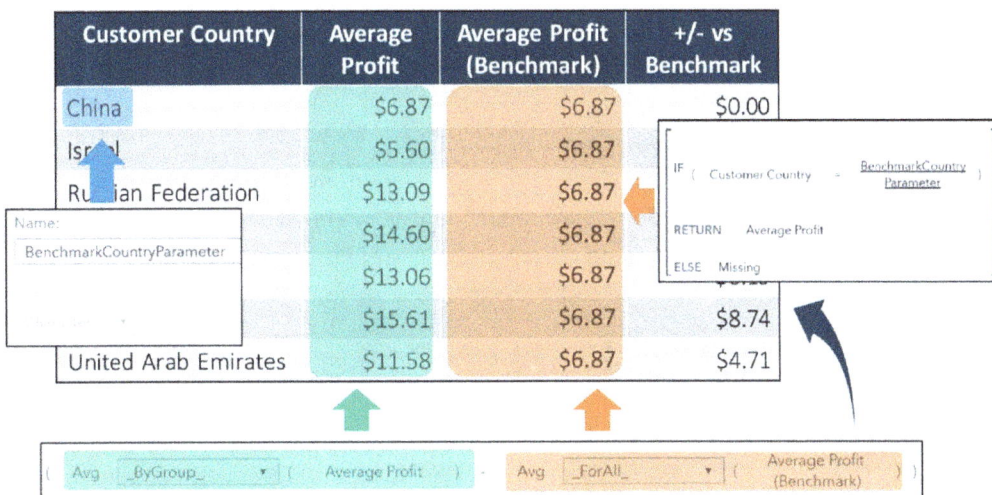

Demo 13.2: Using a Character Parameter in a Calculation

This demonstration illustrates how to create a character parameter, populate the parameter with a control object, and apply the parameter to a calculation.

1. From the browser window, sign in to SAS Viya.
2. In the upper left corner, click **☰** (**Show list of applications**) and select **Explore and Visualize**. SAS Visual Analytics appears.
3. Click **All Reports**.
   a. Navigate to the **Courses/YVA285/Advanced/Demos** folder.
   b. Double-click the **VA2-Demo9.2** report to open it.
4. Create a character parameter for **Customer Country**.
   a. In the left pane, click **Data**.
   b. Right-click **Customer Country** and select **New parameter**.
   c. In the Name field, enter **BenchmarkCountryParameter**.
   d. For **Type**, verify that **Character** is specified.
      The New Parameter window should resemble the following:

Name:
BenchmarkCountryParameter

   Type:

Character ▾

   ☐ Multiple values

   Current value:

   Note: Current values do not need to be specified for character parameters.

   e. Click **OK**.
      The Data pane should resemble the following:

∨ Parameter
[x] BenchmarkCountryParameter ≫

5. Modify the control object to populate the parameter.
   a. On the canvas, click the drop-down list control to select it.
   b. In the right pane, click **Roles**.
   c. For the **Category** role, select **Add ⇨ Customer Country**.
      Note: This populates the drop-down list control with values from **Customer Country**.
   d. For the Parameter role, select **Add ⇨ BenchmarkCountryParameter**.
      Note: This updates the parameter with the selected value of **Customer Country**.
      The drop-down list control should resemble the following:

Select a benchmark country (required):
China ▾

   e. In the right pane, click **Options**.

f. View the options in the Drop-Down List group.

> ∨ Drop-Down List
>
> ☑ Required
> Background color:
> ☐

This drop-down list is set as **Required**, meaning that a country must be selected.

6. Modify the calculated item for the average profit of the benchmark country.

a. In the left pane, click **Data**.

b. In the Measure group, right-click **Average Profit (Benchmark)** and select **Edit**.

The expression should resemble the following:

> IF (Customer Country = " China ")
>
> RETURN   Average Profit
>
> ELSE   Missing

China has been hardcoded into the expression. We need to replace this with the new parameter.

Note: Because we are looking at average profits, the ELSE condition needs to be a missing value and not zero. Missing values are ignored in the average, but zeros are not.

i. Right-click **China** and select **Replace with ⇨ BenchmarkCountryParameter**.

The expression should resemble the following:

> IF (Customer Country = BenchmarkCountryParameter)
>
> RETURN   Average Profit
>
> ELSE   Missing

ii. In the bottom right corner of the window, click **Preview**.

a. In the Parameter Configuration on the right side of the window, enter **Germany**.

The preview should resemble the following:

Average Profit (Benchmark)	Customer Country	Average Profit
$10.60	Germany	$10.60
($0.20)	Germany	($0.20)
$19.60	Germany	$19.60
.	Denmark	$5.60
.	Denmark	$7.00

Note: Average Profit (Benchmark) will contain the value of the average profit for the benchmark (or selected) country.

    b.   Click **Close** to close the Preview Result window.

   iii.   Click **OK** to update the calculated item.

7.   View the aggregated measure that calculates the difference of average profit for the benchmark country from the average profit for each country.

    a.   In the Aggregated Measure group, right-click **+/- vs Benchmark** and select **Edit**.

       The expression should resemble the following:

(Avg	_ByGroup_	▼	(	Average Profit	)	-	Avg	_ForAll_	▼	(	Average Profit (Benchmark)	)	)

Note: +/- vs Benchmark calculates the difference in the average profit (for each country) from the benchmark country. The aggregation context for the **Average Profit (Benchmark)** value must be _ForAll_ because this value needs to be calculated and compared to every country in the report object.

    b.   Click **Cancel** to close the aggregated measure.

8.   Modify the roles for the bar chart.

    a.   On the canvas, click the bar chart to select it.

    b.   In the right pane, click **Roles**, if necessary.

    c.   For the **Measure** role, select **Frequency** ⇨ **+/- vs Benchmark**.

       The bar chart should resemble the following:

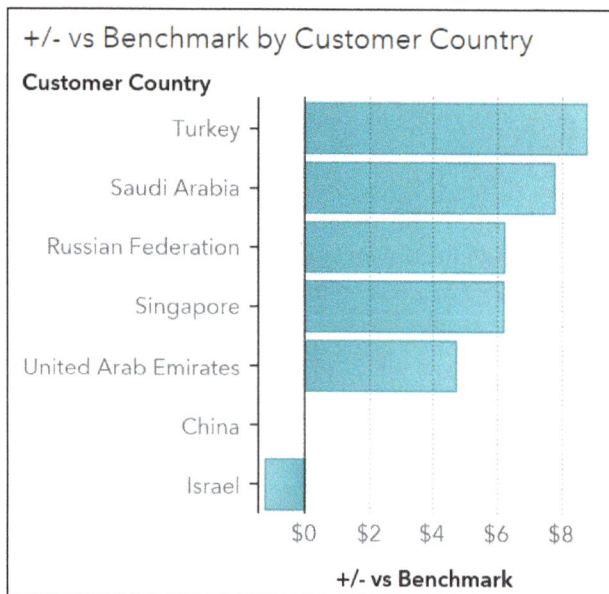

9. Modify the roles for the list table.
    a. On the canvas, click the list table to select it.
    b. In the right pane, click **Roles**, if necessary.
    c. For the **Columns** role, click **Add**.
    d. Select the following measures:
       Average Profit (Benchmark)
       +/- vs Benchmark
    e. Click **OK**.

       The list table should resemble the following:

Customer Country ▲	Average Profit	Average Profit (Benchmark)	+/- vs Benchmark
China	$6.87	$6.87	$0.00
Israel	$5.60	.	($1.27)
Russian Federation	$13.09	.	$6.22
Saudi Arabia	$14.60	.	$7.74
Singapore	$13.06	.	$6.20
Turkey	$15.61	.	$8.74
United Arab Emirates	$11.58	.	$4.71

   With China selected as the benchmark country, the **+/- vs Benchmark** values are updated to compare average profit for each country to the average profit for China. In this instance, only one country (Israel) has a lower average profit than China.

10. In the drop-down list control, select **Russian Federation**.

    The bar chart should resemble the following:

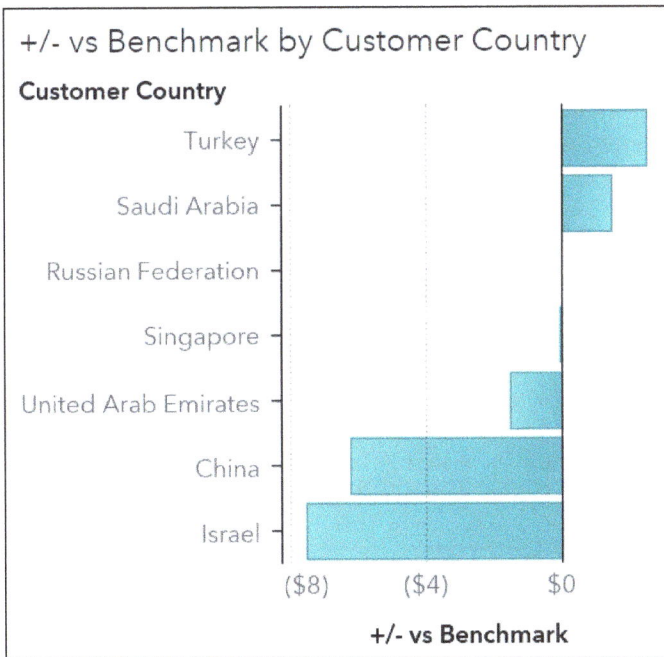

+/- vs Benchmark by Customer Country

The list table should resemble the following:

Customer Country ▲	Average Profit	Average Profit (Benchmark)	+/- vs Benchmark
China	$6.87	.	($6.22)
Israel	$5.60	.	($7.49)
Russian Federation	$13.09	$13.09	$0.00
Saudi Arabia	$14.60	.	$1.51
Singapore	$13.06	.	($0.03)
Turkey	$15.61	.	$2.52
United Arab Emirates	$11.58	.	($1.51)

With Russian Federation selected as the benchmark country, the **+/- vs Benchmark** values are updated to compare average profit for each country to the average profit for Russian Federation. In this instance, four countries (China, Israel, Singapore, and United Arab Emirates) have a lower average profit than Russian Federation.

11. Save the report.

End of Demonstration

Figure 13.4: Practice Scenario: Customers

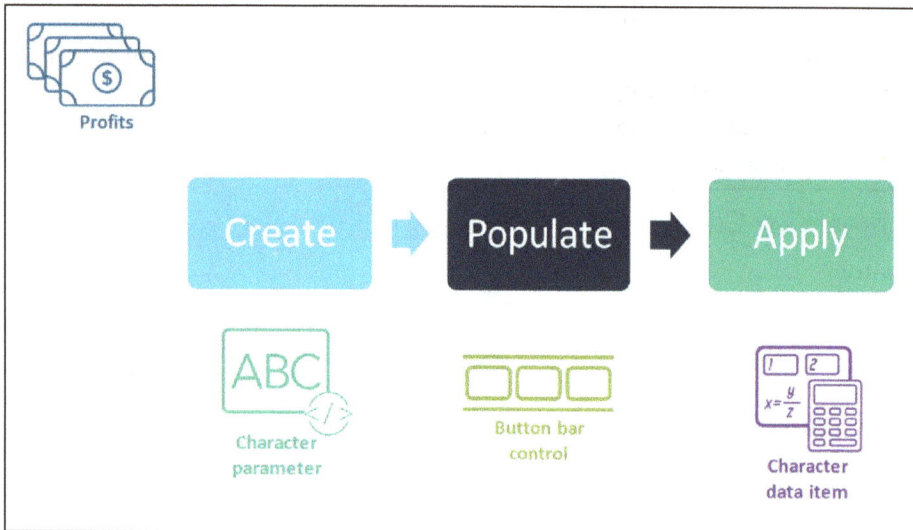

Figure 13.5: Practice Scenario: Customers

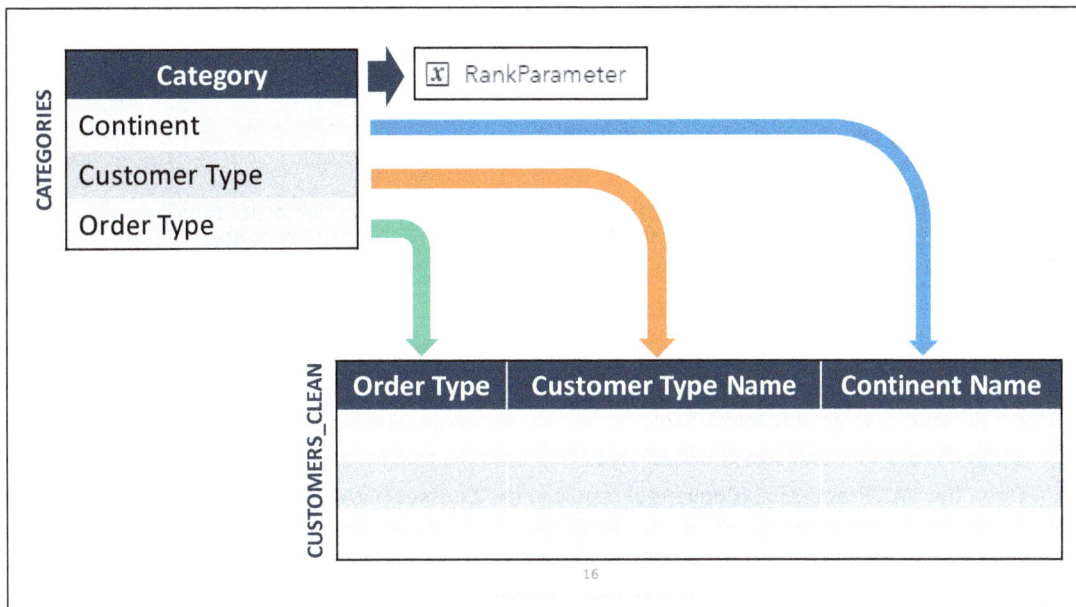

We will load a small table to CAS that contains one data item that has the values *Continent*, *Customer Type*, and *Order Type* and use that data item to create the parameter.

Note: As an alternative, you can create a simulated data item that contains the values *Continent*, *Customer Type*, and *Order Type*. An easy way to do this is to create a custom category that produces those values. The custom category can be based on any category data item that contains at least three distinct values. However, because this simulated data item is based on a category data item in the CAS table, you need to be very careful when adding actions between objects, as the action will use the underlying data item. The challenge practice explores this option.

Practice 13.2

1. **Using a Parameter to Select Your Metric**
   a. Open the browser and sign in to SAS Viya.
   b. Open the **VA2-Practice9.2** report in the **Courses/YVA285/Advanced/Practices** folder.
   c. Answer the following questions:

   What are the names of the data sources used in the report?

   Answer:

   Which data source contains a data item named **Category**?

   Answer:

   How many distinct values does **Category** have?

   Answer:

   What are the distinct values of **Category**? Do these match data items in the other data source?

   Answer:

   d. Create a parameter (**CategoryParameter**) from the **Category** data item.
   e. Create a calculated item (**Selected Category**) that returns the appropriate category based on the selected value of the parameter.

   Hint: The new calculated item should be associated with the data source that is used to create the bar chart.

   f.   Add a control object to the canvas to populate the parameter.

      Hint: Make the control object required so that a report viewer must choose a category.

   g.   Modify the bar chart to use the selected category.

   h.   Answer the following questions:

      What type of parameter did you create? Why?

      Answer:

      Which continent has the highest profit? Which customer type? Which order type?

      Answer:

   i.   Save the report.

Challenge (Optional)

1.   **Using a Parameter in an Advanced Rank**

   a.   Open the browser and sign in to SAS Viya.

   b.   Open the **VA2-Practice9.2 (Challenge)** report in the **Courses/YVA285/Advanced/Practices** folder.

   c.   View the rank on the bar chart and answer the following question:

      What measure is used to rank the bar chart?

      Answer:

   d.   Create a custom category (**Measures List**) that contains the following values:

      Unit Actual

      Unit Discards

      Unit Capacity

      Hint: This custom category can be based on any category data item.

   e.   Create a parameter (**RankParameter**) from the custom category.

   f.   Create a calculated item (**Rank By Measure**) that returns the appropriate measure based on the selected value of the parameter.

   g.   Modify the control object on the canvas to populate the parameter.

      Hint: The control object is required, so a report viewer must choose a measure.

   h.   Modify the rank to use the selected measure.

   i.   Answer the following questions:

      What type of parameter did you create? Why?

      Answer:

      What are the top 10 units by discards? By capacity?

      Answer:

      What happens if you add a filter action between the control object and the bar chart? Why?

      Answer:

   j.   Save the report.

      `End of Practices`

13.3 Using Date Parameters

Data parameters are useful if you want to select two independent date periods for comparison. This is not the same requirement as filtering the report between a start and end date. This report requirement is such that a report user can select two independent dates in the source data to be able to analyze the change in related variables such as Expense magnitude for different aggregation levels, such as Region, Product Line and Product. Or you might need to create a calendar that shows values of a variable a number of days after a specific date. In both these examples, because the user would like to specify a date, we will need to create a date parameter (DateParameter). To populate this parameter, we can use a text input control to enter a date directly. We will apply the parameter to an advanced filter that filters the calendar.

Figure 13.6: Using a Date Parameter Example

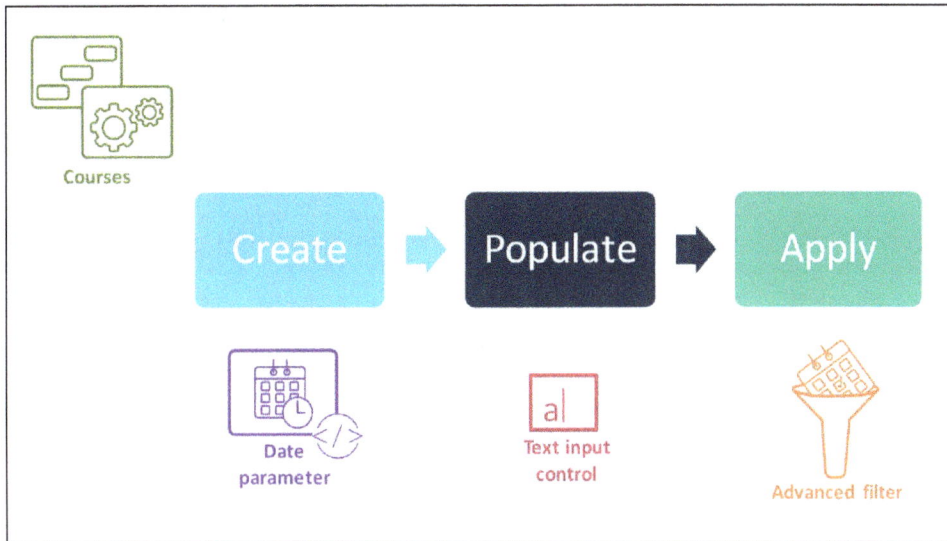

Demo 13.3 describes how to create a date parameter, populate the parameter with a control object, and apply the parameter to an advanced filter.

Activity 13.1

Which comparison operator enables you to select a range of dates?

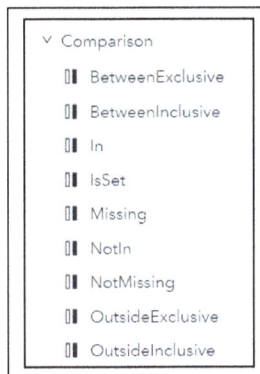

Demo 13.3: Using a Date Parameter in an Advanced Filter

This demonstration illustrates how to create a date parameter, populate the parameter with a control object, and apply the parameter to an advanced filter.

1. From the browser window, sign in to SAS Viya.
2. In the upper left corner, click ☰ (**Show list of applications**) and select **Explore and Visualize**.
    SAS Visual Analytics appears.
3. Click **All Reports**.
    a. Navigate to the **Courses/YVA285/Advanced/Demos** folder.
    b. Double-click the **VA2-Demo9.3** report to open it.

4. View the date parameter.
    a. In the left pane, click **Data**.
    b. In the Parameter group, right-click **DateParameter** and select **Edit**.

    Name:

DateParameter

    Type:

    Date ▾

    ☐ Multiple values

    Minimum value:

17Oct2006	📅

    Maximum value:

31Aug2018	📅

    Format:

DATE9 (Date with Month Name)	✎

    Current value:

04May2011	📅

    Note: The minimum and maximum values for the parameter match the span of dates available in the table.

    c. Click **Cancel** to close the parameter.
5. View the control object that populates the parameter.
    a. On the canvas, click the text input control to select it.
    b. In the right pane, click **Roles**.

    The Roles pane should resemble the following:

    ˅ Category

        📅 Event Delivered (Start) Date

    ˅ Measure

        ✚ Add

    ˅ Parameter

        x DateParameter

    ˅ Hidden

        ✚ Add

    Entering a date in the text input control updates the current value of **DateParameter**.
6. View the advanced filter on the schedule chart.
    a. On the canvas, click the schedule chart to select it.
    b. In the right pane, click **Filters**.

c. Next to the **Selected Date Plus 90 Days** filter, click ⋮ (**Options**) and select **Advanced edit**.

The expression should resemble the following:

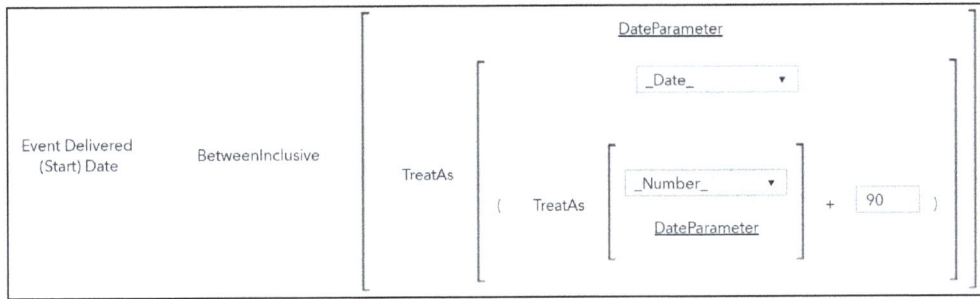

This filter looks for all **Event Delivered (Start) Date** values between the selected date (**Date Parameter**) and the selected date plus 90 days.

Note: DateParameter must be treated as a number to add 90 days. The result must then be treated as a date to use in the BetweenInclusive operator with **Event Delivered (Start) Date**.

d. Click **Cancel** to close the Edit Filter Expression window.

7. Test the parameter.

a. In the text input control, enter **11Jan2012** and press Enter.

Note: Dates must be entered in the format ddMmmyyyy because that is the format specified for **Event Delivered (Start) Date**. As an alternative, a single-point slider control can be used to specify the value of the parameter.

The schedule chart should resemble the following:

b. Clear the text input control and press Enter.

The schedule chart should resemble the following:

Because the text input control has a missing value, the parameter also has a missing value, so the filter expression does not return any data.

8. Modify the advanced filter on the schedule chart.
   a. On the canvas, click the schedule chart to select it.
   b. In the right pane, click **Filters**.
   c. Next to the Selected Date Plus 90 Days filter, click ⋮ (Options) and select **Advanced edit**.
      i. Right-click the expression and select **Copy**.
      ii. Right-click the expression and select **Clear**.
      iii. On the left side of the window, click **Operators**.
      iv. Expand **Boolean**.
      v. Double-click **IF...ELSE** to add it to the expression.
      vi. On the left side of the window, expand **Comparison**.
      vii. Drag **IsSet** to the **condition** field for the IF operator in the expression.
      viii. Right-click the field (for the IsSet operator) and select **Replace with** ⇨ **DateParameter**.
      ix. Right-click **condition** for the RETURN operator and select **Paste**.
      x. On the left side of the window, expand **Comparison** if necessary.
      xi. Drag **NotMissing** to the **condition** field for the ELSE operator.
      xii. Right-click the **number** field for the NotMissing operator and select **Replace with** ⇨ **Event Delivered (Start) Date**.

      The expression should resemble the following:

      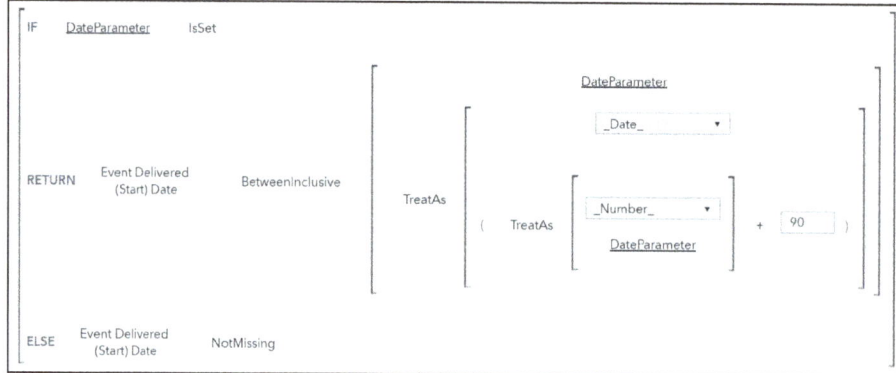

      xiii. Click **OK** to update the advanced filter.

      The schedule chart should resemble the following:

      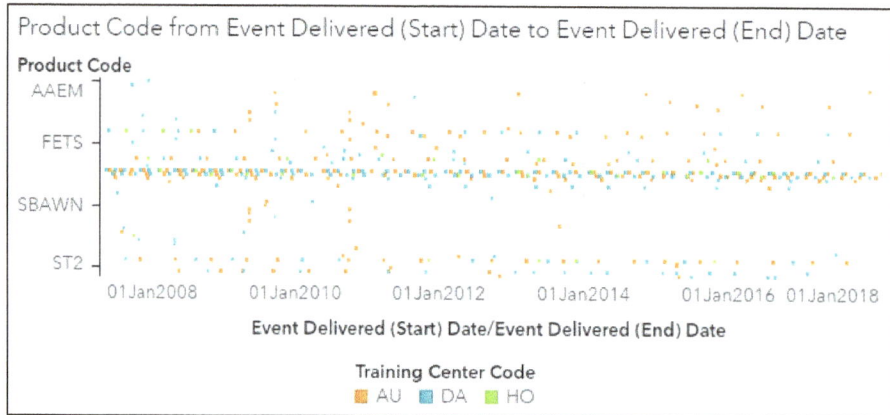

      When no value is specified for the parameter, all the data is displayed.

9. Save the report.

End of Demonstration

Figure 13.7: Practice Scenario: Toy Customers

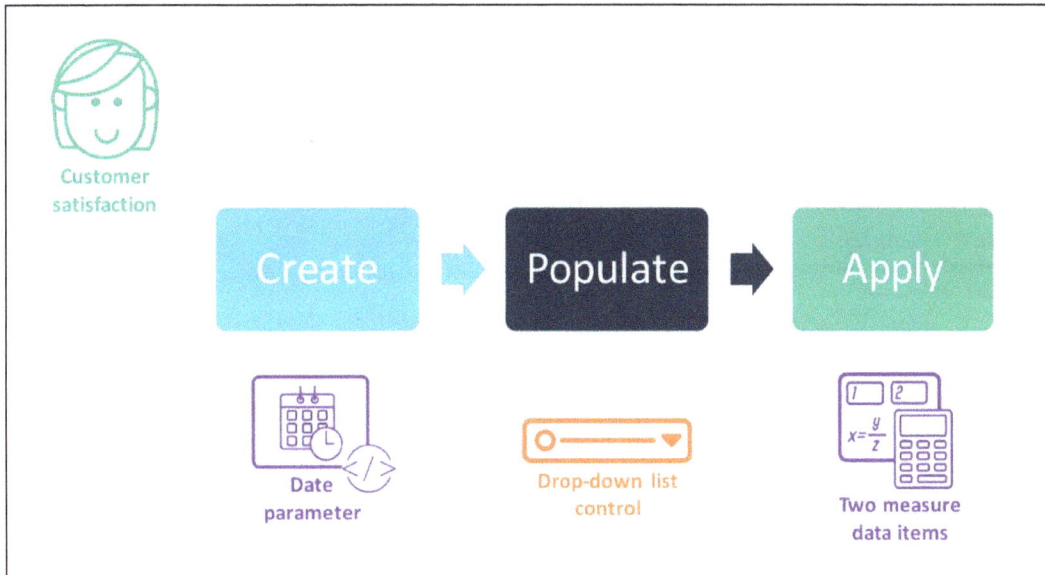

Practice 13.3

1. **Using a Parameter in a Calculated Item**
   a. Open the browser and sign in to SAS Viya.
   b. Open the **VA2-Practice9.3** report in the **Courses/YVA285/Advanced/Practices** folder.
   c. Create a parameter (**DateParameter**) from **Transaction Date**.
   d. Add a control object to the canvas to populate the parameter.

      Hint: Make the control object required so that a report viewer must choose a measure.

      Hint: Because there is only one year of data, add a filter so that the report viewer cannot select January.
   e. Create a calculated item (**Selected Month**) that returns customer satisfaction for the month specified by the parameter.
   f. Create a calculated item (**Prior Month**) that returns customer satisfaction for the month before the month specified by the parameter.
   g. Modify the targeted bar chart to compare the selected month to the prior month.
   h. Answer the following questions:

      What type of parameter did you create? Why?

      Answer:

      For February, does the customer satisfaction for any product line exceed the prior month?

      Answer:

      For April, does the customer satisfaction for any product line exceed the prior month?

      Answer:
   i. Save the report.

Challenge (Optional)

1. **Modifying a Calculated Item**
   a. Open the browser and sign in to SAS Viya.
   b. Open the **VA2-Practice9.3 (Challenge)** report in the **Courses/YVA285/Advanced/Practices** folder.

c.   Answer the following questions:

What format is used for the date data item?

Answer:

In the drop-down list control, select **Jan2013**. What target values are displayed in the bar chart? Why?

Answer:

d.   Modify the calculated item (**Prior Month**) to return the correct values when January is selected.

e.   Save the report.

End of Practices

Appendix: Solutions

Chapter 1

Solutions to Activities and Questions

Quiz 1.1: Correct Answer

Which of the following statements is true?

a. All users have the ability to create reports.

b. Administrators control access to reports.

c. Only administrators can create reports.

Administrators manage role-based capabilities, which control the application features that each group of users can access.

Security also enables the administrator to control which data sources, plans, and reports each group of users can access.

Practice Review

Figure A1: 1.1 Viewing a Report in Visual Analytics - Solution

What links are available for the Product Analysis page?

Links:
Double-click a product group in the bar chart to view details about products in that group.

Figure A2: 1.1 Viewing a Report in Visual Analytics - Solution

Which product category has the fewest number of orders? The lowest total profit?
Indoor Sports has the fewest number of orders (11,755).
Team Sports has the lowest total profit ($133,185.52).

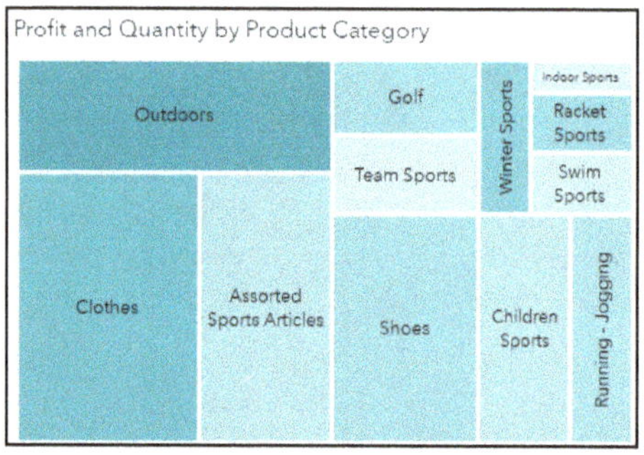

Profit and Quantity by Product Category

Product Category	Quantity	Profit	Number of Orders ▲
Indoor Sports	23,245	$160,689.61	11,755
Racket Sports	41,683	$836,949.47	20,589
Swim Sports	43,323	$244,196.15	20,796
Winter Sports	55,750	$1,067,262.44	26,174

Product Category	Quantity	Profit ▲	Number of Orders
Team Sports	76,736	$133,185.52	34,197
Indoor Sports	23,245	$160,689.61	11,755
Swim Sports	43,323	$244,196.15	20,796
Children Sports	149,142	$429,751.38	71,045
Assorted Sports Articles	241,308	$461,488.46	116,267

Figure A3: 1.1 Viewing a Report in Visual Analytics - Solution

Which product groups are included in the Indoor Sports category?

Fitness, Gymnastic Clothing, and Top Trim

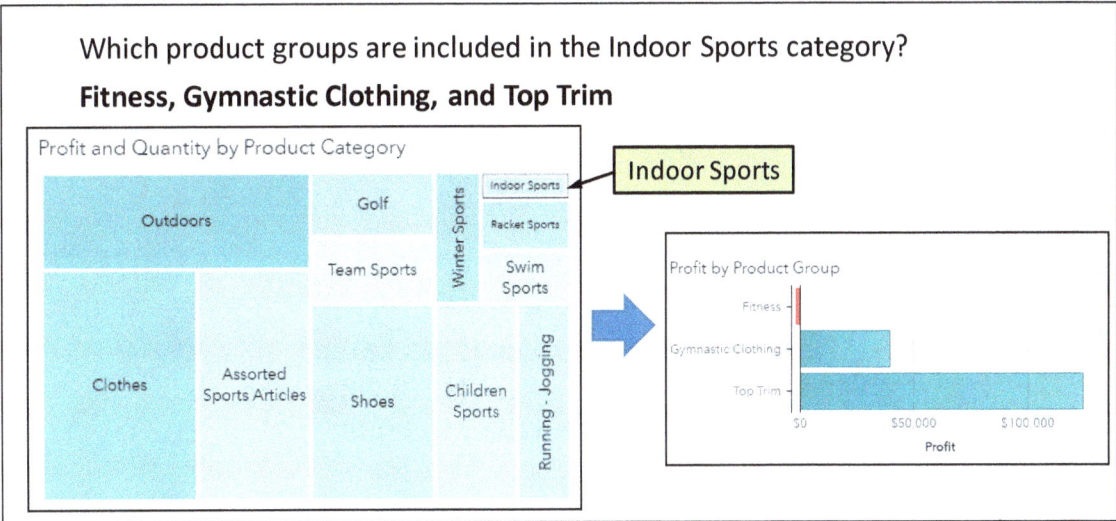

Figure A4: 1.1 Viewing a Report in Visual Analytics - Solution

How many products are in the Fitness product group?

45 products

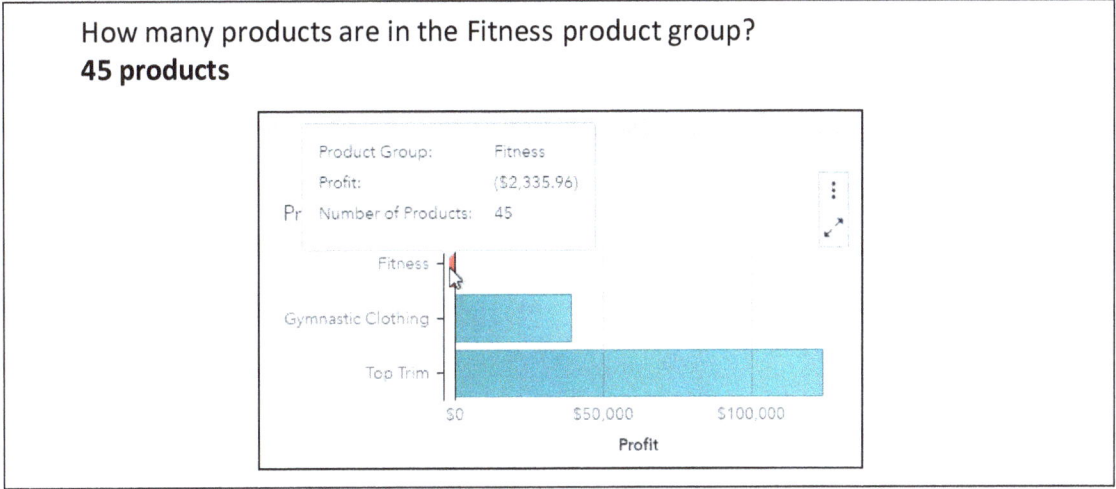

Figure A5: 1.1 Viewing a Report in Visual Analytics - Solution

Do any fitness products generate a loss?

Yes, the following fitness products generate a loss:

Supplier Name	Product Group	Product Name		Profit ▲	Number of Orders
TrimSport B.V.	Fitness	Letour Mag Plus Bike-Buy Now Paper	445	($31,748.60)	318
TrimSport B.V.	Fitness	Letour Spinner Bike	111	($1,745.10)	75
TrimSport B.V.	Fitness	Letour 757 Home Exerciser	44	($1,331.50)	31
TrimSport B.V.	Fitness	Lift Weights 15 Kg Dumbbell	363	($541.26)	223
TrimSport B.V.	Fitness	Weight 1.5 Kg	49	$4.90	29
TrimSport B.V.	Fitness	Weight 0.5 Kg	144	$28.80	90
TrimSport B.V.	Fitness	Weight 2.5 Kg	147	$29.40	100
TrimSport B.V.	Fitness	Abdomen Shaper	315	$31.50	214
TrimSport B.V.	Fitness	Hiclass Stepper	59	$35.40	39
			Sum: 10,752	Sum: ($2,335.96)	Total: 6,213

Click to sort in ascending order.

Figure A6: 1.1 Viewing a Report in Visual Analytics - Solution

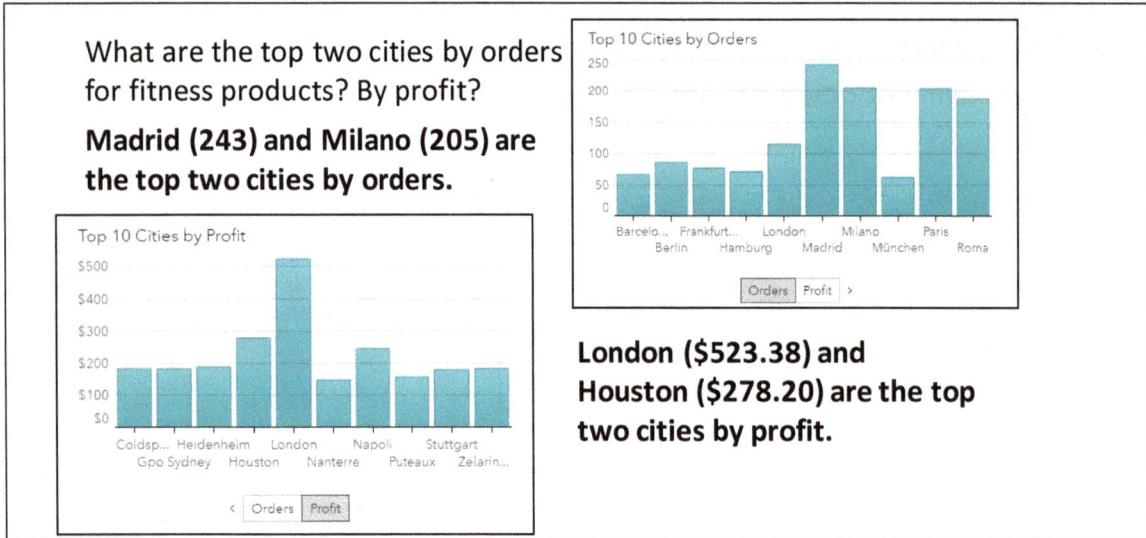

What are the top two cities by orders for fitness products? By profit?

Madrid (243) and Milano (205) are the top two cities by orders.

Top 10 Cities by Orders

Top 10 Cities by Profit

London ($523.38) and Houston ($278.20) are the top two cities by profit.

Figure A7: 1.1 Viewing a Report in Visual Analytics - Solution

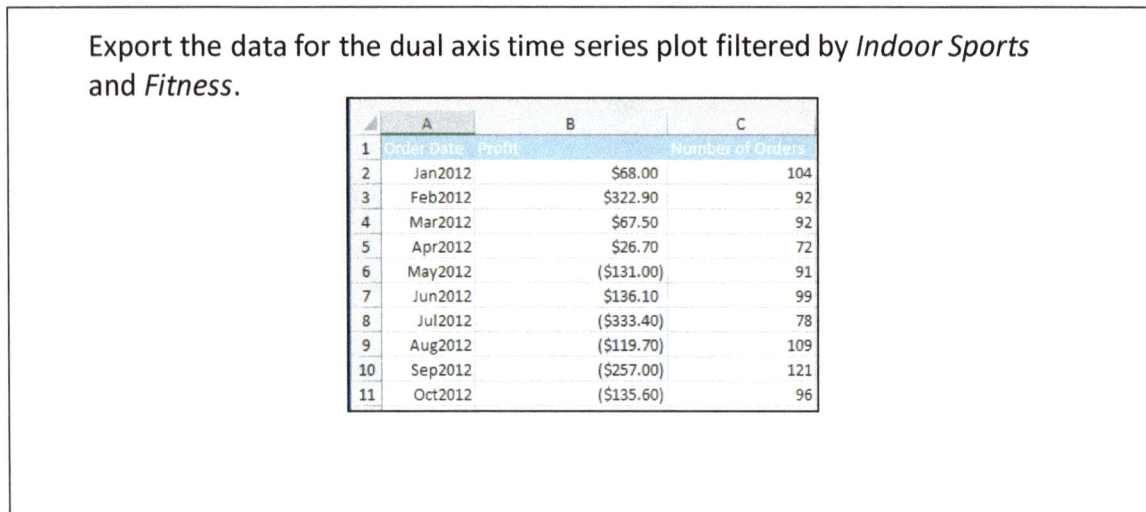

Export the data for the dual axis time series plot filtered by *Indoor Sports* and *Fitness*.

	A	B	C
1	Order Date	Profit	Number of Orders
2	Jan2012	$68.00	104
3	Feb2012	$322.90	92
4	Mar2012	$67.50	92
5	Apr2012	$26.70	72
6	May2012	($131.00)	91
7	Jun2012	$136.10	99
8	Jul2012	($333.40)	78
9	Aug2012	($119.70)	109
10	Sep2012	($257.00)	121
11	Oct2012	($135.60)	96

Chapter 2

Solutions to Activities and Questions

Activity 2.1: Correct Answer

Given the values for **Quantity**, **Total Revenue**, and **Unit Cost**, how would you calculate **Profit**?

Quantity	Total Revenue	Unit Cost
1	$191.00	$160.90
4	$499.20	$107.20
1	$173.00	$145.50
1	$56.90	$51.90
4	$740.40	$155.40

Profit = Total Revenue - (Unit Cost * Quantity)

Practice Review

Figure A8: 2.1 Accessing and Investigating Data - Solution

View the Data pane and answer the following questions:

How many unique values does **Company** have? **12**
Job Title? **Nine**

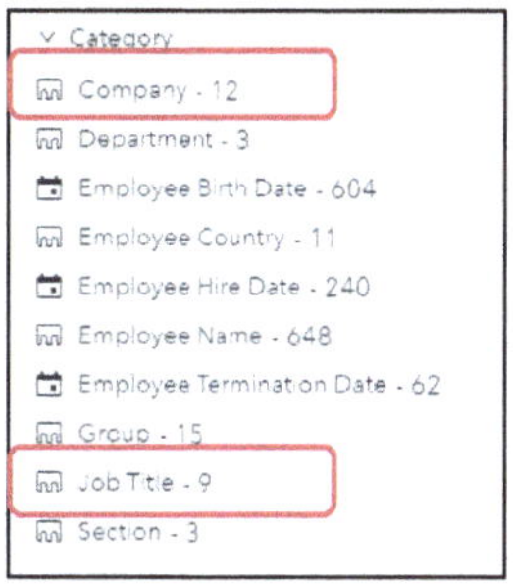

What is the type (or classification) of **Employee ID**?
Measure

∨ Category
- Company - 12
- Department - 3
- Employee Birth Date - 604
- Employee Country - 11
- Employee Hire Date - 240
- Employee Name - 648
- Employee Termination Date - 62
- Group - 15
- Job Title - 9
- Section - 3

∨ Measure
- Annual Salary
- Employee ID
- Frequency
- Levels of Management

Figure A9: 2.1 Accessing and Investigating Data - Solution

View the list table and answer the following questions:

What is the case of **Employee Country**?
Lowercase

Employee Country
au
au
au
au

Which employee represents sales over the internet or through the catalog?

Internet/Catalog Sales

Employee Name
Internet/Catalog Sales
Sian Shannan
Petrea Soltau
Caterina Hayawardhana
Fang Wilson
Koavea Pa)
Leonid Karavdic

§sas

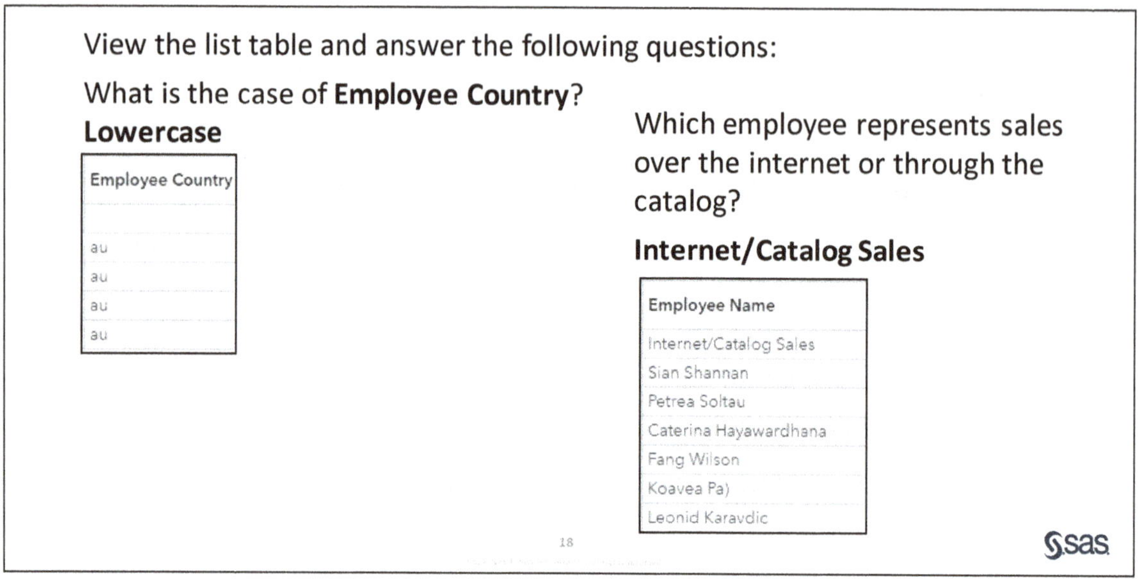

Figure A10: 2.1 Accessing and Investigating Data - Solution

Which data item can be used to determine whether an employee is active (currently employed) or retired (formerly employed)?
If Employee Termination Date is missing, the employee is active (currently employed).

If Employee Termination Date is *not* missing, the employee is retired (formerly employed).

Employee Termination Date	
.	← Active
30Jun2010	
.	
.	
31Jan2010	← Retired

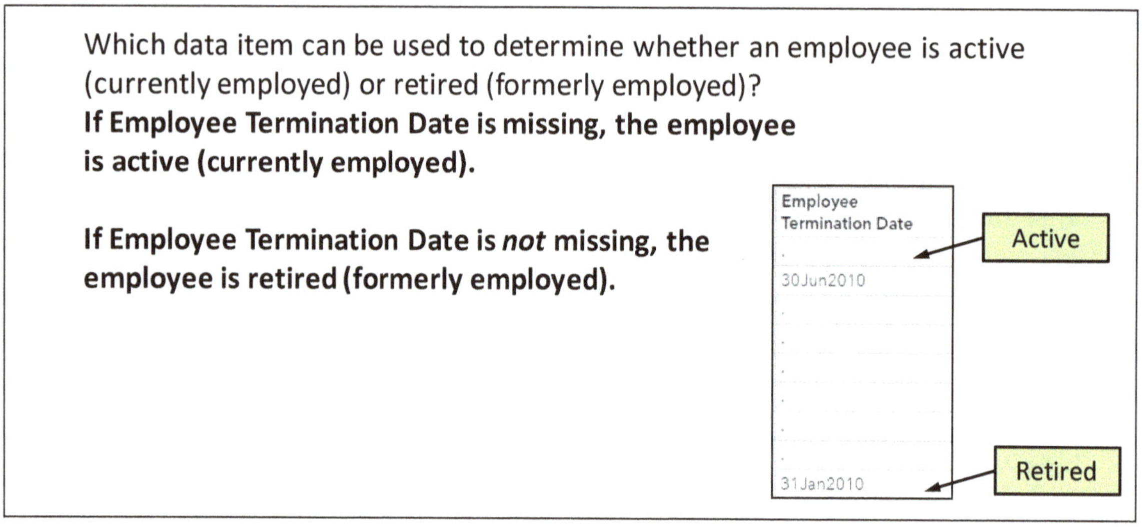

Figure A11: 2.1 Accessing and Investigating Data - Solution

View the crosstab of **Department** and **Job Title** and answer the following question:

Which department contains the missing job title?
Stock & Shipping

Department ▲	Job Title ▲	Frequency
Purchasing	Purchasing Agent I	1
	Purchasing Agent III	2
Sales	Sales Rep. I	215
	Sales Rep. II	172
	Sales Rep. III	113
	Sales Rep. IV	49
	Temp. Sales Rep.	70
	Trainee	25
Stock & Shipping	(missing)	1

We will filter the table to include only employees in the Purchasing and Sales Departments.

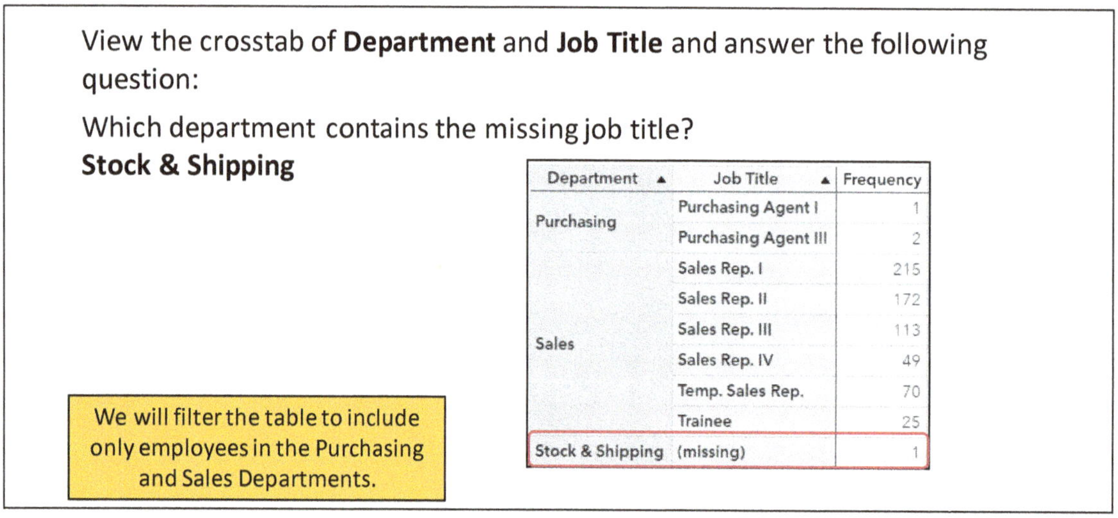

Figure A12: 2.1 Accessing and Investigating Data - Solution

Create an autochart of **Company** and answer the following questions:

What is the largest company, based on the number of employees?
Orion USA is the largest company (120 employees).

The smallest?
Logistics is the smallest company (one employee).

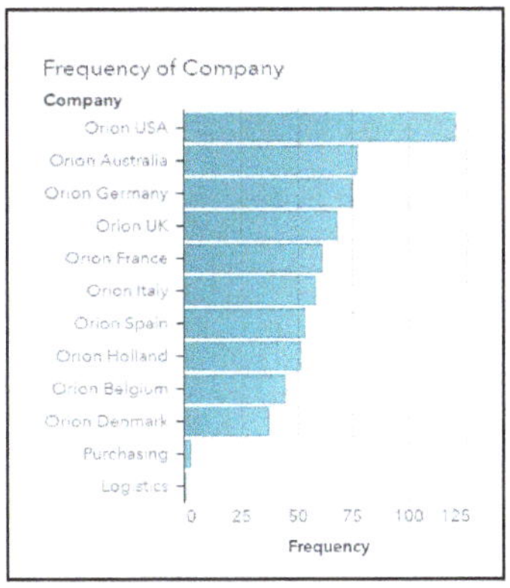

Figure A13: 2.1 Accessing and Investigating Data - Solution

View the measure details (from the Data pane) and answer the following questions:

What is the minimum total profit generated by an employee? **11.10**

The maximum? **19,146,779.62**

The average? **109,148.07**

The total profit generated by all employees? **70,727,947.65**

Name	Minimum	Maximum	Average	Sum
Total Orders	1.00	186,636.00	1,152.80	747,012.00
Total Products Ordered	1.00	235,699.00	1,468.63	951,669.00
Total Profit	11.10	19,146,779.62	109,148.07	70,727,947.65

Figure A14: 2.1 Accessing and Investigating Data - Solution

View the properties of the result table and answer the following question:

How many rows are in the **EMPLOYEES** table after the actions of the plan are applied?

647 rows, one for each employee at Orion Star

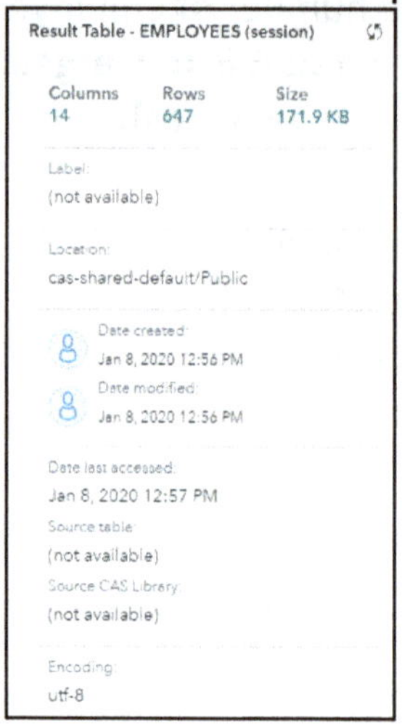

Result Table - EMPLOYEES (session)

Columns	Rows	Size
14	647	171.9 KB

Label
(not available)

Location:
cas-shared-default/Public

Date created:
Jan 8, 2020 12:56 PM

Date modified:
Jan 8, 2020 12:56 PM

Date last accessed:
Jan 8, 2020 12:57 PM

Source table
(not available)

Source CAS Library:
(not available)

Encoding:
utf-8

37

Figure A15: 2.1 Accessing and Investigating Data - Solution

View details about the steps performed in the plan and answer the following questions:

How many convert column actions were performed? On which column (or columns)?

One convert column action (Employee _ID)

Which column was changed to uppercase?

Employee_Country

Figure A16: 2.1 Accessing and Investigating Data - Solution

What filter was applied to the table?

Department in ('Purchasing', 'Sales')

What is the name of the new output table created from the plan?

EMPLOYEES_CLEAN

Chapter 3

Solutions to Activities and Questions

Activity 3.1: Correct Answer

Match each new data item with the type of calculation.

_B_ Gross Profit Margin (Total Profit/ Total Revenue)

_A_ Date (from month, day, year)

_A_ Hemisphere (from continents)

A. calculated item

_B_ GDP Growth (year-over-year)

B. aggregated measure

_B_ Number of Employees (distinct count)

_A_ State Abbreviations (uppercase)

§sas

Activity 3.2: Correct Answer

Given the values of **Employee Hire Date** and **Employee Termination Date**, how would you calculate **Years of Service**?

Active employees:

YOS = (Today – Employee Hire Date)/365.25

Retired employees:

YOS= (Employee Termination Date – Employee Hire Date)/365.25

Use the IF... ELSE operator to perform different calculations based on a condition.

Employee Hire Date	Employee Termination Date
01Dec2004	28Feb2007
01Nov2005	. ← Active
25Jan2005	.
01Mar2005	28Feb2010
31May2005	31May2012
11Dec2005	.
01Sep2002	.

Retired

Activity 3.3: Correct Answer

Each report object has a threshold for how much data it can visually display. Many report objects will not display high-cardinality data items with a large number of unique values.

What are some examples of high-cardinality data items?
Examples: Employee ID, Street Address, Customer Name, Birth Date

What are some examples of low-cardinality data items?
Examples: Country Name, Age Group, Job Title, Order Type

Quiz 3.1: Correct Answers

Which graph would help you determine whether a measure is normally distributed?

a. distribution plot

b. box plot

c. histogram

d. normality plot

Which object can use a data item that has a classification type of geography?

a. crosstab

b. geo map

c. table

d. bar chart

All these graphs can use a data item that has a classification type of geography. The geo map requires it.

Practice Review

Figure A17: 3.1 Working with Data Items - Solution

What is the classification of **Employee_ID? Manager at 1. level**?

Employee_ID has a classification of category.

Manager at 1. level has a classification of measure.

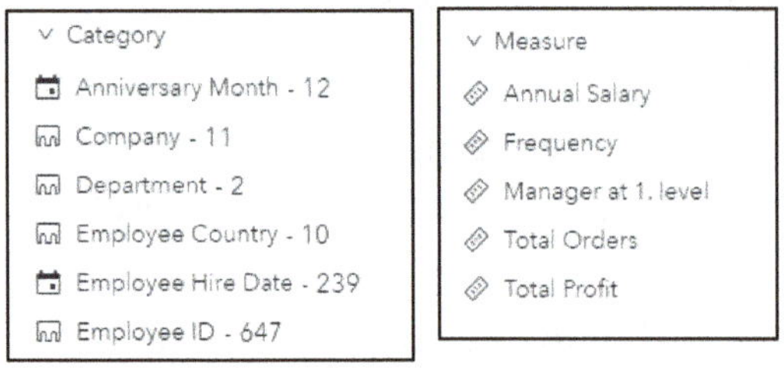

∨ Category	∨ Measure
📅 Anniversary Month - 12	◈ Annual Salary
ᵬ Company - 11	◈ Frequency
ᵬ Department - 2	◈ Manager at 1. level
ᵬ Employee Country - 10	◈ Total Orders
📅 Employee Hire Date - 239	◈ Total Profit
ᵬ Employee ID - 647	

What does the **Frequency** data item represent?

Frequency represents the number of employees.

Figure A18: 3.2 Exploring Data: Part 1 - Solution

Into which range do the majority of salaries fall?

More than 75% of salaries fall within the $25K to $30K range.

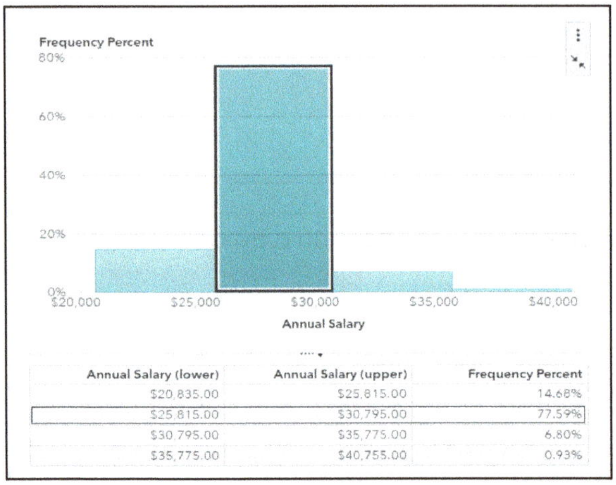

Annual Salary (lower)	Annual Salary (upper)	Frequency Percent
$20,835.00	$25,815.00	14.68%
$25,815.00	$30,795.00	77.59%
$30,795.00	$35,775.00	6.80%
$35,775.00	$40,755.00	0.93%

Figure A19: 3.2 Exploring Data: Part 1 - Solution

In which department are a majority of our salary costs spent? **Sales**

For which job title? **Sales Rep. I**

What could be some reasons why salary costs are so much higher for this group? **Most likely because there are more employees with this job title.**

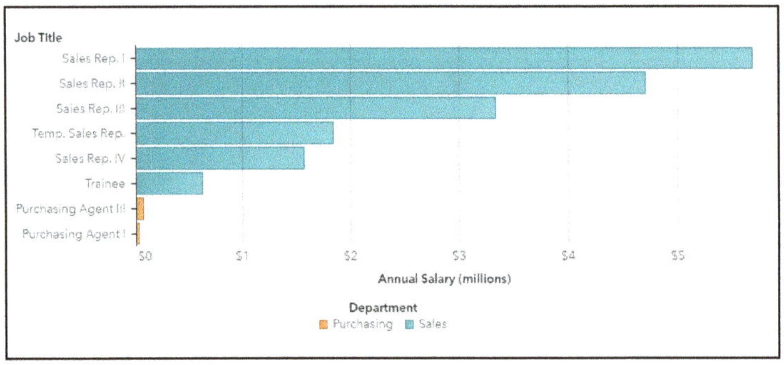

Figure A20: 3.3 Exploring Data: Part 2 - Solution

Which job title has the highest average salary?
Purchasing Agent III

The lowest?
Trainee

Job Title	Minimum	Lower Whisker	First Quartile	Average ▲	Median	Third Quartile
Trainee	$21,615.00	$24,015.00	$24,515.00	$25,260.80	$25,405.00	$25,580.00
Temp. Sales Rep.	$21,580.00	$25,020.00	$25,735.00	$26,317.43	$26,407.50	$26,910.00
Sales Rep. I	$20,835.00	$25,010.00	$25,795.00	$26,417.79	$26,495.00	$26,980.00
Sales Rep. II	$26,015.00	$26,015.00	$26,600.00	$27,373.58	$27,325.00	$28,005.00
Sales Rep. III	$25,005.00	$28,040.00	$28,525.00	$29,457.35	$29,500.00	$30,070.00
Purchasing Agent I	$31,760.00	$31,760.00	$31,760.00	$31,760.00	$31,760.00	$31,760.00
Sales Rep. IV	$30,150.00	$30,150.00	$30,890.00	$31,880.51	$31,605.00	$32,210.00
Purchasing Agent III	$34,270.00	$34,270.00	$34,270.00	$35,070.00	$35,070.00	$35,870.00

Which job title has the highest number of outliers?
Sales Rep. I

Figure A21: 3.4 Creating Data Items - Solution

Employee Status – Custom category

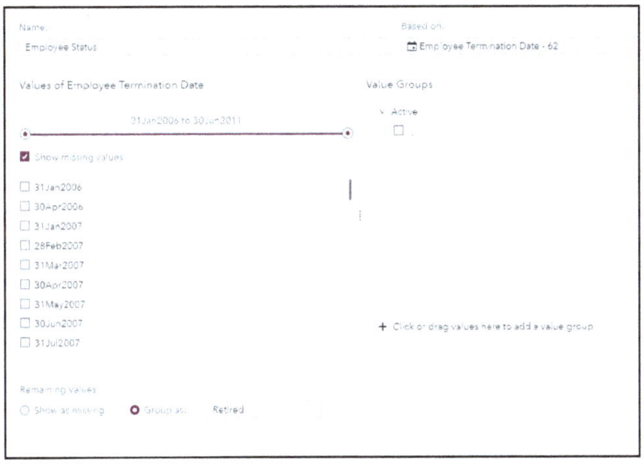

Employee Status – Calculated item

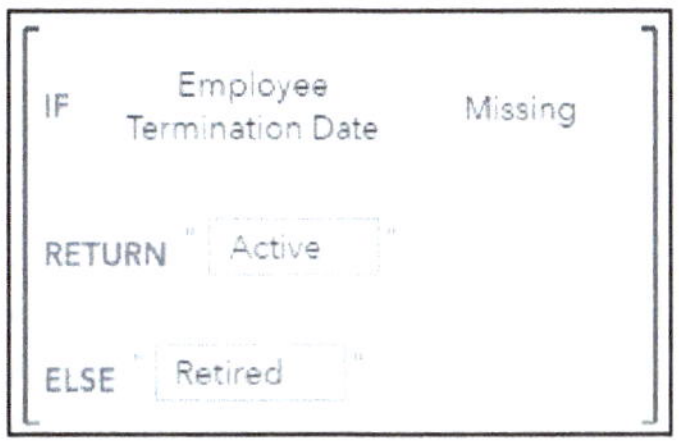

Figure A22: 3.4 Creating Data Items - Solution

Which job title has the highest years of service among active employees?
Purchasing Agent III

Among retired employees?
Sales Rep. II

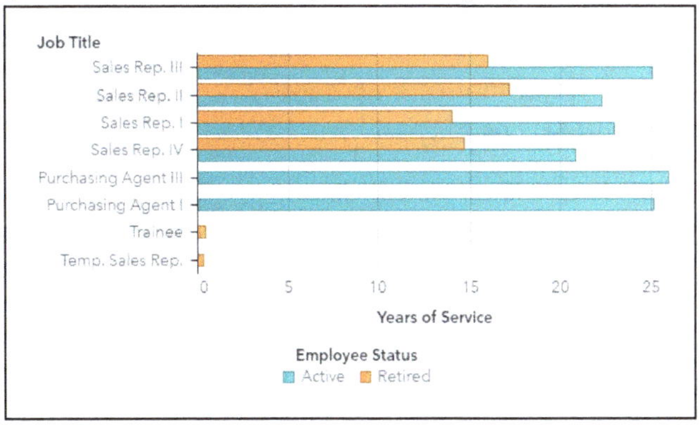

Figure A23: 3.5 Applying Filters - Solution

Add a data source filter to filter for active employees in the Sales Department.

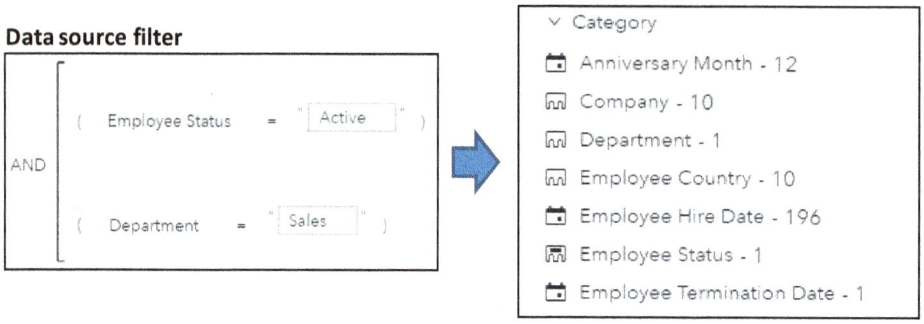

Data source filter

AND

(Employee Status = " Active ")

(Department = " Sales ")

∨ Category

📅 Anniversary Month - 12

📊 Company - 10

📊 Department - 1

📊 Employee Country - 10

📅 Employee Hire Date - 196

📊 Employee Status - 1

📅 Employee Termination Date - 1

Figure A24: 3.5 Applying Filters - Solution

Which two countries generate the highest profit?
United States and Germany

Why do they have such high profits?
These countries have more employees.

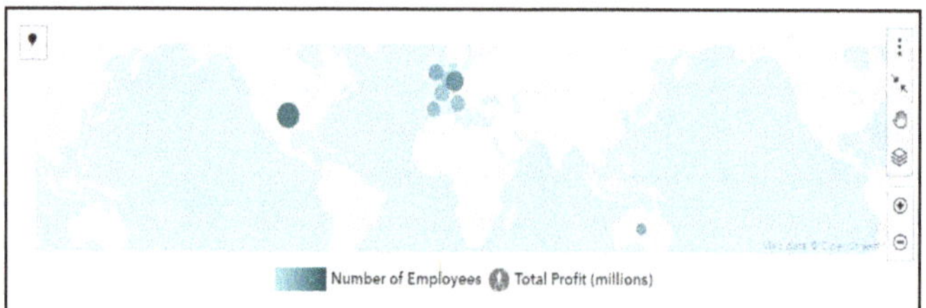

Number of Employees | Total Profit (millions)

Employee Country	Total Profit ▼	Number of Employees
US	$9,490,871.30	73
DE	$6,705,983.90	60
FR	$5,475,320.86	38

Figure A25: 3.5 Applying Filters - Solution

Which country has the highest average profit?
France

Highest number of employees?
United States

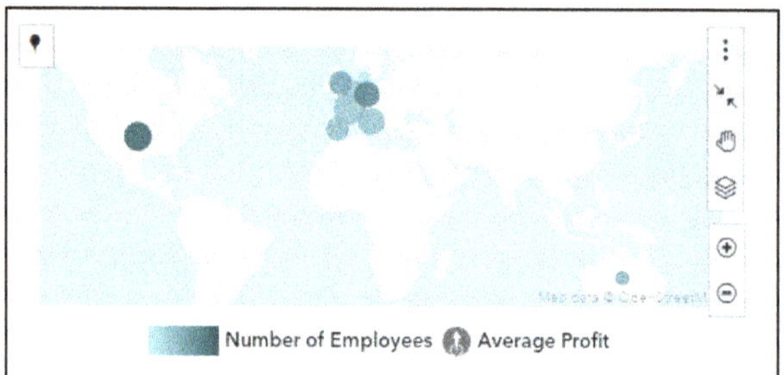

Number of Employees | Average Profit

Employee Country	Average Profit ▼	Number of Employees
FR	$144,087.39	38
US	$130,011.94	73
IT	$120,524.99	39

Figure A26: 3.6 Analyzing Data - Solution

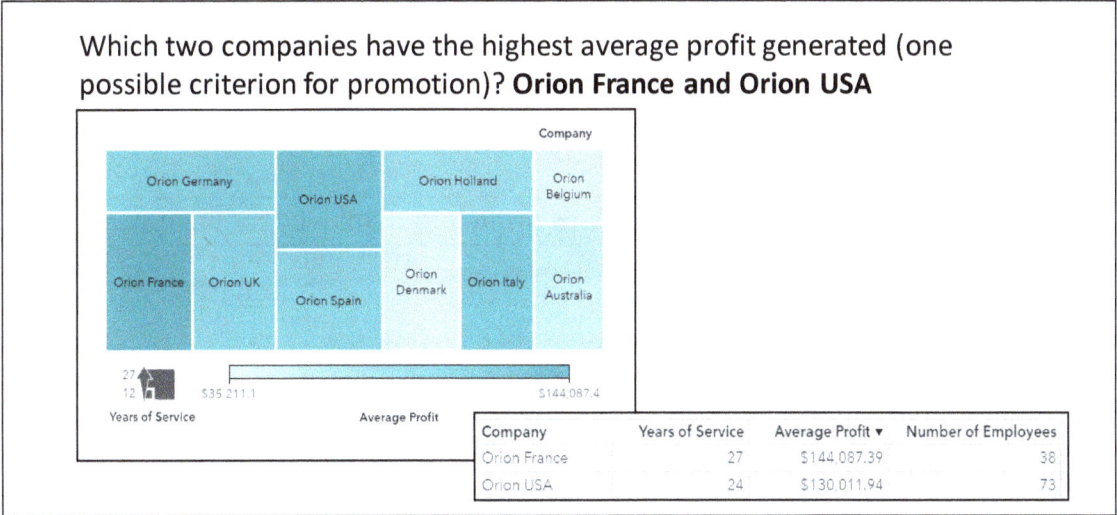

Which two companies have the highest average profit generated (one possible criterion for promotion)? **Orion France and Orion USA**

Company	Years of Service	Average Profit ▼	Number of Employees
Orion France	27	$144,087.39	38
Orion USA	24	$130,011.94	73

Figure A27: 3.6 Analyzing Data - Solution

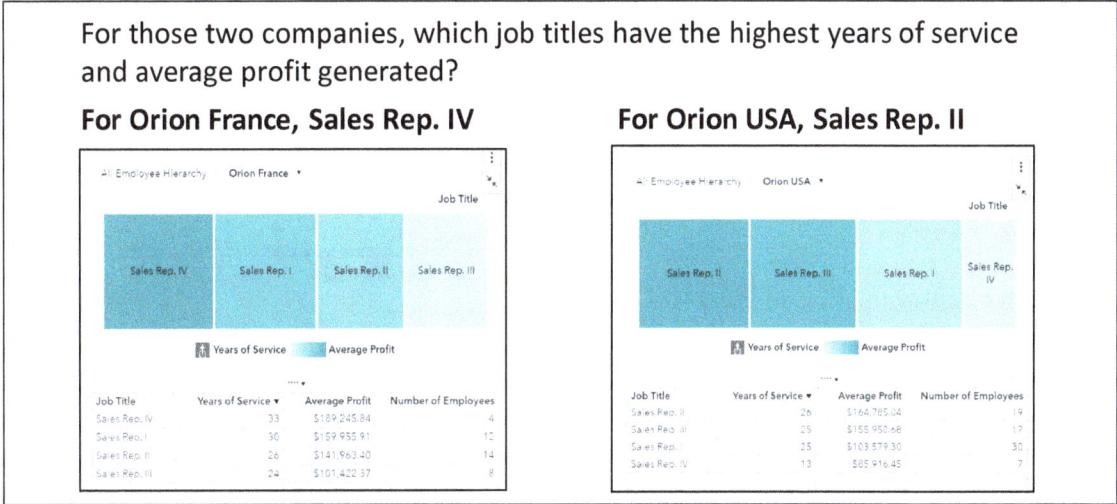

For those two companies, which job titles have the highest years of service and average profit generated?

For Orion France, Sales Rep. IV

Job Title	Years of Service ▼	Average Profit	Number of Employees
Sales Rep. IV	33	$189,245.84	4
Sales Rep. I	30	$159,935.91	13
Sales Rep. II	26	$141,963.40	14
Sales Rep. III	24	$101,422.37	8

For Orion USA, Sales Rep. II

Job Title	Years of Service ▼	Average Profit	Number of Employees
Sales Rep. II	26	$164,785.04	19
Sales Rep. III	25	$155,950.68	17
Sales Rep. I	23	$103,579.30	30
Sales Rep. IV	13	$85,916.45	7

Figure A28: 3.7 Adding Data Analysis - Solution

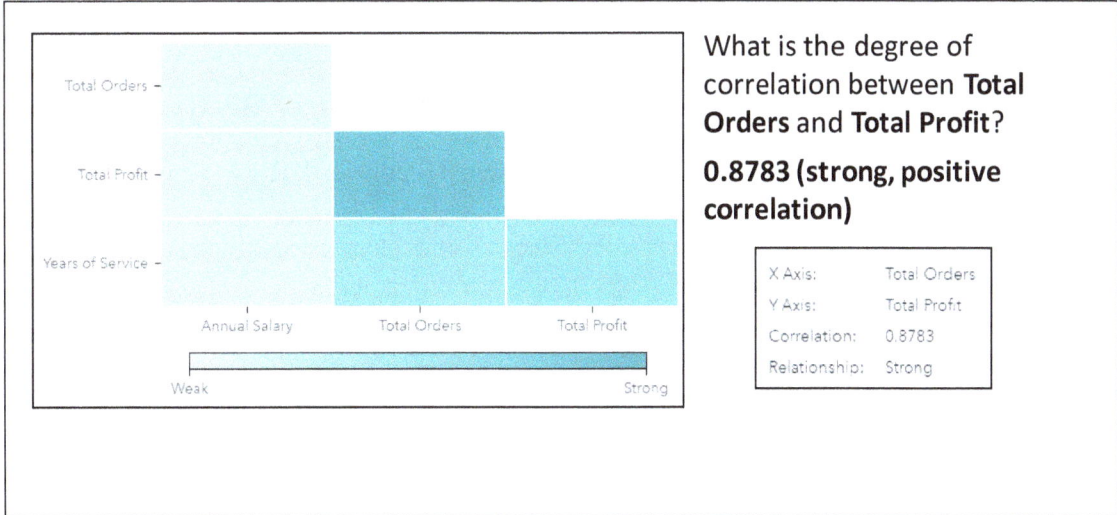

What is the degree of correlation between **Total Orders** and **Total Profit**?

0.8783 (strong, positive correlation)

X Axis:	Total Orders
Y Axis:	Total Profit
Correlation:	0.8783
Relationship:	Strong

Chapter 4

Solutions to Activities and Questions

Quiz 4.1: Correct Answer

What type of chart would you use to show profit information by continent?

a. bubble plot

b. pie chart

c. bar chart

d. treemap

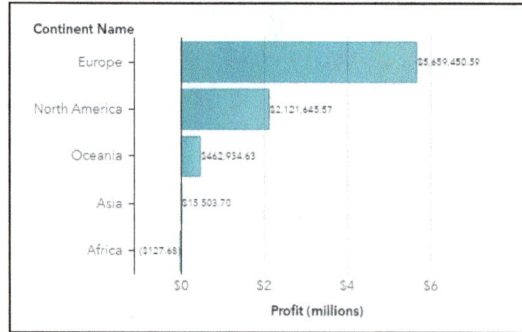

Bubble plots require three measures.

Pie charts and treemaps cannot display negative values.

Practice Review

Figure A28: 4.1 Creating a Simple Report - Solution

Which country has the highest average profit? **Germany (DE)**

Employee Country	Average Profit ▼	Number of Employees
DE	$101,306.73	75
FR	$101,282.97	61
IT	$101,143.68	58

Employee Country	Average Profit ▲	Number of Employees
DK	$30,493.46	37
BE	$32,199.92	44
AU	$42,026.84	77

The lowest? **Denmark (DK)**

Which country has the highest number of employees? **United States (US)**

Employee Country	Average Profit	Number of Employees ▼
US	$96,861.47	123
AU	$42,026.84	77
DE	$101,306.73	75

Employee Country	Average Profit	Number of Employees ▲
DK	$30,493.46	37
BE	$32,199.92	44
NL	$67,704.25	51

The lowest? **Denmark (DK)**

§sas

Figure A29: 4.1 Creating a Simple Report - Solution

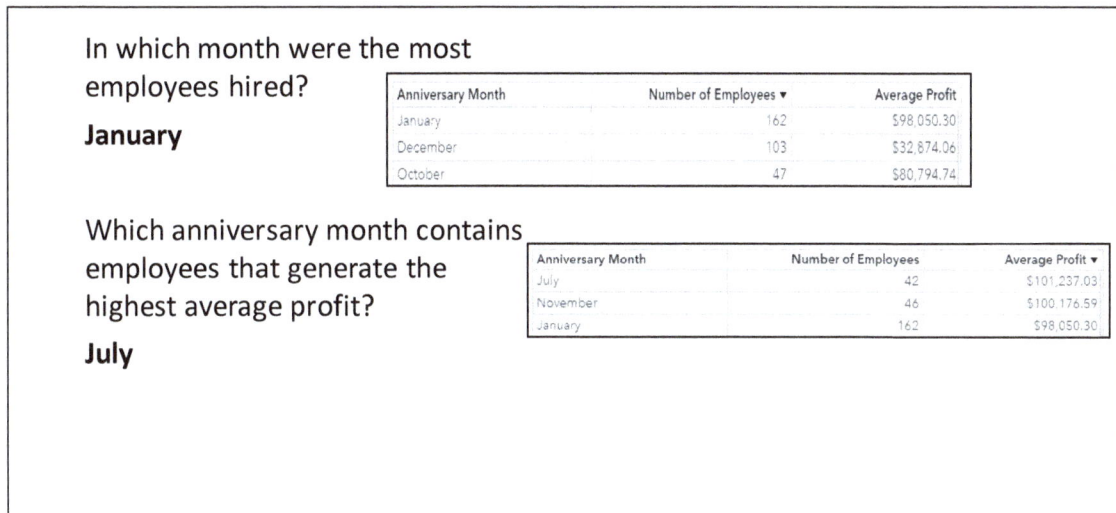

In which month were the most employees hired?

January

Anniversary Month	Number of Employees ▼	Average Profit
January	162	$98,050.30
December	103	$32,874.06
October	47	$80,794.74

Which anniversary month contains employees that generate the highest average profit?

July

Anniversary Month	Number of Employees	Average Profit ▼
July	42	$101,237.03
November	46	$100,176.59
January	162	$98,050.30

Figure A30: 4.2 Working with Pages - Solution

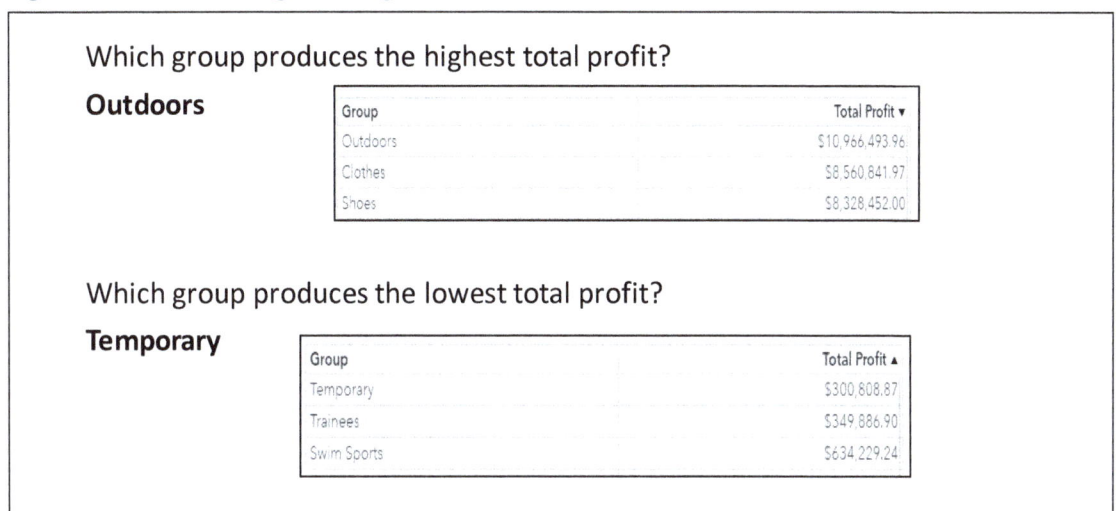

Which group produces the highest total profit?

Outdoors

Group	Total Profit ▼
Outdoors	$10,966,493.96
Clothes	$8,560,841.97
Shoes	$8,328,452.00

Which group produces the lowest total profit?

Temporary

Group	Total Profit ▲
Temporary	$300,808.87
Trainees	$349,886.90
Swim Sports	$634,229.24

Figure A31: 4.2 Working with Pages - Solution

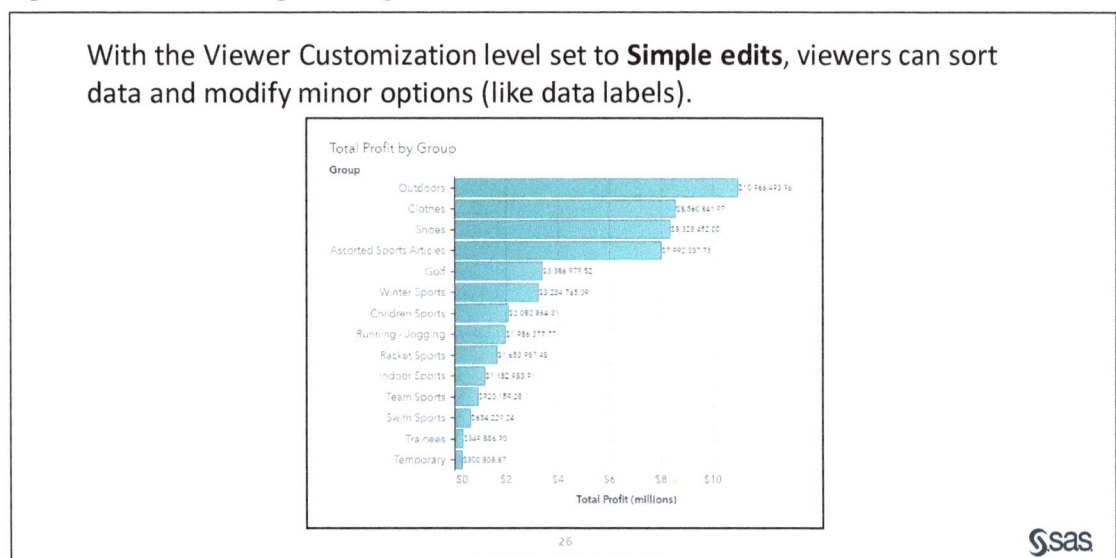

With the Viewer Customization level set to **Simple edits**, viewers can sort data and modify minor options (like data labels).

Figure A32: 4.3 Working with Prompts and Actions - Solution

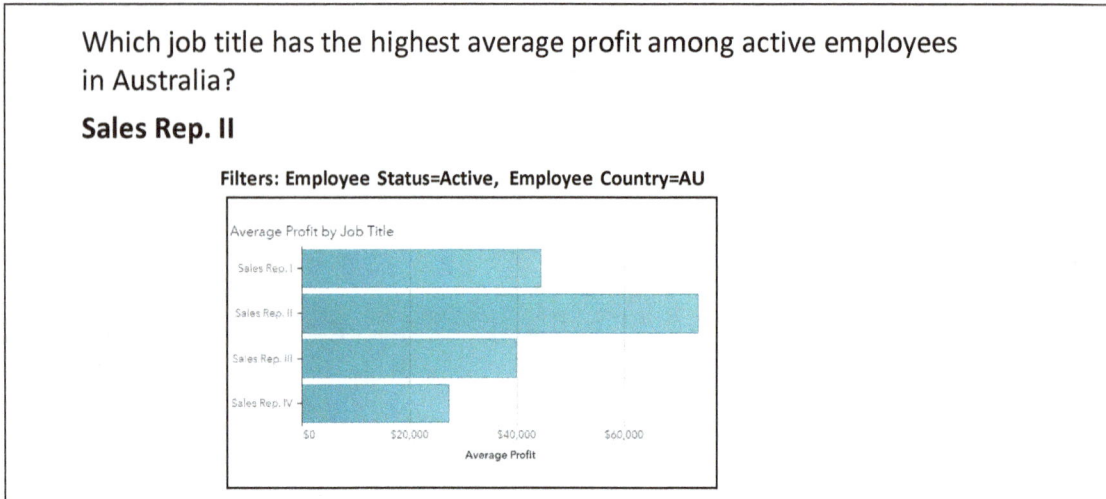

Which job title has the highest average profit among active employees in Australia?

Sales Rep. II

Filters: Employee Status=Active, Employee Country=AU

Average Profit by Job Title

Figure A33: 4.3 Working with Prompts and Actions - Solution

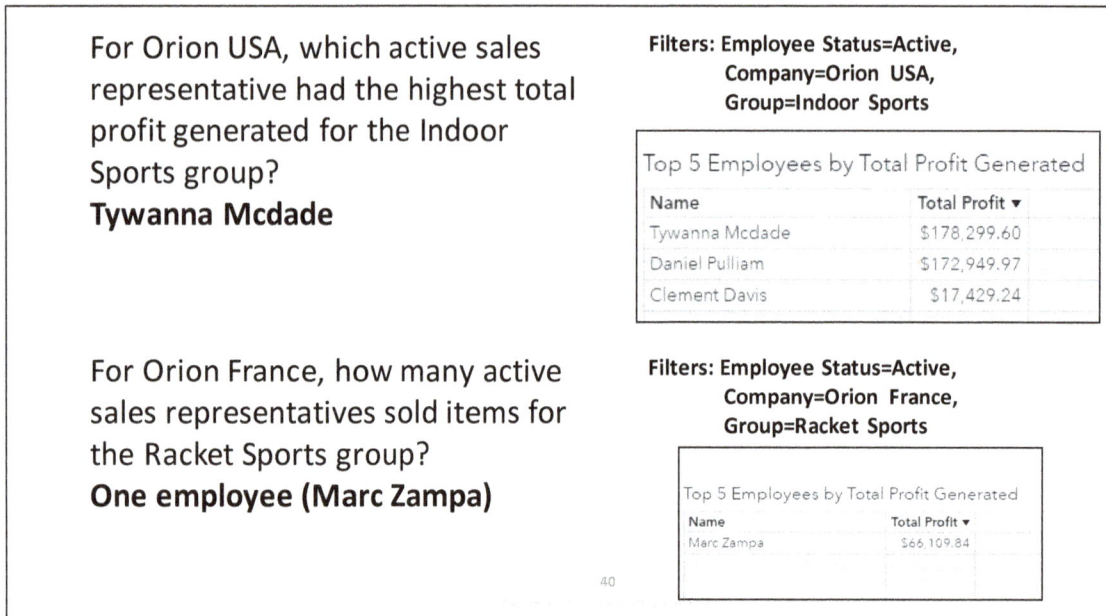

For Orion USA, which active sales representative had the highest total profit generated for the Indoor Sports group?

Tywanna Mcdade

Filters: Employee Status=Active,
Company=Orion USA,
Group=Indoor Sports

Top 5 Employees by Total Profit Generated

Name	Total Profit ▼
Tywanna Mcdade	$178,299.60
Daniel Pulliam	$172,949.97
Clement Davis	$17,429.24

For Orion France, how many active sales representatives sold items for the Racket Sports group?

One employee (Marc Zampa)

Filters: Employee Status=Active,
Company=Orion France,
Group=Racket Sports

Top 5 Employees by Total Profit Generated

Name	Total Profit ▼
Marc Zampa	$66,109.84

40

Figure A34: 4.4 Working with Hidden Pages and Page Links - Solution

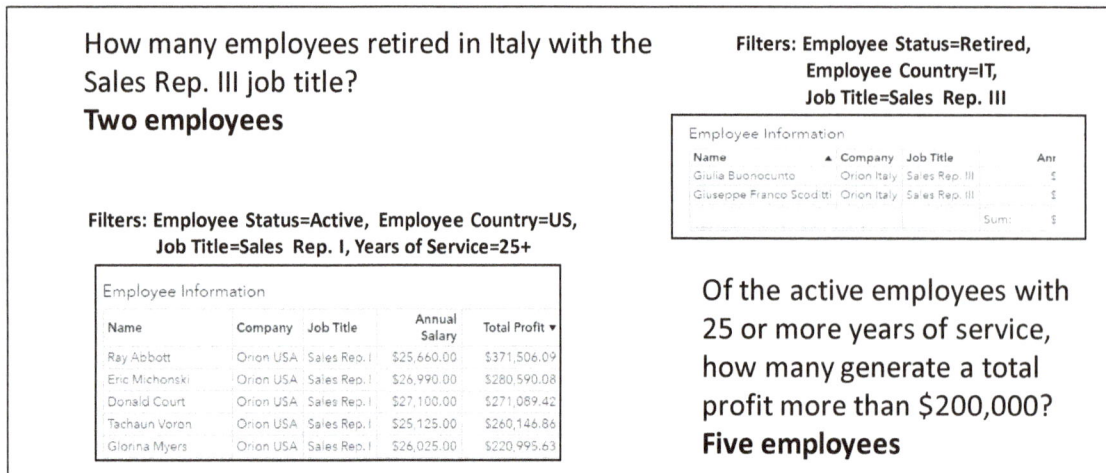

How many employees retired in Italy with the Sales Rep. III job title?

Two employees

Filters: Employee Status=Retired,
Employee Country=IT,
Job Title=Sales Rep. III

Employee Information

Name	▲ Company	Job Title	Anr
Giulia Buonocunto	Orion Italy	Sales Rep. III	$
Giuseppe Franco Scoditti	Orion Italy	Sales Rep. III	$
		Sum:	$

Filters: Employee Status=Active, Employee Country=US,
Job Title=Sales Rep. I, Years of Service=25+

Employee Information

Name	Company	Job Title	Annual Salary	Total Profit ▼
Ray Abbott	Orion USA	Sales Rep. I	$25,660.00	$371,506.09
Eric Michonski	Orion USA	Sales Rep. I	$26,990.00	$280,590.08
Donald Court	Orion USA	Sales Rep. I	$27,100.00	$271,089.42
Tachaun Voron	Orion USA	Sales Rep. I	$25,125.00	$260,146.86
Glorina Myers	Orion USA	Sales Rep. I	$26,025.00	$220,995.63

Of the active employees with 25 or more years of service, how many generate a total profit more than $200,000?

Five employees

Figure A35: 4.5 Working with Report-Level and Graph-Level Display Rules - Solution

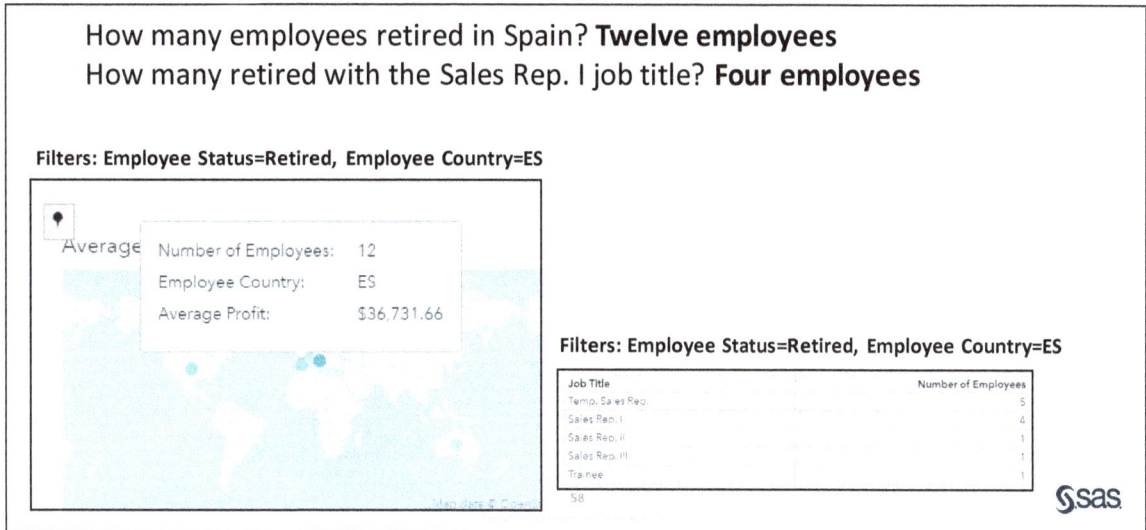

How many employees retired in Spain? **Twelve employees**
How many retired with the Sales Rep. I job title? **Four employees**

Filters: Employee Status=Retired, Employee Country=ES

Number of Employees:	12
Employee Country:	ES
Average Profit:	$36,731.66

Filters: Employee Status=Retired, Employee Country=ES

Job Title	Number of Employees
Temp. Sales Rep.	5
Sales Rep. I	4
Sales Rep. II	1
Sales Rep. III	1
Trainee	1
	58

§sas

Figure A36: 4.5 Working with Report-Level and Graph-Level Display Rules - Solution

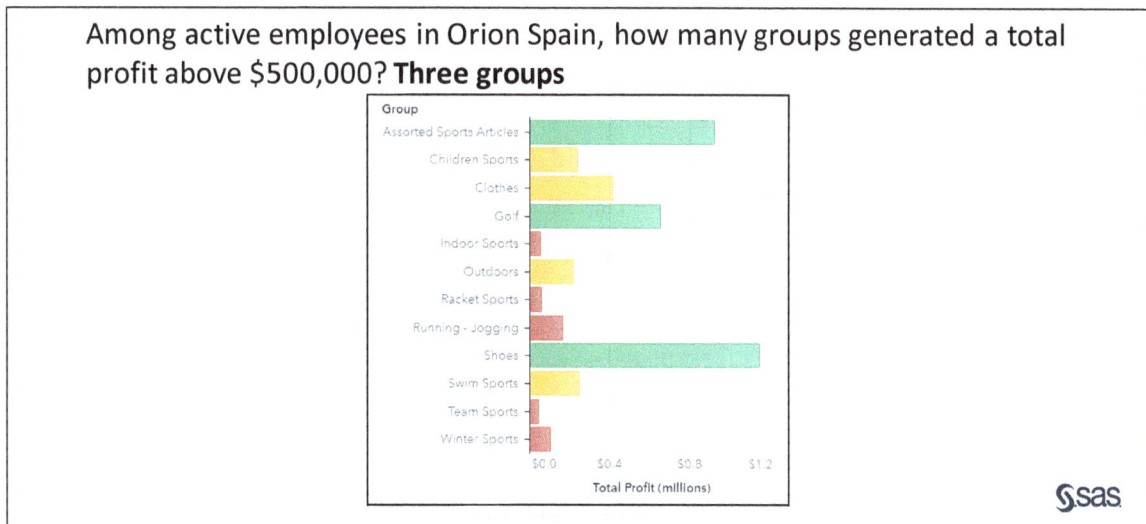

Among active employees in Orion Spain, how many groups generated a total profit above $500,000? **Three groups**

Group	Total Profit (millions)
Assorted Sports Articles	
Children Sports	
Clothes	
Golf	
Indoor Sports	
Outdoors	
Racket Sports	
Running - Jogging	
Shoes	
Swim Sports	
Team Sports	
Winter Sports	

§sas

Chapter 5

Solutions to Activities and Questions

Activity 5.1: Correct Answer

What is the predicted customer satisfaction for the following factors? 45%

What values for the most important factors should be used to predict?

What is the prediction for Customer Satisfaction?

Customer Country

AR

45%

Product Line

Figurine

The predicted Customer Satisfaction for this case is 5.139% lower than the observed average Customer Satisfaction of 47.15%. Most observations (55.87%) have a lower Customer Satisfaction than this predicted case. The prediction is based on an automatically selected Decision Tree model.

Product Cost of Sale

15

Customer Distance

2.0

Use an *automated prediction* object to predict a response variable using adjusted values of underlying factors.

Product Price (target)

4

§sas

The automated prediction object runs several models to predict a specific response variable using most of the data items in the table. A champion model is chosen, and the model prediction and relevant underlying factors are displayed (ordered by their relative importance values). The default model prediction is calculated by using the median values of measure factors and the most common value of category factors. You can then adjust the values of the underlying factors to determine how the model prediction will change with each adjustment.

For category response variables, the following candidate models are run:

- logistic regression (binary response only)
- gradient boosting
- decision tree

The champion model is chosen based on the highest accuracy, which is 100 – misclassification rate.

For measure response variables, the following candidate models are run:

- linear regression
- gradient boosting
- decision tree

The champion model is chosen based on the lowest average squared error (ASE).

Practice Review

Practice 5.1: Solution

What is the average **Customer Satisfaction** value? **47%**

What are the top three factors most related to **Customer Satisfaction**?

What factors are most related to Customer Satisfaction?

Customer Country	
xyCustomer Lat	
xyCustomer Lon	

Which factor best differentiates the highest and lowest **Customer Satisfaction** values? **Customer Distance**

What are the characteristics of Customer Satisfaction?

Customer Satisfaction ranges from 19% to 100%. Average Customer Satisfaction is 47%. Most cases (202K of 252K) have a Customer Satisfaction between 30% and 71%. Customer Distance best differentiates the highest (top 10%) and the lowest (bottom 10%) Customer Satisfaction cases. There are 14K cases that might be outliers, with Customer Satisfaction above 85%.

§sas

What is the customer distance for the highest predicted customer satisfaction (96%)?
Customer distance is less than 5.5

What are the groups based on Customer Distance by the average value of Customer Satisfaction?

High   Low   >

96%   If Customer Country is CO, MA, NG, or PE, Customer Distance is less than 5.5, then the 4.9K cases have a predicted Customer Satisfaction of 96%.

What are the groups based on Customer Distance by the average value of Customer Satisfaction?

<   High   Low

31%   If Customer Distance is greater than or equal to 50, then the 300 cases have a predicted Customer Satisfaction of 31%

For the lowest predicted customer satisfaction (31%)?
Customer Distance is greater than or equal to 50

§sas

Which range of **Customer Distance** contains the most observations?
Between 3 and 8

		Customer
Customer Satisfaction (lower):	33%	ce?
Customer Satisfaction (upper):	38%	
Customer Distance (lower):	3	
Customer Distance (upper):	8	
Frequency:	19,237	

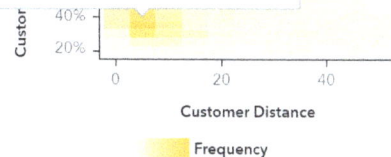

Which factor best differentiates the highest and lowest **Product Sale** values?
Product Price (target)

Customer Distance

Frequency

What are the characteristics of Product Sale?

Product Sale ranges from 0 to 162. Average Product Sale is 25. Most cases (202K of 252K) have a Product Sale between 3.9 and 62. Product Price (target) best differentiates the highest (top 10%) and the lowest (bottom 10%) Product Sale cases. There are 22K cases that might be outliers, with Product Sale above 71.

§sas

Chapter 6

Solutions to Activities and Questions

Activity 6.1: Correct Answer

Which options are available for modifying the case of columns?

Uppercase and Lowercase

Case:

Uppercase ▼
Uppercase
Lowercase

If SAS Data Preparation is licensed, then you have access to more advanced options using the Casing transform.

Quiz 6.1: Correct Answer

To create a geo map, you need a geographic data item.

Which geographic areas would require a geographic data provider or latitude and longitude in data? (Select all that apply.)

a. voting districts
b. cities
c. sales regions
d. school districts

Latitude and longitude in data

Latitude

Longitude

Geographic data provider

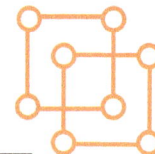

To use custom polygonal shapes, a geographic data provider must be defined.

Note: Special user permissions are required to define and edit geographic data providers. The **/maps/providers** URI controls the access to polygon provider. For more information, see "Access to Functionality" in the *SAS Viya Administration: Identity Management* documentation.

Practice Review

Practice 6.1: Solution

What is the name of the source table for the plan?
FACILITY_TOY

How many rows are in the source table?
35.2K rows

How many columns?
28 columns

Source Table - FACILITY_TOY

Columns	Rows	Size
28	35.2 K	12.9 MB

Label:
(not available)

Location:
cas-shared-default/Public

Date created:

Date modified:

Encoding:
(not available)

Tags (0):
No items have been added.

17

How many unique values exist for **Facility Continent**?
Six unique values

Column	Unique
◈ FacilityContinent	0.02% (6)

What is the average number of products produced by each unit?
The minimum? The maximum?
Average=6.86, Minimum=1.00, Maximum=55.00

Column	Mean	M.	M.	S..	S..	Minimum	Maximum
⊞ UnitActual	6.86			8..	0..	1.00	55.00

Result Table - FACILITY_TOY (session)

Columns	Rows	Size
28	26.1 K	9.6 MB

How many rows are in the result table?
26.1K rows

What is the name of the result table for the plan?

Saved table (FACILITY_... ▾	Run Profile
Input table (FACILITY_TOY)	
Saved table (FACILITY_TOY_AMERICA)	

FACILITY_TOY_AMERICA

How many unique values exist for
Facility Continent?
Two unique values

Column	Unique
◬ FacilityContinent	0.01% (2)

What is the average number of products produced by each unit? **6.73**

Column	Mean
⊞ UnitActual	6.73

What does this tell you about production in the Americas compared to production in other continents?
This is below the average for all continents (6.86), so production in the Americas is below that in other continents.

19

§sas

Note: No solutions are provided for the alternate practices (optional).

Practice 6.2: Solution

What percentage of data items are mapped? **89%**

Name:		89% mapped
Facility Country		
Based on:		
☑ Facility Country		
Geography data:		
Geographic name or code lookup ▾		Map data © OpenStreetMap
Name or code context:		1 of 1 unmapped values:
Country or Region Names ▾		Venezuela

How many facilities are in the United States within 250 miles of Topeka, KS? **Eight**

All Facility Hierarchy › United States ▾

NEBRASKA · Moline · Kirksville · ILLINOIS · INDI·
United States of America · E·· · Poplar Bluff · K·
Enid · Fayetteville · TENNES·

⊙ Facility Employees   Unit Actual

32

Chapter 7

Practice Review

Practice 7.1: Solution

How many columns are in the source table?
Nine columns

Source Table - MVAINJURIES90		
Columns	Rows	Size
9	118	16.5 KB

MVAINJURIES00.sashdat

Details   Sample Data   Profile

#	Name	Label	!
1	Date		

Date profiled:
(none)

Columns	Rows
9	--

How many columns are in the **MVAINJURIES00** table?
Nine columns

Practice 7.2: Solution

Which algorithm is selected for the forecast?
Seasonal Exponential Smoothing

Results	Dependent Variables Results	Forecast Summary

Dependent Variable	Algorithm
Injuries from Motor Vehicle Accidents	Seasonal Exponential Smoothing

Which measures, if any, were selected as underlying factors and applied to the forecast?
Tourism Index (Difference from previous period)

§.sas

Which algorithm is now selected for the forecast?

ARIMA

Algorithm

ARIMA: Injuries from Motor Vehicle Accidents ~ P = 2 + INPUT: Lag(11) Tourism Index

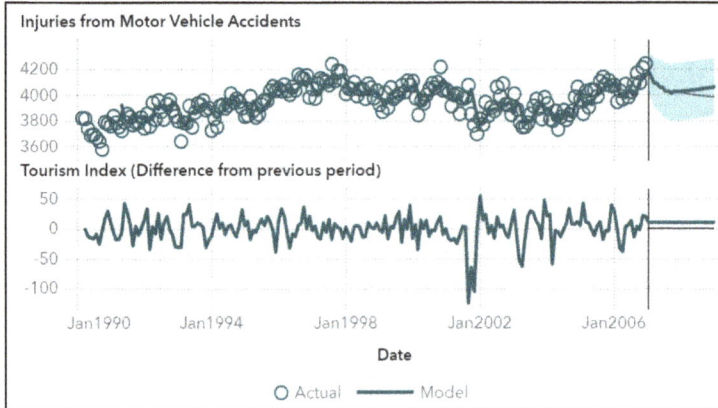

Injuries from Motor Vehicle Accidents

4200
4000
3800
3600

Tourism Index (Difference from previous period)

50
0
-50
-100

Jan1990   Jan1994   Jan1998   Jan2002   Jan2006

Date

○ Actual —— Model

How does increasing the underlying factor impact the forecast?

Increasing the number of tourists increases the number of injuries from motor vehicle accidents near the end of the next year.

§sas

Chapter 8

Practice Review

Practice 8.1: Solution

Which states did Hurricane Matthew hit in 2016?
Florida, Georgia, South Carolina, and North Carolina

What was the maximum wind speed?
145 mph

How was Hurricane Matthew categorized?
Tropical, Hurricane, and Extratropical

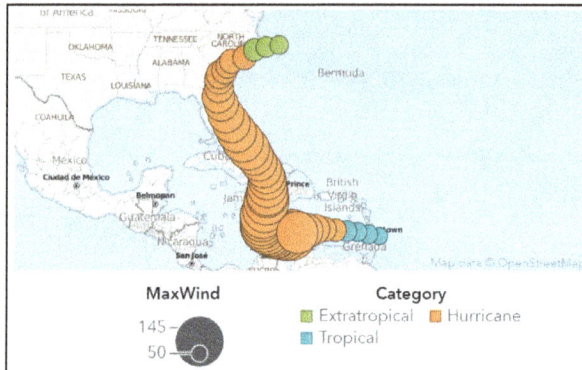

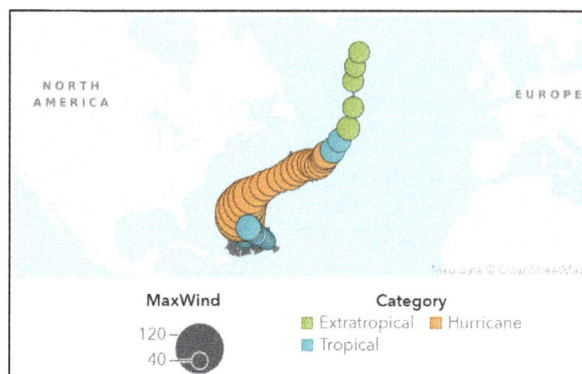

MaxWind

145
50

Category
■ Extratropical ■ Hurricane
■ Tropical

Which states did Hurricane Nicole hit in 2016?
None

What was the maximum wind speed?
120 mph

How was Hurricane Nicole categorized?

Tropical, Hurricane, and Extratropical

NORTH
AMERICA

EUROPE

MaxWind

120
40

Category
■ Extratropical ■ Hurricane
■ Tropical

Note: No solutions are provided for the alternate practices (optional).

Chapter 9

Practice Review

Practice 9.1: Solution

How many unique courses did students attend?
391 unique courses, including PG1

> ∨ Category
> 🏠 Course Code - 391

What information is displayed when you place your mouse pointer on ⓘ
in the lower right corner
of the object?

> One or more paths that tied for the ranking are not shown.
> An artificial sequence order was generated for 5 paths that contains simultaneous events.

This means that there are students who attend multiple classes that start on the same day.

What do you think this means?
Some training packages include access to an instructor-led class and a self-paced e-learning class. There could be simultaneous events if students activated the e-learning on the day on which the instructor-led class started.

10

§.sas

With which course do a majority
of students begin?
PG1 (SAS Programming 1)

> 9595   5748
> **PG1**   EG1   INTRO   BASIC

Of those students who start with PG1, how many have not taken another class?
9,595 students

Of those students who start with PG1,
what is the next course that most are
likely to take?
PG2 (SAS Programming 2)

> 9595
> **PG1**
> 5045
> 40...
> **PG2**   EG1   SQ1   ST1   MC1

How many students take this course?
5,045 students

Are there any students who take PG1 twice? **Yes**

How many students do this? **56 students**

Why might this be the case?
There could be a number of reasons why students take PG1 twice. For example:

- **do not use the tool and forget the material**

- **retake it as a refresher course**

- **start the free e-learning course and switch to an instructor-led course later**

- **take class initially for a project and then retake for certification attempt**

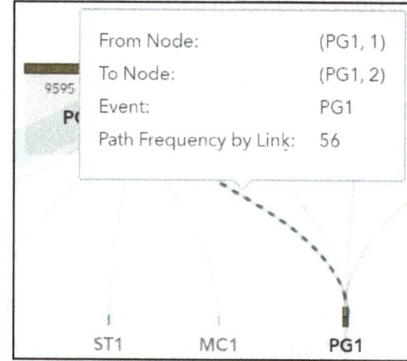

From Node:	(PG1, 1)
To Node:	(PG1, 2)
Event:	PG1
Path Frequency by Link:	56

ST1   MC1   PG1

Chapter 10

Solutions to Activities and Questions

Activity 10.1: Correct Answer

What three things are required for the text topics object?

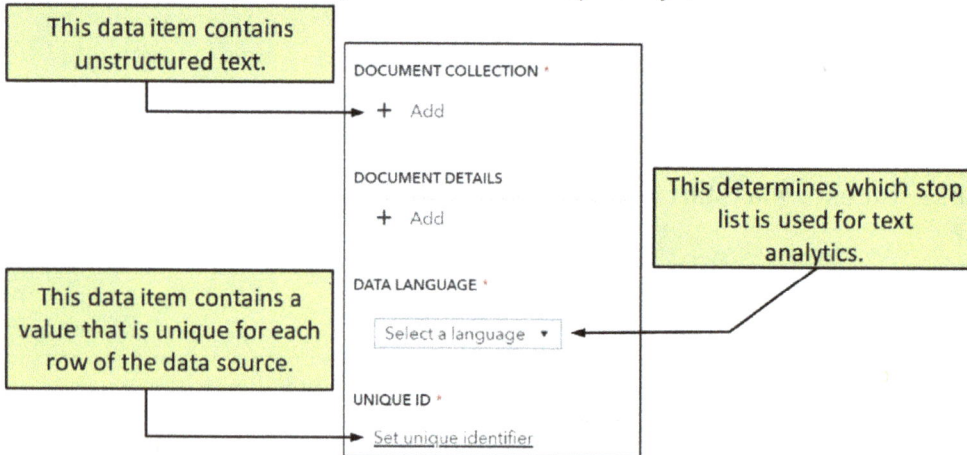

This data item contains unstructured text.

DOCUMENT COLLECTION *

+ Add

DOCUMENT DETAILS

+ Add

This determines which stop list is used for text analytics.

DATA LANGUAGE *

Select a language ▾

This data item contains a value that is unique for each row of the data source.

UNIQUE ID *

Set unique identifier

Practice Review

Practice 10.1: Solutions

Which data item would be the unique identifier column?
Course Code, because it has many unique values and acts as an identifier for the course information

⌄ Category
⊞ Attendee Type - 739
⊞ Course Code - 1.1K
⊞ Description - 1.1K
⊞ Learn How To - 806

Which data item would be the document collection?
Description, because it contains unstructured text

Which sentiment (negative, neutral, or positive) is assigned to a majority of course descriptions? **Neutral**

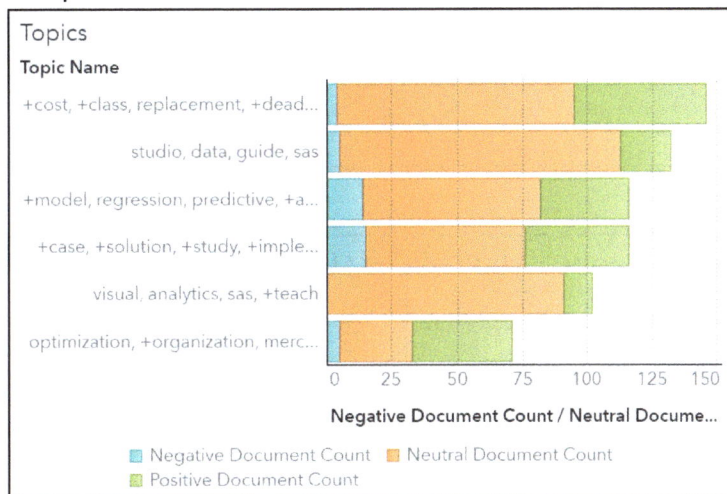

Topics

Topic Name

- +cost, +class, replacement, +dead...
- studio, data, guide, sas
- +model, regression, predictive, +a...
- +case, +solution, +study, +imple...
- visual, analytics, sas, +teach
- optimization, +organization, merc...

Negative Document Count / Neutral Docume...

- ■ Negative Document Count
- ■ Neutral Document Count
- ■ Positive Document Count

How many documents are in the **visual, analytics, sas, +teach** topic?
102

Topics	Terms	Text Topics Summary		
Topic Name	Negative...	Neutral...	Positive...	Document...
visual, analytics, sas, +teach	0	91	11	102

What are the top two terms for all topics?
course and sas

Topics	Terms	Text Topics Summary
Term	Document count	Role
course	862	Noun
sas	764	Proper noun

Does that make sense given the data?

Yes, because these are descriptions for SAS courses

Chapter 11

Practice Review

Practice 11.1: Solution

Are there any jobs that do not exist in Europe?
Purchasing Agent I and Purchasing Agent III

Are there any jobs in which Europeans make more than other continents (on average)?
Europeans in Sales Rep. IV and Temp. Sales Rep. make more (on average) than other continents.

Job Title	Salary (Europe)	Salary (America/Oceania)
Purchasing Agent I	.	$31,760.00
Purchasing Agent III	.	$35,070.00
Sales Rep. I	$26,390.00	$26,486.37
Sales Rep. II	$27,348.50	$27,444.33
Sales Rep. III	$29,444.13	$29,489.39
Sales Rep. IV	$31,997.35	$31,615.67
Temp. Sales Rep.	$26,344.35	$26,265.83
Trainee	$24,704.29	$25,477.22

Practice 11.2: Solution

Where are the top five products produced? **Lima and Caracas**

Product Code	Frequency	Facility City
PELIMA..-TAF	245	Lima
PELIMA..-TGM	246	Lima
VECARACA-TAF	260	Caracas
VECARACA-TGM	265	Caracas
VECARACA-TSA	231	Caracas

Practice 11.3: Solution

The expression should resemble the following:

(Sum _ByGroup_ ▾ (Unit Actual) / Sum _ByGroup_ ▾ (Unit Capacity))

The crosstab should resemble the following:

Unit ▲	Unit Actual	Unit Capacity	Yield Rate
Total	176007	429427	40.99%
NBD000020	31	348	8.91%
NBD000028	743	2784	26.69%
NBD000036	1541	2964	51.99%
NBD000044	1773	3048	58.17%
NBD000066	929	1980	46.92%
NBD000094	36	408	8.82%
NBD000111	936	2004	46.71%

Practice 11.4: Solution

The expression and the list table should resemble the following:

Selects interval based on level displayed in object		
CumulativePeriod	_Sum_	
	Profit	
	_IgnoreAllTimeFra...	
	Order Date	
	Inferred	
	ByYear	
	0	Starting point
	3	
	Full	

Order Date ▲	Profit	Cumulative Profit
Jan2012	$118,773.87	$118,773.87
Feb2012	$106,735.23	$225,509.10
Mar2012	$84,893.31	$84,893.31
Apr2012	$94,871.26	$179,764.57
May2012	$118,248.93	$298,013.50
Jun2012	$159,343.43	$457,356.93
Jul2012	$140,479.12	$597,836.05
	$151,644.75	$749,480.81
	$74,120.37	$823,601.18
Oct2012	$80,908.90	$904,510.08

§sas

Practice 11.5: Solution

Solution

Aggregation type	_Sum_	
Direction of aggregation	Profit	Measure
AggregateCells	default	
	start ∨ 0 ∧	Starting point
Ending point	current ∨ 0 ∧	

What is the total profit for all countries?

$8,259,406.82

United Arab Emirates	$544.17	$5,336,061.08
United Kingdom	$861,804.13	$6,197,865.21
United States	$2,061,541.61	$8,259,406.82

§sas

Note: No solutions are provided for the challenges (optional).

Chapter 12

Solutions to Activities and Questions

Activity 12.1: Correct Answer

Which Date and Time operator could be used to calculate the date value for four years prior to today? **DateFromMDY**

DateFromMDY	Month (DatePart (Now ( )))
	DayOfMonth (DatePart (Now ( )))
	(Year (DatePart (Now ( ))) - 4)

Activity 12.2: Correct Answer

∨ Numeric (advanced)
- ⊞ Abs
- ⊞ Ceil
- ⊞ Exp
- ⊞ Floor
- ⊞ Ln
- ⊞ Log
- ⊞ Mod
- ⊞ Power
- ⊞ Root
- ⊞ Round
- ⊞ TreatAs
- ⊞ Trunc

Which operator enables a numeric or datetime value to be used as a different type for the calculation? **TreatAs**

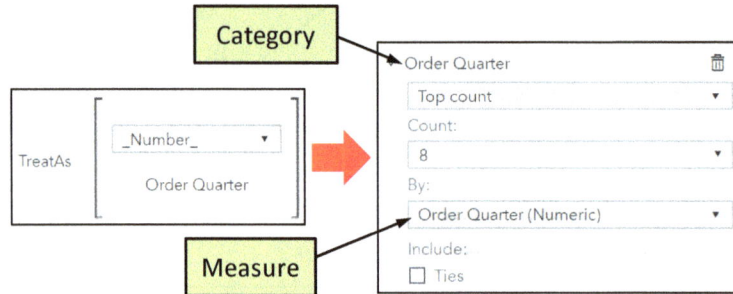

Category

Measure

TreatAs — _Number_ — Order Quarter →

Order Quarter 🗑
Top count ▾
Count:
8 ▾
By:
Order Quarter (Numeric) ▾
Include:
☐ Ties

Because ranks use measures for the BY variable, we need to convert date values to numbers to show the last eight quarters.

Practice Review

Practice 12.1: Solution

What is the range for **Quantity**?
1 to 10

> ∨ Quantity 🗑 ⋮
> ☐ Filter aggregated values
> 1 to 10
> ●━━━━━━━━━━━●
> ☑ Include missing values

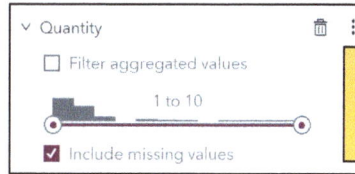

> The range represents the values for **Quantity** in each row of the table.

What is the range for aggregate **Quantity**?
2 to 393,350

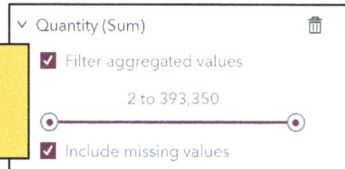

> The aggregated values are based on the other columns included in the list table.

> ∨ Quantity (Sum) 🗑 ⋮
> ☑ Filter aggregated values
> 2 to 393,350
> ●━━━━━━━━━━━●
> ☑ Include missing values

How many countries have a total quantity greater than 100,000?
Seven

Country ▲	Quantity
France	188K
Germany	212K
Italy	166K
Netherlands	105K
Spain	160K
United Kingdom	178K
United States	393K

> The list table uses the abbreviated numerical value of quantity.

Practice 12.2: Solution

To which product line does the Running - Jogging category belong? **Sports**

Which product groups are in the category? **Jogging and Running Clothes**

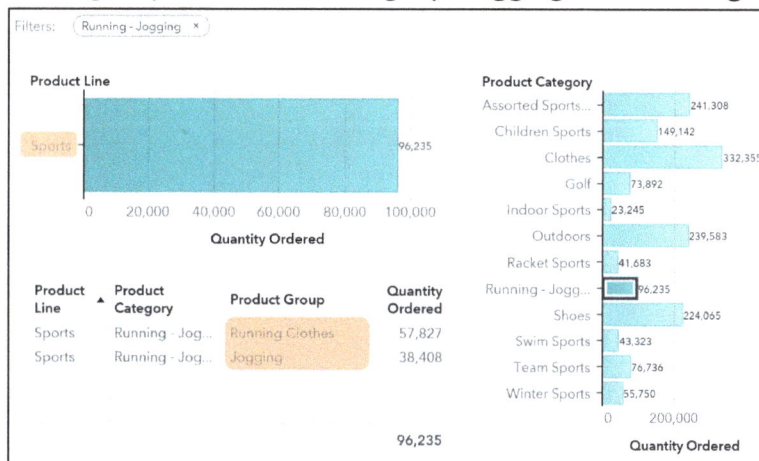

Filters: (Running - Jogging ✕)

Product Line

Sports ▌96,235

0   20,000   40,000   60,000   80,000   100,000
Quantity Ordered

Product Line ▲	Product Category	Product Group	Quantity Ordered
Sports	Running - Jog...	Running Clothes	57,827
Sports	Running - Jog...	Jogging	38,408
			96,235

Product Category

Assorted Sports...	241,308
Children Sports	149,142
Clothes	332,355
Golf	73,892
Indoor Sports	23,245
Outdoors	239,583
Racket Sports	41,683
Running - Jogg...	96,235
Shoes	224,065
Swim Sports	43,323
Team Sports	76,736
Winter Sports	55,750

0   200,000
Quantity Ordered

Note: No solutions are provided for the challenge (optional).

Practice 12.3: Solution

Which data source is used for the treemap?
PRODUCTS_CLEAN

Which data source is used for the list table?
EMPLOYEES_CLEAN

Which data items can be used to map the two data sources?
**Product Category from PRODUCTS_CLEAN and
Group from EMPLOYEES_CLEAN.**

Which employee makes the highest salary (of those who sold Indoor Sports products)?
Alexei Platts

What is the job title of the above employee?
Sales Rep. IV

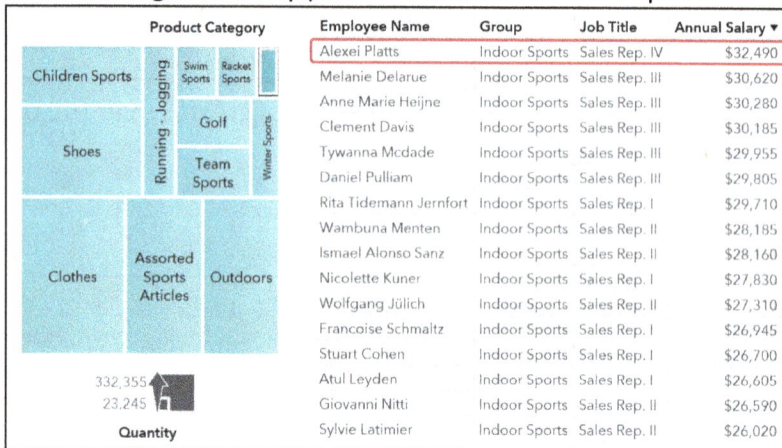

Employee Name	Group	Job Title	Annual Salary ▼
Alexei Platts	Indoor Sports	Sales Rep. IV	$32,490
Melanie Delarue	Indoor Sports	Sales Rep. III	$30,620
Anne Marie Heijne	Indoor Sports	Sales Rep. III	$30,280
Clement Davis	Indoor Sports	Sales Rep. III	$30,185
Tywanna Mcdade	Indoor Sports	Sales Rep. III	$29,955
Daniel Pulliam	Indoor Sports	Sales Rep. III	$29,805
Rita Tidemann Jernfort	Indoor Sports	Sales Rep. I	$29,710
Wambuna Menten	Indoor Sports	Sales Rep. II	$28,185
Ismael Alonso Sanz	Indoor Sports	Sales Rep. II	$28,160
Nicolette Kuner	Indoor Sports	Sales Rep. I	$27,830
Wolfgang Jülich	Indoor Sports	Sales Rep. II	$27,310
Francoise Schmaltz	Indoor Sports	Sales Rep. I	$26,945
Stuart Cohen	Indoor Sports	Sales Rep. I	$26,700
Atul Leyden	Indoor Sports	Sales Rep. I	$26,605
Giovanni Nitti	Indoor Sports	Sales Rep. II	$26,590
Sylvie Latimier	Indoor Sports	Sales Rep. II	$26,020

Product Category treemap: Children Sports, Running - Jogging, Swim Sports, Racket Sports, Shoes, Golf, Team Sports, Winter Sports, Clothes, Assorted Sports Articles, Outdoors

332,355
23,245

Quantity

Chapter 13

Solutions to Activities and Questions

Activity 13.1: Correct Answer

Which comparison operator enables you to select a range of dates?

BetweenInclusive

				DateParameter			
Event Delivered (Start) Date	BetweenInclusive	TreatAs		_Date_ ▼			
			(TreatAs	_Number_ ▼ DateParameter	+	90	)

25

Ssas

Practice Review

Practice 13.1: Solution

What is the expression for the display rule on the treemap? **When Quantity is less than 50,000, the tile is colored red.**

Quantity by Product Group

Display Rules

Quantity by Product Group ▼

+ New rule

Object

Quantity

▪ Quantity < 50000

What is the range of **Quantity** in the treemap?
478 to 127,765

127,765
478
Quantity

8

Ssas

What type of parameter did you create?
Numeric

Why?
You need the report viewer to enter a number to update the treemap.

How many product groups have a
quantity less than 2,500?
Three

Less than 500?
One

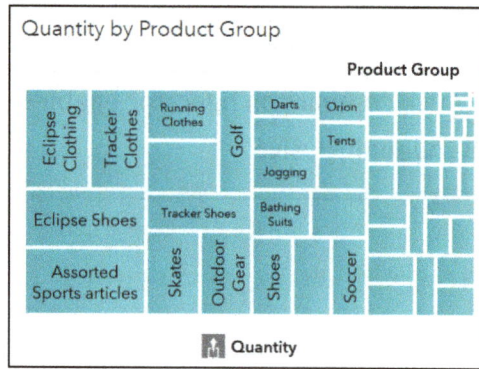

Practice 13.2: Solution

What are the names of the data sources used
in the report?
CATEGORIES and CUSTOMERS_CLEAN

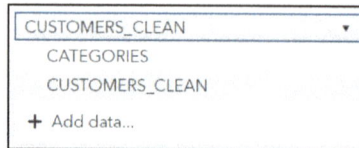

Which data source contains a data item
named **Category**?
CATEGORIES

How many distinct values does **Category** have?
Three

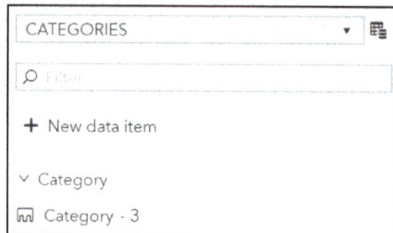

What are the distinct values of **Category**?
Continent, *Customer Type*, and *Order Type*

Do these match data items in the other data
source? **Yes**

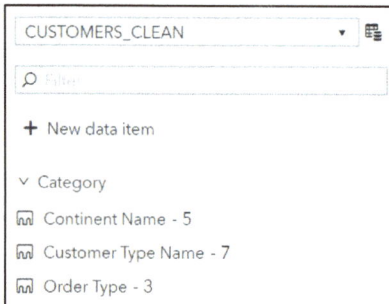

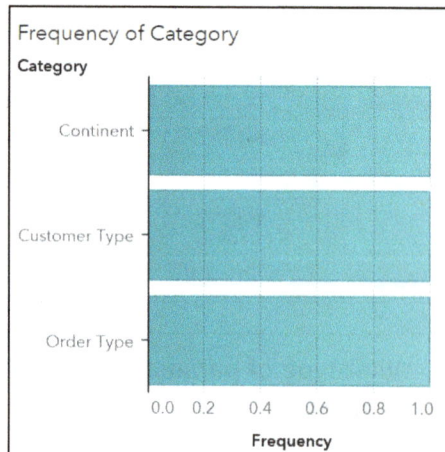

What type of parameter did you create?
Character

Why?
Because the parameter is based off Category (a character data item), you need to create a character parameter.

Which continent has the highest profit?

Choose a category to view in the bar chart below:

| Continent | Customer Type | Order Type |

Selected Category

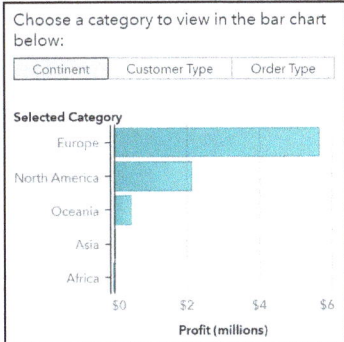

Profit (millions)

Which customer type?

Choose a category to view in the bar chart below:

| Continent | Customer Type | Order Type |

Selected Category

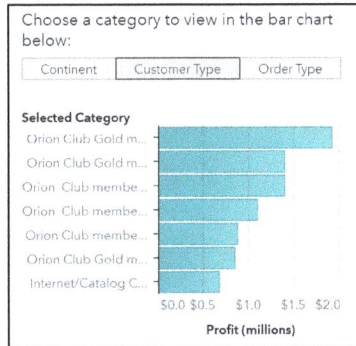

Profit (millions)

Which order type?

Choose a category to view in the bar chart below:

| Continent | Customer Type | Order Type |

Selected Category

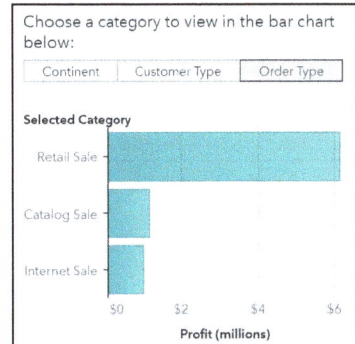

Profit (millions)

§sas

21

Practice 13.3: Solution

What type of parameter did you create?
Date

Why?
Because the parameter is based off Transaction Date (a date data item), we need to create a date parameter.

For February, does the customer satisfaction for any product line exceed the prior month?
Yes, for Game, Plush, Promo, Kiosk, and Bead

Selected Month by Product Line to Prior Month

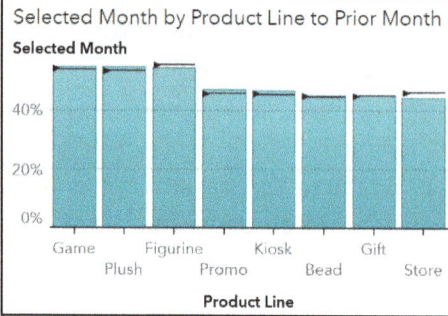

For April, does the customer satisfaction for any product line exceed the prior month?
No

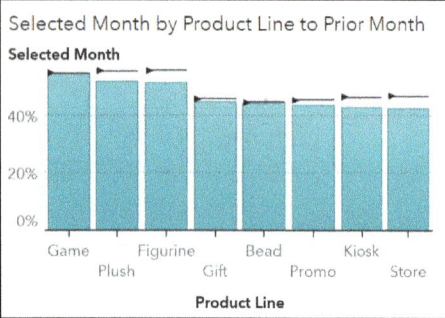

Note: No solutions are provided for the challenges (optional).

www.ingramcontent.com/pod-product-compliance
Lightning Source LLC
Chambersburg PA
CBHW081045220326
41598CB00038B/6986